David W Taylor

Our War
The History and Sacrifices of an Infantry Battalion in the Vietnam War
1968-1971

David W. Taylor

WAR Journal Publishing

Medina, Ohio

Published by:
War Journal Publishing LLC
P.O. Box 10
Medina, Ohio 44258-0010

© 2011 by David W. Taylor
All rights reserved. No part of this book may be reproduced or utilized in any form or by any means, electronic or mechanical, including photocopying, recording or by any information storage and retrieval systems, without written permission from the publisher.

Library of Congress Cataloging-in-Publication Data
LCCN: 2011920663
Taylor, David W. 1946 –

Our War – The History and Sacrifices of an Infantry Battalion in the Vietnam War – 1968-1971
David W. Taylor

Includes bibliography, references and index

1. Vietnamese Conflict, 1961-1975, Campaigns Vietnam, Wheeler/Wallowa, Burlington Trial, Task Force Cooksey, Golden Fleece, Russell Beach/Bold Mariner, Geneva Park, Nantucket Beach, Accelerated Pacification
2. Vietnamese Conflict 1961-1975
3. United States Army. Infantry Brigade, 198th – History
4. Vietnamese Conflict, 1968-1971 – Personal Narratives, American
5. Taylor, David W. 1946 -

ISBN 978-0-9832683-0-7

Printed in the United States of America
First Edition, Second Printing

Printed in 2011

Maps designed by Frank R. Mika

CONTENTS

DEDICATION — v

ACKNOWLEDGEMENTS — vi

PREFACE — xv

Chapter 1: GENESIS — 1
June 1965- October 1967

Chapter 2: REPORT FOR DUTY — 12
October 1967 - March 1968

Chapter 3: LANDING ZONE GATOR — 28

Chapter 4: IN-COUNTRY — 39
March – June 4, 1968

Chapter 5: THE PROFESSIONALS — 66
June 5-July 10 1968

Chapter 6: TASK FORCE COOKSEY — 97
July 11-September 17, 1968

Chapter 7: GOLDEN FLEECE — 128
September 18, 1968 – January 12, 1969

Chapter 8: RUSSELL BEACH — 167
January 13 – February 9, 1969

Chapter 9: EXTENSIVE PACIFICATION — 206
February 10 – May 13, 1969

Chapter 10: GENEVA PARK   251
May 14 – July 14, 1969

Chapter 11: NANTUCKET BEACH   297
July 15 - August 31, 1969

Chapter 12: CLEAR, HOLD AND PACIFY   339
September 1 – December 31, 1969

Chapter 13: RETRIBUTION   383
January 1, 1970 – March 31, 1970

Chapter 14: DEATH AND DESTRUCTION   424
April 1 - June 30, 1970

Chapter 15: TACTICAL HEGEMONY   465
July 1 – September 30, 1970

Chapter 16: BEGINNING OF THE END   506
October 1 – December 31, 1970

Chapter 17: END OF THE TUNNEL   546
January 1 – February 28, 1971

Chapter 18: FINAL SACRIFICES   585
February 29 - May 22, 1971

Chapter 19: REVELATION   629
May 1971 – March 2011

Appendix A: LEST WE FORGET   655

BIBLIOGRAPHY   661

INDEX   677

DEDICATION

Dedicated to the men who served in the 5th/46th Infantry Battalion of the 198th Light Infantry Brigade, Americal Division in the Republic of South Vietnam.

And a special thanks to Sergeant Randy Backovich, one of my squad leaders, whose tenacity on June 3, 1969 saved my life. I will be forever grateful.

ACKNOWLEDGEMENTS

In 1999 I attended my second Americal Division Veterans Association (ADVA) annual reunion, held in St. Louis, Missouri. When I entered the main hospitality room I noticed a small group of vets sitting at a table looking at a crude drawing of a firebase. When I heard the words, "LZ Gator" I realized they were fellow veterans of the infantry battalion I had served with and immediately approached them to join in the conversation. Among those present were the battalion's first chaplain, Jim Cosner, and Ed Davis who served with Delta Company as a rifleman. They were trying to remember the outline of Gator's perimeter and where everything was positioned inside the base camp.

Landing Zone (LZ) Gator can best be described as a hollowed-out bowl inside a low-lying hill. It was just a big patch of dirt, an unremarkable chunk of Mother Earth. It may not seem very important to most; but to the infantrymen who lived there it was all important, for some nearly sacred. Because that's what infantrymen do, they occupy and move across dirt.

I added my recollections of where things were located inside the LZ perimeter, vividly remembering and pointing out the location of my unit, Charlie Company. Since I had revisited that hill in early 1997, I was also able to fill them in on what "Gator" looked like so many years after the war ended. Then out of my mouth came something unexpected. "You know, I think I'm going to write a book about the history of the battalion in Vietnam."

Our small group at the table reminisced about our tours of duty with the battalion and the many memories that would never leave us. I told the group that I was honored to have served in the battalion as a rifle platoon leader and I felt the history of our efforts, the struggles and sacrifices, the laughter and sorrow, deserved to be told. As we concluded and departed for lunch, Ed Davis placed his hand on mine and stared into my eyes with the intensity of a laser and said, "Dave, tell them our story." And in that instant I knew I would.

"Tell them our story." Those words stuck with me for many years and they triggered in me a resolve to make my planned historical account more personal. When I returned home from the reunion, I hit the ground running and set about trying to create a cohesive story, replete with eye witness commentary about our collective war as a battalion.

To that end I located and interviewed, directly or indirectly, many battalion vets and read reports, periodicals and pertinent books. The culmination of it all is this book, a detailed history of the 5th/46th Infantry Battalion's combat experience in the Vietnam War and some of the personal stories of the soldiers who fought in this war.

As an author, this endeavor required me to relive my own personal experiences when serving with the battalion. As a soldier and a writer it has not been easy.

My key source documents were the Battalion S-2/S-3 Daily Staff Journal and "Officers Duty Log" (DA Form 1594). Each day during the war, the 5th/46th Infantry Battalion (and other battalions as well) recorded the day's incidents as they were radioed from the field by the unit. This could be from a squad, platoon or company, at the time the incident was occurring. "Incidents" included firefights, sniper fire, encounters of mine and booby-traps, logistical problems, combat air-assaults, etc. Everything called in was recorded in the Journal, including dates, times, locations, and brief summaries of what happened. Naturally these written entries could not convey the turmoil and sacrifice experienced by the soldiers making these reports. The soldiers were often under enemy fire as they radioed for fire support to crush the enemy or called for dustoffs to remove our dead and wounded.

The soldiers recording these incidents in the Daily Journals were junior officers and sergeants who had, for the most part, experienced similar incidents themselves and were now serving their time in the "Rear" while finishing their tours of duty. These events were recorded on paper at the battalions Tactical Operations Center (TOC) at LZ Gator and later, at LZ Beach when the battalion relocated to Chu Lai in late March 1970. At times they were also recorded at "Forward TOC's" in the field, such as LZ Bowman or the Ky Tra Outpost west of Chu Lai.

A typical day of journal entry review involved the reading of thirteen to thirty pages, depending on the level of enemy contact. My task as a writer was to read every journal page for the three years the battalion served in Vietnam. It necessitated reading over 23,000 pages of documentation and trying to place things in perspective while trying not to be overcome by the events unfolding before my eyes in the terse descriptions written on each page.

The battalion's documentation allowed me to position units and their locations on the maps I had custom made for the book. Most of the soldiers who served did not know where they were when an incident occurred. Instead, they were focused on their task, to cross a field, move down a trail or enter a hamlet. Their location on a map was not important. What lay ahead of them was most important, possibly booby-trapped hedgerow or an ambush beyond the bend of a trail. Life and death hung in the balance.

It is not possible to cover every soldier's story or capture all the personalities, successes and failures that comprised our battalion's collective "march" into history. It is also not possible to cover in detail every personal sacrifice that was made, especially by those who gave the ultimate sacrifice. But I made it an objective to mention the death of each soldier who died while serving with the 5th/46th Infantry Battalion. Some soldiers received more explanations of the circumstances surrounding their deaths than others. For these others, I simply could not locate comrades who were at their side when they fell.

Consequently some accounts of our fallen may seem brief, perhaps matter-of-fact or clinical. But this does not belie the true feelings I experienced writing about each one of them. In many cases my sources of information were limited. For some of our fallen comrades whose fatal wounds were so severe I saw no need to elaborate. Yet, in some cases readers may believe I was too graphic. I believe it is important that the hell of war be understood by non-veterans who read this book, and so I have written what I have written.

There are many topics often discussed when one talks or writes about the Vietnam War. These include the nature of the enemy, the terrain, personalities of leadership, examples of bravery and cowardice, sex, drugs, racial tensions, etc. I have covered all of these as they pertained to the 5th/46th Infantry Battalion in what I believe is a balanced manner.

Veterans of the battalion who read this book may not always agree with my description of events. In my seven years of interviewing those who served in the battalion, I found that impressions of what happened in certain incidents occasionally differed among the participants. The old axiom, "I only knew the war as it looked from my foxhole", rings quite true. I have attempted to be as accurate as possible and my descriptions for the most part reflect the consensus of these recollections. In other actions, where I only had one witness to an event, if his description corroborated what was recorded in the battalions journals and met my requirement of what was realistic based on war experience, it was included.

Along these lines I wish to point out something that some battalion vets may not accept but which is absolutely true. In a number of operations where the battalion operated deep in the mountains, vets insisted they had crossed the border and were operating inside Laos. This is simply not true. The Battalion's Daily Staff Journals are very specific about operational locations, locations of fire support bases, the ranges of the artillery from those bases to support the soldiers on the ground, etc. I tracked it all from the large laminated field maps taped to my home office wall. The battalion was never in Laos; it simply did not happen. Nor, I might add, would the Americal Division have attempted anything so politically suicidal as by sending soldiers into Laos by their own decision.

In veteran-authored books on the Vietnam War, various words have become standard in lexicons about Vietnam, but have been spelled differently. For example, the word "Hooch" has been often used when describing a dwelling in a hamlet, but has been spelled variously as Hootch, Hooches, etc. For my purposes I decided to use the word Hooch in the singular and Hooch's in the plural. Similarly the word "ville" was used by soldiers to describe a cluster of hooch's. Most often these clusters of hooch's were actually a sub-hamlet that was searched by the soldiers while on patrol. The true sense of the word - "ville" connotes a village, a larger demographic grouping of hamlets, sub-hamlets and people. But for the grunts that entered a sub-hamlet, that was their "ville" and so be it.

The issue of referencing locations is complicated. Vietnamese and American names for specific Vietnamese administrative divisions of populations did not always match, particularly at the sub-hamlet level. In the larger scheme South Vietnamese administrative divisions started at the Province level. The province of Quang Ngai, headquartered in Quang Ngai City, was the primary area of operation for the battalion.

Within each Province were districts with a district administration, such as the town of Binh Son which served as the administrative center for the geographic district in its area. Within the district were various villages, one of the most famous being Son My, because it was within this village's territory the My Lai massacre took place. Son My was composed of four hamlets: (1) Tu Cung, (2) My Khe (also known as Truong Dinh), (3) My Lai and (4) Co Lay. Within each hamlet were sub-hamlets, all geographically separated apart from each other, and it is at this level the average soldier is most familiar. The My

Lai hamlet was composed of six sub-hamlets, My Lai (1) thru My Lai (6). My Lai (4) was the location of the infamous massacre. My Lai (1), once a large population center, was known as "Pinkville" because the maps issued to U.S. forces identified this populous sub-hamlet in pink. Various commentaries about the My Lai massacre use the title "Pinkville" as though it and My Lai (4) were one in the same. They were not.

One more comment about hamlets. In this book I have made numerous references to sub-hamlets, either the hamlet itself or a location nearby, such as "one-half mile southeast of Liem Quang (1)". I do this to be as precise as possible so the reader understands the location of the incident being described. The reader may tire of so many precise location references, but I wanted the battalion's veterans to know where their missions or incidents occurred. These locations are taken directly from the Daily Journal reports. To further help the reader understand distances, I have not used the distance description of kilometers (one thousand meters) which was used in Vietnam. I decided readers will gain a better appreciation for distances with the more common expressions of "miles" or "yards".

One more comment on words and descriptions. Each book about Vietnam may vary somewhat on the use and spelling of the common lexicon of that war. For example, the enemy is alternatively spelled as Viet Cong or Vietcong. I have chosen the later. Grunts often referred to the enemy as "Gooks", "Slopes" or "Dinks". Unless quoting a soldier directly, I have stayed with the terms, "enemy", NVA (North Vietnamese Army), VC or Vietcong.

At times I also use the word "insurgent" as an oblique reference to the quandary Vietnamese peasants experienced. They faced the challenge of intense pressure from the enemy to support them with food, shelter and labor, while at the same time they faced American firepower and Vietnamese Army interrogations if they supported the enemy. Given a choice, many peasants wanted to be simply left alone in their ancestral sub-hamlet.

Yet one must be careful here. The large coastal peninsula from Chu Lai to Quang Ngai City was an area where Communist loyalties remained strong because of the French Indochina War experience. Then too, the populace's loyalty to its ancestral home was also very intense. These conflicting loyalties contributed to the difficult challenge the 5th/45th Infantry Battalion faced conducting combat operations in their area.

Mention of the large coastal peninsula discussed above requires an important caveat. On many occasions soldiers of the 5th/46th and other battalions who served there referred to this large plain as the "Batangan Peninsula". Even General Norman Schwarzkopf made a reference to the large peninsula as "The Batangan" in a TV documentary. However, this large coastal area was NOT officially the Batangan. The Batangan Peninsula was the small promontory northeast of Pinkville that extended into the South China Sea. On some terrain maps it is labeled as the Binh Duc Cape. Marine CAP 142 was established on the northern half of the Batangan and CAP 143 on the southern half. The western edge of the Batangan is identified by an imaginary demarcation line starting with the Chau Binh hamlets in the north and ending with Pinkville in the south.

I make note of this important distinction so the reader will not be confused by my descriptions of terrain and my labeling of the Batangan Peninsula on many of the maps in the book. I spent an afternoon interviewing the former Major Ken Mink, who was the battalion's operations officer during Operation Russell Beach (the Marines titled their portion as "Operation Bold Mariner"), in January and February 1969. Operation Russell Beach / Bold Mariner was the largest combined amphibious / ground operation in the Vietnam War. Mink was emphatic that the Batangan was the small peninsula on the cape which the operation was to cordon and squeeze, and not the coastal peninsula from Chu Lai to Quang Ngai. This was also the understanding of Brigadier General Howard Cooksey who had overall control of the operation as well as LTC Ron Richardson, commander of the 5th/46th, the controlling ground battalion for the operation.

Whether subsequent discussions of ground operations by other units in the area broadened the interpretation of the "Batangan" is probably immaterial at this point. I simply wish to point out to the reader my frame of reference.

There are many people who have helped me with this book and to all I am profoundly grateful. Most important are the battalion's veterans who have volunteered detailed information about ground operations and by so doing, opened old memories and old wounds, things deeply buried for so many years, in order to give me the descriptions I needed. I know many suffered sleepless nights afterward, trying to put the old memories back into the box. I am very grateful for their contribution.

Larry Swank saved me two years of effort putting this book together. He is one of the principals in a database management company in Maryland who arranged for two University of Maryland students to copy the remaining year and one-half of Daily Journals I needed from the National Archives. He had this data printed and filed by month, ready to be used, with backup disks. Larry was an artillery officer forward observer with the 1st/6th Infantry Battalion in our brigade, and was awarded a Silver Star for Valor. He is a patriot and an American hero. I can't thank him enough.

One of my goals was to mention each and every soldier who was killed in the battalion. Dick Arnold of the Coffelt Database, known as The Virtual Wall® (www.virtualwall.org), was very helpful in cross referencing my list of the battalions killed in action and found some errors. I believe I now have every man killed accounted for. If I missed someone the error is mine and mine alone.

A number of people have encouraged me throughout the process to continue writing despite the personal pain it caused me and others. Bob Chappell of Bravo Company was an early supporter of the book and connected me with his comrades to start the process of interviews and information gathering. Bob commanded Bravo after the original commander was severely wounded. Based on my research of his service in Vietnam I believe he deserved to be awarded two medals for valor; but was not. His men respected him in Vietnam and still do today. Had he not encouraged his men to open up to me, I may have become discouraged early in the process and not continued with the book. Thank you Bob.

Lieutenant Colonel David Lyon (Colonel-Retired) was the battalion's first commander and granted me personal interview time and access to his documents. This was very helpful to me in the launching of my research and gave me the impetus to see this through. Thank you Colonel Lyon. Likewise my first oral history interview was with Ken McCarley at his home. After an hour of discussion, I noted my tape recorder had not recorded the conversation. Ken smiled and said, "Let's do it again." In many other interviews I never made that mistake again. Thank you, Ken, for your help, understanding and encouragement.

Robert Wight of Delta Company had difficulty concentrating on his college studies after Vietnam and took time off in 1970 to write his memories of Vietnam. He did so when these memories were very fresh and authored a 257-page typewritten unpublished memoir which he graciously provided to me. His observations, particularly about the challenges of Accelerated Pacification, were invaluable. Robert is an excellent writer, and has proofed my work whenever asked. I am exceptionally grateful to him for his assistance and hope he will choose to, someday, publish his memoirs.

Unfortunately, because of the length of time required to write the book, some of the vets who assisted me have passed on to their final roll call before publication. California native Leo Pillow of Delta Company, a man small in stature but with a giant heart called me every few weeks to check on my progress and offer me more information or provide other vets for me to contact. He did not live to see the finished book.

Major Ken Mink (Retired Lieutenant Colonel), the battalions Operations Officer (S-3) in the later part of 1968 and early 1969, possessed an intimate knowledge of the battalion's operations and operational area. I spent several hours in his Gettysburg, Pennsylvania home soaking up his descriptions of operations as seen at the battalion command level. Unfortunately, a year later he died, much too young for a man who devoted his adult life to the service of his country.

Doug Herier, who served with the 1st/14th Field Artillery Battalion, graciously accepted me into his southern Ohio home for an afternoon as we talked about artillery operations in support of Operation Russell Beach. He too has passed on.

In addition to Leo Pillow and Bob Chappell, there are a number of other vets who have been very helpful in providing me with the names and contact points of battalion vets to interview regarding the battalion's operations. Every battalion vet mentioned in the bibliography has been most helpful but some standout for their ability to connect me with many others: Tom Brissey, Bob Chappell, Lee Gunton, David Hammond, Richard Totten, Robert Wolf and William Tunnell (son of one of Echo recon's original soldiers).

I believe every writer needs someone or something as a "Gut-check" to keep him on a path towards completion and to be honest in his assessment of what he feels and wants to express. Several of the aforementioned individuals have helped in that role; but I want to single out two other vets as well. Ken Teglia, a Forward Observer for Charlie Company has proofed portions of my book and has been an excellent "sounding board" on how to place the experiences of war on paper. He is finishing his own memoir of war which will be published soon. His memoir concerns a unique teaching assignment he was selected to present to incoming Americal Division soldiers. It is interspersed throughout with accounts of his experiences in the field with Charlie Company in early 1970.

Likewise there is Robert Romaniello, a Vietnam veteran in my hometown of Medina, Ohio who served in the Army and was stationed at Marble Mountain near Danang. Robert is completing his own memoirs of his time in Vietnam and it will be published shortly. Our home town is a typical small Midwest town with a town square, gazebo, and a laidback atmosphere. One block off the square is an Irish pub called "Sully's" where Robert and I would meet for lunch and discuss our books, our Vietnam experiences, and the craft of writing. I have enjoyed those lunches immensely. Both Ken and Robert are excellent writers. I have been enriched by their friendship and their forthcoming books will be great additions to the Vietnam War dialogue.

Thanks as well to Terry Shoptaugh, Corinne Edgerton, Kirstin Bohm, Katie Hamness and Jody Bendel for help in preparing the book for publication.

Last but not least I want to thank my wife Susan for enduring the many, many hours I spent off alone in my home office working on "The Book". As a New Jersey native I was sent to Walson Army Hospital at Fort Dix, New Jersey after being shot up in Vietnam. Sue was an Army Nurse taking the Operating Room Course at Fort Dix when we met in October 1969, and we fell in love. We were engaged in January 1970 and married the following July.

We had an Army saying back in the 60's, "If the Army wants you to have a wife they'll issue you one." Well, that's just what the Army did and 2011 marks forty-one years of our married "Duty Assignment". I don't know what she saw in that young First Lieutenant whose left side was marked with an eight-inch scar from an AK-47 round and whose lower right leg was disfigured by another AK-47 round that smashed the tibia and fibula, but I'm glad she "took me in." It's been a good tour of duty for the past forty-one years. Thank you.

And so, the book that follows is the culmination of many years of personal effort and the cooperation and support of many. Writing this detailed history did not come easy. My desire and hope is that this book will supplement the personal memories of the soldiers who fought under the 5th/46th Battalion's credo as "The Professionals". Let it also serve to forever keep alive the memory of their courage, struggles, and sacrifices.

PREFACE

Late in the afternoon on June 2, 1969 I was called to the Tactical Operations Center (TOC) on Landing Zone (LZ) Gator for a mission briefing. The next morning three platoons from our company (Charlie) plus two platoons from another company, each platoon reinforced with combat engineers, would air-assault to the Tra Bong Road approximately six miles south of LZ Gator. The mission was simple. Each platoon was assigned a section on the Tra Bong Road, from the district town of Binh Son by Highway One, and west for sixteen miles to the Tra Bong Special Forces camp at the foot of the Annamite Mountains. We were to clear the road of mines and enemy forces, to enable an engineer unit, which had improved the Special Forces camp defenses, to depart the camp and move back to Highway One.

The Tra Bong Road was also known as the "Cinnamon Road" because in French colonial times there was a cinnamon plantation in the mountains and the dirt road, when dry enough, would allow the cinnamon to be transported to the coast and exported back to Europe. My platoon, the second platoon of Charlie Company, was tasked to land halfway between Binh Son and Tra Bong and move east to link up with another platoon moving west from Binh Son. Each platoon element had a portable mine detector to facilitate road clearing.

Premonitions come in many forms. On that morning of June 3 I decided not to eat breakfast in the mess hall at LZ Gator before being picked up by the Huey helicopters for our one day mission. Usually I ate a hearty breakfast because I did not eat in the daytime Vietnamese heat. But on this day, something told me not to eat breakfast and I did not. Little did I know that in five hours I would be on an operating table at a division hospital in Chu Lai. Surgeons don't like to operate on people who have a lot of food in their stomach. It is not optimal.

We lifted off in the early light and my platoon with attached engineers landed at our sector along the Tra Bong Road. We immediately pushed east but the movement was slowed because the engineers were discovering mines which had to be destroyed in place. Moreover, the desire to not miss anything kept our movement at a snails pace.

After an hour we started receiving sniper fire from a tree line, just one-quarter mile south of our location. Everyone went to ground. I stood up and slowly walked to the front of my column, figuring the sniper would have to be one lucky son-of-a-bitch to hit me at that distance. I received no fire and everyone rose up and continued to move. This happened several times and, with the slow and deliberate effort of mine sweeping, my platoon was falling behind its scheduled link-up. My Company Commander, Captain Dan Porter, flew over in a Huey and the bird's door gunners helped by firing their M-60 machineguns into the tree line. But the sniper fire persisted.

A short time later I received a call from a Light Observation Helicopter (LOH or sometimes pronounced as a "Loach") which was flying from the east, following the Tra Bong Road to our position. Behind it was a Cobra Gunship. The LOH pilot radioed "I understand you are having some problems?" I radioed an emphatic "roger that" and asked him to check the wood line south of my position. As he turned south over the dry rice paddy he radioed, "Oh, there's one … an NVA in uniform! He just went down a hole. I'll mark his position with a smoke grenade." The smoke soon billowed up only two hundred yards from our position. I was stunned. The small scrub brush in the dry paddy was enough to provide some concealment for a number of enemy soldiers.

The LOH reached the tree line and I watched it circle overhead. He radioed "I see NVA uniforms on a clothes line. I'm going in for another look." My stomach tightened, this was not good. An instant later I heard a large explosion and saw the LOH plummet into a rising cloud of dark smoke. The Cobra gunship watched his comrade crash and immediately poured 40mm cannon fire into the foliage around the downed bird. The pilot was also on my radio frequency shouting, "Bird is down! Bird is down!" My heart sank. I had directed that observation helicopter into the enemy's nest and now he was shot down. There definitely were more than snipers nearby.

Just then the battalion commander, Lieutenant Colonel Wagner landed on the dirt road with Captain Porter and ordered: "Lieutenant, I want you to take a team on my bird to protect that crew until I can get reinforcements here." My eyes shifted to my company commander, whose face had an expression of anger and sorrow. Thirty-one years later at a reunion with Porter I would learn why. Porter had argued with Wagner not to send me in because, "Once you've sent him in you've lost all control." Porter argued to wait for the armored personnel carriers coming from the east. They were with the road-clearing element from Binh Son. I could have placed my platoon on the tracks and gone in by land. Wagner overruled Porter. I had my orders and I followed them.

My eyes quickly scanned my platoon and I yelled as I selected my troops to get on the commanders Command and Control (C&C) helicopter. I needed an M-60 machinegun for firepower; "Italiano, Sandman, on the bird!" Harry Italiano was one of my machine gunners and Mitchell Sandman his assistant gunner. As Italiano passed me he gave me an anguished look, a look that told me "you are choosing me to die." I also called for Sergeant Michael Scherf, a squad leader and an excellent soldier. If I got hit, he could take over.

I turned to my radio telephone operator (RTO), PFC Robert Zimmerman, and said, "Let's go!" Zimmerman was new to my platoon and Charlie Company. He was a scientist, just a dissertation short of a PhD in Chemistry when he was drafted into the Army. When he was assigned to me I asked him, "Which professor did you piss off?" This was Zimmerman's first time in the field and I thought I would try him as an RTO on this "simple" one-day mission. In five minutes he would be fighting for his life. As we started towards the helicopter another squad leader, Sergeant Randy Backovich, ran up to me, "Do you need some more help?" Puzzled that anyone would volunteer when surely the enemy would be waiting for us, I replied, "Yeah, get on the bird!" It was a decision that would save my life.

We ran for the helicopter and in seconds we were airborne and heading for the wood line. The Cobra Gunship continued to blast the area around the downed LOH as more Cobras were racing to the scene. I yelled to my team, "When we hit the ground get under some cover and cover me. I'll search the area!" I didn't want everyone moving around, offering too many targets. The optimum plan was to jump from the bird while it hovered, help get the downed pilot and his crew chief on board, and get out. The lone Cobra followed us as our bird descended to the crash site.

Our Huey approached the downed LOH and the pilot observed a small ditch nearby. He elected to drop us above the ditch so we could rapidly seek some cover. This was a decision that kept us all from being annihilated. I was the first out, jumping from the right side, and running to the downed LOH. The Cobra behind us opened up with his mini-guns, spewing out 40mm grenade fire, the rounds exploded all around me as I ran, but I was just outside their killing range.

Backovich, Scherf and Zimmerman followed me out the right door and jumped into the ditch. Italiano and Sandman jumped out the left side and were cut down by enemy fire. They never made the ditch.

Their bodies were pummeled with automatic weapons fire. The bullets tore into their flesh and bones with such ferocity that they severed some limbs. The battalion commander's pilot was shot in the leg as he hovered. Worried that his bird would be shot down on top of those in the ditch, he ordered his co-pilot to pull pitch and get out. We were on our own.

I reached the two bodies closest to the downed LOH which had landed on its side. Both men had exited the bird and moved a short distance from it before they were cut down. They were badly burned from the explosion. Their bodies were riddled with bullets. I turned to go back to the ditch when I saw another soldier lying ten feet away. How could this be? An LOH or "Loach" was a small helicopter, not much more than a bubble of Plexiglas, with usually one pilot and a crew chief sitting up front, with little room behind their seats for another passenger.

I moved quickly to the other passenger. He was a tall and stocky-built soldier with blond hair, lying face down. The mid-section of his uniform was bloodstained, and I saw a wound across his neck. It was obvious the enemy had been using him for target practice until our helicopter landed to offer up fresher targets. I thought he was dead and turned to leave when I saw his hand slowly make a fist, release itself and make a fist again. He was signaling me he was alive but too weak or too afraid to move.

Unknown to me because I was preoccupied with the grave situation before me, the rest of the team in the ditch was under heavy fire. Sergeant Backovich eyed the machinegun which lay in the open next to the bodies of Italiano and Sandman. He needed that gun for more firepower and leapt from the ditch to retrieve it. As he bounded the short distance to grab the gun, an NVA soldier moved out of the nearby brush with the same objective. Backovich was faster on the draw and cut him down with his M-16, grabbed the machine gun with a full belt of ammo, and bounded back to the ditch.

About then a burst of AK-47 fire whizzed past my head, coming from bushes twenty feet in front of me. Still crouching, I fired my M-16 into the bushes, emptying the magazine of its eighteen rounds. I quickly reached to my side to get a new magazine but suddenly I was knocked to the ground by a giant sledgehammer in the form of an AK-47 round that tore through my left side, slicing it open, and leaving an eight-inch long gash. I reached for my rifle which had spun out of my hands. I was now flat on the ground, and forced a new magazine into my weapon. Instinct told me I was outgunned and too vulnerable in the open. I could not possibly drag the wounded soldier to the ditch; he was too heavy and the effort would slow me down. I would surely be killed.

    I decided to return to the ditch which would hopefully take the enemy fire off of the wounded soldier and place it on us until we could get help. Running and zigzagging the thirty feet or so to the ditch, I fired behind me as I yelled to Scherf and Backovich, "Cover me!" With bullets whizzing past me I reached the edge of the ditch. In my mind I cursed the enemy and laughed, "Ha you bastards, I made it!" Just then another AK-47 round tore through my lower right leg, entering one side and exiting the other, smashing my tibia and fibula. I tumbled into the ditch, landing face up with my leg bones sticking out of the skin, the muscle and flesh throbbing uncontrollably from the trauma to the leg. My lower right leg had turned to jelly.

    Scherf was closest to me in the ditch. On his other side crouched Backovich and then Zimmerman at the far end. I yelled to the RTO to radio our hopeless situation, even though Backovich had already done so. It seemed hopeless to me because I could not fire my weapon. Firing my weapon gave me courage, and without my ability to do so, I had nothing. Fighter/bomber aircraft were flying overhead, ready to drop five hundred-pound bombs and the Forward Air Controller asked Backovich on the radio, "Where do you want it?" Backovich's reply was short, "Everywhere, they're all around us. Just drop it"

    Scherf crawled to me in the ditch. I was in intense pain and going into shock if not there already. I asked him to take a bootlace out of one boot and tie my two lower legs together to stabilize my right leg which was now useless. It helped ease the pain that ran through my body with every twitch of the splattered bones. He looked at me to assure me everything was going to be OK, that he would get us out of this mess. But his head was tilted little too far up, slightly over the lip of the ditch, and he caught an AK-47 round in his right cheek. He placed his hand on his head, as though he had a headache, slowly lowered his head to my feet, and died.

    Shortly thereafter, the three Armored Personnel Carriers (APC's or "tracks") that Captain Porter had opted for us to use, came crashing through the brush. With five hundred-pound bombs being dropped and the roar of approaching APC's, the enemy started to melt away. I learned the next day that our division headquarters had detected radio intercepts from the geographic grid in which we were located (6/10ths of a mile by 6/10ths) that were the signature of an NVA Regimental Headquarters radio. At this time in the war the enemy did not mass its forces in one location; American fire power was too great. But the NVA headquarters had been near, and we never received that intelligence report for the road clearing mission.

The soldiers from the tracks were in no mood to stay long. They were still receiving harassing fire. They wanted to load the living and get out quickly. I refused to move unless the dead were included. I was in too much pain to be lifted out of the ditch by hand. Two soldiers brought out a folding stretcher, lifted my body into it and wrapped the sides around me to stabilize my body. All of us, dead and wounded were placed inside one track with the back ramp left open. The bodies from my platoon and the LOH were stacked on the ramp to provide us cover from snipers. On the short ride back to the Tra Bong Road I told Backovich I was putting him in for a medal. He replied, "I'll trade it for a couple days back at Gator!"

When we reached the road a Medevac helicopter was waiting. The dead were placed on the floor and I was placed on a rack inside the bird with the unidentified soldier from the Loach. That soldier, still alive but in intense pain, was placed under me on the floor. The medic on board looked solemnly at the lifeless bodies, hoping one of them would move. I told him with tears in my eyes, "They're all dead" he looked back at me, "I know."

That afternoon after surgery I was visited by my company commander and first sergeant. The next morning the battalion commander made a visit with the battalion surgeon. He told me "I stayed up all night wondering if I had made the right decision." Unaware of the "discussion" he had with my company commander, I told him, "Sir, if I were shot down I'd surely want someone to come in and get me quickly." He thanked me for that. But I wish he would have taken option two and waited for the tracks. I could have remained in Vietnam with my men instead of leaving after only four and a half months of duty. It haunts me to this day.

I did not write home that I was wounded until I was at an intermediate hospital at Camp Zama, Japan. I had signed a release not to notify my parents of any wounds unless they were life threatening. A Chaplain convinced me to write home. I felt I was coming home too early, I had failed.

In late June 1969, when I lay in Walson Army Hospital at Fort Dix, New Jersey, having been transported from Camp Zama, Japan, I questioned if I had ever served in Vietnam. Yes, I had been shot in the left side and then the lower right leg, but was it all real?

The sweet smell of freshly cut grass wafted into my hospital room at Fort Dix and the melodic lyrics of the song "Love (Can Make You Happy)" from someone's radio filled the air. I was at peace in that hospital room. Vietnam seemed somewhere on the dark side of the moon. I thought of the statue of "Atlas Shrugged" and how the weight of that world had been taken off of my shoulders, albeit at a price. There were no more sleepless nights waiting to be hit in small perimeters, no unyielding heat, and no anticipation of what lay ahead as my platoon patrolled our assigned terrain. And, in that hospital room, there were no more mines.

It was twenty-eight years later, April 1997, when my plane glided into Hanoi, The Socialist Republic of Vietnam's runway, and I used my window seat to take in as much as I could. I was returning to a land that, since being flown out in early June 1969, had seemed like only a mirage. As I debarked from the plane in Hanoi I saw security officials and wondered what my reception would be. How much hassle would there be with luggage inspection? We had, after all, bombed this city and its surrounding area for many years, and unexploded bombs were still being discovered in fields around the capital city.

As I approached the customs official my mind froze. His face. There he was. I remembered seeing him before. There was a Newsweek article in the mid-1960's with a cover story and photo titled, "The Face of the Enemy". The picture showed a Vietcong being pulled from a tunnel, his shock of thick black hair caked with mud. His eyes were black and stern as he was pulled from the tunnel by a South Vietnamese soldier, ready to give his captive whatever fate he deemed appropriate. The enemy soldier was not cowed. The customs official in front of me, asking for my passport, was the same man; his shock of black hair, stern eyes and confidence unnerved me. But he never gave me a look, just stamped my passport and waved me through. No luggage was inspected. I was free to grab a cab and find my hotel.

The next day I flew the short hop to Danang and was picked up by my guide and deposited at the "Modern Hotel" (Tan Tien) by the Han River. From there I took day trips to the usual tourist sites, Hue, Hai Van Pass, Marble Mountain, Hoi An, Tu Duc Tombs and sites in Danang.

During time not reserved for formal tours, I walked around Danang, sometimes riding in a cyclo, a small carriage peddled by an enterprising Vietnamese. Once I even took the cyclo tour late at night, observing what the city's residents did at night. At no time did I feel threatened. It would not have been the same in many large stateside cities.

Two blocks from my hotel was a large Catholic Cathedral, white and pristine, built by the French back in 1926. The grounds of the cathedral contained a parochial school, offices, and a large grotto made in the image of Lourdes, France, where the blessed Mother Mary appeared. I walked there in the late afternoon of each day of my stay in Danang and prayed the Rosary, then went to daily Mass. The Mass was sung in its entirety except for the homily (sermon). It was not crowded, I was the only westerner, and my presence was noticed, but not dwelled upon.

And then my last day in Danang arrived. I became increasingly nervous because the next day my driver was to take me down Highway One to Chu Lai. I had my map from the war and I wanted to stop at Landing Zone (LZ) Gator which I thought should be easily recognizable from the road. Beyond that we would be heading down the coastal road to visit Quy Nhon and Nha Trang, after which I would fly to Saigon. Gator troubled me. Questions raced through my mind. Could I handle walking on that sacred soil again? What would it look like? What feelings would it arouse in me? What about the hamlets just north of Gator, Tri Binh (5) and Tri Binh (1)? One was controlled by the enemy and the other controlled by the government. Were they still there? Could I approach them? How would I be received?

My anxiety urged me on to the cathedral earlier than usual. This time, I decided, I would pray the Rosary inside the church and meditate until Mass. As I approached the cathedral's doors, a lone figure standing in the doorway intently watched my approach. He was a young man, perhaps in his thirties. He directed me to follow him. I pointed to the Rosary in my hand and motioned I wanted to go inside the church. He gently swiveled his head side to side in the universal sign for "no" and gestured with his hand to follow him. I followed, not knowing why.

We entered a building adjacent to the church, and I followed him down some halls, passing from one section of the building to another, moving deeper into the structure in what reminded me of the catacombs of Rome. Finally we entered an office and across that room sat a grey haired, elderly Vietnamese priest. His black shirt and white "collar" clung tightly to his body; perhaps the Bishop? My young escort spoke a few words to the priest who then slowly rose and approached me, my Rosary sitting limp in my hands. With kind eyes and a gentle touch he removed the Rosary from my palm and took it over to some holy water, blessed it and returned it to my still open hands. Then, to my surprise, he embraced me. At that moment a country that was once for me a killing ground, became a healing ground.

The next day I traveled south and by mid-morning stopped along the highway just past the Americal Division's former base camp at Chu Lai. My map and my mind clearly identified the hamlet of Tri Binh (5), west of the highway, across a quarter of a mile of open rice paddy. It was exactly as I remembered it from so long ago; tall palm trees, mud and thatched homes tightly knit together, a world unto itself.

And I remembered. We had just come back from a mission in the 1st/52nd Battalion's area of operation, working as a company-sized patrol because of a North Vietnamese Army Regimental threat in the area. I received my first Purple Heart on that mission after my grenadier stepped on an anti-personnel mine sending small bits of shrapnel into my temple, neck and ear. A quick dustoff to the hospital to remove the shrapnel - that is, what they could find at the time - and it was back to the field. After returning to LZ Gator the company commander told me not to get too comfortable. I had to walk my platoon off Gator the next morning, sweep through Tri Binh (1) at the northern edge of the firebase, then move on to Tri Binh (5) to remain a week as a show of force. The enemy had threatened to destroy the hamlet because it supported the South Vietnamese government.

Our week in Tri Binh (5) was idyllic. The villagers allowed me to take possession of a vacant stone building for my headquarters. This was where I needed to be because it was located on the western side of the hamlet, near thick trees and vegetation; I expected the enemy to focus its initial attack in this area. There was a courtyard of hard dirt in front of the building and we made a deal with a mama san, that each night she would take our C-rations, keep half of them for herself and use the other half to prepare a large bowl of steamed rice with herbs and spices for our evening meal. I can still taste those savory meals to this day.

A stream running though this hamlet completed this postcard setting. We set out ambushes at night along likely enemy avenues of approach. To supplement the hamlets defenses, villagers kept nightly watch from bamboo platforms, which overlooked the extensive rice fields supporting this ville. If approaching intruders were detected, small gongs would be tapped, an early warning system which would direct a squad of my soldiers to the area of concern.

One night while I walked the perimeter I sat on a platform next to an old man. I wanted him to know I cared for him and his fellow villagers. He offered me rice bread and tea and I offered him cigarettes. Even though we could not communicate, each of us understood our mutual role in the defense of this hamlet.

Now, twenty-eight years later I had journeyed from the other side of the world and the other side of my life and was approaching this hamlet again. At the side of the road where my driver parked the car, facing Tri Binh (5) in the distance, was, as luck would have it, a small Coke stand. I asked my driver to bargain with the owner of a motor scooter, to take me to the ville because it required moving over a narrow rice paddy dike which the car could not navigate. I was eager to go and the scooter owner could sense it. We settled on $3.00. Off I went. I motioned from the back of the scooter where I wanted to go. We maneuvered around the northern side of the hamlet to get to the western end and there it was before me, the stone building I had stayed in so long ago.

I was so filled with emotion I could not approach it. The memories hit my gut, they were too strong. Children moved back and forth, the villagers noticed my presence but did not stare. The memories flooded back as we drove through the hamlet for fifteen minutes, exiting on its southern side. Someone once wrote "You can never go home again." Well, for fifteen minutes on the back of a simple motor scooter, I had gone "home".

We continued in the car for a short distance and arrived in the small ville once known as "Nuoc Mau" between LZ Gator and Highway One. I had seen Gator's hilltop from Tri Binh (5) and my heart was pounding. Now we were in Nuoc Mau at the base of its hill. After parking the car my driver spoke briefly to one of the residents to clear the way for me to walk up the hill. We walked on a dirt road the short distance that led to my former base camp. About one-third of the eastern half of the base had been sheared off, robbed of all its soil, undoubtedly for road projects through the years. My driver motioned towards the hill at its base and said, "You go ... twenty minutes OK?"

I followed a dirt path on the southern edge of the base of the perimeter and followed it past small desolate gardens. Finally the path ascended and I soon found myself passing over what used to be the VIP helicopter pad. Some of the pad's asphalt was still visible though conquered by grass and weeds.

I moved across the top, anxious to see the bunkers once again, or what remained of them. My eyes scanned the area but there was nothing. Years of monsoon rains had transformed the earth. The fields of fire beyond the perimeter, from the military crest to the bottom of the hill were overgrown with trees and bushes. I had to look hard to find the indentations in the clay soil where bunkers once stood, the sure sign that an Infantry unit at war once held this land. The force of Gods hand – nature- had erased everything. Birds whistled a faint chirp, a soft breeze blew across my face, not enough to ease the scorching heat of the blistering sun, and small wild-flowers dotted the gently slopping perimeter that once held concertina wire and claymore mines.

But I found nothing. There was nothing to tell anyone that brave men once occupied this hill, defended Nuoc Mau below and, from our helicopter pad flew to distant locations to fight the enemy. And there was nothing to note that soldiers experiences on and off this hill shaped them for the rest of their lives. No markers to say, "OK, the United States Government lost the war but we gave it our best. Peace be with you." I sat down on the parched earth and understood for the first time in my life, the emptiness of war. I took out my Rosary and offered a Decade of Hail Mary's. For whom I prayed I don't know. Maybe for me, maybe for those who served here, for every soul who died here, or maybe for the peace that had now come to this hill and to this land.

When I returned home, my wife and I became empty nesters. The children had moved out to proceed with their lives. My business career was coming to an end. Retirement would mean having the chance to do other things with my life. Being with other vets prompted a desire, unhindered by the chore of raising a family, to think about those I served with. After my return trip to Vietnam more questions nagged my mind. What happened to my men after I was wounded and sent to Japan? What other missions did they have to endure? Did the battalion acquit itself well in the war? Where else did it go? What did they experience? How did it all end? What happened in the battalion before I arrived?

When I joined the battalion in late February 1969 at LZ Gator, the men of the battalion appeared tired and reserved. The battalion had just concluded an operation known as "Russell Beach". The area they had "pacified" was known as the "Batangan Peninsula". The name was spoken in hushed tones. No one wanted to return there, yet we were all destined to go back.

Two years after my return trip to Vietnam I made the decision to write a book about the battalions Vietnam War history and its sacrifice's in Vietnam. Like our return missions to the Batangan Peninsula, you the reader will not have an easy time going back. But you who choose to read this book are destined to do so.

*"However, take care and be earnestly on your guard not to forget the
things which your own eyes have seen,
nor let them slip from your memory as long as you live,
but teach them to your children and to your children's children"*

Deuteronomy 4:9

1 – GENESIS

In the beginning, there were the Marines. Commencing in June 1965 Major General Lewis Walt, Commander of the III Marine Amphibious Force (III MAF), was accountable for the I Corps tactical area of responsibility (TAOR) in The Republic of South Vietnam. Walt pursued an "enclave strategy" that called for securing his coastal bases along the South China Sea by combining both pacification and military efforts. The military efforts would be offensive operations within a fifty mile radius of his coastal bases. From his perspective, pacification was preferred as a first priority to stabilize the densely populated rice bowl area south of Danang. As Walt noted, "With one hundred thousand people within 82mm mortar range (Communist mortars) of Danang, I had to be in the pacification business."

His overall goal was to secure the entire I Corps coastal plain, which lay between his two largest enclaves, Danang in the northern sector, where the Marines first arrived in Vietnam in March 1965 and Chu Lai in the southern sector, which became an operational base three months after their arrival.

The establishment of Chu Lai as a coastal base was made on the recommendation of Marine Lieutenant General Victor Krulak, the Commander of Fleet Marine Force, Pacific. He saw the sandy coastal area as an ideal location for a short airfield for fighter/bomber aircraft to provide tactical air support. The name "Chu Lai" was not Vietnamese. Krulak was given that name as a young Marine officer stationed in China prior to World War II. The Chinese characters that approximated the Chinese pronunciation of his name, when spoken in Vietnamese, were "Chulai", which meant "little man." Krulak was small in stature, five feet, five inches tall, but was a Marine Corps legend. His Naval Academy classmates had dubbed him "Brute."

General Walt's strategy in the I Corps area consisted of a three-pronged approach: Search and destroy operations for main-force enemy units, counter-guerilla operations, and pacification, with an emphasis on pacification. An integral part of his pacification program was the establishment of the "Combined Action Program", which at its core were Combined Action Platoons" (CAP's), a squad of Marines assigned to a Vietnamese Popular Forces (PF) platoon who were local militia trained to protect their local hamlets. In General Walt's thinking, a major Communist military unit (Vietcong (VC) Main Force or North Vietnamese (NVA) unit), would only be engaged when a "clear opportunity" existed to attack that unit on terms favorable to the Marines. Walt's initial plan was to secure the entire coastal plain of I Corps by the end of 1966.

Walt had the Third Marine Division and the 1st Marine Aircraft Wing (MAW) as his major subordinate commands. However, by August 1965 he also commanded the 1st Marine Division in Chu Lai. That same month Walt was presented his "clear opportunity" to engage the Communists in an area eight miles southeast of Chu Lai on a small coastal peninsula called the Van Tuong Peninsula.

In early August 1965 General Walt's intelligence group began receiving reports that the 1st Vietcong (VC) Regiment was moving into the Chu Lai area. The 1st Regiment was "born" in late 1962 in the Communist's Military Region V, an area encompassing Quang Nam and Quang Ngai Provinces, including the region around Chu Lai. The enemy regiment consisted of three main force battalions of veteran soldiers. Many of their commanders were also experienced from fighting against the French in the early 1950's.

More intelligence flowed into Walt's headquarters and by mid-August intercepts of enemy radio communications placed the 1st VC Regiment near the village and hamlet areas of Van Tuong. The hamlets of Van Tuong village included the Van Tuong's, the Nam Yen's, An Thoi's and An Cuong's.

The radio intercepts were supplemented by more intelligence provided by a defector of the 1st Regiment who was captured by Army of Vietnam (ARVN) soldiers. The defector was a seventeen-year-old private by the name of Vo Thao. Thao also confirmed the 1st Regiment was massing southeast of the headwaters of the Tra Bong River in the

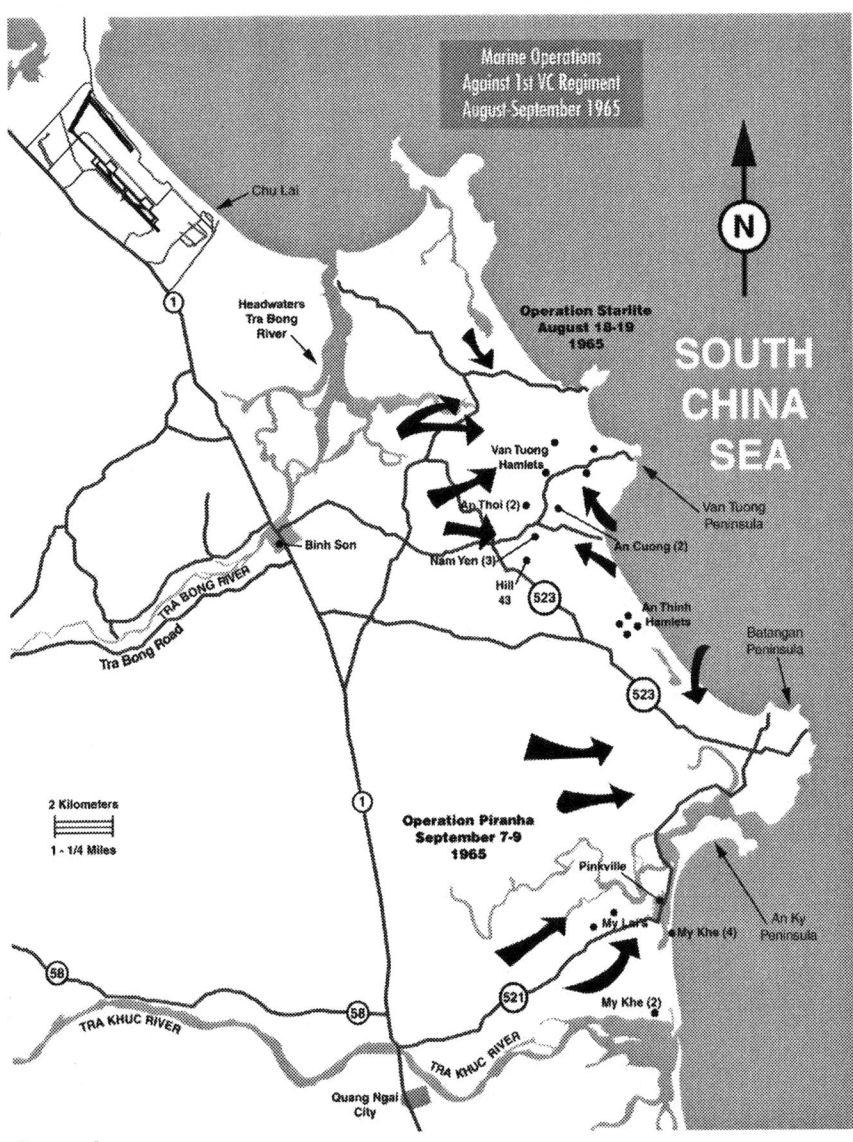

Genesis

Van Tuong hamlets in preparation for a major assault on the Marine base at Chu Lai.

Thao's background hinted of the many dilemmas of the Vietnam War. He had many relatives on both sides of the fight. One uncle fought as a Vietcong while two other uncles worked for the ARVN and/or the Americans. His step-father was an ARVN Sergeant. Thao wanted to return home on leave to see his family but his VC Commander refused. He falsified his leave papers to get away and defected.

Thus from Thao's report and other intelligence, "Operation Starlite" was launched and fought viciously on August 18-19, 1965. Starlite was the first major battle of the Vietnam War. The Vietcong chose to stay and fight, underestimating the heavy air, ground, and sea power of the Marines. The enemy suffered heavy losses. The Marines killed six hundred and fourteen VC by body count, took nine prisoners, detained forty-two VC suspects, and captured one hundred and nine assorted weapons. They virtually destroyed the 60th VC Battalion and badly mauled the 80th Battalion, the two main-stay battalions of the 1st VC Regiment, at a cost of forty-five Marines killed and two hundred and three wounded.

Three weeks later intelligence reports indicated the remainder of the 1st VC Regiment had moved eight miles farther south to another peninsula, the "Batangan", to regroup and recover. The Marines set out to destroy the remainder of the 1st VC Regiment in "Operation Piranha", fought during September 5-9, 1965. Piranha did not achieve the same results for the Marines as Starlite, but the operation destroyed a number of caches, tunnel complexes and a small enemy hospital. Along with the South Vietnamese soldiers who supported them, the allied forces also killed one hundred and seventy-eight VC and captured or detained three hundred and sixty VC or suspected VC. Friendly casualties were relatively light, two Marines and five South Vietnamese killed, fourteen Marines and thirty-three South Vietnamese wounded

Later, it was learned that a portion of the 1st VC Regiment had not participated in either the Starlite or Piranha battles, and was positioned west of Chu Lai. It would provide the basis for recovery and replenishing the regiment's empty ranks. The VC learned a key lesson from Starlite that limited their losses in Piranha. They would never again mass their forces near coastal areas where they could be squeezed against the sea by land forces and then pounded by naval gunfire, air strikes and artillery.

Because of Starlite and Piranha the Local Force (LF) 48th Vietcong Battalion, which assumed control of the area from the 1st VC Regiment, also changed its tactics. The 48th Battalion operated mostly in squad and platoon-size units of six to thirty soldiers, who lived in the large coastal plain from Chu Lai to Quang Ngai City. They only massed their forces when attacking preplanned targets and rapidly dispersed their forces when they were attacked. Their primary defensive "firepower" was to come in the form of mines and booby-traps.

General Walt's initial plan for his III MAF was to secure the entire I Corps coastal plain by the end of 1966. But progress toward this goal was hindered by circumstances that would shape the conduct of the Vietnam War for years to come. First came the major political unrest throughout South Vietnam in the spring of 1966. The chaos that resulted brought the pacification effort to a complete halt. Second, despite fierce fighting by the Marines and the resulting setbacks for the VC and NVA, the Communist command in Hanoi continued to absorb their losses and channeled more arms and soldiers down a steadily improved and growing "Ho Chi Minh Trail". The "trail" was an intricate network of jungle roads and trails from North Vietnam through the country of Laos and into the I Corps area.

From September 1965 to March 1966, the dry season provided optimal conditions for North Vietnamese laborers along the trail to add sixty miles a month of new "roadway". In February 1966 North Vietnams Regiment 18B crossed into South Vietnam, with the 24th Regiment not far behind them. In all, fifteen more enemy regiments with smaller support units would enter the south in 1966.

Secretary of Defense Robert McNamara, the "Whiz Kid" from Ford Motor Company, had an answer for this growing problem of troop infiltration. His was not a tactical but a technical solution: The construction of a physical barrier across the Demilitarized Zone (DMZ), which would separate North and South Vietnam, from the South China Sea west into Laos, where much of the trail network had been constructed. McNamara's "brain trust" had conceived of the idea in 1965 and it became known in planning circles as "The McNamara Line". It was a technical solution by "the best and the brightest" that on the surface also provided a political solution. The "Line" would curb the rapid escalation of American manpower to Vietnam. But the military chain of command rejected the concept as militarily impractical and a violation of the 1962 Geneva accords. Highlighting the impracticality of the

McNamara Line was the estimate of a two to four year construction time-frame, requiring two hundred and seventy-one battalion months of engineering work, two hundred and six thousand tons of construction materials, and the commitment of a significant number of troops to defend it.

Even though the idea was scrubbed, work did begin in April 1967 on an anti-infiltration system, or "electric fence". It was designed to counter enemy infiltration and provide early warning of any possible direct NVA invasion. It was partially completed and somewhat successful where it did exist. The project, however, was terminated because of the continued buildup of US forces along the DMZ. This build-up took away the manpower that was needed to construct and protect McNamara's "fence".

In October 1966, with no other solution in mind to counter the growing threat of an NVA invasion, the Marines were forced to shift more of their limited forces north towards the DMZ. This task fell to the Third Marine Division, which shifted its headquarters from DaNang to Phu Bai, near the ancient city of Hue. This move left the First Marine Division with the responsibility for all of the remainder of I Corps south of Thua Thien Province. Clearly the Marines were stretched thin. The Communist's chief strategist, General Vo Nguyen Giap looked at the Marine's predicament and gleefully observed, "The Marines are being stretched as taut as a bowstring".

The first Army combat units were introduced in October 1966 into the I Corps area under the overall operational control (OPCON) of the Marines, to help bolster the firepower of the Marines along the DMZ. This support included several batteries of 175mm and 105mm self-propelled howitzers. This added support proved to be of small comfort in thwarting the growing North Vietnamese threat. Intelligence indicated the enemy was shifting its forces to the I Corps area, with force strength increasing from twenty-three main force battalions in the summer of 1966 to fifty-two battalions by the end of the year.

The early months of 1967 saw continued and increased combat along the DMZ. In late February, General William Westmoreland, Commander of Military Advisory Command Vietnam (MACV), authorized the Marines to fire into and north of the DMZ, against military targets. This "bold" move by the Marines was answered by equally bold and heavy enemy artillery barrages against Marine bases near the DMZ.

Military intelligence indicated a major enemy offensive was in the works along the DMZ and Westmoreland instructed his MACV staff to plan for a task force of four Army Brigades (later reduced to three) for deployment into the I Corps area to bolster the Marine units. The NVA expedited this effort in April 1967 by launching several damaging attacks against Army of South Vietnam (ARVN) units near La Vang. The Marines also engaged elements of the 18th NVA regiment above Khe Sanh resulting in a week of fierce fighting. Westmoreland decided it was time to act. Army Major General William Rosson was assigned Command of a new I Corps Army Task Force designated "Task Force Oregon". Rosson began planning efforts in mid-February 1967, assembling a small group of officers and enlisted men to be the nucleus of a planning staff. Westmoreland supported this effort by sending specific instructions to all his major subordinate commands. Those units selected for Task Force Oregon would continue normal operations but be prepared to move immediately when the Task Force was officially a "go".

The initial brigades selected were the 1st Brigade, 101st Airborne Division, the 196th Light Infantry Brigade (separate) and the 3rd Brigade, 25th Infantry Division (later designated 3rd Brigade, 4th Infantry Division). Other adjustments were made to ensure the "Task Force" had all the capabilities of an infantry division.

The selected task force base of operations was the coastal enclave of Chu Lai, still being defended by the Marines. By early 1967 the Chu Lai base became one of five "Minor Support Bases" established in South Vietnam. "Major Support Bases" were Saigon, DaNang, and Cam Rahn Bay. As a "minor support base" Chu Lai was, nonetheless, quite large. The base offered twenty-six million square meters of cleared land, base housing for 1,595 officers and 10,337 enlisted, and 101,881 square feet of covered storage space with a fresh water capacity of 4,520 gallons/day. Base facilities included an airstrip to handle jet fighters; four ramps for Landing Ships - Tank (LST's); three ramps for Landing Ships -Utility (LSU's); a barge discharge pier; and a pipeline for off-shore discharge of petroleum, oils and lubricants.

Deployment of Task Force Oregon to the Southern I Corps area began on April 12, 1967 and became operational on April 20 under the OPCON of the III MAF. In carefully scheduled increments battalion combat teams were sent to the Chu Lai airfield. Heavier support loads went up the coast by LST. On April 26 the responsibility for the defense of the Chu Lai Base and the surrounding tactical area of responsibility

(TAOR), was passed from the Marines to General Rosson. The arrival of the Task Force in Chu Lai allowed the Marines to concentrate their forces farther north, where the enemy build-up was of growing concern.

Shortly after its arrival in Chu Lai the task force was eager to prove its operational mettle and swung into action. The 196th Brigade began operations near Chu Lai, in Quang Tin and Northern Quang Ngai Provinces, while the 3rd Brigade, 4th Infantry Division conducted search and destroy operations against NVA and main force Vietcong battalions in Southern Quang Ngai Province. In May 1967, the 1st Brigade, 101st Airborne Division arrived in Duc Pho, the southern boundary of Quang Ngai Province and began operations in the jungles and mountains to the west. These operations established an abundance of landing zones and firebases in areas that had been relatively untouched by ARVN forces.

Westmoreland's premonition about the deteriorating I Corps situation (backed by strong intelligence) proved to be on target. Not only were the Marines under increased pressure in the Northern I Corps area, but Task Force Oregon, operating in the Southern I Corps, soon had their hands full as well.

Ground combat in Vietnam intensified over the next few months and by the summer of 1967 additional Army forces were being readied for the ever-growing requirement for boots on the ground in Vietnam. In July 1966 the US Army's 11th Infantry Brigade – a unit that had not seen active service since World War I – was reactivated at Schofield Barracks, Hawaii. The brigade took advantage of its location and trained in the rugged and thickly vegetated terrain of the Koolau Mountains on the island of Oahu. It was one of the few Army units to have such training before deploying to Vietnam and adopted the moniker, "The Jungle Warriors".

By May 1967 the Pentagon announced another brigade was to be formed for Vietnam duty. Its origins stemmed from the cavalry reconnaissance troop of the 99th Infantry Division, which saw service in Europe in World War II. The 3rd platoon of that troop was redesignated as the Headquarters element for a newly formed 198th Light Infantry Brigade and was activated at Fort Hood, Texas. Its initial organizational strength came from the 3rd Brigade of the 1st Armored Division. At Fort Hood the brigade organizationally picked up the 1st/52nd Infantry Battalion, the 1st/46th Infantry Battalion and the 1st/6th Infantry battalion.

Soldiers, supplies, and training support for this new brigade came mostly from the 1st and 2nd Armored Divisions stationed at Fort Hood. The Army was stretched to the limits for infantry personnel and some soldiers who were trained in tank warfare at Fort Hood were redesignated as infantry. This, combined with the influx of draftees who had just finished their basic and Advanced Individual Training (AIT), made up the pool of deployable personnel for the brigade. Filling a new brigade was not made any easier with President Johnson's political strategy of requiring a very limited call-up of the Reserve and National Guard. Adding to problems was a limited pool of Vietnam-experienced NCO's and Officers. Many career soldiers had just finished tours, were already deployed in Vietnam, or were completing their active duty.

This manpower situation tested the mettle of the 198th Brigade's leadership. The 198th picked up one intact unit, H Troop of the 17th Cavalry, which was stationed at Fort Hood. The brigade's first commander, Colonel James R. Waldie, was another Fort Hood contribution, having commanded the 3rd Brigade, First Armored Division at Fort Hood. But unlike the 11th Brigade, the 198th trained for jungle fighting at Fort Hood with its wide plains and desert-like terrain.

Lieutenant Colonel Elbert (Bert) Fuller was assigned as S-3 (operations officer) for the brigade. Although forced to train on the open plains of Texas, Fuller made the best of what he had. He planned five infantry battalion field training exercises (FTX's) and two brigade-size exercises using the assets of an aviation battalion from Ft. Bliss, Texas. "Live fire" exercises, including tactical air and artillery support, provided the infantry units additional valuable training. Realizing Green Berets would be operating in its assigned area in Vietnam; the brigade also used its assigned engineer company to build a mock Special Forces camp on Cow House Creek at Ft. Hood where units practiced relief operations.

Two months after the brigade was formed, and while it was still training for Vietnam duty, Fuller took an advanced planning group in mid-July to Vietnam to make arrangements for its arrival. The brigade shipped from Fort Hood in mid-October 1967 and arrived in Danang, South Vietnam. From Danang the brigade moved by troop-ships to Chu Lai, arriving on October 22. Task Force Oregon had been transformed into The Americal Division.

The Americal Division was first formed in World War II in the Southwest Pacific, the only Army division to have a name, not a number. It fought with the US Marines throughout the war, beginning with the heavy fighting on Guadalcanal. With the newly formed Americal Division still organizing itself in Vietnam, no division-sponsored combat training center for in-country orientation had yet been established at Chu Lai. General Howard Johnson, Chief of Staff of the Army at the time, mandated a month of in-country training before a newly-deployed brigade was to be employed in full combat. Thus, in short order the 198th Brigade was transferred from their collection point at Chu Lai to LZ Carenten, an abandoned village near Duc Pho.

The 198th was assigned to the 3rd Brigade of the 4th Infantry Division, which was involved in on-going operations. The 198th trained with them in patrolling, communications, firebase organization and in other areas. The few career officers in the ranks of the 198th at that time were the "glue" that enabled it to get established in Vietnam. That asset would diminish over time with the constant turnover of officers.

The 198th Brigade returned to Chu Lai in November, ready for its permanent assignment. They didn't have far to go. Chu Lai sat on the eastern side of Highway One, the main north-south transportation artery in the country. On the western side sat a collection of low-lying hills, which had been occupied by the 196th Light Infantry Brigade. With the 198th now ready to go, the 196th was sent north to relocate at LZ Baldy, near the city of Tam Ky. This move allowed the 196th to relieve the 1st Brigade, 101st Airborne Division, which left I Corps in late November. When the 198th moved in to replace the 196th they did so quickly. Fuller, in recognition of the up-thrusting bayonet on the brigade's shoulder patch, named their base "LZ Bayonet", a name that remained until the division began its stand-down four years later.

In December 1967 the 11th Infantry Brigade deployed from Hawaii to join the Americal, and also trained in the Duc Pho area under the sponsorship of the 3rd Brigade, 4th Division. They assumed responsibility for the Duc Pho area in early January 1968, allowing the 3rd Brigade to return to the II Corps area.

One more battalion was to be added to the newly-formed Americal Division and take its place in the 198th Brigade. This was the 5th/46th Infantry Battalion which was activated at Fort Hood just as Colonel Waldie and his Brigade were getting ready to deploy to Vietnam. The 1st/46th Battalion that deployed with the 198th was to be sent to the 196th Brigade and the 5th/46th would replace it. The first assigned commander of the 5th/46th was Lieutenant Colonel David Lyon, a West Point graduate and expert in staffing procedures. He arrived at Fort

Hood a few days before the 198th's departure. His time with Colonel Waldie was brief and Waldie's guidance to him was succinct: "Train your battalion and I'll see you in Vietnam."

2 – REPORT FOR DUTY

David K. Lyon was drafted into the Army as a private in 1944. By 1948 he won an appointment to West Point and four years later was commissioned a second lieutenant, Infantry. Lyon was sent to the Korean conflict as an infantry platoon leader in 1953, and returned the following year as a company commander. Advanced schooling marked his next ten years of service (Graduate school - Purdue University; Professor of Electrical Engineering and Nuclear Physics – West Point; Amphibious Warfare School and the Army's Command & General Staff College), as well as an increasingly higher level of staff officer assignments.

By 1967 he was completing a three-year assignment at the Combat Developments Command but as yet, no assignment to the heavy fighting in Vietnam. Lyon had not been enthusiastic about Vietnamese Army advisory roles offered him but realized something had to be found soon or his chances for promotion to full Colonel would pass him by. The offer he waited for came in August 1967 from the Infantry Assignment Desk in Washington: "Would you be interested in training an infantry battalion for Vietnam?" Lyon eagerly said yes, and less than thirty-days later he brought his "Rush Orders" to Fort Hood, Texas with the specific assignment to "activate, organize, train and eventually deploy" the 5th/46th Infantry Battalion to Vietnam.

Lyon was informed his battalion would be assigned to the 198th Light Infantry Brigade, which had just completed its training for Vietnam and the brigade was earmarked to serve in the newly activated Americal (23rd) Infantry Division. When Lyon arrived at Fort Hood, his commander, Colonel James Waldie, with the rest of his 198th Brigade, was leaving for Vietnam. Lyon arrived at the building reserved for his battalion headquarters, in Fort Hood's 2nd Armored Division area, and found an empty building. The 2nd Armored Division was assigned as the "host command" to get his battalion ready for Vietnam. There were a few soldiers "assigned on paper" to the battalion, but none to be seen.

By the fall of 1967 many of the career infantry and artillery officers needed for the training of a new infantry battalion for the Vietnam War had already served or were deployed in combat. As the buildup for Vietnam reached its zenith, the reality for Lyon was not good. Qualified officers and equipment were now in scarce supply. At Fort Hood five armor branch officers, trained in tank warfare, were detailed to be infantry officers to help him fill his officer ranks.

As officers and noncommissioned officers (NCO's) processed into the battalion, Lyon took stock of what he had. In his view most of his officers were either gung-ho or at least willing to give it their best effort. A few were reluctant and it was apparent in their attitude towards training. A few of his sergeants, the Noncommissioned Officers (NCO's) who are the guts of any Army unit, were looking at a second Vietnam tour, but most had never been there. A few had seen combat duty during the Korean War. Lyon and his officers believed that most of the enlisted soldiers being assigned to the 5th/46th were more or less resigned to their circumstance and would do well under able leadership.

Captain Kenneth W. McCarley arrived as the battalion's first assigned Captain and was appointed as Alpha's Company Commander. McCarley was armor branch, not infantry, and served a tour in Germany where a drastic draw down of troop strength was in motion in order to support the Vietnam commitment. One-third of the soldiers in his Germany-based unit were sent to Vietnam, one-third detailed for training for Vietnam, and one-third remained to continue their Cold War mission in Europe.

McCarley looked forward to deploying to Vietnam with a trained unit, rather than going as a replacement officer. This gave him the opportunity to build cohesiveness and espirit-de-corps in his company. Ideally he wanted to be elsewhere to train his soldiers, such as the wooded terrain at Fort Benning, Georgia. The question on his mind and the minds of many of his men was, "why are we training on the open plains for jungle warfare?"

The battalion filled its ranks with soldiers reporting to Fort Hood during the growing anti-war movement in the country. Lyon and his company commanders did not view this as much of an issue. The soldier's general isolation from the civilian world during the time necessary for them to complete basic training and advanced individual training (AIT) had insulated them from the anti-war chorus.

Another early arrival to the 5th/46th was Captain Roger Dimsdale. Dimsdale, as a junior Captain, was assigned as the battalion staff S-2 (intelligence) officer. As an early arrival he didn't have much to do but observe the soldiers processing in. In his view they were every bit as good as any other unit he would serve with in the Army until retiring as a Colonel. He stated "some bright ones, some not so bright, all racial compositions – a cross section of America."

Because Lyon did not know any of the assigned officers, he went by seniority for assignments. Senior Captains were given company commands; the next in seniority became battalion staff officers. Most of the battalion's lieutenants were freshly minted from Fort Benning's Infantry Officer Candidate School (OCS). A few were prior service sergeants who saw the war as an opportunity for advancement in the Army and entered OCS when the college education requirements were relaxed. Nicknamed "Benning's School for Boys", Infantry OCS would serve as the primary source of platoon leaders for the 5th/46th in Vietnam.

Peacetime units in the Army had trained clerical staff to properly process soldiers in an orderly fashion. For the newly-formed 5th/46th Infantry Battalion, NCO's and officers rapidly processed in together as quick as the Army could find them, which caused the inevitable confusion. Soldiers, who had experienced an orderly transition from one training assignment to another, faced a disorganized 5th/46th battalion that was rapidly put into place and expected to go to war.

Roger Stanford was a medic at a Fort Hood Medical Battalion. In October 1967 he was awoken one night about midnight by the 2nd Armored Division Band, which was playing "Georgia Girl" as soldiers of the 1st/46th Infantry Battalion, part of the 198th Brigade, was loading on busses for their departure to Vietnam. Stanford thought, "Those poor bastards, they're going to Vietnam!" One week later he was assigned to the 5th/46th and preparing for the same fate. Stanford was the 13th soldier to sign into the battalion.

The day after Lieutenant Colonel Lyon signed in to take command he drove to Fort Worth, Texas to pick up his personal belongings. As he left Fort Hood's front gate he picked up a hitch-hiker, a young private taking a weekend leave. Both Lyon and the private were in civilian clothes. The private told Lyon, "I just got assigned to some outfit called the 5th/46th Battalion. Boy are they all screwed up. Nobody knows what is going on." A few days later Lyon returned and while in uniform he inspected some barracks. He saw his hitchhiker, and the private recognized him. The young private's mouth dropped as Lyon approached him. Lyon smiled, "Good to see you again".

Junior officers assigned to the battalion came from all types of assignments. Second Lieutenant Robert "Bob" Chappell was assigned to a mechanized infantry battalion at Fort Hood when the 5th/46th started its build-up. Chappell enjoyed riding armored personnel carriers but thought that flying helicopters would be more to his liking and applied for flight school. His battalion commander, a southerner, was one of a rare breed born and bred for Army life. He had served in the enlisted ranks during World War II with the First Infantry Division, achieving First Sergeant at the age of twenty-one, before receiving a battlefield commission. When Chappell's flight school application reached the WWII veterans desk, the second lieutenant was called in for a "chat". The battalion commander reminded Chappell he was wearing the crossed rifles of infantry on his collar and reminded him "Only fairies and Yankees fly helicopters!" Five days later he was assigned to the 5th/46th as the interim commander of Bravo Company. Chappell would command the company in Vietnam the following August.

Chappell surveyed the situation in Bravo Company as officers, NCO's and enlisted soldiers continued to arrive and fill his company's ranks. He thought to himself, "I'm in deep shit". He realized they were starting from scratch and wondered why he hadn't volunteered for Vietnam as a replacement, getting a platoon with an experienced platoon sergeant and squad leader's in-country. Bravo filled its ranks but had only one NCO with Vietnam experience. Chappell found him, "a drunk and drug-addicted loser." The battalion's young officers from Infantry OCS who had trained intensely for Vietnam at Fort Benning, were not comfortable with most of the Korean War NCO's they found in their midst. To the Vietnam-oriented lieutenants, dialogue and mindset were barriers when dealing with most of the Korean War sergeants. To Benning's "Boys", it was apparent most of the older sergeants were too conditioned to conventional war and too advanced in age for the rigors of jungle fighting. The younger offices did not see much of a "fit".

Captain James Lamb reported in and was assigned to command Bravo and Lieutenant Chappell was assigned as the company's executive officer. Lamb was the only company commander with any Vietnam experience but his experience had come as a Vietnamese Army and National Police advisor, not with a US Infantry unit. Lamb was viewed as not being a "hands on" leader and avoided field training duty with his men. His men began to lose confidence and respect for Lamb as a leader. This problem would only intensify in Vietnam.

Captain Al Chioffe arrived in early October and was assigned the command of Echo Company. The E Companies of infantry battalions are round-out companies, not organized as regular infantry companies but possessing special assets, including the battalions Reconnaissance (Recon) Platoon and the heavy 4.2 inch mortar platoon.

Chiofee was blessed with several good platoon leaders. His mortar platoon leader, Second Lieutenant Armando Ramirez was as good as they came and he not only trained his heavy (4.2-inch) mortar platoon to a high level of proficiency but assisted the line companies with the training of their 81-millimeter (81mm) mortars as well. Chiofee's recon platoon leader was Second Lieutenant (2LT) Charles Mrdjenovich, an "Army Brat" (father in the regular Army) who entered active duty while living at Fort Bragg, North Carolina. Chiofee found Mrdjenovich to be gung ho but also hard headed, not willing to accept suggestions regarding the training of his platoon.

In addition to the leadership issues Chiofee had with Mrdjenovich, he also had concerns about his platoon sergeant, a Korean War vet. Still haunted by his brutal experiences in Korea, the platoon sergeant was apprehensive that his traumatic experiences in Korea would be repeated in Vietnam. His apparent unwillingness or inability to pass on his experiences to Mrdjenovich, and the platoon leader's unwillingness to take advice, were potentially fatal weaknesses in a combat situation. Twenty-three days after arriving in Vietnam, Echo's recon platoon was virtually wiped out, and 2LT Charles Mrdjenovich would become the battalion's first officer killed in action (KIA).

Training plans were prepared, facilities readied and personnel assigned as the battalion's training began in late October 1967. Southern Texas experienced a very cold winter in late 1967 and early 1968, which made nights on the Texas plains miserable. A few days of moderate weather could rapidly change to freezing cold winds with the arrival of a cold front. To husband valuable training time, the companies bivouacked in the field during the week and returned to the main post area only on the weekends. Fort Hood's cold weather made it difficult mentally and physically to prepare for the rigors of a jungle environment. One soldier recalled his training, "Picture men who are suppose to be guarding a jungle-style perimeter huddled in connected shelter-halves, trying not to get frostbitten".

2LT Terry J. Care arrived in the battalion in mid-October. Another graduate of "Bennings School for Boys" he was typical of many OCS officers at the time. Not sure of which path to take in life, he placed his fate in the Army infantry and the distant challenge in Vietnam. He and thirteen of his OCS classmates were sent to the 5th/46th at Fort Hood. Asked where he wanted to be assigned he remembered an old Latin saying, "You're the safest in the middle". Thus he chose Charlie Company. His Commander, Captain Larry Johnson asked, "what platoon do you want?" he replied, "Second platoon".

Care's platoon had only twelve men. He quickly read their minds and in turn his men looked at him closely when he arrived at their barracks, thinking "So this is the guy who is taking us to Vietnam?" Care was equally apprehensive and thought, "These men are my own age and some older; if they only had an idea of the doubts in my mind." But Care and his men were drawn to their Company Commander from the very beginning. Tall (6'4") and lanky, Larry Johnson was a natural leader who exuded confidence. He appeared to his men as competent, knowledgeable, and very sure of himself. Care also had confidence in his battalion commander, LTC Lyon, and liked him immediately. "He was very much in charge, interested in all of us as a person with the understanding that we were not going to be friends, but that I was going to be one of his lieutenants."

Like many of his fellow junior officers, Care was not enamored with the training at Fort Hood, having received more Vietnam-oriented training in OCS. "There was a universal feeling the training we were getting was not preparing us for what we were going to do", he remembered. M-16's, the assigned weapon for duty in Vietnam were used only on the rifle ranges. M-14's were carried on field exercises with no blank ammo available. At times, this was reminiscent of the early training days of World War II when soldiers had to scream "bang-bang" on maneuvers until live rounds could be obtained.

Career Sergeants, "Lifers", were assigned to the battalion but many rotated out with physical profiles rendering them "unfit" for combat or with other "issues" that earned them a transfer. In Charlie Company's First Platoon, the soldiers went through four to five platoon sergeants who, once assigned, worked quickly on transferring out once they learned their destination was Vietnam. The platoon's morale was at rock bottom. Another platoon sergeant, a Staff Sergeant was seriously overweight. Morale plunged further. It was apparent to all he could get his men killed in Vietnam. At a time when soldiers were to prepare for war, there was almost open rebellion. The Staff Sergeant was assigned a squad in the platoon, but after a few weeks in the field in Vietnam, he was sent to another unit to avoid being killed by his own men. After he was transferred, he was killed during an enemy attack on a firebase.

Then the platoon was assigned Sergeant First Class Kenneth Stretch. Stretch assembled his platoon and talked about the difference between "lifers" and career soldiers, and that he was a career soldier. He demonstrated that immediately in his leadership and earned the respect of his men. He arguably became the best platoon sergeant in the battalion.

The battalion's reconnaissance platoon viewed Fort Hood as a "holding area", with little relevance to its mission in Vietnam. But Lyon did what he could for this special platoon that would be his "eyes and ears" in Vietnam. The platoon was sent to train at the 82nd Airborne Division Raider School at Fort Bragg, North Carolina from mid-November to mid-December 1967. Green Berets assisted in their training, teaching map and compass navigation, patrolling, and escape and evasion techniques. One Green Beret told the inexperienced soldiers about being overrun in Vietnam. He was seriously wounded and feigned death among the defenders bodies, while an enemy soldier sat on him to eat his meal.

The recon platoon returned to Fort Hood ready mentally, physically and tactically to face its challenge in Vietnam. But it was the impulsive and stubborn platoon leader who would bring chaos to his platoon shortly after arriving in Vietnam. One of the recon soldiers who received training at Fort Bragg was Private James Rudd, a young black soldier who quickly absorbed everything he was taught. He was the fastest runner on the physical fitness test at Fort Bragg, strong but reserved, not brash. One Green Beret, impressed by what he saw remarked, "This soldier is a super-nice kid. If anyone comes back alive from Nam it will be him." Rudd would die four months later because of a tragic decision made by his platoon leader, a decision that ignored the lessons learned at Fort Bragg.

Fort Hood's headquarters gave priority of its resources to the 5th/46th Infantry Battalion but the resources were subjected first to the priority of the Army's needs in Vietnam, making the best intentions of Fort Hoods commanders fall short in providing equipment to the battalion. The soldiers trained with what they had. Lieutenant Care saw in his men a profile that was mirrored throughout the battalion: "An education level of ten to twelve years, most nineteen to twenty-two years of age, a few college drop-outs, virtually all draftees. However, most were determined to do their job as best as possible and get out".

Private First Class Ron Van Avery was an exception. At the age of twenty-three he was older than most, and was married with four children. The six foot, three inch Oregon native was drafted into the Army while holding a steady job and encountered another Oregon draftee, Ron Cannon, at the Portland, Oregon Induction Center.

Cannon and Van Avery became close friends as they moved through each step of military training until their joint assignment with the 5th/46th Recon Platoon at Fort Hood. Dubbed "The Old Man" Van Avery served as big brother and father figure to many in the platoon. When Cannon received a "Dear John Letter" at Fort Hood from his girlfriend, Van Avery comforted him. "Hey, you're with us now, not her! And we're taking care of you and you're taking care of us!" Van Avery never stopped singing his favorite tune at Fort Hood, "Daddy's Home". The 1961 hit, sung by Shep and the Limelites, allowed him to think about what he wanted to do with his family when he finished his Army service.

One month after arriving in Vietnam, Van Avery gave the ultimate sacrifice for his country; Ron Cannon nearly lost his own life that same day. Thirty years later he reconnected with his best friend through the faces of Van Avery's children. Like Cannon, others who gathered in the battalion to train for war were unaware their destinies to fight in Vietnam would change them forever.

In early December 1967 word came to Lyon that President Lyndon Johnson would visit the battalion on December 12 to review the troops. The presidents visit was labeled as a "hush-hush/do not discuss" event for presidential security but the battalion practiced their "stand in review" for two mornings, including how to "break ranks" and "gather round" the Commander-In-Chief. Johnson was expected to call the men closer together after his review to talk to them about the importance of their mission in Vietnam. It was all heady stuff and the battalion's soldiers were appreciative. Rumor had it that the Commander-In-Chief would also have lunch with them as well.

The parade ground bleachers were filled with families of the soldiers and individuals from the larger Fort Hood community. The battalion arrived early that morning in starched fatigues and shined boots. There was a strong, cold wind that blew across the parade ground and the color guard struggled to hold their flags steady. The soldiers were mindful that Johnson's helicopter arrival would give the president his first view of the battalion while he was above them. The soldiers wanted to look their best. There was a sense of duty and honor that had entered their hearts. After an hour at attention the president had still not arrived and the soldiers were placed at parade rest. Medical personnel were to the rear of the formations to tend to some soldiers who passed out while standing too long in the cold.

Johnson finally arrived in an Army jeep with Lieutenant General G.R. Mather, the III Corps Commander and Commander of Fort Hood. The jeep pulled to the front of the battalion formation to pick up its commander, LTC Lyon, for the review. The Secret Service saw Lyon's 45-caliber pistol holstered on his side which made them wary, and they tried to stop him. Lyon, fed up with the long delay, stepped past them into the jeep. General Mather told the harried agents, "This is how it's done in the Army" and the jeep pulled away. The President of the United States passed in review of the last battalion of the newly formed Americal Division. Johnson's eyes looked somber, staring straight ahead, not a glance or acknowledgement to the soldiers he passed. The soldier's hearts sunk. 2LT Donald Wilson watched the jeep pass by and was shocked as he looked at Johnson's face. "It was ashen and quite wrinkled. He looked old beyond his years."

In seven to eight minutes it was over. Lyon stepped out of the jeep, and without a word, the president rode off. Lyon surveyed the faces of his battalion and knew his troops felt anger and betrayal. The president had just lost over nine hundred votes. Lee Gunton, a private in Charlie Company from Euclid, Ohio was more succinct: "A sorrier son of a bitch I have never known." Four days after the battalion arrived in Vietnam, on March 31, 1968, President Lyndon Baines Johnson told the nation he would not seek reelection.

The challenges to Lyon as he prepared his battalion for war were many. He faced the lack of ammunition for training, a compressed training schedule, a continuing rotation of personnel in and out of the battalion, a desert-like climate for jungle training, and minimal availability of helicopters for airmobile training. He had only two assets: First, the Commander of the 2nd Armored Division at Fort Hood, Major General Joseph A. McChristian, was fully committed to seeing the 5th/46th Infantry Battalion deploy at full strength. McChristian ultimately stripped his own units of personnel and equipment to ensure this happened. Second, Lyon had "can-do" company commanders and platoon leaders and enough competent NCO's to provide core leadership at the company level. To further enhance his readiness, he sent eight enlisted soldiers and eight lieutenants to the Army Ranger School at Ft. Benning, from mid-January to early March 1968.

By early December 1967 Lyon had ten more Lieutenants than required, but kept them for his company commanders to evaluate and to "pick the best of the bunch" for Vietnam. But as the battalion focused on preparing for war, it was not immune to the personnel issues experienced by Army units in the late 1960's.

Fort Hoods Criminal Investigation Division (CID) checked the barracks periodically, as they did throughout Fort Hood, for signs of marijuana. During a search they spotted a soldier dropping a small bag in a garbage can. This black soldier had boasted to everyone that H. Rap Brown, a leader in the "Black Power" movement of the 60's, was a personal friend of his. The CID analyzed the bag and found nothing more than ordinary grass seed. The word soon got out that "someone was going to get his ass kicked". Rap Browns "friend" had spent good money for nothing.

Other "confessions" came from soldiers harboring doubts about Vietnam combat. One soldier claimed an incestuous relationship with his mother. Lyons office received a call from another, claiming he was homosexual and was attracted to the hitchhiker picked up by Lyon. He added, "That company commander in Charlie Company doesn't look bad either."

A few others were badly influenced by family and civilian friends who were eager to see them avoid Vietnam duty. Charlie Company had such a soldier. From the day he joined the battalion he was sick and always hyperventilating. His wife called twice a day, everyday asking the company to get him help. Medical personnel never found anything wrong. He deployed with the battalion. After his first two months in Vietnam, Lyon reviewed an award recommendation from Captain

Johnson for this previously "chronically sick" soldier. Johnson noted, "The minute this kid was away from his wife he became a model soldier."

Training was rigorous but not totally relevant to Vietnam. Some of the training sergeants at Fort Hood had been to Vietnam and changed their class curriculums to reflect the realities of Vietnam. It was typical for a class taught by combat vets to begin with, "For training purposes, I'll tell you how the Army say's how to do it ... but then I'll tell you how it's done in Vietnam". The trainers could readily identify recalcitrant soldiers with poor attitudes and pulled them aside. "You'd better work with your buddies and pull your load because they will be the one's to come to your aid, not your momma!"

A major problem arose in early 1968 that sapped more time and energy from the battalion's effort to prepare its soldiers for war. It began in Captain Lambs Bravo Company, which received a sudden influx of personnel. It was as though manna was flowing from the Army Gods in heaven. 2LT Wesley Bradford reported to Lamb, "Sir, I have an interesting situation. I have four soldiers with Master's degrees and one CPA. Best that I can tell I am on the lowest rung of the ladder when it comes to a college education in the platoon." Lambs First Sergeant, Charles Cotton confirmed the findings, "You have a well educated company sir, in fact, for your two company clerks, one has a doctorate and the other a masters degree." It was soon determined the battalion had received an influx of one hundred and forty OCS applicants who had not been sent to Officer Candidate School due to cutbacks in the program or had been "boarded out" of OCS.

By the time Bravo Company discovered this problem, the OCS-denied soldiers had already written to their congressmen and a full investigation was under way. The soldiers' complaints were not with the 5th/46th but with the Army. Most had been lied to. Once it was determined their complaint was legitimate, one hundred and twenty-three opted for another unit assignment. The balance remained with the battalion. Their tours in Vietnam would be as enlisted soldiers, not junior officers. For those denied the OCS experience there was some expressed contempt for their supervisors, the junior NCO's who graduated from Fort Bennings Noncommissioned Officer Instruction Course (NCOIC), known as Noncommissioned Officer "Shake & Bakes". The NCOIC was the enlisted counterpart to the OCS program, with the goal of turning out a high number of junior leaders in a wartime environment.

Table of Organization
(Authorized Strength)

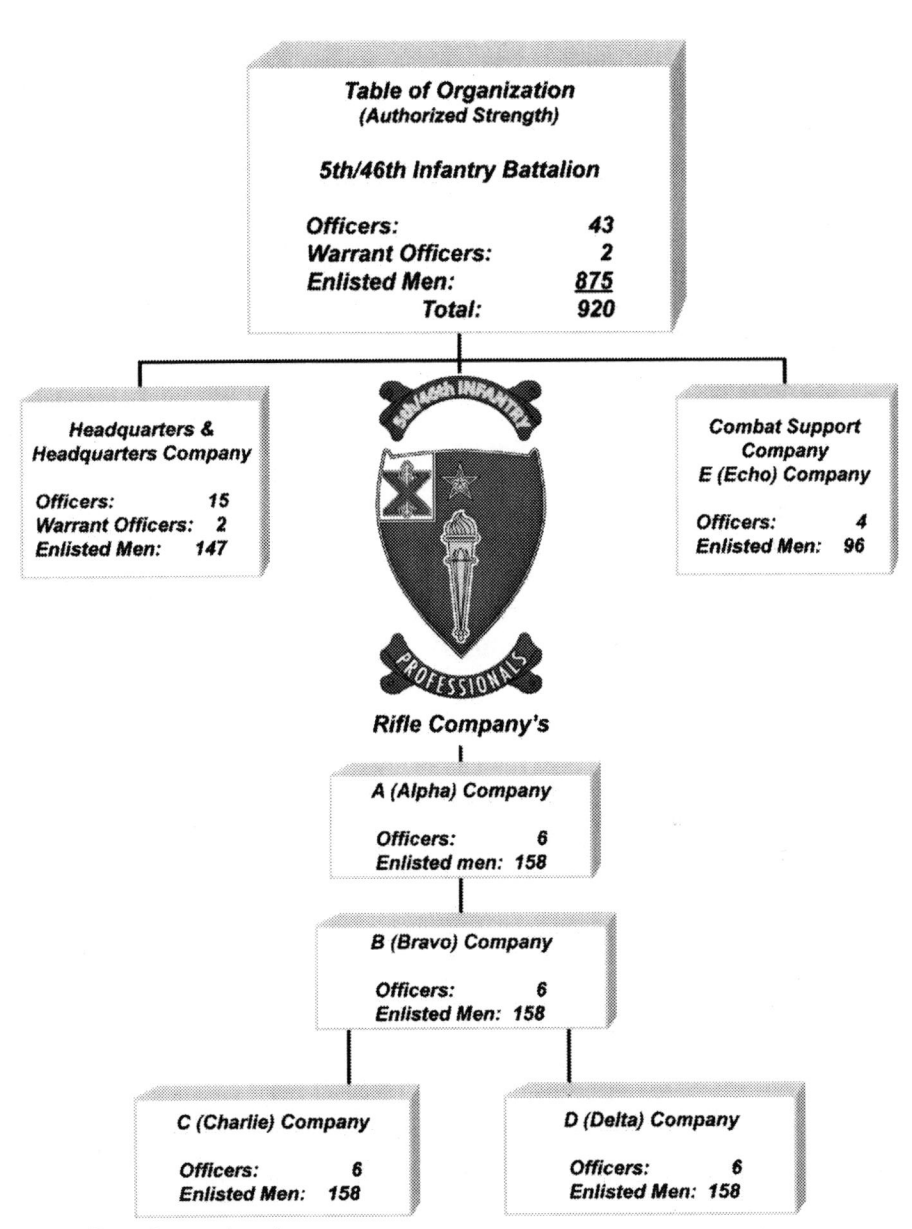

5th/46th Infantry Battalion

Officers:	43
Warrant Officers:	2
Enlisted Men:	<u>875</u>
Total:	920

Headquarters & Headquarters Company

Officers:	15
Warrant Officers:	2
Enlisted Men:	147

Combat Support Company
E (Echo) Company

Officers:	4
Enlisted Men:	96

Rifle Company's

A (Alpha) Company

Officers:	6
Enlisted men:	158

B (Bravo) Company

Officers:	6
Enlisted Men:	158

C (Charlie) Company

Officers:	6
Enlisted Men:	158

D (Delta) Company

Officers:	6
Enlisted Men:	158

Battalian Organization

One hundred and forty other soldiers eventually left the battalion before it deployed to Vietnam, yet the battalion departed for Vietnam at full strength. Some arrived just before the battalion shipped out from Fort Hood, their only preparation having been their Basic and Advanced Individual Training (AIT). For these soldiers, preparation for Vietnam would be "on-the-job-training". Bonding with their squads and platoons would have to be worked out in the combat zone.

While Lyon was dealt a good hand in junior leadership, he did not fare as well with his senior staff. His Executive Officer (XO) and Operations Officer (S-3), both at the assigned grade of Major, were Armor officers with little infantry experience. Some battalion officers viewed the XO as "willing but not bright". The S-3 was "not a self-starter without his wife's thumb on him." Their ineffectiveness was felt throughout the battalion, and other staff officers could sense the tension between Lyon and his two senior staff officers. Lyon excelled in staff management and took a more direct role in the XO and S-3 duties. The two majors resented it and shared a mutual dislike for their commander, finding comfort at the Officers Club bar for lunch each day, which, as one staff officer dryly noted, "Adversely affected their energy levels in the afternoon."

Lieutenant Colonel David Lyon's battalion in total was the hand he was given from the Army's deck of cards and he decided to make the best of the hand he was dealt. Lyon reasoned if he wished to improve his hand and throw away a card or two, the next ones dealt to him may not be any better. With training time at a premium, and his deployment to Vietnam rapidly approaching, Lyon moved forward, looking to improve his situation once he arrived in Vietnam.

Lyon's leadership style with his company commanders was "hands off". As a young Army Captain with his first company command, he had an overbearing battalion commander who tried to insert himself in all things. Lyon resented this intrusion and swore he would not do the same to his own company commanders. His commanders had a great amount of autonomy, which frustrated the battalion staff. This was reflected in the lack of effective communications between the staff and company commanders several times at Fort Hood and early in Vietnam.

The early training of the battalion, which was influenced at the company level (squad, platoon and company tactics), went as well as could be expected with the limitations of Fort Hood. Company commanders thrived on Lyon's style and freedom of action, with his only directive being "Get your company trained."

The attitude of the battalion's soldiers was mixed. Those boarded out from the OCS program felt they were better trained than their NCOIC squad leaders. Many of the enlisted soldiers had just completed their Basic and AIT training and accepted the training they received at Fort Hood as appropriate for Vietnam duty. Others had lingering doubts about the realism of their tactical training. Platoon leaders worked to build as cohesive units as possible. Some worked harder than others. Company level officers, captains and lieutenants, generally went "by the book" out of necessity.

The battalion's company-level officers and NCO's provided the basic expertise expected by the Army for its infantry soldiers. All companies successfully passed their squad, platoon, and company training tests. But when all the pieces had to come together, Lyon's senior staff officers, primarily due to the incompetence of the Executive Officer (XO) and Operations Officer (S-3), did not operate effectively as a battalion unit. The 5th/46th failed its first battalion-level training test and had to repeat it. The infantry companies and platoons were ready to give Vietnam their best effort, but, as one company commander noted, "collectively, there was chaos" in trying to work as a battalion, with poor coordination between the company commanders and the battalion's staff.

Captain McCarley commanding Alpha Company had taken advantage of his autonomy and tried to "Vietnamize" his training at Ft. Hood. Imbued with the many months of Vietnam doctrinal training at Benning's OCS, his company left the pup tents in the field and moved out with just ponchos. "Our objective" he recalled, "was not to be found by the 'enemy' if we could possibly do so."

After the 5th/46th failed its first battalion-level test, McCarley had seen enough. He had a long talk with Lyon about his concerns over the competence of the XO and S-3. Faced with an impending departure to Vietnam, Lyon was not willing to change anything at that late date. McCarley told him he wanted out of the command assignment. He would not follow the directions of the XO or S-3 who, in his opinion, might get his soldiers killed unnecessarily. He told Lyon, "I see a court martial in my future by refusing to obey the S-3. That wouldn't be good for me, you or the battalion".

Lyon relented and assigned Captain Herbert Erb, Assistant S-3, to take command of Alpha. Erb was one of the few in the battalion who served a tour in Vietnam. He was a junior Captain and had deployed to Vietnam with the First Air Cavalry Division in August 1965 as a lieutenant, serving with the division's pathfinder detachment, returning in August 1966.

In February and early March, 1968, the battalion made final preparations for its deployment. The battalion faced an Inspector General ("I.G.") review of its records and equipment. The battalion's executive officer discovered his motor pool officer had been negligent and replaced him with Second Lieutenant Don Wilson. Wilson found that "Most of the vehicle paperwork had not been maintained, including the receipt for new equipment. We ended up 'recreating' vehicle log books, reconstructing maintenance records, and quickly ordered parts for vehicle repairs which had not been made. Excess parts, particularly tire patches, proved valuable as barter in Vietnam. We barely finished before the final I.G. inspection".

With training almost completed, apprehensiveness among the soldiers grew as they had more time on their hands to ponder their future. With the battalion's departure drawing near, the leadership at Fort Hood remembered the turmoil caused when the 198th Brigade shipped out the previous October. At that time some in the brigade developed a "nothing to lose" attitude as it prepared to depart for war. The soldiers commenced a massive drinking binge. Military Police (MP's) intervened and fighting broke out in some units. Now, six months later as the 5th/46th Infantry Battalion prepared to depart, the soldiers observed a nearby unit practicing riot training. They were not aware of what had happened the previous October but sensed a message was being sent to them that everyone would depart peacefully.

As time grew short at Fort Hood, the natural anxiety of going to the war increased. PFC John Migacz from Colonia, New Jersey and two friends decided to "wash away" their anxiety at the Enlisted Club. Staggering back to their barracks one evening they were stopped by the Military Police (MP). The soldiers gave the MP's lots of lip and finished with Migacz peeing on the rear tire of the MP's squad car while his good friend, Terry DeMott, urinated on the front tire. Another friend, George Vander Dussen laughed so hard in his drunken stupor he fell down. They were certain they would all be placed in jail. After watching them relieve themselves one MP remarked, "Going to where you men are being sent is worse punishment than anything we could do" and they drove off. In less than two months Migacz would walk into a minefield and lose a leg. DeMott would go to his rescue risking his own life and carry him out. Vander Dussen would be killed two months later.

Captain McCarley, after relinquishing his command of Alpha Company became the battalion's S-4 (logistics & supply) officer and Movement Officer for its deployment to Vietnam. LTC David Lyon, commanding the 5th/46th Infantry, had prepared his battalion for war as best as he could under the circumstances of an Army stretched thin in late 1967-early 1968. For the officers and men of the 5th/46th it was now time to walk through the gates of destiny. In February 1968, as they completed packing for their departure, South Vietnam came under a country-wide attack with a massive Communist offensive during the Vietnamese New Year called "Tet". Anti-war protests in the USA began to reach a fever pitch. In the midst of it all, Lieutenant Colonel David Lyon turned to his new S-4 and gave his usual succinct direction, "Captain McCarley, move my battalion to Vietnam."

3 – LANDING ZONE GATOR

Seven miles southeast of the Americal Division headquarters at Chu Lai sat a low-lying hill on the western edge of Highway One. Highway One (known as QL1 on the maps and division operational orders), was the main highway of the Republic of South Vietnam, running north and south down the eastern coast of the country. The hill by Highway One was not high in elevation but held a commanding view of everything around it for miles. A soldier standing on its forward slopes could face east and admire the headwaters of the Tra Bong River two miles away, which opened up from the South China Sea at the southern edge of the massive base at Chu Lai.

The hilltop view also extended southeast over the flat coastal lowlands which enveloped the Tra Bong River's tributaries. Two major "headlands" dominated the coast, the Son Tra Promontory at the southern tip of the Chu Lai Bay by the South China Sea and the Batangan Peninsula twelve miles northeast of Quang Ngai City. These coastal lowlands east and immediately west of Highway One held the population centers and rice-growing areas in the region. Fertile rice paddies were nourished by silt from mountain runoff, a product of the eastern watershed of the Annamite Mountains to the west. Wooded sanctuaries, open fields of dry ground and numerous hedgerows of thick vegetation were interspersed among the acreage of fertile paddies.

A soldier looking west from the hilltop could also view the eastern slopes of the Annamite Mountains six miles away, officially known as the Chaine Annamtique (Annamese Range) with some peaks over eight thousand feet high. The mountain range was bounded on the west by the western watershed of these mountains and the Laotian border. The Chaine was home to primitive Montagnard tribesmen, elephants, tigers, clouded leopards and several types of venomous snakes, including the King Cobra. It was also the well-camouflaged lair of the enemy. North Vietnamese Army (NVA) soldiers prepared logistical depots, hospitals and barracks to support their aggression against the South Vietnamese. They and the Vietcong used a well-developed system of high-speed trails and swift rivers, primarily the Tra Bong River, to move people and supplies rapidly to and from the Piedmont and coastal population centers.

The eastern slopes of the Annamite Chaine extended to Highway One before the land transitioned to the coastal lowlands. This rolling terrain was known as the Piedmont. The Piedmont was marked by a series of low-lying hills one thousand feet or less in height which dominated the transition from the mountains to the sandy coast. In the Piedmont, small, scattered hamlets peppered the area. Hamlets increased dramatically in size and density as the land flowed east to the coastal lowlands.

The Piedmont, with its low-lying hills provided soldiers excellent observation points and areas on which to locate fire support bases. Hilltop-based artillery or mortar positions could cover enemy routes of access or egress into the coastal lowlands. Vegetation in the Piedmont varied from short grass to tall "elephant grass", to thick bushes and trees ten to fifteen feet tall. The lowlands east of Highway One were represented by a large coastal peninsula stretching north to south from Chu Lai to Quang Ngai City, a distance of eighteen miles.

This land east and west, north and south of the hilltop where the soldier would have to live and fight was a mixture of contrast and contradiction. While it was blessed with over one hundred inches of rain annually to water fertile fields of rice, desert-like cacti existed near the swamps or rice paddies. The temperatures on the coast or in the valleys of the Piedmont could soar to over one hundred degrees. Yet the hilltops in the Piedmont only a few thousand feet above sea level or the mountains in the Chaine, shrouded in clouds and rain and whipped by high winds, drove temperatures to bone-chilling lows. The cold and driving monsoon rains came abruptly, causing temperatures to plummet, but also switched just as quickly, back to searing heat. The rapid changes stressed soldier's bodies, leaving lean, muscular men wet and racked with pain, their skin rotting from fungus and water immersion, along with their ever present fatigue.

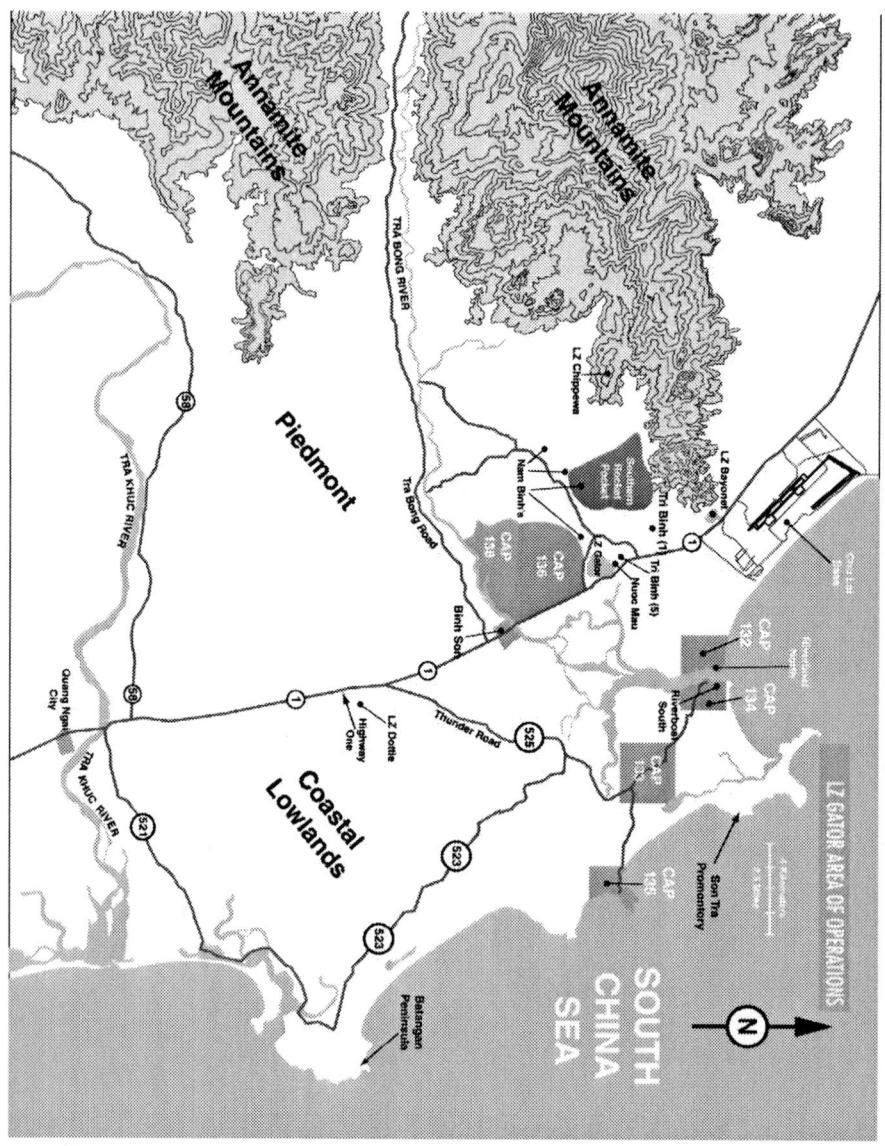

Landing Zone Gator

On the fertile ground surrounding the hilltop lived the people of the area. Their circumstances and loyalties were as varied as the country they lived in. Their villages, hamlets and sub-hamlets were of varying sizes and political loyalties, although they shared a common culture and a dedication to their ancestral homes and the lands within their immediate geographic area. Some of the area's inhabitants were fervently communist and supported the communist insurgents. Others favored the South Vietnamese Government which held nominal control of the land. These people were caught in a paradox that the soldiers assigned to the hilltop also faced. Differences in political allegiances were matched each day with a common desire to survive the harshness of their war-torn condition, feed and grow their families and worship their ancestors.

Hamlets were small, independent clusters of homes surrounded by rice paddies. Several sub-hamlets made up a hamlet. Each sub-hamlet was composed of a few thatched dwellings of clay, bamboo and grass, and was politically and culturally connected to other sub-hamlets in the vicinity. It was this grouping of several sub-hamlets that formed a hamlet and several hamlets formed a village political structure, which covered a larger geographic area. North of the hilltop by Highway One was the area of the Tri Binh hamlet, divided by sub-hamlets of which there were five, and west of the hilltop was the Nam Binh hamlet. The Nam Binh sub-hamlets numbered seven although not all were populated. Both the Nam Binh and Tri Binh hamlets made up the larger village area of Bing Thang.

When the 198th Infantry Brigade arrived in the Republic of South Vietnam late in 1967 it concentrated its operations against the enemy in Quang Ngai Province. First were the North Vietnamese Army (NVA) regulars from the People's Republic of Vietnam (North Vietnam). Then there were main force Vietcong units formed out of the South Vietnamese pro-Communist populace who were supported by Local Force (LF) Vietcong units. The LF units were communist sympathizers who were part-time soldiers and part-time farmers.

The NVA soldier was well-trained and equipped. His training emphasized camouflage techniques which often employed ant hills, grass, trees, brush, stumps and spider holes to conceal his presence. He was usually equipped with an AK-47, a Russian-made Automatic Assault Rifle, along with plenty of ammunition and hand grenades manufactured by the Chinese Communists. When the NVA Soldier arrived in the lowlands after walking down a network of mountain trails, he wore a Khaki uniform and carried a rucksack which contained such articles as another uniform, a hammock, a poncho, a sack of rice, a small entrenching tool and personal pictures of his family. In addition to his AK-47 ammunition he sometimes carried mortar rounds or helped to carry larger rockets for specially-trained rocket troops in his unit.

Main force Vietcong (VC) units were similar to their North Vietnamese allies. They were highly trained with the same equipment as the NVA. They were exceptionally trained in the use of crew-served weapons, such as mortars, and had an advantage over the NVA in that they were usually employed in the geographic areas where they came from. Their knowledge of the terrain was excellent. Local Force (LF) VC units were not as well equipped nor was it required. Their mission was to be the eyes and ears for the NVA and main force VC in their local areas. Their primary weapons were mines and booby-traps, which were used against enemy soldiers and their vehicles. The greatest effectiveness of LF VC was their intimate knowledge of the land which surrounded their hamlets. They knew every trail, every depression, and every bush. Supporting this collective enemy was a vast intelligence and supply network that was highly successful in 1967, spanning across the mountains, piedmont and coastal lowlands.

As early as 1961 weapons and supplies from North Vietnam, via the burgeoning Ho Chi Minh Trail supported insurgent forces in Quang Ngai Province. In the fall of 1962 North Vietnamese Colonel Vo Bam, an early architect of the trail had walked from North Vietnam to Quang Ngai Province in only twenty-six days. By late 1967 when the 198th Brigade arrived in Chu Lai, the trail was well-established and extended much farther south, through Laos into the central highlands of South Vietnam. The enemy threat that existed from Chu Lai to Quang Ngai City would be the primary responsibility of whatever American battalion occupied this low-lying hill by Highway One.

It was on this commanding hill by Highway One that the 1st/6th Infantry Battalion of the 198th Brigade was assigned to improve its position, after some South Korean Marines from the Second "Blue Dragon" Brigade departed. The battalion's primary area of operations was the south and southwest region of the Chu Lai base. The 1st/6th Infantry Battalion, "The Regulars" held a lineage that came from the Sixth Infantry Regiments' long service since the War of 1812, which included several Indian campaigns. The most notable was the Second

Seminole War, when the regiment bore the brunt of the fighting of Lake Okeechobee, Florida on December 25, 1837. Its regimental crest includes an alligator to commemorate that event. Sensing the parallel of being sequestered in a new type of "Indian-Country", the battalion designated its hill as Landing Zone (LZ) "Gator".

LZ Gator's hot and dusty high ground was bulldozed in its center to form a "punch bowl" to allow for interior roads and flat terraces to house the battalion's infantry company's and headquarters elements. The base was roughly one-eighth mile in width from east to west and approximately two hundred and fifty yards from north to south. An artillery battery was located on the eastern end and on the western end stood the battalion tactical operations center (TOC). The perimeter along the "military crest" of the hill (the forward slope of the high ground), contained a system of sandbagged positions overlooking pre-planned "fields of fire". Each field of fire interlocked with the fields of fire from adjacent positions. The terrain that formed these fields of fire was cleared of all vegetation to eliminate any cover or concealment for enemy movement.

Forward of the sandbagged positions were rolls of "concertina", thin metal coils with razor-like blades. Interspersed among the concertina were trip flares to detect nighttime enemy movement. And interspersed within the concertina were claymore mines, officially known as the "M-18A1 Claymore". Each Claymore weighed three and one-half pounds and carried an explosive charge of one and one-half pounds of C-4 plastic explosive. Embedded inside were seven hundred 1/8th-inch steel balls that, when detonated, would blast out to attackers, at a velocity of 3,995 feet per second. Its zone of death gave a high probability of killing an attacking enemy soldier within twenty feet.

Approximately two hundred yards from the base of the eastern side of LZ Gator sat Highway One and a small cluster of thatched and cement dwellings which were collectively called "Nuoc Mau" or "The Ville." The ville of Nuoc Mau grew with the American presence on Gator. A dirt road led from the south-side entrance of Gator's interior bowl, and skirted the southeast edge of the perimeter for one-eighth mile until reaching Nuoc Mau and Highway One. In short order after the 1st/6th arrived with a battalion of American soldiers, Nuoc Mau featured a laundry shop, a tailor and a well-staffed whorehouse.

Nuoc Mau offered something for everyone, including Local Force Vietcong posing as peasants, some of whom would eventually work inside the perimeter of Gator. To "win the hearts and minds" of the local population, American units were encouraged to provide work for Vietnamese civilians whenever possible. The required identification check did not stop the enemy from gaining employment with the Americans, and their access inside LZ Gator would provide excellent intelligence for nighttime attacks.

A short one-eighth mile north of LZ Gator, in the shadow of Gator's hilltop perimeter, sat the hamlet of Tri Binh (5). While the soldiers of LZ Gator were there to guarantee the security of the population around them, and thereby help win the battle for "hearts and minds", the hearts and minds of those living in Tri Binh (5) were firmly implanted in the communist revolution to reunite Vietnam. This hamlet served as a way station for small groups of Vietcong moving across Gator's northern boundary east and west from the Piedmont to the coast. The hamlet was an excellent source of intelligence for the Vietcong because it was a ringside seat for the watchful eyes of the hamlets residents, as it sat in the shadow of the American outpost.

A valley of open patches of ground sat two miles northwest of LZ Gator. The valley terrain was interrupted by hedgerows and tree formations interspersed by well-used trails. This area earned the titles of the "rocket pocket" or "rocket valley". The area was located about six miles southwest of the Americal Division headquarters at Chu Lai. The rocket pocket became the launch pad for Soviet 122mm rockets to be fired into Chu Lai. The simplicity of this weapon was readily evidenced by the effective but simple placement of the rockets in the vertex of crossed bamboo poles or on a mound of dirt. The dirt mound or bamboo poles were arranged to allow for the correct angle and direction of fire. From this valley the target was always the same, the Americal Division's massive headquarters complex in Chu Lai. Soldiers from Gator would patrol the trails and hedgerows of this area for years and the mission would always be the same: "Keep the rockets off the general's back".

The 1st/6th Infantry Battalion occupied LZ Gator for just a short time. By the end of March, 1968 the 5th/46th would take ownership of the hill, and it would serve as the battalion's most permanent "home" during its three years in the Vietnam War. During the twenty-four months the 5th/46th defended LZ Gator, the Vietcong would attack and penetrate its large perimeter numerous times, and the battalion would suffer casualties, including the loss of a battalion commander; Indian country, indeed.

In late 1967 and early 1968 the 1st/52nd and 1st/6th Infantry Battalions were assigned to Northern Quang Ngai Province as part of "Operation Muscatine". Muscatine was the phased relief of the Republic of Korea (ROK) 2nd Marine "Blue Dragon" Brigade which was tasked to deploy north to help the beleaguered US Marines in the Danang Tactical Area of Responsibility (TAOR). The 198th Brigade and the Army Republic of Vietnam (ARVN) 2nd Division began the relief effort in a phased sequence beginning December 20, 1967. On December 26 Muscatine began with Companies A and B of the 1st/52nd Battalion air assaulting on a large coastal plain due east of the district town of Binh Son.

The 1st/52nd fared well, killing thirty-one VC in a sweep of a coastal village on January 3, 1968. But in short order they received a rude awakening to the realities of fighting Local Force (LF) Vietcong in the treacherous coastal lowlands. On January 6, two squads, while pursuing Vietcong soldiers, walked into a minefield. It was not an enemy minefield but a mine field that had been set up by the Koreans, and no plans were left behind to identify its location to the newly arrived 198th Brigade soldiers. Six soldiers were killed in action (KIA) and nine were wounded in action (WIA). The next day, the soldiers killed six more VC, at a cost of one soldier KIA and nine WIA. But the following day seven more soldiers were wounded from mines.

In the slugging match that would ensue over the coming weeks, the newly arrived 1st/52nd proved their mettle in combat. On January 17, the battalions Alpha and Bravo Companies, in conjunction with a company of Army of the Republic of South Vietnam (ARVN) soldiers, accounted for eighty-three VC killed at a cost of five battalion soldiers wounded.

The 1st/6th launched its operations from LZ Gator in early 1968 to complement the 1st/52's control on the coastal lowlands east of Highway One. The 1st/6th focused its operations west and south of the highway. Its assigned area began north of Gator at the southern edge of the 198th Brigade headquarters at LZ Bayonet. Its southern boundary was four and one-half miles further south from LZ Gator at the Tra Bong River, which extended west into the mountains and east to the South China Sea. The 1st/6th also had to watch their western flank for any major attack from NVA regulars who could swiftly move out of the mountains. To accomplish their mission, the battalion worked off of two firebases, LZ Gator and LZ Chippewa. Chippewa sat on one of the

Piedmont's low laying hills six miles west of Gator along the eastern slopes of the Annamite Chaine.

After one month of "In-Country Training", the 198th Light Infantry Brigade was considered "trained" and in November 1967 the brigade headquarters moved into a large firebase formed out of high ground across Highway One opposite from the Division base at Chu Lai. The 196th Brigade had controlled this high ground and was moved further north to Landing Zone Baldy, north of Tam Ky City. The 1st/46th Infantry Battalion, which had trained with the 198th at Fort Hood, was released from the brigade and assigned to the 196th. This left the 1st/52nd and 1st/6th, along with H Troop of the 17th Cavalry as the primary combat elements of the 198th until the 5th/46th finished its training at Fort Hood and could join them in the spring of 1968.

The 1st/52nd Infantry Battalion worked in its assigned area of operations (AO) from the southern edge of the division's Chu Lai headquarters south to the Tra Bong River tributaries east of Highway One, and the other coastal lowlands moving east to the South China Sea. The battalion was also given the mission of establishing a waterway patrol base at the mouth of the Tra Bong River (south of Chu Lai) which was adjacent to a refugee-fishing village.

This base was divided into two sectors, designated "Riverboat South" (east of the headwaters) and "Riverboat North" (on the western side). Enemy "rules of engagement" did not offer much latitude for the civilian populace. Vietnamese were not to leave their villages from sundown in the evening to dawn in the morning. Anyone moving on the waterway was presumed to be Vietcong. While this was the general rule for all American infantry, it created hardships in the "hearts and minds" battle as fishing boats sometimes returned late from rough seas and could be mistaken as Vietcong sampans moving men and equipment.

Alpha Company of the 1st/52nd secured LZ Paradise, another small outpost of land along the South China Sea which overlooked a small refugee village. From the headwaters of the Tra Bong and to the coast, the battalion provided reaction forces for six Marine "Combined Action Platoon" (CAP) teams (more would be established) located throughout the area. These were Marine General Lewis Walt's frontline soldiers for pacification. Marine CAP units were usually made up of six to eight Marines who lived in hamlets with local Vietnamese defense forces, known as Popular Forces or "PF's". These Vietnamese were not regular army but local irregular soldiers who never left the immediate area of their village. They were generally poorly trained and lightly armed. Their effectiveness depended on the steady hands of the Marines who worked with them.

Throughout the northern area of the large coastal lowlands east and west of Highway One around the district town of Binh Son, CAP teams depended on the American Army units in their area, such as the 1st/6th and 1st/52nd Battalions for protection. The relationship between the CAP Marines and soldiers of the Americal proved to be one of cooperation but fraught with confusion at times.

At this early juncture of the 198th Brigades entry into the Vietnam War, the biggest obstacle was not the enemy but the presence of many mines left by the South Korean Marines. The five Korean battalions operated from thirteen fire-support bases of varying sizes, in the area now occupied by the 198th. Each small fire-support base was defended by a perimeter of mines. The Korean brigade headquarters was four and one-half miles south of the district town of Binh Son, just east of Highway One. This base would eventually be named LZ Dottie when the Americans took over.

The introductions of the Korean military in Vietnam was intended to "Asianize" America's involvement in Vietnam and bring hope of "Asian understanding Asian". But reality quickly replaced political intentions. The Korean and Vietnamese languages were completely foreign to each other and the Korean demeanor was much more authoritative than the Vietnamese. Moreover the "shoot first and ask questions later" attitude of the Koreans was not conducive to the "winning of hearts and minds" part of their mission in Vietnam.

Korean Marines had little tolerance or empathy for the Vietnamese. Widely known for their brutality as a means to control the area they occupied, the Korean Marines' typical response to enemy fire from a hamlet meant its wholesale destruction. In late January 1968, as the battalions of the 198th brigade moved in to replace them, the Korean Marines headed north to Hoi An near Danang, to assist American Marines who were coming under increased pressure from the NVA. The maps of their mined areas were allegedly turned over to the G-3 (Operations) of the Americal Division, but none were ever found.

The mines of the Korean Marine Brigade, whose locations were unknown to the Americans replacing them, provided a supermarket of mines for the Vietcong to retrieve and transplant throughout the area. Those not retrieved served the Vietcong equally well by remaining buried and unmarked, causing many casualties for Americal Division soldiers who were destined to cover the same ground, month after month, year after year, replacement after replacement. The constant shifting of American units in and out of this area of operations only increased the probability of mine injuries or death for troops traversing its terrain. Also, the scheduled replacement of small unit leaders each six months, if not sooner due to other reasons, insured a lack of "institutional memory". The large coastal lowland between Chu Lai and Quang Ngai City was one of the most mine-infested areas of the Vietnam War.

Into this deadly situation arrived the soldiers of the 5th/46th Infantry Battalion at the end of March 1968. Its soldiers, trained on the open plains of Fort Hood Texas, would occupy LZ Gator and in short order, be assigned the area previously covered by both the 1st/6th and 1st/52nd Infantry Battalions and before them, the Korean Marine (Blue Dragon) Brigade. With the gift of thousands of mines, the Vietcong were ready to receive their new adversary.

4 - IN-COUNTRY

Second Lieutenant Donald Wilson, Headquarters Company of the 5th/46th Infantry Battalion began his battalion's march to war on February 20, 1968. Wilson was the first to depart Fort Hood with a detail of three enlisted soldiers and the battalion's general cargo. Their destination was the Republic of South Vietnam. They traveled by rail and the soldiers and their cargo arrived in Oakland, California on the 24th.

While they waited in Oakland for the equipment to be loaded on a transport ship, Wilson frequented the military base's Officers Club. Over a few drinks he met a Colonel who was assigned to the base and had lost a son in Vietnam. The thought of another battalion of soldiers being sent to the war, and the impending loss of other parents' sons that would surely follow, weighed heavily on the Colonel's mind.

The Lieutenant and the Colonel drank steadily, one in anticipation of going to war and the other, anticipating the sacrifices that would surely follow. The Colonel decided to do what little he could do to help the young officer. He took Wilson to what he described as a "surplus equipment storage area" and encouraged the Lieutenant to "pick out whatever you think your battalion needs". Wilson helped himself to desks, a U.S. Navy trailer-mounted generator, several 5K and 10K generators, and over ten refrigerators. All items, he thought, would come in handy for the battalion's field headquarters. With a wink and nod from the Colonel, the right-handed Wilson used his left hand to sign the receipts, insuring his signature was barely legible.

On March 3, Wilson and his men departed by sea for Vietnam with more equipment than he was authorized at Fort Hood. Seven days later the battalions advance party of four officers and one sergeant flew to Vietnam, arriving at the huge logistical base of Cam Ranh Bay on March 12. The next day they caught a plane for the Americal Divisions headquarters in Chu Lai. The main advance-planning group of Lieutenant Colonel Lyon, nine officers and ten enlisted men departed Fort Hood by C130 cargo plane on March 13. They arrived in Chu Lai on the 16th and moved directly to the 198th brigade headquarters at LZ Bayonet. Lyon was told by Colonel Waldie, the brigade commander, his battalion would be assigned an area of operations in the "Southern Chu Lai Sector", and be based on a hilltop designated "LZ Gator" after the required in-country training for his soldiers.

The same day Lyon received his briefing, two major events were occurring which would affect the tactical course of America's war effort and ultimately America's support for the war. First, a massacre was taking place by American soldiers in a series of sub-hamlets called the My Lai's, centered in the sub-hamlet of My Lai (4).

The second event was that General Creighton Abrams officially replaced General William Westmoreland as the new commander of the Military Advisory Command Vietnam (MACV). Abrams immediately began a shift in the war's tactical focus from search and destroy missions with an emphasis on body counts that Westmoreland pursued, to one of increased pacification and securing the Vietnamese population.

Abrams realized the search and destroy approach, the "War of the Big Battalions", was very costly in terms of time, effort and resources. The enemy had learned well the harsh lessons of remaining to fight in large formations against superior American firepower. By avoiding the enemy in large battles, the NVA and main force VC could attack the ARVN and Americans using smaller and more dispersed units. Moreover, by avoiding frequent contact the communists could allow their enemy to become complacent, which improved the enemy's chance of success when choosing to attack. Additionally the enemy chose to make up for its lack of firepower with a heavy reliance on mines and booby-traps. The change in tactics dictated by General Abrams and the concomitant change in tactics by the enemy, would define the kind of war the 5th/46th would have to fight in Vietnam.

Lyon was briefed that the northern boundary for his assigned area of operations would start at LZ Bayonet and follow a line moving east to the southern perimeter of the division base at Chu Lai. His eastern boundary would be the South China Sea along the coastal lowlands. His area of responsibility extended south to the provincial capital of Quang Ngai City and west into the Annamite Mountains, as far west as he needed to go to find the enemy. This assigned area, without even penetrating the mountains, was approximately two hundred and sixty square miles.

On March 28, 1968 Bravo and Charlie Company arrived in Chu Lai and immediately moved to the Americal Division's newly developed Combat Training Center (CTC), along the Chu Lai beach. The battalion's general cargo arrived in Chu Lai the following day. That same day an AC-141 cargo plane landed in Chu Lai with the battalion's air cargo and sixty-two soldiers from Headquarters Company and Echo Company. The cargo was trucked down Highway One to LZ Gator as the soldiers were shuttled to the CTC. Delta Company and the balance of the Headquarters Company arrived at the CTC on March 30. Alpha Company, the last to leave Fort Hood, arrived in Chu Lai on March 31.

The 5th/46th Infantry Battalion was now fully deployed to the war zone. On March 31, 1968, the day their deployment was completed, their Commander-in-Chief, President Lyndon Johnson, who practically shunned them during his visit at Fort Hood, announced he would not run for reelection to the presidency.

Each soldier's arrival in Chu Lai presented to him a searing image. Captain Ken McCarley, the S-4 in charge of supplies and logistics, was dumbfounded at the "insane civilization" he found at the massive Americal Division headquarters, an infantry division supposedly at war. His eyes surveyed the Officer and NCO Clubs, snack stands, a large shopping facility, an American Express branch office and a "business as usual" attitude for thousands of Navy and Army personnel assigned at the sprawling base. The soldiers arriving from Fort Hood expected nothing but foxholes and sandbags. What they found was staggering stink and heat, with "the smell of burning shit everywhere" and the constant threat of enemy rockets. Dennis Hughes of Bravo Company found the heat so oppressive he wondered if he could actually breathe for the next twelve months under such conditions.

When Charlie Company's aircraft made its approach to the Chu Lai airstrip, Lieutenant Terry Care and some of his soldiers were concentrating on a serious game of craps on the floor of the planes' tail section. As a Sergeant began to pour a new round of screwdrivers with their smuggled vodka and orange juice, the plane was ordered to take a steep dive to approach the runway. The nose dive was a standard procedure to avoid possible ground fire and it promptly ended the craps game. The hasty landing began a new game of chance that for some would hold dire consequences. Soviet-made 122mm rockets from Rocket Valley were exploding on the airstrip as the plane came to a stop on the runway. The soldiers hustled off the aircraft and were welcomed with blasting hot air and the smell of shit. They ran to some bunkers until the rocket fire ended.

The obligatory one week of in-country orientation at the CTC in Chu Lai was limited to two days for most of the battalion. This policy change would have serious consequences. Bravo and Charlie Company were moved quickly out of the CTC upon Alpha's arrival and trucked seven miles down Highway One to LZ Gator to strengthen its defenses. The rumor for the hasty move, heard by some soldiers in the battalion, was "they were urgently needed in the field". And the rationale given for the missed orientation at the CTC was, "On the job training is always the best training." The rapid move to LZ Gator was ill advised. The soldiers were scheduled to receive special training on mines and booby-traps when the class was abruptly cancelled to load them on waiting trucks for their trip to LZ Gator. Bravo Company was to experience the first casualties in the battalion from mines and booby-traps.

On April 4 at 9:16PM, the battalion formally entered the 198th Brigades radio net and announced its Tactical Operations Center (TOC) on Gator was ready and the battalion was operational. Ten minutes later Vietcong snipers opened fire on the bunker line. John Migacz and Dennis Hugues had walked over to an experienced soldier eating a can of peaches on the bunker line. He was one of the few remaining 1st/6th soldiers on the perimeter to be replaced by the 5th/46th. They were peppering him with new-guy questions when they heard some buzzing sounds pass over their heads. They asked the soldier, "What was that?" He casually replied in a southern drawl, "Ya'll bein shot at." The next day all the battalion's infantry companies completed their two days of "combat orientation" in Chu Lai and arrived at Gator.

Captain McCarley as the battalion S-4 had his hands full. LZ Gator was in a shambles. Sandbags around the perimeters' edge were piled only two to three high. The previous occupants, the 1st/6th, knew they wouldn't remain on Gator very long and made little effort to improve its defenses. McCarley realized he not only had to quickly unpack his equipment from Fort Hood but scrounge additional equipment he was not authorized in order to make Gator secure as a permanent base. McCarley also discovered that his cargo had been pilfered in Chu Lai

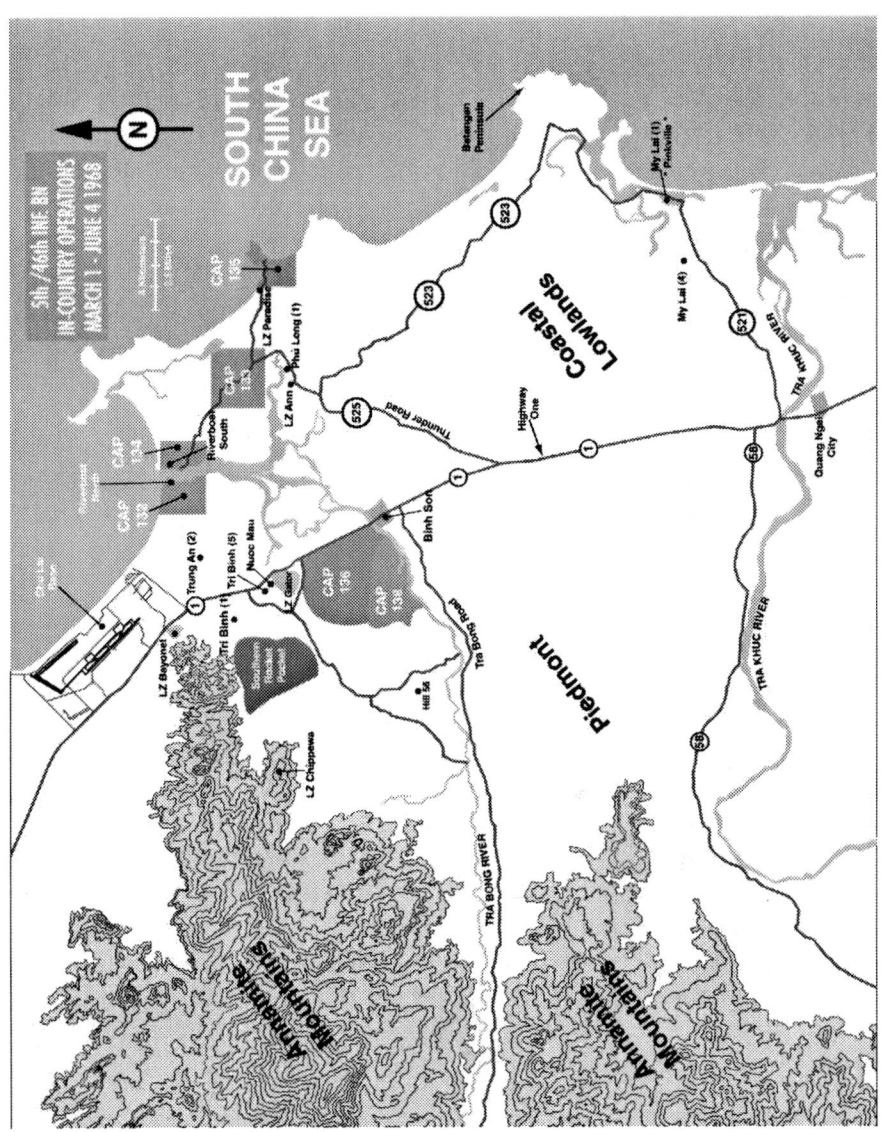

In Country

before it was shipped to Gator. He set about making up for the shortfall by wheeling and dealing back at the division's massive base, with the same people who caused his shortfall in the first place. McCarley's personal shopping list made up for the authorized equipment that he was missing and the unauthorized equipment he needed to make Gator a more functional base camp.

The supply systems of military units at war have always operated at two levels, "official" and "unofficial". McCarley, as a newcomer to the division's logistics system had to take shortcuts. While visiting the Chu Lai base during daylight hours, he took note of where the extra items he needed were located. McCarley had too little time to develop the relationships needed to "wheel and deal", so he returned in the evening to get his fair share during off duty hours. This entailed making the round trip in the dark up and down Highway One, at a time when all bets were off for security in the countryside. There was a significant risk of ambush along the seven mile stretch on Highway One from Chu Lai to Gator. Since the sound of his trucks made it obvious he was on the move, he developed his own brand of psychological warfare. McCarley kept radio music from his trucks blasting like he was running a high school prom night and the headlights were kept on against all tactical wisdom. His hope was to make the VC think his group was either crazy or deliberately drawing them into a trap. His ploy worked. The supply runs at night were never ambushed. Thirty-two years later McCarley recalled with satisfaction, "The VC left me alone".

"On-the-job training" for the 5th/46th Battalion was tasked to the 1st/6th and 1st/52nd Battalions which had only four months of in-country experience themselves. Delta Company of the 1st/52nd began integrating the battalions Echo's recon platoon and elements of Bravo Company into observation posts (OP's) and patrols near the headwaters of the Tra Bong River. They added some guard duty at the main bridge on the northern edge of Binh Son.

In early April, Alpha Company patrolled the Tri Binh hamlets north of LZ Gator searching for VC in conjunction with Bravo Company, 1st/6th. By mid-April its range of operations extended to the headwaters of the Tra Bong River and LZ Paradise on the coast. Paradise contained a small landing zone which sat on a low-lying hill located on the edge of a steep cliff overlooking the sea. The cliff theoretically protected their northeast from attack. The compound was small, approximately one hundred yards square, surrounded by concertina wire and sandbagged bunkers. All food and water were choppered in. Approximately four hundred yards southeast of Paradise sat a small refugee village protected by Marine Combined Action Platoon (CAP) 135.

Bravo Company remained on Gator but sent out elements to support the 1st/6th on the tributaries of the Tra Bong River. Captain Larry Johnson's Charlie Company was airlifted to LZ Chippewa, along the eastern edge of the Annamite Mountains, to assume responsibility for that small hilltop position. Chippewa provided excellent observation of the countryside. He immediately pushed out his platoons west and north into the surrounding hills for signs of the enemy and to occupy various observation posts (OP's). Johnson also sent patrols several miles northeast into Rocket Valley just northwest of Gator. In short order Charlie Company located many caves and tunnels in the surrounding hills, some with weapons and equipment, but absent the VC and NVA who occupied them. Delta and Echo Companies remained on Gator to defend the firebase. Echo's recon platoon led by Second Lieutenant Charles Mrdjenovich was now given the opportunity to perform reconnaissance patrols around LZ Gator in the terrain of war, not the chilly plains of Texas.

Echo Company's 4.2-inch heavy mortars were zeroed in and ready for action. Captain Carl Koppeis, Delta Company's commander became responsible for much of the bunker line on Gator but was handed a quandary that was to dog all rifle companies assigned to that task. He was stretched thin with too many missions that reduced his strength to adequately accomplish any of them. His 2nd platoon was assigned security operations in Nuoc Mau, the small village at the base of Gator by Highway One. The 4th platoon was sent to the district town of Binh Son, three miles south on the highway, to support the 1st platoon, H troop, 17th Armored Cavalry (three armored personnel carriers – APC's or "tracks") to secure the all-important bridge over the Tra Bong River at the towns northern edge.

On April 7 Bravo Company got the nod to deploy to LZ Ann, a small, low-lying hill five miles due east from LZ Gator. Alpha Company experienced sporadic contact with several VC on the north side of Tri Binh (5) while Delta on the bunker line faced the south side of the same hamlet. The bunker line was hit with three satchel charges tossed by Vietcong sappers. This was the first attack by sappers against LZ Gator and there would be two more years of sapper attacks to endure while the battalion held Gator's perimeter.

Sappers were specially-trained enemy soldiers who could crawl slowly for hours, clothed only in shorts. They were trained to feel their way through defensive perimeters laced with metal concertina wire, flares and Claymore mines. Their mission was to attack perimeters at night, usually under the cover of an enemy mortar or rocket attack, and destroy bunkers, artillery or communications facilities with satchel charges. These experts in night movement felt their way past the claymore mines or trip flares that guarded the defensive bunker lines. Their satchel charges were bags of explosives designed to blow holes through defensive wires or knock out bunkers as they penetrated the defensive perimeter. The stealth of sappers was legendary and their tactics, deadly.

On April 8, Bravo Company on LZ Ann received word from Captain Dimsdale, the battalion's intelligence officer (S-2), that elements of the 48th VC Battalion and 95th Sapper Company were two and one-half miles southeast of their position. Combat training in Chu Lai for new arrivals had included a sapper demonstration by an NVA soldier who had previously surrendered. The demonstration on how the enemy could silently kill was part of the training missed by Bravo in their two day orientation. Bravo's patrols spotted five Vietcong northeast of Ann near a large tunnel. It fell to Bravo to begin destroying this first tunnel of what would be hundreds of tunnels, large and small, the battalion would find in its long tenure on the coastal lowlands.

Captain Dimsdale was not happy with the radio communications he monitored from the field. Poor radio security and confusion over radio frequencies and procedures initially dogged the infantry companies and platoons. It was a direct result of the battalion headquarters' coordination problems with field operations in its first field test on the plains of Texas. This problem had to be solved quickly in the enemy terrain of Quang Ngai Province.

By April 10, a short six days after becoming operational the 5th/46th Infantry Battalion was spread far and wide; it's on-the-job training had rapidly morphed into a "trained" status, far short of the prescribed one-month mentoring by an experienced battalion. The battalion's "mentors", the 1st/6th and 1st/52nd were now needed elsewhere to fight in their own slice of the war.

Captain Erb's Alpha Company conducted search and clear operations southwest of Gator and southeast of Chippewa on the flat plains just north of the Tra Bong River and west of the district capitol of

Binh Son. Alpha also kept an eye on two Marine Combined Action Platoon (CAP) teams, 136 and 138 west of Binh Son, who were coming under increased pressure from the Vietcong. In addition smaller elements operated off LZ Paradise along the coast in platoon-size patrols during the day and squad-size ambushes at night.

Erb, one of the few officers in the battalion who had a previous tour in Vietnam, saw the coastal lowlands as a "meat grinder". In his prior tour with the First Cavalry Division, his battalion moved in large groups throughout the central highlands spoiling for a fight with the North Vietnamese Army. Now Erb's troops were operating in platoon-sized patrols in heavily mined terrain. He tried to obtain armored personnel carriers (APC's) whenever possible, to improve his soldier's odds against the anti-personnel mines. But riding APC's to night ambush positions was not tactically sound and his men had to walk through heavily mined terrain. It was a frustrating mission for the young Captain and not the Vietnam he expected to see on his second tour.

Captain Lamb's Bravo Company on LZ Ann was also stretched thin. His 2nd platoon supported the pacification camp at Riverboat South and part of his 1st platoon reinforced Marine CAP Team 133 north of LZ Ann. The balance of Bravo conducted road-clearing operations on Provincial Route 525, the widened dirt path which served as a road in their immediate area. The "road" passed by the south side of LZ Ann and north to Riverboat South. Because the road was heavily mined and ambushes were frequent, it earned the moniker of "Thunder Road".

Bravo's 1st Platoon found itself in a small hamlet where Marine CAP 133 was also headquartered. Their perimeter was protected by concertina wire, flares and claymore mines. One of Bravo's squads was tasked to join in a patrol with the Marines to a nearby hamlet. The Marine point man heard an unusual amount of noise in the "Ville" and the patrol quickly bounded into its midst. Behind one thatched building they found a clearing with bowls of rice arrayed in a circle on the ground. The "picnickers" had hastily departed.

The Marines placed Bravo's inexperienced soldiers on security and Bravo's troops watched the CAP Marines scream at and rough up the villagers. They threw a grenade down a well and burned the thatched dwelling that hosted the meal of the quickly departed enemy. The patrol then departed and shortly after the Marines explained their rage to Bravo's squad. The hamlet had been listed as supposedly under the protection of the Marine CAP but was, in reality, filled with communist sympathizers. They had interrupted a group of Vietcong having an evening meal. As they walked back to the CAP headquarters the patrol was fired on by the same Vietcong who escaped. Bravo's soldiers spotted three of them and opened fire. The VC disappeared and the patrol moved on to their camp. The Marines smiled as Bravo's soldiers exchanged war stories with the rest of their platoon. It was their first combat action.

On April 10 Delta's 2nd platoon moved by Huey Helicopter from their bunker line on LZ Gator to Trung An (2), one and one-quarter miles south of Chu Lai's southern perimeter. They landed on a tall, sandy knoll to replace another platoon that had been positioned there. The 2nd platoon leader, Second Lieutenant Sidney George, was pleased with his commanding view of the terrain. He had a very defensible position for his first time in the field.

Shortly after arriving a Vietnamese teenage boy approached George and introduced himself as "Pete". He spoke in broken English and told Lieutenant George he was available to help his platoon find the Vietcong. George was wary, the young boy's eyes shifted constantly and the Lieutenant surmised he probably worked for the VC. But George went along with the boy's offer to lead them to some weapons and ammunition. George sent a squad with "Pete" who led them to old, unusable ammunition, which the soldiers blew in place with some C-4 explosive. George, a Texas native, thought the whole thing was a ruse, using a "find" of old munitions to build confidence with his soldiers.

While "Pete" was gone two Marines from CAP 132 introduced themselves to George and asked for three to four men to form a blocking position for a planned night ambush. George did not think the plan had much chance of success but saw a training opportunity for his men. Flushed with forty-three soldiers in his platoon, he gave the Marines a squad of ten men plus an M-60 machine gun team which made the short-handed Marines very happy.

That night the Marines placed the squad in two blocking positions. They made contact with the enemy as the Marines and their Popular Force (PF) militia drove the Vietcong to them. George's squad killed nine VC. Early in the morning "Pete" reappeared on the sandy knoll, disappointed that Lieutenant George had not discussed the ambush mission with him. The Texan Lieutenant looked him squarely in the eyes and told him nothing military would ever be discussed with him. "Pete" was never seen again. George quickly recognized this war would be fought like his Texan forefathers fought the Comanche Indians.

He never used the same night position twice nor traveled the same route twice. But one month later, another platoon occupying this same sandy knoll experienced heavy casualties from a booby-trapped 500-pound bomb.

First Blood

On April 11, Bravo's soldiers found another large tunnel in the hamlet of Phu Long (1). It was large enough the radio report said, "That a two hundred pound man could get into it". Lieutenant Ray Craig's platoon set out to destroy as much as possible of the tunnel. While directing the operation he hit a mine which sheared off his left arm. Craig became the battalion's first officer casualty. Craig, a black soldier, was a former NCO who completed Infantry Officer Candidate School (OCS) at Fort Benning. His prior enlisted service made him a solid junior officer. After his surgery Lyon visited him in the hospital at Chu Lai and presented his Purple Heart. Before leaving the hospital the battalion commander was reprimanded for his lack of protocol, "Colonels", he was told, "Don't give Purple Hearts. Generals do."

Working close to Craig was Lieutenant Mike Kuhn's platoon, which was searching another portion of the same hamlet. At Kuhn's side was Private Richard Atwood, his radio telephone operator (RTO), from Cleveland, Ohio. Both Kuhn and Atwood were tall and lanky, and physically resembled each other. Atwood lived in a large family and had moved in with his older sister and husband to ease the hardship on his mother. When Atwood reached his late teen years he realized he was being a financial burden on his sister's young family as well and he joined the Army. Atwood turned eighteen years of age when the battalion departed from Fort Hood. His comrades bought him his first official beer in Alaska when their aircraft stopped for refueling.

Kuhn, like other platoon leaders, was always at risk from snipers. His RTO's radio and the long, distinguishing antenna, served as a bull's eye for Kuhn. As they emerged from behind a hooch, Atwood walked in front of his platoon leader and a sniper's bullet, intended for Kuhn, cut into his stomach. In less than ten minutes Kuhn had a dustoff land to rush his RTO to Chu Lai but Atwood died on the bird before it reached the hospital. Private Richard Atwood, barely eighteen years of age, became the 5th/46th Infantry Battalion's first soldier killed-in-action (KIA).

The soldiers had noticed several farmers leaving a rice paddy when they approached the hamlet but they were too inexperienced to connect the dots. They took out their revenge on two water buffalo, the hamlets prized possessions, and also opened fire on the tree line from where the shots were fired. Bravo's First Sergeant drove a jeep down a rough path from LZ Ann. The jeep towed a "Quad 50" (four synchronized 50-caliber machine guns behind an armor plate). Although the sniper probably had departed, the tree line was obliterated with the Quad 50 to send a message. The newly arrived soldiers had some revenge by killing the water buffalo and demonstrating their superior firepower, but the shadowy enemy would respond with their own special brand of firepower, planted just below the ground.

The next day Bravo's soldiers hit another mine, wounding five soldiers, two of them seriously. The mine was a 105mm-artillery shell previously fired for illumination. It had been retrieved by the VC, packed with C-4 explosive and metal fragments, and rigged with a trip wire. C-4 was a new plastic explosive that came into its own for the Vietnam War. The plastic high explosive was packaged in 1" x 1" x 6" blocks that could be cut and molded like clay, into any shape. It could even be burned without exploding for those troops who ran out of the heat tablets to warm their C-rations. This use was, of course, frowned on. The C-4 was detonated by a combination of extreme heat and a shock wave, usually accomplished by a detonator placed inside the plastic.

The Vietcong did not kill any of Bravo's soldiers with the mine, but succeeded in removing some of their adversaries from the field. This scenario would be replayed many times as the battalion patrolled the coastal plains. The use of mines and booby-traps was a deadly tactic that remained effective because of the skill used in planting them and the constant rotation of new, uninitiated American soldiers in and out of the foreboding coastal lowlands over the next three years.

Typical of the improvised mines on the coast were empty artillery shells loaded with metal fragments and C-4 explosive, inserted with a homemade a pull-type friction fuse. Usually a hole twelve inches deep and twelve to eighteen inches in width and length was dug. At one end of the hole the explosive and the shell were buried. A piece of string or trip wire was tied to the fuse and secured at the other end of the hole on a small stake. The hole was covered with small twigs or thin bamboo stalks and not heavily covered with dirt, to increase the blast effect of the explosion. Noting the habits of unseasoned or careless soldiers, the

Vietcong often placed their deadly traps on trails, even minor footpaths, or old positions that had been used by the Americans.

Worse still were the "command detonated" mines; large explosives buried and detonated not by trip wires or pressure devices, but by a guerilla hiding nearby, holding a detonation device, connected by buried wire to the explosive. Maximum casualties could be gained since the guerilla could pick the precise moment to detonate the mine when most of his enemy was in the kill zone.

American hand grenades (M-26) or Chinese Communist (Chicom) grenades were widely used. The M-26 was secured on one side of a trail and a trip wire connected to the grenade's safety pin was secured at the other side of the trail. Chicom grenades had no pin to pull. The wily Vietcong would attach a friction fuse to the grenade's cap, activating the grenade when a wire was pulled. The M-14 mine was a small plastic mine containing two ounces of plastic explosive. Approximately two inches in diameter and two inches thick, it rarely killed but disabled soldiers with injuries serious enough to remove them from the field.

The M-16 "Bouncing Betty" mine was a holdover from the Chinese Communists of the Korean War. Weighing approximately eight pounds and resembling a tomato can, it was armed with a pressure-pull fuse. When a soldier stepped on the pressure device it activated the fuse and the main part of the mine was thrown into the air approximately three feet, waist high for most soldiers, and exploded.

Empty C-ration cans, or used claymore mines, or expended artillery shells and other refuse of war became weapons of death. On April 19, Charlie Company's 1st platoon, operating five miles southwest of LZ Gator located a booby-trap made from a C-ration can with a bamboo handle attached to a trip wire. Ten miles further east of Charlie, Bravo's soldiers working south of LZ Ann found four M-14 mines rigged with beer cans. Both mines were destroyed, but the battalion's patrols were playing a game of Russian Roulette with their movements in enemy territory that usually won some casualties for the Vietcong. The next morning Alpha's third platoon hit a Bouncing Betty mine, wounding four. At 11:00AM, Bravo's first platoon lost a man who stepped on a M-14, blowing a hole in his left foot. At 6:29PM, three of Alpha's soldiers went down from a Bouncing Betty with groin, head and arm wounds. At 7:00PM, another Alpha soldier stepped on a mine, blowing off his foot and injuring a soldier nearby. Other soldiers close by were hit by another mine which wounded three. Thirteen soldiers were taken from the field in one day and not one enemy soldier was killed or captured.

The mines quickly took a toll on the psyche of the battalion's soldiers. North of LZ Ann were several low-lying hills that Bravo Company had been warned to stay off, because they were laden with mines. Nevertheless, Bravo's Commander, Captain Lamb, wanted the hills to be checked to see if there was any enemy activity. He remained on LZ Ann while the 1st and 2nd squads of the 1st platoon were sent to take a look. The squad leader for the first squad was a "lifer" who had been around since the Korean War, and never recovered from the trauma experienced in Korea. He had been demoted and promoted so many times it was said he had three complete sets of dress uniforms with different ranks. Now just a buck Sergeant, he was one of the older sergeants at Fort Hood, and the men had no confidence in his leadership.

While on the hills the 1st squad heard an explosion from the 2nd squad's area which was followed by gut wrenching cries of agony. A booby-trapped claymore mine had been command detonated, taking out a three man machinegun crew and several others. The 1st squad moved to assist the 2nd, with John Migacz taking point as usual. He hadn't moved far before he stepped on an anti-personnel mine, blowing off his foot. Suddenly the sound of exploding mines seemed to be everywhere. Everyone froze into place. Migacz's comrades Dennis Hughes and Terry DeMott went to his aid. As they carried his body in a poncho to a chopper for a dustoff, Migacz stared at his comrades while clenching his teeth in pain and warned, "Don't walk off this hill-make them send choppers."

Their squad leader was on the radio with Lamb reporting that seven men had been dusted off and they were in a dangerous situation. Lamb told him to "Walk back".

"Saddle up, we're hiking back to Ann."

"No way" said DeMott, "Make them send choppers, it's too fucking dangerous".

The shaky squad leader responded, "You know that ain't gonna happen, get your fucking equipment on and let's go. We got our orders!"

The young soldiers weren't buying it. "No way, make them send choppers, it's too fucking dangerous". The sergeant threatened his men then made a gesture that he was moving out, but no one followed.

He radioed Lamb again, "Captain says they can't send choppers, we have to hoof it".

Still the men resisted.

DeMott retorted, "We've left enough body parts on this piece of shit hill and we're going back with all that we have left."

Another call to the company commander and the old and hapless sergeant told his men, "Captain says you'll be in deep shit if you don't saddle up right this fucking second, and that's a direct quote". The men on the hill cackled. Someone yelled, "What's he gonna do? Send us to Nam?" Finally Lamb, aware he had a mini-revolt on his hands, relented and choppers were sent in to get them. The birds would not touch the ground because of the mines. They hovered a foot off the turf and the emotionally drained soldiers climbed on and departed the hill. Nothing was said when they arrived back at LZ Ann.

The stark reality of combat quickly became embedded in the psyche of the soldiers. Harry Ehret was a medic in the Headquarters Company Medical Section who volunteered to come to Bravo Company while one of Bravo's medics returned to LZ Gator for observation, after being hit in the head with shrapnel. Ehret met up with another medic friend in the company, who deployed to Vietnam as a conscientious objector (CO). The CO was now carrying an M-16, .45-caliber pistol and machete.

On April 21, Alpha, working off LZ Paradise on the coast, suffered four more wounded from mines, two with their feet blown off. Bravo took an additional two casualties from mines. But it would be Echo Company's Recon Platoon on that same day, operating in the Piedmont west of Highway One that experienced the terror of mines rise to a new level.

Second Lieutenant Mrdjenovich's battalion reconnaissance platoon had been screening the southern boundary of the battalion's area of operations along the north side of the Tra Bong River west of Binh Son. Since arriving in Vietnam the recon platoon adeptly applied its training from Fort Bragg's Raider School. They moved in small groups, making their way through dense brush rather than exposing themselves on trails or natural openings, which were likely areas for mines or ambushes.

But Mrdjenovich did not bond well with his men, other than his RTO, PFC Ronald Van Avery, the tall, six-foot three inch intellectual soldier whom the platoon leader liked. The soldiers in the platoon knew their craft well and performed well, yet their platoon leader was aloof and did not acknowledge their performance to build esprit in the platoon. Nor did he accept suggestions from his men who were adapting well to their job. Mrdjenovich always had to be in complete control and did not acknowledge the excessive toil his platoon expended to operate more securely. Mrdjenovich was tolerated by his men but not well liked. Then he became impulsive. Not satisfied with the slow pace of movement through thick brush, he directed that all movement be made in the open, even on trails if necessary. "From now on" he declared, "We'll be a walking ambush."

By mid-morning on April 21, Mrdjenovich made the decision it was already time to start moving to a night defensive position. Hill 56 was nearby, a low-lying hill that had been used repeatedly by the South Korean Marines and by the American Marines before them. All the collective tactical knowledge of Vietnam combat told the platoon leader never to occupy the same position twice. But Mrdjenovich directed his platoon to return to the hill.

As they reached the base of the slightly elevated terrain, the point element surveyed the concertina wire that had been placed around the hill by the Korean Marines. One section that crossed the main path leading up the hill had been open the week before. Now it was closed. Things just didn't look right and they told their leader they were wary of what might await them. Mrdjenovich rebuffed them, "Get up the hill and move into the positions you occupied last week."

The hilltop had little vegetation and one tree. Scattered about were a number of old sand-bagged bunkers. PFC Ron Cannon was in the point element. Once on top of the hill his section crossed over to the other side, with Cannon seeking the shade of the tree. It was his same defensive position as in the previous week. This opened him up to friendly sarcasm from his comrades, "There he goes again, always getting the shady area!"

Once Mrdjenovich with his RTO and another soldier, SP/4 James Rudd, reached the top they moved to the dilapidated bunker which served as the command and control position. The platoon leader let his heavy rucksack slide off his back and took a step back. The still, hot air hovering over Hill 56 was violently shaken by a loud explosion. Mrdjenovich was slammed to the ground, riddled with shrapnel. PFC Van Avery, leaning next to him, caught the full blast of the mine which tore away much of his face and chest. SP/4 Rudd, the affable and physically fit soldier who Fort Bragg's Green Berets were sure would be the one to survive his tour, was also torn apart with shrapnel. All three died within minutes.

The reaction was predictable, just as the enemy planned. Soldiers rushed to help their comrades and two more mines were set off in rapid succession. Twelve more soldiers were wounded. More soldiers took steps to help their comrades but froze. The hilltop was littered with trip wires attached to mines. Where there were no wires it was assumed the ground held pressure plates just below the surface to detonate more mines. The hill was littered with homemade mines, made from explosive-packed C-ration cans left by prior units.

SP/4 David Tunnel was in the rear element, and reached the top of the hill just as the mines exploded. Seeing the carnage he screamed, "Stay down! Stay down!" PFC Carl Williams had a sucking chest wound. PFC Oral Brenner was hit in the throat with shrapnel that he spit out. The heat of the metal fragment that penetrated his neck cauterized his wound. Tunnel went to Williams to help keep him alive. He heard Van Avery murmur nearby as he slipped away.

PFC Cannon began to move back over the hilltop to help his comrades but was told to freeze in place. Another soldier screamed on the radio to the battalion headquarters on LZ Gator, his panicked voice and incoherent speech betrayed a state of shock. His eyes surveyed the carnage in front of him as he tried to talk but his panicked hand would not release the "push to talk" button on the radio, making it impossible for Colonel Lyon to talk to him. Lyon finally was able to communicate with the soldier and he knew in an instant he had a debacle on his hands. He ordered Charlie's Company Commander on LZ Chippewa, Captain Johnson, to fly south and take control of the situation.

Dustoffs came in. The first one landed by chance where no mines were located. Each succeeding Huey landed on the same position, not willing to change the landing spot or the pattern of movement required for the soldiers to reach them. Johnson landed just before the second dustoff arrived. It was now 11:35AM and he realized that the recon platoon was tactically finished. Virtually every man had been wounded. After the more serious wounded had been dusted off to Chu Lai, he called for more Hueys to take the remaining soldiers back to LZ Gator.

SP/4 Tunnell continued to exert control over the traumatized platoon, taking care to ensure that no one moved unless absolutely necessary. After most were lifted out he moved to within twenty yards of PFC Cannon and told him to "head up the hill." Tunnell pointed out another trip wire to Cannon which glistened in the sun. Cannon, keeping his eye on the wire rose up from under the shade tree and took a step forward. The deadly hill belched some more buried hell and claimed another victim. Cannon had stepped on a pressure-release mine which threw him fifteen feet into his shade tree, his body somersaulting then slamming back to the ground. His right foot was sheared off leaving nothing but a denuded bone six inches above his ankle.

Standing next to SP/4 Tunnell was PFC Johnny Winn. Tunnell and Winn were best of friends, both hailing from Alabama, but exact opposites in temperament. Winn was a hard drinking devil-may-care soldier who would never rise above the rank of PFC. His drinking and hard-living would lead to an early death after the war. Tunnell was reserved and religious, the son of a preacher. It was the kind of friendship only made possible by the crucible of war. Winn went to work immediately on Cannon. He patched up his shattered, bloodied body, wrapped him in a poncho and carried Cannon past the trip wires to a dustoff. Cannon was the last casualty to be dusted off. The dustoff pilot, Major Patrick Brady, had already been recommended for the Medal of Honor for heroics while previously rescuing many other wounded of the Americal Division. Brady would receive the Medal of Honor and the Distinguished Service Cross during his tour supporting the Americal. For his part, SP/4 William Tunnel was awarded the Bronze Star for Valor on Hill 56.

After the hill was evacuated, it was determined that weapons, ammunition and unexploded mines still littered the hilltop. Helicopter gunships raked the hilltop with 40mm grenade fire followed by artillery fire from the battery of 155mm Howitzers on LZ Gator which pummeled the hill. Later jet fighters dropped 500-pound bombs and napalm. Second Lieutenant Charles Mrdjenovich, twenty-one years of age and married from Fayetteville, North Carolina became the first officer of the battalion to be killed in action. Dying with him was PFC Ronald Van Avery, age 23 and married from Portland, Oregon and SP/4 James Rudd, age 20 and single, from Halifax, Virginia. Thirteen others were severely wounded and loaded in the dustoff's to Chu Lai. The remainder of the recon platoon suffered shrapnel wounds which were patched up back at LZ Gator.

LT. Terry Care's platoon from Charlie Company had been patrolling to the east off of LZ Chippewa, looking for VC in the Tri Binh hamlets just north of LZ Gator. Johnson alerted him on the radio that Echo Recon was in serious trouble. Care changed one of his radio's frequencies to pick up the radio traffic from the battalion and he immediately sensed something terrible had gone wrong. His platoon was under the flight path of the dustoff helicopters that were making the flights from Hill 56 to Chu Lai. He heard that "the 6" (Mrdjenovich) was in bad shape and instinctively knew he wouldn't make it.

As the Huey flew over Care's position carrying his friend's body, Care's mind returned to Fort Hood, forty-eight hours before the battalion departed for Vietnam. He, Mrdjenovich, and another officer had gone to the Officers Club for one last soiree. In short order all three were pleasantly drunk. After securing a car they drove to nearby Copperas Cove and pulled into a driveway of a home that Mrdjenovich remembered belonged to a friend. Knocking on the door he received no answer so he let himself in to use the bathroom. Care soon heard a loud bang from the bathroom and opened the door to see his buddy jumping off the toilet to kill cockroaches on the floor. How they safely returned to Fort Hood escaped his mind. It was the last time they had been together.

The next morning Care was back on Chippewa when Echo's Company Commander, Captain Al Chiofee, came out to tell him, "You're working for me now". Care was brought back to LZ Gator to take over the demoralized soldiers of the recon platoon. Care saw that the platoon had been under strength to begin with and most everyone who remained had been wounded. In his first week with the platoon, he waited for the mental and healing process to continue, and for additional soldiers to fill his platoon. LTC Lyon told each of his infantry companies, Alpha, Bravo, Charlie and Delta to "Send four to five of your best soldiers to recon". As they arrived Care sized up the replacements coming to him and sensed he was actually getting someone else's "screw-ups". He confirmed this later with his fellow officers on Gator.

Care's new "recruits" looked a bit wild to him and he found out in the coming weeks just how wild they could be. Half of those coming to him had been previously wounded, and the other half was close to being sent to an Army jail for discipline problems. Given the unique requirements of the recon platoon and its mission, he tried to turn his situation into an advantage with his suspect mix of soldiers. Gathering his soldiers together on Gator, he told them "It's us versus them. You've fucked up and can't get any lower in this battalion than being assigned to recon. But we are not just some other grab-ass platoon. We are the bastards of the battalion with a unique mission and we'd better be proud of it because no one else cares." This new identity struck a chord of pride with his men and attitudes slowly began to change. Most times Care moved his men in teams of six or seven men rather than the entire platoon, moving mainly at night, always with a heightened sense of security. His men felt safer operating with a smaller footprint than as a platoon. In short order the battalion's recon platoon became effective again.

Two days later on April 23, the 2nd platoon of Alpha Company walked into a minefield. But the platoon leader, Second Lieutenant Richard Knight Jr. remained calm. One soldier hit a small "Toe-Popper" mine and the platoon realized they had walked into a mined area. Knight had everyone freeze in place. PFC Robert Cummings carried a portable mine detector and after each mine was detected, Knight personally dug it up. Each mine found was marked with toilet paper from a C-ration box until the platoon leader could get to it. The ground yielded shell casings, discarded C-ration cans and metal fragments. Knight meticulously dug each piece of metal out of the ground working under the hot sun all afternoon while his men remained in place. As clear paths started to open up, the men near them walked out of the mined area. The mines were blown in place by Knight with small chunks of C-4.

Shortly after the incident Lieutenant Knight was wounded at another location and evacuated back to the United States. Early in 1971 he returned to Vietnam and the Americal Division as a Captain, and became a company commander in the 1st/46th Infantry Battalion. Knight was killed on March 22, 1971 in the infamous attack on Firebase Mary Ann.

The Depth of the Enemy

By April 24, only twenty days after the battalion declared itself operational, the 5th/46th was strung out in a variety of missions. Vietnamese Provisional Reconnaissance Units (PRU's) were periodically assigned to the battalion's patrols in the field. PRU's were local Vietnamese who were light infantry soldiers but well trained in Ranger tactics and interrogation methods. They operated among the local hamlets to eliminate Vietnamese peasants identified as Vietcong Infrastructure (VCI). The VCI were the communists that lived in sub-hamlets and, in many cases even local villagers were not aware of their communist allegiance. The VCI were deeply embedded in the fabric of South Vietnamese society and provided the leadership for the insurgency.

VCI were classified in categories of A, B or C. "A" indicated key insurgency leaders in a village or hamlet organization. Category "B" identified active supporters of the leadership who carried out their directions, to keep the key leaders submerged in anonymity. Category "C" was low-level support cadre such as women who would shop in the marketplace to obtain medicine for the Vietcong.

The Republic of South Vietnam was comprised of forty-four provinces. Ten provinces accounted for half of the Vietnam War's combat deaths and five of those provinces were in the I Corps Tactical Zone. The 5th/46th was assigned to the southern part of I Corps. Two I Corps provinces, Quang Nam and Quang Ngai were among the provinces where the VCI was the strongest. Quang Ngai province would account for six percent of all combat deaths in Vietnam. By early 1968 it was estimated enemy strength in Quang Ngai Province was between ten-thousand and fourteen-thousand individuals of which two to four thousand were regular forces, three to five thousand were guerillas and five thousand were peasants sympathetic to the insurgency who carried out support functions, such as carrying supplies.

The PRU worked with the battalion's soldiers off and on for the three years the battalion was in Vietnam. The PRU's first mission prior to 1966 was to provide counter-terrorist teams. They were used to capture prisoners and documents using village sweeps, and locate VCI personnel.

After 1966 the American Central Intelligence Agency (CIA) took control of the PRU in South Vietnam to support "Operation Phoenix", a concerted effort to wipe out the Vietcong Infrastructure with ruthless intensity. American soldiers did not make many distinctions among the populace other than a Vietnamese with a weapon was the enemy and if he or she, or their children did not have a weapon, they should be watched carefully.

Under CIA tutelage, the PRU took a "rifle shot" approach to their mission, carefully targeting hamlets where VCI were known to exist. At times they operated alone, and on other occasions they worked with American troops for added protection, while searching targeted hamlets. Most soldiers of the battalion were unaware of the CIA ties with the PRU and its real mission. They viewed them as point men or additional reconnaissance assets.

The deadly February 1968 TET offensive began when the battalion began to deploy to Vietnam, and had it exposed many of the VCI who chose to rise out of anonymity, because they were confident of a general populace uprising which would lead to victory. Now the PRU set out, using CIA "Black lists", to destroy those who were identified and had survived the fighting. Provincial Interrogation Centers (PIC's), located in the district towns of Binh Son, Son Tinh and Quang Ngai City, were used to extract information from the captured VCI. These interrogations often directed the PRU to other targets. One of the attributes of the PRU which made them effective was the requirement they be from the same province in which they operated.

By the summer of 1968 control of the PRU began to shift from the CIA to the Vietnamese government in Saigon. A total change in control was completed by the following summer. By July 1969 control would flow down to the provincial capitals such as Quang Ngai. With the Vietnamese government directing the PRU, Vietnamese control of the PRU at the Province level went to the highest bureaucratic bidder in the province, who wished to use this highly trained asset for his own agenda. Targeting of VCI continued, but with the provincial Vietnamese in charge was expanded to include extortion, bribes and the elimination of political enemies. Many of the battalion's soldiers who worked with the PRU considered them real "bad asses".

The Vietcong Communists likewise had their own VCI-type hit list to eliminate pro-government leaders at the village or hamlet level. The communists listed their targets in Categories I, II and III.

Category I was Vietnamese who "give information to the enemy (South Vietnamese or American forces) that is harmful to the revolution. Such comrades are traitors and should be eliminated."

Category II were Vietnamese who had brief contacts with the enemy and "who gave a small amount of information not generally harmful." These Vietnamese were to be "re-contacted (with caution) for possible reeducation and a return to the revolution."

Category III were "former comrades who left the revolution but had not cooperated with the enemy. Every effort should be made to re-contact and reactivate such comrades."

In operations against the NVA and VC scout dogs were assigned to the battalion's platoons operating both on the coastal lowlands and in the mountains. The 198th Brigade's Scout Dog Platoon resided on LZ Bayonet and consisted of forty dogs, primarily German Shepherds trained in Malaysia.

"Kit Carson" Scouts, were NVA defectors who were also assigned to the battalion's platoons to help capture and interrogate prisoners. "Kit

Carson's" were an early innovation of the U.S. Marines who, after their arrival in Vietnam, found that some NVA defectors could be "turned" to work for the Americans. The hard life of the NVA in the mountains and the massive fire power brought against them by American units were persuasive reasons for a few NVA to change sides. The Vietnamese Army (ARVN) did not trust NVA prisoners but the Marines treated them with respect and cultivated them as a valuable asset that in turn, kept the NVA prisoner out of the cells and torture chambers of ARVN prisons.

With an assigned tactical area of operations (AO) of two hundred and sixty square miles, the 5th/46th Battalion's tactical mission included defending its fire bases, manning observation posts (OP's), searching and destroying tunnels and enemy caches, and hitting the enemy in night ambushes. Its pacification mission was focused on protecting villagers harvesting rice and offering medical aid to Vietnamese villagers when it was practical to do so. These missions had the goal of establishing control over the hostile landscape and "winning the hearts and minds" of the populace to some small degree.

For the 198th Light Infantry Brigade this effort was carried out under Operation Muscatine, with its operational objective of establishing control of Northern Quang Ngai province from the departed Korean Marine (Blue Dragon) Brigade. Muscatine began on December 20, 1967 while the 5th/46th was still at Fort Hood and ended on June 10, 1968. During Muscatine sixteen soldiers in the brigade were killed and ninety-five wounded. Muscatine accounted for two hundred and forty-four enemy dead, fourteen enemy prisoners and fifty-one weapons captured. But to the soldiers on the ground, Muscatine was not found in their vocabulary. Their daily mission was simply to survive the heat, the snipers and deadly mines.

As the field experience of the 5th/46th Infantry Battalion grew, so too did the sophistication of the enemy. Bravo's second platoon tripped a Bouncing Betty on May 1, which was connected to an 81mm mortar round lying twenty feet away. PFC Danny West was killed from the explosion. West was age 20 and single from Fort Smith, Arkansas. Another soldier lost both legs in the explosion and two more received shrapnel wounds. Three days later the platoon ambushed fifteen Vietcong. Most slipped away but some were wounded and left trials of blood after dropping their loads for a fast escape. The soldiers retrieved a Bangalore Torpedo, four satchel charges, grenades, mines, ammunition and clothing. Bangalore Torpedoes were tubes of bamboo or metal pipe filled with high explosives and used during night infiltrations to blast holes through defensive wire, which allowed sappers to pass through.

On May 4, 1968, with just one month of experience in the field, LTC Lyon received word from the brigade commander, Colonel Waldie, to be prepared to send an undetermined part of the 5th/46th to an area northwest of Chu Lai, outside the battalions assigned AO. On May 10, Lyon started consolidating his men closer to LZ's Chippewa, Riverboat South, Ann and Gator to make it easier to be picked up for the move north. The soldiers swept the areas close to these bases with day patrols and night ambushes but did not venture too far in order to be ready for the move north. The battalion's control over its assigned AO was tenuous at best after only a month but now Lyon faced the prospect of ceding the gains made by the battalion in support of another mission. Local intelligence reports added to the possibility of increased vulnerability once the battalion left the area. Marine CAP Team 136, operating one mile south of LZ Gator, captured an NVA soldier on May 14. He was carrying a detailed drawing of LZ Gator's defensive positions, including bunkers, artillery emplacements, and mortar positions.

The movement north began on May 17 when Bravo deployed two platoons West and Northwest of Chu Lai and came under operational control (OPCON) of the 1st/46th Infantry Battalion, which was heavily engaged in "Operation Burlington Trail" north of Chu Lai. Two days later Captain Lamb left his fourth platoon on LZ Ann and took the balance of Bravo to join up with his departed platoons.

Alpha's company commander, Captain Erb, had to split his company resources into smaller groups, perhaps beyond prudence, to meet all his missions. LZ Paradise's defense was reduced to one platoon with two armored personnel carriers ("Tracks") from the 1st platoon, H troop, 17th Armored Cavalry. Each track had a heavy mortar (4.2-inch) for fire support. He sent some soldiers to support Bravo's 4th platoon on LZ Ann and the balance of Erb's company secured RiverBoat South. Charlie Company, out west on LZ Chippewa, held the Chippewa perimeter with one platoon and the company headquarters element. The rest of the company was spread far and wide in the Annamite Mountains, Rocket Valley, and the hamlets north of Gator to ferret out the VC. At 9:30AM May 19, Charlie's 2nd platoon medic was shot near the hamlet of Nam Trung, three and one-half miles south of Chippewa. SP/4 Grant Newell, age 24 and married from Xenia, Ohio died from his wound.

Delta Company continued to man the bunker line at LZ Gator and send patrols into Rocket Valley, the Tri Binh hamlets north of Gator, and out to the headwaters of the Tra Bong River, where increased Vietcong activity was reported. At 4:45PM on the 24th, Alpha's grunts came under automatic weapons fire just north of Phu Long (4). SP/4 Gerald Parmeter, age 20 and single from Cazadero, California was wounded in the firefight and dusted off. He did not survive his wound.

Two days later on May 26, the massive Chu Lai base came under attack from eight 122mm Soviet-made rockets which slammed into the base. Four rockets hit the airstrip, three landed in another sub-sector and one on the beach. Radar detected the launch area for some of them and counter-battery fire from heavy mortars and 8-inch artillery from LZ Bayonet responded. Most of the rockets were fired from the southern boundary of the 1st/46th Battalion's AO, but the battalions hands were full with Operation Burlington Trail farther west and north of Chu Lai. Charlie Company choppered its 2nd platoon off Chippewa and flew it north to search the hills around rocket valley. The platoon found some rocket canisters but nothing else. That same day Bravo's 1st platoon, also patrolling in the same area to free up the 1st/46th Battalion, lost it's third soldier, PFC Daniel Powell, age 19 and single, from Artesia, California.

Powell had had several premonitions in his dreams about his death. Weeks earlier he mentioned to his buddies that Richard Atkins, the battalions first KIA, also had a dream he would die in Vietnam. The platoon was content to be in rocket valley, as it was "easy duty" compared to operating in the mine-laden coastal lowlands. While on a hilltop watching for VC, Powell detonated a mine. The Korean War squad leader he had argued with on the hill just north of LZ Ann in mid-April, when Captain Lamb told them to walk back, was also wounded. The squad leaders arm was almost severed and hung by a thread of muscle. A new soldier, PFC Woodrow Davis, lost a leg. Seven soldiers were dusted off. Powell died shortly after the bird left the ground. Woodrow Davis was convinced he was going to die despite a relatively clean amputation of his leg. On June 15 he succumbed to his wounds. Davis was age 20 and single from Holly Hill, South Carolina.

After their comrades were dusted off the remaining members of the platoon realized they made an unforgivable blunder. They had been on the hill before and unknowingly returned a second time. The ground was torched to mark it for the future. The Platoon leader radioed his company commander to have his platoon removed from the field so it could recover. His men heard him say on the radio, "But sir, you don't realize how few of us are left." He listened for a moment then composed himself and turned to his men. "Listen up ... saddle up ... we're moving out, they need us farther north."

On June 4, the Americal Division Commander, Major General Koster and the Deputy Commander for Operations, Brigadier General Young, paid a visit to Lyon on LZ Gator to discuss the problem of enemy rockets being fired into Chu Lai and the problem of "infusion". By now the battalion had worked out most of its own field standard operating procedures (SOP's) and was becoming more effective operationally. But they were about to get their hands tied once again. The newly-formed Americal Division faced major personnel problems in meeting the twelve-month rotational policy of its soldiers. Control of the rotational "hump" with the two recently arrived combat brigades, the 11th, and 198th, was particularly acute and required the transfer of personnel among the division's brigades. The "infusion" program was designed to reduce the potential impact of a large number of personnel in the same battalion reaching their end-of-tour date at the same time.

The Infusion Program, and the receipt of a large number of replacements from the United States, created considerable personnel turbulence in the 198th and 11th Infantry Brigades. The consequences were more acute for Lyon and the 5th/46th Battalion because it had not arrived until the end of March 1968 and was the most recent battalion in the division to enter the war. Like its sister battalions, new arrivals to the 5th/46th had to be integrated and oriented to their new company commanders, platoon leaders, sergeants and the operating procedures of the unit. Unlike other battalions, the 5th/46th was still working out some of those procedures, and its leaders were just becoming acclimated to their missions. It is a testament to Lyon and his junior officers that the battalion functioned as well as it did. In short order it would be called upon to assume the role of a highly experienced maneuver battalion against an experienced and determined enemy far away from their assigned area of operations.

June 4, 1968 marked the battalion's second full month since becoming operational. Its "on-the-job training" had come hard. The Vietcong, suffering from hard blows from the 1st/52nd and the U.S. Marines, now operated in smaller groups, allowing mines and booby-traps to accomplish what their open formations could not do under the weight of American firepower. The battalion's success with its rapid integration into its assigned AO came at a high price in pain and sacrifice in the field. As the battalion S-3 Daily Staff Journal closed its entries for the day, its two-month tally sheet listed enemy losses as only thirteen killed and eleven captured. Battalion losses were eight killed and one hundred and twenty five wounded in action, most by mines on the coastal lowlands east of Highway One. Now with its newly assigned mission, the casualty toll was about to rise.

5 – THE PROFESSIONALS

Operations for the Americal Division varied based on the enemy situation, the terrain the enemy occupied and availability of soldiers to meet a particular threat. To counter enemy threats, several operations often overlapped each other. Some operations concluded while others had just begun. Infantry and artillery battalions, used in support of these operations, were themselves subject to orders directing them to support others within and outside their own areas of responsibility.

Operations "Wheeler" and "Wallowa", undertaken by the 196th Light Infantry Brigade when they were a separate brigade, were combined on November 11, 1967 to form Wheeler/Wallowa. This occurred when the Americal Division, formally Task Force Oregon, absorbed the 196th into the division's organization. The objectives for Operation Wheeler/Wallowa were to locate and destroy enemy forces in the Que Son and Hiep Duc Valleys, to provide security to Tam Ky, the capital city of Quang Tin Province, and to secure a portion of Highway One north of the city.

Another major operation, Operation Burlington Trail, began on April 8, 1968 with three objectives: Open the twelve miles of Provincial Route 533 from Tam KY to Tien Phuoc; neutralize the NVA forces in the area; and extend the South Vietnamese Army's (ARVN) presence into the Tien Phuoc Valley. Tien Phuoc was the district capital in Quang Tin province and the site of a US Army Special Forces outpost. Quang Tin's southern boundary and Quang Ngai's northern boundary were joined together at the southern rim of LZ Bayonet and the Americal's headquarters in Chu Lai. The 5th/46th was responsible for the northern half of Quang Ngai province just south of Chu Lai, but could be tasked to cross boundaries and head north whenever additional forces were needed to fight the NVA.

Wheeler/Wallowa was not only the name of an on-going operation, but referred to the geographic area that encompassed both it and Operation Burlington Trail. Burlington Trail was conducted in the southern portion of the Wheeler/Wallowa AO. Initially the 198th began the operation with the 1st/46th and 1st/6th Infantry Battalions along with elements of the 1st/14th Artillery Battalion, the 1st Squadron, 1st Cavalry and the 2nd ARVN Division. By mid-June heavy casualties and an expansion of the operational area required support from the 5th/46th Infantry Battalion as well.

Burlington Trail

On June 13, the balance of Bravo Company of the 5th/46th which had been securing LZ Ann, was lifted off to join its two other platoons up north near Tam Ky. The following day Charlie Company assembled on LZ Gator for the same purpose. In their short amount of time on Gator, Charlie's soldiers worked on their equipment, requisitioned replacement parts for anything broken, cleaned and checked their ammo and looked forward to a night of sleep on cots after forty-five days in the field.

In the afternoon Sergeant Ed Arndt's soldiers walked past the mess hall and saw some Igloo-type water coolers filled with ice water. They stopped to get a drink. The mess sergeant came out and screamed at the grunts to stay away from the coolers, they were for his KP's. Arndt told his bone-tired soldiers to "Leave the Motherfucker Chicken-shits alone." To Arndt the slight wasn't worth a fist-fight. There wasn't a great deal of love lost between some of the rear-echelon troops in the battalion headquarters on Gator and the field soldiers. Those who worked at the company level, such as clerks, supply personnel, etc. generally had a great deal of respect and empathy for their fellow soldiers who went to the field and worked hard to support them. A number of them felt guilty not being field soldiers.

Charlie moved by Chinook Helicopter from LZ Gator to Tam Ky. From there it combat air-assaulted in Hueys to the field. Charlie Company lifted off on June 15 using a total of fifteen Hueys in flights of three. Arndt was in the first ship along with Mike Ayers, a machine gunner, and two other men from his squad. As their bird descended onto the LZ with two other Hueys behind them, they heard a series of "clacks", ground fire coming up at them, and saw their aircraft commander jerking his head, looking around quickly in all directions, as though his head was on a swivel. Their bird touched down and Ayers started to exit with his machine gun amidst the enemy fire. A door gunner grabbed his rucksack and pulled him back into the chopper. The LZ was too hot and the three lead birds quickly took off and flew back to Tam Ky, while artillery and jet aircraft pounded the site. Later the three birds returned and Arndt's small group established a base of fire on the ground while the next group of three Hueys landed and disgorged more soldiers. Three more birds followed the first two lifts, each group of soldiers enabling Charlie Company to expand the perimeter on the LZ.

The operation was another day of hell in intense heat and Charlie's soldiers quickly ran low on water. They filled their canteens from pools of stagnant water lying in bomb craters, cupping their hands over the canteen mouth while filling them, to keep leaches from entering. One of the gunships supporting the air-assault had a mechanical problem and landed on a small hill near the LZ. Arndt's squad was ordered to secure the downed gunship. The pilots told them to remove the remaining rockets from their launch pods so a Chinook could come in and sling load the gunship to fly it back to Chu Lai. The soldiers nervously asked the pilot "What would happen if one of the rockets cooked off on us?" The pilot retorted, "Nothing, as long as you can run real fast and keep up with it".

LTC Lyon moved his consolidated command group to LZ Bowman in the 196th AO to coordinate a joint sweep of the area by Bravo and Charlie once both companies arrived. The two companies moved out in separate groups. Charlie moved into some jungle terrain and started up the side of a mountain for a couple hours. It was ordered to stop so an air strike could be dropped on the thick terrain to its front. The soldiers felt shards of metal from the air strike falling on them through the heavily canopied jungle. After the jets left Charlie's point element with Sergeant Arndt, could hear voices ahead. Arndt radioed back, asking if there were any other "friendlies" in the area. The answer came back, "No." Arndt was instructed to move forward and take a closer look. He and another soldier crawled to within twenty yards of the voices and saw a black-skinned soldier in jungle fatigues. Arndt radioed back to his platoon leader who told him to "blow him away." Charlie's

Tam Ky

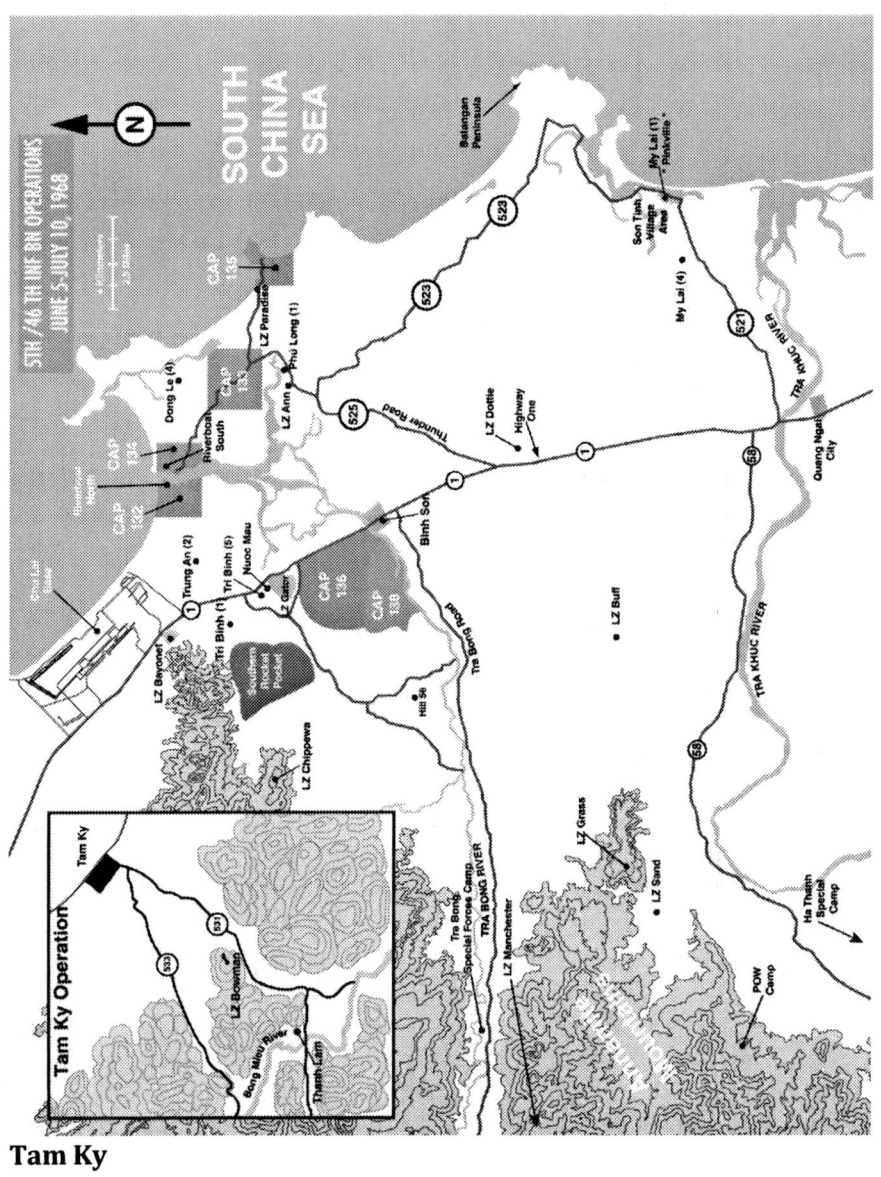

commander, Captain Johnson thought better of the plan and told them to check on the radio it was determined that the men in front of Arndt were from Bravo Company, who were supposed to be five miles further away. A minor disaster was averted.

The battalion's move north from the Gator AO left one platoon from Delta Company and a mortar squad from Echo Company to secure LZ Chippewa. Alpha Company was in sole possession of the northern half of the coastal lowlands from Chu Lai to Quang Ngai, and could only count on support from the four Marine CAP teams in the immediate area. There were some armored personnel carriers from H troop, 17th Cavalry, and Swift Boats from the riverine patrols at the headwaters of the Tra Bong River further north. Alpha soldiered on, relying on its junior leaders and the courage of its individual grunts. The term "grunt" was common slang to describe the average infantryman, denoting the groan let out when the heavy rucksacks of ammunition, food, and water were lifted on the backs of weary soldiers.

Typical of Alpha's dogged efforts on the coast was the experience of the 1st platoon led by Lt. Henry Stauffer. On June 12, his grunts engaged in a shoot-out with VC at Dong Le (4). Stauffer was hit with shrapnel in the back, shoulder and head and dusted off. He later returned to the field. In the heat of the fight PFC Wayne Decker charged the insurgents in a one man assault with grenades and rifle fire, but was shot in the head which caused massive brain damage. He died the next day and was posthumously awarded the Silver Star. Decker was age 20 and single from Elkhart, Indiana.

Shortly after Charlie was moved north to Tam Ky, Alpha got the nod to be prepared to do the same while it continued its mission on the coast. If Alpha moved north there would be no Army troops left in the area. Engineers began destroying LZ Ann; there was simply no one left to defend it. Alpha's soldiers had been stretched thin with patrols around Ann and were happy at the prospect of leaving the hilltop. It was as unpleasant a place as could be found. Grunts woke at night to find rats crawling on their faces. They left food for the rats apart from the sleeping area to steer them away. Destroying the bunkers gave the grunts their last revenge. With .45 caliber pistols in hand they shot the rats as they scampered out of their bunkers. Two days later, while still dismantling Ann, Alpha gave up its first platoon to fly north and lend support to some H Troop, 17th Cavalry soldiers engaged in the

Burlington Trail operation. The remainder of Alpha continued to dismantle Ann and patrol around LZ Paradise.

As previously mentioned, immediately after landing in the LZ Bowman area, Bravo and Charlie pushed west in a shoot and run contest with small elements of the VC and NVA. Their success would mostly come from what they found and not from the number of enemy they killed. The ground around Bowman offered the prospect of engaging tough main force VC and NVA, something the battalion had not experienced in the LZ Gator area. Despite the prospect of facing main-force NVA regulars, the soldiers were happy to be removed from the mines of the coastal lowlands. Intelligence reports indicated at least two Vietcong battalions (409th Sapper Battalion and 70th Main Force Battalion) and the 40th NVA Battalion were in the area. Shortly after the 5th/46th arrived, villagers reported large enemy formations moving west, trying to escape to the mountains.

On June 16, Captain Johnson's Charlie Company found One thousand, four hundred and seventy-five pounds of rice on top of a high hill two and one-half miles southwest of Bowman. The next morning they descended the north slope of the hill and walked into an abandoned NVA base camp containing twenty-five bunkers and tunnels, all recently occupied. Sensing that Charlie might be on to something, Bravo Company was sent to join the search on the north slope while Charlie Company backed out to search the southern slope. Two days later on the 18th, the hill revealed more evidence it had been a major staging site for the VC and NVA. Charlie's troops detained a VC suspect who led them to a mortar cache with a complete 81mm mortar, base plate, sighting mechanism and mortar rounds. Bravo's soldiers located more tunnels that contained fifteen dead NVA and scattered rocket canisters. By the end of the day Bravo found two thousand, three hundred pounds of rice and Charlie located two thousand, seven hundred pounds more. These stocks were airlifted to the Tien Phuoc Special Forces camp.

Just a few days after the 5th/46th entered the Burlington Trail operation, alarm bells were sounding off on its home turf. Intelligence reports indicated that the NVA located in the mountains west of Binh Son, near the Tra Bong Special Forces camp, threatened to attack the district capital of Binh Son. On June 19, Bravo and Charlie assembled on Provincial Route 531 in order to be picked up by Hueys and returned to Tam Ky where they would fly by Chinook to the LZ Gator area. Route 531 was a dirt road just over a mile south of LZ Bowman, cutting through a narrow valley north of the hill that had provided the bonanza of enemy equipment the day before. The primitive road was the only flat ground in the area that could serve as a pick up zone (PZ). Adjacent to the dirt road near the PZ lay a small hamlet.

The task to extract Bravo and Charlie fell to the 71st Assault Helicopter Company. The company was organized with three platoons. Two were troop-carrying UH-1Ds and UH-1Hs, Hueys. The Hueys' only protection was two M-60 machine guns, one on each side of the bird, manned by door gunners. These two platoons were known as the "Rattlers". The other platoon, the "Firebirds" flew UH-1C helicopter gunships. Their primary mission was to support the Hueys or "slicks" when they were landing or picking up troops. When not supporting Rattlers, the Firebirds flew missions of opportunity to seek out the NVA and VC wherever they could find them.

At 4:55PM on June 19, the Rattlers entered the narrow valley to pick up the waiting troops, with the Firebirds close behind. Bravos 3rd platoon under 1LT Bob Chappell was to be extracted first. As Chappell and his RTO with another grunt approached their slick, Captain Lamb followed, deciding to get on the same bird with his two RTO's. Chappell noticed the "Peter Pilot" (co-pilot) had written in a grease pencil on his windshield, "WO (Warrant Officer) Charley Cotton – SHORT – 15 days and a wakeup". As Chappell rounded the front of the Huey to get on board he acknowledged the message to the short-timer with a thumbs-up. Cotton returned a big smile and laughed.

The bird lifted off the ground but only climbed a few hundred feet when it received heavy automatic weapons fire. Chappell was sitting on the floor, behind the aircraft commander's seat with his legs crossed indian style. Two rounds came through the floor between his crossed legs and through the roof. The troopers could hear loud popping sounds hitting the aircraft. Suddenly the Huey started to roll to the right and descend. Chappell looked over his shoulder and saw WO Cotton slumped over the controls which caused the bird to weave in the air and lose altitude. One of Lambs RTO's, Private Kim St. Bernard reached over his shoulder and grabbed Cotton, pulling him back in his seat. This allowed the aircraft commander, WO Benny Goodman, to regain control of the chopper just as the engine started shutting down. St. Bernard's quick action saved the lives of everyone on board. The terrified grunts sat helpless as the pilot tried to set the bird down with no engine power and incoming enemy fire. He landed it hard in a dried-up rice paddy next to the hamlet. The passengers made a fast exit from the bird, taking the M-60's with them to set up a hasty perimeter by a rice paddy dike. WO Cotton had received a mortal wound from an enemy bullet which came up through his window and penetrated his skull.

The Firebirds flying above were enraged. No sooner had the troops exited the aircraft than the gunships came in and unloaded everything they had on the hamlet next to the road. Rockets, 40mm grenades, and machineguns obliterated the small group of dwellings. Whether the gunfire had actually come from the hamlet or not, the Firebirds were not in a guessing mood, and wanted swift revenge for the loss of their fellow aviator. A Rattler slick came in and picked up Cotton's body with the rest of the aircraft's crew and flew off. Chappell, Lamb and four others set up their six-man perimeter in anticipation of a ground attack, while the Firebirds hovered above. In an hour the rest of Bravo and Charlie walked to their location, tired and drained from humping their heavy loads. PFC William "Joe" Scurlock, one of Charlie's medics, was called over to a hooch on the edge of the hamlet. "Hey doc we got one for you to patch up!" Scurlock walked over and entered the hooch. A boy six or seven years of age lay in a hammock with his brains dripping on the ground. Scurlock walked back out, cursing his buddies for their sick joke.

It was late afternoon and Bravo and Charlie Companies set up a defensive perimeter in the hamlet for the night. As dusk approached the soldiers, still digging their fighting positions, watched an old woman approach them in a ghost-like trance, carrying the dead boy in her arms. The top half of his head was missing and his skin was a pale gray from blood loss. She cried, cursed and then said nothing, staring straight-ahead as she walked through the perimeter. The soldiers stopped digging and froze as they watched her pass by. Scurlock, the medic trained to save life was remorseful, "This was someone's child, not another enemy gook."

The following morning the grunts were lifted off to Tam Ky and then back to LZ Gator. While Bravo and Charlie had been patrolling the hills northwest of Tam Ky, Alpha Company had continued its work on the coastal lowlands with aggressive patrolling and the defense of LZ Paradise. The dismantling of LZ Ann was completed June 15. Delta secured LZ Gator but provided twenty grunts to the military police (MP) patrolling the headwaters of the Tra Bong River in 17-foot Boston Whaler patrol boats, using Riverboat South as a base. Each Whaler had a

M-60 machine gun mounted in front of the control consol for added firepower. Patrolling the Tra Bong River was hazardous duty. Two boats were used on each mission, each carrying two MP's, two Delta soldiers and a Vietnamese interpreter. At times the river narrowed to only six to eight feet of navigable water, making the boats sitting ducks for ambushes from the shoreline.

At one point or the other, many of the battalion's grunts took a turn at Riverboat South. When they were not on a hazardous river patrol, duty was more like a Rest & Recuperation (R&R). They performed guard duty at night but during daylight the grunts swam in the river using air mattresses as floats and fished with hand grenades. The grunts had Vietnamese kids clean their fish, allowing them to keep the "leftovers" after filleting the main parts for the soldiers. In short order the grunts noticed their fillets were getting thinner, and the "leftovers" had increased in size.

Delta's second platoon operated in the hills nine miles northwest of Gator to detect any major enemy movement from the mountains while LT. Care's Echo Recon Platoon continued its squad size missions west of Gator and far south on the northern edge of the Tra Bong River. The recon grunts would soon receive lots of company because that was the area Lieutenant Colonel Lyon was told to move to next.

Vance Canyon

On June 20, the battalion regrouped on LZ Gator to prepare for a new mission, known as Operation Vance Canyon. The 1st/52nd Battalion having returned from Operation Burlington Trail, was directed to take over the defense of Gator while the 5th/46th operated further south. The 1st/52nd, commanded by LTC Elbert Fuller, was tasked to cover the 5th/46's area (LZ's Gator, Chippewa and the coast), as well as LZ Dottie south of Binh Son and LZ Buff, their own battalion base camp. Buff was eight and one-half miles south of Gator, and five and one-half miles west of Highway One. Buff's low-lying hill mass had no symmetry and resembled a large lump of rolling high ground. Someone, not enamored with its character as seen from the air, referred to it as a "big, ugly fat fucker" and hence it's name, LZ Buff. Fullers successor to command the 1st/52nd, LTC William Stinson, would be killed in March 1969 and Buff was renamed LZ Stinson.

For Lyon's soldiers, it was just another one-night stand at Gator to clean equipment, reload, and return to the bush. 1LT Terry Care moved his recon platoon south to the Tra Bong Special Forces camp, which sat in the shadow of the Annamite Mountains. Care was directed to plan advance reconnaissance missions with the Green Berets and their Nung mercenaries in advance of the battalion's air assault into the area the next day.

A Green Beret A-Team of twelve men, Detachment A107, manned the Tra Bong camp. The camp was built in August 1965 as part of an early effort to form civilian irregular defense groups (CIDG) among the indigenous Montagnard tribesman (known as "Yards") living in the mountainous regions. The "Nungs", a Vietnamese minority group of ethnic Chinese descent, were also used. Nungs had a reputation as fierce fighters. With Green Beret training and leadership, the CIDG's original mission in the early 1960's was to serve as a strike force of "VC Hunters". With the growth of the Ho Chi Minh Trail and increased infiltration from North Vietnam, a shift in mission gave a greater importance to border surveillance which led to the subsequent construction of this camp in the Southern I Corps. Special forces, with their CIDG mercenaries were tasked to work with the 5th/46th Battalion in their "hunter" role for the Vance Canyon mission.

To Care's reconnaissance platoon, the Tra Bong Special Forces Camp looked like a junkyard. The defensive positions on the perimeter were "textbook", very strong and sound. But the interior was a collection of mortar pits, generators, chickens, Montagnard children running about, and bunkers placed in all directions. The CIDG soldiers and their SF advisors carried every type of weapon issued since World War II. When Captain Chiofee, Echo Company Commander visited the camp, he commented on the erratic camp organization. His Special Forces contact answered dryly, "The CIDG's live here and that's how they like it."

In the early morning of June 21, the battalion combat air assaulted south of the camp into designated landing zones. Alpha and Delta inserted into LZ Manchester five miles southwest of the Tra Bong camp. The soldiers jumped off the birds onto patches of grass which appeared to be knee-deep, but were over six feet high. With sixty-pound rucksacks on their backs, a number of ankles and knees were injured. The troops rested momentarily and lit up cigarettes. One soldier tossed a lit cigarette into the grass which burnt some nearby vegetation. The smell perked everyone up. It was a large patch of marijuana.

The hill mass designated LZ Manchester was covered with grass but contained ample flat ground at the top to hold a battery of artillery which could support the mountain mission. While the position was prepared for the artillery, Bravo landed at "LZ Grass", seven miles southeast of the Tra Bong camp to set up the initial artillery position with three 105mm howitzers from B Battery, 1st/14th Artillery. The guns at Gator and Chippewa were simply too far out of range to be of help in this operation. Joining Bravo Company were two CIDG platoons. Charlie Company landed at "LZ Sand" in a narrow valley just southwest of the high ground occupied by Bravo. One platoon of CIDG was inserted with them.

Care's recon platoon, having reached the Tra Bong Camp the night before, was able to partake in the traditional drinking party the CIDG and Green Berets staged before each mission. At first light on the 21st, they moved out of the camp with Care commanding his recon platoon, and a Green Beret Sergeant named Kennedy leading his platoon of Nungs. They headed southwest along a trail network into the mountains. Care's grunts developed an immediate fondness for the Nungs as they watched them operate and the two forces complemented each other in a variety of ways. The Americans had to carry C-Rations; meat packed in cans which was extremely heavy for a long patrol. The Nungs carried Chinese noodles plus the lightweight, freeze-dried rations known as "LRRPs" or "LURPs" provided by the Special Forces. But the Nungs craved the heavier C-rations and the meat inside. It didn't take long for swaps to take place among the grunts and Nungs until everyone was satisfied. Nungs also carried a coconut candy wrapped in a natural paper that dissolved in the mouth. Care's troops thought the candy was quite good.

The combined recon force moved through the triple canopy jungle led by the CIDG platoon, across leech-filled streams, the air heavy with dampness from rain and mildew. At one point the patrol held up at a trail intersection. It had stopped long enough to cause some concern, so Care and Kennedy moved to the front of the column to check the situation. Through an interpreter Care learned that the Nung pointman had come to this same intersection five years before and had been ambushed. He was carefully discerning which way to go. Care shook his head thinking, "These guys have been doing this for five years and most of us will be in the field less than a year".

On June 22, Bravo and the three howitzers were moved from LZ Grass to LZ Manchester after that hilltop was cleared and a tactical headquarters set up for LTC Lyon. Bravo took two platoons to secure the perimeter and a CIDG platoon of Montagnards joined them. Although Manchester was a primitive firebase there were an ample number of "REMF"S", Rear Echelon Mother Fuckers", who dropped in to see the "war". Bravo's hardened grunts looked at perimeter duty as a drag, "chicken-shit" duty with battalion staff officers walking about, acting as though they understood field duty. Bob Chappell, who commanded one of the platoons, found the Montagnards to be, in some respects, like kids, ready to steal anything that was not nailed down. On patrol they were deadly careful, but on a night perimeter they lit up fires that had to be constantly extinguished to keep the enemy from using them as aiming points for their mortars.

Charlie Company exited LZ Sand after shooting a fleeing Vietcong. It moved up the rugged terrain southwest of Sand, in the direction of Alpha and Delta. Charlie was destined to repeat its success at finding things, as it did near LZ Bowman, but got off to a bad start for reasons beyond its control. On the previous day Bravo's LT. Chappell tried to assist the battery commander of the howitzers on Manchester, when he was sighting in his guns. Chappell noticed the battery commander was using the wrong hilltop on his map to denote LZ Manchester. Chappell, the lieutenant with field experience, couldn't make the Captain change his coordinates and walked away disgusted. The Captain proceeded with his task; neither sought to seek an arbitrator and Charlie Company would pay the price.

At 8:44AM on the 23rd, Charlie Company's point platoon commanded by Lt. Donald Wilson reached a creek bed at the bottom of a ridge when it came under heavy automatic weapons fire, wounding one soldier. The platoon immediately deployed to both sides of the creek bed and soldiers were hit by command detonated mines which wounded five more. Sargent Martin Jordan moved among the wounded, giving medical aid while under constant fire. PFC William Scurlock, the platoon's medic, moved forward into the kill zone to administer medical aid and direct the bandaging of others. With bullets zipping out of the dense terrain all around them Jordan and Scurlock stabilized the wounded, and carried the most seriously wounded over five hundred yards to where a dustoff could land. Both soldiers were awarded Bronze Stars for valor.

The enemy fire continued and Lt. Wilson called for an artillery fire mission from the Manchester battery. The guns, registered on the wrong hill, dropped their rounds on Charlie's soldiers, wounding an additional five grunts including Wilson. Chappell, monitoring the radio traffic calling for a dustoff, knew immediately what had happened. He radioed the battalion S-3 Operations Officer, Major Carl Koppeis concerning the cause of the errant rounds. In short order a helicopter arrived on Manchester and the Artillery Captain was ushered out. For the balance of the day and through June 24 the three-company force, Alpha, Bravo and Charlie searched the mountains but met light resistance. They found some way-stations for guerillas that were on the move which included ammunition, small corn fields, pigs and chickens.

On June 25, Charlie ran into a force of VC, killing three and capturing two AK-47's rifles, four grenades and some clothing. The next day they found thirty-one automatic weapons, a recoilless rifle, mortar rounds, three light machine guns and a large stack of ammunition. The following day at noon on the 27th they entered what appeared to be a small POW camp containing nine buildings enclosed by a bamboo fence seven feet high. The fence was intertwined with concertina wire to prevent those inside from escaping. A center platform six feet high served as a guard tower. Two hooch's outside the compound appeared to be the guards sleeping quarters while the buildings inside the fence were constructed with doors which could only be locked from the outside. The grunts also found inside the compound several wood stocks for hands and legs, reminiscent of those used by the early American Pilgrims.

At 7:30PM just two miles west of Charlie Company, Alpha, also operating on a hill mass, came upon a hooch with punji stakes and sleeping mats. After ninety minutes the company carefully picked its way another three hundred yards farther north and walked upon a large building with several bundles of punji stakes six to seven inches long. Punji stakes were another weapon of the Vietcong. Punji pits were dug into the ground and the bamboo stakes, with pointed ends up, were anchored into the ground at the bottom of the hole. Light twigs and leaves covered the opening. A grunt stepping on this trap would plunge his foot into the hole and be stabbed by the sharp bamboo, sometimes causing horrific wounds. A tunnel was also discovered in the small camp, functioning as a bomb shelter. A few feet away was a classroom with two rows of seats on each side with a couple of tables, a blackboard and chalk.

On June 28, Charlie's grunts located another weapons cache with AK-47 automatic rifles, light machine guns, a 60mm mortar, rocket launchers and ammunition. Alpha likewise continued to find evidence of recent enemy presence, locating a tunnel complex with VC propaganda, an NVA personnel roster, and newspapers. Alpha moved west one-half mile on a densely-covered ridgeline when it received automatic weapons fire from a squad-size element, wounding three grunts. The dense terrain made it difficult to pursue their foe. The best Alpha could accomplish was to call a dustoff for its wounded soldier and request some rocket fire from helicopter gunships circling overhead. That evening LZ Manchester received automatic weapons fire and incoming grenades along its perimeter.

The next day Charlie's grunts found a small Vietcong training center in the rugged terrain which included an obstacle course made of bamboo and wire. It had all the markings of a permanent facility. A further search found numerous foxholes, an obstacle wall, and practice grenades made of wood. They destroyed the camp and moved southeast for one-third of a mile, across a ridgeline to the top of another hill, where they found a larger base camp. Fortunately for Charlie's soldiers, who were exhausted and under strength, the camp had been abandoned recently. The complex consisted of two hooch's and approximately one hundred foxholes, each with a tunnel behind it. The tunnels were deep enough for three to five soldiers to quickly escape if air strikes fell on their position.

June 30 brought another day of discovery for Alpha and Charlie as they searched the mountainous terrain nine miles south of the Tra Bong camp. By noon Charlie's grunts moved two-thirds of a mile north from their previous position and located another base camp with thirty small hooch's, each large enough to house seven to eight soldiers. It had been occupied two-three days before, with its tenants moving out after the 5th/46th air assaulted into the area. Alpha, operating two and one-half miles southwest from Charlie found an NVA hospital complex complete with beds, bomb shelters and assorted items such as crutches, but minus hastily removed medical supplies and patients. The grunts marveled at the complexity of the camp, finding central heating and running water systems. A large oven-like structure sat in the middle of the camp with small covered ditches leading to the hooch's. The covered ditches provided hot air to be "piped in" during the chill of the mountain nights. Running water was provided by a system of bamboo pipes, all gravity fed.

For the nine days the grunts of the 5th/46th scoured the mountainous terrain they confirmed what intelligence reports had indicated. This was an elaborate base camp area spread out across approximately fourteen square miles of rough terrain. The battalion's presence disrupted enemy plans for a push east for an assault on the district town of Binh Son. The battalion also lucked-out with the enemy choosing to retreat further into the mountains to avoid a major fight. The ante on combat for the battalion however would soon be upped for its weary troops.

LTC Lyon received word from the 198th Brigade at LZ Bayonet to be prepared to move again, this time back to the Muscatine (Coastal lowlands) AO, no later than July 2. While most of the grunts began consolidating on Manchester to lift off to the coast, Captain Erb of Alpha thought he could find more enemy camps and requested an extension of his time on the ground. This did not go over well with his troops who needed a rest. For the next three days they moved further east and southeast in the mountains down to the Ha Thanh Special Forces camp, located in another mountainous valley sixteen miles west of Quang Ngai City. Although coming under sporadic shoot and run contact, Erb's quest in the mountains yielded no more discoveries and further weakened his men for a major fight that was soon to come.

While on their extended mountain trek, resupply in the dense terrain was extremely difficult. There was little water in their part of the mountains. Soldiers dipped their canteens into craters left by B-52 Bomber Air Strikes, bringing up water full of large green leeches. The water was strained through poncho liners to remove leeches, mosquitoes and other bugs. Alpha Company had a choice to blow some trees with C-4 explosive to bring in supplies or have some Hueys hover high overhead and drop cases of C-rations. They chose the later. One "lifer" platoon sergeant, who had not been liked since Fort Hood, yelled at his men to get close to trees as the resupply came tumbling down. The sergeant was hit with a case of rations which required his men to level some trees anyway for a chopper to fly in. He was never seen again.

On July 1 Delta, Charlie and Echo Recon converged on pick-up zones for the move back to the coastal plains. Chinooks were detailed for the pick-up with fire support from three Huey gunships. Extraction would be from the same narrow valley Charlie Company had set down in ten days earlier, on LZ Sand. In the extraction process, one Chinook collided with a gunship in midair. The gunship spun in circles until its pilot regained control and set it down by autorotation but the Chinook broke in two and plunged to the ground. As it fell soldiers on the ground watched two crewmembers fall from the bird and tumble down into the trees, getting impaled on the branches. Three other crew members went down inside the bird. After much effort the bodies of all five crewmembers were recovered. Delta was lifted to LZ Buff, along with the mortars from Echo Company to support the 1st/52nd, which was stretched thin on its headquarters perimeter. Bravo remained on Manchester to provide security while the firebase was torn down and the artillery extracted.

BATTLE OF PINKVILLE

On July 4, Bravo arrived at LZ Dottie and pushed off to the northwest for a reconnaissance in force, their platoons separated but in close proximity to one another. Supporting them were APC's or "tracks" from the 2nd Platoon, H Troop, 17th Cavalry. Bravo was glad to have them, the soldiers walked in the tread tracks made by the armored personnel carriers, to avoid anti-personnel mines. But in war tragedy is ever present and fate sometimes overrules precautions. When Bravo's soldiers pulled into a night position, soldiers threw their rucksacks from the tracks, to prepare their fighting holes for the night. One rucksack had a hand grenade attached to a strap. The rucksack hit the ground and the grenade's corroded pin snapped causing an explosion. Seven grunts in the immediate area were wounded, three seriously. A scout dog resting nearby was killed. One of those wounded was PFC George Vander Dussen. The medics evaluated him and found a small puncture wound to his lower back which entered his kidney. He was quickly dusted off but an infection set in that could not be healed. Vander Dussen died six days later on July 10. Vander Dussen was age 21 and married from Artesia, California.

Charlie Company was tasked to help secure LZ Dottie while running local patrols and night ambushes in the area. Sergeant Arndt's squad was one of those remaining on Dottie to help defend the perimeter. The landing zone was defended by Charlie Company of the

1st/20th Infantry Battalion of the 11th Light Infantry Brigade, part of a "Task Force Barker". The 11th Brigade at this time controlled the southern part of the coastal lowlands down to Quang Ngai City as part of the "Muscatine" operations.

Charlie Company of the 1st/20th was commanded by a Captain Ernest Medina. Sergeant Arndt spoke to members of Medina's company and developed some home town banter with some of the soldiers from Tennessee. Arndt was introduced to a platoon Sergeant from middle Tennessee, Arndt's home turf and he proceeded to tell Arndt a story about going into a village south of LZ Dottie and killing everyone, including women and children. Arndt didn't believe him. He had been exposed to other "stories" of VC being thrown from helicopters, summary executions, etc. The person telling the story was never there, but his buddy knew a guy who knew a guy who saw it. He didn't believe the sergeant. The thought of those actions was abhorrent to him. Months later Arndt would meet the same sergeant again at Fort Campbell, Kentucky. Both were getting early outs from the Army, Arndt because of wounds and the other for "compassionate" reasons. The platoon sergeant walked away from Arndt as soon as he saw him.

Echo's Recon Platoon also joined the battalion on Dottie and moved east to screen the area with patrols and night ambushes. On July 5 the tracks that worked with Bravo Company continued to set off anti-personnel mines in front of the grunts as they walked behind on the tread path made by the APC's. But by 3:00PM Bravo's luck ran out when a soldier in the fourth platoon, SP/4 Thomas Van Guilder hit an anti-personnel mine. The explosion propelled him six feet into the air. Both he and Sergeant Billy Hooker standing next to him received leg wounds. Fragmentation vests shielded their bodies from multiple metal fragments which ripped into their vests. Van Guilder's leg wounds were very serious. The platoon leader, Sergeant First Class Albert Stephens, rushed forward. Another soldier standing next to Stephens, SP/4 Roosevelt Hurst turned away after the explosion and walked back a few steps to sit on a dike and bend over. Van Guilder's first words to Stephens were, "Sarge, I know my left leg is gone, but how about my right?" Stephens looked at his right leg which was completely mangled but told him he would make it, less he go into shock. A dustoff was called. The platoon medic called Stephens attention to SP/4 Hurst sitting on the dike. Hurst had shunned wearing the hot and bulky protective vest and was seriously wounded with a sucking chest wound. Van

Guilder, Hooker and Hurst were dusted off. Van Guilder would lose both legs at the hip and Hurst died in route to the hospital. SP/4 Roosevelt Hurst was single and age 21, from Saraland, Alabama.

At 11:00AM the 198th Brigade Commander's attention was drawn to a report from an American ARVN advisor, flying in a helicopter up the coast to Chu Lai, who observed a large group of Vietcong in uniform just north of a coastal enclave known as "Pinkville" - My Lai (1). "Pinkville" was so designated because of the solid pink color on operational maps, which denoted a large concentration of people in the hamlet. Pinkville was situated six miles northeast of Quang Ngai City, with Provincial Route 521, a dirt road, linking Pinkville to Quang Ngai.

The battalion was about to be dropped into a deadly cauldron caused by a long and brutal history of the area which would ultimately make the My Lai hamlets and the area northeast of them on the Binh Duc Cape, the Batangan Peninsula, the most heavily mined area in the Vietnam War. Quang Ngai Province historically had a long history of supporting rebellion. After World War II when the French tried to reestablish itself in Indochina, Quang Ngai became a Viet Minh stronghold for the expulsion of the French. As early as 1948 Ho Chi Minh considered Quang Ngai Province free from French rule. When the country was divided in 1954 under the Geneva Accords into North and South Vietnam, hard-core Viet Minh remained behind in the area and by the early 1960's, a whole generation of young Vietnamese had grown up to carry the fight to "liberate" Quang Ngai.

In the "Strategic Hamlet" program of the early 1960's, the villagers of Son My, with the hamlets of the My Lai's comprising part of the village, were resettled and the hamlets burnt to the ground by ARVN soldiers to prevent their use by the communists. Most villagers drifted back to their homes and rebuilt hooch's to live under both Vietcong and government control. Their desire to live on their ancestral land was paramount.

A number of VC and NVA regiments had operated in Quang Ngai Province prior to the formation of the Americal Division. However, the 48th Local Force (LF) Battalion became the principal threat in the southern Quang Ngai Province and the Son Tinh District. The district boundaries were north of the Tra Khuc River and Quang Ngai City, stretching west of Highway One to the mountains, and east of Highway One to the coast. My Lai(1), Pinkville, where the large group of Vietcong were spotted from the air, was but one sub-hamlet among four hamlet

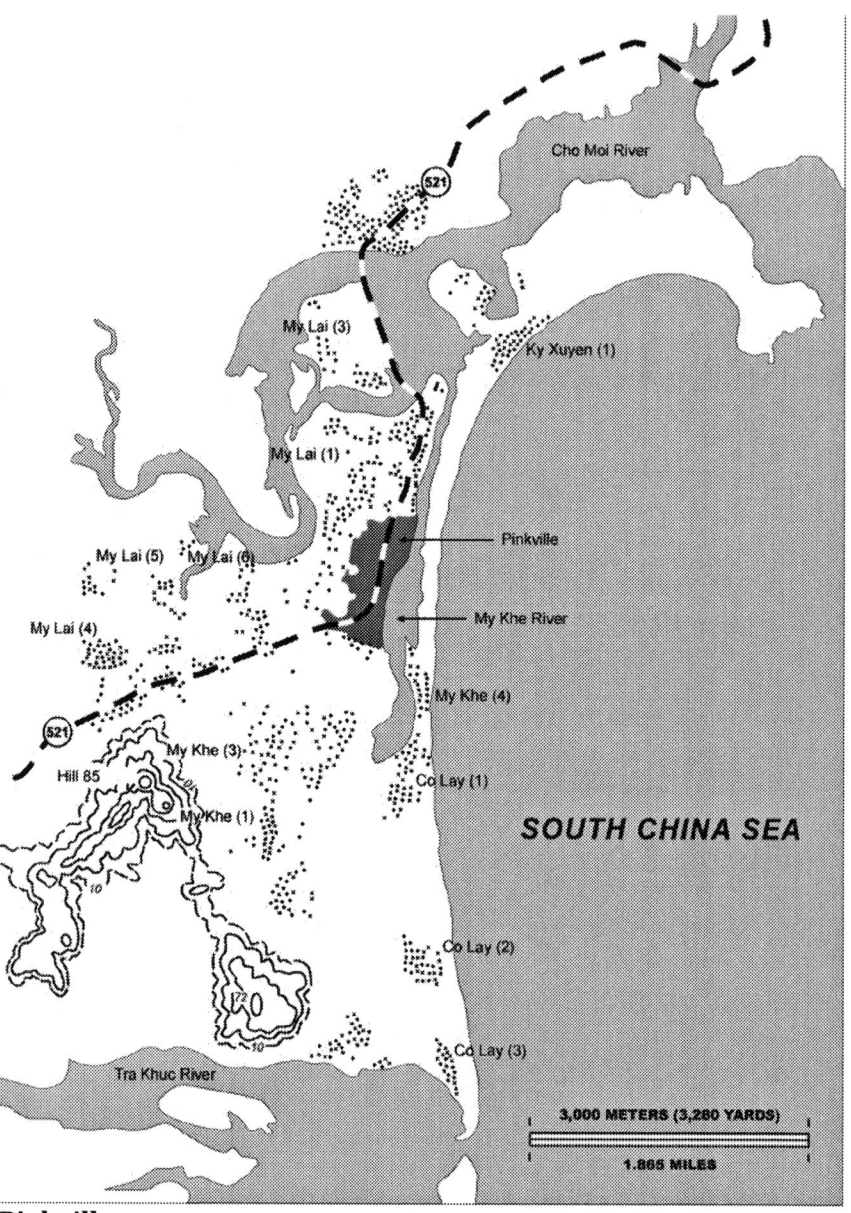

Pinkville

groups, the My Lai's, My Khe's, Co Lay's and Tu Cung's which comprised the village of Son My.

Enemy local force battalions normally recruited from a particular district and limited their operations to the local area. But the 48th LF Battalion stretched itself even farther, operating north in Binh Son District which was the principal operating area of the 5th/46th Infantry Battalion. The 48th Battalion lived with local villagers in hamlets or in well-developed tunnel systems in order to conceal their presence. They operated in typical guerilla fashion, "farmer by day and fighter at night." Their headquarters was reported to exist in fortified underground positions northeast of the Pinkville area, on the smaller but geographically well defined Batangan Peninsula.

During the TET offensive of February 1968, the 48th LF Battalion overran the Regional Force/Popular Force Training Center near Son Tinh but was eventually driven out by soldiers of the 2nd ARVN Division. In the fighting the 48th suffered about one hundred and fifty casualties, including the battalion commander and two company commanders killed with a third company commander captured. After TET, remnants of the 48th retreated into the mountains to rest and reequip or melted into the hamlets on the Batangan. The long and bloody history of Son My village in the Son Tinh District of Quang Ngai Province was soon to add another blood-stained page with the arrival of the 5th/46th on July 5, 1968.

At 11:00AM on the 5th, after the American advisor spotted the formation of Vietcong just north of Pinkville, the 198th Brigade Commander became eager to bag the enemy formation. Although the 5th/46th located on LZ Dottie was exhausted from the Burlington Trail and Vance Canyon missions, the operation was organized quickly. Air strikes, artillery and helicopter gunships were laid on and LTC Lyon was told to stand by. Alpha Company, coming in from the Ha Thanh Special Forces Camp, was the only unit not strung out on patrols. Although its strength was down to eighty-four grunts, Lyon told Captain Erb to get ready as a reactionary force. Erb's troops were bone tired from the extra trek in the mountains. What Alpha desperately needed was some rest. What they got was an air assault into one of the deadliest hamlets in the Americal Division's AO.

At 6:30PM on July 5, Erb's troops were air assaulted to the beach just north of the Pinkville hamlet, near where the VC formation had been spotted. Gunships prepared the LZ with heavy rocket fire, and then shifted fire to the west and south. Erb's troopers were carried in on five slicks in three lifts. His soldiers found enough light in the waning daytime hours to see the enemy fire coming up to their helicopters. Yet it was dark enough to see the muzzle flashes across the ground below them.

Sergeant Bob Cummings, a squad leader in the second platoon turned to one of his men, Bob Salter, and asked, "How can a chopper tell if it is being fired at with all this noise?" At that instant they heard loud "cracks" of bullets zinging by. They also saw tracers that seemed to be curving up to meet them. Cummings turned to Salter, "Oh, so that's how you tell." Salter, sitting in the open doorway was getting "edgy" and began firing down on the enemy as Cummings held the straps on Salter's rucksack to keep him from falling out. They landed on a narrow peninsula running north from Pinkville, a beach enclave with the South China Sea on the east and the My Khe River on the west. The river ran south through Pinkville, creating a canal between the beach and the hamlet. During the air assault, gunships protecting the slicks killed eight Vietcong and set off a total of seven secondary explosions in the area, indicating caches of enemy ammunition. Jet air strikes were made before the gunships arrived, killing more insurgents. Alpha would later find bodies everywhere.

LTC Lyon, flying in his command & control bird, surveyed the area where the gunships were hitting their targets and his bird took hits from automatic weapons fire. The chopper lost oil pressure and emergency lights came on, followed by a loss of power. Lyon's pilot landed the bird by autorotation, essentially guiding it to the ground with dead engines, onto the beach near Alpha's troops. By this time Erb had placed his second platoon five hundred yards south on the sandy beach, only five hundred yards from the north edge of Pinkville. Immediately after Lyon's bird landed the second platoon received heavy machinegun fire from the hamlet. Lyon's crew removed the two M-60 machine guns from the chopper and prepared a defensive position. Within twenty minutes another bird arrived to take Lyon and his crew back to LZ Dottie and Erb was tasked to guard the aircraft until the next day. It was now 7:40PM. Sergeant Cummings soon learned that shit falls downhill quickly. Erb tasked the 2nd platoon leader, Richard Horne Jr., to secure the ditched chopper. Horne in turn ordered Cummings' squad to get it done. Noting that the downed helicopter was not within the defensive lines of the rest of Alpha, Cummings squad dug deep holes and remained awake all night, their position completely exposed.

As they prepared their night defenses, Alpha's troops found a reinforced bunker system three hundred yards away but they had no demolitions to do much about it. More enemy fire hit Alpha at 11:00PM, requiring a dustoff for two grunts with head wounds but artillery fire discouraged any enemy night attack. At midnight Erb received a warning from the brigade headquarters at LZ Bayonet, "You are in a heavily booby-trapped area. Expect to find yourselves completely encircled. This comes from a commander who worked in your area before".

By 7:30AM on July 6, Erb moved his headquarters element and second platoon into the hamlet of Ky Xuyen (1) which was close to where he landed on the beach. His third platoon was more than a half mile south on the beach-like peninsula. The first platoon was tasked to move north from the third to link up with Erb. The troops with the headquarters element were busy in the hamlet finding tunnels, bunkers and munitions. An Explosive Ordnance Demolition (EOD) team was choppered in from Gator to help out. Crater charges were used to destroy the enemy munitions. But there was so much destruction lying on the ground that logs and trees were blown sky high, the soldier's eyes following the timber going up then dodging the logs when they fell to the ground. There was simply no place to take cover on the sandy beach.

Dead bodies were everywhere. The battalion had initially reported the eight dead VC from the gunships prepping the landing zone but Alpha's grunts were finding many more with weapons. No one was interested in reporting body counts beyond the original eight previously reported, and didn't give any additional reports because no one asked for them. Most dead were partially buried in destroyed bunkers but not all were combatants. In one bunker lay a young, beautiful Vietnamese woman with her left breast exposed and a baby still suckled to it. Both were dead.

By 2:30PM, the engineers destroyed a cesspool of bombs and bomb-making equipment, including an unexploded five hundred pound bomb from an air strike. Thousands of flies were everywhere amidst the carnage, the dead bodies now rotting in the sun. If a soldier opened his mouth for any reason, flies flew in. Before soldiers could get their canteens to their mouths to drink water, flies flew inside the canteens. If they tried to open a can of C-rations, two layers of flies were on the food instantly. They were everywhere, landing on their sweat-soaked bodies and crawling into eyes and ears.

The next day Erb moved his troops farther south on the sandy beach to the northeast corner of Pinkville. The canal separating the beach from the hamlet was only thirty yards wide and a small footbridge connected both sides. At 10:05AM, Alpha came under heavy fire from the hamlet. After establishing a base of fire from the beach, Erb was ordered to attack the hamlet. He sent small groups of grunts by leaps and bounds over the footbridge to establish a position on the other side at the edge of the hamlet. Gunships were requested to help in the attack but none were available.

Alpha had little choice but to press the fight forward since its position on the beach left it too exposed. Once soldiers on the other side gained a foothold, Erb and a larger group of grunts dashed over the bridge to add weight to the fight. The Vietcong got what they wanted. Their trap was set and the bridge exploded from a command-detonated mine. In an instant bodies were lying in the water and on the beach, seventeen grunts wounded, including Richard Horne a platoon leader and Erb, the company commander. Alpha's grunts received a shocking blow that traumatized everyone. Loyalty to one another, and guts and determination took over in the midst of the disaster.

Although SP/4 Donald Hess's face was bleeding from a shrapnel wound, he grabbed another injured grunt and carried him back to the beach while under heavy fire. He went forward to bring another grunt back and treated both, giving comfort to his traumatized buddies. SP/5 Jon Kester was a medic who caught shrapnel in the right eye and over most of his upper body. Ignoring his wounds he organized a medical treatment effort on the beach while under fire, advising the other grunts on the use of field dressings, morphine syrettes, splints and tourniquets. His direction provided order and comfort amidst the chaos. PFC Stephen Richards, another medic was unable to move because of serious wounds but yelled out instructions for other grunts to efficiently use his supplies. He was able to able to hang on long enough until a dustoff took him back to the hospital in Chu Lai but he succumbed to his wounds twenty-one days later. Richards was 20 and married from Burlington, North Carolina. He was posthumously awarded the Silver Star.

Sp/4 Carl Roegner, an RTO, had been hit in the face but waved off any medical aid while calling in dustoff support. PFC Kenneth Steele, another RTO was wounded in the face and foot. Under the heavy automatic weapons fire coming from the hamlet, he made two trips, carrying two wounded grunts fifty-five yards away from the demolished bridge back to the beach. SP/4 John Bridges had not been wounded but exposed himself repeatedly under the heavy fire to get off effective shots with his M-79 grenade launcher. He crawled thirty yards to grab an aid kit left in the open and brought it back to treat the wounded. Staff Sergeant William Weber was in the first group that had crossed the bridge. When the bridge exploded he directed fire on the enemy positions. Realizing more effective action was needed, he led his team to assault a gun position in the hamlet. SP/4 Charles Bennett was up with him, firing his M-79 grenade launcher. Both soldiers were cut down by enemy fire. Webber was age 21 and married from Denville, New Jersey and Bennett was age 20 and also married, from Calhoun, Georgia.

Those on the hamlet side of the canal were supported by jet aircraft, which dropped five hundred pound bombs on the hamlet. By 1:30PM, the balance of Alpha consolidated back on the beach side of the canal in preparation for a counterattack and to secure the dustoffs for their wounded. Another air strike was made west of the canal at 1:48PM, to suppress the fire still coming from that direction. Clearly Alpha, and by extension the battalion, had hit a hornets nest in Pinkville.

At 2:00PM, the 2nd and 4th platoons from Bravo and one platoon from Charlie Company lifted off Dottie and were deposited on the western side of Pinkville as a blocking force. Likewise the 1st and 3rd platoons from Bravo, under the command of the 3rd platoon leader, Bob Chappell, were set down one-half mile southwest of Pinkville, in an open but dry rice paddy near the sub-hamlet of My Khe(3). This insertion was to prevent enemy escaping in that direction. Chappell and his men were girded for heavy fighting. Intelligence had reported there were "absolutely no friendlies" in the area. Yet as their Hueys descended to their landing zone he saw women and children working in the rice paddies. In the paradox that was Vietnam, he was shortly involved in heavy fighting as the "civilians" quickly melted away.

My Khe (3) was nestled in a grove of trees one thousand yards southwest of Pinkville. Directly west of the hamlet was an open rice paddy designated as the soldier's landing zone and one thousand yards southwest of their LZ stood a high hill, designated Hill 85, which dominated the area. By 2:30PM, the blocking forces were in place and the soldiers were greeted by heavy automatic weapons and mortar fire. Sergeant First Class Stephens, commanding the fourth platoon, remembered it was "a hornet's nest" with enemy fire specifically targeting those around the antennas of radios.

The first lift of birds carrying Chappell's contingent to the My Khe position carried a new replacement, Sergeant Mitchell Samples, a tall, lanky country boy from Braxton County, West Virginia. Samples was a graduate of Fort Benning's "shake and bake" Noncommissioned Officer Course (NCOC) who felt he was ready for Vietnam and, like many trained junior leaders for that conflict, wondered how he would do. As his Huey approached Pinkville he was pumped up thinking, "Finally I'm going to be doing the real thing". It didn't take long for him to understand "the real thing". As his chopper approached the LZ, the entire lift of four Hueys came under heavy fire. When his bird was ten feet off the ground Samples jumped, not waiting any longer for enemy bullets to find him in the door.

As bullets whizzed around him Samples was still intrigued by it all. "Finally I'm in combat after all that training", he mused, "I finally get to shoot at someone instead of some target at Benning." Ten minutes into the fray his focus intensified. The grunts were pinned down by automatic weapons fire coming from a clump of trees two hundred and fifty yards to their northeast, and in a direct line with Pinkville. Casualties were mounting from mortar rounds being walked onto their position. The cries of the wounded and screams on the radio for support girded Samples. He looked one hundred yards to the east where a wood line stood and which stretched towards the location of the enemy automatic weapons fire. He turned to a grunt next to him, one of the few he had time to meet since joining the platoon, and said, "Grab that M-60 and follow me."

The two of them began crawling toward the wood line, while using paddy dikes for cover. Other grunts hugged the earth and watched, their eyes collectively asking, "What the hell are they doing?" As Samples and his assistant passed their platoon sergeant, the sergeant said nothing, but his eyes sent the message, "Well, whatever you want to do, I hope it works." Once they reached the wood line they found a small footpath and cautiously moved toward the enemy fire. They could see a large mound of dirt, behind which were eight Vietcong in black pajamas, firing at the exposed grunts. The two maneuvered to the right rear of the position where they found the mound was open in a crude bunker-shaped position. They opened fire with their M-60 machine gun and killed four, while two jumped into a hole inside the mound and two more took off running. The two soldiers rushed the mound and both tossed in hand grenades, killing the two remaining VC.

Samples had a radio on his back and called his platoon, telling them they had silenced the position. The response was immediate, "Get out quickly, gunships are coming in to pour fire on your area". Both grunts, exhausted, ran back down the footpath. They could feel the gunships raining fire down on the enemy to their backs. Halfway back to their starting point in the tree line they came under sniper fire, then a grenade was tossed on their path. The concussion blew Samples on top of the machinegun. Neither man could hear because of the explosion but they picked themselves up and continued running back to their platoon.

Chappell moved his troops closer to the My Khe (3) hamlet to get out of their exposed position in the paddy but they came under more automatic weapons fire which caused more casualties. He moved his troops into a shallow creek bed where there was some measure of cover while he called in artillery fire. The wounded were placed in a small bomb crater, which offered slightly better protection. As a dustoff came in for the wounded, two more mortar rounds hit the lip of the crater, hitting those already wounded and wounding a few more. Chappell's grunts were moving the wounded to another spot when he heard the dustoff coming in and the pilot came up on his radio frequency. The Huey was approaching from behind the soldiers and the pilot came in fast. Just as he turned sideways to flare and land his bird, Chappell heard "thunk – thunk" in the distance and screamed to the pilot, "Get the hell out – we have incoming!" As the pilot pulled pitch to rise up two mortar rounds hit just below the "chin bubble" of his Huey, the Plexiglas situated below the pilot's legs. The exploding mortars smashed part of the chin bubble as the pilot gained altitude to escape the fire. But he was determined not to be denied his patients. With complete disregard for the mortars, which had now targeted his landing spot next to the wounded, the pilot made another pass coming in low from the opposite direction and landed. It was 5:10PM, the wounded were loaded on board, and the bird took off just as two more mortar rounds landed behind him. On his way out he spotted the mortar tube and its VC crew on top of Hill 85 which overlooked the whole scene. Bravo's soldiers were sitting ducks. Chappell called in artillery fire on the hill and requested an air strike as well. Colonel Lyon, flying above, relayed the request but was told to wait for "political clearance" for the jets, since the area was under Vietnamese Army (ARVN) control.

Helicopter gunships continued to pound the Pinkville area throughout the afternoon, moving from Alpha's position in the north to Bravo's blocking positions west and southwest of the hamlet. After watching the courage of the dustoff pilot and receiving additional close-in support from gunships, Chappell thanked a gunship flying overhead, saying, "This is a hell of a way to make a living!" LTC Lyon who monitored the gunships' frequency immediately cut in, "Yeah, but its honest work!"

Late in the afternoon a much needed supply of water and ammunition was kicked off a resupply Huey coming in at fifty knots of speed and eighty feet off the ground. The bird took enemy ground fire all the way. The supplies landed behind the grunts in the open paddy as the VC continued to rain automatic weapons fire on them from My Khe (3) to their front. Chappell and some of his soldiers ran out under fire to pull the supplies back to their position while other grunts laid down a base of fire on the hamlet. Among those retrieving supplies was SP/4 Donald Wilson, who took an enemy bullet in his armpit and died instantly. Wilson was age 20 and single from Portage, Indiana. Sergeant David Holman carried another wounded soldier under fire one hundred yards back to cover where he could be treated.

Armored personnel carriers from H Troop arrived by nightfall to help solidify Chappell's blocking position. More ammunition was dropped by a Huey at 11:04PM and the bird backhauled the remaining five wounded grunts and SP/4 Wilson's body. Sergeant Samples would be awarded the Silver Star for his efforts on his first day in the field. Bronze Stars would be awarded to Samples' partner who charged the mound, as well as Sergeant Holman and SP/4 Wilson (posthumously). Chappell's troops continued to receive fire throughout the night until "spooky", a DC-3 cargo plane, converted with a large mini-gun out its side door, came on station. Spooky dropped flares and then followed with highly accurate and devastating fire around the grunts. The roar of fire from the huge guns belching down to the earth sounded like a freight train coming through the sky. Chappell was pleased. There would be little sleep that night but the flares were as useful as the firepower. Each flare lasted fifteen minutes long, longer than artillery flares, which gave his soldiers ample vision to detect a possible ground attack.

The fight at Pinkville on July 7, 1968 was hard fought, and undoubtedly the enemy had suffered enormously from direct fire and air strikes. Since no bodies were recovered at the mound Samples and his gunner knocked out, and Alpha had not been able to enter Pinkville, the true extent of enemy casualties was unclear. Battalion losses for the day totaled three killed in action (KIA) and twenty-five wounded. Enemy losses were "unknown". Twenty years later one of the soldiers from H Troop who supported Bravo's efforts characterized the Pinkville fight as "A cluster fuck from the pits of hell."

The battalion's mission for July 8 was to "exploit" the contact it had made on July 7. LTC Lyon requested help from an ARVN unit garrisoned just three miles west of Bravo's position along Provincial Road 521 at a crumbled French fort known as "The Citadel". He reasoned the additional soldiers would help him encircle the Pinkville area and prevent VC from slipping away. But Lyons' efforts to get help from the ARVN at the Citadel did not bear fruit. Too many levels of political clearance got in the way. During the heavy fighting the prior day the ARVN chose to sit it out and let the Americans do the heavy lifting. By 7:14AM, the air strikes requested by Chappell the day before were placed on Hill 85 and My Khe (3) for good measure. They were dropped after ample time had elapsed for the enemy to retreat and reposition themselves in other locations, and keep their mortars for another attack.

In lieu of getting no ARVN support, Delta Company was relieved of its duties on and around LZ Buff, and air assaulted southeast of My Khe (3) and (1) and southwest of My Khe (4), which sat along the coast. Their mission was to close the noose south of the Pinkville zone and provide some relief to the weary troopers of Alpha and Bravo. The air-assault was conducted in an orchestrated fashion, the slicks carrying Delta flying in an east-west direction while the jets conducting air strikes flew north-south. All of Deltas grunts were on the ground by 7:45AM. Pinkville now had the bulk of the 5th/46th on its doorstep. Alpha remained northeast on the narrow peninsula, Bravo west and southwest, and Delta to the south.

Shortly after Delta was on the ground another jet air strike with napalm was placed on My Khe (4) as Delta's grunts started moving north between the My Khe hamlets. At 8:20AM, they came under sporadic automatic weapons fire from My Khe (1) but continued forward using fire and maneuver with support from gunships. Along the way they found evidence of enemy positions, including an enticing love letter from a soldier to a female in Hanoi dated June 28, 1968. The mix of enemy they faced included some NVA along with hard-core Vietcong. Because of periodic sniper fire and Vietcong shoot and run tactics, Delta moved cautiously.

Delta was spread out in platoon formations east to west between the three My Khe's and was very wary of mines and booby traps in its area. Unlike Bravo, they had no armored personnel carrier support. During its patrolling Delta uncovered one thousand pounds of rice found in haystacks in a graveyard. Moving slowly, Delta's move north covered no more than one-half mile. Despite the air strikes and availability of gunships and artillery, Delta was finding what Bravo and Alpha knew only too well, that they were operating in an area densely seeded with mines. As nightfall arrived, Delta saturated its patrol area with defensive positions, listening posts and ambushes. Its area of responsibility stretched from the southern point of Pinkville, now one-half mile to their north, the My Khe (1) hamlet three hundred yards to the west and My Khe (4) one-half mile to the east on the coast.

July 8 also saw the death of another brave Bravo soldier although it occurred thousands of miles away. SP/4 Roland "Mike" Sheredos had been wounded by small arms fire in late May when most of Bravo Company deployed north from LZ Ann to be under the operational control of the 1st/46th Infantry Battalion in Quang Tin Province near Tam Ky. Sheredos was stable enough in Chu Lai that he had been airlifted to an Army hospital in Japan where he succumbed to his wounds. He was age 24 and married from Long Island, New York.

Dawn on July 9 found the battalion still surrounding Pinkville, conducting probing patrols against the hit and run actions of the enemy. The closer the battalion's grunts got to the Pinkville enclave, the more numerous were the mines and booby traps. All of Bravos troops were now consolidated, along with the platoon from Charlie Company, on the southeast edge of the Pinkville/My Lai (1) hamlet area. Bravo's soldiers took full advantage of the armored personnel carriers (APC's) working with them to avoid mines. Although standard procedure was to follow behind the APC's, walking in the depression made by the carrier's treads, it was tricky business at best. Jim Tuckers 2nd platoon was several hundred yards north of Route 521 where the road entered a hamlet. At 8:15AM a track leading Tuckers grunts hit a mine, a buried 105mm artillery shell, which cracked the transmission block of the APC. No soldiers were injured.

Twenty minutes later Tuckers pointman, Sergeant Nirenstein, led the platoon and walked behind an APC moving toward some hooch's where they had received sniper fire. Nirenstein was a model soldier, carrying a shotgun whenever he volunteered for point. Tucker was not far behind him. Stopping for a moment to assess the situation and get better footing between the depressions made by the treads, Nirenstein was thrown into the air by a booby-trapped mortar round. Both of his legs were sheared off by the blast, one above the knee, the other below. Tucker was hit with fragments to his head, arms and legs. Lyons' command and control Huey was flying close by and landed among the carnage. It loaded both soldiers on the bird along with one of Nirenstein's feet still in its boot. Nirenstein remained fully awake with the help of morphine and kept very positive while Lyons' Huey made full throttle back to Chu Lai and a surgical table. Automatic weapons fire and sniper fire continued to come from a stand of hooch's nearby. By mid-morning they were destroyed. Shortly after, Bravo's troops found a two hundred and fifty pound bomb ready to be planted by the VC. It was blown in place with C4 explosive.

Captain Yanessa's Delta troops kept patrolling in its sector without the protection of APC's, which made its movement very tenuous. He was assigned some Vietnamese National Police to question the villagers they encountered and by 11:05AM they were working inside My Khe (1), finding some old men whose sons, they acknowledged, were VC and "Fighting in the mountains". The 4th platoon searched My Khe (3) and located a tunnel with mines and a cache of one thousand pounds of rice hidden in the walls of a hooch. By 12:30PM, grunts were carrying the rice to a pickup point between both hamlets, careful not to walk on trails and keeping ten feet apart while wearing flak jackets. Despite these precautions, the soldiers set off two mines, wounding three, one with a traumatic amputation of his lower left leg, just below the hip.

Delta's first platoon worked the coastal area one-half mile away, in the hamlets of Co Lay (1) and (2). They found rice caches, an 8-inch artillery round and two 105mm artillery rounds as well as two 81mm mortar rounds. As night fell, defensive positions were established, defensive artillery fires preplanned, and ambush positions laid out. Alpha Company, still on the sandy peninsula northeast of Pinkville, pulled out in the evening back to LZ Dottie. Its company strength was no more than seventy soldiers, less than half of its authorized strength. It never fully recovered from its drubbing on July 7, and for the rest of the Pinkville fight, sat on the sandy peninsula primarily as a blocking force while evacuating soldiers each day for heat exhaustion. It no longer had the strength or ability to go on the offense.

The deadline that had been set by the 198th Brigade headquarters for the Pinkville operation, "To find, fix and kill the NVA and VC forces in the area", was midnight, July 10. Lyon's troopers were still encountering sporadic rifle fire and evidence of enemy activity, although the tempo of enemy contact had steadily lessened after the full impact of air strikes and helicopter gunship support over the prior three days. LTC Lyon wanted to extend his time in the area to get the job done, but brigade headquarters said "no", citing "Major changes were coming". His troops were to be extracted as soon as possible on the 10th and returned to LZ Dottie.

At 7:50AM on July 10, Bravo began consolidating its platoons near My Lai (6) for an extraction, even while sniper fire continued in the area. Captain Lamb sent his attached armored personnel carriers south to pick up Delta's troops, still operating in the My Khe hamlets. Three Chinooks flew in to extract Delta at a consolidated pickup zone at 10:30AM, and they extracted Bravo thirty minutes later. As a farewell, the Vietcong fired on the helicopters, hitting two Chinooks carrying out Delta and one that carried out Bravo. Some of Bravo's soldiers remained with the APC's of H troop until the extraction was completed, then headed west on Route 521 to Highway One to complete their departure. By 1:30PM, this rear guard was back on Highway One, heading north to LZ Dottie. Lyon was on his way to LZ Bayonet for a conference with the brigade commander and other battalion commanders about another move north, to a "LZ West", under operational control of "Task Force Cooksey". The battalion was being summoned back to the Tam Ky – "Burlington Trail" area.

6 – TASK FORCE COOKSEY

Americal Division operations in the Que Son – Tien Phuoc terrain west of Tam Ky were having the intended impact on the enemy. Increasingly the NVA could not secure the rice supply necessary to sustain their force in the mountains west of Tam Ky. The Que Son – Tien Phuoc area was the operational area of the 196th Light Infantry Brigade although no brigade could sustain itself indefinitely in a major operation without battalion support from other brigades.

Division intelligence reports in early July 1968 indicated a major enemy force was in the Phuoc Chau Valley south and southwest of Que Son – Tien Phuoc. This valley provided a fertile rice bowl and was therefore a priority for the enemy to control. The intelligence reports were backed up by increased enemy contact in the area. In early July air cavalry helicopters came under repeated heavy automatic weapons fire from the high ground north of the valley and west of the Thanh River, which lay west of Tien Phuoc and south of Hiep Duc. On July 16, a Huey attempted to insert a Long Range Reconnaissance Patrol (LRRP) in the same area and came under heavy fire. The intensity of the ground fire gave credence to the possible location of the 33rd Anti-Aircraft Battalion of the 2nd NVA Division. The LRRP team and the Huey aircrew spotted one hundred and fifty to two hundred NVA in green uniforms. Subsequent over-flights in other choppers spotted groups of twenty to thirty NVA moving through the area and follow-on air strikes resulted in secondary explosions, indicating the presence of enemy ammunition storage sites.

Task Force Cooksey, named for Brigadier General Howard Cooksey, Assistant Division Commander for Operations, was formed to meet the new threat. Task force planning set into motion an elaborate scheme of maneuver which would require a number of Americal infantry battalions as well as two battalions of the 2nd ARVN Division. Cooksey would use these forces in an orchestrated manner to search, find and destroy the enemy, provide blocking forces, secure landing zones and fire bases, and stand by as reaction forces. The 5th/46th would serve in all of these roles. For the grunts of LTC Lyon's battalion, participation in Task Force Cooksey would require another mountain exercise testing their endurance in rugged terrain under stifling heat, with the possibility of encountering well-trained and well-equipped North Vietnamese Army regulars. This would be the trade-off for relief from the Pinkville mission and the carpets of mines which took such a heavy toll on the coastal plains.

POCAHONTAS FOREST

Task Force Cooksey would control two operations at the same time. First was "Burlington Trail" whose primary objective was to keep Provincial Route 533 open from Tam Ky to Tien Phouc. The second operation was "Pocahontas Forest" which was to be conducted from July 5 to August 2, 1968 and was aimed at neutralizing enemy forces in the Hiep Duc Valley. The terrain in the rugged mountains and dense jungle that covered Hiep Duc and the terrain south of it provided easy concealment for the enemy. The terrain hid numerous enemy base camps, communications routes, both land and water, logistical sites, and troop assembly areas.

Americal Division intelligence reports indicated the 2nd NVA Division had two regiments in the area, the 1st Main Force VC Regiment and the 3rd NVA Regiment. On July 6, when the 5th/46th was heavily engaged in the fighting around Pinkville, the Americal Division launched an attack to begin Phase I of Pocahontas Forest. It included the 4th/31st Infantry Battalion of the 196th Light Infantry Brigade and two battalions from the 11th Light Infantry Brigade, the 4th/21st and 4th/3rd.

On July 11, after just one night of rest on LZ Dottie, the 5th/46th closed in on its new AO west of Tam Ky to join the Pocahontas operation. Alpha Company had been beefed up in strength to ninety-four soldiers. Bravo Company was operating with seventy-eight, and thirty-two more were attached to them from the 3rd platoon, F Troop, 17th CAV. Charlie had one hundred and thirteen soldiers and Delta counted one hundred and eighteen. Delta was the "fattest" company in the battalion, but still far short of the authorized full strength of an infantry company at one hundred and sixty-four. Echo's Weapons Company, by design a smaller unit, had seventy-eight soldiers to man its headquarters element, heavy mortar platoon and recon platoon.

Alpha Company was tasked to secure LZ West nineteen miles west of Tam Ky. LZ West would be Lyon's initial command post in the operation. It was situated on the top of a massive hill complex and held a commanding view of the valley on all four sides. Five miles further west was the strategic town of Hiep Duc. Charlie Company pushed out as a reconnaissance in force in a valley north of LZ West. Delta secured LZ Polar Bear II, a hilltop approximately three and one-half miles southwest of LZ West and reconnoitered the valley east of Hiep Duc and west of LZ West, along the Chang River. Bravo Company secured two artillery fire bases, LZ's Craig and Karen, on high ground one mile east of Hiep Duc. Both LZ's held a commanding view of the valley around the town as well as Provincial Route 534. The battalion's combat supplies, such as ammunition and C-rations, were located on LZ Baldy which straddled Highway One, approximately fourteen miles north of Tam Ky.

On July 15, Delta Company spotted small groups of NVA and was hit with fire from enemy-controlled 60mm mortars. The NVA were playing shoot and run which confirmed to Delta's troops they had just moved into a unfriendly neighborhood. At 1:13PM they encountered two squads of NVA. With the assistance of helicopter gunships to take care of the threat, Delta moved into the hamlet of Phu Huu (2), just one and one-half miles southeast of LZ Polar Bear II. The soldiers found a tunnel complex with gas masks, NVA uniforms and two thousand, five hundred pounds of rice. Over the next few days Bravo's 1st and 2nd platoons discovered two thousand pounds of rice, uniforms and cooking equipment; Bravo's 3rd platoon captured four VC near the sub-hamlet of An My (1). Echo's Recon platoon raided some hooch's and captured three VC, killing another while a fourth insurgent escaped. Interrogation of the prisoners revealed a large base camp and aid station were located five miles south of Hiep Duc.

Shoot and run skirmishes continued resulting in more NVA and VC supplies being found, prisoners taken and some battalion casualties, but no deaths. Bravo's soldiers captured a VC squad leader who, while being interrogated, revealed aid stations and base camps were located farther west along the Laotian border. Then on July 17, LTC Lyon received a Warning Order to "Be prepared to move the battalion from its present area and be prepared for heavy rucksack loads of ammunition and rations for three days." Intelligence reports indicated a possible move of the NVA south and east from the border region into the battalion's AO.

Typical of enemy contacts were the actions of the 2nd and 3rd platoons of Bravo on July 21. The company made a river crossing the night before, and the two platoons took a much-needed break at noon. PFC Christopher George, who carried an M-79 grenade launcher, was out on flank security during the break. This black soldier was from Trinidad. He had a strong British accent and flew the Trinidadian flag over his bunker on LZ Gator. George suddenly motioned to the platoon leader to come over, holding up four fingers. His leader, thinking there were four enemy soldiers soon realized he was looking at four feet. George had taken a break next to two NVA soldiers sleeping in their hammocks. He and his comrades moved in. George grabbed an AK-47 just as one of the NVA woke up and went for the other weapon. George backhanded him with his M-79 and knocked him out. The other NVA jumped from his hammock, took two steps to flee and was dropped by the Platoon Sergeant with a short burst from his M-16. Hoping he would live to provide much needed information; he provided a quick death rattle and died. The other NVA, sporting a big welt on his head from the M-79, was dazed and confused. As his head was bandaged, soldiers radioed the company interpreter who tried to question him over the radio. The prisoner indicated quite a few of his comrades had been killed in the 1968 Tet Offensive the previous February and March. A Huey came in and took him out to gain more information using ARVN interrogators. The prisoner's time for "hard knocks" was just beginning.

That same morning two Vietcong females carried white flags and weapons and approached some Delta Troops on LZ Polar Bear. They reported two NVA Companies were hiding one and one-half miles west of their position. The NVA mission, according to the two females, who were tired of their deprivation in the field, was to attack Polar Bear and LZ O'Conner in the near future. Air strikes were called in on the suspected location and the jets received light weapons fire when they dropped their bomb loads.

Two days later Bravo Company walked off LZ Sooner, a firebase seven miles north of Hiep Duc, which had become the new battalion command post (CP). The valley below them supposedly contained NVA according to some NVA prisoners. Close to the valley floor Bravo met a Special Forces Mike Force of American Advisors and Nung mercenaries, all wearing tiger-striped fatigues. Lieutenant Chappell asked the SF sergeant in charge for any information he may have about the area. The response was one of arrogance and no willingness to help Chappell's grunts. This attitude was the same as Chappell had experienced at the Tra Bong Special Forces camp in mid-June, and there was no love lost for the Special Forces by Chappell, an infantry officer and a grunt who shared the same risks as these Nung advisors.

Moving in company formation, Bravo received sniper fire almost immediately and this continued throughout the day. The soldiers were edgy and didn't have a good feeling about the valley. Their night defensive position (NDP) was made tight. At 2:00AM, AK-47 fire and fire from an M-79 grenade launcher hit a platoon listening post (LP). As the LP moved back into the perimeter the enemy fire followed them and engulfed the company. Well-placed fire from the enemy M-79 gunner, something any American commander would be proud of, began picking locations inside Bravo's perimeter. Bravo's CO, Captain Lamb, had selected a CP in a small, furrowed garden plot. As the fire came into the perimeter he kneeled to grab his radio handset when an M-79 round landed next to him, the shrapnel hitting the side of his face. Others around him were also wounded. Lamb began screaming orders for a medic, drawing in more fire. He was not a popular commander among his men, never leaving LZ Ann as one example, while his men trudged around in the heavily mined terrain around it. In the river crossing the night of July 20, Lamb required his RTO to carry his rucksack while he floated across on a poncho raft, and his men walked through the water.

LT. Chappell had to get Lamb out before one of his men shot him in the dark. Sensing the incoming fire was not a major attack, Chappell managed to calm the perimeter into a cease-fire. Bravo still had another ambush position in front of its perimeter and the outpouring fire, plus Lamb's screaming, simply aided the enemy in directing their fire. Once Bravo's fire stopped, the enemy fire did as well. Chappell called in a dustoff in the dark of night understanding there was the possibility of drawing more fire, but knowing he had to get Lamb out with his head wound, plus six other wounded members of the command group. The dustoff was completed without a hitch, and Chappell took command of the company. He would effectively lead Bravo from that point on until his field duty was over. He was one more unheralded tribute to Fort

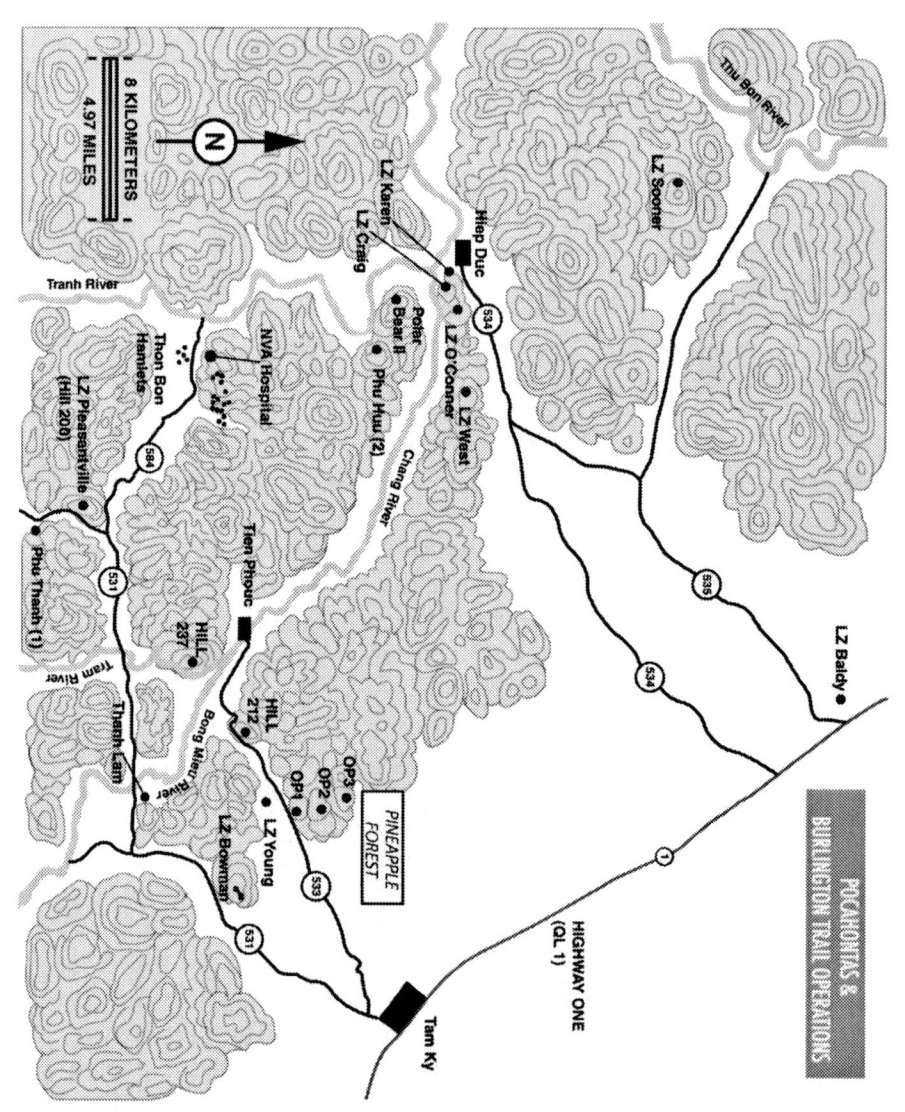

Pocahontas and Burlington Trail

Benning's "School for Boys", it's Infantry OCS. At the age of twenty-one he was now responsible for more than ninety soldiers in the field. He later mused, "A little over two years prior, I was barely responsible for myself."

The 5th/46th continued its daily mission of protecting its assigned firebases with aggressive patrolling in the rugged country around Hiep Duc. While the battalion was not ignorant about enemy intentions, it increasingly appeared that the devastating effects of the TET offensive had limited the NVA and main-force VC to primarily platoon and squad-size assaults.

Like their wily foe, the grunts of the 5th/46th were worn down from unending field duty and continuing pressure to gain hegemony over its enemy. A growing number of soldiers attempted to find jobs in the rear, or get a respite from the field by any means possible. For some, even a job as a door gunner on a Huey, exposing one's self to direct fire on combat assaults was deemed better than being a grunt in the boonies. Increasingly grunts were going to the rear for a variety of excuses, and to "sham" as long as they could. LTC Lyon looked at his diminishing numbers in the field and found it unacceptable. He had his staff on LZ Gator collect everyone. Those who did not have a specific reason to be there were sent back to the field. Lyon let it be known that everyone's "ghosting" or "shamming" days were over and for added measure, told his staff if they did not control it, they would be in the field as well.

"Ghosting" however was a phenomenon characteristic of life in a war zone and plagued all infantry battalions in Vietnam. Attrition in the field resulted from combat casualties and illness such as heat, infections and chronic diarrhea. Some grunts desperately sought a respite from arduous field duty. Any excuse counted. And those who were evacuated for legitimate reasons sometimes looked for ways to extend their stay in the rear after they were judged fit enough to return to the field. Jobs were created at LZ Gator, such as in company supply rooms and the resupply point on the helicopter pad. These were given to those grunts that had given their best in the field but had been worn too thin to be effective anymore. The selections were usually made by the Company First Sergeants, who knew the men intimately, their morale, and their needs. Still, the illegitimate "ghosters" or "shammers" had to be continually weeded out as their means for avoiding the field became more sophisticated. On August 5 for example, the battalion's executive officer sent thirteen soldiers of Bravo Company and twelve from Delta, back to the field.

Burlington Trail

Early August saw the battalion deploy south from the Hiep Duc operations to the area around the Special Forces camp at Tien Phuoc. The Pocahontas Forest operation was ending and the focus shifted to the Burlington Trail mission. The Tien Phuoc Special Forces camp was established in November 1965 as a strategic outpost between the mountainous border area to the west and the fertile "rice bowl" area leading east to Tam Ky. The camp was commanded by a Special Forces "A-Team" detachment, A-102, which also advised a Vietnamese Special Forces detachment at the camp. The Vietnamese commanded an irregular battalion-sized force of Vietnamese CIDG, with some Cambodians and Montagnards. There were three companies of CIDG with one recon platoon.

Typically two Green Berets and two Vietnamese Special Forces counterparts took company-size elements to the field. At times, they reinforced Americal units operating in the AO with reconnaissance and knowledge about their "backyard" since the Americal battalions rotated in and out of the AO. The Americal also supported the Tien Phuoc camp with an artillery battery, Quad-50 heavy machine gun crews, and personnel to keep the airstrip functional.

Although the 5th/46th was operating in Quang Tin province, the move to Tien Phuoc brought the battalion back under the control of the 198th Brigade. The battalion descended onto the Tien Phuoc air strip via Chinook (CH-47) helicopters and brought with them rations and ammunition, trucks and jeeps for the battalion's support company, engineers and another artillery battery for direct fire support.

On August 5, General Cooksey landed at Tien Phuoc to assess the progress of his task force in protecting the rice harvest and seeking out the NVA. Hill 237, a scant two miles southeast was rumored to hold an enemy element and Bravo's grunts were sent to check it out the following day. Seven miles due south a B-52 ("Arc Light") strike was in the planning and the Echo Recon Platoon was tasked to go out, monitor the strike, and assess the damage. "Arc Light" was the code name for the devastating air strikes from B-52 Stratofortresses, flying from long distances to drop their heavy loads on suspected concentrations of the enemy. Because of the large load of bombs, targets selected were usually in mountainous terrain away from villages or hamlets. The battalion's CP was displaced to Hill 200, seven miles southwest of Tien Phuoc which overlooked Provincial Road 531.

US Marines, South Vietnamese Infantry (ARVN), and Americal Division units had worked the area around Tien Phuoc for many months. Despite the lush green countryside, seemingly undisturbed, the footprints of past operations were apparent. Before Lyon's group could land on Hill 200, the battalion's new command post required engineers to remove unexploded cluster bomb units (CBU) from previous air and artillery strikes, before the troops could settle in. Not sure if all the unexploded ordnance was destroyed on or around the hill, the soldiers had to walk carefully on the hilltop. Hill 200 was dubbed "LZ Pleasantville".

Closer to Tien Phuoc, Bravo climbed Hill 237 to search for enemy and found instead an abandoned ARVN outpost, complete with concertina wire and eight bunkered positions connected by trenches. A large pile of abandoned 81mm and 60mm mortar rounds were discovered on the open ground and stored in a bunker. Bravo's soldiers were incensed. The careless ARVN had left another "supermarket" of mines for the VC.

Chappell called for re-supply and requested ten pounds of C-4 explosive to destroy the abandoned munitions. What arrived was a crate of one hundred pounds of C-4, enough to do serious damage to the entire base complex in Chu Lai. Chappell and his artillery forward observer (FO) (normally a lieutenant, Bravo Company had a buck sergeant) looked at each other wondering whether someone in the rear was smoking marijuana to send so much explosives. Their puzzled faces turned to smiles and they proceeded to do what grunts do best, blow things up.

After allocating a small amount of the C-4 for each grunt to use for heating their C rations, all the abandoned ordnance was piled inside one bunker and rigged for detonation. The soldiers moved two hundred and fifty yards off the hill thinking that would be a safe-enough distance. Chappell and his FO smoked a cigarette and placed bets on the amount of boom they would get. With the grunts cleared, the fuse was set and the two ran to take cover with the rest of the troops. The ground roared and trembled causing a mushroom cloud of dust, dirt and logs which began falling to the earth all around Bravo's troops. Fortunately for Chappell, the new commander, no one was injured. Radios started to buzz from Tien Phuoc asking, "What the hell is happening over there?" Chappell chortled "There must have been more mortar rounds than we thought". He led his troops away with the new mission to secure the battalion CP on LZ Pleasantville, leaving behind one hill in Viet Nam several feet shorter than nature had intended.

LTC Lyon's first order of business on LZ Pleasantville was to search the area around his new neighborhood to insure no large force of NVA was lurking nearby. Provincial Road 531 snaked its way south past the battalion CP at the eastern base of the hill and continued one and one-half miles south, flanked by hills on each side, past a narrow valley which opened to the east. At that point Route 531 continued south to Hau Duc. The valley moved east to the Tram River. Alpha Company was sent to patrol an area two miles northwest of Pleasantville along Route 584. In this move Charlie Company remained one mile behind Alpha. Both units were in close proximity to come to each other's support if needed. Delta was sent south from Pleasantville to follow the general trace of Route 531 while the Echo Recon Platoon also walked south but then turned east to recon a narrow valley near the Tram River.

It was Recon's eastward movement that would draw first blood for the battalion in the Tien Phuoc AO. Barely had it moved east into the narrow valley when it entered the abandoned hamlet of Phu Thanh (1). Just then two jets soared overhead heading east towards Tam Ky. To the grunts surprise two Vietcong exited a hooch to watch the jets fly by. Private Larry Olsen and two comrades were on the point and opened fire. They immediately came under heavy fire from more VC inside the dwelling. Olsen's buddies were pinned down and unable to move, but the private crawled to where he could bring the dwelling under effective fire. The VC thought it was too effective and three Vietcong charged him from the hooch, but Olsen cut them down. He crawled back to guide his platoon leader forward. In short order the grunts secured the hooch, finding another dead VC and capturing three females and one male, along with weapons, maps and mortar aiming stakes. For his aggressive action, Olsen was awarded the Silver Star.

Delta's 3rd platoon, located to the west, captured a NVA soldier who was assigned to the 145th NVA Battalion, whose mission was to control the narrow valley. The prisoner was defiant, expressing high morale for his unit, which he claimed took part in overrunning the Kham Duc Special Forces camp the previous May. The Special Forces never reconstituted the camp after losing it. The prisoner was sent to Tam Ky for more questioning

The heat, rugged terrain, and heavy loads carried by the battalion's grunts were taking its toll. Each day on the Tien Phuoc operation one or two grunts were dusted off with fever from malaria, heat stroke, or infections. Dysentery was also common, but did not guarantee a trip out of the field. Grunts simply had to gut their way through it, suffering uncontrolled movement of their bowels as they walked, drinking water and popping pills until the medicine eventually caught hold.

By now the battalion's Burlington Trail operation was one of small contacts, mostly by sniper fire, by an enemy too weak or too smart to avoid direct engagement with a battalion on the prowl. Alpha in its westward move killed one VC while his two NVA comrades escaped. The enemy left behind equipment, diaries, maps and about thirty women and babies, living in a trench under thick vegetation. Charlie Company, screening Alpha's rear, found fortified positions with foxholes, ammunition and equipment, but absent any VC or NVA soldiers. Among its find was five thousand pounds of rice and corn, cached for future use.

By mid-August Lyon had pushed his battalion to the rugged terrain northwest of LZ Pleasantville, where the prisoners and detained "civilians" captured by Alpha indicated more NVA were located. The location given by the prisoners was four and one-half miles northwest of the battalion's CP and eight miles southwest of Tien Phuoc. It was the same valley that had received so much attention in mid-July when the LRRP team and Hueys came under heavy fire. The valley tracked roughly east to west for five miles until it reached the Tranh River, which flowed south through dense mountainous terrain. The valley floor contained the Thon Bon, Thon Mot, Thon Nam and Thon Sau hamlets, running west to east in that order. The hamlets were sparsely populated. Intersecting the valley was Provincial Road 584 and dispersed throughout the valley were tributaries of the Tranh River. The valley floor varied in width from one-half to one mile.

The battalion moved into this valley "rice bowl" to conduct a "reconnaissance in force". Alpha moved west on the north side of Route 584 which was only a mud road gutted with holes and ditches. Charlie moved in tandem on the south side, lagging slightly behind Alpha. Delta, minus its third platoon, followed Charlie. Delta's third platoon, reinforced with CIDG from the Tien Phouc camp, followed Alpha north of the road. Echo Recon also patrolled on the battalion's southern flank, staying south of Charlie but moving in the same westerly direction.

On August 14, refugees reported there were large VC food caches near the Thon Bon hamlets, which were located close to the Tranh River on the western end of the valley. They also reported a large concentration of NVA soldiers and a supposed NVA hospital in the rugged hill country north of the valley floor near the Tranh River and the Thon Bon hamlets. In their sweep west, the battalion's soldiers encountered sporadic action; VC who had seen enough and wanted to surrender did so along with civilians who wanted to be evacuated from the pressures of the enemy. A few NVA and VC who resisted with sniper fire were killed for their effort.

The soldiers of the 5th/46th moved slowly, killing or capturing the enemy generally one at a time, as they moved west. Once the 5th/46th reached the Thanh River, Charlie Company swung north towards the Thon Bon hamlets. Lt. John King's 3rd platoon took the lead to search for the NVA hospital. Two local civilians pointed to the location of a concealed trail that led the way. King's soldiers were about to witness an exceptionally harsh lesson of mans inhumanity to man. At 1:00PM on August 16, King's platoon found the hospital, precisely where the refugees said it would be. Moving quietly and cautiously they caught one NVA off guard and shot him as they worked their way into the complex. Fire pits for cooking were still warm to the touch and the soldiers felt they were being watched. Four hogs roamed the camp area and, among twenty hooch's, lay dead VC who had not been buried and two very emaciated women who appeared to be suffering from malaria.

King's grunts found tunnels that contained operating and recovery rooms, with fresh blood-stained bedding. It was obvious the hospital had been abandoned recently and the patients and staff had fled into the surrounding terrain. The tunnels also revealed medical supplies, such as penicillin, sleeping tablets, aspirin, dysentery tablets, scissors, forceps and surgical gloves.

Once the battalion's interpreters arrived, the emaciated women, thought to be enemy nurses, proved to be local villagers who told a grisly story. With barely audible voices, the two women cried, "Vengeance for me, kill my captors!" They were victims of "blood draining." Wounded NVA soldiers suffering from severe blood loss were "hooked up" to these women for an expeditious transfusion. Both women had lost so much blood they couldn't hear or eat and could barely talk. Each weighed less than 50 pounds and they were evacuated to the division's 27th Surgical Hospital at Chu Lai.

One of Charlie's medics, Joe Scurlock, carried one of the women down the trail to a pick-up zone. When the dustoff arrived, the woman clung to Scurlock and wouldn't let go. Scurlock would remember forty years later "You could tell they felt secure around us, they didn't want to leave our side."

The women said the NVA had escaped a few days before the grunts arrived. As King's troops searched the area they found twenty graves, five of which were freshly dug. Bones were strewn about as evidence of many amputations. Intelligence officers were flown in and estimated the hospital's capacity at four hundred patients. Among the documents found was a North Vietnamese letter of commendation to the director of the hospital commending him for his efficiency.

As Charlie moved north at the western end of the valley, Echo Recon continued moving west. At 2:30PM on the 16th, when Charlie discovered the grisly evidence at the hospital, Echo was one mile east of the Thanh River and one-half mile south of the valley road. Always small in number (it only had twenty-one soldiers in the field at this point) the Recon platoon had a nose for trouble and, more often than not, found it. It killed two NVA in a small base camp and found a tunnel which concealed a large cache of rice.

The following day Lyon tasked Lt. Care and his recon platoon to push farther north, following the Thanh River into the mountains. That morning the lead man pointed to four VC walking through the thick vegetation wearing black pajamas and carrying AK-47's. There was too much vegetation between them and the enemy to provide effective small arms fire. Care realized that calling artillery would be time-consuming and would alert the VC to the American's presence. Care pushed his troops north, hoping to intersect them later with an ambush.

By 2:00PM, the recon grunts advanced to a point where the river entered mountainous terrain. The river slowly lost itself in a narrow gorge on both sides of their position. Care knew this gorge-like terrain offered little space to maneuver, and was a perfect ambush site. Just as the thought entered his mind, the grunts received a heavy volume of automatic weapons fire from twenty feet away, on the opposite side of the narrow river. With bullets kicking up twelve inches in front of them, Care saw one of his Sergeants get hit, and ran to his aid. The enemy broke contact and the grunts started down a trail, in the direction of the enemy. Part of the lead element walked on the right flank of the trail and found Chinese (Chicom) grenades. It was apparent they had interrupted the enemy's work at preparing booby traps.

Charlie Company's 1st platoon was sent from the abandoned NVA hospital, less than one-half mile to the east, to assist the recon platoon. Lt. Harold Aldrich, new to the field, led the 1st platoon. By 4:00PM they moved in behind the recon grunts. Lee Gunton, an experienced rifleman who came over with the company from Fort Hood, told his buddy next to him, "We are either going to find nothing or every gook in the world is around the next corner." With those words spoken, heavy enemy fire broke out and three members of the first platoon immediately went down with wounds. Three soldiers from recon were also wounded, including Care and his RTO. Automatic weapons fire poured from a tree line thirty to forty feet to their front. Gunton's squad, led by Russ "Pappy" Welder, took cover behind a small mound of dirt. Lt. Aldrich yelled, "Prepare to assault!" Gunton, only three men away from Aldrich told another grunt, "Tell him only the Marines do that." They assaulted none-the-less and luck was with Gunton, whose rifle jammed after firing only two rounds. When they reached the tree line the firing stopped and the enemy pulled back. It was apparent the force firing on them was a small, harassing force, but they were well-positioned north, west, and south of the beleaguered soldiers at very close range with good camouflage and excellent fields of fire.

Harassing fire broke out time and time again at very close range, making every grunt a hero just by his participation in the event. Sergeant Larry Thomas, a squad leader with the recon platoon was at the point of the file when the fire fight first began. He insured a strong base of fire was placed on the insurgents as he crawled from man to man. With their ammunition getting low, he made it back to LT. Alrich's platoon, which was also under fire, to obtain extra ammo and bring it back to his troops. When his platoon leader, Lt. Care, was wounded, he moved to take command of the platoon and keep the unit in check. Thomas was awarded the Bronze Star for valor for his leadership.

The enemy fire steadily rose in intensity and Lyon lost no time in requesting air strikes before the situation worsened. Napalm and five hundred pound bombs were requested, especially for the northern side of their position, on the steep ridgelines rising up from the river. At 5:00PM, an Air Force Forward Air Controller (FAC "23") flew overhead and radioed help was on the way. The process took time to develop from the air, but the grunts knew that with the FAC above, control of the fire fight would shift to them. By 5:45PM, jet aircraft were dropping their ordnance, with helicopter gunships firing machine gun and cannon fire in between the sortie's made by the jets. The FAC orchestrated the air support while the grunts sought cover. The heavy gun support from the air, both jets and gunships, were fired at "Danger Close" range. One canister of napalm was dropped behind Gunton and his squad, hitting the ground and skipping over them, before exploding. Both the aircraft and helicopters took enemy fire as they made their strikes. At 6:30PM FAC 23, low on fuel, checked out and FAC 19 continued coordinating the strike for twenty more minutes.

Charlie Company's commander, Larry Johnson, arrived with more troops to take control of the ground operation. A dustoff was called for the wounded. LT Care was placed on the dustoff's crowded floor, his head hanging below one of the door gunners and his M-60, who was returning machine gun fire on an enemy gun position that was attempting to destroy the dustoff. The M-60, just inches above the platoon leaders head, caused excruciating pain in his ears. As the bird pulled pitch to gain altitude, the enemy obliged Care by placing an AK-47 round through the door-gunners wrist, which stopped the firing. The remaining grunts on the ground searched the area while jets patiently circled above. The enemy fire ceased. Various positions were found with overhead cover, revealing well-established observations posts to thwart the advance of an approaching force.

During a break the next day, Charlie's newest platoon leader, Lt Aldrich, asked his squad leader "Pappy" Welder, how he had done the previous day. Pappy took a long puff on his cigarette and said, "Well sir, you fucked up." Aldrich asked "How?" "We don't assault over here. That's what we have artillery and aircraft for." The platoon never assaulted a tree line again and Aldrich, in the words of his men, "Became a hell of a leader once he got the swing of things." Aldrich lost a leg two months later, when his RTO stepped on a mine. Amidst all the heavy fighting in the valley, the battalion took an unexpected casualty on August 17 when PFC Paul Meaux, 23 and single, from Kaplan, Louisiana died of natural causes at the 2nd Surgical Hospital in Chu Lai.

The morning of August 18 found Charlie Company and the recon platoon west of the NVA hospital and east of the Thanh River, the distance between the two points being not more than one mile. East of the hospital were Delta's third platoon with some Special Forces CIDG troopers, looking for NVA in the hills. South of Charlie and Echo was Alpha Company, searching near the hamlet of Thon Bon (4). They moved north into the canyon-like terrain just east of Charlie and the recon platoon. Aerial reconnaissance flying over the area spotted fresh trails, trenches and tunnel openings.

Alpha's move north would guarantee it a share of the action. At 3:15PM, they were hit by a small group of VC resulting in one Vietcong killed, one captured and the third fleeing. Alpha unfortunately suffered three wounded in this shootout and one, PFC Bruce Poulson, died of his wounds. He was the only fatality during the battalion's trek through the Tien Phuoc Valley. Poulson was 21 and single, from Corona Del Mar, California. During the firefight valor was present as usual. PFC James Hackett moved from a sheltered position and killed the Vietcong who pinned them down. He then treated a wounded comrade in the open while under fire. Two months later he received the Bronze Star for valor. Among the captured equipment were AK-47's, hand grenades, gas masks and numerous medical supplies.

As the battalion continued its recon in force, LTC Lyon continued orchestrating its movements on LZ Pleasantville and in the air. Each contact with the enemy seemed to heighten the smell of blood for the commanders above him. The brigade commander, the generals from division headquarters and even some generals from MACV headquarters in Saigon flew in to get briefed. Lyon's command & control helicopter (C&C) worked overtime, taking him to the field daily to talk to his company commanders, bringing in supplies and soldiers returning from Gator and hauling out wounded GI's. Lyon also grew impatient with his rear support. His company commanders complained that requested supplies were not making it out to the field. Lyon's ass chewing to his staff officers on Gator was direct and attention getting, "Start doing your job or you go to the field as a rifleman".

The intelligence received from scattered villagers throughout the valley confirmed the 5th/46th was making its presence felt. Refugees moving east from the Thanh River reported approximately one hundred NVA killed or wounded from the heavy bombing brought on by Care's recon platoon and Charlie Company. Dead bodies were hastily buried by the enemy in the craters created by the five hundred pound bombs. Enemy wounded by Delta's 3rd platoon with its CIDG contingent were reported by villagers as dying in abandoned hamlets. Seriously wounded enemy soldiers used their last ounce of strength to reach empty hooch's where they could be found and buried by passing villagers.

The bulk of Delta Company had been following Charlie Company's general movement westward but south of the valley road. Lyon had his battalion's heavy mortars (4.2 inch) moved to the western end of the valley for more immediate indirect fire support. They were located within a small perimeter one-half mile south of the valley road in the hamlet of Thon Bon (3), approximately one mile east of the Thanh River. Part of Delta Company provided perimeter defense while the balance of the company pushed north towards the NVA hospital, in search of small groups of VC and NVA.

The VC and NVA in the Tien Phuoc Valley were a tenacious lot. Despite the thrashing they received, they lingered and attempted to draft more recruits from the isolated hamlets. Those villagers who resisted were forced to leave. The enemy's presence forced refugees seeking protection into the American's perimeter established for the mortars. The soldiers didn't want them as there was no certainty there were no VC in the group. For their own security, the grunts had to place the refugees outside the perimeter as the villagers pleaded to be relocated. Task Force Cooksey sent in Chinooks to pick them up. It had become clear the VC and NVA, not in a strong position before the 5th/46th entered the valley, had been further decimated in the five days since the battalion arrived. The battalion's sweep at this point had been largely completed and plans were made to pull the battalion out for another mission. To further assist the reconnaissance effort in the mountainous region by the Thanh River, the division laid on a mission for chemical defoliation of the area, scheduled for August 22. The division chemical officer assured the battalion "The spray is not harmful to humans."

LZ Bowman

On August 21, the battalion was extracted from the Tien Phuoc Valley by Chinook helicopter with Alpha, Charlie, Echo's heavy mortars, and the battalion headquarters set to take up residence on LZ Bowman. Bravo and Delta were lifted to LZ Young. Delta's grunts received a farewell with enemy ground fire as their Hueys lifted off the valley floor. The CIDG working with Delta's 3rd platoon returned to the Tien Phuoc Special Forces camp and the Echo Recon Platoon, worn thin, returned to LZ Gator for a "stand down". LZ Young was situated five miles due east of

Tien Phuoc and Bowman was another three miles further east; the two firebases were almost in a direct west-east line from Tien Phuoc.

The next day the battalion's participation in Task Force Cooksey was officially terminated but it continued its "Burlington Trail" missions. These included protecting road networks between Tam Ky and Tien Phuoc as well as becoming the primary reaction force for any major attack on Tam Ky. LZ Bowman was far from ideal as a battalion headquarters and firebase. It was composed of two high points and a long saddle between, causing dead spots in fields of fire along the perimeter. Ideally, one high point, with interlocking bunkers or fighting positions located where the hill started sloping downward (the "Military Crest") offered the best defensive terrain. Bowman was not to offer anything close. Moreover, units moved in and out of Bowman frequently as they rotated in continuous operations, with no steady ownership to make significant improvement in its defenses. To add to Lyon's woes, elements of the 5th ARVN Regiment, headquartered in Tam Ky, had defended part of Bowman before the battalion arrived and their sector of the perimeter was left in exceptionally bad shape.

Lyon lost no time in getting to work. On August 22, the battalion's first full day on Bowman, Alpha began improving its defenses while also sending out local patrols. It had ninety-five grunts to do the job, less than two-thirds of its assigned strength. Bravo, with eighty-two soldiers pushed off LZ Young for a combat sweep one mile northwest of the base and also manned observation posts (OP's) to provide early warning for any enemy movements to Bowman. Charlie Company, at a strength of ninety-two, patrolled one and one-half miles south of Bowman in a narrow valley that was intersected by Provincial Road 531, which led east to Tam Ky. Its mortar platoon remained on Bowman. Delta, with ninety-two soldiers, secured LZ Young and patrolled beyond its perimeter. Echo Company brought its 4.2-inch heavy mortars to Bowman and helped secure the perimeter. It counted sixty soldiers with its recon platoon still back on Gator.

The battalion's newest officer, Major Grady Tittle, joined Lyon when he arrived at Bowman. Tittle was assigned as the Executive Officer (XO), second in command. He was one of the battalion's few officers in 1968 that had a prior Vietnam tour, serving with the 25th ARVN Infantry Division as an advisor. As nightfall arrived on August 22, Title and Lyon, who had been feeling ill all day, were in their bunker some fifty feet away from the Tactical Operations Center (TOC). The battalion's

Communications ("Commo") Officer, Captain Wilburn Gideon had responsibility for the night shift at the TOC. Lyon rotated that duty among the S-3, Assistant S-3, Commo Officer and S-2, so each could get some sleep for their daytime duties. Gideon was one of the original officers at Fort Hood. A gifted officer, he was very religious and married with children.

At 10:00PM the perimeter received thirty to forty rounds of AK-47 fire coming from the northeast. By 11:25PM, Bravo reported sniper fire on its night defensive position and ten minutes later Delta received fire along its perimeter at LZ Young. The tired grunts would get no respite sitting on this firebase and the worst was yet to come. At 2:00AM, August 23, 82mm mortar rounds began dropping just outside Bowman's perimeter on the northwest sector. In quick order, the rounds were "walked" inside the perimeter directly to the TOC. Simultaneously sappers came through the wire, blowing large holes with Bangalore Torpedoes. Once they were pushed under the concertina wire which surrounded the perimeter, the sappers pulled charges that set off explosions, blowing a wide opening. Sappers rushed through the openings and attacked the TOC, the radio switchboard bunker, and the fighting and sleeping bunkers that stood in their way.

Lyon awoke at the first incoming mortar rounds and instinctively ran to the bunker door in his shorts, leaving his flak jacket under his cot. As Tittle rose from his cot in the same bunker he moved toward Lyon. Lyon turned toward him and saw a hand toss in a grenade through a bunker aperture. In a stroke of divine providence the grenade rolled under Lyon's flak jacket as it blew up. Tittle was between the exploding grenade and Lyon. He caught shrapnel in the legs and feet when the flak jacket was blown to pieces all over the bunker. Both continued to run to the TOC.

Before the sappers attacked Lyon's bunker, they had headed straight for the TOC. A sergeant in the headquarters section had been outside the TOC and saw the enemy approaching. At a moment that called for valor, he chose the act of a coward and hid. Captain Gideon heard explosions and raced outside the TOC to check on his switchboard bunker, a move that silhouetted him against the light in the TOC, and he was cut down by Ak-47 fire. Gideon was 27, and his wife and children lived in Dillen, Texas. A satchel charge of explosives was then thrown inside the TOC. Lyon's radio operator, Specialist Forth Class Roger Moll, was also killed with an Ak-47 round to the head while on top of his sleeping bunker nearby. Moll was 20 and single, from Bay City, Michigan.

With Alpha's troops manning most of the perimeter, Echo's grunts along with headquarters personnel formed a reaction force and swept through the headquarters and TOC area firing at fleeting targets. Ten Bangalore Torpedoes had been used to create holes in the perimeter and, by individual count, fifty grenades and twenty RPG rockets had been fired on or inside the perimeter in a matter of a few minutes.

Adding to the mayhem was the loss of radios that were blown up in the TOC, making communications with artillery support, gunships, medevac's and the other companies in the field, difficult at best. LZ Young also came under mortar fire at the same time Bowman was hit. This was done in typical NVA fashion, to try to suppress the artillery fires from Young, which would have supported Bowman.

Bob Cummings from Charlie Company had spent the whole day placing trip flares in front of his bunker because it was in such a poor location. Then at dusk a Chinook flew in low over his head and ignited every one of the flares. One of the soldiers in his bunker was a man with a very low IQ, one of Secretary of Defense McNamara's "Project 100,000" soldiers, a project to place low IQ men in the Army, thinking they could handle Army tasks, and get a start on life.

Cummings referred to him as "Dipshit." When the attackers came inside the wire Cummings placed "Dipshit" at the bunker entrance to guard his back while he and another soldier climbed on top of the bunker to throw grenades as fast as they could. Later he found "Dipshit" inside the bunker whimpering under a bunk instead of guarding their backs. Cummings came close to killing him and no one would have been the wiser. The three Alpha grunts that were killed that night were Cummings good friends. After the attack, "Dipshit" was assigned to drive a garbage truck in Chu Lai.

Sergeant Terry Miller was in the radio switchboard bunker with one of his three men. The others were on the perimeter. The switchboard team reported to Captain Gideon who was a father figure to them. Miller's team was responsible for connecting the bunkers and fighting positions to a SB22 switchboard hooked to field phones located in each position. Miller had spent the early evening calming SP/4 Moll who was new and had been with the battalion for only two weeks. They talked about cars and which ones they would buy when they returned home "to the world".

When the attack came Sgt. Miller quickly awoke and protected the entrance to his switchboard bunker. A Chicom grenade was tossed in by an attacker who ran by, which landed on a shelf in the bunker. Millers mate, Eddie Baun, was at the switchboard when it blew. The shrapnel from the grenade hit Miller in the back. The back of Baun's head was peppered with shrapnel which would take three years to work its way to the surface for removal. Baun glanced at a wood beam above his head which held a large piece of shrapnel. The radio beside him was destroyed. Miller continued to fire through the bunker entrance to keep the enemy at bay but then the two decided to exit their death trap and take their chances outside. Miller, a young sugar beet farmer from Montana moved from position to position in his commo section to keep watch for attackers.

Major Tittle, with bleeding foot and leg wounds, helped to reestablish order in the TOC, getting communications going again, and moving among the wounded rendering first aid, as AK-47 and RPG fire landed around his area. He encountered the sergeant who had gone to ground and allowed the death of Gideon. Tittle told him to get out of his sight. He was later transferred off of Bowman for his own safety.

Staff Sergeant Drexel Ray, the battalion's Chemical NCO encountered a Vietcong who was ready to toss a grenade inside the bunker he shared with a liaison officer. Caught by surprise, the Vietcong dropped the grenade and aimed his AK-47 at Ray and the officer. Lunging at the VC, Ray knocked the weapon from his hands. In the ensuing struggle the VC broke away and ran towards the perimeter. Sergeant Ray gave chase and tackled him just short of the perimeter. Ray's prisoner would be the only one taken that night. After placing him under guard Ray moved to the TOC to help establish order.

Lyon's Command Sergeant Major of the battalion, Walter Edge, a soldier's soldier ran from his bunker to the perimeter and saw explosions and "little people" darting in and out of the shadows (the command later estimated about twenty infiltrators). He grabbed the headquarters soldiers in the area and formed a reaction force, starting at the TOC then moving out amidst the explosions to seek out the sappers.

Specialist Fourth Class Matthew Spearing in the headquarters element was fifty feet from the switchboard bunker with one of Millers line men, John Savoy. He heard a grenade tossed into his bunker but the two exited out the back just as it exploded. For Spearing, there would be no roaming around. The VC came to him. Savoy's weapon was damaged in the blast and Spearing had only one full magazine. Spearing heard voices and movement to the front of his bunker. He peered around the side of the bunker and a jolt moved up his spine. A group of attackers came up to the front of the bunker and poured automatic fire inside the front aperture. Assuming they had killed everyone inside, the enemy moved forward by the side of the bunker.

Spearing took a couple deep breaths to try to control the panic he felt and moved around the corner in a crouch to face the enemy. Dropping to one knee he fired in two and three round bursts, hitting the first two VC who were only four feet to his front. The rest fell to the ground, yelling and screaming as they returned fire. Why Spearing was not hit will remain one of life's mysteries. Spearing fired off several more bursts and the enemy scattered, electing to throw hand grenades. One grenade landed at Spearing's feet but it was a dud. After that the enemy stayed clear of his position. By steady nerves in a chaotic situation he and others helped turned the tide. Tittle, Ray, Edge and Spearing were awarded Bronze Stars for valor. Many more medals were earned, but in the fog of battle and the rush to continue operations, deserving soldiers would not see the awards they were entitled to.

LTC David Lyon also entered the TOC after his bunker was pulverized, still in his shorts. The first order of business was to get continuous illumination rounds shot in the air to give soldiers on the perimeter better visibility. With the help of a flashlight he and his staff established communications with brigade headquarters and LZ Young. Within thirty minutes aircraft dropping flares were over Bowman as Alpha Company swept the perimeter and reaction forces searched inside the LZ. At 4:30AM Charlie Company was told to move north before first light to search the southern area around Bowman. The Echo Recon Platoon at LZ Gator was ordered to saddle up and was brought in to add to the search.

The dustoffs descended onto Bowman with no lights, flares were allowed to burn out before the loading of the dead and wounded was attempted, to keep the enemy mortars from zeroing in on the dustoffs. Lonnie Loftis's bunker was the closet to the Headquarters bunker, just below the perimeter. He and a few others carried Captain Gideon's body to the helicopter pad on a cot. They stumbled many times trying to walk over the many boulders on the LZ. One medic said, "You're wasting time, he's dead." Another medic replied, "No, he still has a pulse." When they arrived at the pad they could hear choppers overhead but could not see them. One soldier volunteered to lie on his back on the pad with a strobe light on his chest, so the birds could see where to land. The dustoff's landed on top of him, but their landing struts missed him each time and he was not injured.

By 5:00AM it was over. Three soldiers from Alpha Company and Gideon and Moll from Headquarters Company were dead and twenty-six wounded, including fourteen from the Headquarters Company and nine from Alpha Company. Alpha's dead were Sgt. Robert Salter, 22 and single from Parish, Alabama; PFC Joel LaRoche, 21 and single from Huntington Beach, California and PFC Steven Vinter, 25 and single from Sacramento, California. Lying along the perimeter and among the interior bunkers were three unexploded Bangalore Torpedoes, twenty-six hand grenades and two AK-47 rifles. Charlie Company was brought back onto Bowman on the morning of the 24th but by noon it was transferred off Bowman in support of the 3rd/1st Battalion, 11th Infantry Brigade which was preparing for a NVA threat against Quang Ngai City.

LZ's Young and LZ Bowman continued to receive sporadic mortar fire. Lyon was sure a major attack was still in the works. He requested the brigade supply twenty airplane-type flares for lighting the perimeter at Bowman, along with a chemical specialist to advise on the condition of CS Gas dispensers and the installation of "Foo-gas", napalm-like containers which were hidden forward of the perimeter and ignited when under major ground attack. He also wanted engineers to survey the hapless LZ and get earthmoving equipment to improve its fields of fire. Throughout the night VC and NVA were reported around the perimeter. Echo's Recon Platoon dispatched an ambush team southeast of Bowman's saddle. No sooner had it departed the perimeter than it encountered two VC in a gun-fight.

The next day, August 25, the ante was raised for all Americal soldiers in the Tam Ky area. The 2nd Platoon of A Troop, 1st/1st Cavalry Regiment and the 3rd/4th ARVN Cavalry had intercepted a NVA Regiment moving in from the mountains towards Tam Ky through an area known as the Pineapple Forest, a rectangular area one and one-half mile from south to north and roughly four miles west to east. The forest began at the mountain's forward edge on the western side and ended two and one-half miles outside the provincial capital of Tam Ky. The dense mountains leading up to the heavily foliaged Pineapple Forest, offered a fast track corridor of cover and concealment for NVA to attack the provincial capital. The 196th Infantry Brigade, "The Chargers", set out to meet the NVA head-on with the 1st/1st Cavalry Squadron in the lead.

To support the heavy fighting now underway in the Pineapple Forest, Echo's Recon Platoon pushed north of Bowman to provide Observation Posts (OP's) to watch for NVA trying to move south towards Bowman. Bravo, still further north was tasked to create blocking positions and OP's on the hilltops located on the southeastern tail of the mountains, southwest of the forest. Chappell's Bravo Company humped three hours to get to LZ Young for water re-supply on their way north, but there was little to be found. Chappell did find some in a can that had been presweetened with Kool Aid. It tasted nasty but he filled his canteen and the troops headed off the LZ, with a promise they would be re-supplied with water while enroute to their OP's. Chappell would later regret his decision to drink the Kool Aid.

During Bravo's trek north, intelligence reports estimated three hundred NVA were moving out of the Pineapple Forest towards Bravo's planned OP's. At 3:10PM Bravo encountered five NVA just north of their sector killing one soldier wearing a pith helmet who appeared to be a commander with a pistol and maps. While Delta was under mortar attack on Young, Bravo patrolled its OP area and the soldiers on Bowman tried to improve the firebase's pitiful conditions. One of the dilapidated bunkers they inherited collapsed on two soldiers who were assigned to the artillery battery.

August 26 saw Bravo Company making increased contacts with the NVA. They had been reinforced with some CIDG to supplant their own dwindling numbers, now at seventy-eight grunts in the field. Chappell established three OP's: OP #1, with six of Bravo's grunts and forty CIDG sat on a knob overlooking Provincial Road 533 which led to Tam Ky. One mile north from OP #1 sat OP #2 (Hill 97), which was Chappell's Company base with thirty-five grunts, overlooking a vast expanse of terrain leading northeast up to the Pineapple Forest, only one and one-quarter miles away. Three-quarters of a mile farther north sat OP #3 which 1LT. Jim Tuckers 2nd platoon manned, reinforced with some CIDG.

After arriving at their OP's, Bravo observed NVA stragglers moving past their hill-top positions, moving away from the drubbing they were getting from the 1st/1st Cav in the Pineapple Forest. Tuckers platoon captured an NVA fleeing from the battle with a head wound. He was snatched for questioning. All of Bravo's soldiers had front row seats for the battle, watching air strikes, helicopter gunships, jet bombers, and artillery concentrations throughout the day.

At 7:15PM, OP #2 spotted six NVA moving up the side of a small hill. Chappell told his FO, the same sergeant that helped him blow the top off Hill 237, to call in some artillery. The sergeant called for a Controlled Fragmentation (COFRAM) round, also known as a "firecracker." It had a veritable timing (VT) fuse which exploded about 250-feet above the ground, dispersing small bomblets. The bomblets landed over a wide area and exploded upon hitting the ground. Knowing six NVA would not justify the expense of granting such ordnance, the six NVA were inflated to a company of NVA when the sergeant requested the fire mission.

Delta's soldiers heard loudspeakers in the early evening outside its perimeter on LZ Young, with the enemy communicating anti-American propaganda and exhorting the CIDG to defect. Artillery was called in and the public broadcast stopped. Lyon ordered all defensive perimeters on one hundred percent alert from 1:00AM-5:00AM, then two-thirds alert until daylight and one-third alert during the day. The following morning CIDG patrols from Bravo's OP's searched the area of the COFRAM strike. They did not find NVA bodies but lots of blood and flesh were splattered about. Brigade Intelligence called Lyon to advise him that the NVA soldier captured by Tuckers platoon was from the 70th Battalion, 21st Regiment, 2nd NVA Division. This was a unit not normally found in that area which supported the belief the NVA had been reinforced for a major attack on Tam Ky which was now being stopped in its tracks in the Pineapple Forest.

On the evening of August 27, Chappell faced a third night of OP duty. He remembered his Fort Benning tactics training to avoid sitting on a position too long, particularly with main force NVA units nearby. The NVA surely knew where he was. He requested permission to move but permission was denied. That night Chappell placed a listening post (LP) about eighty yards down the hill by a trail. At 2:30AM, the LP, which had only three soldiers, Sgt. Kenneth Turner and SP/4's Paul Ciglar and Morris Dyes, heard Vietnamese voices approaching. The LP wanted to come in as the voices were getting closer. Chappell, who was sick all day and feverish, crawled to the south side of his OP where the three soldiers would pass through. The LP blew their claymore mines and bounded up the hill shouting, "LP coming in … don't shoot!" Moment's later grenades began exploding, the perimeter opened up and the top of the hill caught fire.

Chappell crawled back to his position to call in illumination rounds. Figures kept darting in and out of the shadows and NVA ran across the top of the hill. Chappell moved along the small perimeter with his RTO, passing out ammunition. His thirty-five soldiers fired away at the NVA coming up the hill with the enemy moving in small groups. A few Chicom grenades exploded on the perimeter's edge. They were poorly made and had minimal effect, but did wound the RTO. When Chappell reached one of his M-60 machinegun positions, he found the gunner dead and the assistant gunner severely wounded, hit with shrapnel in the stomach, ripping open his intestines. The M-60 was missing. After bringing the wounded grunt back to his small CP, Chappell and the medic took turns holding the mortally wounded soldier as he lay in a fetal position, calling for his mother, until he died. The NVA exacted a price for Bravo's effectiveness in manning the OP's. Five soldiers were wounded and two were killed in action on OP #2: PFC Clay Holt Jr., the machine gunner, age 24 and married from Marshall, Missouri, and his assistant, PFC Tom Thomas, age 22 and single from New Philadelphia, Ohio.

At 8:25AM, the grunts searched the base of their hill and the immediate area, finding blood trails, fifteen Chicom grenades, a satchel charge, and a basket loaded with ordnance. With small consolation, Tuckers platoon also found eight uniformed NVA bodies with weapons near their OP, a result of their artillery fire mission called two evenings prior. Charlie Company, which had returned from Quang Ngai City, reinforced LZ Young and sent their 2nd platoon to reinforce Bravo on OP #2. Chappell again asked to relocate but was nixed. With his fever worsening, he was no longer in any condition to stay in the field. He was picked up by a Command & Control (C&C) helicopter flying nearby, obviously of some high ranking officer because it sported carpeting on the Hueys floor. No sooner had they lifted off than Chappell defecated on the carpet, unable to control himself. Back at Chu Lai the doctors determined he had amoebic dysentery, with the contaminated Kool Aid as the source.

On the afternoon of the 28th, Delta's position on LZ Young was heavily mortared and small arms fire swept across its perimeter. Delta's counter battery fire from mortars and artillery on Young had no effect. This reinforced the belief that there was a cave complex one and one-half miles north, the location of the artillery fire. Air strikes were called to do what Artillery firepower could not do. For the next three days patrols of the battalion continued to find individual bodies of VC and NVA, as well as blood trails and small caches of ammunition. Bravo was finally pulled off its OP's and returned to Bowman for some rest, then it replaced Delta on LZ Young while Delta and Charlie moved south on platoon-sized sweeps. On August 31, the well-established Special Forces camp at Tien Phouc received an early morning barrage of 40-122mm rockets, 82mm mortar fire and recoilless rifle fire, killing three and wounding thirteen in the camp.

On September 1, PFC Edward Jackson of Echo Company, age 18 and single from Athens, Texas stole a 1-3/4 ton truck on Hill 54, an artillery support base north of Chu Lai. As he drove the truck from the hill it overturned and killed him.

At 3:00AM on September 4, Delta's night defensive position (NDP) near the hamlet of Thanh Lam was attacked, just east of the Bong Mieu River, two and one-half miles south of LZ Young. PFC Edward O'Dea was part of a listening post forward of the perimeter. When the LP radioed enemy movement, Delta's CO called in preplanned artillery fire. The NVA quickly moved closer to the perimeter, a well-developed "hugging tactic" to avoid defensive fires. This left the LP no choice but to open fire and expose it's position. The enemy returned fire on the LP as it skirted the OP position and continued heading for the perimeter. Although wounded, O'Dea took charge and led his comrades back to the perimeter, passing the attacking NVA in the night and reaching the perimeter first. His initiative earned him a Bronze Star for valor. Probing of Delta's perimeter continued throughout the night but close-in artillery support and a tight perimeter kept the NVA at bay.

At noon the NVA opened up with well-placed 60mm mortar rounds. Seven rounds hit the perimeter's edge and five rounds landed inside the small perimeter near the command group. Delta's CO was wounded and 1LT Robert Porter took command, exposing himself to hostile fire while checking on his perimeter's defense and calling in dustoffs. He would be awarded a Bronze Star for his valor but for Porter and his grunts, their hilltop position was a slice of hell on earth. Bodies were shredded with shrapnel and men went into shock while mortar rounds continued to explode.

All routine dustoffs were cancelled in the area and diverted to Porter's beleaguered troops while gunships sought out the mortar positions. For PFC Jim Wagner it was his first firefight and he was terrified. The Cobra gunships came in low and behind Wagner, belching their mini-guns and grenade fire on the enemy outside the perimeter. Wagner thought the Cobra fire was enemy fire and they were being overrun until he looked up. Wagner recalls, "They made a frightening noise but made a definite impact as things stated to calm down." Delta, unable to dig in because of the rocky ground, had remained at their NDP too long, allowing the enemy to sight their mortars and pound their position. In the short span of thirty minutes, twenty-seven soldiers were wounded and evacuated, effectively cutting Delta's strength by one-third. After the headquarters section was dusted off, Wagner was given a PRC-25 radio and told "You are now an RTO". Wagner replied "I don't know how to be an RTO". He was asked, "Didn't you go through Infantry AIT (Advance Individual Training)?" He replied, "Yes." "Well then, you know enough."

Flying overhead was Brigadier General Howard Cooksey and newly arrived Captain Michael Smith. Smith had just reported into the division looking for a company command and Cooksey, who had been his brigade commander in Korea, invited Smith to fly with him for the day. Learning of the carnage with Delta Company, Cooksey told Smith, "I've just found you a company" and dropped him off at Delta's position. Smith met 1LT Porter and assumed command.

Alpha conducted a recon in force one-half mile southwest of LZ Young, while Bravo continued to improve its defenses with daytime patrols in the vicinity. Charlie Company secured LZ Bowman while Delta, depleted in numbers, screened the terrain two and one-half miles southwest of Young. They continued to find small pockets of NVA, calling in artillery fire to disperse them, and located enemy equipment scattered about. In one hooch they snatched a female who was surrounded by a cache of NVA helmets and gear. Echo Recon began a three-day sweep south of Bowman, along Provisional Road 531.

In the first half of September 1968 the 5th/46th Infantry Battalion aggressively continued its patrolling, killing NVA and VC as they found them in small groups or one by one. It was evident these seasoned grunts were taking their toll on the enemy, not with major fire fights but by denying the initiative to the enemy and depleting his strength one body at a time. Intelligence reports indicated a major attack had been planned for LZ Young. This information came to light because of the aggressive patrolling by the battalion. Soldiers found abandoned bunkers, medical equipment, clothing and ammunition. Civilian villagers in the area reported small groups of NVA and VC looking for food while evading Lyon's troops. Here and there NVA and VC bodies were discovered, with wounds that had led to fatalities from loss of blood or infections. With heavy packs, constant movement, and little time to sleep, the battalion's soldiers trudged on, averaging one dustoff each day for malaria, dysentery, or heat exhaustion. Another chemical defoliation mission was flown in the area on September 15, to "assist" the grunts in their work.

By September 14, plans began to take shape to move the battalion back to its old Area of Operations in Quang Ngai Province. The 1st/52nd, which had back-filled the 5th/46th on LZ Gator, would replace the 5th/46th and take its turn in the Burlington Trail Operation. Bravo Company of the 5th/46th was the first to be extracted and it was moved by Chinook Helicopter to LZ Chippewa.

On September 17, Delta continued its patrolling one and one-half miles west of LZ Young in the village of Phuoc Lam, during the final hours of the battalion's stint in the Burlington Trail operation. Delta's grunts discovered one thousand pounds of rice at noon, which struck a nerve with the hungry NVA nearby and prompted a firefight. The grunts continued their search in the area, finding lots of blood trails.

At 5:50PM, they came under heavy mortar and small arms fire. When a Huey carrying ammunition came in to drop its load, SP/4 Albert Rose, an 81mm mortar gunner, ran to the chopper to unload the much needed ammunition. Realizing his fellow grunts were running out of M-16 ammunition, he ran along Delta's hasty perimeter resupplying his fellow grunts, all while enemy mortar rounds were exploding. During the fire fight his luck ran out when an exploding mortar round killed him. He would be posthumously awarded a Bronze Star for his efforts to keep his fellow soldiers supplied with ammo. Rose was 21 and single, from South Lyon, Michigan.

Although seriously wounded, PFC Robert Breedlove placed suppressive fire on the enemy while moving from position to position giving medical aid to the wounded. He was awarded a Bronze Star; SP/4 Gary Collins and SP/5 Robin Hauck continually exposed themselves to hostile fire while moving to secure more ammunition from the supply point. Both were awarded Army Commendation Medals for valor.

While Delta was being pounded by mortars, an engineer platoon close by (Alpha Company, 39th Engineer Battalion), was pinned down by heavy enemy fire. The ARVN's were securing the area for the American engineers to complete some road work. When some enemy fire began the ARVN soldiers, without notice, picked up and moved back around a hair-pin curve in the road. Once they were out of sight, in the words of one engineer, "All hell broke loose." In short order the engineers lost communications with their company and battalion headquarters and took heavy casualties. Panic set in. Smith's RTO was able to make contact with the platoon on its internal frequency and got a desperate plea for help.

Flying overhead was Lieutenant Colonel Ronald Richardson who had just assumed command of the 5th/46th Infantry Battalion. Richardson and Smith agreed to send Delta's 3rd platoon in the night to link up with the engineers and the rest of Delta would move at first light. Initially the 3rd platoon leader and platoon sergeant refused to move at night but Smith offered some serious persuasion and they went, even though the enemy situation was unknown. The platoon linked up with the engineers in the dark and dustoff's were brought in during the night to begin evacuating the many dead and wounded.

Early in the morning the rest of Delta closed in on the engineers' position and continued the evacuation of the dead and wounded. Among the dead NVA was a large man Captain Smith believed to be a Chinese advisor. He had a small bullet hole in the forehead while the back of his head was missing. During Delta's two days of combat on September 17-18, including the rescue of the engineers, over forty NVA were killed and nine US soldiers killed, eight of which were from the engineer platoon and one (SP/4 Rose) from Delta Company.

It was during Delta's fight to rescue the engineers that the 5th/46th's new battalion commander, LTC Ronald Richardson, made an aerial reconnaissance when he heard Delta's calls for fire support. Flying to the scene of the action his bird was hit by ground fire and it limped back to LZ Young. It was a fitting introduction to a new battalion commander in the Burlington Trail Operation.

Lieutenant Colonel David Lyon finished his one-year tour of battalion command, roughly six months of preparing it for war at Fort Hood, Texas and six months of steady combat in Vietnam. As was often the case in Vietnam, the battalion commander's departure was swift, during an on-going operation, with little or no coordination with his replacement. During Lyon's command tenure, twenty-six of his grunts were killed by hostile fire, one of natural causes and one by accident and two hundred and eighty-three had been wounded, including himself. Through infusions, combat injures, wounds and rotations, many of the original soldiers who came from Fort Hood were now gone, yet a sufficient number remained to mentor the steady stream of replacements coming in. Soldiers with six weeks of field duty were considered "seasoned" and they mentored new replacements as well. Soldiers with six months of field duty under their belts were considered "survivors".

On September 18, Alpha and Delta Company's, still engaged with the NVA, called in artillery strikes on Hill 212 (Nui Xau), a source of persistent mortar fire. A sweep of the hill uncovered five NVA killed and many blood trails. A helicopter pilot flying two miles northwest of LZ Young at 10:00AM radioed excitedly that he saw, "Camouflaged graves – twenty-five NVA uniforms hanging out to dry - tunnels - hooch's and too many spider holes to count!" But it was time for the 5th/46th to withdraw, and that find would be the task of the 1st/52nd Battalion to pursue which they did, finding an abandoned NVA base camp. By afternoon on the 18th, the 5th/46th returned to its LZ Gator area of operations. On its last morning of the operation, five more soldiers were wounded while engaging the enemy as helicopters came in to take them back to Gator. Delta was sent to secure LZ's Dottie and Buff, previously occupied by the 1st/52nd Infantry Battalion.

7. GOLDEN FLEECE

Consolidation

On September 18, 1968 the 5th/46th Infantry Battalion resumed responsibility for their old stomping grounds, "The Southern Chu Lai AO", which covered the terrain from LZ Gator moving south to the Tra Bong River and east, covering the coastal lowlands down to Quang Ngai City. Alpha Company secured LZ Chippewa and set out to improve its defenses with sixty-seven grunts on the line while twenty-seven other soldiers patrolled the nearby high ground to pick up any enemy movement. Alpha was also tasked to lend any support needed to the Marine Combined Action Platoon (CAP) 133 out on the coastal plain.

Bravo Company was tasked to secure LZ Gator. They had a "foxhole strength" of one hundred and twenty-one but also sent squad-size patrols beyond its perimeter in daylight reconnaissance and nighttime ambushes. Three grunts manned Observation Post (OP) 3, a relatively open area astride a dirt road and a tributary of the Cap Da River, 1/3-mile northeast of LZ Gator. Nestled near the OP were small fishing hamlets. The area was a convenient causeway for Vietcong and NVA migrating between the coastal plain east of Highway One and the mountains west of the highway, passing through the friendly embrace of the villagers of Tri Binh (5), which sat in the shadow of LZ Gator. Four grunts held OP 5 located two and one-half miles north of Gator, west of Highway One and just north of Tri Binh (1). A low stretch of high ground provided OP 5 a long view looking south through the Tri Binh hamlets west of Highway One and the sandy terrain east of the highway which held the headwaters of the Tra Bong River.

At 12:30AM on September 19, OP 3 received small arms fire from the direction of a nearby hamlet as well as ten to twelve rounds of 60mm-mortar fire. Seven of the rounds landed inside their small perimeter, wounding some of the defenders but causing no deaths. At 1:30AM the grunts searched the north side of the perimeter and found a dead Vietcong with a Bangalore Torpedo. In his effort to blow-up the OP he was killed by his own mortar fire.

Bravo's duty on LZ Gator gave its soldiers some opportunity to wind down, which included visiting the ville of Nuoc Mau at the eastern base of Gator next to Highway One. One of things Nuoc Mau offered was an opportunity for soldiers to get some "Boom Boom" at the ville's whore house. The experience was always educational for new soldiers to the battalion. One sergeant, who had seen nothing but field duty since arriving two months prior and his two comrades, also relatively new to Vietnam, ventured down into the ville after a long overdue shave, shower and hot meal. They carried their M-16's with several clips of ammo, the rule for all grunts. Entering the front of the hooch serving as a whorehouse, the Mamasan greeted them and the three soldiers nervously argued a price, settling on $5.00 per man. A blanket separated the front of the hooch from the back. Having been paid, the Mamasan raised the blanket and the three soldiers nervously went to the back.

The three soldiers debated who would go first, aware that they couldn't waste time since Military Police (MP's) from LZ Bayonet frequently raided the facility. One solder volunteered to go first and the other two stood guard with M-16's while their companion took his clothes off. The Mamasan giggled during his encounter but the other two soldiers remained unsettled. The first customer finished and then the Mamasan said, "Sergeant, now your turn." The sergeant started to undress while he watched the Mamasan wash something in a dish pan. She removed a very wet and dripping condom the first customer had just used and handed it to the next customer. The sergeant lost interest quickly and could not get his "Old George" up even if he wanted to. The soldiers departed more quickly than they arrived. The first customer chided his buddy for chickening out and going for seconds, until the sergeant told him his condom was washed and was probably used many times before him. For the immediate future, in addition to worrying about mines, snipers and mortar rounds, the soldier worried about what he might come down with until the period for infection passed.

Charlie Company was assigned the mission of moving back to the dreaded coastal lowlands to secure LZ Paradise with seventy-six grunts, and secure Riverboat South with twenty-five. Charlie could also count on support from the armored personnel carriers, "tracks" of the 3rd Platoon, H Troop, 17th CAV. On September 18, their first day back on the coast, Charlie's grunts on patrol one and one-half mile west of Paradise hit a mine, wounding three grunts and their Vietnamese interpreter.

Delta Company relinquished fifty-seven of its grunts to LZ Dottie just three and one-half miles south of Binh Son, to help bolster it's defense as an artillery fire support base. One other rifle platoon and their weapons platoon, down to a mere thirty-seven soldiers combined, was dispatched to help defend LZ Buff south of the Tra Bong River, the base camp of the 1st/52nd Infantry Battalion while that battalion conducted operations in the Tien Phouc area.

Echo Company's heavy mortar platoon (4.2 inch), placed twenty-nine of its soldiers on LZ Chippewa to help provide for its defense as well as support LZ Buff to its southeast. A small section of eighteen men were sent to support CAP 133 with two 4.2 inch tubes to augment the smaller 60mm mortars used by the Marines and the Vietnamese local forces. Echo's Recon platoon set out to screen the area south and east of Chippewa.

With the battalion's grunts spread thin throughout their AO, the VC would provide equal opportunity attacks to all of them. On September 22 at 2:30AM, LZ Dottie was hit by well placed mortar fire which damaged a 155mm howitzer, four 5-ton trucks, two 2-1/2 ton trucks, and two jeeps. Under their mortar barrage a Vietcong squad penetrated the artillery portion of the perimeter, and destroyed two ammunition bunkers. One dead VC was found inside the perimeter with a bandoleer of ammo around his waist, hand grenade in his hand and RPG's lying around him. The attack on Dottie was the typical diversion to silence or keep occupied the artillery battery that provided fire support to Binh Son a short distance north.

LZ Gator was also hit by enemy 82mm mortar fire starting at 2:05AM. The first rounds were directed at the artillery battery on Gators northeast corner, and then fires were shifted to sleeping quarters within the LZ with approximately twenty rounds fired in total. Under cover of the mortar fire, ten to twenty sappers attacked Gators perimeter with RPG fire and hand grenades, infiltrating the bunker line near the artillery battery and on the southern edge of the perimeter, near the dirt road from Nuoc Mau. One Bravo soldier was killed in the attack, PFC Willie Ray Lay from Fairhope, Alabama. He had been in Vietnam less than a month. Lay was age eighteen and single. Two other soldiers were wounded and one 155mm Howitzer was damaged along with six vehicles. Two enemy sappers were captured.

With Dottie and Gator somewhat neutralized, Binh Son was hit with a ground attack at 4:10AM. The Vietnamese Popular Force (PF) militia guarding the town received seventy-five rounds of recoilless rifle fire, 60mm and 82mm mortars and intense automatic weapons fire accompanied by the ground attack on their compound. The primary VC objective was to rescue VC prisoners held in a large compound next to the PF headquarters. But when the VC reached the prisoner compound and told them to leave, the prisoners, tired of the austere field duty of guerillas, refused. Their "rescuers" set out to slaughter them. Buildings which covered four city blocks were set on fire as satchel charges were thrown throughout the town. That night the grunts on LZ Dottie lost one killed and two wounded. The Vietnamese in Binh Son lost approximately forty killed and thirty wounded.

Battalion intelligence estimated CAP teams 133, 135 and LZ Paradise were next on the enemies list for attack. The grunts patrolled aggressively around their assigned defensive positions, the only sure way to try to deny momentum to the enemy. Here and there they found elusive pockets of VC or NVA, killing some and detaining others. The heavy fall monsoon rains were also taking their toll, causing foot disease among the troops while sandbags on bunkers fell apart from rot. The weather also hindered the effectiveness of their 81mm and 4.2 inch mortar fires, with atmospheric conditions causing rounds to glide off course.

On September 23, a "short round" fired from an 81mm mortar on LZ Paradise landed on a bunker, killing one soldier, PFC Teodoro Santellan, and wounding another. Santellan was from Delta Company and had only been in country twenty-two days. He was twenty years of age and single, from Grant, Michigan. Dustoffs for malaria continued, with snakebites not uncommon and four Alpha grunts required dustoff from massive bee stings. Whatever could happen to an infantry unit in Vietnam was happening to the grunts of the 5th/46th. The 198th Brigade headquarters saw its field strength diminished in all its assigned battalions, so the 198th Brigade policy now required all grunts finishing

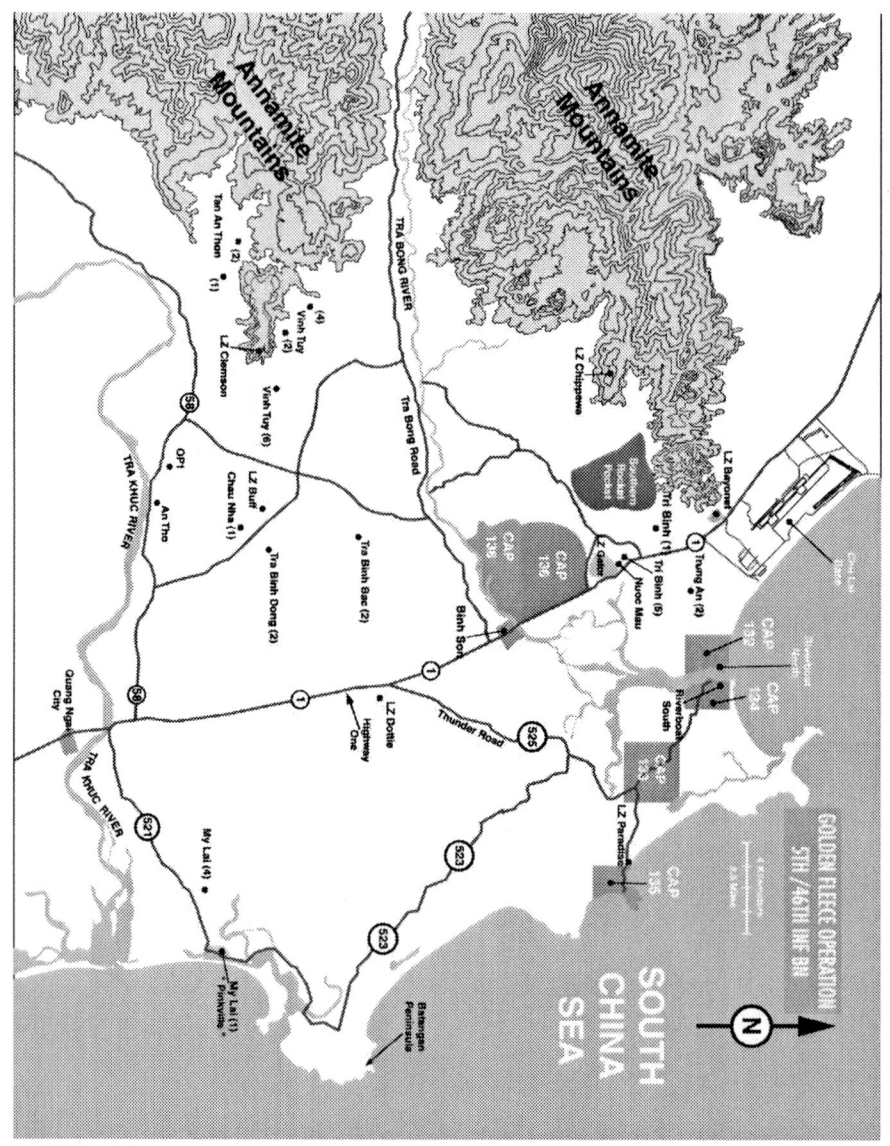

Golden Fleece

their Vietnam tours to remain in the field until seven days remained prior to their rotation home.

One of the most puzzling units the battalion worked with was the 635th Military Intelligence (MI) Detachment which resided, in part, on LZ Gator. Battalion staff officers found the MI "spooks" odd to deal with, never knowing who they were talking to. They wore no rank and used aliases. 1LT Schulte's S-5 Civil Affairs crew encountered them from time to time as they traveled from hamlet to hamlet. His men over time got to know most of them but the spooks usually moved from hamlet to hamlet on their own but seemed to cling to Schulte's men when too many VC were in the area.

Charlie Company, working on the coast, was managing to keep its casualties low by remembering the lessons learned from its July duties in the area. But on September 26, the company Forward Observer (FO) stepped on an M-16 mine booby-trapped to a 105mm artillery round. It should not have happened. The 2nd platoon was on patrol, rounding a bend on a trail. The point element spotted a mine, by-passed it carefully, and passed the information down the line behind it. Along the line was a grunt that paused, out of breath from his heavy load and the heat. The grunts behind him thought the entire element stopped so they stopped as well. This caused a physical and communications gap in the patrol file. Realizing the point element had not stopped, the grunts bypassed the resting soldier and moved on, unaware of the mine that had been spotted. 1LT Fisk, the Company FO from the 1/14th Artillery Battalion stepped on the mine. The hastily called dustoff was just as hastily cancelled. Fisk's traumatic amputation of his lower torso allowed him to live only a few minutes.

With the impending fall rice harvest, intelligence reports from the Marine CAP teams told of VC and NVA squads setting up tax collection points, requiring fifteen pounds of rice and twenty-five percent of the money the villagers collected from rice sales. These Marine CAP Teams were at the forefront of village life in their assigned areas and were valuable sources of intelligence. The CAP concept was "Vietnamization" at its core, long before President Nixon would coin the term. But at times the CAP teams generated their own unique set of problems to the 5th/46th. Occasionally they called for fire support when the battalion thought none was justified. But, by and large, they made a solid contribution to the battalion's war effort. A typical night was September 27. At midnight CAP 137 came under small arms fire but held their perimeter with M-60 machine gun fire and 60mm mortars. Twenty-five minutes later CAP 134 heard dogs barking in their assigned hamlet. They opened fire on two Vietcong squads attempting to infiltrate the hamlet and killed three. These small "Fort Apache's" in the Chu Lai area brought security where it counted, at the village and hamlet level. The CAP's were a credit to the Marine Corps legacy and demonstrated foresight and expertise in counterinsurgency warfare.

SP/4 Howard Davis from Bakersfield, California served with the battalion's 4.2-inch mortar section at CAP 133. He and his fellow soldiers got along well with the Marines and added some strength to their thin numbers while providing fire support, mostly with night illumination rounds and harassment & interdiction (H&I) fires. Both squads of mortar men lived in two small barracks-type buildings with cots, a basketball court outside, and a horseshoe area.

Davis found the Marines to be highly competent, all were volunteers chosen for the CAP mission. Their primary advantage was they stayed in the same area and became very familiar with the terrain and the people. They bolstered that familiarity with the help of the local PF forces they worked with. On one mission the Marines captured some high ranking VC in a village ambush and occasionally some of Davis's comrades would go on patrols with the Marines, to act as Forward Observers or to relieve boredom.

Davis found it a bit odd the hamlet near their small base was split in half. The PF's and their families lived on one end. At night they closed a gate between them and the other half of the hamlet. Davis was told the other half housed the VC sympathizers. Strange times in a strange war.

While never strong enough to attack a VC-controlled hamlet, the Marines applied guerilla tactics against the guerillas. This included the decision to rustle a cow from the VC controlled hamlet of Dung Le (4). Davis was in a bunker on the east-end of the low-lying hill, which held their small base camp, on the night of the operation. They were told the time the heist would take place so they wouldn't shoot the returning Marines. Davis heard the mooing of the cow being kidnapped from the enemy hamlet. He then heard a large "clop, clop, clop" as the VC cow broke loose from the Marines and lumbered back to the hamlet. The Marines walked back empty handed.

Late September the NVA and VC increased pressure on the 5th/46th firebases and Marine CAP Teams, attempting to bottle-up the grunts while the enemy coerced the Vietnamese in the rice fields. On

September 28 at 2:12AM, LZ Gator was hit with thirty-two 82mm mortar rounds coming from one-half mile north of the perimeter. Remarkably, no one was wounded but LZ Chippewa had a tougher time one hour later.

At 3:42AM, Alpha's grunts manning the Chippewa perimeter were also hit. Well-placed mortar fire was followed by a sapper ground attack. One bunker was hit by a satchel charge. In such an attack, each soldier must respond in heroic fashion or face certain death in the dark. SP/4 Jack Vater was one of three grunts in the bunker that was hit. All three were wounded. Despite his painful wounds he treated his companions and was wounded a second time by an enemy grenade. He continued to treat his comrades and helped move them to the dustoffs when they arrived. PFC Francis Davidson had been wounded by the mortar fire on the perimeter but realized that Vater's bunker next to him had received a direct hit. Despite his own wound and the small arms fire coming across the perimeter, he headed for the bunker and saw two attackers ready to throw grenades to finish the wounded grunts. One was thrown (the one that hit Vater) before he could get a bead with his M-16, but Davidson cut down both of the enemy. He also helped to move the wounded to a dustoff. Both Vater and Davidson would receive Bronze Stars for valor. Six of the enemy attackers on Chippewa were killed and one captured. Five Alpha grunts were wounded. In the early morning hours Alpha's Forward Observer spotted three NVA entering a mud hooch just one and one-quarter mile southwest of the perimeter. He called in artillery fire and scored direct hits with the first rounds.

Operation Golden Fleece

Operation "Golden Fleece" referred to rice denial operations against the enemy and was first established when the Marines arrived in the I Corps area in 1965. Golden Fleece operations were used throughout the I Corps area by Marines and the Army alike. In September 1968 another Golden Fleece mission was developed by the Americal Division and 198th Brigade Headquarters to place command emphasis on "denying rice to the enemy, protecting the Vietnamese in their rice harvest efforts, and increasing the South Vietnamese Government's influence over rice harvest areas." The targeted areas were the Ly Tin and Binh Son Districts. Ly Tin was located two and one-half miles north of the Chu Lai base on Highway One which was the stomping grounds at the time of the 1st/6th and 1st/46th Infantry Battalions. The district town of Binh Son, two and one-half miles south of LZ Gator on Highway One, resided in the 5th/46th Battalion's operational area.

Two-thirds of the Binh Son District's land area and one-fourth of the population were under partial or complete Vietcong control. While the population under government control was relatively secure in their densely populated villages and hamlets close to Highway One, these safe havens were primarily refugee camps away from the land that had be farmed. This required the farmer to move through VC/NVA controlled areas to harvest the rice in outlying paddies. For their harvesting efforts, the government imposed a measure on the amount of rice the civilians could return to their home. The quota was roughly one pound of rice per day per person and could not exceed a thirty-day supply. This was to prevent the VC from raiding hamlets and securing larger stores of rice. Rice above that amount was "excess" and had to be sent to government storage areas in and near Binh Son. Rice could also be temporarily stored in Marine CAP compounds before being transported to government storage areas.

Both the Ly Tin and Binh Son Districts were historically rice deficient as a whole with just a few small areas that proved an exception. Historically, even during times of relative peace, the population of these districts had to struggle against possible starvation due to the unyielding mountainous region to the west and the South China Sea to the east. The narrow green plain between offered little fertile soil to be used for farming and was only fifteen miles wide at the most. To add to the Vietnamese worries, the October harvest, normally a small harvest, was expected to be smaller than usual in the fall of 1968 due to an exceptionally dry year. With some fertile areas controlled by the VC and the limited farmland in general, the available rice supply for the population had to be supplemented with rice from the USA.

South Vietnamese government forces assumed responsibility for protecting the harvested rice in storage compounds in or near Bihn Son. These "forces" were primarily composed of National Police Field Force (NPFF), Revolutionary Development workers (RD's), Popular Force Militia (PF's), village self-defense teams, Marines in CAP Teams and South Vietnamese soldiers, when required. The interrelationship of these forces was complex and did not always work smoothly.

National Police did not participate in field duty and were not trained for it. These were "day people", who specialized in intelligence and operated in the hamlets only temporarily, with minimum arms to defend themselves. Their interest was not the Vietcong operating in the field as much as the people who connected the VC with the villagers and with those who supplied intelligence, food and recruits for the VC units. The RD's, in theory, helped the villagers in their daily work tasks, demonstrating that the South Vietnamese government cared for them and that the Vietcong were to be shunned. The concept of RD operations called for the PF's to protect them. The PF's worked in the hamlets and directly with the Marines in the CAP teams. Their effectiveness varied in relationship to the leadership of the Marines in each CAP Team or other American advisors.

Caught in the middle of all of this were the Vietnamese themselves. Within each hamlet could be found pro-government and pro-VC civilians. Some were ardently on one side or the other but most walked a thin line, careful not to be showing too much friendliness to the Marines or PF's, aware that spies may target them as being too supportive to the government. Each hamlet could harbor dedicated, stay-behind agents who were members of the "Viet Cong Security Section". No one in the hamlet, including guerillas, knew exactly who they were. "Security Section" Communists targeted villagers of influence who held a pro-government bias, for assassination. These deeply submerged agents were careful to not even participate in Vietcong attacks, always remaining in the shadows of their anonymity.

"Concurrent with present operations", the 198th Brigade orders read, "the 5th/46th Battalion will conduct search and clear, cordon and search and saturation patrolling around assigned rice growing areas in the Binh Son District." The movement of harvested rice in large bags also offered the enemy an opportunity to smuggle mortar rounds and ammunition across the district. The battalion's grunts were tasked to assist in manning check points for this purpose but also to assume the "heavy lifting" by patrolling and ambushing known enemy exfiltration routes leading from rice producing areas.

As the battalion ramped up for its additional missions it remained thin in strength and was saddled with mission overload. October 6 saw Alpha on a search and clear mission five miles south of LZ Chippewa and five miles southwest of CAP 132, searching for VC infiltrators into the rice fields around Binh Son. They counted ninety-seven "packs" (grunts), only fifty-nine percent of authorized strength. Bravo secured LZ Gator's perimeter with one platoon on Chippewa but it also periodically air assaulted into areas to assist in cordon and search operations. Bravo's field strength on Gator was down to sixty-seven soldiers. Every rear echelon soldier on Gator had to take up perimeter security duties in the evening after a full day of work in the hot sun. Charlie Company had seventy-two soldiers on LZ Paradise with one platoon at Riverboat South numbering thirty-two grunts. Delta secured LZ Dottie with one of its platoons assigned to defend LZ Buff.

Over the coming weeks Delta would also be tasked to support the 11th Brigade in their on-going operations further south in the Duc Pho area. Echo's Recon Platoon operated three miles west of LZ Chippewa deep in the mountains, with only twenty grunts in the field, screening for any NVA movement that might threaten Chippewa. After only three days they were further reduced to fourteen soldiers in the field due to injury and sickness. The Heavy Mortar Platoon kept a section of sixteen soldiers with CAP 133 and the balance of the platoon on LZ Chippewa. The harsh conditions of field duty remained the ally of the NVA/VC and assisted in the attrition of the battalion's strength in the field, beyond what the enemy could not accomplish on its own. In four short days from October 6-10, seven grunts were dusted off with malaria, most had temperatures of 104, and another grunt passed out from a scorpion bite.

The provincial authorities in Binh Son forecasted the rice harvest would begin on October 13 or 14, but the maneuvering for leverage between the enemy and South Vietnamese Government began in early October. Increased pressure on CAP Teams 133 and 134 called for a cordon and search operation which saw Bravo Company air assaulting into the area two miles north of Cap 133's AO as a blocking force. Delta Company back-filled them on LZ Gator's perimeter. Sweeping up from the south to take advantage of Bravo's blocking force, in a "hammer and anvil" tactic, were the Marines and PF's of CAP 133 along with the 1st platoon of Charlie Company and "Tracks" from the 2nd platoon, H Troop of the 17th Calvary.

The battalion's S-5, 1LT Dan Schulte flew reconnaissance flights by Huey during the pre-harvest and harvest periods, identifying the status of the areas of large rice crops. Each day he identified the rice paddies ready for harvest and then the battalion S-3 section would schedule the search and capture missions to confiscate any excess rice from the enemy. Excess rice was moved to the Binh Son District Headquarters and eventually on to the Quang Ngai Province storage centers. Schulte felt blessed, his job was easy because once the rice was spotted, it fell to the battalion's grunts and the Marines in the CAP teams to confiscate and transport the excess rice to Binh Son.

In their sweep on October 3, the Marines found a large cache of mines including fifty Bouncing Betty mines and a booby-trapped 105mm artillery round. Across the rice-producing areas, enemy activity intensified. CAP 137, working with Rural Development (RD) cadre, was engaged in a firefight. A helicopter gunship flying over CAP 136's area spotted three hundred VC two and one-half miles east of their zone. Firefights in the hamlets against attacking VC took their toll on villagers as dustoffs were routinely called for civilians wounded in the crossfire. Each dwelling in a hamlet held a family bunker. When they anticipated a firefight because of VC or government forces in the area, the villagers scrambled into their bunkers which were large, thick mounds of earth, hollowed in the center.

In this war for hegemony over the rice collection effort, no one was spared. A small bridge was being repaired one and one-half mile South of Binh Son. On October 3, an American Engineer Sergeant working on the bridge lost his toes and half of his left foot from an M-16 mine planted twelve inches off the highway. The main bridge on the north side of Binh Son was always under heavy guard at night by local defense forces (CIDG) with munitions support from the 5th/46th, such as Claymore Mines. One morning, civilians driving by the CIDG position in a small-motorized cab ran over a detonator attached to the claymore's which the CIDG's had erroneously faced the wrong way. Thirteen civilians were wounded and four killed due to this carelessness.

At 12:30AM October 8, VC opened fire on a CAP 134 patrol of Marines and PF's. While searching for the source of the gunfire the patrol heard laughter and singing. They called in artillery fire and searched the area, capturing twenty VC suspects and finding numerous blood trails and enemy equipment with blood on it. Two days later, part of Charlie Company was working with CAP 137 near the hamlet of Phu Long (5), two miles northeast of Binh Son, when it came under enemy fire at dusk. One Marine and two PF's walking point hit a bobby-trapped 81mm mortar round, killing all three. LTC Richardson, flying nearby in his command & control (C&C) helicopter, landed in the booby-trapped area and picked up the bodies, returning the PF's to Binh Son and the Marine to Chu Lai.

Three days later Richardson's C&C would land again to pick up a Bravo soldier who stepped on a mine. Oblivious to the risks, the 5th/46th commander would land his C&C time and time again to pick up his wounded, bring in ammunition, and lend support on the ground when one of his patrols was in trouble. On October 13, Charlie Company, while supporting CAP 135 just south of Paradise, lost another soldier, PFC Halpenny, who was killed and two others wounded in a firefight. PFC Jerry Lee Halpenny was 23 and married from Enterprise, West Virginia. Refugees told the CAP teams that VC morale was low because of little food and medical supplies due to the aggressive patrolling by battalion grunts and the CAP teams.

To exert pressure against the Golden Fleece operations, the enemy once again attacked Binh Son on October 14, with the Vietcong demonstrating their ingenuity to make a profound statement. Metal boxes four to six inches square, each containing ten to fifteen pounds of explosives were tied with a pull rope. More deadly than satchel charges used for bunkers, these munitions were used for larger targets to destroy morale. Attackers were able to penetrate the town, destroying the Buddhist Temple and causing damage to the Catholic Church before being driven off.

Mid-October saw Alpha, Bravo and Charlie Companies committing elements to the cordon and search of hamlets east of Binh Son in conjunction with CAP Teams 133, 134 and 135, and Tracks from the 2nd Platoon, H Troop, 17th CAV. Alpha located a large tunnel complex on the north ridge of Hill 106 in Phu Long (5) with evidence the VC had just fled. A large cache of mines was found but PFC Andrew Gilmore stepped on an M-14 mine which blew off his foot. The rice harvest was reaping a heavy price.

Increased emphasis was placed on a Vietnamese Informant Program (VIP), which had existed for some time but the 5th/46th Infantry Battalion took it to a new level. This program was intended to elicit civilian information regarding VC and NVA activity and arms caches. While some pertinent information was obtained, the program routinely yielded one or two munitions along with information necessary to build a larger picture of the enemies' intentions. Items turned in were usually unexploded mortar or artillery rounds which meant less material for the enemy to make mines. Exchange rates for types of information or material (arms and ammunition) were published in the hamlets. Several "turn-in days" were established, with the most successful turn-ins occurring on LZ Dottie.

Prior to departing for LZ Dottie to monitor a scheduled turn-in day, 1LT Schulte was advised by the "spooks" of the MI Detachment that the VC had placed a reward on his head during his trip to reach Dottie. Schulte departed Gator anyway and noticed as he drove down Highway One to Dottie that Richardson's Huey was following him overhead, the two M-60 door gunners at the ready. Schulte surmised the battalion commander had received the same information and was covering his back. He arrived safely at Dottie.

Villagers were compensated for turned-in munitions found in the fields. Schulte noted that the monetary compensation fed the program, "If one satisfied customer returns to his hamlet he usually comes back the next time with twenty friends, all with something." The battalion's grunts on LZ Dottie became a convenient repository for the civilians in the area. During early October they received one thousand five-hundred and eighty loose rounds of ammo, six hundred and ten M-60 machine gun rounds, nine artillery shells, ten pounds of C-4 explosives, four anti-personnel mines, two claymore mines and various dud rounds from 60mm and 80mm mortars and 105mm howitzers. The soldiers on Dottie decided to destroy all the turned-in munitions at one time. When the explosion occurred, the concussion was felt as far north as the giant base at Chu Lai, ten miles away. The rear echelon troops in Chu Lai went on alert.

On October 19, Charlie Company, while sweeping west of Binh Son along the Vietcong's infiltration corridor, took five casualties from a delay-type mine. It was primarily SGT Edward "Buzz" Gabbert's squad that was hit, but it included his platoon leader, LT Aldrich, whose right leg was sheared off by the blast. Aldrich's RTO, SP/4 John Horton, was just behind Aldrich and was killed by a piece of shrapnel to his chest. Horton was age twenty-one and single from Suffern, New York. Gabbert froze his men in place while he walked through the mined area to recover the wounded. Platoon medic PFC Ernest Biscamp assisted.

The intelligence coming out of CAP 136's area indicated local guerillas were forming to blow bridges and culverts along Highway One. On October 24, a highway culvert was blown one and one-half mile south of Binh Son and another explosion blew a hole in the highway one-half mile north of the town. Adding to the enemy pressure to stifle the movement of harvested rice, the heavy rains made Highway One around the Binh Son area almost impassable.

Lieutenant Colonel Richardson decided to send Bravo Company west of Binh Son as well, as his antenna was up after the increased contact made by Charlie Company. Bravo was pushed farther west than Charlie, a distance of eight and one-half miles west of Binh Son and two and one-half miles south of the Tra Bong River around the hamlets of Vinh Tuy. Bravo screened the area for enemy infiltration that was moving from the mountains to the Binh Son rice fields, and it also served as an early warning for any attack against LZ Buff, just five miles to their east. On October 26, early morning sniper fire greeted them in the Vinh Tuy neighborhood. By early afternoon a firefight broke out, causing two casualties, which Richardson's C&C promptly picked up. The following day, as Richardson's Command & Control bird monitored the extraction of Delta Company on the coast, it was hit by ground fire, along with the helicopters picking up Delta.

Richardson flew west to cover the activities of Bravo Company just as it became engaged in a firefight. Bravo had placed a cordon around Vinh Tuy (4) and proceeded to search the hamlet when it received fire from three positions. In short order four grunts were down with stomach and leg wounds. PFC's John Vest, Paul Moore and Dalton Adams rose to the occasion and took care of the wounded in the kill zone. Adams was the trained medic but the other two took their limited medical training to heart and performed as trained. Moore moved the wounded to an extraction point while the other two sheltered the ones waiting to be evacuated. Richardson had his C&C land and jumped out while under fire to assist PFC Moore in the loading of the wounded. The battalion commander took his grunts to a Chu Lai hospital and Vest, Moore and Adams moved back to their platoon to take care of normal business. All would receive Bronze Stars for valor.

Under the pressure of artillery fire support, the VC that Bravo encountered melted back into the mountains with just one body to be found but, as usual, lots of blood trails were left in their wake. Richardson had Delta Company move west to join in the fray and placed his Echo Recon Platoon east of Bravo and Delta, one and one-half miles northeast of LZ Buff, to help observe known infiltration routes.

By October 28 the battalion, undermanned as usual, protected artillery firebases, secured the rice harvest, and hunted for VC. Alpha defended LZ Gator and provided security for engineer units and civilian contractors repairing Highway One in the Binh Son area. Bravo continued its rice denial operations west of LZ Buff. Charlie Company helped defend LZ Dottie with its headquarters element and two platoons while its two other platoons defended LZ Buff. Delta worked southwest of Buff, moving in a northwesterly direction towards Bravo. Both companies tried to cover a low-lying rice harvest area approximately two and one-half miles wide and five and one-half miles long, running southwest to northeast, bounded by LZ Buff to the east and the Annamite mountains to the west. Echo's recon platoon patrolled a corridor three miles southwest of Binh Son, staging OP's and ambushes and looking for VC that might make it past Bravo and Charlie on their way to Binh Son.

    On October 28, just seven months after the battalion's arrival in Vietnam, the Echo Recon platoon was to lose its third platoon leader, and, like its first, from the scourge of mines on high ground. One recon grunt on a four-man OP tripped a wire attached to two Chicom grenades, wounding all four. Arriving on the scene, Lt. Donald Penney established some order and then realized they were in a minefield. He set up a line of five grunts to pass equipment out of the mined area. To collect some equipment out of reach he moved on his own while the others remained in place. Doing so he tripped another bobby trap consisting of a M26 grenade armed with a pressure release device. He took the full impact of the blast but another grunt was wounded as well. The two were dusted off while others, less seriously wounded, elected to stay with their comrades. Penney died enroute to Chu Lai in the dustoff. He was age twenty-four and married from Willseyville, New York. The battalion closed out the day with nine wounded and one officer killed in action. One Vietcong was killed.

    As the calendar turned to early November the 5th/46th Battalion continued its aggressive posture to control it assigned area and deny the Vietcong and NVA the means to capture meaningful supplies of rice. "Shoot and run" actions continued to characterize the contact made by the enemy. Alpha Company patrolled the area west of Binh Son with cordon and searches, observation posts (OP's) and night ambushes. Bravo defended Gator's perimeter with day patrols and night ambushes beyond the perimeter to deter attacks. One of Bravo's platoons was sent to support CAP Mobile Training Team 2 (MTT-2) in the area immediately west of Binh Son and Highway One. Other Bravo troops were siphoned off of Gator for local security around engineer units rebuilding or improving Highway One. Charlie defended LZ Dottie while two of its platoons were posted on LZ Buff to help secure its perimeter. Delta still patrolled the area south of Alpha, but readied itself to relieve Charlie on Buff and Dottie, when it came their time to take a break from the heavy "humping" in the field.

On the evening of November 1, Staff Sergeant Everette Rice, along with his squad in the 2nd platoon of Charlie Company, were inserted at night three miles northeast of Dottie to support a Long Range Reconnaissance Patrol (LRRP) which had been observing increased Vietcong activity in the eastern boundary of the Binh Son rice bowl area. The following day Rice, a career soldier, kept his squad in check as a VC platoon-sized force approached his position. They were not close to his position but close enough that his grunts opened up with their M-16's and M-60 machine gun. Rice knew the VC would turn and run and was on the radio as soon as the ambush was sprung, calling for artillery support. His M-60 gunner cut down several VC, including a NVA soldier with grey uniform, pack and rifle. Two other VC were cut down as they tried to retrieve the bodies of their comrades. By Rice's estimate his squad accounted for six of the kills and five came from the artillery. The methodical nature of Rice's actions accounted for eighteen enemy killed in two days with no friendly casualties. But to get an exact body count would require crossing an open rice paddy and exposing his men to unnecessary risk, something Rice was not willing to do. Accordingly brigade headquarters gave all the credit for the enemy KIA to the artillery. Scratching his head at the unfairness of it all, Rice moved his troops onward looking for more VC.

As is so often the case, the "unconventional warfare" the battalion's grunts found themselves fighting, often took unconventional turns for each small unit trying to stay alive in the field. A small squad from Bravo Company set up a night ambush northwest of Gator around Tri Binh (5), which was a "way station" for the VC. While hunkered down at night waiting for the VC to come in range, a villager's pig charged the ambush, forcing the grunts to open fire and reveal its position. A KIA of one enemy pig was not claimed.

Charlie Company, having switched missions with Delta, was engaged in numerous shoot and run incidents with fleeing VC in the narrow rice bowl southwest of Buff. After clearing out some VC from a hooch, it found two women and three children with one thousand, five-hundred pounds of rice that was stolen and had been carried to the base of the mountains. Charlie's 2nd platoon killed one VC while the 1st platoon captured another. After moving out of a night ambush they found a cache of clothes, rice, punji stakes and documents. The 3rd platoon, patrolling one-half mile south of the 1st, engaged some VC who quickly ran, leaving their equipment behind. Inside one VC pack was a bag of rice, poncho, hammock, small bottle of medicine, fishing hook with cord and a diary. The grunts were making their mark against a main force VC unit.

Alpha's platoons patrolled two miles north of Charlie, near Buff, searching hamlets and finding military age males for questioning. In a war that had been waged for years with the South Vietnamese Army drafting everyone eligible, no one of military age was to be found in remote hamlets unless they were absent from the military (highly doubtful) or, more likely, were main force Vietcong. The "rules of engagement" in the battalion and among the Marine CAP teams was quite simple. "Engage (shoot) any military-age male that is evading." Alpha picked up four detainees, one whom tried to escape and was shot in the leg and lower hip. All were lifted out by helicopter for questioning.

On November 7, Charlie's 2nd platoon lost two grunts to a mine. While setting up a machine gun position, one grunt sat down on a Bouncing Betty mine. Richardson's C&C picked up PFC's William Meinecke and John Schaffer, both twenty years of age and single, for dustoff. It was in vain. Both died enroute to the 27th Surgical Hospital in Chu Lai. Meinecke was from Milwaukee, Wisconsin and Schaffer from Altus, Arkansas.

Alpha continued its operations and some additional troops became available to them on LZ Gator. One was PFC Gary Cardinal who had just returned from R&R in Hawaii. He stepped out of a jeep on Gator still in his Class B Khaki uniform, excited to talk about his R&R when his platoon sergeant yelled, "Get your God dam ass changed and geared up and get on the helo pad, we're moving out now." His fellow grunts didn't think he'd have a chance to catch up. As the last chopper took off from the pad at Gator, the grunts saw Cardinal running to the pad, pushing his arm through his field shirt while running with his rucksack and rifle over his shoulder. The Huey set back down and he jumped on, happy he was able to make it. When they landed in the field Cardinal's mind was still in Hawaii, telling his buddies about having his own bathroom, hot showers, food on demand, beaches and the great time he had with his family and girlfriend.

That evening, just past midnight, Alpha's 1st Platoon moved in to cordon and search the hamlet of Tri Binh Bac (2), two miles north of Buff. Cardinal's platoon sergeant picked up an old man to walk the trail in front of them, confident he knew where any mines would be. In short order the old man refused to go any further. He muttered some words but no one was able to understand them. The platoon leader wanted the column to continue moving and so they released the peasant. As he walked away the grunts saw him shaking nervously and muttering as the patrol moved cautiously forward. They moved a short distance down a trail that led to the hamlet where a small picket fence stood in the way, apparently to prevent water buffalo from coming into the hamlet. Half of the platoon stepped over the fence when a command detonated mine exploded. Six grunts were wounded, but their lives were saved by the flak jackets they were wearing. As was often the case, even with flak jackets, the smallest piece of shrapnel might hit a vulnerable artery unprotected by the thick and hot armored vests, such as the neck, or under an armpit, causing a mortal wound. PFC Garryl "Gary" Cardinal, 20 and single, received such a wound and was killed on his first day back from R&R. Cardinal was from Montrose, Minnesota.

The platoon called in a dustoff and returned the way they came in. The platoon sergeant immediately went to the hooch where the old peasant lived. His men could hear the sergeant yelling and the old man screaming, and when the sergeant came out there was silence. Then the hooch was set on fire, the old man never came out. No one said a word, no one dared to, as they watched the hooch burn. Then they loaded their rucksacks on their tired bodies and started out in a new direction.

PFC Wilson "Willie" Lavender carried Cardinal's rucksack with his buddies blood was all over him. When the sun came up, the blood jelled and he couldn't get rid of it. Sand took it off his hands but it lingered on his clothes and even when it dried, he could still smell it. Thirty-five years later he would still smell it.

At 8:00AM, Alpha's 2nd Platoon set in a blocking position to cordon and search the hamlet of Chau Nhai (1), a mere one-half mile southeast of LZ Buff. PFC Gregory Beeman was shot in the back by a sniper but blasted away with his M-16 causing the sniper to flee. The platoon, like other battalion patrols, was plagued by sniper fire wherever it moved. In the absence of elusive VC males, women were equally skilled in setting mines and booby- traps. Alpha shot a woman in the leg attempting to flee from her handiwork, having laid out a booby-trapped area. She was picked up by a utility helicopter and taken to the 27th Surgical Hospital to have her wounds dressed, then to be questioned.

Further east on the coast, CAP 133 engaged a VC squad which was concluding a meeting in Trung Hoa (1). Fourteen VC were killed and eight wounded. Sgt. James Wyant, one of the Echo mortar platoon grunts assigned to the CAP, was wounded. Among the captured equipment was surgical equipment appropriate for a doctor, paper, rifles, grenades and clothing. The captured papers revealed a Vietcong infrastructure that was still very much intact. The documents included an invitation from the district VC Office to hold a class on how to send messages. Every hamlet was to send one man to the district office (Trung Hoa 3) to meet at a female's house ("Can") to be shown where to go for the training. This was to occur the following day in the hamlet of Lac Son, three miles to the south. The instructions added, "Each man will bring his own food for the one day class."

Throughout the coastal lowlands east of Binh Son's rice bowl the Vietcong remained tenacious. Not only were the battalion's grunts and CAP teams seeing daily contact, but aero scouts in light observation helicopters (LOH) continued to spot pockets of NVA/VC moving throughout the area. Gunships were called if available. Jet air strikes were also used to support the artillery, mortars and gunships, which in turn supported the direct fire of the grunts on the ground.

The saturation of all this ordnance caused its own problems. Jets hit a hill mass two and one-half miles northeast of Dottie, dropping five-hundred pound bombs on a suspected bunker complex where VC were spotted moving in and out. Complicating the strike was the fact that six of the bombs were duds which required more strikes to destroy the unexploded ordnance, or it would be used by the VC for more command-detonated mines. As grunts checked the targeted area, tunnels were found. But there were far too few troops to destroy them or adequately search them, and other missions compelled the soldiers to move on. As happened so often, command reliance was on spotting and killing the enemy, with their tunnel systems and bunkers being too numerous to be destroyed completely. It was pre-ordained that every new rotation of troops to the battalion area would encounter, in their own time, the same tunnels, always occupied by VC.

Charlie's 2nd platoon spotted eight NVA just west of CAP 133's AO. Three were killed by the platoon, five killed by artillery and

Richardson, flying above with a nose for trouble, shot one from his bird. Lieutenant Colonel Ronald Richardson, commanding the 5th/46th Infantry Battalion, was plagued by the same constraints as his predecessor, LTC Lyon. The requirement to secure multiple firebases tied up at least half his battalion on hilltops. LZ's had to be secured to protect headquarters elements, supplies and munitions, and the critical artillery batteries of 105mm and 155mm howitzers, necessary for grunt support and for mutual fire support to each LZ in case of attack.

Hunter-Killer Teams

LTC Richardson, like LTC Lyon before him, was burdened with marginal missions such as railway bridge security even though the trains never ran during the war. Richardson constantly worked at getting his troops pulled off of no value targets, those certainly not worth a soldier's life.

Company-size operations were becoming rare unless operating close to the mountains, where the risk grew for a major attack from NVA main force units. Patrolling occurred primarily at platoon level to expand the reach of the grunts. Richardson's grunts became adept at cordon and searches of hamlets, with a SOP that took note of the "lifestyle habits" of the VC. Whether operating as a company or platoon, the cordon was established not later than midnight, earlier if possible. Knowing that visiting VC would leave the hamlets after midnight and before daylight, this gave the grunts an opportunity to bag some in ambushes as they departed the hamlets. Moving into a cordon earlier than 10:00PM was problematic, as the waning daylight might reveal their movement, and the villagers were still actively moving in and around their hamlets. Searches of hamlets began just before daylight, so at first light the troops could provide a "wakeup call" for villagers harboring VC.

Richardson was also convinced that if his troops were to take the initiative from the VC, more night operations, particularly ambushes, had to be used. The enemy's movement in large groups was severely constrained during daylight hours due to the vigilance of helicopters constantly flying over the area. Major movements of NVA/VC had to be made at night and the battalion commander wanted to be part of that action. Recognizing his battalion's manpower limitations in covering the large area he was assigned, and the heavily mined areas on the coast plus the large number of small bands of VC which moved at will, his solution came in one word: "Slurps".

Referred to as "SLRPS" (pronounced "Slurps"), Special Long Range Patrols were a combination of the lightly armed Long-Range Reconnaissance Patrols used by the division's LRRP's to search deep in enemy territory, and the heavily armed "Hunter-Killer Teams", teams which sat in one spot and never moved, waiting for targets. Later the SLRPS would be referred to as simply "SRP's" (Short Range Patrols) in reports. The grunts referred to their small groups as "Hunter Killer Teams" although they would move more often than the original hunter-killer concept required. Richardson knew larger company and platoon-size patrols played to the advantage of the VC. With plenty of targets, the VC laid low, sniped at grunts and set mines where these larger formations most likely would move. Richardson wanted to saturate areas with smaller teams to reduce enemy movement during day and night. Placing teams in locations, usually on some high ground that offered cover and concealment as well as good observation, reduced the necessity to constantly move. And, in Richardson's mind, if they weren't moving, they weren't walking into mines.

A typical SLRP team numbered 10 to 13 men. Richardson wanted smaller teams but higher-echelon policy required a reinforced squad in the field at a minimum. This size however proved optimal as it allowed the battalion commander to run his teams without outside support. Two Huey helicopters were available to him each day. One was his command and control ship and the other was tasked for resupply of his units in the field. With a 13-man team, seven grunts were placed in the resupply bird and six on the C&C with himself. The battalion commander led the way for the inserts, so he could personally decide if the area was too hot for his team. The Hueys would drop down several times, before and after the actual drop-off, to conceal the exact location from enemy eyes in the area.

The team leader was usually a squad leader, a sergeant or staff sergeant, but from time to time the platoon sergeant or platoon leader led the way. If possible a trained sniper, a graduate of the Americal's sniper school in Chu Lai, would also accompany the team. Trained snipers in the battalion carried a 7.62mm M-14 "accurized" rifle, using an "Adjustable Ranging Telescope" (ART) and special 7.62mm M118 National Match Ammunition collectively designated as the XM21.

Starlight scopes were also assigned for use during periods of limited visibility.

Each SLRP team carried two M-60 machine guns, two grenadiers with M79 grenade launchers and the best riflemen in the platoon, using M-16's. The team was equipped to maximize their ability to "reach out and touch someone" and place out heavy firepower. Teams were inserted into the field "heavy". Priority was to carry enough ammunition to sustain the team if attacked by a larger force of NVA or VC, until help could arrive. Each of the M-60 machine gunners carried two thousand rounds of ammunition and soldiers with the M-16's, and snipers with M-14's carried a minimum of twenty magazines of eighteen rounds each. A large number of claymore mines were included for the defense of their very small perimeters as well as for night ambushes. Each man carried as many as ten hand grenades.

Battalion intelligence decided where teams would be placed based on patterns of VC movement. While a small piece of defensible high ground provided a "base perimeter", SLRP teams would move short distances from the base to set up multiple OP's and ambushes. To expand their kill area, preplanned artillery fire was called in under the guise of interdiction fire. A couple rounds, disguised as "harassment and interdiction fires", were fired to determine accuracy. Other preplanned rounds were then "dry fired" between the SLRP and the artillery battery, the battery marking their azimuths and elevations to hit additional targets without firing the rounds. This completed a complex target list of locations and trail networks the SLRP could call immediately, by pre-planned numbers, for rapid fire-support. This allowed SLRP's to be effective if VC were spotted beyond the range of their own weapons. If a larger force attacked the SLRP team, they would pull back to their patrol perimeter and adjust the preplanned artillery fires on the attackers.

In short order Richardson found his SLRP perimeters would have to be moved every one to two nights, at least a distance of fifty to one hundred meters. The VC became very adept at attacking the teams at night with grenades and small arms fire but the movement of the SLRP perimeter after dark, even for a small distance, confused the enemy.

On November 13, 1968, two of Delta's SLRP teams sprung an ambush on ten to eleven VC carrying weapons on a trail. The following day Bravo placed two SLRP's one and one-half miles west of LZ Gator around the hamlet of Nam Binh (7), which was a way station for VC approaching to hit the Gator perimeter. The teams captured two enemy insurgents, one a messenger and one a nurse, complete with a medical kit and papers which identified a PF Platoon Leader in Nuoc Mau who was targeted for assassination. Another Bravo SLRP team, operating two miles southeast of Binh Son spotted twenty VC outside its effective small arms range walking on a trail that had been targeted with preplanned artillery fire. The first barrage fired, killing seven. The second barrage wounded more as the enemy tried to drag its dead comrades away.

In the early morning hours of November 17, Binh Son was again hit by mortar fire followed by a ground attack. Soldiers manning the southern edge of the Gator bunker line had front row seats as they watched enemy mortar fire come from the southern edge of Nuoc Mau, supposedly under the battalion's control, exploding in Binh Son. As the enemy mortar fire came from Nuoc Mau, two company-size VC elements attacked the district town from the southeast but the PF and RF forces stood their ground. At daylight, fifty-six dead VC were found and thirty taken prisoner along with numerous AK-47's, B-40 rocket launchers and one hundred and fifty Chicom grenades. The Popular Forces estimated the average ages of the dead VC were fourteen to sixteen. One PF militiaman was killed, eight wounded and eighteen civilians were killed.

Four days later a Bravo Company SLRP spotted six VC carrying weapons, packs and mortars out of range of their small arms fire. Additionally they were walking so fast artillery fire could not be adjusted. A Charlie SLRP missed twelve VC in the same manner but the next day killed one and wounded three. One of the wounded dropped his backpack and ran, but the team captured the other two carrying four SKS rifles, medical kits and grenades. As usual, blood trails were found in the direction of the fleeing VC.

A squad from Alpha's third platoon had hunkered down on a rock-piled hilltop when they spotted a few VC/NVA walking in the valley below. The few became a few more and then over a dozen. The squad leader called in artillery, citing "gooks in the open" and after the first marking round of White Phosphorus ("WP", "Willy Pete") landed, the guerillas scattered for cover. The squad leader, SSG Ken Turner, adjusted the fire by one hundred meters and called a "fire for effect". In seconds a salvo of high explosive air bursts (COFRAM rounds) detonated over the enemy, exploding again and again as they attempted to run. The platoon watched the show in amazement atop their high perch. Twenty-two enemy bodies were found. This was an example of a SLRP at its best.

On November 23, at 7:10PM, the 198th Brigade commander directed all bases to be on one hundred percent alert from midnight until 4:00AM based on "increased observations of groups of VC who might be gathering for an operation against one of the brigades firebases." The 5th/46th hunkered down for a long night as they tightened their defenses on LZ's Gator, Dottie and Buff. It was to be a long night. Fifteen minutes later brigade headquarters alerted the battalion that a truck loaded with beer had overturned on Highway One, three miles north of Quang Ngai City and five miles south of LZ Dottie. Four armored personnel carriers were sent from LZ Dottie while one truck of RF/PF soldiers were sent up from Quang Ngai City to secure the beer. By 8:40PM, the combined force reached the beer truck and stayed with it for the night. This was an unnecessary example of joint Vietnamese-American cooperation. No attack ever came so the question never had to be asked if the beer was worth the loss of life.

For the remainder of November, SLRP's continued to keep the VC at bay, killing a few but wounding many more. The VC were aware of the general presence or likely locations of SLRP ambushes and tended to detour around their previous routes while totally aware they were not escaping the observation of the grunts. Increasingly the VC seemed to prefer taking their chances with indirect artillery fire, and hoped to escape it when the rounds were adjusted on them. The SLRP'S main drawback was that not enough sergeants were skilled in calling and adjusting artillery fire. Richardson had his company FO's train them in the basics.

As the battalion continued its operations, casualties due to mines decreased, owing to the seasoned experience of the grunts on the ground. This was primarily due to experienced junior sergeants serving as squad leaders and, in some cases, platoon sergeants, who had survived the early initiation of combat. But the battalion's assigned area was so saturated with mines and booby traps, the principle means of resistance for the Vietcong, that casualties were inevitable as a course of pursuing the war.

On November 29 an Alpha SLRP, the 3rd squad of the 3rd platoon was low on water. Re-supply by a Huey was unthinkable as it would give away their hilltop position. Three grunts volunteered to slip down to a stream near a hamlet to fill the SLRP's canteens. While moving to the stream PFC John Gaston detonated a trip wire. The rest of the SLRP heard the explosion and saw a cloud of black smoke. All three soldiers were wounded and loaded on a dustoff but PFC John Rufus Gaston Jr., age twenty and single from Washington D.C. died of his wounds. Another soldier, Raymond Mailloux, was wounded severely and sent home. The other soldier on the detail, Tom McMullen, returned to the field the following week.

Their hill-top position now exposed, the squad moved out after the dustoff departed. Late in the afternoon they moved deep into some thick elephant grass near the base of another hill. Hilltops were now obvious targets for the enemy. The center of the foliaged area was set in a depression, where they chose to remain as a good defensive position. Silence was the order of the night. Early in the morning the SLRP team heard a group of enemy soldiers talking and then a hail of bullets slammed into the grassy area. The depression the grunts were in allowed the bullets to zip over the SLRP defenders, the enemy bullets slicing through the thick grass, looking for the flesh of their nemesis. No one moved and no one fired back. Later in the day another large patrol of VC/NVA passed by, looking for the SLRP team. They too fired into the elephant grass, but the depression in the ground kept the heavy fire from hitting them. Still later another group passed by, firing into the thick elephant grass. The patrol kept silent.

For over thirty-six hours the SLRP team remained silent while a total of over one hundred enemy probed their position at various times. Each man kept to his own thoughts as the SLRP team chose silence over annihilation. PFC Barry Sweigart penned his thoughts as he lay silently in the grass (next page).

The following day everything was quiet and the SLRP team slipped out of its position and moved to another site.

The end of November found Alpha manning LZ Gator's bunker line with its 3rd platoon and two of its 81mm mortars from the weapons platoon, helping to defend LZ Paradise. Other squads were assigned to guard bridges on Highway One and one SLRP was sent to the coast just north of CAP 133's AO. Bravo also defended Gator while sending three SLRP's to the field. Charlie Company continued its defense of LZ Dottie while posting three SLRP's out in the bush. Delta defended LZ Buff because the 1st/52nd continued its operations up north in the Tam Ky AO, but Delta's commander sent out three SLRP's to areas where Aero Scouts (light observation helicopters) had spotted VC on the move. Echo Company divided its heavy 4.2-inch mortar platoon in three sections in defense of LZ Gator, CAP 133 and LZ Buff.

LIVING AND DIEING (SIC)
"Take a man then put him alone
Put him 12,000 miles from home.
Empty his heart of all but blood
Make him live in sweat and mud".

"You "peace boys" vent from your easy chairs
But you don't know what its like over here.
You have a ball without half trying
While over here the boys are dying.
You burn your draft cards and march at dawn
Plant your flags on the White House lawn".

"You all want to ban the bomb
There is no war in Viet Nam (sic).
Use your drugs and have your fun
Then refuse to use a gun.
There's nothing else for you to do
I'm supposed to die for you".

"I'll hate you till the day I die
You made me here (sic) my buddy cry.
I saw his arm a bloody shred (sic)
I heard them say, "This one is dead".
It's a large price to pay
Not to see another day".

"He had the guts to fight and die
He paid the price but what did he buy.
He bought your life by giving his
But who gives a damn what a soldier gives.
His wife does and maybe his mom
But they're about the only ones

Charlie Company at LZ Dottie continued to receive the refuse of combat, brought in by Vietnamese civilians in exchange for Vietnamese currency ("Piasters") under the VIP Program. On December 1, 1968 a designated "turn in day", 69,400 Piasters were paid out for:
18 M-16 mines
11 Claymore mines
75 M-26 hand grenades
24 M-14 mines
31 M79 grenade launcher high explosive rounds
1 M72 Light Antitank Weapon (LAW)
10 Improvised Vietcong grenades
26 60mm high explosive mortar rounds
87 81mm high explosive mortar rounds
12 pounds of TNT explosives
10 105mm high explosive artillery rounds

Approximately 1,000 rounds of small caliber ammunition and one VT (Veritable Timing) artillery fuse were also turned in.

Two and one-half miles northeast of Dottie, Charlie Company's 3rd platoon SLRP spotted three VC moving among a group of villagers in the field. The grunts and VC fired at each other and, as so often the case, the civilians bore the cost of combat. Two females were shot in their legs and dusted off. A captured Vietcong informed the 198th Brigade intelligence section that he worked for a hidden aid station northeast of LZ Dottie. His story to his interrogators confirmed the effectiveness of the battalion's SLRP operations. Back on November 23 when a Charlie Company SLRP fired on VC with small arms and preplanned artillery fires, a search had turned up the usual, no bodies, just blood trails. This captive was one of those who helped carry the bodies away for burial. He claimed eight VC were killed outright and six more killed from the artillery fire. These kills did not show up on the battalions "body count", even after the POW's story, but Richardson knew his SLRP's were making an impact.

While Charlie's SLRP's working off Dottie were having an impact against the enemy, some of its soldiers on Dottie worked with less focus. On December 4, several Charlie soldiers working in the motor pool apparently had been drinking. One witness said they saw SP/4 William Hodges pull a pin on a grenade and hold it until it went off, killing him instantly. Two other PFC's in the motor pool were wounded and two vehicles damaged. A bottle of whiskey was found near the men. William Jeffrey Hodges was age twenty-one and single from Silver Spring, Maryland.

On December 6, PFC Frederico Matias-Santana, part of a five day Delta SLRP, volunteered to slip down to a stream to refill canteens. The SLRP had been sitting in ambushes around the hamlet of Tra Binh Dong (2), only two miles east of LZ Buff. Matias-Santana tripped on an M-16 mine. His wounds were severe, and he didn't survive the trip on a dustoff to Chu Lai. Matias-Santana was 20 and single, from New York City.

On December 13, a Delta SLRP team working off LZ Buff bumped into Vietcong wherever it went. One mile southeast of the firebase a third platoon SLRP engaged VC at 11:00AM, suffering one wounded, which Richardson's C&C Huey promptly picked up and flew to Chu Lai. Later, two other SLRP's engaged thirteen VC four miles west of Buff, killing four. Richardson, with his nose for trouble, flew over the fight and his door gunner killed another of the enemy.

At times the wily VC seemed clueless. One SLRP team on high ground spotted two VC with weapons and packs one-half mile to their front, walking around as if on a Sunday stroll. As the team leader, Sgt. Dennis Brayboy noted, "They acted as if they owned the place." As he was calling in an artillery fire mission, eight more VC appeared and joined the first two. The first artillery rounds were two hundred yards off mark but a quick adjustment brought it in on target, including some air bursts, which sprayed the area with shrapnel. The VC did not seem to realize they were being observed. As darkness approached, the team continued to call harassment fire on the same area to discourage other VC from retrieving the bodies. When the patrol reached the scene the next morning blood trails abounded, all leading northwest to the mountains.

The Binh Son districts' VIP policy for civilians to exchange munitions for money continued to pay big dividends although the battalion's grunts noticed some deterioration in the quality of the merchandise. While some munitions were functional, many were old and corroded, leading the grunts to question when they would start getting some of the "good stuff" still cached in tunnels and underground bunkers. But on December 14, Christmas came early to the grunts during another turn-in day for LZ's Paradise and Dottie.

LZ PARADISE
1   Booby-Trap
19   M79 Rounds
3   155mm Artillery Rounds
3   155mm Howitzer Artillery Rounds
8   M26 Hand Grenades
2-1/2 Pounds of TNT
1   B40 Rocket
4   81mm Mortar Rounds
5   4.2-Inch Mortar Rounds

LZ DOTTIE
10   M16 Mines
1   M72 Light Anti-tank Weapons (LAW)
51   M79 Rounds
3   M79 Canisters
14   81mm Mortar Rounds
44   60mm Mortar Rounds
11   Claymore Mines
36   M26 hand Grenades
2   White Phosphorus Hand Grenades
11   Vietcong Improvised Hand Grenades
1,276   M-60 Machinegun Rounds
310   M16 Rifle Rounds
7   105mm Howitzer Artillery Rounds
1   155mm Howitzer Artillery Round
25   M14 Mines & 1 VC Improvised Mine
1   3.5-Inch Rocket launcher

On LZ Paradise a CAP Marine dropped an M-79 grenade round at the turn-in point and it detonated, lightly wounding several of the battalion's soldiers working with the Marines. The Company Commander of the wounded troops had to fill out an accident report. When he reached the section on the report asking for the "corrective action to be taken to prevent a recurrence", he simply typed, "Don't stand next to Marines when they are handling ammunition."

The battalion's grunts paid many Vietnamese piasters for weapons and munitions turned in by civilians, but the battalion's SLRP's continued to receive bigger dividends in accomplishing the objectives of Operation Golden Fleece. The SLRP teams prevented the enemy's disruption of the rice harvest. But the Vietcong remained active and elusive as they adjusted to SLRP tactics, careful to stay out of the range of their small arms fire.

On December 16, a Delta 1st platoon SLRP spotted forty VC on the move five and one-half miles southwest of LZ Buff near Tan An Thon (1). The enemy was out of small arms range. Gunships in the area were immediately called but were just as quickly cancelled by brigade headquarters because the SLRP was not in direct contact with the enemy and the birds were needed elsewhere. Frustration mounted among the grunts, whose carefully concealed observation points were paying off in terms of spotting large enemy formations either out of range or too large to handle themselves. Gunships were rarely available and artillery was called in, often with unknown results because the grunts were too small in number to search the impact zones. Thirty minutes later the same SLRP team saw two VC run into an unoccupied and dilapidated hooch. Artillery fire destroyed the hooch but no bodies were found.

Although SLRP's had limited mobility, those fortunate enough to fly over the AO had ample opportunity to observe VC movement throughout the area. Aero Scouts flying in their light observation helicopters (LOH) increasingly became the eyes of the SLRP's after artillery fire missions. The LOH's were effective in searching areas to shoot fleeing VC and NVA or to "snatch" others that were wounded or unarmed, both male and female. Richardson's C&C bird also joined the hunt and picked up detainees for questioning while shooting others who chose to run from the small arms fire of the SLRP's. The battalion commanders C&C Huey always flew "nap of the earth", moving just over treetop level, coming in fast, confusing the enemy soldier who could hear the approaching aircraft but, at a low level had no idea from which direction it was coming. This gave Richardson and his crew the element of surprise balanced against the danger of flying at treetop level.

Boredom was a fact of life for the battalion staff back on LZ Gator. Major Ken Mink, the battalions S-3 of operations, saw their duty on Gator as "long hours of boredom punctuated by moments of sheer terror when Gator would get hit". Life on Gator for support troops was routine but hectic and their morale ebbed and flowed based on the casualty reports and successes from the troops in the field. In the words of one staff officer, "in good times morale was high, in bad times it really stunk". But morale was almost always upbeat under Richardson and he ensured his soldiers had little time on their hands, with a series of tasks always at hand. Aggressive but smart tactics also brought results in the field and the soldiers wanted to feel that progress was being made in exchange for the heat and smell, and lack of sleep they endured.

The Black Power movement had found its way to Gator, owing to the rotation of newer soldiers from the states, who had been immersed in the anti-war rhetoric and affected by the killing of Martin Luther King. There was enough slack time for the disgruntled who resented being in Vietnam to ease their predicament with pot and soul music. This also occurred when grunts came in from the field to man the bunker line, but their pot smoking was more occasional than regular, except for the malcontents working on Gator, who performed their jobs with little gusto. It was a situation that began to plague all infantry battalions in Vietnam.

Priority for work on Gator always went to the troops in the field, especially in places such as the resupply point on the helicopter landing pad. Each day was a flurry of activity with Hueys landing with light casualties and taking off with supplies. Support soldiers who worked the pad were usually grunts who had done their time in the field and needed a rear assignment for a variety of reasons. They understood what it was like out in Indian Country and worked with a sense of commitment.

When a rifle company returned from the field for a rest, either by chopper or walking in, the rear troops on Gator stood their distance, admiring and perhaps fearing in a way, these Spartans in their filthy garb who were thin, tired and worn. The field soldiers looked worn but they were not broken and were not to be trifled with. LZ Gator was a slice of heaven, where there were no mines, no booby traps, and no nightly ambushes. Bunker duty at night and daytime jobs like filling sandbags, and the threat of mortar or sapper attacks were a fair trade for showers, hot meals, cold beer, nude pinup photos from Playboy Magazine, loud music and an occasional "weed" for some.

Mink allowed his junior officers in the S-3 to go "dink hunting" when "things got bad morale wise" and he felt his men were losing their edge. The twenty and twenty-one year old helicopter pilots also wanted to let off steam after days of routine flying, acting as taxis for troops or shuttling supplies to the companies in the field. The best target area was usually the coast east of Highway One, much of which was designated as a military "free fire zone". Military aged males were considered "bad guys" because the war had been in progress so long either the ARVN or the enemy had laid claim to all of Vietnam's youth. Mink, his officers and helicopter pilots often flew over the area late afternoons, hoping to catch VC moving to night positions before it got dark. Flying a "nap of the earth" pattern, their approach could not be determined by the VC on the ground, and so they had an edge in the hunt. The bored staff officers had enough successes finding Vietcong in groups of one or two, to make the effort a good diversion.

Alpha operated SLRP's four miles north of LZ Buff along the southern rim of the Tra Bong Road, in conjunction with CAP teams that had moved west from Binh Son. This area tended to be more populated with hamlets and was a major corridor for VC and NVA moving swiftly from the mountains to Binh Son. But with population comes the scourge of more mines and on the morning of December 17, PFC Grayson Craft, age 19, stepped on an M14 mine which killed him and wounded two others. Craft was single from Magee, Mississippi.

Richardson was concerned about a buildup of VC and NVA southwest of Buff, where the Delta SLRP had previously spotted the forty Vietcong. One of the Aero Scouts had also snatched an unarmed VC who reported an NVA hospital was in the same area. Accordingly, Richardson had Charlie Company on LZ Dottie bring in its far-flung SLRP's and saddle up for a company-wide air assault into the Buff area for a closer look. By noon on December 18, they had reached the hospital but saw it had long-since been abandoned. Detainees in the area reported that groups of NVA south of their location had been moving west back into the mountains. The following morning Charlie's grunts drove off some VC with small arms fire and found spider holes and an abandoned bunker. Delta, defending Buff, also placed SLRP teams around Charlie Company's patrol area to increase the chances of bagging some larger formations.

In the early morning of December 20, Charlie's 1st platoon had an unexpected visitor walk into its location, a narrow valley near the hamlet of Tan An Thon (2). Although wearing a uniform and carrying a rucksack, the soldier had no weapon, making the catch easy and therefore highly unusual. The prisoner was taken to Gator for questioning. Staff Sergeant Everett Rice of the 2nd platoon, also on the valley floor, took half of the platoon on an ambush in the early morning hours. No contact was made and he returned to the patrol base. Rice, the consummate professional, was the grunt who bagged eighteen VC in early November on the coast. His platoon leader, 1LT Thomas Sikes from Jacksonville, Florida took the other half of the platoon for a recon in late morning. Sikes elected to climb the steep ridges moving north off the valley floor. He chose to be the point man. The area had thick foliage, not jungle terrain but densely packed trees which were ten to fifteen feet in height. A narrow trail ran up the middle, not a good route but Sikes chose to use it. When he had advanced a scant one-half mile up the ridgeline, he walked into an ambush. Sikes was killed immediately by a command-detonated mine used to spring the ambush and a squad leader, Sergeant Vincent Daiello from New York City was shot in the head. Daiello was 24 and single, Sikes was 23 years of age and married with a newborn son he had never seen.

Sike's patrol came under heavy automatic weapons fire only fifty yards from their front. Another soldier was wounded in the foot. Rice collected the other half of the platoon and went to its support. With his half of the platoon, Rice took control and directed heavy suppressive fire on the enemy until gunships came on station to force the attackers to withdraw. A dustoff arrived and dropped off two stretchers, electing not to stay on the ground because of enemy fire. It pulled pitch and rose to the air to wait until the relief force could get up close and recover the bodies. Sergeant Lee Gunton's squad was given the task and brought the bodies back to where the dustoff could land. Gunton covered the bodies with ponchos. When the chopper landed he placed the stretchers on the bird but the poncho over Sikes blew off revealing a midsection devoid of a stomach. The seasoned medic on board turned and vomited. Rice moved what was left of the platoon down to the valley floor. He earned his second Bronze Star for valor in just six weeks.

At 6:15PM, Charlie's headquarters element and 1st platoon were sweeping the same narrow valley floor when they opened fire on two VC to their front. One VC fell and the grunts tried to flank the other who was hiding when they ran into more fire which wounded two grunts in the legs. Gunships once again arrived to take care of business and the attackers melted away. At 6:00PM the next day, the grunts found fifteen foxholes close to where 1LT Sikes had been killed. Nine fresh graves were also found along with interlocking trenches, chickens, some cows, metal engineering stakes and communications wire. By all indications it had been part of a battalion-size base camp. Apparently Sikes had stumbled on to a rear guard protecting the camp.

Delta's platoon operated one mile due east of the base camp Charlie discovered, and spotted four Vietcong dragging two bodies at 6:40AM the following morning, December 22. As usual, the VC were too far away to engage with small arms so artillery fire was called. The grunts moved forward, finding no bodies but many bloodstains on the grass where the artillery rounds had landed.

The extent of the battalion's operations on a day-to-day basis is difficult to chronicle. Each company, platoon and squad had a unique story to tell while being fully occupied with its mission to seek out the enemy. Alpha, responsible for the security of LZ Gator lent its 1st platoon to assist a CAP team near the Tra Bong Road. Its 3rd platoon helped secure LZ Dottie to allow Charlie Company to patrol the valley floor west of Buff. Another squad manned OP 5. All the soldiers on LZ Gator working rear echelons jobs during the day now had to man the bunkers for security at night, to support the few remaining Alpha soldiers available for bunker line duty.

Delta's troops spotted Vietcong dragging some bodies eleven miles south of Gator in the early morning while Alpha's 2nd platoon moved into Tri Binh (4) one-half mile north of Gator and engaged three VC in a shoot-out, killing one, a VC nurse who carried medical supplies, soap and documents. One mile north of Gator, Echo's recon platoon found four aiming stakes stuck in the ground with burnt grass, homemade wood carrying handles and communications wire. This was obviously a launching site for Soviet-made 122mm rockets which were fired periodically into the division's base complex in Chu Lai.

The area west and north of Tri Binh (4) was tagged as rocket valley or the rocket pocket and the source of constant irritation for the Americal Division Headquarters. When the 5th/46th aggressively patrolled this corridor, rocket attacks ceased. But the enemy was patient enough to wait for the battalions soldiers to move elsewhere so they could move back in to launch more rockets. From the pocket location, rockets were only three and one-half miles from the southern edge of the runways on Chu Lai and five and one-half miles from division headquarters along the rocky cliffs of the shoreline.

On December 23, as the battalion's first Christmas in Vietnam approached, Alpha's 1st platoon spotted two VC one mile east of Tri Binh (4) and moved in behind them. One Vietcong started to run and the other reached for a carbine. Both were cut down. The following day, Christmas Eve Day, Charlie's 1st platoon SLRP walked into an ambush in the hamlet of Thanh Tra (3) three miles west of Gator at 11:20AM. One command-detonated 81mm mortar round triggered the ambush, critically wounding PFC Ambrose Tannasso, age 20 and married, from

Randolf, Massachusetts and another soldier near him. Richardson's C&C once again was first on the scene to pick up his wounded grunts for a rapid dustoff. As his helicopter banked northeast at one hundred feet to head for Chu Lai it was hit with small arms fire, damaging the fuel tank and rotary blade. The bird barely made the short hop to LZ Gator where the wounded were transferred into a utility helicopter. Tanasso died at the 27th Surgical Hospital.

Ten hours later division headquarters requested an immediate report on enemy activities from its infantry battalions, such as movements, attacks and mine incidents. The Communists had declared a cease-fire beginning 6:00PM on the 24th until 6:00PM Christmas Day. Out on the coast in CAP 133, Echo Mortars' soldiers were hit with small arms fire at 5:55PM Christmas Eve. Howard Davis grabbed his M-16 and saw a man running from the ville where the firing came from. Davis fired in front of the insurgent, the bullets splashing into the rice paddy the insurgent attempted to cross, the zip-zip-zip of bullets in front of him sending a clear signal he would not get far. The insurgent stopped and the Marines ran out to grab him. Davis figured he gave himself a Christmas present. He didn't have to kill the enemy soldier.

Christmas provided the grunts in the field a respite from the war but "defensive patrols" continued to prevent attacks on their positions or rockets being fired onto Chu Lai. One incident of sniper fire interrupted Christmas Day but the battalion enjoyed its first day of "Peace on Earth" since arriving in Vietnam. But by the afternoon of the 26th it was business as usual with Charlie's 2nd platoon spotting six Vietcong three miles southeast of Gator. The usual procedure ensued; artillery fire was called while other Charlie grunts encircled the area and the 2nd platoon moved in. No bodies were found, but ample blood trails indicated accurate artillery fire. Richardson had established a small firebase, LZ Clemson, three and one-half miles due west of LZ Buff, with a couple 105mm howitzers to support his troops operating in the area. On New Years Eve he and his S-3, Ken Mink, sat on Clemson and watched the sky light up from tracers and illuminating rounds, up and down Highway One nine miles to their east as their troops on Dottie and the ARVN's celebrated the evening.

Delta Company spent Christmas split between LZ's Buff and Dottie. On the 27th, the company closed Buff since the 1st/52nd Battalion, which nominally used Buff as "home", was still engaged in Task Force Cooksey activities west of Tam Ky, and there was no one left to defend Buff. Richardson wanted Delta in the field rather than be tied up defending a hilltop. First, all but twelve of Delta's soldiers were picked up by Chinook and taken back to LZ Gator. The remaining grunts, including the company commander, Captain Mike Smith, set explosives to destroy the bunkers and wire fences on the perimeter. One explosion blew a metal engineering stake high into the air, which then sailed back down to earth as a deadly spear thrust. It landed just between the commander and his RTO. As the remaining twelve were extracted on Hueys the VC gave them a parting "farewell" with sporadic small arms fire. The company's first sergeant mounted the engineer stake in cement at company headquarters on LZ Gator, for posterity.

Early January 1969 saw the battalion continue its hunt for VC and NVA. The Golden Fleece rice denial operation morphed back to the battalion's standard cordon and search, search and destroy and SLRP operations. On January 1, Charlie's 3rd platoon, still patrolling west of Tri Binh (4) in the southern sector of the rocket pocket, made contact with four VC, three in uniform and one in black pajamas, wounding one. They followed blood trails into the hamlet only to meet villagers who would not assist in finding the enemy.

Alpha, working west of LZ Buff in the same narrow valley that LT. Sikes from Charlie Company was killed, had moved six miles deeper into the mountains where the valley narrowed considerably and was intersected by a small stream bed. Alpha's mission was to screen the southern sector of the mountainous region with Delta following the same trace one-half mile further north while a Special Forces CIDG patrol from the Tra Bong camp was beating the rugged terrain further north of Delta, all looking for NVA. The terrain Alpha worked in could not have been worse from a tactical standpoint, with sharp ridgelines rising up north and south of their position and little maneuver space for the grunts, who faced a wall of high ground around them.

A Special Forces sergeant with a small team of CIDG irregulars made his way to Alpha's position where he was supposed to join Alpha in a night defensive position (NDP). The sergeant told Alpha's commander they should move to higher ground, citing the NVA were all around them and they were too vulnerable in the narrow valley. Alpha's commander was hearing none of it, pulled rank on the sergeant and argued their night position would stay where it was. The Green Beret sergeant moved his small group of irregulars away from the NDP in disgust. At 12:30AM, the company was hit with rocket propelled grenades (RPG) which killed PFC Richard Seely, age 21 and single from Berwick, Pennsylvania and wounded five others.

The battalion's chaplain, Captain James Cosner, had joined the company in the field for a few days and noticed one of the wounded during the attack was in an exposed position. While under RPG fire, Cosner moved him to a sheltered position and gave him first aid. He moved to another grunt to give first aid and offer encouragement while medics attended to others, including Sgt. Michael Bastian, who had a serious head wound. Dustoff was called at 12:40AM, January 2, but the rugged terrain stalled an extraction until one hour later. Cosner continued to expose himself to help load the wounded, which were flown to the 312th Evacuation Hospital. Cosner would receive a Bronze Star for valor for his night's work. Sgt. Bastian, 22 and single, from Sewell, New Jersey had one hundred days left in-country. He died twelve hours later. The Neurosurgeon who performed the surgery felt compelled to write his parents a letter later that evening, noting in part, "He passed away quietly without awakening from his sleep. He felt no pain. I hope this information helps you. Father Kirchner anointed Michael when he first came into the hospital."

Delta on January 1 located a small NVA/VC base camp and hospital consisting of fifteen large huts, each about 20 x 30 feet in size, plus a mess hall with running water. The camp had been recently occupied. It was burned to the ground.

Alpha and Delta Companies were pulled back to LZ Gator for a brief rest to prepare for future operations. Alpha's commander was relieved of his command in February after an investigation, for his poor performance in selecting an indefensible night position. Bravo Company remained at Gator with primary responsibility for perimeter defense. Charlie returned to LZ Dottie and Echo's 4.2-inch heavy mortars remained split between LZ Gator and CAP 133. Richardson sent out SLRP's from LZ's Gator and Dottie as well as platoon-size reconnaissance patrols.

On one of these patrols a squad from Charlie's 3rd platoon found a skeleton in a hooch only one-half mile east of Dottie, with seven bullet holes in its skull. South of LZ Buff a forward observer team protected by some PF soldiers sat on a high perch of rock three miles south of the LZ, known as OP 1. They had a commanding view for miles, including provincial road LTL/58 which passed by on the southern edge of their hill. At 12:45PM January 5, the OP spotted six VC walking with weapons one and one-half miles east of their perch, just north of the road, near the hamlet of An Tho. Richardson's C&C flew south to check it out and found one VC carrying a basket along the way. The insurgent was cut down by door gunners as the Huey proceeded south.

Richardson's ariel recon found no VC in the area but the next morning a patrol from Delta arrived to take another look and at 9:40AM came under heavy fire. Richardson again flew over the action and his bird was hit in the rotary blade and door from ground fire. Artillery fire was called after which Delta's troops moved in again. But they came under heavy fire again, wounding a grunt in the neck and the platoon leader in the elbow. When another grunt dropped to the ground to place effective fire, he was bitten by a centipede and suffered convulsions. Gunships arrived to level the playing field while a dustoff picked up those wounded under fire. Finally the patrol moved into the hamlet, discovering eight females, two of whom had minor wounds. Documents were found in a fortress-like hooch, surrounded by barbed wire. Richardson brought the wounded females up to Gator for treatment and questioning.

Two days later Delta's patrol moved one mile farther east of An Tho and at noon spotted another six to eight VC with weapons, packs and a nasty attitude. Gunships were called in but even after their heavy concentration of fire, snipers restricted the movement of the grunts, proving as often was the case, wherever VC were seen, there were more around unseen. The forward observers on OP 1 continued to spot small groups of VC for Delta's troops but the limited number of grunts available, limited time, and large expanse of terrain gave the VC a decisive advantage in escaping and evading. On the afternoon of January 8, the remaining Delta soldiers in the LZ Buff area were lifted out to return to LZ Gator to join the rest of the battalion for a short period to rest, refit and prepare for a major operation around a place called "The Batangan Peninsula"

8 – Russell Beach

Well before the 5th/46th Infantry Battalion's arrival in Vietnam, the 48th Local Force Vietcong Battalion, considered by some to be one of the most effective Vietcong military units in the war, held a strong base of operations northeast of Quang Ngai City on the Binh Duc Cape, known as the Batangan Peninsula.

The 48th's ranks' were decimated in early 1968 from the February 1968 TET offensive when it attacked Quang Ngai City. A regiment of the 2nd ARVN Division counterattacked, making the 48th pay a significant price in dead and wounded, particularly in its leadership ranks. To many Vietcong, TET 1968 was an unforgettable slaughter by South Vietnamese and American firepower. Moreover, many peasants of Quang Ngai Province lost faith in the Vietcong's ability to "liberate" a large area of the province. "Revolutionary morale" would never be the same.

But rejuvenation is a hallmark of guerilla movements; and no one did it better than the 48th Local Force Vietcong Battalion. While it would never fully recover its strength from it's loses in TET, the battalion continued to be the beneficiary of enough popular support in hamlets in the coastal area to make it a potent enemy force. The 5th/46th further diminished the strength of the 48th Battalion in its Golden Fleece operations, but supplies and NVA regulars continued to infiltrate from the mountains to provide political and military support.

The primary route of enemy infiltration generally ran from the mountains eastward along the trace of the Tra Bong River, sliding past Binh Son and Highway One, and moving eleven miles onto the coast by the South China Sea. Another migration route lay northeast of LZ Gator, where the VC and NVA slipped out of the mountains west of LZ Chippewa, passing through with the assistance of villagers in Tri Binh (5), then across Highway One and into the coastal area near CAP 133.

Operation Golden Fleece and its effort to secure the rice harvest was a lesson to the 5th/46 Infantry Battalion, the Marine Combined Action Platoon (CAP) teams and the Military Advisor Teams in Binh Son and Quang Ngai as to the tenacity of the VC in the 48th Battalion. The numerous tunnel complexes the enemy used throughout the greater coastal area could not be adequately dealt with, owing to limited time and limited troops from the battalion. Some of the heaviest fighting during Golden Fleece fell to the CAP teams who were on the front lines of village life as the VC fought for hegemony in the coastal hamlets. Golden Fleece highlighted the reality that the southern doorstep of the Americal Division was still very much under the control of the VC and far from being "pacified". And the heart and soul of that resistance appeared to emanate from the Batangan Peninsula. The Americal Division set out to change this condition, once and for all.

The plan to trap and destroy the VC and pacify the Batangan Peninsula depended on two major operational forces: "Operation Russell Beach" involved American Army and ARVN forces, and "Operation Bold Mariner" brought in Marine Battalion Landing Teams (BLT) and the Navy. Both came under the nominal control of Brigadier General Howard Cooksey, the Americal's Assistant Division Commander for Operations, who activated his familiar"Task Force Cooksey" for the large-scale operation.

The task force's objectives were to first, "Find, fix and destroy enemy local force (LF) units; second, support an accelerated pacification campaign by conducting search and screening operations to capture or destroy the Vietcong Infrastructure (VCI), enemy caches, other materials and fortifications in the area; and third, Conduct an extensive pacification program in the area" after the enemy was neutralized. Pacification was to be the long term solution to providing security and relative calm to government protected hamlets.

While the Vietcong menace permeated throughout the large coastal area, intelligence reports indicated the mainforce command structure, major storage areas, heavy weapons and the bulk of forces were concentrated on the Batangan Peninsula with a strong supporting infrastructure in the area around My Lai (1) (Pinkville), extending south and northeast on the coast.

Russell Beach was planned by the 198th Light Infantry Brigade, but the 5th/46th Infantry Battalion was to be the key maneuver element of this multi-battalion, multi-service operation since it was to be conducted within the battalion's assigned operational area. The overall Task Force was composed of two Marine landing forces, the 2nd/26th and 3rd/26th Marine Battalion Landing Teams (BLT), supported by the III Marine Amphibious Force (MAF) off the coast. The Marines planned to strike from the sea using landing craft and assault helicopters. One reinforced battalion from the 2nd ARVN Division and the 5th/46th and 4th/3rd Infantry Battalions from the Americal Division, would represent the Army forces coming in from the land side. The 4th/3rd would be on "loan" from the 11th Infantry Brigade in Duc Pho. Further backup would come from three Army artillery batteries, one Army cavalry troop of armored personnel carriers and one ARVN cavalry troop.

   The concept of the operation was simple enough: encircle the Batangan Peninsula in a large "half-moon" cordon from the coastal area south of Pinkville to the coast six miles further north, sealing off the Batangan with a massive use of manpower. The cordon would be gradually tightened in a phased operation, slowly moving east to "squeeze" the enemy further east onto the Batangan Peninsula and pin their backs to the sea. This was a very conventional way of dealing with an unconventional enemy like the 48th LF Battalion and portions of the 38th VC Battalion which was also thought to be in the area.

   The key to the cordon's success was to prevent the landward or seaward escape of the Vietcong and its deep infrastructure which existed in the hamlets and in extensive tunnel networks. US Naval forces using swift boats were tasked to provide coastal surveillance and serve as a blocking force to prevent Vietcong from escaping in small boats down the coast. The Americal Division knew the peninsula could not be pacified overnight, and believed the overall objectives would take approximately three months to accomplish. The operation was divided into five phases, with the large-scale tactical operation (Phase III) lasting approximately fourteen days. The plan was as follows:

   PHASE I (1-6 days before "D-Day") would be the staging of units for commitment into the area and to conduct of "economy of force" operations. This called for the 5th/46th to conduct operations west, north and south of the Batangan Peninsula, using SLRP's (Modified Hunter Killer Teams). The SLRP's, along with platoon and company-size elements, were to "herd" VC units from north, south and western boundaries towards the area to be cordoned. At a minimum, it was hoped these actions would keep VC units from migrating west out of the coastal area, to keep more enemy inside the cordon to kill when all friendly forces arrived.

A "cover and deception" plan was also carried out. Visual reconnaissance and fire support missions were oriented to indicate the operations objective would be in the Mo Duc District of Quang Ngai province, approximately eleven miles southeast of Quang Ngai City, in the American's 11th Brigade area of operations (AO). The Mo Duc area presented a credible ruse. It contained a hotbed of Communist resistance which boasted, among other things, to be the birthplace of North Vietnam's Prime Minister, Pham Van Dong (Duc Tan Village – Mo Duc District). To add credibility to this deception, the Marine Amphibious Force, backed by a large portion of the US 7th Fleet, including the USS New Jersey, would pummel the Mo Duc area, along with air strikes at previously identified hard core VC locations pinpointed by 11th Brigade intelligence. The sea forces would then move swiftly to the north, off the coast of the Batangan for the real operation.

PHASE II (D-Day – January 13, 1969) called for the "cordon" to be established on the land-side of the targeted area, along with Psychological Operation (PSYOP) speakers and leaflet drops to provide instructions for refugees to comply with the collection procedures.

PHASE III (D+1 to D+15) called for a "Detailed search operation, to be conducted by all ground forces to locate enemy local force units and destroy or capture VCI, hamlet guerillas, and materials or fortifications in the AO. The ground forces would also screen civilians and assist in their evacuation to holding areas outside the assigned area of the cordon".

PHASE IV: (D+15 to D+75 – estimated) was to "Conduct extensive pacification programs and assist GVN (South Vietnamese Government) in reestablishing government control in the AO".

PHASE V: (D+76 – est.) "Turning over responsibility for territorial security to GVN forces."

Herding the Enemy

On January 3, 1969, two SLRP's from Charlie Company were inserted north and east of LZ Dottie to observe the enemy (mostly VC reinforced by some NVA regulars) and direct blocking fires to prevent

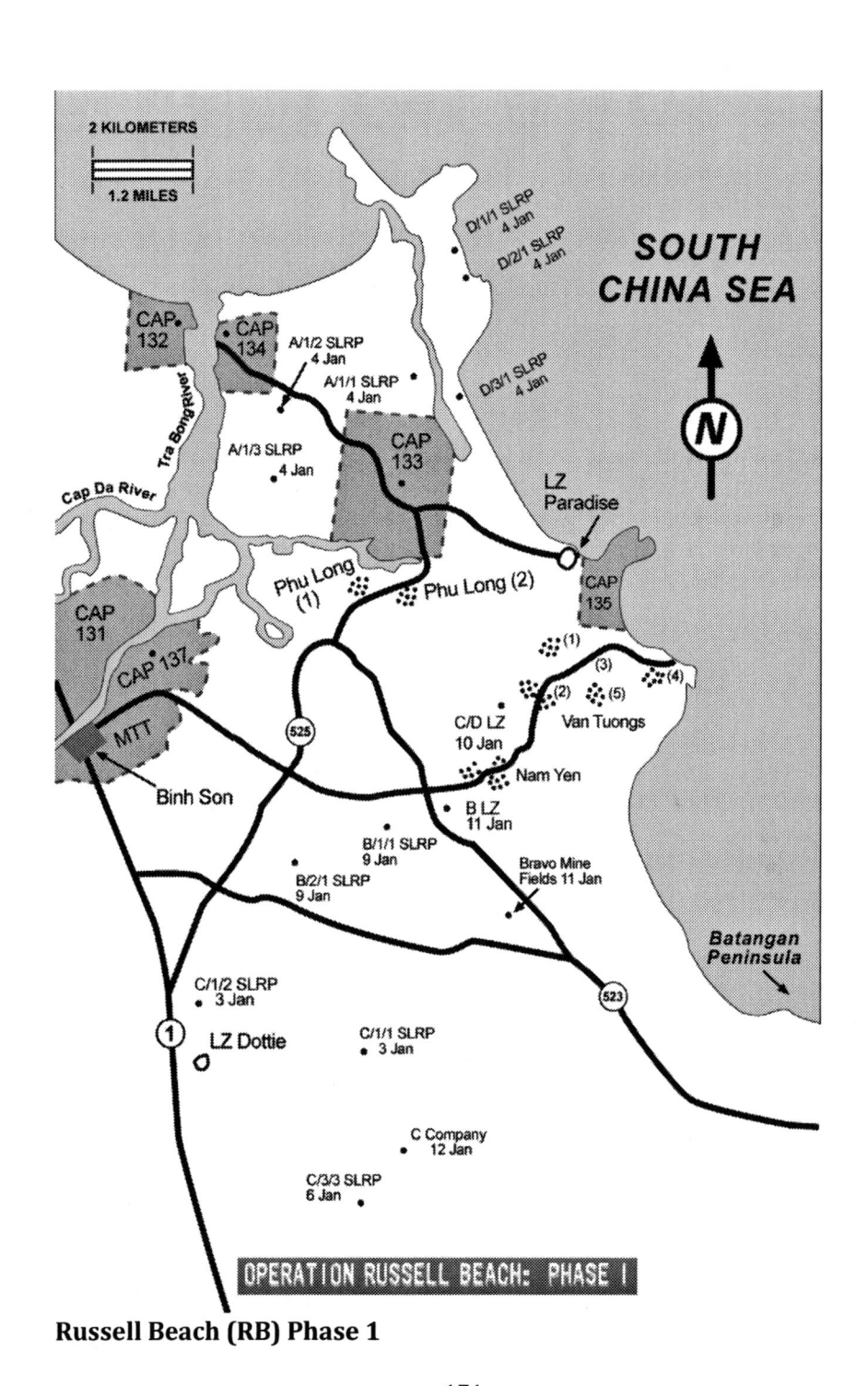

Russell Beach (RB) Phase 1

their western movement across Highway One. The following day Delta Company inserted three SLRP's along the far north shoreline of the South China Sea, east of CAP's 133 and 134, to force the enemy to shift farther south towards the targeted area of the Russell Beach operation. The SLRP's were tasked to spot enemy activity and use artillery to force their movement south, away from the punishing indirect fire. Alpha inserted two SLRP's west of Delta to improve the observation and interdiction of any northward movement of VC. Alpha also airlifted a SLRP to CAP 134, which then walked south to fill a gap between the other two SLRP's.

On January 5 at 3:25AM, SLRP A/1/3 (Alpha, 1st platoon, 3rd squad) heard movement six hundred and fifty yards southwest of their position and called in artillery fire. SLRP A/1/1 to their northeast received approximately forty rounds of small arms fire from two hundred yards south of their position which wounded one soldier. Again artillery fire was called in. These contacts gave the operations planners confidence the SLRP's were shaking the bushes and that the VC were rattled by their presence. The hope for operational planners was that the SLRP's would provide the enemy enough motivation to keep moving south.

The next day another SLRP (C/3/3) was added southeast of LZ Dottie to improve the observation of the southern sector of the targeted area. SLRP C/1/2 had to be withdrawn to Dottie, having been discovered by Vietnamese civilians. The Delta and Alpha SLRP's continued to receive light contact as they disengaged; a sure sign that they were exerting some pressure on enemy movement in the area.

During this time frame when the entire focus should have been on "herding" the enemy, the battalion was stretched to the limit. They defended LZ's Gator and Dottie, sent numerous SLRP's to herd the enemy in preparation for Operation Russell Beach but were tasked with other search and clear operations as well. For example, on January 6, a reinforced platoon from Alpha and one from Delta was sent far south into the 1st/52nd Battalion's area of operation, just north of the Tra Kuch River, seven miles west of Quang Ngai City.

At 9:35AM, Delta's platoon came under enemy fire near the hamlet of An Tho. The soldiers were promptly pinned down in the open by small arms fire. LTC Richardson, ever present with a nose for trouble, flew over the area. His helicopter was hit in the rotor blade and the door near his seat. On the ground PFC Jason Woody, a platoon machine gunner, maneuvered to a vantage point where he could pour fire on the insurgents to allow his comrades to move to cover.

Two squads then moved to assault the enemy position but were pinned down again. Woody once again exposed himself to enemy fire to move to another vantage point where he could place suppressive fire on the enemy to allow the squads to withdraw. Three soldiers were wounded but none killed. Artillery and gunships were called in. For his valor that morning, Woody was awarded the Bronze Star.

That same day the plan to herd the VC into the Russell Beach target area was stepped up a notch from SLRP teams to larger sweeps. Charlie's 2nd platoon was air lifted to CAP 134 (Riverboat South) to connect with the Marines and popular force (PF) soldiers of CAP's 133 & 134 and two tracks from the 2nd platoon, H Troop, 17th Cav. The small task force set out to sweep east, then south to CAP 135 on the coast to push any remaining enemy farther south.

By January 7, final plans were made for the Russell Beach "D-Day", which was scheduled for January 13. Most of the 5th/46th units operating in other areas were pulled back to Gator to prepare for Phase II, the establishment of a large cordon, the most lengthy tactical cordon to be used in the Vietnam War. On the 8th, Alpha and Delta's SLRP's were extracted and flown back to Gator in preparation for an air assault on D-Day in company-size assault elements.

At high noon on the 8th, a Charlie Company soldier stepped on a mine, causing massive injuries to his body. Charlie's commander, 1LT Jim Fraser, called for an immediate dustoff. Army photographers had been assigned to each rifle company to document the Russell Beach multi-service operation and as the medics feverishly worked on their comrade to keep him alive, Charlie's assigned photographer began snapping photos, thinking this was what he was supposed to do. Soldiers near their wounded buddy were incensed at this abrupt intrusion while their comrade fought for his life and turned to attack the photographer. The company's forward observer, 1LT Bill O'Neill, personally intervened, "Back off, the kid is just doing the job he was ordered to do". The grunts walked away in disgust while the photographer kept shooting pictures as tears streamed down his face, unable to comprehend the totality of the moment.

The soldier was dusted off to the hospital ship USS Sanctuary offshore, which was the primary support hospital for the Russell Beach operation. Days later Charlie's First Sergeant, Adolf Smith, was able to hitch a ride to the vessel to visit his soldier. The explosion had left him blind and had blown off both his legs and one arm. The critically wounded soldier had only one question for his First Sergeant, "Why didn't my buddies do the right thing and kill me, instead of saving my life?"

On January 9, Task Force Cooksey was activated at 1:30PM. At 6:45AM that same morning, Alpha air assaulted just south of Phu Long (1) to move east and conduct a cordon and search of Phu Long (2). This effort was made to bag some Vietcong moving from the Riverboat South sweep begun on the 6th, and push the VC farther south in the direction of the Batangan. The Phu Long hamlets had long been a contentious area for the Marine CAP's. LTC Richardson, flying above to watch the insert, spotted two VC evading and his door gunners cut them down. By 11:25AM, Alpha had the hamlet cordoned but came under enemy fire. They killed another VC. While searching the hamlet, Alpha's grunts found two 105MM-Howitzer artillery rounds, captured one VC and detained four other suspected VC. Alpha then walked to CAP 133 to be extracted by Hueys and return to Gator. That same day Bravo inserted two SLRP's to improve observation and containment of the target area.

In an effort to continue pushing the enemy south, the morning of January 10 saw Charlie and Delta Companies air assault to cordon and search Van Tuong (2), one and one-half mile southeast of Phu Long (2). The hamlet was part of the Van Tuong Peninsula, a potential base area for the VC. The GI's found one thousand pounds of corn and seven VC suspects. One of the "suspects" turned out to be a Vietcong nurse and another was a member of the "VC Youth Organization." Having received nothing more than sniper fire, Charlie and Delta finished their work and moved northeast towards CAP 135 for extraction to Dottie. On their way they walked into a mined area and suffered two casualties from an M-14 mine. While backing out of the minefield to evacuate their casualties, the grunts came under small arms fire and another soldier was wounded. By 6:30PM, they were finally lifted off from their day's work. As small compensation, the C/3/3 SLRP near Dottie killed three VC dressed in camouflaged uniforms, as they moved west through the SLRP's kill zone. The SLRP team retrieved two AK-47 assault rifles and twelve hand grenades.

The following day at 7:30AM it was Bravo's turn to air assault and do some "herding" near the Nam Yen hamlets, south of the Van Tuongs, moving south in a sweep of the area. Its SLRP's (B/2/1 and

B/1/1) linked up with them for the mission. At 4:37PM, Bravo's grunts were hit by small arms fire and an apparent enemy mortar round, killing two men: Bravos artillery forward observer, 1LT Danny Clark of South Hill, Virginia and Sp/4 Matthew Thorton, age 20 and married, of Alexandria, Virginia. Clark had reached for his RTO's radio handset to call in supporting fires and when his knee touched the ground he was engulfed in a tremendous explosion that literally blew him apart. He had triggered a pressure-release mine that was initially thought to be a mortar round. Five others were wounded. When a dustoff arrived it received more fire and was unable to land. While moving to a better spot for another pick-up, Bravo's grunts moved into another mined area, setting off three more mines and wounding seven more soldiers. This time gunships escorted the dustoffs into the LZ firing on suspected VC positions, killing at least one insurgent. Two dustoffs came in and picked up nine wounded along with Clark and Thorton. Richardson's command & control (C&C) bird picked up three more slightly wounded the next morning. The mine field had unnerved Bravo's commander who froze and could not take charge during the action. Richardson relieved him of command.

Throughout the ordeal valor was required by all to keep from panicking in the minefield as well as respond to enemy fire. SP/4 Edward Floyd was one of those wounded but moved through the minefield to render first aid while directing the fire of his squad against the VC. When the dustoffs came in, he carried several of the wounded out of the minefield for pick-up. He would be awarded the Silver Star. First Lieutenants Stephen Mennuti and Lawrence Russell, both wounded took charge in the absence of any direction from their company commander and placed effective fire on the VC while aiding the wounded. Both were awarded Bronze Stars.

Many of Richardson's C&C flights included his battalion surgeon, Captain Wayne Secrest. Unlike the battalion's first surgeon, who refused to leave LZ Gator unless directed to by LTC Lyon, Secrest at times acted more like a combat medic than a doctor. He felt he could do more in the field with his medics than sitting on Gator and cajoled Richardson to let him ride in his bird. His willingness to place himself in harms way created a close relationship with Richardson. Because Richardson picked up so many of his wounded, having a doctor on board provided an added benefit.

On January 12 Charlie Company, supported by tracks from the 2nd platoon, H Troop, 17th Cav, screened the southern sector of the Russell Beach AO. One of the tracks hit a large mine (five hundred pound charge), which destroyed the armored personnel carrier and killed one of the Cav soldiers. Three Cav grunts and four from Charlie Company were wounded.

D-day for the Russell Beach/Bold Mariner Operation arrived the following day, January 13. LTC Richardson had harbored reservations about the entire operation, not from a unwillingness to fight but the fact that it involved the ARVN who would most certainly be compromised by a Vietcong agent within their ranks. The enemy agent would undoubtedly tip off the Vietcong Infrastructure. This could mean the big catch of VC they hoped for would likely not materialize. But orders were orders and Richardson was determined to make the operation successful.

At 8:00AM, Bravo Company combat air assaulted in Hueys into a cold LZ amongst the Phu My hamlets, one and one-half miles north of My Lai (1) (Pinkville). One-half hour later, Charlie and Delta Companies air assaulted approximately one mile due west of Bravo at the western edge of the Phu My hamlets. Delta set out to search Trung Son (1) before moving east. The company made enemy contact immediately and SP/4 James Wagner, a radio/telephone operator (RTO), moved to a vantagepoint to pinpoint the enemy fire and call in gunships. By so doing he was wounded but remained in place to direct the gunships. In the process he was wounded a second time. Delta's CO, Captain Michael Smith directed suppressive fire and while under enemy fire loaded his three wounded on a dustoff. Wagner and Smith were awarded Bronze Stars for valor.

Charlie Company was further north of Delta and moved east to form a long cordon line tying in with Delta to its south, who in turn tied in to Bravo further south. Their target was the Phu My hamlets, to root out VC suspects and move any detainees to the battalion collection point nearby. Coinciding with their insertion, Alpha of the 4th/3rd Infantry Battalion (11th Brigade) flew up from LZ Bronco at Duc Pho, and landed just south of Pinkville at the Co Lay (1) hamlet, to seal the cordon at the coast. The 2nd Battalion of the 5th ARVN Regiment had secured the area.

The Marine 3rd/26th Battalion Landing Team (BLT) air assaulted from their off-shore ships, after the completion of a Navy bombardment and air strikes on targeted shore landing areas and on the designated LZ's for their helicopters, along the coast north of the Batangan. For the Marines, coming back to this area was Deja Vu. The Van Tuong hamlets just north of their designated LZ's were the scene of the first major battle of the Vietnam War in August 1965. Three battalions of Marines fought against approximately one-half of the 1st Vietcong Regiment under "Operation Starlite." The intense fighting yielded many casualties for both sides, but the Vietcong were heavily bloodied because they chose to resist against the superior firepower of Marine artillery, air strikes and naval guns.

Several weeks after Starlite the Marines launched "Operation Piranha", to flush out the remnants of the 1st Vietcong Regiment. Operation Piranha focused on the Batangan Peninsula, the precise squeeze point the 5th/46th Battalion now aimed for. During Piranha, two Vietnamese battalions, one infantry and one of marines pushed up from Quang Ngai City into the My Khe's, My Lai's and Pinkville area, while the US Marines moved in from the north. Piranha yielded one hundred and seventy-eight VC killed-in-action (KIA) while suffering only two Marines and Five Vietnamese KIA. After the one-two punch of Starlite and Piranha, the VC learned to never again mass its forces on the Batangan or anywhere on the larger coastal plain. The coastal area largely became the responsibility of the 48th Local Force Vietcong Battalion.

In three hours and twenty minutes Marine helicopters transported over nine hundred Marines of the 3rd/26th BLT and support forces to their landing zones on D-Day. The day was not ideal for the aviators, with a five hundred foot overcast ceiling and only one mile visibility, which held up the Marine's insertions by helicopters.

Richardson's troops faced the same problem. The Army's younger Warrant Officer (WO 1) pilots were only Visual Flight Regulated (VFR) trained, while commissioned officer pilots and more senior WO's were rated for instruments, which were now required to fly in the dense and overcast weather. As a result, many of the WO's scheduled to fly the air assault were not "rated" to fly in the weather that awaited them. Richardson was anxious to get his troops in on time. The commissioned officer pilots volunteered to lead the way for the assault which would allow the WO's to follow, as ducks in a row, keeping "visual" distance of the bird in front of them while flying under the low clouds. Where there is a will there is a way and the WO's were up for it. The 5th/46th Infantry Battalion went in on time, the only battalion in the operation to do so. The rainy monsoon season would make the operation miserable for all, on the ground and in the air but the operations planners did see one key benefit to the weather. The heavy rains would prevent the enemy's use of its tunnel systems as most would be flooded. By 3:00PM on D-Day all the Russell Beach and Bold Mariner forces were in their assigned cordon positions.

Cordon and Search

After landing in the Phu My hamlets, Richardson's Bravo Company moved in to form a cordon between the western end of the Chau Me Dong River and link up with other battalion forces to the south. At 10:30AM, some Vietnamese detainees spoke of a Vietcong company that left the area earlier, moving east to the Dong Xuan hamlets.

Delta Company made enemy contact at high noon on the western edge of the Phu My's receiving RPG and small arms fire. Artillery and gunships were summoned. Four soldiers were wounded and PFC Harry Dorsey, 21 and single, from Nesmith, South Carolina, was killed. VC mortar fire, RPG's and small arms fire throughout the day plagued Charlie and Delta Company's, especially Delta's soldiers, many of whom were pinned down by close-in enemy fire. The thick scrub brush interrupted with rain-swollen rice paddies made excellent defensive terrain for the Vietcong.

Delta's Senior RTO, SP/4 Wagner was wounded and Captain Smiths other RTO, Richard "Bird" Ellashek endured heavy fire in the enemy's effort to knock out Delta's communications. His PRC 25 radio took a hit by an Ak-47 round but still functioned. Delta's command group was hit hard. Its Artillery Reconnaissance Sergeant was also wounded. Total casualties were now at one killed and six wounded. When a dustoff braved enemy fire to land, two soldiers panicked under the intense and close-in enemy fire, threw aside their rucksacks and started climbing on the helicopters struts. Captain Smith pulled out his 45-caliber pistol and ordered they drop off or he would shoot them. He had to keep his men from becoming unglued. The soldiers complied and returned to their positions. A short memorial service was held that evening for PFC Dorsey when Delta linked up with Charlie for their night defensive position. Such an intense day required some closure.

Russell Beach (RB) Phase II

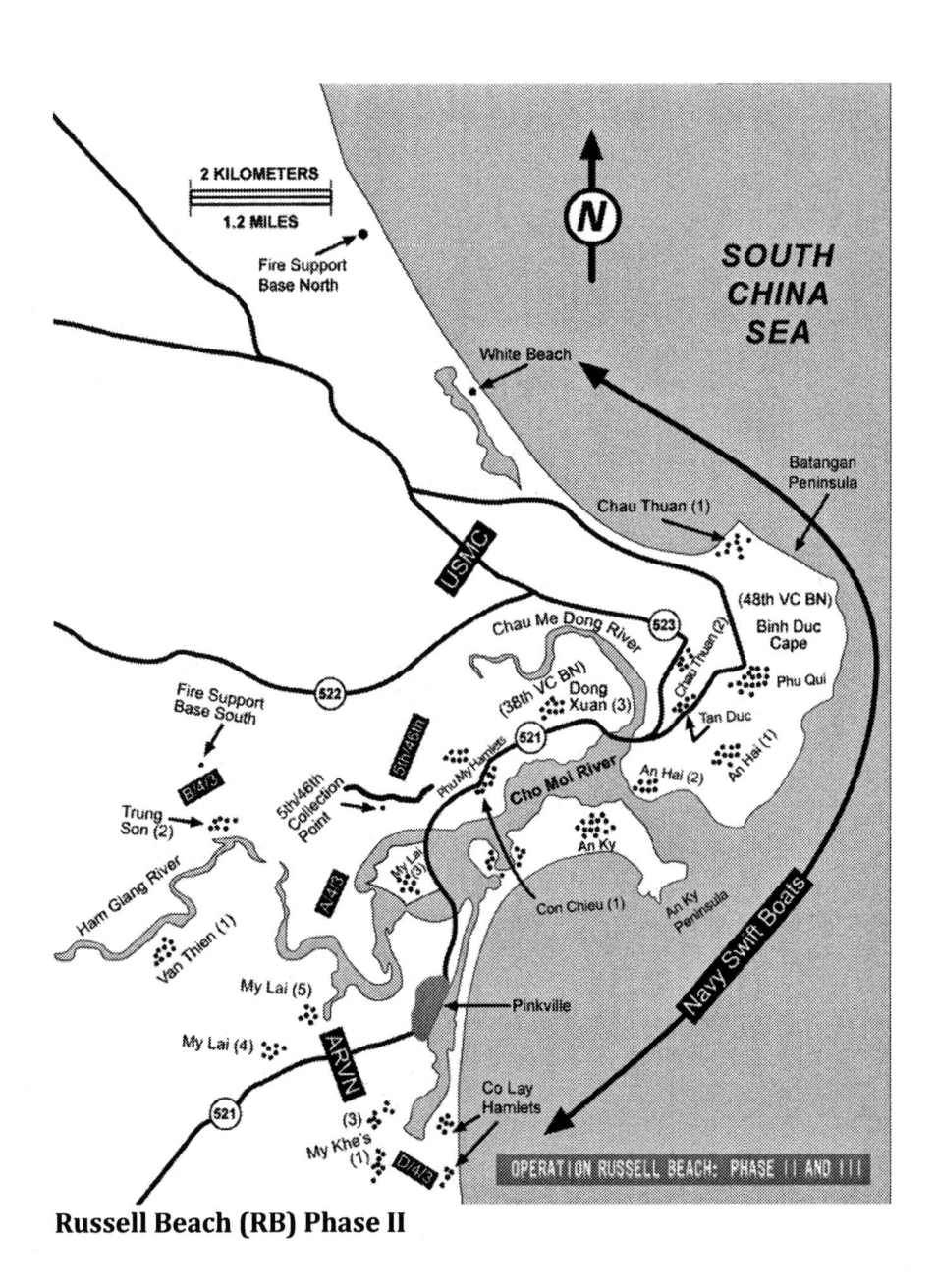

Part of Charlie Company's troops accompanied tracks from the 2nd Platoon, H Troop, 17th Armored Cavalry as they moved east on Provincial Road 522 to join the operation. The tracks rumbled past the hamlet of Duyen Loc, which straddled the dirt road three miles west of the Phu My's and a track hit a large mine which wounded eight soldiers, four from Charlie Company and four from H Troop. One Cavalry soldier was also killed.

Two fire support bases (FSB's) were established to provide close-in artillery support. FSB North sat three and one-half miles south of LZ Paradise on the coast and was tasked to support the Marine portion of the cordon. FSB South, supported the Americal soldiers and the ARVN, and was located just one and one-half mile northwest of the Phu My's. Richardson was determined not to let the enemy slip through the cordon. Air Force flare ships flew over the entire cordon line each night of the operation, extending the night into 24-hour daylight, dropping as many as 600 flares per night. Mindful that a VC "payback" could come to the battalion in the rear, Alpha Company and Echo's Recon platoon remained on LZ Gator for perimeter security. Alpha's first platoon augmented the defenses on LZ Dottie.

Sgt. Doug Herier, an Ohio native, served with A Battery, 14th Artillery on LZ Gator. His battery of 105mm Howitzers hooked out of Gator on Chinooks, carrying them to FSB North to support the Marines after they landed in the area. The battery dug in on the beach with difficulty, as the sand was unstable, but they solved the problem by filling empty ammo boxes with sand to keep the walls of their positions from caving in. The Marines had a mortar platoon nearby but no artillery, hence Herier's free government ride to the beach. Herier was the Chief of Section, Gun #3, the "base piece" for registering fire missions for the battery. The Marines set up a perimeter around him, bringing ashore their "ugly duckling" Ontos tracks, light anti-tank vehicles to help with perimeter defense. The M50A1 Ontos ("Rifle, Multiple 106MM, self-propelled, M50), packed plenty of firepower to defend the battery. Developed for exclusive use by the Marines, they mounted six M40-106mm recoilless rifles and four 50-caliber spotting rifles. Herier felt fairly secure with this heavy protection until their first fire mission called for the use of "charge one" powder, which placed their rounds just a short distance ahead of their perimeter, where the sandy beach meshed with the hard dirt of the mainland.

While A Battery hooked off to FSB North, B Battery hooked to FSB South, and was joined by elements of B Company, 26th Engineer Battalion, to rapidly build a defensible perimeter. Bravo Company of the 4th/3rd was tasked to provide perimeter security. FSB South would also become Richardson's tactical command post for the operation. The battalion's staff moved off Gator by Chinook with heavy metal Conex containers to be used as the Tactical Operations Center (TOC). The launch of the Russell Beach/Bold Mariner operation was relatively seamless considering the fact that although Task Force Cooksey had nominal control of all forces, the Marines and ARVN largely kept their own independence of action.

Armed Propaganda Teams (APT's) from Quang Ngai and 198th Infantry Brigade Psychological Operations (PSYOPS) Teams conducted loudspeaker broadcasts from helicopters. The Hueys were specially equipped with an improvised one thousand watt transmitter hooked up at LZ Bayonet. The flights flew over the cordoned area throughout the operation, up to eight hours each day, sometimes flying as low as four hundred feet. The Hueys carried NVA deserters serving as Kit Carson Scouts and Vietnamese Interpreters. Their broadcasts from the air advised the villagers where to move, how to move and what to bring (clothing, identification papers and one day's supply of food).

At this early point of the operation the cordon was at its largest, spanning over seven miles of terrain covered by US infantry, ARVN soldiers and US Marines all closely linked together. Refugees and detainees passing through the ground forces were evacuated to a Combined Holding and Interrogation Center (CHIC) northwest of Quang Ngai City at Son Tinh.

On day two, January 14, the Vietcong, stunned by the massive incursion onto their turf, attempted to organize a resistance. Alpha of the 4th/3rd detained forty-one civilians but in the process tripped a booby-trap which wounded three soldiers. On the morning of the 15th, ARVN intelligence reports identified one hundred and fifty VC of the 48th LF Battalion located on the Batangan just north of Chau Thuan (2) and a smaller element of the 38th LF Battalion was near Dong Xuan (3). Intelligence reports coming from the 4th/3rd confirmed the VC 48th Battalion was on the Batangan and that support elements of the 21st NVA Regiment were trapped inside the cordon as well. With this news the operations planners held out hope another possible Piranha victory was in the works.

Delta Company was on the northern flank of the battalion's portion of the cordon, with the Marines tied in to their left (north) flank. Delta's grunts employed two portable mine sweepers as they moved cautiously forward. Their commander, Captain Smith watched the Marines move forward on his flank probing for mines with nothing but bayonets on poles, like they did in World War II. Smith took pity and loaned the Marines one of his hand-held mine sweepers. Over the course of the operation, the Marines would encounter a significant share of the enemy's mines and suffer heavy casualties.

By noon on January 15, the battalion's soldiers began receiving sniper fire across their long cordon. No other operation in the Vietnam War would be like Russell Beach/Bold Mariner. Charlie, Delta and Bravo Company formed one single line over one and one-half mile in length, with each soldier able to see a soldier to the left or right of him, close-in, so as to not miss tunnels below. They moved forward slowly, searching every possible spider hole, tunnel or suspected enemy bunker. The movement was slow and tedious by design, hampered by heavy rains which caused hardship for the grunts as well as their enemy. The 198th Brigade Commander reinforced his edict that each element was to move no faster than the slowest element. Liaison officers were positioned with the Army, ARVN and Marine elements, to ensure communications about their joint movements would not be confused. Richardson emphasized to his company commanders, "We're in no hurry, take your time and do it right."

The first refugees to arrive at the battalion's collection point were confused and scared. The VC had warned them not to leave, telling them they would be sent far south to Cam Ranh Bay to work as laborers. Medical teams evaluated each refugee to ensure none had a serious disease since they would be closely quartered at the CHIC in Son Tinh north of Quang Ngai City. When peasants were transferred from the battalion collection point to the CHIC by Chinook helicopter, the refugees were certain upon arrival they were at Cam Ranh Bay and refused to leave the helicopters. The province chief walked out to each arriving helicopter to talk to the villagers, convincing them they were "only" twelve miles from their homes.

But to the hamlet peasants, twelve miles were a life's journey away from their ancestral home and most peasants rarely ventured more than two miles from their hamlet. Their most important tie to hamlet life centered on ancestral worship of those who worked the land before them. This took precedence above all else. The South Vietnamese Government ignored this basic tenet of their own culture and that longing to occupy ancestral lands would later strain the 5th/46th Battalion's pacification efforts. A slow but steady migration back to hamlets would follow for many months after the cordon phase of Russell Beach was completed. As one American intelligence officer noted, "Vietnamese villagers were the world's most flexible peasantry."

Bravo Company continued walking east, ever so slowly, and picked up three Chieu Hoi's (VC deserters) on the fourth day of the cordon. Two of them turned in their M1 Carbines. The third carried a picture of a fellow Vietcong, a boy of nineteen, who Bravo's soldiers immediately recognized as the boy who cut their hair at the barbershop on LZ Gator. These Chieu Hoi's repeated earlier reports that the 48th VC Battalion and elements of the 38th Battalion were withdrawing to the Batangan Cape on the coast, laying mines as they withdrew. Further questioning by the Vietnamese revealed stories of enemy deprivation and heavy losses. The 38th and 43rd Vietcong Battalions were merged because of heavy loses three months prior in the Golden Fleece Operations. They were now supporting the 48th Battalion by carrying supplies. Two NVA advisors were assigned to each Vietcong company in each battalion.

Two hours later Bravo found more VC hiding in a flooded tunnel. They were afraid to emerge for fear of being shot and had no guidance from their superiors on where to go. They were finally coaxed out; having been in the water for days one soldier noted their skin looked like "shriveled prunes".

Delta of the 4th/3rd searched the Co Lay hamlets south of Pinkville and found two thousand pounds of rice, anti-personnel mines and hand grenades hidden in caves. To further tighten their part of the cordon, Alpha, 4th/3rd crossed the western reaches of the Cho Moi River by swimmer assault boats to move onto the island containing the hamlet of My Lai (3). They were hit with automatic weapons fire along the way. Once reaching the hamlet, they evacuated thirty-two Vietnamese and found two Vietcong previously killed by artillery along with seven metal containers holding fifteen hundred pounds of rice. On January 17 LTC Richardson's Bravo Company of the 5th/46th retrieved two VC with enemy medical supplies from another flooded tunnel.

After three days on the beach at Fire Support Base (FSB) North, Sgt. Herier's 105mm Howitzers were now increasing their shells to

"Charge 3 rounds" from the charge 1 rounds fired when they first arrived. This gave the artillery men confidence that the Marines were making progress moving inland. He and his fellow artillery grunts were now feeling comfortable and safe and they had no problems with their beach duty. Each night the USS New Jersey fired her 16-inch guns over their heads in support of the Marines, and Herier could hear the twenty-four hundred-pound projectiles "whooshing" though the air, reminding him of Volkswagens being tossed overhead.

But at daylight they received word their beach duty was over, they were flying to FSB South. Herier had a premonition things would turn sour for them. It started on their chopper ride to the new base, when their only medic was hit in the buttocks from ground fire. Soldiers on FSB South had spotted a group of VC crossing the Ham Giang River, moving into Trung Son (2), one-half mile south of their location. Rules of engagement prohibited firing into a hamlet unless fired upon. A Huey swooped down over the hamlet to draw fire while the troops on the perimeter cheered on the Vietcong, encouraging them to open fire on the bird. The Vietcong obliged and the Huey received automatic weapons fire. Herier watched a two and one-half ton ("Deuce and a half") truck with mounted "Quad 50's" (4-50 caliber machine guns in tandem) back up to the edge of the hill and placed fire on the hamlet. The 105mm howitzers joined in with their fire as well. The hamlet was in the ARVN sector of maneuver and the ARVN's later moved in to check out the destroyed hamlet, finding nothing. But the exercise was a great morale boost for the troops on the hill who were getting tired of constant sniper fire.

Fifty minutes into January 18, Bravo's SP/4 William Rollins was hit in the chest by a gunshot. He was dusted off by 1:25AM to the 312th Evacuation Hospital in Chu Lai but succumbed to his wound. Rollins was age twenty and single from St. Mary's, West Virginia.

At 4:55PM the same day FSB South received seven 60mm mortar rounds inside their perimeter. The timing could not have been more fortunate for the Vietcong. Brigadier General Howard Cooksey, Task Force Commander, had just arrived to get a briefing on the operations progress. The briefing area was situated on the southeast edge of the hill, overlooking the cordoned area leading to the coast. The briefing was almost complete when the officers heard an explosion on the northern side of the perimeter. It occurred next to a soldier setting out a claymore mine for night defense. The group walked over, finding the soldier with a serious head wound and thought he had inadvertently set off his claymore. As they watch the medics attend to the man, another explosion went off in the middle of the hilltop. They then realized the first explosion was a marking round for enemy mortars and everyone except the medics scattered for cover.

General Cooksey and Major Ken Mink, the battalions operations officer found a pit close by and the two large men found themselves together in a four foot deep by five foot-wide garbage dump. Realizing it did not offer much cover, each sprang from the pit to find more suitable space. Mink ran for a foxhole close to their TOC and saw his battalion commander headed for the same spot. Mink jumped in first with LTC Richardson right behind him. More mortar rounds could be heard exploding the split second they jumped into the hole and Mink heard the round with his name on it explode behind him. LTC Richardson's caught some shrapnel in his leg.

Eight soldiers, mostly from the 4th/3rd were wounded, but the battalion's SSG Freddie Bonetti, 32 and married, a career soldier from Brady, Texas, was killed. Bonetti was assigned to the 5th/46th TOC and ran for cover just when a round landed about ten yards from him, rendering him unconscious. Major Mink held the unconscious soldier in his arms as medics feverously looked for the wound. They found a small shell fragment the size of a pencil eraser that hit him in the back of the head, just under his helmet, in a vital area. Mink's RTO had been eating chow on top of a covered foxhole when a round landed three feet from him. He was thrown three feet straight up but the sandbagged culvert he used as overhead cover took the blast. He lost one eye from shrapnel. The 4th/3rd troops responsible for perimeter security suffered the most casualties because they had failed to dig in properly, feeling safe since the hilltop was positioned well behind the operations cordon. Serious work was begun building perimeter bunkers.

January 19 saw the cordon tighten ever so slowly as Bravo, Charlie and Delta continued to push east through the Phu My hamlets to Provincial Road 521, north of Pinkville. At 6:40AM, the Marines, only two-thirds of a mile farther north received enemy fire. Bravo spotted two hundred Vietnamese in the area of Dong Xuan (3) moving north at 4:00PM. The Marines, moving from the north to close on that area, kept the refugees from escaping. Bravo detained sixty-eight Vietnamese in a make-shift holding area until Regional Force militia (RF's) could move them farther west to a collection point. Along the way the soldiers and

Marines found small caches of grenades, anti-tank mines, claymore mines and ammunition, but the hoped-for large gunfight against the enemy had not yet materialized.

At 8:45PM, some hope was raised that a clash might still be in the works. Information obtained from a captured VC Tax collector/Paymaster (carrying 86,000 Piasters) indicated a large force of three hundred VC had left the An Ky area, a small peninsula east of the Cho Moi River, the prior day. According to the POW, the unit's commander and political officer had been killed by artillery fire the previous night.

About this time a platoon from Bravo Company was assigned the task of escorting twenty-five to thirty refugees west to the battalion's collection point. Sgt. Mick Samples was part of the designated platoon. Samples had operated south of this area, near Pinkville on his first day in the field back on July, 1968. That had been another major battle the battalion fought against the 48th VC Battalion where Sample's earned the Silver Star and Purple Heart for assaulting a bunker. After walking most of the day, the platoon and their refugees stopped to set up a night perimeter, with the refugees, all women and children, placed in the center.

At 1:00AM, Samples heard some noises from the refugees and walked over to quiet them down, fearing they were signaling their location to the VC. He discovered one of the women had just delivered a baby she had been carrying in labor during the day. The other women helped with the delivery. Samples, a country boy from West Virginia who knew hard times was astonished. The mother giving birth did not whimper or moan while in labor and he never heard the baby cry.

The next day at noon, the patrol reached the battalion's collection point with their refugees. In addition to temporary shelters for the refugees, a lightly constructed enclosure surrounded by chicken wire held captured VC and NVA. Sample's comrades goaded him into trying to get the captives to talk. The easy-going country boy went into the enclosure and pushed them around, half-heartedly pulling out his bayonet at one point. The enemy was not cowered. Leaving the enclosure he laughed, "Well, I guess they won't talk." Watching Sample's antics close by was a squad of a Vietnamese Provincial Reconnaissance Unit (PRU). They proceeded to show Samples how it was done Vietnamese style and entered the enclosure with heavy switches from nearby trees, beating the prisoners unmercifully and drawing blood.

As the platoon rested they also watched the PRU take babies and children from the recently arrived women to place them on helicopters, telling them they would be dropped from the sky if they didn't give information about the VC. An interpreter assured Bravo's grunts the helicopter would circle the area and then return with the children. "It's a technique we try on every new group of refugees" he said. Sample's men saw enough and started their walk back to their company, mulling over silent babies born in the night and now this, not sure if any humanity existed anymore in Vietnam.

First light on January 20 saw Bravo Company forming the left (north) side of the battalions' cordon line, about one-quarter mile west of the Dong Xuan (3) hamlet area. Delta was center of sector, east of Phu My (2) and Charlie closed the southern flank East of Phu My (1), tying the long line to Provincial Road 521. Supporting them was the 2nd Platoon, H Troop, 17th Cav. Farther south were the ARVN who worked through the My Lai hamlets. The ARVN spotted a squad of VC using refugees to escape east. As Bravo began exploring the western edges of Dong Xuan its 2nd platoon at 9:36AM, found three tons of rice and salt. All three companies were kept busy demolishing tunnels. It was dangerous work. At 11:12AM, Charlie required a dustoff for two GI's who were wounded, one in the leg and one in the chest, while blowing a tunnel. Another two grunts in Bravo were wounded when a claymore mine accidentally exploded.

The flow of refugees continued and a number of them reported that the headquarters element of the 48th VC Battalion was entrenched in tunnels by Chau Thuan (1) at the edge of the Batangan Cape. Other refugees being processed told of an underground dispensary along the southern edge of the Cape. Engineers attached to Bravo were kept busy and by 4:00PM, had destroyed ten bunker complexes and two hundred feet of tunnel, while avoiding booby-trapped grenades left by the VC. Not to be outdone, Charlie at 4:30PM, found ten tons of salt and one thousand pounds of rice in dispersed caches around Con Chieu (1). The villagers and VC had fled east, leaving their cattle behind to wander. Other detainees told of a large number of VC and some refugee casualties when the USS New Jersey fired on the An Ky Peninsula the night before.

The Naval support from the USS New Jersey was problematic. Her one ton-plus shells did not impact like artillery shells but rather careened to the ground, sliding across the soft soil before belching their explosive power across a wide area, obliterating everything in its path.

The battleship's guns did not lend themselves to the pinpoint accuracy of 105mm Howitzers, especially in a war where enemy positions were situated next to hamlets with peasants. The Batangan Peninsula was treacherous, but it was not Iwo Jima. To the extent possible, the 5th/46th Battalion's staff tired to direct the New Jersey's fire to the unpopulated areas, even if they held no tactical value.

Delta began January 21 by detaining sixty Vietnamese and one Chieu Hoi who were transferred to the battalion's collection point. This raised the total for the battalion's refugee list at that point to one thousand, eight hundred and thirty-four Vietnamese. About fifteen claimed to be Chieu Hois and more detainees, once questioned at the CHIC, were confirmed as Vietcong attempting to escape the cordon. One Chieu Hoi took a Delta patrol to a tunnel to retrieve rifles, ammo and training documents and described his guerilla life in the area. He was a member of a fifteen-man team in Son Quang (My Lai area) which had access to three WWII vintage BAR's, twenty-two M2 Carbines with fifty rounds per weapon and seventy to eighty hand grenades. Mines in the area were planted by VC "engineers" and marked with bamboo for the local peasants. Whenever ARVN or Americal troops entered the area, the bamboo markers were removed. This Chieu Hoi reinforced what other POW's had already said, that the 48th Vietcong Battalion was low in strength and numbered around two hundred guerillas due to recent casualties. The defector pointed to the Batangan Cape where, he said, "The battalion was dug in".

Other Chieu Hoi's reinforced the view the 48th Battalion was on the Cape with several light machine guns, carbines, AK-47's, SKS rifles and lots of ammunition. Delta worked at full speed, processing refugees while searching abandoned tunnels and caches, all while being harassed by sniper fire. At 2:50PM, Delta's 2nd platoon leader was shot in the leg by a sniper. At 7:00PM, some fifty Vietnamese emerged out of holes on the northwest edge of the An Ky peninsula. Two were confirmed VC after being questioned by Kit Carson Scouts.

The battalion's S-2 (Intelligence) officer, Captain Harmon, worked the battalion collection point with Lieutenant Schulte, the S-5 (Civil Affairs). Refugees were screened for intelligence, their medical condition and to cull out VC suspects. Harmon and Schulte worked in tandem but were constantly harassed by sniper fire with little security to count on. When LTC Richardson arrived to check on their work, Harmon requested an infantry squad be sent for more protection but the battalion commander refused, saying there was no need. As his chopper lifted off the ground he received automatic weapons fire. One round hit his Huey, piercing the floor and coming up between his feet. Harmon and Schulte had a reinforced squad by nightfall.

While most of the 5th/46th worked in the muddy fields of Operation Russell Beach, Alpha, back on Gator, took an aggressive posture to patrol beyond Gator to keep the VC from attacking the landing zone. They were also tasked to man OP 5 again, the familiar spot by the railroad tracks and Highway One, north of Tri Binh (1) and one and one-quarter mile south of LZ Bayonet. At 4:17AM on January 22, the Vietcong attacked Alpha's small group on OP 5 with five rocket propelled grenades and small arms fire. Three minutes later radio contact with the OP was lost. Two armored personnel carriers from LZ Bayonet scrambled down Highway One while gunships and flareships circled overhead in support.

A reaction force from Gator arrived, finding three Alpha grunts dead: PFC's Marvin Erickson, 21 and married from Ashland, Wisconsin, Gary Payne, 19 and single from Tucker, Georgia and Tyrone Wright, 21 and single from Philadelphia, Pennsylvania. Wright, a black soldier, had complained the day before he was "not being treated right" in his platoon. The company commander transferred him to another platoon which by grim luck had been assigned the OP duty. Three other Alpha grunts were wounded, along with two PF's. Three dead Vietcong were found nearby with two AK-47 assault rifles, an RPG Launcher and Chicom grenades. The next day another dead VC would be found over two and one-half miles farther south, the local villagers admitted he was killed in the attack the night before.

Back on the Batangan, Bravo had collected one hundred and thirty-five men, women and children by 9:10AM for relocation. Charlie, still working near the Phu My's, received heavy sniper fire and, deciding it had enough, unloaded with the 50 caliber machine guns from the two tracks that worked with them. Later more fire came to Charlie's grunts and they responded with artillery. A sweep of the area found two dead VC.

Richardson's Command & Control Huey flew one mile east of My Lai (3) over a "cleared" (empty) hamlet when it took heavy automatic weapons fire. Gunships came on station and poured heavy fire into the ville. The cordon tightened in several areas which freed up some troops for patrols and ambushes behind the cordon line. By so doing, a platoon from Charlie Company of the 4th/3rd bagged three VC trying to slip through the cordon.

By 8:00PM, Bravo and the engineers attached to them destroyed sixteen bunkers. One bunker produced a secondary explosion, indicating a cache of ammunition was beneath the bunker floor. That evening FSB South was hit again with eight mortar rounds which wounded eleven 4th/3rd grunts on the perimeter.

By January 23, ten days after D-Day, constriction of the cordon enabled the 2nd/26th Marine Battalion Landing Team to depart, leaving the 3rd/26th Marine BLT in place. The Marines had taken numerous casualties from land mines in their sector. To hold down casualties, APC's and tanks from the 1st/1st Armored Cavalry (A Troop, 1st Squadron, 1st Cavalry) were deployed to work with the Marines. To save time coming overland, the tracks were sent by LCM's and LCU's down the coast, coming ashore at the same spot the 2nd/26th BLT was departing. One of the tanks began to sink in the water by the beach as it crossed over a large pothole. The tank floated to the side then sank up to the top turret. The tankers set out to follow SOP and blow it in place when the officer in charge arrived and told them to "do better". They eventually pulled it out.

The 5th/46th operations officer, Major Mink, had ample occasions to observe the Marines and was non-plussed about the Leatherheads. "Good fighters", he observed, "they were reliable. If they said they would do something, or be at a spot at a certain time, I could depend on it". But with the Marines came big egos and they seemed, at least to their Army counterparts, to relish having their operating conditions miserable. The 5th/46th Battalion had to support them once with food because they would only request ammo from their own re-supply birds. The Marines were limited with re-supply by helicopters and so ammo had the priority over feeding the troops. Initially they were offered the battalion's copy of an enemy mine overlay but the Marines declined until they started drawing casualties from mines.

The 3rd/26th Battalion Landing Team (BLT) commander, a Lieutenant Colonel, had no Command and Control Huey like Richardson of the 5th/46th or the commander of the 4th/3rd from the 11th Brigade. The Marine commander's view of what awaited him ahead was only what he could see from the ground and his maps, just as in WWII. LTC Richardson lent him his Huey so he could fly over his area of advance and get a better feel for what lay ahead. Richardson's TOC consisted of a metal CONEX container located on top of FSB South. The Marine BLT "TOC" consisted of the battalion Commander and his S-3 officer pitching their shelter-half tents together.

Another insight into the Marine way of "doing business" came from 1LT Michael Kuhn. Kuhn was one of the original officers of Bravo Company who came over from Fort Hood. He was fulfilling his staff duty after time in the field before rotating home. He was "volunteered" to be a liaison officer with the Marines, flown out to the USS Enterprise and made the assault landings when the Marines came ashore.

While walking to a briefing on the Enterprise the Navy enlisted braced themselve's against the wall when an officer passed through. Kuhn was surprised at this eighteenth century behavior; he was used to sleeping with his enlisted in prone fighting positions. At the battalion briefing he was surprised only three companies would make the assault while the other two would be held in reserve on the ship. Kuhn asked "why?" and a staff officer whispered, "Don't speak to Marine Colonels unless spoken to". The Executive Officer of the Battalion Landing Team confided to Kuhn, "We have two companies in reserve because we don't have enough equipment for them."

Kuhn found out the Marine's were short of helmets and other basic gear. He made a radio call to LZ Gator which in turn was passed to the Seabees at Chu Lai with a list of what was needed, plus Kuhn's own booze order. A short time later Army Hueys landed on the deck of the ship, disgorging all the equipment. Kuhn was below deck at the time with some junior Marine officers when a Bird Colonel burst into their room and got into Kuhn's face shouting, "What's going on?" Kuhn explained his actions were part of his liaison role and the Colonel snarled, "Mr. Kuhn, you're a son of a bitch!" and stomped out. Kuhn thought he was in serious trouble but the Marine Lieutenants laughed, "No, he was paying you a compliment."

Despite the 5th/46th Battalion's ever tightening cordon and heavy fire support, the Vietcong were still able to exert their presence by firing mortars from inside the cordon to the battalion's rear. At 2:10AM the battalion's refugee collection point received ten mortar rounds and small arms fire which wounded one soldier. Sniper fire continued to harass the group assigned to sort out the daily arrival of refugees. Captain Harmon called in artillery fire at times to keep the enemy off his back, calling it in so close to his position that the battery was reluctant to fire but did so at "danger close" distances, which kept the VC at bay.

Throughout the following day intelligence reports continued to point to elements of the 48th and 38th Local Force Battalions still inside the cordon, but Chieu Hoi's were beginning to indicate some VC had already slipped through, as far as two miles west of the Phu My's with other small groups of VC getting away as far west as LZ Dottie. In response Alpha's platoon on LZ Dottie added patrols to their southeast in the direction of Russell Beach. Refugees at the CHIC also indicated a minefield was located at the northern end of the Batangan Cape, directly in the path of the line of march for the Marines who were moving in from the north.
     From the onset of Operation Russell Beach the Marine CAP Teams came under increased pressure from the VC in an effort to try to relieve the pressure being exerted on the Batangan Cape. But the CAP Marines held their own in their personal hamlet wars. Flying over the coast and the Russell Beach operational area became an aviator's dream. Pockets of VC appeared everywhere, attempting to escape or trying to maneuver around their enemy for a rear attack. The numbers were small, usually the enemy traveled in groups of two to three guerillas. Once the birds spotted their prey, they swooped down low so the sound of the "thump, thump, thump" of their rotary blades would not reveal the direction from which they were coming. The Russell Beach operation brought excitement to those supporting the operation from the air. At day's end after flying re-supply missions bored chopper pilots went "VC hunting". At 9:35AM the morning of January 24, LTC Richardson's C&C spotted a VC with an M1 rifle, ammo belt and two grenades. Swooping down low, the Huey's door gunners opened up. Another VC entered the list of enemy KIA.
     On January 25, the battalion's collection point was once again hit by another barrage of six-60mm mortar rounds which wounded a Delta grunt. Intelligence from two Chieu Hoi's continued to point to the concentration of VC on the Batangan Cape and NVA regulars who were manning the mortars. In an ominous sign of what was happening, these Chieu Hoi's indicated they were able to escape through the cordon by taking water routes at night, slipping down the Cho Moi and Chau Me Dong Rivers. But these insurgents decided to surrender. At 4:35AM Delta Company of the 4th/3rd laid an ambush on the southern bank of the Cho Moi River to stem the ex-filtration of the enemy. A sampan was seen in the dark heading south, floating by with ten VC inside. The ambush blew apart the small boat. One VC body was recovered and the rest were

presumed wounded and drowned. By late morning Delta found another dead VC in a tunnel nearby, along with seven hundred pounds of salt and a gas-powered engine. By 5:00PM that day, they captured another five Vietcong, a sub-machine gun and two grenades.

The CAP Marines continued to hit back at sporadic VC attacks in their areas. CAP 135 found and destroyed twenty-seven bunkers, which caused thirteen secondary explosions near Dong Le (5), the area that had just been swept by Charlie's 2nd platoon with two tracks from H-Troop on January 6-7. The CAP Marines also killed five VC and captured five more. Their fellow Marines in the 3rd/26th BLT, busily squeezing the northern sector of the cordon under "Bold Mariner" - were not as lucky. As they squeezed their cordon, I and K Companies walked into a mined area north of Provincial Road 523, and detonated five anti-personnel mines, which killed one Marine and wounded thirty-nine others.

More reports from refugees revealed wounded VC were hiding in underground tunnels in Dong Xuan. In some cases the refugees passing this intelligence were returned to the area by Huey to point out locations of tunnels for the grunts. At 3:25AM on the 26th, as flare ships continued to turn the night into day, Bravo's soldiers in Dong Xuan heard a baby crying and found a trap door leading to a tunnel. Inside they found an old man, old woman, a young man of seventeen and a baby. The 3rd/26th BLT also picked-up some Chieu Hoi's who were promptly sent to the CHIC. The Chieu Hoi's gave locations of tunnels, mines and booby-traps in an area yet to be reached by the Marines.

The 5th/46th was making steady progress moving east in their sector with no barrier in front of them except the Chau Me Dong River at the point it flowed into the Cho Moi River. Beyond the river lay the Batangan (Binh Duc) Cape where the 48th LF VC Battalion was reportedly entrenched. It was time to add some muscle for the final push. Alpha of the 4th/3rd took over the defense of LZ Gator so LTC Richardson's Alpha Company could hook out on Chinooks from Gator to FSB South, then by Huey to join the cordon. They landed by Provincial Road 521 just south of Dong Xuan.

Where "Pacification" Begins

The die was now cast to begin the final tactical phase of the Russell Beach operation and determine if the VC were trapped in such substantial numbers that they would be forced to fight, giving the ARVN

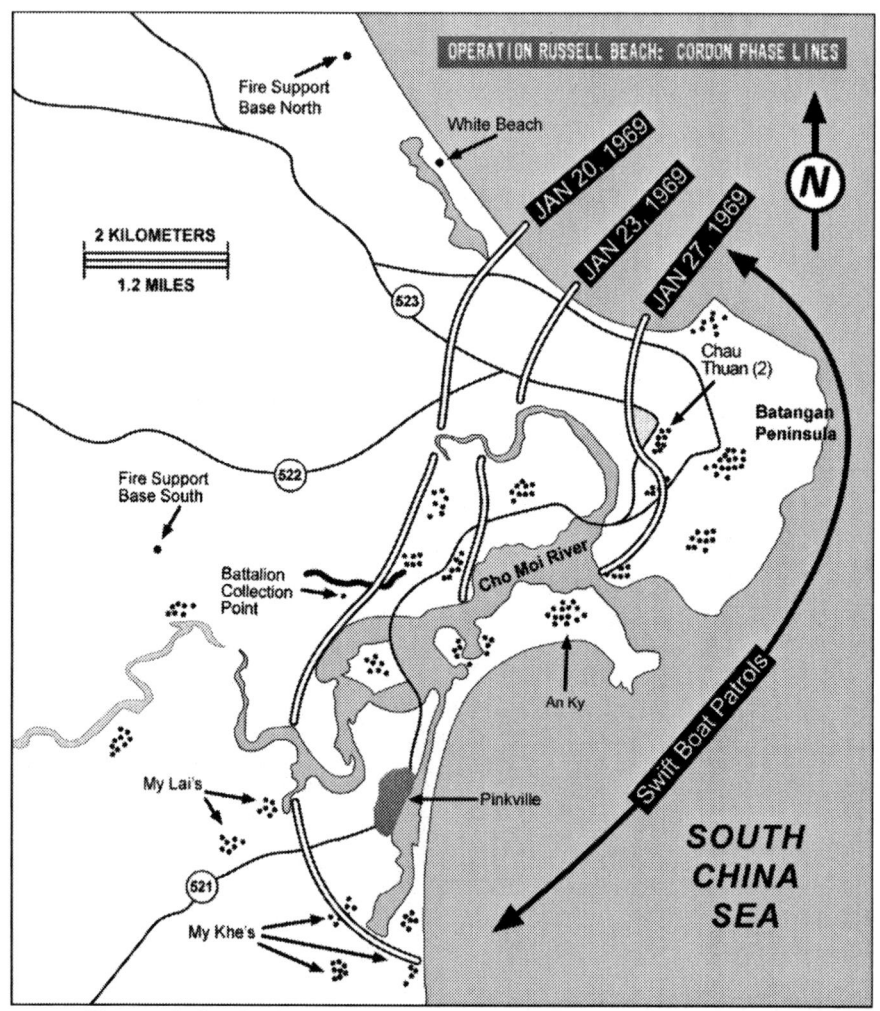

Russell Beach (RB) Phase Lines

and Americans another Piranha-style victory. The VC, with their mines in place, were ready. At 7:30AM on January 27, Bravo, Charlie and Delta air assaulted across the Chau Me Dong onto the Batangan. Alpha remained near Dong Xuan in reserve. Charlie landed on the southern edge of the Cape while Bravo took the center of sector near Tan Duc. Delta held the northern line of the battalion's cordon on the Batangan, positioning itself on the southern edge of Chau Thuan, where intelligence had pointed to the location of the 48th VC Battalion. They linked up west of the hamlet with the southern flank of the Marine's 3rd/26th Battalion Landing Team. Just north of Chau Thuan stood the tanks and armored personnel carriers of the 1st/1st Cav. One platoon of its Alpha Troop was placed in support of each of the battalion's rifle company's.

By 11:30AM on the 27th, Delta found one dead VC stripped of clothing. Delta's soldiers judged by the size of holes in his body he was killed by 50 caliber fire from one of the tracks of the Cav. At 3:45PM, Delta hit a large mine, tripped by a scout dog which killed PFC Thomas Graham, age 20 and married from College Park, Georgia. Two attached engineers were also killed and nineteen others wounded. The scout dog was also killed and its handler wounded. One of the wounded was medic PFC Harold Thetford who ignored his wounds and moved through the minefield to treat as many as he could while shouting instructions to other soldiers on how to treat those he couldn't get to. He was awarded a Bronze Star for valor. The most critically wounded were picked up by Marine helicopters and moved to the hospital ship "Sanctuary", just offshore.

That evening LTC Richardson picked up Delta's commander, Mike Smith in his C&C and flew out to the Sanctuary to visit Delta's wounded. Smith was a hard driver who rarely ate during the day. He was humbled in the presence of his wounded, especially the young dog handler. The young soldier grabbed the bar above his bed and chinned himself up, showing Smith "how easy it is." Smith saw that both of the soldier's legs were missing and the Captain passed out from shock, lack of food, lack of sleep and days of mines. After he recovered he returned to his company to report on the status of his men. It was a very tough day for the infantry company commander. Three killed, nineteen wounded and one specially trained dog lost.

At 6:25PM, a Charlie soldier hit another large mine in the hamlet of An Hai (2), the blast shearing off both the soldiers' legs while wounding two others. Another medic, SP/4 John Schwall stopped the heavy bleeding of the double amputee and attended to the other wounded while moving around the mined area. He too received a Bronze Star for Valor.

The following day on January 28, Delta found fourteen tunnels near Chau Thuan. Delta's attached engineers carefully searched and destroyed them; one was rigged with a booby-trapped grenade. Another had a false bottom that exposed a ten foot by twenty foot room. The tunnels were well constructed, typically with a ten foot ladder that led from ground level down to a large room where other tunnels led off in different directions. Bravo Company, center of the battalion's cordon, found ten bunkers each capable of holding fifteen to twenty insurgents. Their engineers also blew a tunnel, which led to two rooms. A secondary explosion indicated a cache of ammo stashed inside. Bravo also picked up twenty-seven detainees who were transferred to the CHIC. Throughout the day the company kept busy processing detainees, destroying tunnels, watching for mines and receiving sporadic fire. At 8:25PM, enemy fire killed Sgt. Lewis Callaway, age 26 and single from West Point, Georgia. He was first hit by two enemy grenades then shot in the right side. Callaway was promptly dusted off to the 27th Surgical Hospital, but died enroute.

January 29 would see more casualties from mines, the primary "determined resistance" the VC had planned. The previous day one of the 1st/1st Cav tracks hit a mine with no injuries or damages. This day another track near Chau Thuan (2) hit another mine which blew off some pads of the tracks' treads but again no injuries. Late afternoon at 5:45PM, while Alpha started setting up their night position, a GI from the weapons platoon tripped a mine which wounded three more. Company medic PFC Ray Essemacher treated all three who were sent offshore to the hospital ship.

The battalion's morale was slowly morphing into in a perpetual state of fear. Fear that every step would lead to lost limbs, disfigured bodies or death. And that fear did not let up at night when they were stationary. Alpha's PFC Bob Wolf, a married soldier, lay on the rocky red soil during the night, watching the aircraft drop their flares to illuminate the darkness, wondering if he was destined to survive or die at the young age of nineteen. As his eyes watched the flares slowly descend to the ground he heard a loud "swish" go by his head, then a "thud". He reached out and touched a hot piece of shrapnel that had landed just inches from his throat. Then he heard a quiet voice inside his head saying, "You will not die". Wolf survived his tour without a wound.

Wolf and his companions in Alpha Company had no problems with their bunker-line duty on Gator. But here, in the terrain around the Batangan they were on the dark side of the moon. Wolf could still remember it thirty-four years later, "I recall seeing lots of smoke. Smoke all around me. Smoke from hamlets burning, smoke from grenades and artillery rounds exploding. Smoke from air strikes. I recall hearing lots of automatic weapons fire. Constantly. I recall hearing artillery rounds exploding. Constantly, all day and all night long. I recall trying to dig a foxhole in the barren, rocky soil but I couldn't dig any deeper than six inches. There was no protection".

Just after midnight, ten minutes into January 29, Charlie Company of the 4th/3rd was hit by a mortar barrage and then a ground attack by approximately fifteen sappers. Six Vietcong were killed in the attack. The attack came at Charlie's night defensive position at Dong Xuan (3), west of the Chau Me Dong River. At 10:00AM, the soldiers found a cache disguised as a grave which contained two 30-caliber machineguns and a 60mm mortar with two hundred rounds. At 10:30AM, the Marines of K Company, 3rd/26th BLT, operating on the coast near Chau Thuan (1), tripped a booby-trapped 105mm howitzer round which killed four and wounded two.

On January 30, Delta of the 5th/46th started producing early, finding sticks of dynamite buried in a small grave at 9:55AM. At 10:20AM, they found five more graves of cached ammunition with two mines guarding them. Delta's attached engineers used a bangalore torpedo to clear the area. The enemy was losing its valuable stocks of arms and ammunition to the approaching grunts of the 5th/46th but it came at a high price with mines and booby-traps. The enemy's efforts also included treachery.

During the morning, Alpha was sent a Chieu Hoi who volunteered to take them to the rest of his comrades who wanted to surrender. Alpha's first platoon, led by Lt. Darrel Porter, got the mission. The platoon sergeant was Sergeant L.D. Loftis, another shake & bake from Fort Benning who had moved up the ranks by virtue of his proven competence and attrition from casualties of higher ranking NCO's. The day before, Staff Sergeant Ray Utley, who outranked Loftis, arrived to take over the platoon. But Utley, who was beginning his second Vietnam tour, prudently told Loftis to continue as platoon sergeant until he got his feet wet with his new unit.

Loftis assigned the 3rd squad to take the point with the Chieu Hoi up front leading the way. His best friend, PFC Lee Hamilton Harra was in the 3rd squad and joked that he would take the point as he was the best point man in the platoon. And so he did. Porter and Utley were close to the front of the platoon file walking with the point squad while Loftis took the "drag", towards the rear of the formation, where the platoon sergeant usually walked. The front of the column reached the east side of the Chau Me Dong River, near Tan Duc. The river was swollen because of high tide, causing the column to double back on itself. The platoons' maps showed both sides of the path they were on were mined. Loftis moved up to the front of the column, screaming about "the cluster fuck" he saw with all his men milling around. Porter told him the Chieu Hoi had just gone into a tunnel to get his VC comrades and he wanted someone to checkout another tunnel five feet away.

Loftis, frustrated at the "cluster fuck" he saw, took off his rucksack, pulled out a flashlight and his unauthorized .38 caliber pistol, and entered the other tunnel. Just as Loftis' body entered his tunnel the Chieu Hoi came out of the other and stared at SSG Utley who had just unknowingly placed his rucksack on a pressure-release device hooked to a 105mm Howitzer round. The Chieu Hoi knew it was there and had hoped someone would trip it when he was in the tunnel. He saw Utley move to lift his rucksack and the Chieu Hoi quickly went into a fetal position on the ground. The ground erupted with a giant explosion. Loftis came out of his tunnel to find chaos. PFC Harra was killed outright, his body so close to the blast it was powder burned. Lt. Porter and platoon medic Don Sheffield were both wounded. SSG Utley, on his first day in the field of his second Vietnam tour, lost both legs. Sgt Gregory Sikora and PFC Joseph Salopek standing on top of the tunnel where the round exploded also lost both legs.

The blast knocked out both platoon radios. Loftis positioned the rear squad, which had been out of the blast area, for local security, while others tended to the wounded, including the platoon medic, SP/4 Donald W. Sheffield. Sheffield was seriously wounded from the blast but moved among his comrades rendering first aid until he collapsed from his injuries. He was awarded a Bronze Star for valor. Loftis and one other soldier ran towards the remainder of Alpha, which had been operating with APC's. Alpha's CO, who would soon be relieved as a result of the investigation of the debacle on January 2, became concerned from the lack of communications and was moving in the direction of the First Platoon. The commander rounded up his company medics and those from the Cavalry unit to race to the scene on the tracks.

PFC Essenmacher, one of the medics, moved up on one of the tracks and saw what he thought was an odd scene, wounded men laying on a "trail below ground level". The impact of the explosion was so great that it opened up the roof of the tunnel to daylight. Essenmacher and others began patching up the wounded, then hoisting them up to others who carried them to waiting dustoffs. Three were sent to the hospital ship Sanctuary, three others to the 312th Evacuation Hospital in Chu Lai and two soldiers with minor wounds elected to stay in the field. Those carried to the USS Sanctuary were placed on LTC Richardson's command and control helicopter when he arrived in the midst of the carnage.

Richardson walked around the mined area with his M-16, offering encouragement. The men were amazed to see a Lieutenant Colonel put himself in harms way walking over the dangerous ground. Richardson's pilot was extremely low on fuel, but even with his low fuel alarm sounding off he took off none-the-less with his precious cargo and managed to set down on the hospital ship just when the chopper ran out of fuel. Richardson stayed with Alpha's grunts until his pilot could refuel to pick him up.

PFC Harra's body was not accepted by Alpha's commander as being him because the dead soldier was black and Harra was white. Loftis assured him the dead soldier, his best friend, was Harra, the blast having powder burned much of his body, blowing away most of his stomach area and one leg. No one was luckier in the platoon than another soldier, Vernon "Bud" McFarland, who had chosen to sit down just when the Chieu Hoi was emerging from the tunnel. The blast went over McFarland's head. Thirty-seven years later McFarland still has nightmares about that day. The Chieu Hoi, also low to the ground, escaped the blast but after such treachery, did not get the privilege of living.

At 5:20PM, another 1st/1st Cav track hit a mine, but the mine was designed for personnel, not vehicles. They quickly made repairs and moved on. With small comfort, Alpha Company at 7:00PM found another dead VC whose head had been blown off, apparently dead for several days. He was wearing an officer's belt.

The 4th/3rd Battalion was not having it any easier. At 1:00PM, their Charlie Company detonated a Bouncing Betty mine, wounding five. When they were not finding dead VC from artillery strikes, the VC were mortaring them, which prompted more calls for artillery. Four Vietcong were captured. The hard-luck Marines of K Company hit another booby-trapped 8-inch Howitzer shell, which killed one Marine and wounded twenty others.

January 31 marked the fifth day since the 5th/46th Battalion crossed the Chau Me Dong to constrict the cordon and close in on the remaining one and one-half to two miles separating them from the coast. The final distance would not get any easier. At 2:17AM, Charlie Company called for a fire mission from the 105mm Howitzers on FSB South. Sgt. Herier's gun, as usual, registered the mission with an airburst round of white phosphorous ("Wily Pete"). One of the other guns was having trouble with its Pantel Sight and the Corporal in charge of the gun requested his gun be put out of action for the mission. He was overruled by a hardcore Master Sergeant "Lifer", and was told to fire anyway. The gun's rounds dropped short and Charlie Company's PFC Bobby Anthony, 19 and single, from Cherryville, North Carolina was hit with exploding shell fragments to his body and head. He was dusted off to the 312th Evacuation Hospital but died on the chopper.

Delta Company at 9:25AM found an old man, and an old woman who was missing a left foot. They reported that thirty VC in uniform were waiting until the battalion reached the coast, and then they would set off a carpet of command detonated mines. At 11:56AM, Bravo found a tunnel near An Hai (1). Cots and bottles of medicine were found with steps leading farther into the ground. By 1:50PM, their discovery yielded five more tunnels, each ninety feet long and each with branches of other tunnels which were one hundred feet long. Throughout the tunnels were cots, packs of medical supplies and straw mats. Sleeping and eating areas were discovered. It appeared they had not been occupied for some time. While on the move a soldier standing by Delta's commander stepped on a Bouncing Betty, which popped up to waist level in front of both of them. It was a dud and failed to explode.

Each hamlet the soldiers entered in the Russell Beach area appeared haunted. To the battalion's grunts these were not the same hamlets they encountered elsewhere in the war. There was something spooky about the area, the paths, the trees, the hooch's, and the people. The reputation of the Batangan and the area around the My Lai's would continually haunt the battalion until it left LZ Gator and be assigned a new area of operation one year later.

The soldiers lived in paralyzing fear with each step they took. This kept the soldiers on edge, each step they took was a roll of the dice to see who won and who lost. There was no patience for pacification. Not here. Hamlets were burned if weapons or VC were found. The extent to which this happened depended on the attitude and leadership of each company and platoon, but the harshest response to the conditions of the Batangan came from a platoon of Alpha. The platoon leader was brave and daring but psychologically spent from the pressures of the past month. He collected ears from the Vietcong he killed and he operated on a short fuse.

In one hamlet his platoon was welcomed as friends by the peasants, and the soldiers had a supply of C-Rations flown in for their benefit. Here was kindness by peasants not often experienced and the platoon relished some measure of humanity. At dusk as they were about to leave the hamlet, the platoon found a hidden AK-47 Assault Rifle. The platoon leader's mental light switch was turned off. He ordered his men to burn the hooch's in the hamlet and they proceeded from hooch to hooch to burn everything in sight. The old women and young children sat weeping as their homes went up in flames.

At 2:00PM on January 31, Alpha's Executive Officer (XO), 1LT Irvin Prosser, Jr. of Saquoit, New York arrived to pay the troops and boost morale. This 22 year-old officer, who was single, had survived his six months in the field as a platoon leader and convinced his commander to keep him as company Executive Officer rather than assigning him a rear job. He was well respected by the men and was determined to remain with Alpha as long as he could. Alpha was woefully short of men and worn out and Prosser used the payroll excuse to come out to the field to see how his men were doing. In November, Prosser had stepped on two Bouncing Betty (M-14) mines, back to back, but both proved to be duds. On this day however, his luck would run out.

After paying two platoons, Prosser moved with a squad across a rice paddy to pay the others. The path they took had been used by soldiers that day at least three times. Prosser stepped on a Bouncing Betty mine and was critically wounded. Aid man PFC Essenmacher and another medic placed field dressings on his back and then "log rolled" him onto a poncho to help secure the dressings. Prosser stopped breathing and CPR was started. Two large-boar IV's were established.

LTC Richardson's C&C landed with the Battalion Surgeon, Captain Wayne Secrest. Prosser was placed on the helicopter and Essemacher jumped in. Both Secrest and Essenmacher took turns giving CPR on the short flight to Chu Lai, but 1LT Prosser was pronounced dead on arrival. Prosser's death still brings tears to his men forty years later.

At 4:10PM, another 1st/1st Armored Cav track hit a mine which damaged the track pads but caused no injuries. Delta at 6:16PM captured two Vietcong, ages twenty-five and thirty. Two others, ages ten and thirteen, ran away but one was shot as he disappeared into the bushes. Once back at the CHIC the captured VC gave information about tunnels where more Vietcong were hiding. Richardson sent a chopper to return them to the field.

At 1:55AM, February 1, 1969, the battalion received a message from the III MAF noting the day was the one-year anniversary of the infamous TET offensive of 1968 and warned that major installations could be attacked. At first light Delta received the Vietnamese detainees returned to them from the CHIC, who led the troops to a tunnel in Chau Thuan (2). They found an additional thirty refugees, among which four were identified as hardcore Vietcong. At 1:00PM, the Marines of K Company hit another booby-trapped 105mm round which wounded eleven.

February 2 saw no American injuries. Five tunnels were destroyed, one VC was found dead from previous artillery fire and the grunts found ten more VC killed throughout the area. On February 3 LTC Richardson's C&C came under fire, which had been almost a daily occurrence for him during most of the operation. The battalion commander's Huey flew low and fast and his door gunners bagged another VC. A track from the Cav hit a mine wounding five of their soldiers. The 4th/3rd discovered five hundred pounds of rice and medical supplies, killed one VC, and captured nineteen VC suspects for the CHIC. The Marines killed three more Vietcong.

On February 4, Task Force Cooksey officially reached the eastern coast of the Batangan Peninsula and the cordon was terminated. Delta Company moved to the flat terrain around Chau Thuan (2) in a quasi cornfield where work was immediately begun on what was to be a textbook landing zone to create a permanent presence on the Batangan Peninsula. Bunkers were carefully laid out, allowing interlocking fires with interior bunkers for command and control. All bunkers were constructed to withstand heavy mortar and rocket barrages. LTC

Richardson, grateful for the strong operational support of the 176th Assault Helicopter Company (AHC), whose moniker was "The Minuteman", named the LZ in their honor.

February 5 saw Charlie Company picked up for a much needed "standdown" (rest & recuperation) on the beach in Chu Lai. Alpha was pulled out and picked up perimeter responsibility for LZ's Gator and Dottie. Bravo supported Delta on LZ Minuteman while it was under construction, with heavy patrolling in the surrounding area. Echo's Recon platoon moved from LZ South to LZ Gator and Echo's heavy 4.2-inch mortars moved off of Gator to Minuteman. The 4th/3rd continued to secure LZ South and patrol the area around it to prevent more mortar attacks. Its soldiers detained more wandering peasants who were trying to remain in their ancestral area. More Vietcong were killed as they attempted to evade capture. The 3rd Platoon, H Troop, 17th Cav was detached from the Marine 3rd/26th BLT as the Marines prepared to depart the operation. H Troop drove their tracks to LZ Minuteman to assist in its defense.

As Minuteman was being constructed the 5th/46th Infantry Battalion was given "ownership" of the Batangan Peninsula. The soldiers continued to find VC despite the heavy, multi-battalion operation just concluded. On February 6, the 4th/3rd, operating around LZ South, found six hundred pounds of rice and medical supplies while killing three VC and capturing three more. M Company of the 3rd/26th Marine BLT saw a Chieu Hoi come out of the brush to surrender even as the Marines were loading on vessels to depart from the operation. Delta's soldiers on Minuteman were plagued with enemy shoot and run activity while Bravo found more tunnels just east of Minuteman that were previously undiscovered. The tunnels showed recent occupancy. Sporadic small arms fire plagued them through the night. It was apparent to the grunts the enemy's resistance on the Batangan was far from over.

Early morning on February 7, Bravo's second platoon found a dead Vietcong who had been shot the previous night. During the day they captured two more, one a female found in a tunnel with an AK-47, 81mm mortar round, two grenades and a blasting cap with a time fuse. Close by were five male suspects who were sent to the CHIC. As the engineers on Minuteman constructed the LZ, their bulldozers hit mines while moving dirt to lay foundations for bunkers. Delta's soldiers wondered what kind of firebase they were building. Did anyone want to be on it? The 4th/3rd began closing down FSB South and prepared to move back to the Duc Pho area.

The following day Charlie returned from their stand down in Chu Lai and occupied LZ's Gator and Dottie while Alpha took its turn resting on the Chu Lai beach. The 4th/3rd completed the closing of LZ South and was lifted back to Duc Pho, leaving its Bravo Company to provide security for the Vietnamese at the CHIC northwest of Quang Ngai in Son Tinh. The day was also marked by tragedy. Artillery fired from LZ Dottie mistakenly killed two young boys, wounded another and killed a cow in the field southwest of Dottie near Highway One.

February 9 saw Bravo Company capture six more VC only one-half mile southeast of Minuteman, by talking them out of tunnels. Three were females. Along with the prisoners came a carbine, medical bags and surgical equipment. By 1:00PM, the Marines had completely departed the Bold Mariner /Russell Beach Operational Area, the 4th/3rd Infantry Battalion was gone and Task Force Cooksey was deactivated. Control and ownership of the operation was back in the hands of the 198th Brigade and the 5th/46th Battalion. The large hoped-for battle with the 48th Local Force VC battalion had not materialized. While many were killed, intelligence suggested that many more slipped down the Cho Moi River north of An Ky before the final push on the Batangan, and simply melted away. The hoped-for results of another Operation Piranha were not to be.

Operation Russell Beach had a dual focus of destroying the Vietcong as well as resettling the area's population. Operation Piranha in 1965 had one objective, destroying the remnants of the 1st VC Regiment. Piranha yielded one hundred and seventy-eight VC killed and three hundred and sixty suspected enemy captured. Only two Marines and five ARVN were killed with fourteen Marines and thirty-three ARVN wounded.

By the time Phase IV, the final phase of Russell Beach was concluded on July 21, 1969, Operation Russell Beach accounted for one hundred and fifty-eight VC killed by body count with one hundred and four captured, as well as two hundred and fifty-seven other members of the VC infrastructure detained. There were thirty-eight Chieu Hoi's. The operation uncovered thirteen tons of rice, fifteen and one-half tons of salt and one hundred and fifty-three mines, grenades and mortar rounds. Over twelve thousand civilians were moved from the cordoned area to the Quang Ngai City area and some back to refugee camps on the

Batangan coast, the An Ky Peninsula and one across Route 521 opposite My Lai (4). These camps would come under the protection of newly established Marine CAP teams.

The friendly cost was high, with thirty-one Americal soldiers killed and one hundred and seventy-seven wounded. Marines on the cordon operation suffered twenty-five killed and seventy-seven wounded. But for now on February 9, 1969, a new phase, Phase IV of Russell Beach had begun, the "Extensive pacification and assisting the South Vietnamese Government in reestablishing control." But to the grunts of Bravo and Delta left on the Batangan, nothing would change. Daily life was to offer more mines, tunnels and Vietcong.

9 – Extensive Pacification

For the 198th Brigade planners, Phase IV ("Extensive Pacification") of Operation Russell Beach began February 10. This phase was designed to "Provide a shield for the establishment and expansion of South Vietnamese pacification efforts to include the resettlement of refugees evacuated from the cordoned areas". Original estimates showed a population between 10,000 and 15,000 villagers existed in the Russell Beach area of operation. By the end of July 1969 over twelve thousand refugees were evacuated by most accounts. But for the weary eyes, minds, and bodies of the soldiers of the 5th/45th Infantry Battalion a new operational phase was non-existent. Their daily routine remained the same, killing, interdicting, wounding and capturing the enemy and discovering more caches and tunnels, detaining more refugees and suffering more casualties from mines.

Before first light on February 10, Bravo's 1st Platoon, screening outside Minuteman, captured two VC and at 8:30AM the 2nd Platoon captured two more. Bravo's troops and the ARVN from the 2nd/5th Battalion found a recoilless rifle with ten rounds in the same area. Bravo and the ARVN argued over bragging rights to who found it but the ARVN walked off with the weapon.

The bulk of the ARVN forces continued to work in the contentious area of the My Lai hamlets which had been their primary area during the cordon phase of Operation Russell Beach. Intelligence reports indicated two platoons of the 48th LF VC Battalion were two and one-half miles northeast of where FSB South had been located. The Vietcong were dressed in peasant clothes, trying to escape from the area.

At 3:45PM Bravo found ten men, ten women and two boys, all considered VC suspects, hiding in a tunnel close to LZ Minuteman.

The following day the rhythm continued. Bravo found five more detainees, one male, and four females. The ARVN identified them as NVA regulars. A document identified one as an NVA squad leader. By days end Bravo's efforts accounted for fifty-seven more detainees and a collection of over four hundred armor-piercing .30 caliber machinegun rounds, rucksacks, carbines and mines.

February 11 saw three platoons of Alpha air assault back to the Batangan to relieve Bravo, now scheduled for their stand-down in Chu Lai. Alpha Company also had a new company commander, Captain Ben Anderson, a graduate of the US Naval Academy who decided after graduating that he liked the Army better. Anderson set about getting Alpha back into shape, discipline-wise and morale-wise. Before Bravo departed the Batangan on the morning of the 12th, it picked up another thirty-one detainees, seventeen of whom were men, seven young girls and seven women along with medical supplies, grenades, ammunition and two M2 carbines.

ARVN soldiers searching near Dong Xuan (3), which had been the cordon's front line back on January 23, and which was declared "cleared", engaged twenty VC in a firefight and killed four. One, a Vietcong officer, was captured. Reports from the CHIC at Quang Ngai indicated a number of previously detained Vietcong suspects were indeed, Vietcong, including a large number of women. Many claimed they joined the VC in their hamlets in January 1968, in anticipation of the "great victory" the Vietcong promised in their February 1968 TET offensive. Most of the women served as ammo bearers and saw their ranks decimated in the TET fighting.

Marine CAP teams east and west of Highway One came under increased attack. On February 15, the enemy attacked the hamlet of Phuoc Thuan, about two miles west of Binh Son, destroying a school, dispensary, and hamlet administrative building. ARVN soldiers on the periphery of the Batangan continued to find more enemy and equipment in areas that had been "swept clean" during the Russell Beach cordon. Five ARVN were wounded in a firefight near Tan Duc. Intelligence reports from hamlets that leaned towards the government confirmed an increase of enemy movement away from the Batangan Peninsula moving west through its two major infiltration corridors, south of Binh Son and north of LZ Gator. After completing its stand-down in Chu Lai, Bravo

Company flew to CAP 133 to sweep south and try to intercept the VC moving out of the coastal area.

Intelligence reported a noticeable increase of activity of NVA and Vietcong northwest of Gator. Villagers reported the VC were being integrated with NVA regulars to form provisional units. Listening Posts (LP's) for early warning were placed beyond Gator's perimeter. Intelligence received on February 17 pointed to an NVA Company two miles northeast of Gator, which would attack the battalion within the next two weeks. The 5th/46th Infantry Battalion was viewed by the enemy as its major nemesis in controlling the large amount of terrain from Chu Lai to Quang Ngai, especially on the coastal plains.

Three days after replacing Bravo on the Batangan, Alpha discovered more supplies in tunnels and caches. They collected ten mines, five VC prisoners, fifteen grenades, four hundred pounds of rice and corn, one hundred pounds of salt, eighty mortar rounds and uncovered seven more tunnels. One tunnel contained an underground eating area for twenty soldiers. Another tunnel concealed a small hospital dug two levels below the surface with medical supplies and beds. Yet another tunnel was dug even deeper which revealed four separate levels. The tunnel yielded two hundred pounds of rice, fresh eggs, fifty pounds of salt, three hundred pounds of corn, an NVA dress uniform and an underground lavatory complete with fresh human feces.

On February 18, Alpha found large amounts of rice, corn and salt which had been scattered during Operation Russell Beach several weeks prior. The crops had already been salvaged by the VC and the peasants who remained in the area. This time the food caches were destroyed. Aircraft flying the coast spotted rice and laundry drying out in the open in Chau Thuan (1), a hamlet that was supposedly cleared of all refugees. Like the Phoenix rising from the ashes, the enemy and peasants were returning.

That evening CAP Marines and their PF's engaged a reinforced company of Vietcong two and one-half miles southeast of Dottie. One Marine was killed and two were wounded. The following morning Bravo found a wounded VC on the Batangan who was dusted off to the 312th Evacuation Hospital in Chu Lai for medical treatment and questioning.

The hospital's care for wounded enemy prisoners presented its own set of problems. POWs were placed in a Vietnamese ward among civilians recovering from everything from infections, friendly fire incidents, serious diseases or pre-mature births. Often the families of the civilians accompanied the patient to the hospital, feeding them and sleeping with them in the same bed or under the bed. American nurses felt the cold stare of Vietcong and NVA prisoners. Military Police were placed at the entrance to the ward to prevent the prisoners from attacking nurses and the Americal's soldier-patients in nearby wards from attacking the prisoners.

The VC prisoner sent in by Bravo had been found in Dong Xuan (3) on the Batangan, in a grey uniform with full field pack, including medical kit, penicillin, canteen cup, poncho liner, toothbrush, extra clothing and two syrettes, all in good condition. Enemy reinforcements were now flowing from the mountains to the coast, guided by the VC who managed to escape the Russell Beach Cordon. Alpha, less its 4th Platoon, was placed under operational control to the 1st/52nd Battalion for an additional mission. The 4th Platoon assisted in the defense of LZ Gator.

On February 22, Bravo Company engaged three VC in a firefight at 1:25PM. At about the same time one track from the 3rd Platoon, H Troop, hit a booby trapped 105mm Howitzer round, wounding three of its troopers. One suffered a broken hip, another with a fragmentation wound in the head and the third, a broken ear drum. At 6:15PM a headquarters grunt on LZ Gator was killed with his own M-16 by accident. A round hit him in the chest. SP/4 Albert McCullough was age twenty-one and single from Bridgeport, Connecticut.

At 1:15AM on February 23, the battalion became the first target of the new enemy buildup. LZ Gator was hit with a heavy barrage of mortar fire (60mm and 82MM). Bunkers on the south side of the perimeter, by the main gate, were hit with rocket propelled grenades, small arms fire and sapper assaults.

Two soldiers were guarding bunker #1, which straddled the main gate into Gator. The two soldiers were generally viewed as less than stellar in their performance. One of them was a black soldier who viewed himself as a black revolutionary and refused to fire on the enemy when his platoon had been in firefights in the field. This night his attitude would have been the same had the enemy been at a distance. But they were assaulting his position, intent on killing everyone they encountered. That made it personal. The two soldiers put up a wall of fire and stopped the VC from getting past their bunker.

Bunkers #2 and #3, just to the west of #1, received direct hits from RPG fire. In one bunker PFC Gerald Gwaltney, single and 20 from

Newport News, Virginia was killed outright. His bunker companion, stunned by the blast, ran from the bunker and headed for higher ground near the battalion mess hall. Some soldiers by a mess hall fighting position saw the survivor stumble by, confused and deaf from the explosion.

A reaction force was formed quickly and returned to his bunker. By this time an estimated squad of sappers had already pushed into the firebase from various openings in the perimeter created by RPG fire or satchel charges. Cries of wounded soldiers could be heard along the bunker line as VC darted in and out of the shadows. Any shadowy figure without a helmet on his head was shot. The reaction force arrived at Gwaltney's bunker and shot it out with two VC. One was killed and the other wounded. The soldiers found Gwaltney's body near the wounded VC and they promptly strung up the Vietcong with commo wire, hanging him on the spot, one grunt muttering "Sorry about that!" An officer came by to check on the perimeter and told the troops to "Cut the dink down and be quiet about it".

Fighting inside Gator's perimeter continued with enemy mortar fire lasting until 2:30AM. When it was over, two battalion soldiers were killed and twenty-two wounded. In addition to Gwaltney, SFC Herbert Grant from Headquarters Company was dead. He was a career soldier from San Rafael, California, who was age thirty-five and married. The artillery battery of 105mm Howitzers at the eastern end of Gator overlooking Nuoc Mau was also hit hard. Seven attackers in total were killed and three AK-47 assault rifles and one RPG launcher were recovered. Another Vietcong was found wounded. At first light a sweep of the perimeter uncovered forty Chicom grenades, three Bangalore Torpedoes and three 82mm mortar rounds.

Thirty minutes after the attack began; LZ Dottie was also hit by 82MM-mortar rounds, RPG and small arms fire. Charlie's 1st and 4th (mortar) platoons were on the perimeter to buttress the thin ranks of artillery and support personnel defending Dottie. To their credit the defenders prevented any penetration of their perimeter. At first light, they searched beyond the wire finding fifty-three home-made "Beer Can" type grenades, eight Chicom grenades, three Bangalore Torpedoes, eight NVA pistol belts, two B-40 rockets, propaganda leaflets, an AK-47 assault rifle and a bullet riddled pair of black pajamas. Several blood trails led away from the perimeter.

The early morning of February 23 saw a general offensive throughout the battalions AO. In the battle to "win hearts and minds", the NVA and VC demonstrated they could still exert deadly force, even after their losses in the Russell Beach operation. The CAP 135 refugee village on LZ Paradise was hit by small arms fire and a ground assault. One VC grenade was tossed into a hooch which killed the hamlet chief and six others. CAP 138 by Binh Son was hit by mortar fire but suffered no casualties. An unexploded satchel charge was found outside its perimeter. The Mobile Training Team (MTT) south of CAP 138 was also hit with mortar fire, but received no casualties. CAP 136, north of 138, was shelled as the VC entered Phy Lo (1) near the CAP compound and destroyed a clinic. The VC took two male prisoners and distributed propaganda leaflets as they left. Local peasants estimated there were twenty Vietcong in the attack. CAP 131 also received small arms fire but no ground attack. A sweep of the area revealed propaganda leaflets written in both Vietnamese and English.

Alpha Company was released from operation control of the 1st/52nd Battalion on February 22. At first light on the 23rd they followed a blood trail south of Gator to the hamlet of Nam Binh (3) and surrounded it, requesting the Vietnamese National Police to search it. By 10:30AM, the search was complete but no VC suspects were apprehended. The grunts did locate one of the mortar sites used to fire on Gator the night before. Charlie's first platoon assisted a mine-sweeping team on Highway One between LZ Dottie and Binh Son. At 3:35PM, they search Long Hoi (3) and found one dead Vietcong. Villagers indicated a VC mortar platoon had passed through after the night attack on Gator, moving east.

Bravo Company, operating just west of LZ Minuteman, continued to find VC suspects and supplies. One soldier hit a mine wounding him and two others. One of those critically wounded was the platoon medic, SP/4 Edward Gilliard. PFC Santo Gerace moved to help the wounded. Gilliard, immobile, shouted directions to Gerace who treated Gilliard and the other two, moving from man to man while disregarding potential mines. Richardson's helicopter picked up the wounded and Gerace was awarded a Bronze Star.

The enemy continued to probe the perimeters of LZ's Gator and Dottie while attacks continued in the hamlets under the protection of the CAP teams. On the 25th of February Alpha's 2nd and 3rd Platoons patrolled north of Gator. Its 1st platoon assisted engineers as they rebuilt the Binh Son Bridge over the Tra Bong River, which was hit hard by the VC in the early morning of the 23rd. Alpha's 4th platoon remained on Gator's perimeter. Bravo patrolled west of Minuteman with support from the tracks of the 3rd Platoon, H Troop while Delta continued Minuteman's defense and construction. Charlie Company held the perimeter at LZ Gator with its 2nd and 3rd platoons while the 1st and 4th Platoons secured LZ Dottie. Echo's Recon Platoon moved to the area around Dottie to interdict any further sapper attack on its perimeter.

On February 27, the Russell Beach area claimed another casualty. PFC Michael Rommel of Bravo Company stepped on a Bouncing Betty mine near Chau Binh (1) and was killed by shrapnel to the head, throat and upper body. Rommel was age twenty and single, from Clarksville, Indiana.

March 2 saw another combat death for Bravo. Its wounded medic, SP/4 Gilliard, who had given instructions to PFC Gerace on how to treat the wounded, including himself, succumbed to his wounds. Edward Gilliard was twenty-one years old and single was from Heidelberg, Mississippi. Early March was relatively calm for the battalion but intelligence reports pointed to frequent movements of up to company-size groups of NVA and VC trying to assemble for another attack on LZ Gator, LZ Dottie or the district capitol of Binh Son.

In addition there was an increased threat of Soviet 122MM-rocket attacks on the Americal's headquarters in Chu Lai. Delta was sent to sweep the "rocket pocket" northwest of Gator in hopes of eliminating that threat. CAP 135 on the coast received intelligence from villagers that three to five hundred NVA and VC were massing in the Van Tuong area for a major attack. The villagers were fearful they would be drafted as ammo bearers and would therefore face the consequences of American firepower. The Vietcong made it clear they would kill anyone refusing to go. The Vietcong moved into Le Thuy (2) and reaction forces were sent from CAP's 133 and 135 to flush them out. Villagers told the CAP Marines the enemy had moved into caves in the area to wait for orders to attack.

The Van Tuong Peninsula, site of the first major battle of the Vietnam War, continued to be a major staging area for the Communists. Southwest of Van Tuong near the hamlet of Tam Hoi (2), villagers reported the Vietcong were digging more than sixty empty graves for their soldiers in preparation for an attack on Binh Son. A CAP patrol also found fifty-two freshly dug and empty graves prepared near Dong Phuoc

(2), two miles northwest of Dottie and two and one-half miles southeast of Binh Son. More than anything else, the preparation of advance grave sites was a sure sign the enemy was preparing to attack shortly, before the winds and rain could fill in the pre-dug graves.

On the 3rd and 4th of March mortar fire support for the soldiers on LZ Minuteman was moved to a new fire support base on Hill 26, the high ground on the tip of the An Ky Peninsula, one and one-half miles south of Minuteman. Echo's Recon Platoon was airlifted from Gator to Hill 26 followed by Echo's heavy mortar platoon (4.2-Inch) and a squad from B Company, 26th Engineer Battalion. The mortar platoon was later augmented by a battery of 105mm howitzers from the 1st/14th Artillery. Hill 26 provided more defensible terrain for the mortars and artillery and a broader area of coverage to offer fire support, to include the Batangan Peninsula, the My Lai hamlets and My Khe hamlets south of Pinkville on the coast.

The month of March was generally marked by a low intensity of guerilla activity as the enemy regrouped for further attacks. Contact with VC and NVA was sporadic as the 5th/46th continued its patrolling, ambushes and firebase protection throughout its AO. Intelligence reports however continued to point to more major attacks on LZ's Gator, Dottie or Minuteman.

As night crossed into the early morning of March 14, the battalion sent its soldiers on smaller unit patrols and ambushes, trying to saturate the areas of known enemy movement while at the same time being tied down with too many site protection missions and other defensive positions that had to be protected. Alpha's 3rd Platoon set out ambushes east of Tri Binh (1), across Highway One. The 2nd Platoon did likewise in conjunction with CAP 133. The 1st Platoon patrolled three miles due east of Binh Son while the 4th remained on Gator's perimeter. Bravo continued its operations on or near LZ Minuteman. Charlie Company defended Gator, less its 1st and 4th Platoons which defended LZ Dottie.

Because of the increased threat of enemy attacks, LZ Gator was augmented with AN/PPS-5/4 Radar units on its bunker line. During the night when curfews restricted any movement outside hamlets, radar operators began picking up groups of individuals walking beyond Gators perimeter, far from any of their ambush teams. Charlie's mortar platoon leader worked with the radar team by calling in mortar fire on radar "signatures" of enemy movement. His 81mm tubes on Gator were registered well and the radar detected the enemy scattering when the mortar rounds fell. Flare rounds were also called to light the sky.

After two nights of this Harassing and Interdiction (H&I) fire, a local villager complained a flare round landed on his hooch and burned it to the ground. H&I's were a handy excuse for villagers to collect money from the battalion's Civil Affairs officer for "damages" incurred. The distance between where the flares landed and the burned hooch took an enterprising villager (or VC) some initiative to drag the round over one-half mile to his dwelling and then set it ablaze.

Charlie Company was also assigned to secure a quarry site used by Seabee engineers working on Highway One north and south of LZ Dottie. Delta's platoons patrolled west of Gator near the now abandoned LZ Chippewa to intercept any enemy moving out of the mountains. Echo's recon platoon laid in ambushes around Chau Thon (2) on the Batangan Peninsula while Echo's heavy 4.2-inch mortars occupied Hill 26, in support of Bravo and the ARVN.

At 9:35AM on March 14, an Alpha soldier stepped on a Bouncing Betty that did not detonate. At 2:40PM one-half mile farther northeast another grunt stepped on a mine which wounded five, including one soldier, PFC William McFarland, with a sucking chest wound. Richardson's Command & Control bird flying nearby landed quickly to pick up McFarland but he died. William McFarland was age twenty and single, from Lancaster, Pennsylvania.

In the midst of the battalion's usual hectic activity, LTC Ronald Richardson's tenure as battalion commander came to a close. He was rotated to the division headquarters to become the Division's Assistant G-4, and on March 15, LTC Alfred Barnes took command of the battalion. Barnes was a black officer which was rare in the Army at the time for senior field grade ranks. The 198th's brigade commander, Colonel Robert Tully, told Barnes he was getting a "Hot shot battalion." This respectful comment no doubt coming from the battalion's arduous experience on Russell Beach, its performance under Task Force Cooksey and its "Hunter-Killer (SLRP) teams. Tully himself was no stranger to combat, having commanded the 2nd/5th Battalion of the 1st Cavalry Division in 1965 during which he led his battalion to the relief of LTC Hal Moore's battalion at LZ X-Ray in the famous battle of the Ia Drang Valley.

Tully made it a point to tell Barnes that "Battalion Commanders are not dustoff pilots" and that he didn't want him emulating Richardson's habit of landing in the middle of firefights. Both Tully and

Barnes had stuttering problems, making radio communications between them interesting. While Barnes was inheriting a "hot shot" battalion he was also following in the footsteps of the six foot, five-inch Richardson, who was highly regarded by the officers and enlisted men in the battalion, who witnessed his constant presence in the field, many times at risk to himself.

But Barnes was no stranger to combat and was a pioneer for black officers in the Army. He graduated from Howard University, an all-black college, in 1948 and was commissioned out of its ROTC program. In June 1950 he accompanied the first contingent of American troops into the Korean War and served in five major campaigns as a platoon leader and infantry company commander, earning two Silver Stars, three Bronze Stars and the Purple Heart.

Although he was quite capable and held a caring concern for his soldiers, he also preferred a more "spit and polish" command style with shaving required each day in the field and jungle fatigue shirts to be worn at all times. This did not go over well with the battalions soldiers in the hot and humid climate of Vietnam, either in the field or while working on Gator. LTC Richardson had favored a more hands-off approach with his company commanders, allowing them to put their own stamp on their units as long as they were performing and getting the job done.

Under Barnes, most officers and senior NCO's attempted to adapt by buffering their own policies at the company level from his more stateside, "by-the-book" style. Many soldiers continued to wear t-shirts with towels around their necks while humping their heavy rucksacks on patrol. If told the battalion commander was on his way out, the jungle fatigue shirts came out of the rucksacks and were worn for the visit.

Similar to LTC David Lyon, Barnes tended not to "mix it up" with enlisted soldiers. His uniform was always pressed and rarely soiled with sweat, a symbol not well accepted because it sent a message he was not spending enough time in the field with his troops. For these reasons he was generally not well liked by the grunts in the field and worst, not respected. Barnes' staff generally felt he was a good commander but he needed to "lighten up" on protocol for a battalion at war.

Barnes early on made a point with his company commanders that he thought the battalion's soldiers were not receiving the decorations they deserved compared to other battalions in the division. For example, after the heavy night attack on LZ Gator on February 23 in which some grunts shot it out face-to-face with the enemy, no valor awards had been submitted. In this respect he was correct. Indeed, during the tours of duty for the battalions original solders from Fort Hood, the number of deserving valor awards lacked behind those of the sister battalions in the 198th Brigade.

Enemy mines and booby traps remained a constant threat but on March 17 Delta Company suffered eleven soldiers wounded by friendly 81mm mortar fire. Operations in the Marine CAP areas were stepped up as the enemy attempted to re-establish their control lost by Operation Russell Beach. On March 21, the Vietcong attacked the hamlet of Phouc Hoa (1), inside CAP 133's area. The hamlet was hit with fifty to seventy 82mm and 60mm mortar rounds, after which an estimated company of VC swept though the hamlet, throwing grenades and satchel charges into the dwellings. The Popular Force (PF) Militia were vastly outnumbered and fled, leaving a few Marines to fight it out on their own. One wounded Marine feigned death as he was searched by the VC. The attackers captured a PRC-10 radio, M-60 machine gun, a WWII vintage Thompson Sub-Machine Gun (a favorite weapon of the PF), one carbine, one M1 rifle, a 60mm mortar and two M-16's. Nine days later a Chieu Hoi VC Sergeant indicated the attack had not been carried out by the Vietcong but fifty NVA regulars.

Deadly "Pacification"

On March 18, the Americal and 2nd ARVN Division realigned their division boundaries to conduct both independent and combined operations, often over the same terrain, in an effort to speed up pacification efforts as well as begin the process of eventual ARVN control of the Americal's area of operations. General Abrams' edict for accelerated pacification, with the ARVN in South Vietnam taking up more of the load, began in the I Corps of Vietnam in the second half of 1968. The 1st ARVN Division in the northern portion of I Corps earned an enviable reputation for getting this done. But the 2nd ARVN Division headquartered in Quang Ngai City, whose area of responsibility covered the Americal's area, required much more prodding.

The 198th Light Infantry Brigade realigned its boundaries in conjunction with the 6th ARVN Regiment of the 2nd ARVN Division to form a common Operational Zone (OZ), which replaced the Americal's Tactical Area of Responsibility (TAOR) concept of operation. The 198th

OZ with the 6th ARVN Regiment was called Geneva Park. In the same manner the OZ for the 196th Brigade was dubbed "Frederick Hill" and the 11th Brigade's OZ was "Iron Mountain". To maximize the fire power of the US and ARVN forces, and to prevent friendly-fire incidents, Fire Control Areas (FCA) were established whereby the FCA Commander would be whichever unit commander occupied the forward operating base within the FCA. In the case of a joint ARVN/US collocation, the commander of the major unit on the base would control the use of all artillery.

The realignment goal was "To place ARVN units in a more favorable position to provide security for the local population after the withdrawal of American military forces". A key element to accomplishing this goal was the establishment of Revolutionary Development Areas (RDA), where both civil and military activities would be aimed at "Restoring, consolidating and expanding the Government of Vietnam (GVN) controlled areas."

Within the 5th/46th Battalion's former TAOR, the target RDA's were the areas around Pinkville, the Batangan Peninsula, the hamlets immediately east and west of Binh Son and on the upper coastal area near the Van Tuong Peninsula. To "win hearts and minds", RDA's would also be required to more carefully develop Controlled Fire Zones (CFZ) to reduce friendly fire incidents on the civilian population. To make all of this happen, liaisons were required between the battalions of the 198th Brigade (1st/52nd, 1st/6th, 5th/46th) and the 6th ARVN Regiments' battalions. Two ARVN battalions were assigned to the 5th/46th area of responsibility because of the many contentious RDA's to be covered in the 5th/46th area and the continued infiltration of NVA to help the VC take control of that area. The principal liaisons established were

1st/6th ARVN with 1st/6th Inf. BN.
2nd/6th ARVN with 5th/46th Inf. BN.
4th/6th ARVN with 5th/46th Inf. BN.
3rd/6th ARVN with 1st/52nd Inf. BN.

Soviet 122mm and 140mm rocket attacks were firing into the Americal's division base at Chu Lai with more regularity. Units of the 2nd NVA Division were tasked to infiltrate into the "rocket pockets" or "rocket valley's" with VC main-force or local force units to lend their expertise in the use of these rockets. The 5th/46th was tasked to handle the southern rocket pocket just northwest of LZ Gator. The 1st/6th Battalion was tasked to handle the northern rocket pocket west and northwest of LZ Bayonet.

March 20 saw Delta's 3rd platoon moving to LZ Minuteman to secure engineers who were building a road near a resettled "New Life" Hamlet. The rest of Delta was tasked to saturate the rocket pocket west of Gator with patrols and ambushes to "Get the rockets off the general's back."

On March 21, Delta's first platoon found a rocket site, a simple platform of bamboo with string tied to aiming stakes. The soldiers drew a compass azimuth through the vertex of the crossed poles where the rocket had been placed. It pointed directly to Chu Lai. Burnt holes on the ground indicated the rocket had already been launched. More sites would be discovered by the battalion's soldiers and found in the same condition after the rocket had been fired. The simplicity of launching this deadly weapon and the wide choice of terrain the enemy could use made stopping them extremely difficult.

The next day Charlie Company's CO, Captain Dan Porter set out to check on a small guard detachment (3rd squad, 4th platoon) which oversaw the massive quarry straddling the west side of Highway One one-half mile southwest of LZ Dottie. The construction workers hauling rocks from the quarry had been harassed by VC sniper fire and the 3rd squad was placed as a guard detachment at the top of the quarry. Porter rode down Highway One on his jeep with his First Sergeant, Adolf Smith, and the jeep driver, SP/4 James Lister. They walked up a narrow path to the top of the quarry to check on their men, and then started back down to their jeep. As they descended the hill, Lister stepped on a pressure-release mine which exploded under his legs. Lister absorbed the full blast. Porter, who was in front of Lister and had stepped over the mine, was shredded in the back with shrapnel but fortunately was wearing a flak jacket which absorbed much of the shrapnel. Shrapnel also hit his feet and the calves of his legs. First Sergeant Smith, a grizzled veteran of Darby's Rangers in World War II, who also served a tour with Special Forces on a secret mission in Laos, cradled Lister, a boy he regarded as his own son and begged him to live. A resupply helicopter flying nearby promptly picked him up but Lister, single and age twenty-one from Burley, Idaho succumbed to his wounds.

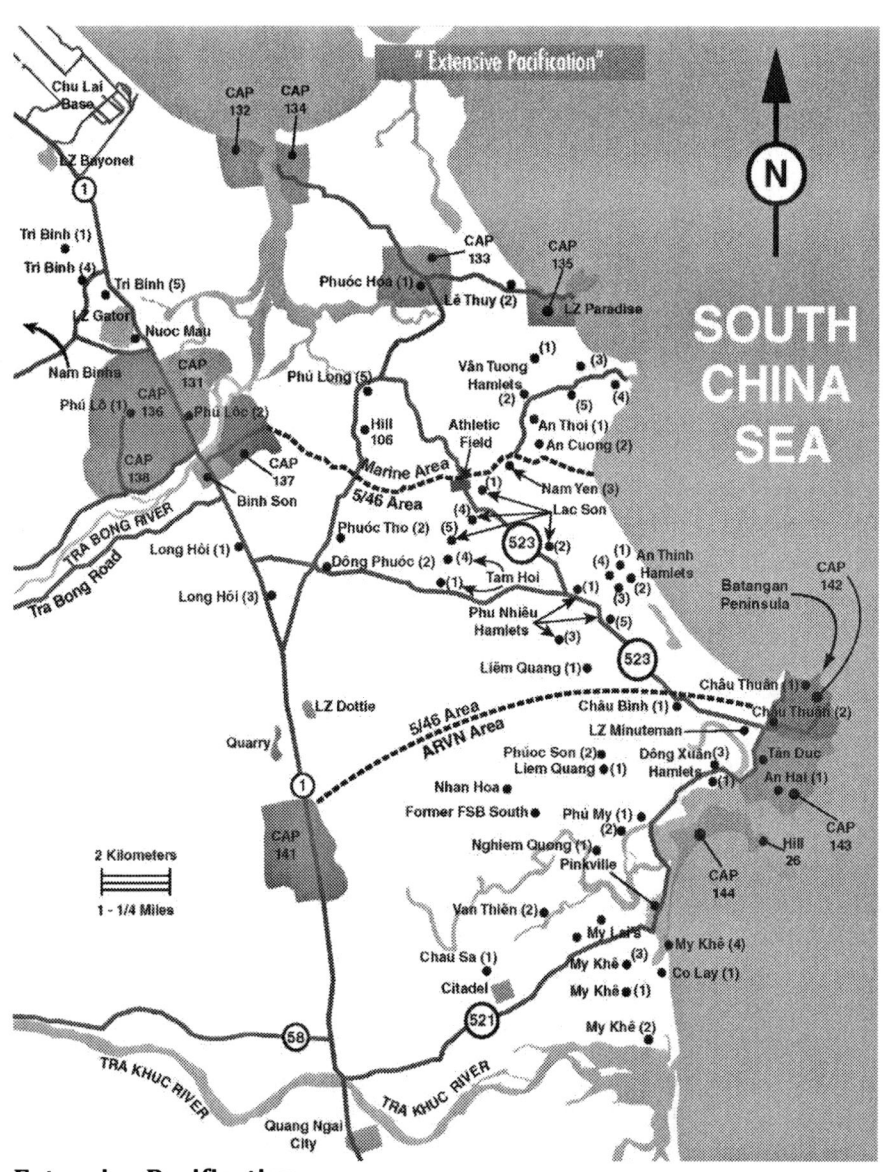

Extensive Pacification

On March 24 Bravo, working on the Batangan with tracks from the 3rd Platoon, H Troop of the 17th Cav continued to patrol the area and improve Minuteman's defenses with their attached engineers. During the sweep, 1LT Curtis Onchi and his platoon paused to take a short break. Onchi's RTO told his platoon leader he had to relieve himself and Onchi moved a few feet to watch the radio. As he sat down he detonated a mine which exploded in front of him, causing massive injuries. Onchi was placed on a dustoff but succumbed to his wounds on the trip to Chu Lai. Onchi was a Japanese-American and a graduate of the UCLA school of Architecture and ROTC. As one soldier fondly remembered, "He was smart, respected, and respectful of others and well liked". Curtis Onchi was age twenty-three and single from Portland, Oregon.

Four days later Bravo's soldiers on LZ Minuteman came under attack with eleven rounds of 82mm mortar fire and thirty-five rounds of 60mm mortar's, seven RPG rounds and small arms fire southwest of the perimeter near Tan Duc. The barrage lasted from 2:25AM to 3:30AM. One Bravo soldier received shrapnel in the shoulder and another was creased by a bullet on the side of the head. Echo's recon platoon had moved from Hill 26 to Minuteman to augment Bravo's patrols and ambushes. One of its soldiers was shot through the thigh during the attack but there were no KIA's. A sweep of the area at first light found ten unfired 57mm RPG rounds and a dead Vietcong in his green uniform with a camouflaged helmet. The large hole in his body left no doubt he was killed by a .50 caliber machine gun from one of the tracks on the perimeter. Several blood trails were found.

The deadly reputation of the Batangan Peninsula continued to grow for the 5th/46th Infantry Battalion. Soldiers became mentally depressed well beyond the normal apprehension usually felt when soldiers returned to the field. LTC Barnes gave "pep talks" to the soldiers during stand-downs in Chu Lai which usually preceded a rotation back to the Batangan. In the minds of many, a Huey ride out to LZ Minuteman was a death sentence. Patrols and ambushes beyond its perimeters were extremely hazardous and tested the leadership of junior officers and sergeants and the mettle of their soldiers. Even within the perimeter of Minuteman, caution was required as time and time again mines were discovered that had been missed by engineers while constructing the LZ. As one Alpha Company soldier remembered it, "Working on the

Batangan would drain your blood. Guys were ghost white when they got the news we were going back there."

Late the afternoon of March 30, Delta was advised they would be lifted out of the rocket pocket for an operation southwest of the Batangan. As in most operations, little time was given for the grunts to pull up stakes and move out. The mortar platoon had developed a secure position with sandbagged mortar positions to provide rapid support to its soldiers. Now their hard work would have to be destroyed to move to another location. There was no time or helicopters available to transport all the mortar rounds back to Gator. The platoon fired off most of their high explosive and white phosphorus rounds to the high ground north of them, where F-4 Phantom jets had made numerous bomb runs during the night.

Illumination rounds were kept despite the heavy loads they presented. They were in short supply and highly prized in a night attack. Everything else had to be destroyed by C4 explosive or by burning. Trash was collected as best as possible. In state-side conditions during peacetime, soldiers formed long lines and walked slowly to "police" a training area before leaving. The soldiers in Nam joked the brass at MACV's headquarters in Saigon would have to have the last soldiers at wars-end form a line at the north end of South Vietnam and "police" the countryside down to Saigon.

Because the rocket pocket was fairly free of enemy activity, large Chinooks lumbered out to pick up the grunts. Delta walked one-half mile to a pick-up site, laboring under their usually heavy rucksack loads but with the added base-plate and tube of an 81mm mortar and extra illumination rounds.

Preparation for Delta's mission was feverish on LZ Gator, the routine for most companies when preparing for another combat assault. As soon as word got out they would be going back out "Near the Batangan" there was a rise in sick calls and mysterious ailments. A night on LZ Gator afforded a cold shower and one to two trips to the Mess Hall which had a reputation for being the best in the brigade. Supplies were turned in upon arriving at the company area but reissued shortly after. They included C-rations, ammunition for the M-16's, water, fragmentation grenades, smoke grenades, Light Anti-tank Weapons (LAW's -ideal for enemy bunkers)and of course personal items such as cameras, writing paper and cigarettes. The tradeoff was always the same, how much to carry for comfort and how much to carry for survival. It was the job of the platoon leaders, platoon sergeants and squad leaders to insure their soldiers opted for "pushing power" with ample ammunition.

On the morning of March 31 Delta rose well before dawn to make a "last call" at the mess hall, then "rucked-up" in the company area. It was a scene repeated hundreds of times for the soldiers of the 5th/46th Infantry Battalion. Last minute checks were made to insure each man carried enough ammunition. The call to "haul ass" came and the long line of soldiers slowly trudged up to the lower landing pad, on the southwest side of Gator, where enough space was available for several Hueys to land at one time. The smaller "VIP" landing pad just above was reserved for the battalion commanders' Huey as well as visitors from the brigade or division.

The sullen and sober-faced soldiers arrived at the pad and were placed in groups of seven to swiftly load each Huey that would land. The wait began as final radio checks were made by the platoon leaders. Sometimes the company jeep brought some soldiers up to the pad who languished too long at the mess hall, some still carrying cartons of milk or other tidbits of food. They were greeted with friendly jeering by their comrades. The First Sergeant made sure they didn't miss the pleasure of another free helicopter ride to the bush, all expenses paid.

Soldiers sat on the pad of black asphalt in platoon and squad groups. By 10:00AM, the sun had enough time in the sky to melt the black tar so it could stick to the soles of boots. Each man sat and rested against his rucksack, alone in his thoughts, comforted only by the physical presence of his comrades and the knowledge he will not make the trip back to the bush alone. And he must go because his comrades were going as well.

Suddenly the radio cracked with a sound too static for most to understand, but its sound indicated something was up. Then the cry, "Birds in-bound!" The men rose up on their feet and with great difficulty, slung their heavy rucksacks onto their backs. The rucksack frames were too big for most men and grunts knew they would have to endure the metal frames bumping into their tired bodies with each step they would take in the field. It was another point of torture to go along with the heat, thirst, hunger, mines and booby-traps. The first lift of Hueys arrived and the company headquarters, the weapons platoon and one other rifle platoon were the first to go. The birds would return for two additional lifts.

Delta's mission was to land three miles northwest of Pinkville and four miles southwest of the Batangan, to push the Vietcong into an ARVN blocking force situated between Delta's landing zone and the Batangan. On this air-assault no artillery would be fired to soften the landing zone and the door gunners would not open up with their M-60's upon its approach, all in hopes of surprising the enemy. The plan worked and the company landed "cold", no enemy fire.

As the first lift landed the soldiers spotted some Vietnamese who ran from the area. Two minutes later Delta received automatic weapons fire and the gunships accompanying the combat air assault went to work. The Cobra's poured fire on the surrounding area each time another lift of troops arrived. By the time all the troops were on the ground the firing subsided. Delta moved out cautiously toward the Phu My hamlets. By 11:00AM they suffered their first casualty, a soldier who stepped on an anti-personnel mine and lost two toes. He was quickly dusted off and the company continued moving northeast.

The next day a Vietnamese Popular Force (PF) soldier stepped on an M-14 mine within the LZ Minuteman perimeter and lost a leg. The refugee camp established just outside the perimeter, where local villagers had been moved back from the detention center near Quang Ngai, had become a camp of squalor and filth. The Vietcong moved in and out of the camp each night with ease, visiting family members.

Delta searched the area near Phu My (1) and killed one VC on the morning of April 2. Charlie Company's squad, which protected the Seabees at the Quarry site by Highway One, watched as a bulldozer uncovered a cache of ammunition when its front shovel scrapped the earth for a load of stones. One Vietnamese man appeared out of nowhere and grabbed some grenades from the cache and ran off. He was captured by the squad.

By late afternoon Delta found a tunnel in Phu My (1) which contained .30 caliber ammunition, an M-72 Anti-Tank weapon (LAW), three hundred and fifty pounds of rice and two empty coffins. Thirty minutes later an eleven to twelve year old girl wandered into their position with burns over her back and on her arms, claiming the VC had killed her parents. The men could not be sure if she was from a VC family and possibly received the burns from a earlier napalm attack, with her parents now sending her forward to the grunts for assistance. The enemy knew the soldiers would give her medical treatment. Her burns were too serious for the medics to treat and she was dusted-off to a Chu Lai hospital.

The following morning Delta, still at Phu My (1) found thirteen 82mm mortar rounds hidden behind an ancestral worship alter in a hooch. This find precipitated a more vigorous search, resulting in three hundred rounds of .30 caliber ammunition and a 57mm recoilless rocket round found inside a freshly dug grave. In a nearby pagoda, enemy documents were also found. Later, Delta found approximately one hundred and fifty females and two hundred and fifty children in two obscure hamlets three-quarters of a mile northwest of Phu My. Alpha's 3rd Platoon, screening north of Gator and west of Tri Binh (4) to prevent rockets from being fired into Chu Lai, provoked a shootout with a group of Vietcong, killing two and wounding five others who slipped away. The platoon captured one SKS rifle and five grenades.

The morning of April 4 on LZ Minuteman started as business as usual. Just beyond the north gate of the perimeter was a large crater, made by the 16-inch shells of the Battleship New Jersey during Operation Russell Beach. The crater became a convenient dump for bombs and other ordnance brought in by peasants from the refugee camps. Periodically the munitions were destroyed by C-4 explosives. This morning the crater was about one-third full of mines, booby-traps, grenades, shells and mortar rounds all which were scheduled to be destroyed that day.

Refugee children always hung around the north gate to get treats from the soldiers. As a large Chinook helicopter landed with its load of cargo, it kicked up a storm of dust on the barren landing pad. The grunts instinctively hid in bunkers or covered their faces to keep the Chinooks from blowing another layer of red dirt on their bodies. The children by the gate, not having a bunker to hide in, jumped into the crater to avoid the whirlpool of dirt. One child triggered a Vietcong grenade which killed him instantly and caused other explosions. Another child suffered a broken arm and his left heel was blown off. Three others were lacerated with fragmentation wounds. The medics bandaged them up, administered blood expander and dusted them off to Chu Lai.

An anniversary for the 5th/46th Infantry Battalion was reached on April 4 which no soldier in the battalion knew about, nor would it have been helpful to know. It was one year prior that the battalion, under LTC David Lyon, established its tactical operations center (TOC) on LZ Gator and entered into the brigade's operational radio net, announcing it was ready to conduct offensive operations in Vietnam. By this day one year later the battalion had lost fifty-nine soldiers to combat action, six more to accidents and suffered four hundred and sixty-three wounded. Over fifty of the battalions wounded were multiple amputations. Most of the wounded came from mines and booby-traps on the coastal plains from Chu Lai to Quang Ngai City and the heaviest casualties came from the Batangan Peninsula and the Pinkville/My Lai area.

On April 6, Alpha moved by Chinook to LZ Minuteman to replace Bravo Company which returned to LZ Gator. Charlie spread its platoons out west of Gator in the rocket areas, to keep the VC from launching more 122mm rockets into Chu Lai. Delta had been picked up in the Phu My hamlets on April 4 to take up the defense of LZ Gator along with protection of the Seabee construction teams on Highway One. Echo's heavy 4.2-inch mortars remained on Hill 26 to support LZ Minuteman and the ARVN and Marine Cap teams which operated in the area.

On April 8, Echo's recon platoon prepared to set out from LZ Gator to patrol west of Binh Son to help prevent the enemy's movement of rice from the lowlands to the mountains in the west. As they began to walk off Gator, LTC Barnes pulled up in his jeep. Jumping out he bore into Sergeant John Forshag, the platoon sergeant, incensed that the platoon had no flak jackets or helmets. The Louisiana native explained dryly, "We're recon we don't wear that stuff ... too noisy." Barnes wasn't buying it and had the recon troops ground their gear and walk back to their company area to get their steel pots and flak jackets. He waited until the troops returned, to insure all had the extra equipment. Later in the field when the platoon's first re-supply bird brought water to them, the helmets and flak jackets were sent back in a red mail bag.

April 9 saw Charlie's patrols in the rocket pocket continuing to make contact with fleeing groups of VC. The wily enemy almost worked with impunity, generally knowing where the soldiers were, and keeping out of range of their small arms fire. While few VC were being bagged, the presence of the soldiers stopped the rocket attacks.

Rockets and Vietcong were not the only nemesis the soldiers faced in the rocket pocket and terrain around LZ Gator. One half of Charlie's 2nd platoon placed in an L-shaped night ambush to cover a trail at a point where it made a sharp turn. The grunts strung a cord across both sides of the "L" to signal each other about enemy movement. In the dark of night an "insurgent" ran across the ambush site and broke the cord, sending a moment of sheer terror into the grunts, waiting for a grenade to explode. The insurgent was a mongoose.

Alpha's PFC Robert Wolf, while on bunker line duty on LZ Gator one night, saw a shadowy "sapper" crawling through concertina wire towards his bunker. He was certain he was witnessing the start of a sapper attack and opened fire. The next morning he discovered the "sapper" was a dead mongoose.

Several months earlier, Alpha grunts were patrolling west of the rocket pocket in the foothills of the Annamite Mountains. After crossing a stream they reached the other side and paused to put on some dry socks. A couple of large monkeys, thought to be Orangutans, came up to two Alpha grunts. One grunt tossed the ape a can of peanut butter and another grunt, "Shorty", told his comrade to "Stop that shit or the whole jungle will be down here!" The bigger of the two Orangutans approached Shorty and just stared at him. Shorty told the animal to "Get the hell out of here or I'll butt stroke your ass!" The Orangutan didn't move so Shorty butt-stroked the animal with his M-16 after which the Orangutan attacked him. As one solder recalled, "The big Orangutan commenced to kicking Shorty's ass; we all had to help him. Boy that monkey sure skinned the bark off of Shorty's butt!"

Another hazard in the field were red fire ants. As one solder recalled, "The first guy may make it pass the ant hills. The second also, but the third guy would throw a sixty pound rucksack in the air screaming after rousting them!" Leaches, deadly centipedes and other creatures rounded out the hazards the soldiers endured in the bush.

Typically each of Charlie's platoons in the rocket pocket divided into two separate patrols during daylight hours, working in close proximity for mutual support. Nighttime saw the platoon split into two to three ambushes, with the ambush teams linking up at a new location in the morning. This was classic anti-guerilla work at the small unit level, not setting any patterns of movement for the enemy, and it paid some dividends.

One night Charlie's 2nd Platoon was informed by the battalion's S-2 that a sapper unit was in their area in the rocket pocket. The platoon could not dig in that night, the soil was too hard. After midnight the men heard movement to their front. Throwing hand grenades did not seem to abate the noise. The platoon moved out in the dead of night, led by their platoon leader and walked to a low-rising hill a short distance away. Once reaching the top, the platoon circled into a defense position. A short time later they heard grenades exploding at their previous position. Slight adjustments usually confused the enemy, which demonstrated little flexibility after meticulously planning its attacks.

Echo's Recon Platoon, now free of their flak jackets and helmets spotted four VC, one and one-half mile southwest of Gator. They killed one insurgent and wounded some others who escaped into the brush. The enemy they encountered appeared to be sappers heading towards LZ Gator. This day ended with the battalion killing twelve VC and NVA, most of them bagged on the Batangan.

The next day Alpha's 2nd Platoon found a stack of .50 caliber armor-piercing rounds, two-155mm artillery rounds, four-105mm artillery rounds, twenty-five 82mm mortar rounds and nine Bouncing Betty mines. Two days later Vietnamese brought in a five hundred pound bomb which had failed to detonate from an air strike.

On April 11, Bravo, now rested and refitted, lifted off LZ Gator on a combat air assault, landing four and one-half miles west of the Batangan and three and one-half miles north of the My Lai hamlets, to support the 2nd/6th ARVN Battalion in a major sweep of the area. This was the battalions' first joint operation with ARVN under "Geneva Park" to assist the ARVN in protecting the resettlement of refugees and seeking out remnants of Vietcong. The following day Bravo received small arms fire and M-79 rounds which wounded four soldiers, three with serious head wounds.

On April 13 Bravo, patrolling near the former FSB South, spotted twelve VC with backpacks and weapons who evaded. Later in the day they were hit by mortar fire which wounded four of their troops. AH-1G Cobra Gunships, "snakes", from the "Blue Ghost" F Troop/8th Cavalry, unloaded their firepower on suspected mortar positions but a sweep of the area revealed nothing.

By April 15, Bravo moved closer to the coast in the vicinity of the An Thinh hamlets, searching for remnants of the 48th Local Force VC Battalion, which intelligence reports indicated had now gathered in the area at an estimated strength of three hundred and sixty-five after being reinforced by the NVA. Bravo's 1st Platoon ran into a group of ten to twelve VC who quickly ran, but one female VC was killed. A sweep of the area revealed trenches, punji pits and stocks of medical supplies. Another dead Vietcong was found with two grenades and notebooks. Vietnamese National Police from Binh Son and a Provisional Reconnaissance Unit (the tough PRU from Quang Ngai) joined Bravo in a cordon and search of An Thinh (2). LTC Barnes C&C Huey picked up nine VC suspects, six were taken to brigade headquarters at LZ Bayonet and three others, two with malaria and one with a gunshot wound, were taken to Chu Lai hospitals.

In the afternoon, a resupply Huey returning from LZ Minuteman spotted five Vietcong near Tam Hoi (1), killing all five. Barnes' C&C went out to take a look and drew more fire. Blue Ghost gunships were called in for extra firepower and an element of Delta was lifted off Gator to search the area. The grunts found nine 82mm mortar rounds, documents, medical supplies and clothing. The war notwithstanding, Barnes staff on LZ Gator also had to manage affairs as though they were a stateside unit. On the 15th, forty officers and senior NCO's were required to complete a twelve-hour block of instruction on "Material Readiness", covering areas such as weapons, vehicles, generators, communications equipment and chemical items. While the enemy maneuvered their way around the battalion's AO, the battalion also had to prepare for an upcoming stateside type Inspector General (IG) inspection of equipment, records management and maintenance.

Delta on LZ Gator's perimeter sent out two eight-man ambushes three hundred and fifty to five hundred yards beyond the defensive wire during the night. Moonlight was low at this time of the month and the extra precaution was needed until the moonlight would return to at least thirty percent visibility. The battalion closed the day with thirteen VC and NVA killed.

On the morning of April 16, two small culvert bridges on Highway One north and south of Binh Son, were attacked. These smaller bridges were guarded by PF militia. The northern bridge, near Phuoc Loc (2) was destroyed after the VC hit a PF platoon with twenty B-40 Rockets, mortars and grenades. Two PF were killed and two wounded. The southern culvert bridge, near Long Hoi (1) was also guarded by a platoon of PF and hit with rocket, mortar and small arms fire but the Popular Force unit held the bridge. One PF and one VC were wounded in the attack.

Five hours later the balance of the PF Company with their advisors pursued the enemy and made contact with a Vietcong company two miles due east of the attack, near Phuc Tho (2). Contact with the enemy was made and broken twice during the fight, but when it was finished one PF and eight VC were killed. The PF's captured a B-40 Rocket launcher, ten B-40 rounds, an AK-47 with twenty magazines, three-TNT mines, three-VC constructed claymore mines, three Bouncing Betty's mines, ten Beer Can-type booby traps, VC clothing, two NVA uniforms, medical supplies, cooking utensils, two hundred pounds of rice and many fuses and blasting caps.

 Bravo, still operating with the ARVN northwest of the Batangan, received heavy small arms and mortar fire in the late afternoon, just north of Provincial Road 523 near the hamlet of Phu Nhieu (1). Close-in air strikes were called and one grunt was wounded by the friendly fire. While under enemy fire and the explosions of the air strike, SFC Charles Gallagher rushed to the wounded soldier who was exposed and carried him out of the line of fire. In so doing he was also wounded. He ignored his wound while tending to the soldier until he was dusted off. Gallagher was awarded a Bronze Star for valor. After the artillery and air strikes, Bravo found two hooch's, each containing a fighting bunker. One secondary explosion during the strikes indicated an ammo cache had also been hit but the Vietcong melted away.

 Intelligence reports indicated a buildup of Vietcong supplied with heavy weapons and rockets were planning to attack the Chu Lai air strip, the village of Nuoc Mau outside the gate of LZ Gator and Binh Son. During the March lull in action, the VC were re-supplied and reinforced by the NVA. The enemy was preparing to regain the initiative with heavy attacks. West of Quang Ngai some PRU forces, regarded by the Americans as the "bad asses" of the Vietnamese regional forces and a unit not to be trifled with, had set out a series of squad-size ambushes in the evening. But at 8:50PM so many VC walked pass their ambush sites they did not open fire for fear of being annihilated. Artillery was called in on the moving formations. The next day, ten of the VC were captured along with grenades and AK-47 ammunition.

 Alpha on LZ Minuteman received small arms and mortar fire that evening which wounded two of its soldiers. During the attack SP/4 Hector Rodriquez realized the lights on the LZ provided the VC with excellent aiming points to "walk" the mortars in. He ran through the enemy fire to turn the generators off which blacked out the LZ. Rodriquez was awarded an Army Commendation Medal with V device for valor.

 The next morning the 1st Platoon of Alpha, patrolling east of Minuteman walked into an ambush, wounding one solder and two PF militiamen. All three remained in the field as "walking wounded". Twenty minutes later contact was again made by Alpha's 1st and 2nd

Platoons, which wounded another grunt. LTC Barnes Command & Control helicopter picked him up. At 10:45AM, two of Bravo's grunts tripped a home-made mine which killed one soldier, PFC Wayne Randall. PFC Randall was age twenty and single from Passumpsic, Vermont. The other soldier was dusted off by a resupply Huey.

By early evening, Bravo called another dustoff for a VC suspect with a head wound and thirty minutes later called still another for one of its own soldiers who suffered a heart attack. At 7:00PM, Alpha's CO, Captain Ben Anderson, making a visual reconnaissance from a Huey near Tan Duc, was hit by small arms fire wounding him in the buttocks. The Huey returned fire, wounded the attacker and swooped down to capture him along with his carbine and two grenades. Anderson returned to Minuteman to get his wound dressed and plan for the next day's activities. It was just another day in an infantry company commander's life.

At 10:10PM, another utility Huey helicopter spotted a Vietcong soldier between Highway One and the Batangan who dropped his equipment and ran at the sound of the bird. The Huey continued on as if he was leaving the area but returned to discover the VC recovering his gear. The insurgent was cut down by a door gunner and the Huey picked up his equipment. Evening "Gook-Hunting" continued to be lucrative for choppers supporting the 5th/46th.

On the morning of April 18 Bravo, as it patrolled west of the refugee camps on the Batangan, found tunnels containing rice, uniforms and mortar rounds. Late that evening while trying to coax the enemy out of a tunnel, a Kit Carson Scout was shot in the hand and First Lieutenant Lawrence Russell was shot in the neck. That stopped the negotiations and two VC were killed in the tunnel. Two hours later Bravo received fire from another tunnel which wounded three more soldiers. One soldier, SP/4 Larry Bleything suffered a head wound. The three wounded were dusted off quickly but Bleything, age nineteen and single from Ottumwa, Iowa was dead on arrival at the 312th Evacuation Hospital. Bravo blew the tunnel in place and retrieved four dead Vietcong.

Early the next day Echo's Recon Platoon was brought out by Huey to support Bravo Company. They were dropped in a small grassy area but the pilots would not land, fearful their helicopter struts might touch off some mines. The troops had to jump off the skids six to eight feet up and by so doing, landed in two feet of mud. This left the grunts stuck like poles in drying cement. With full field gear on, each soldier had to lie on his back and pull each leg out before he could free himself on top of the marsh and carefully walk away.

The undermanned platoon of recon troops was ordered by LTC Barnes to attack up a hill where a possible Vietcong company was entrenched. Barnes, flying overhead, stuttered to the platoon leader, "goo-goo good luck!" Barnes ordered CS gas to be dropped on the hilltop to help make up for the disadvantage of a undermanned platoon attacking up hill against a potential company of VC, but the CS required the recon soldiers to don gas masks in one hundred degree heat while working their way to the top. Fortunately the recon troops found nothing on the hilltop, but no Hueys were available to pick them up. Having left their rucksacks behind for the assault they also had little water left. They were finally pulled out late that night.

Retribution

Intelligence reports indicated sixty NVA sappers from the 60th NVA Battalion had moved down from Quang Tin province and were now located west of LZ Gator near the mountains. One sapper squad was now operating with local VC, staying at Binh Yen (2), two and one-half miles southwest of Gator. The sapper squad had been observing Gator and was predicted to attack the Landing Zone, preceded by a mortar attack sometime mid to late April. LTC Barnes set about reorganizing and reconstructing LZ Gator. New concertina wire was laid on the perimeter and several bunkers rebuilt. Under LTC Richardson's direction, offices for the battalion commander, executive officer and battalion Sergeant Major were separated, to avoid a mortar round wiping out the entire senior staff. Barnes ordered one building constructed to house all three senior leaders so they could be together, to be more "Conducive to proper coordination and management principles."

LTC Barnes' staff repeatedly cautioned their new commander that Gator was ripe for another assault. His sleeping bunker was isolated from the rest of the battalion staff as Richardson had desired but the "civilians" who were working daily inside LZ Gator, part of the "winning hearts and minds" campaign by providing local employment, surely had his bunker pinpointed. Barnes would not move his bunker to the more protected area used by his staff.

LTC Barnes was fortunate to have taken command of the 5th/46th Battalion at near full strength. Unlike the battalion that

Richardson inherited, which was depleted in strength from the exhausting Task Force Cooksey operations in the Tien Phouc and Hiep Duc regions in late summer of 1968, the battalion had recovered its numbers considerably once it returned to working off LZ Gator, despite its losses in Russell Beach.

On April 19, the battalion had thirty-seven of its authorized strength of forty-five officers and warrant officers. Its assigned enlisted strength was eight hundred and seventy-five and the battalion had eight hundred and thirty-three present for duty, a high ninety-five percent of its authorized strength, unusually high for most infantry battalions. But the problem of "Ghosting" and "Shaming" continued, especially when a company was assigned to the Batangan. The strength of soldiers in the field did not reflect the overall assigned numbers of soldiers in the battalion. Soldiers who were convalescing in hospitals or on well-deserved R&R, impacted the strength of field units as well.

Late on April 20, portions of the 2nd and 3rd Platoons of H Troop, 17th Cav entered the rocket pocket area northwest of Gator to replace Charlie's soldiers with the same mission, keeping the rockets from being fired into Chu Lai. Several tracks of the Cav met up with Charlie's 2nd Platoon one-half mile north of Phuoc Binh Toy (1). Charlie's 2nd Platoon leader, 1LT David Taylor thought it odd that armored personnel carriers, "tracks", would be assigned to such a mission. The terrain limited and channeled the track's forward movement. Their presence also deprived them the advantage of silent movement that Taylor's soldiers had.

That night the tracks circled into a 360-degree defensive position with Taylor's troops hunkered inside the circle on the ground. An AC-130 Gunship ("Puff the Magic Dragon", "Snoopy" or "Shadow") flying south of their location began spitting out its deadly fire in a "recon by fire" mission over a "Free-Fire Zone" (no friendly forces or villagers identified in the area). Its second burst of fire came close to Taylor's position and the tail end of its mini-gun burst came across the small perimeter. Taylor rolled off his poncho liner to grab a flare just as a round hit where he lay. It was nothing short of a miracle that none of his grunts on the open ground were hit.

One round from the Gunship entered the opened top of a track, ricocheting and wounding a soldier inside. Taylor popped a flare, hoping the AC-130 would veer off or its next burst of fire would wipe them out. Fortunately the bird moved away, the pilot not sure if the flare was from

VC or friendly soldiers. PFC Harold Stone from H Troop was wounded in the track and dusted off at 3:20AM.

That same evening on the Batangan Peninsula, Alpha's roving patrol spotted twenty lights and heard Vietcong with microphones, calling for refugees to surrender to the VC. Echo's 4.2-inch mortars on Hill 26 fired on the noise, which silenced the nighttime recruiting campaign.

On the morning of April 22 Charlie Company was lifted off by Chinook to the brigade's stand-down area on the Chu Lai beach, before its rotation to the Batangan. Shortly after Charlie exited the Rocket Pocket one of the tracks of H Troop, that was left to continue the rocket mission, hit a mine. At 3:30AM on April 23, "Shadow 47", the same AC-130 gunship which had almost wiped out Charlie's 2nd Platoon flew a mission three miles southeast of Binh Son and hit pay dirt. Its recon by fire struck a VC position with cached ammunition, the secondary explosions, six in all, rose one hundred feet into the air.

April 25 saw Bravo's 3rd and 4th Platoons supporting the ARVN as a blocking force by the Ham Giang River just west of Van Thien (2). The ARVN had been contributing to the pacification effort and recovered the bodies of twenty-eight VC they killed the day before. Bravo's platoons spotted three VC crossing a small foot bridge and took them out, capturing two AK-47's, ammo and grenades. Bravo's 1st and 2nd Platoons screened the area further north with tracks of the 2nd Platoon, H Troop, 17th Cav.

While near the hamlet of Liem Quang (1) northwest of the Batangan, Bravo's platoons were hit with heavy fire from a bunkered position in the hamlet. One grunt was wounded on the open ground and pinned down. PFC Donald Cook ran through enemy fire to drag him to cover, earning a Bronze Star. Sergeant Marion Brunson led a team with SP/4's Victor Justiniano and Steven Sumner in a charge to take out the enemy position and killed three Vietcong. Brunson was awarded a Bronze Star and Justiniano and Brunson received Army Commendation Medals with Valor devices. Bravo's soldiers also captured three VC in the hamlet. Bravo's total for the day was six VC killed and three captured, with three of its own soldiers wounded. The helicopter gunship's that supported Bravo killed another VC.

By day's end, Charlie Company replaced Alpha on LZ Minuteman. Alpha's 3rd platoon was sent to reinforce Bravo while the rest of the company went to Chu Lai for a standdown. Bravo continued to support elements of the 3rd Battalion, 6th ARVN Regiment as they swept the area west of the Batangan in support of rice denial operations during the spring harvest. Delta secured LZ Gator and other positions along Highway One. Echo's recon platoon patrolled the area around Dong Xuan (2) on the western edge of the Batangan.

Late in the evening of April 26, the recon platoon set up a night position in abandoned stucco hooch on the southern edge of Dong Xuan (3). Dong Xuan was infamous for VC activity and the recon troops thought they might bag some in the Ville. All was well but the platoon's radio operator (RTO), responsible for providing situation reports (SitRep's) to the battalion's TOC on Gator, fell asleep. For one and one-half hours the TOC tried to reach its recon platoon. LTC Barnes ordered artillery to be fired around their position, thinking they were under attack. Flare ships and gunships were summoned from LZ Bayonet until contact was finally established with the recon unit.

The next day Barnes flew out to the recon position and held an inquisition. The quick thinking RTO who fell asleep had been carrying a bad radio handset in his pack and placed it on the radio, claiming it was the culprit for non-communications with the TOC. Barnes took the handset with him to have it checked out by his commo section, which they confirmed had been shorted out. The RTO dodged a court martial and never fell asleep again during his watch.

During his fly time around the Batangan and his visit to Bravo and the recon troops, Barnes C&C Huey spotted four VC evading in Liem Quang (1). His door gunner opened up and killed two of the insurgents. The bird landed and captured another. During the snatch shrapnel from ground fire wounded the crew chief. At 3:15PM LTC Barnes chopper spotted three more VC sitting on a rice paddy dike, one wearing a green uniform and two in black pajamas. They had been carrying seven sandbag-style backpacks. Barnes' door gunners opened up and killed two of the enemy.

Barnes, still not trusting his maverick reconnaissance platoon, placed them under the control of Bravo Company, in part because he was still not buying the "defective radio" story. The recon grunts set up a night position but they were not where they thought they were. With the hazard of navigating in the flat rice paddy terrain with few terrain features to recognize, they called in the wrong coordinates.

Bravo, located nearby, had plotted recon's position as a likely area of enemy approach to their own position, and called in a white phosphorus ("Willie Pete") round to mark preplanned defensive fires. Bravo was content the recon troops were somewhere else. As a result the recon soldiers were showered with white phosphorus. This required recon's Sergeant John Forshag to bring in a dustoff at 9:15PM by placing his strobe light inside a helmet held over his head, to keep the enemy from spotting it. The dustoff could see the strobe light blinking from up in the air and hopefully the Vietcong could not. Two recon soldiers with phosphorus burns were picked up.

April 28 saw Bravo's 2nd Platoon pay a heavy price for water. While walking down a trail to a stream to fill their canteens, a soldier tripped a pressure release device wired to an 82mm mortar round. Eight soldiers were wounded. The casualty list spoke volumes for the treachery of the area and the heavy price to be paid when ignoring a key edict of counter-guerilla operations: "Stay off the trails".

(MFW = Multiple Fragment Wound)
PFC Pleasant, MFW, both legs, right arm, partial amputation of leg
SP4 Hgene, MFW both legs, left shoulder and chest
PFC Maysonett, MFW both legs, left arm
PFC Decker, MFW both legs
PFC Mills, MFW right arm, left leg
SGT Bryant, MFW both legs
PFC Gomez, MFW chest, right thigh and face
PFC Parson, MFW both arms, both legs, chest and abdomen

As April came to an end, General Creighton Abrams, who replaced General William Westmoreland as MACV Commander, made it increasingly clear to all US forces in South Vietnam he wanted to move away from "the war of the big battalions." Large scale operations were becoming more infrequent, owing to the heavy losses of the NVA/VC from TET 68. Abrams wanted more platoon and squad-size patrols, with company-size operations only taking place when intelligence reports indicated there may be an NVA Regiment in the area. Moreover, Abrams wanted to "take the night away from the enemy" not only with static ambushes but night patrols as well.

The 5th/46th Infantry Battalion took up the challenge in the rocket pockets and throughout the Piedmont area. The roving night patrols made sense, except on the Batangan Peninsula. Daytime patrols there were hazardous enough, night patrols were unthinkable. "Night patrols" on the Batangan quickly morphed into static ambushes. In some cases where team leadership was not strong the "Ambushes" were set up just beyond Minuteman's perimeter.

At 9:30AM on April 30, Charlie Company's Sgt. John Charnisky stepped on a mine rigged to a 105mm Howitzer round. The explosion sheared off both his legs and sent additional fragmentation wounds into his left hand and face. The following day, May 1, two platoons from Charlie set out with a Chieu Hoi defector, some PF soldiers and an interpreter to allow the Chieu Hoi to lead them to a cache of ammunition and several VC comrades he said he could talk into surrendering.

The patrol walked up a low hill covered by hedgerows and small scrub brushes near An Hai (1). Staff Sergeant Benjamin Green was acting platoon leader of the 2nd Platoon while its platoon leader was in the hospital with malaria. Green and his RTO, PFC Jim Starck, were about twelve men back from the point. The humid coastal air hung heavy over the patrol, until it was violently interrupted by a large explosion and the instant screams of men in pain. Starck expected small arms fire to open up, sure that they were caught in an ambush, but no enemy fire came. He moved forward to see his comrade PFC John Lucibello lying in agonizing pain, his right leg sheared off by a large piece of shrapnel. Others were lying by Lucibello's side. Starck saw a dazed look on Lucibello's face and feared he was going into shock. He offered him some "Goofy-Grape" Kool Aid from his canteen, trying to keep him calm.

SSG Green grabbed the radio handset off Starck's back and called for dustoff's. The Hueys in the area quickly came in but the crater made by the explosion made it hard for a chopper to set down. As the casualties were patched and prepared for evacuation the uninjured grunts faced outward, waiting for an attack to come. SSG Green stepped off the path to make room for transport of the injured when a large blast sent Starck flying into the air, tossing him on a small bush, his face staring at a giant centipede on a branch in front of his face.

Starck recovered and screamed to Green to "Get the wounded on the chopper!" He yelled a second time, angry that Green just sat on the ground acting like he couldn't hear. Starck shouted again asking for some help with Lucibello. Green replied calmly and clearly, "I can't walk, my feet are gone." Starck saw his platoon sergeants feet were gone just above the ankles with nothing left but bloody and mangled flesh. Greens legs would be amputated just below the knees in the hospital. Sergeant Robert Hill, a squad leader also lost his left leg. One of the Huey door gunners jumped out to help get the wounded on board before more mines exploded.

Throughout the melee the 2nd Platoon's medic, PFC Everett Rowles, moved among the wounded despite the mine infested terrain, patching up bodies, stemming the bleeding from traumatic amputations, and keeping the men alive before dustoff arrived. He was nominated for a Silver Star and two weeks later was requested to fly in from LZ Minuteman. Much of his platoon had dysentery and he elected instead to go on a patrol with the men still fit to walk. The general scheduled to give him the award was not pleased and his decoration was downgraded to a Bronze Star for valor.

After forty-five minutes all wounded were dusted off and control was reestablished. Thirteen Charlie Company soldiers were wounded from command-detonated and pressure-release mines, along with two PF soldiers and one interpreter. SP/4's Peter Potenza and Dan Peterson were awarded Army Commendation Medals with valor devices for their steadfastness in the carnage. The casualty list reflected another day of horror on the Batangan:

(MFW = MULTIPLE FRAGMENT WOUNDS)
Sgt. Hougard, MFW both legs, right arm, right foot
SSG Green, traumatic amputation, both legs below knees
SP/4 Gallegos, MFW neck and abdomen
SSG Alan Nascimento, FW face
PFC Starck, MFW both thighs and right leg
SP/4 Lucero, FW left thigh
Sgt Hill, MFW both legs, left hand, amputation left leg
PFC Napier, FW right arm
PFC Hernandez, MFW chest, right shoulder and face
PFC Foster, FW left leg
PFC Lucibello, MFW left leg, amputation of right leg
PFC Delgado, FW left knee
SP/4 Eaves, MFW face and left arm

The remaining soldiers regrouped farther down the trail, but had to return to the scene of carnage to recover the weapons dropped by the wounded soldiers. As PFC Starck moved up the trail with the others he felt a sharp pain from shrapnel to his leg and butt, unfelt before because of the adrenaline running through his system. Starck saw two more unexploded artillery rounds lying in plain view on the trail. Four M-16's were collected and the group backed away from the site. Later Starck was sent to the hospital with shrapnel throughout his lower legs. The Batangan had been a constant curse to him. A few days earlier while filling sandbags on LZ Minuteman he struck something with his entrenching tool. Thinking it was a rock he pounded away with his entrenching tool until he could loosen it from the soil. The "Rock" was a Bouncing Betty Mine with its detonator still in place.

That very same day the battalions S-5 Civil affairs officer went to LZ Dottie to pay for explosives that were turned in by peasants under the VIP program. The refuse of war was never ending. The collection included one hundred and eight small mines, one hundred and forty-eight grenades, eighty-four M-79 grenade launcher rounds, fifty-eight 105mm Howitzer rounds, six 155mm Howitzer rounds, twenty-four blocks of C-4 explosive, sixty-four 60mm mortar rounds, two 82mm mortar rounds, ten veritable timing fuses, two RPG rounds and ten primers for 105mm artillery rounds.

At 6:55AM the following morning, Sergeant Larry Kigar of Charlie Company, a squad leader, patrolled his section of the Minuteman perimeter as he did each morning. Walking ten feet inside the perimeter between his assigned bunkers, he stepped on an old Bouncing Betty mine that had been missed in the construction of the LZ. Although old and deteriorated, the mine exploded, hitting Kigar in his mid-section. Kigar had no reason to wear a flak jacket since he was inside the wire. Kigar died on the dustoff flying him to Chu Lai. Two others in his squad were wounded. Larry Kiger was age nineteen and single, from Baring, Missouri.

On May 2, Alpha Company patrolled the area west of the Batangan in the vicinity of the former FSB South, near the Trung Son hamlets. It found tunnels, blood trails and some Vietcong, killing two and capturing one. The following morning Alpha killed another three VC. Early that evening it air assaulted by Huey to the south of Pinkville near My Khe (2). Alpha passed through the sub-hamlet and moved in a column through a large and dry rice paddy containing an irrigation ditch. A tree line interrupted with several clumps of bamboo, stood to the left of the column as Alpha's grunts humped their heavy loads. The 3rd platoon was the closest to the line of bamboo.

In an instant the company came under heavy automatic weapons fire from the tree line. The company was totally exposed in the open, and took cover as best as possible, some behind dikes and some in the irrigation ditch. The 3rd Platoon got the order to assault the tree line. Machine gunner Jerry Karr started over the lip of the irrigation ditch when he saw three single rounds hit the ground in front of him, each rapidly getting closer, coming straight for him. He slid back into the ditch before getting hit.

Karr started over a second time and someone yelled, "Grenade!" The grenade exploded and two men in front of him were hit. One screamed "I'm blind, I'm blind" but Karr kept running forward with his squad. Karr's squad leader, Sergeant Roy "Arizona" Arnold led the charge and rushed toward a clump of bamboo to their right front where there was no enemy fire, hoping to get into the brush and flank the enemy. As Arnold approached the underbrush, a group of NVA opened fire on him, hitting him six times, the automatic weapons fire zipping up his body, starting at his right thigh above the knee with the last round entering the left shoulder.

During the firefight Alpha's commander, Captain Ben Anderson led an assault on one position, killing an NVA soldier. He then led the assault on another position but the assault was turned back by heavy fire. They were, however, able to suppress the automatic weapons fire coming from concealed positions. Anderson then realized Arnold was hit, and saw him lying in the open. Not realizing he was already dead, Anderson ran out under fire with two others and dragged the body back to cover, even though his bullet riddled body told them he was gone. Roy Arnold was age twenty-one and married, from Holden, Missouri.

A Chicom grenade dropped a few feet near the command group where the three radio operators hunkered down against a low dike, with bullets from AK-47's zinging overhead. One of the RTO's, PFC Tim O'Brien, thought the grenade carried a rather "delicate explosion" but it caused some casualties nonetheless. Under the heavy automatic weapons fire he turned to PFC Wayne "Water Buffalo" Strieff, already a veteran in the company at age nineteen, and asked, "How the hell do they miss?" Strieff grinned, "They ain't aiming!" Strieff clamped his helmet tighter around his head.

When the fight was over Karr and James "The Kid" Rhode were the only soldiers still standing in the 3rd Squad of the 3rd Platoon of Alpha Company. Arnold was dead and the rest wounded. Karr had been charmed in the action. He examined his equipment and found two bullet holes in his rucksack and one in his poncho liner. One bullet had hit a canteen, entered the pack, split a can of C-ration applesauce and exited through another canteen. Karr and "the kid" were transferred to another squad.

For his actions leading his company, Anderson would be awarded his second Silver Star. Alpha suffered one killed and five wounded. They killed three of the enemy and captured one, along with some ammunition, rifles and grenades. The battalion's total wounded for the day included three soldiers from Bravo Company who were manning the bunker line on LZ Gator. Munitions of war do not recognize "friendly soldiers" versus the enemy. Bravo's three grunts were wounded by an explosion while burning grass beyond the perimeter.

Late evening the recon platoon was attached to Alpha to bolster its strength. The recon grunts set up an ambush site one-half mile south of Alpha's position and hit approximately six Vietcong at 10:20PM, slugging it out with rifle fire and grenades. During the night the men of Alpha could hear taunts from nearby VC & NVA regulars. The first and only time during his tour, Karr heard one taunt in English, "GI sucks dick!" The grunts yelled back profanities followed by rounds from their M-79 grenade launchers. In the morning no bodies were found either by Alpha or the recon platoon.

One company of the 3rd/6th ARVN Regiment joined Alpha in the morning in a coordinated effort to sweep east towards the coast near My Khe (2). Alpha Company led the column with the Echo Recon Platoon in the middle and the ARVN bringing up the rear. By dusk on May 4, Alpha came to a small bridge across a narrow tributary. Alpha started taking small arms fire. The recon soldiers turned to see the ARVN behind them bug out. Alpha and the recon troops moved by leaps and bounds, with machine gun fire covering their coordinated movement across the bridge. Jerry Karr from the 3rd Platoon was the lead gunner. His fellow grunts dropped their extra M-60 ammo and two extra barrels by his gun position as they bounded pass him running for the bridge. Karr went through three gun barrels providing the covering fire, switching them quickly when they became too hot to use.

Alpha's troops moved to the left into the remnants of a hamlet while the recon platoon moved to the right. During the intense assault, one sergeant tossed a grenade in a hooch and placed his back to the outside wall, getting peppered with shrapnel in the process. He forgot that grass-thatched hooch's are not masonry.

As darkness approached the recon platoon heard mortars dropping on Alpha's soldiers while recon maneuvered farther to the right across a swampy area of thigh-high water and waist-high grass. Recon slept wet that night, with some mortar rounds coming its way. Before dark Alpha's First Sergeant was hit with an M-79 round and the soldiers blamed it on the recon troops. But recon was out of range of an M-79, proving the errant round came from an Alpha soldier.

The following morning the recon platoon was scheduled to be picked up for a standdown in Chu Lai. While waiting for the choppers they noticed movement to their west in the same direction they had received mortar fire the previous night. One of their snipers saw a moving figure through his modified M-14 sniper scope. He took a shot. Sgt John Forshag saw another figure and took a second shot. A short time later a women came across a dry rice paddy pushing an old man in a wheelbarrow. He had been shot in the abdomen and portions of his intestines were protruding. The women had also been shot just inside her armpit and there was a bullet hole along the side of her breast. The recon soldiers patched them up, called in a dustoff and sent them in to a hospital at Chu Lai. Shortly after, they got their own ride back to Chu Lai for four days of rest and some sanity on the beach. The ARVN had bugged out on them, they had been under constant enemy fire, and it was difficult to distinguish between an enemy with weapons and the enemy without. They were tired, dirty and disgusted with the whole affair.

May 6 saw Alpha picked up by chopper and air assaulted three miles northwest of Pinkville and two miles east of Highway One searching for a Vietcong company reported to be in the area. Charlie Company on LZ Minuteman had to call a dustoff for two Vietnamese children burned by a white phosphorus round they were bringing in for a VIP payment. The ARVN in the area were contributing to protecting the rice harvest effort and showing some aggressiveness, but it would always be at the time and place of their own choosing, when conditions were "right". There was no rush for these soldiers who defended their native land as long as the 5th/46th Infantry Battalion was available to do the "Heavy lifting."hg Acting on an informant's tip, one ARVN platoon raided Phu My (1) north of Pinkville the morning of May 6 and killed four Vietcong.

Dispositions for the battalion at this point showed Charlie working the Batangan Peninsula, Alpha patrolling west of the peninsula in conjunction with the ARVN and Delta coming under Operational Control of the 1st/52nd Battalion minus one squad, which was detailed to live with the villagers of Tri Binh (1), north of LZ Gator. The hamlet was pro-government and the VC had threatened to attack it.

Bravo Company defended LZ Gator and, like all the line companies on bunker line duty, ran the risk of getting too soft back in a relatively "safe haven". Some field grunts gravitated to the soldiers who never went to the field. Marijuana was used, if not in the open, on a common basis at night. The Black Power movement had reached some of the support troops on Gator, which made it uncomfortable for black soldiers coming in from the field. They were cajoled by the "soul brothers" who had rear jobs on Gator to separate from the whites when they were not out in the bush. Barnes, in an attempt to keep the problem under control, had several Military Police from LZ Bayonet reside on LZ Gator, allegedly for main gate security but also to police the growing drug and Black Power issues. Two Bravo soldiers were dusted off at 9:15PM on May 7 for "drug (marijuana) intoxication".

In conjunction with the Pacification Phase IV of Operation Russell Beach, plans were made for Regional Force (RF) Company #228 to occupy LZ Minuteman and provide security for the refugee camps in the area, in conjunction with Charlie Company. The goal was for the RF Company to be eventually weaned off American support and hold Minuteman themselves.

Alpha settled in their night defensive position the evening of May 8, as Sgt. Thomas Markunas talked to Jerry Karr about his wife being pregnant with their first child. Markunas couldn't wait to get home. SP/4 Merricks was holding a lock of hair wrapped with a ribbon he received in a letter. He rolled it in his fingers and placed it under his nose and smiled. Markunas asked him, "What the hell is that. Pubic hair or something?" Merricks just smiled. Karr and Markunas pulled guard until midnight then settled in to get a couple hours of sleep.

On May 9 at 2:00AM, Alpha moved out to surround Chau Binh (1), for a cordon and search at first light. It was reported the VC had come out of the mountains to visit their families in the hamlet. After an hour of movement Alpha, moving in a column by platoon, came to a terraced series of rice paddies. When the last platoon entered the lowest terrace, one soldier stepped on a landmine and the explosion claimed a leg. The nighttime movement stopped until a dustoff could pick him up. Now Alpha's presence was known to the enemy and it started receiving small-arms fire from the hamlet. Illumination rounds were called and Alpha's grunts killed three insurgents and captured three more in the melee.

Just before sunrise Alpha arrived at the hamlet's edge. The 3rd Platoon swept through, moving from east to west, staying off the main trails and moving as best as possible on line, but they were interrupted by bushes and hedgerows. Three 3rd Platoon soldiers moved to the left while Sgt Markunas and SP/4 Merricks moved to the right on another small path. They had not moved far when a large explosion shattered the air. The blasts' concussion knocked the three grunts on the left path to the ground. The three soldiers regained their senses and ran in the direction of Markunas and Merricks, watching palm leaves, branches and other foliage continue to fall to the ground from the explosion.

Other soldiers were closer to Markunas and Merricks and screamed to the three to "Back out, back out!" The three re-established the east side of the cordon. Other soldiers moved to the blast site and picked up what was left of Markunas and Merricks. Merricks had stepped on a pressure-release device connected to a 105mm Howitzer round. Markunas' remains were five to six feet above the ground in foliage. His fellow grunts pulled his body parts down, his head, torso, one arm and a strip of leg with a boot attached to it. One dog tag was in his boot. There wasn't much left of Merricks either. Merricks was black and Markunas white, but each required a careful identification of the skin to decide which body part belonged to whom.

A Huey was called in to pick up the remains. No urgent dustoff required this time, just a helicopter hovering, its struts a few feet off the ground to not set off more mines, while the soldier's remains were brought over on a two foot by four foot piece of board. The grunts carrying the body parts noticed the Huey's door gunner was obviously a "Fucking new guy" an "FNG", as his arms and face were sunburned. FNG's stood out wherever and whenever they were found. The door gunner saw the remains arrive at his side and vomited over his machine gun. The body parts were loaded into one bag and the bird took off. Sgt. Thomas Markunas, age twenty-one and married, father of a child he would never see, was from New York City and SP/4 Alvin Merricks, twenty-three and single was from Orlando, Florida. Both, polar opposites in temperament and backgrounds, answered their final roll call together.

Another Alpha platoon had taken a prisoner that was leaving the hamlet in the dark as the company approached it. In a few minutes they encountered another small group of enemy departing the hamlet which escaped into a rice paddy. Shortly after, the platoon observed still more enemy leaving and opened fire, finding an enemy rucksack that had been dropped. After the explosion killing Markunas and Merricks, the leader of the platoon who carried a shotgun, hit his prisoner so hard the stock of the shotgun broke completely from the gun. Sitting next to him was a soldier who was a former policeman, nicknamed "The Cop", who was troubled by the brutality he was trained not to do as a police officer. The platoon leader, snarled, "Mind your own business cop!" The prisoner was loaded on a Huey to take in for questioning.

Chau Binh (1) was infested with mines and Alpha wanted no more of it. They condemned the hamlet to die. The company backed out and called in an air strike on the cluster of hooch's sitting in the middle of nowhere. The bombs caused three or four secondary explosions from cached enemy ammunition. Napalm was also used. As the last napalm strike was made by an F-4 Phantom, one Alpha soldier saw a defiant enemy solder fire his AK-47 at the approaching F-4, just as napalm landed on top of him. Alpha then moved southwest, sullen they had lost two more good soldiers. The ARVN operating with them also lost two soldiers and eight ARVN were wounded from nearby fighting. Alpha accounted for three VC killed and three captured while the ARVN bagged eight killed and eight captured.

The morning of May 10 began with the brigade commander visiting LZ Gator and presenting the battalion with the brigades "Best Mess Hall" award for April. Colonel Tully was rotating out of Brigade Command and LTC Barnes hosted a farewell party. Captain Jim Woodworth, Headquarters Company Commander, recalled that LTC Barnes was in good spirits that night. After the brigade staff left LZ Gator he continued to pour drinks for his battalion staff, preferring a "Rusty Nail" for himself and inviting his officers to try it. Woodworth remembered, "Barnes had been with us for about six weeks and it was all work with not much interaction with the rest of us. I found it a very pleasant change and felt he was human after all".

In the field the combat mission continued and the day ended when a Charlie grunt stepped on a Bouncing Betty mine near a hedgerow just north of LZ Minuteman. PFC Sam L. Eggert detonated the mine and was killed. Eggert was age 20 and single from Tucumcari,

New Mexico. SP/4 Steven Trapp caught some metal fragments in the chest, but survived.

As mid-May approached, Alpha Company continued its operations west of the Batangan working with the ARVN to locate and destroy VC units by patrols, ambushes and raids. Delta, now released from the 1st/52nd Battalion, fanned out over the rocket areas west of Gator with one squad still protecting Tri Binh (1). Charlie remained on Minuteman and prepared to relinquish control to the PF Company which now manned the bunker line. Bravo Company, along with Gator's support troops, manned the bunkers on the LZ. Ominous warnings from intelligence reports over recent weeks continued to point to impending attacks on static targets in the battalion's area of operations. The warnings would now be proven out with dire consequences.

As evening closed in on LZ Gator on May 11, additional reaction forces were formed on the firebase in response to reports that this night, until 3:00AM next morning, would be "an extremely critical period" because of a "possible nationwide offensive." The bunker line on Gator began with Bunker #1, which overlooked the main gate joining the dirt road which began from the hamlet of Nuoc Mau and Highway One to the LZ. The bunker sequence (#2, #3, etc) followed its way west along the southern end of the perimeter heading up along the western side of Gator, moving on to the northern edge, where the hamlet of Tri Binh (5) sat below the hill and on to the northeast and east, slightly higher ground which held the artillery battery looking down on Nuoc Mau. From the artillery position, the bunker line curved south overlooking the dirt road leading to Gator. The bunker line ended at Bunkers 21 & 21A which also overlooked the entrance to LZ Gator east of the gate, with Bunker #1 sitting just west of the gate.

At 1:10AM, the lights on the bunker line which illuminated the landscape beyond the perimeter went out between bunker's 1 and 15. Elements of the signal company were dispatched to find the problem. Ten minutes later LZ Gator was hit by a heavy barrage of mortar rounds landing in the middle of the base, while RPG and small arms fire hit the southern and western portions of the perimeter. The bunkers located on the southwest edge of Gator were the most seriously hit, as these bunkers were the closest to the battalion's headquarters buildings and the Tactical Operations Center (TOC) at the top of the hill. With the perimeter suddenly dark and under fire, sappers with careful synchronization rushed through openings made by satchel charges, hand grenades and rifle-propelled grenades (RPG's).

Allowing local Vietnamese "Civilians" to work on Gator to do everything from filling sandbags to cutting hair now came to fruition. The sappers knew their way in the dark better than most of Gators defenders, who spent more time in the field than on the LZ. In quick order, sappers rushed LTC Barnes sleeping bunker, killed both of his guards and threw in a satchel charge. Lieutenant Colonel Alfred Barnes, critically wounded, crawled out of his sleeping bunker and into his fighting bunker. The sappers watched him crawl in and threw in another satchel charge which ripped his body to shreds. One soldier would later remember, "We peeled his body parts off the wall".

LTC Alfred Barnes was age forty-one and married, from Montclair, New Jersey. His two body guards were SP/4 Richard Amick, twenty and married from Nashville, Tennessee and SP/4 Charles Wilson Jr., twenty-two and married from Greenwood, Mississippi. LTC Barnes wife would suffer a double blow in 1969. Her husband was killed this night on May 12, and her son, a PFC in the Marines Corps would be killed farther north in Quang Nam province, on August 13.

Simultaneously as Barnes bunker was being hit, the S-5 Civil Affairs building was destroyed, the battalion Executive Officers sleeping area was hit (he was in the TOC) and four buildings belonging to Delta Company were partially demolished. Part of the Radar emplacement was also disabled.

Bunkers 1 through 8 received no enemy fire while men on bunker 9 only received some occasional fire. From that point moving west it got rough for Gator's defenders around the battalion's headquarters and TOC. Bunker 10 received three RPG rounds but all of them missed their mark. It also received small arms sniper fire and its defenders spotted flashes from mortar fire out to their front. Bunker 10A was hit by eight Chicom grenades but suffered no casualties.

The following morning they found two small gaps in the concertina wire where the VC slipped through. Bunker 11 was hit by two RPG rounds and three grenades. The defenders spotted seven VC leaving the perimeter by a perimeter light pole to their right. They fired on the enemy and later discovered blood stains, but no bodies. Bunker 12 received sniper fire and witnessed a stream of possibly thirty VC moving in and out of the perimeter. Once illumination rounds were fired, the sappers' effectiveness was negated and they began to escape the perimeter. Return fire from one bunker wounded one VC, who was seen being dragged away by his comrade. The bunker's defenders would later find blood stains and five homemade grenades in front of their position.

Bunker 13 took three direct RPG hits which wounded three defenders. Despite the destruction of the bunker and the defenders being wounded, they continued to pour out return fire. One dead VC would be found about sixty yards in front of their position with more blood trails leading away. Bunker 14 was hit by two RPG rounds, causing heavy damage and killing one defender, PFC Thomas Cummins, while wounding two others. Cummins was twenty years old and single, from Marysville, California. Later his wounded buddies captured one sapper about one hundred yards in front of their position. Bunker 15 had five RPG's miss their bunker and its defenders spotted one VC throwing grenades. He was fired on as the attacker ran towards Bunker 14 to their left.

Reaction teams moved to their assigned areas of the perimeter to sweep for VC and take care of the wounded. This was as hazardous as walking near mines. The night was dark with fits of light when illumination flares were fired. As the flares descended to the ground, shadows were formed by the flickering light, making it easier for the VC to move from shadow to shadow on their way off the LZ.

As early as 1:30AM, just minutes after the attack began, medics from the battalion aid station were sent to the radar site, LTC Barnes bunker and Bunker's 14 & 14A. SP/4 Larry Medley was assigned to work the ammo dump but left his position to be on a reaction force. Learning that some bunkers were critically short of ammunition he returned and loaded a jeep with ammo, then drove the jeep by himself on the interior roads of Gator to resupply the bunkers. He returned to the dump a second time while the VC were still inside the perimeter, to bring illumination, white phosphorous and high explosive rounds to the mortar positions inside Gator. Medley was awarded a Bronze Star for valor.

Delta, out in the rocket pocket, noticed the heavy illumination which suddenly appeared east over LZ Gator at 1:00AM. Then it saw illumination appear northeast of their position over LZ Bayonet. In short order a progression of night illumination spots appeared from LZ Gator down to Binh Son, LZ Dottie and LZ Stinson. All the bases were hit simultaneously. Deltas leaders knew they were not in a position to cover all the valley trails where the VC might retreat after the attack on Gator and Bayonet. Cobra gunships flew nearby, supported by illumination lighting up the ground, eagerly looking for pockets of VC moving away from the attacks. It made Delta watch the attacks in cold fear, hopeful their night positions had been properly relayed to the right levels of command so they would not be mistaken for enemy. When Delta returned from the field several days later, Delta found the VC had used their company area on Gator as one of two primary paths into the LZ. Their empty platoon hooch's had been heavily damaged.

By 2:00AM, the sapper attacks had terminated but Gator still received sporadic small arms and mortar fire. Reaction teams continued to search inside Gators perimeter for enemy stragglers too wounded to escape. At 3:45AM Bunkers 14A & 15 received more mortar rounds. The defenders watched as the mortars were "walked in" across the battalion commander's helicopter pad and the TOC, both excellent aiming points given by the former workers on LZ Gator. The continuous flashes from the mortar sites revealed that their positions were less than one-quarter mile due south of Gator and two-thirds mile northeast of Gator's perimeter.

By 6:00AM, it was all over. Dustoff's were completed and reaction forces were now searching the terrain forward of the perimeter. While numerous blood trails were found, only two dead VC were accounted for, which interpreters identified as NVA regulars. Another enemy soldier was found wounded and a third was captured. Forward of the perimeter the find included thirty-eight Chicom grenades, two RPG rocket launchers, two RPG rounds, three improvised RPG launchers, one Bangalore Torpedo and two satchel charges. The total cost to the soldiers on Gator was four killed and ten wounded with several bunker and tent areas destroyed.

At 9:30AM, the outgoing brigade commander, Colonel Tully flew in to view the damage and at 10:00AM LTC Ronald Richardson arrived to see what was left of his former headquarters. Richardson lobbied the Division to give the battalion back to him so he could stabilize the situation. But his experience and efficiency did not count as much in the Army's eyes as an opportunity for another officer to get career advancement by commanding a battalion.

At 6:40AM, elements of Delta Company two miles southwest of Gator, in conjunction with tracks of the 2nd platoon, H Troop, found another enemy killed in the attack along with a 81mm mortar base plate, one M-15 mine and one AK-47 assault rifle. Delta's absence from Gator did not eliminate their participation in the attack. At 3:00AM an incoming mortar round hit one of the tracks in the field which wounded four grunts from Delta's 1st Platoon. They were dusted off in conjunction with the dustoffs arriving on Gator.

By mid-morning as the damage was being sorted out on Gator, it was business as usual for the rest of the battalion. The word had spread rapidly about LTC Barnes' death. There was more shock that the VC could have penetrated the LZ with such effectiveness, than the loss of their battalion commander who was not liked by many of the enlisted in the field. When hearing of Barnes death, Alpha's erratic platoon leader threw his helmet in the air and sang, "Ding dong the wicked witch is dead" He promptly put on a prohibited "boonie" soft cap to celebrate.

Much of the animosity with LTC Barnes came from his continued push to place his men back on the Batangan. It would not have been different with any other battalion commander. The Batangan was part of the battalion's responsibility and it had to be pacified. But Barnes gave no slack from what many thought were petty regulations that had no effect on success in the field and therefore was not necessary. Hardened by the carnage of the life they saw and endured, some soldiers felt Barnes' death might somehow help them survive. It was not to be.

One of Alpha's soldiers stepped on another mine before noon, taking off an arm and leg. The enemy pressure continued. Chu Lai received four 122mm rockets, fired from the area west of rocket valley. One hit near the divisions United Services Organization (USO) building, one near the 312th Evacuation Hospital and two overshot their mark and landed in the South China Sea. At high noon Delta's platoons came under fire. One soldier was hit in the head but survived and one Vietcong was killed with the help of gunships. Four of Delta's soldiers were dusted off with heat exhaustion.

At 3:15PM, Major Richard LeBeau, Executive Officer of the battalion, assumed temporary command in the wake of LTC Barnes death. Day turned into night and the battalion's soldiers continued their work at "Pacification". Alpha continued operations on or near the Batangan Peninsula where, if anything could go wrong, it would.

One Alpha platoon passed through an old bombed out hamlet into a large and dry rice paddy. Another Alpha platoon approached on the other side of the paddy. As the grunts set up their lines on the edge of the field, a wounded water buffalo bounded out of the hamlet into the paddy. Water Buffalo were always dangerous to the grunts, but this one was wounded and especially irritated. It seemed the large beasts despised American soldiers worst than the enemy. Someone opened fire to put the buffalo out of its misery and to protect the grunts if it charged them. The platoon on the other side had the same idea at the same time and both platoons fired on each other. A ceasefire was called and the best shot from the platoon, an American Indian, took the beast down with one shot.

Alpha's Jerry Karr remembered two times they had to kill water buffalos. On another occasion in the Rocket Pocket a charging water buffalo had Karr up a tree. As another Alpha soldier, Bill Crawford, recalled, "It always amazed me that some little Vietnamese kid with a bamboo stick would beat them on the butt and it would do whatever he said. But the minute one of those things saw a GI, it turned into a wild beast!"

Bravo Company continued to defend LZ Gator and set about rebuilding the bunkers lost in the attack. Charlie still operated on the Batangan Cape, sending patrols and ambushes off LZ Minuteman. Delta Company continued patrolling the southern rocket pocket and Echo's recon platoon was placed under operational control of the 1st/52nd Battalion while its heavy mortar (4.2-inch) platoon continued to provide fire support to Alpha and Charlie by residing on Hill 26.

In the minds of many soldiers there was no progress at "extensive pacification". With relative ease LZ Gator, their refuge from the field, had been penetrated and their battalion commander slaughtered. Gator had been as close to America as they got. Short rests there brought them hot food, showers, cold beer, tape decks playing Motown Music and pinup posters reminding them of "round-eyed" females waiting back at home.

That mindset was changing. Increasingly for many, progress was to be measured not by how many VC were killed or weapons captured, but by daily survival. And for those on the Batangan, retaining one's arms and legs was a bonus. The only "pacification" a soldier would see would come when he stepped on a "freedom bird" back to "the world".

10 – GENEVA PARK

On the morning of May 14, 1969, the Intelligence, Operations and Civil Affairs staff officers of the 5th/46th Infantry Battalion made a liaison visit to the pro-government hamlet of Tri Binh (1) one and one-half miles north of LZ Gator. The hamlet was still occupied by a squad from Delta Company which helped defend it but the hamlet chief was concerned an NVA soldier was hiding in his hamlet, resting from the attack on LZ Gator. The hamlet chief's dilemma was the same dilemma faced by hamlets throughout the battalion's area of operations. Deltas squad and a squad of PF militia had been searching each hooch and checking identifications. Two military age males were detained and taken to Binh Son for a security check. The District Chief in Binh Son, present for the meeting, said there were nine families in Tri Binh (1) who were VC sympathizers. Additionally there were forty other families who had moved there from other hamlets. The only solution to sorting them out was to conduct a census of all the hamlets' population, compare it to the hamlets' earlier census on file in Binh Son, and isolate the families suspected of supporting the VC. The process would take two days.

The Binh Son District Chief also warned the battalion's staff that children were placing hand grenades into gas tanks on vehicles after the grenade pins were pulled and the handles held by thin rubber bands. Over a short period of time the gasoline would rot the rubber band and the grenade explode. One US advisor had been killed in such a manner in Quang Ngai City. Children were also carefully opening chocolate bar wrappers and replacing the bars with two inches of C-4 explosive and a fuse for a booby traps. Pro-government villagers were the targets.

Intelligence reports pointed to an attack on Binh Son by a portion of a Vietcong Regiment. Small groups of NVA were spotted east and west of Highway One. The VC were reportedly setting up aid stations and positioning nurses near the Batangan Peninsula as recovery measures after the attack.

At 6:00PM, Alpha Company set up a night perimeter around Phu Nhieu (5) northwest of the Batangan. One insurgent stuck his head out of a tunnel and fired on the soldiers then ran away. The grunts spotted a group of twenty to twenty-five VC moving around the village to ambush them. In an attempt to flush them out, some hooch's were set on fire. In short order the company watched the fire get out of control and engulf the hamlet. Alpha moved one-half mile due east and set up a new position for the night. The day ended for Alpha with three of its soldiers wounded by small arms fire, one in the chest, one in the thigh and the other in the left shoulder. All would recover.

The following day intelligence reports from Binh Son indicated Vietcong attacks would be made on the Batangan Peninsula to "rescue" villagers in the "New Life Hamlets", the refugee camps established by the ARVN after the cordon and sweep phase of Russell Beach. The enemy's campaign plan included a reference to the governments "Broken-Down Pacification Plan." The "rescue operations" were set to coincide with Ho Chi Minh's birthday on May 19.

The battle for "hearts and minds" was waged on many levels by both sides of the conflict. The 5th/46th Infantry Battalion conducted hundreds of "MEDCAP's" during its time in Vietnam. These were medical missions to impoverished hamlets to provide medical care and to teach about sanitation and the prevention of diseases. Support of orphanages was also accomplished, and many were helped by grunts that, at the same time, had to survive in the mine-infested terrain around them.

During May, the battalions Chaplain, Captain Charles Adams, a 27—year old Protestant chaplain from Springfield, Missouri, visited the Catholic orphanage in Binh Son. Sixty children were subsisting on one or two bowls of rice a day and sleeping on the floors of a school while rats scampered about. Adams told a group of soldiers on Gator about their plight and they agreed to help. One Sergeant remarked, "Chaplain, those kids have just got themselves some new parents."

Rice that was found from enemy caches was delivered to the orphanage in small but steady amounts, so as to not catch the attention of local authorities. The mess sergeants on Gator set aside surplus food for Adams to take on periodic visits. Forty Army cots were found in Chu Lai and supplied to the children. On paydays in the field a cup was passed for donations. Ten percent of the poker winnings on LZ Gator were also earmarked for the Binh Son orphans. By the end of 1969 under Adam's direction, an eight-room cinder-block structure was erected to house the children and the battalion's contributions averaged four hundred dollars a month.

The morning of May 16 was marked by a memorial service on LZ Gator, to remember Lieutenant Colonel Barnes and the three enlisted men killed in the sapper attack. Brigadier General Clements, Colonel Tully, Lieutenant Colonel Richardson and the Brigade Sergeant Major were on hand, along with one hundred of LZ Gators defenders. During the service Delta's squad in Tri Binh (1) captured a Vietcong female who was sent by chopper to LZ Bayonet to be questioned. Additional intelligence indicated a buildup of Vietcong Company units with NVA advisors who were set to hit Marine CAP teams in the northern half of the large coastal plains beginning at the head waters of the Tra Bong River and ending on the Batangan Cape. A Chieu Hoi defector, a Vietnamese female aged nineteen, gave up and identified herself as a sapper with the Vietcong 95A Sapper Company. She told of the NVA holding squad meetings and propaganda classes and the villagers cooking for them and added, "What the people don't supply in food the NVA take."

On May 17, an eight-year-old boy trudged up Hill 26 carrying a 60mm mortar round to turn in for money. He slipped and dropped the round and it exploded, killing him instantly. Air reconnaissance revealed that the hamlet of Phu My (1), north of Pinkville, largely destroyed during the Russell Beach cordon phase, was being rebuilt by the VC, complete with underground bunkers and two hundred yards of a well-developed trench network.

Interrogation of another VC female revealed she was part of the Vietcong Infrastructure (VCI), residing in Phu Long (1), two miles due west of CAP 135. This hamlet had been firmly controlled by the VC since 1966, despite the numerous incursions by the US Marines and the American's soldiers. One squad of fifteen VC resided there and served as observers and snipers. Whenever Americans approached, the VC fled southwest one and one-quarter miles to the area of Hill 106 for refuge. The woman, age thirty-nine was the Assistant Chief and Secretary of the Women's VC Cadre in the area, part of the VCI. Association meetings

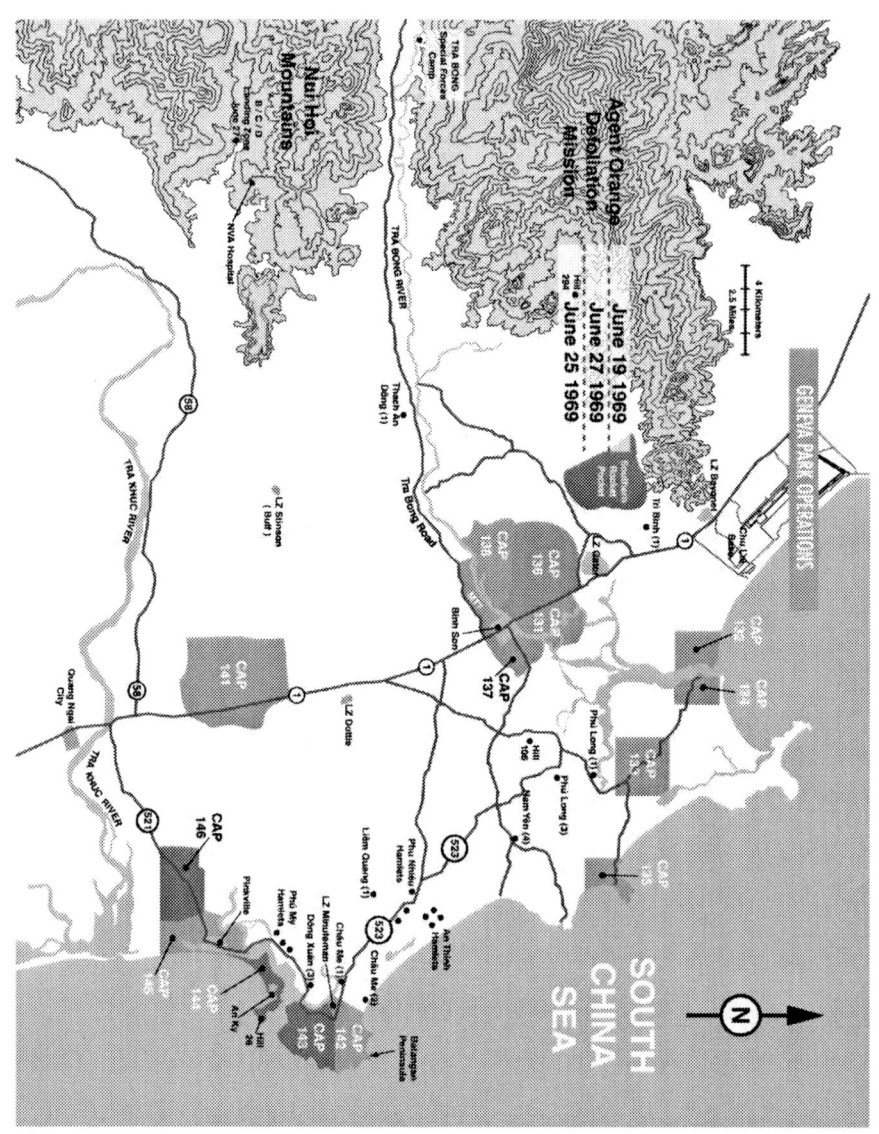

Geneva Park

were held every month, with the main topics being food production and the contribution of money for the hamlet guerillas.

Another captured female was nineteen years old and had been a guerilla since 1967. She began her guerilla career cooking for fighters (for nine months), then became part of the fighting force as an assistant gunner for an M-60 machinegun crew. Three months later she was promoted to squad leader. The units she joined included the 95A Sapper Company which she said, had a strength of about two hundred of which one hundred and fifty had weapons. She operated in Nam Yen (4) and Lac Son (1) hamlets one and one-half miles southwest of CAP 135.

All of this intelligence supported the battalion plans to commit soldiers to the area for a cordon and search. But other intelligence gave the battalion the prospect of catching some bigger fish. A North Vietnamese Regiment was reported to be assembling west of Binh Son for a major attack. NVA were also reported to be in Tri Binh (4) and Nam Binh (7) hamlets, sitting under the nose of LZ Gator. They crossed over Highway One at night to collect rice and money from the hamlets east of the highway in the Binh Nghia area.

The Beginning - "Vietnamization"

On May 20, the battalion received its fourth commander, Lieutenant Colonel Julian F. Wagner. The NVA buildup had preceded Wagner's arrival and, similar to his predecessors, he took command while the battalion was already in motion. Wagner had served as an advisor to the South Korean Army near Danang. His chance to command a battalion in combat opened the door for higher promotion. It was tough at the time for any Army Lieutenant Colonel during the war to make full Colonel without battalion command in the war zone, and so he grabbed at the opportunity.

The opinions on Wagner's leadership were mixed among the officers. Many thought he was a "cowboy", eager to jump into his Command and Control (C&C) Huey each morning and "ride the range". He tended to "shoot from the hip" and make snap decisions without weighing options. His staff on LZ Gator generally relished the fact they were left to do their jobs and had little in common with him to discuss over a beer at Gator at the end of the day. They did the planning, the company commanders carried out their operations and Wagner oversaw his battalion from his Huey. To be sure, Wagner was not afraid to take risks, and would lay himself on the line without hesitation to rescue soldiers or engage with the enemy. For the most part he had good staff officers and company commanders which allowed his style of leadership to be successful. When a few officers had to be relieved for poor performance he did so, but by switching their assignments, not formal relief's of command.

The day after Wagner assumed command found Alpha Company operating southwest of Gator and pushing north into the rocket area, patrolling and setting ambushes. Bravo defended LZ Gator and continued its rebuilding effort after the attack of May 12. Charlie was pulled off LZ Minuteman, leaving it to the ARVN and PF's to defend, and was placed under operational control of the 1st/52nd Battalion in its efforts to find an NVA regiment west of Binh Son before it had time to launch an attack. Two days later Regional Force Company 933 assumed independent responsibility for the defense of LZ Minuteman which was consistent with the "Extensive Pacification" phase of Operation Russell Beach. The takeover of Minuteman also coincided with the Geneva Park operational concept calling for the ARVN to work more closely with the battalion.

Delta served as a blocking force for the ARVN by sweeping northwest of Pinkville in the Phu My hamlets. At one point, a group of ARVN officers came over to Delta to coordinate their movements. PFC Leo Pillow saw an ARVN officer severely beat his own RTO. Pillow, a pensive man, walked over to try to stop it and asked what was going on. His platoon leader told him to get back to his platoon before an incident was created. Later Delta's interpreter told Pillow the ARVN RTO had been AWOL and was getting his comeuppance. The RTO was placed back in the field to serve with no pay.

The next day Delta spotted three VC about two hundred yards away. A new platoon leader asked Delta's commander, Captain John Goorley, to call in an air strike. Goorley would not do it for only three VC and the fact the ARVN were close by. He asked his new Lieutenant if he remembered his fire and maneuver classes in OCS. The response was "Yes." "Well" Goorley responded, "Go do it." Two squads moved forward firing by leaps and bounds; the insurgents were wounded, which was the same as a death sentence for most of the enemy, and scurried away. The troops returned pumped up about their success, finding two weapons and a blood trail.

Echo's Recon Platoon also supported Delta by operating in Phu My (1). Recon's SP/4 Alfred Thomas saw what he thought was a small anti-personnel mine in the hamlet. The area was littered with sandbags from a previous sweep and he picked one up and heaved it on the suspected mine to detonate it. Thomas' suspicions were confirmed but the mine was much larger than he expected. A booby-trapped artillery round exploded with a roar, showering the recon troops with clumps of red dirt. Thomas was seriously wounded and had fragment wounds in the right eye, hand, face and both arms. Recon's platoon leader, Lieutenant Jim Daniels got on his hands and knees and stared in Thomas' face, screaming and telling him what a "stupid ass" he was. Daniels wanted to keep Thomas' mind off his injuries or he would likely go into shock. A chunk of shrapnel seven inches long was embedded in his arm.

When the dustoff arrived, the medic onboard almost vomited as Thomas was handed up on a stretcher, covered with bloody compress dressings. Thomas survived.

Incidents like this were experienced by the men in the battalion on a regular basis; private moments of hell with comrades trying to save each other in the midst of pain, anguish and suffering. Often there would be no medals and no understanding of the anguish endured once the men returned back to "the world." These incidents would only be recorded in the minds of the soldiers who lived it, and the memories would never be erased.

At 4:45PM on May 21, two ARVN companies in the same sweep supported by Delta's blocking force came under heavy attack by two Vietcong Companies. When it was over the ARVN suffered four killed and twenty-five wounded. Twenty VC were killed and one captured. The following day the Batangan claimed more casualties from mines. Filling in the gap from Charlie Company's departure from LZ Minuteman, CAP Marines, Vietnamese PRU and PF militia, along with US Army advisors swept the area just west of the LZ. They walked into a mine field, wounding thirteen and killing an American advisor.

Charlie Company, working with the 1st/52nd Battalion to find and fix the NVA regiment threatening Binh Son, was happy to be away from the mines of the Batangan but got no vacation hunting for the NVA. The area of operation, fifteen miles from the coast, was very hot and barren with little cover and no water. On the morning of May 24, Charlie's second platoon, led by 1LT David Taylor, pointed the company formation as it searched for the NVA. The platoon's point man, William

Watkins, was an experienced soldier, tall, lean and muscular. He sported a Fu Manchu mustache, earning the moniker "Gingus" from his comrades. Watkins stepped on a Bouncing Betty mine and for a split second saw his life disappear, but the mine failed to explode.

A few minutes later Watkins and his side-kick, PFC "Woody" Lambert, who comprised the point element, came to an open area and Watkins spotted NVA at the far side of a large rice paddy. Unaware that he and his comrade had just stepped over another antipersonnel mine, he called for 1LT Taylor who moved forward to call in artillery fire. The platoon leader and RTO behind him also unknowingly stepped over the mine but the grenadier carrying an M-79 behind the RTO, SP/4 Peter Portenza, detonated it, wounding all five. They were dusted off to Chu Lai for treatment but four of them returned to the field the next day. Portenza lost part of his foot from the mine.

Later that morning, the NVA engaged the company with small arms and mortar fire which wounded four more soldiers and killed SP/4 Roy Clark. Clark was a single soldier, aged twenty-three from Culloden, West Virginia. Another soldier was dusted off with heat exhaustion. By 7:40PM Charlie established a night defensive position, but the hard ground prevented any digging of prone positions which would have allowed them to get below ground level. The NVA understood that quite well and hit them with a mortar barrage just one-quarter mile north of their position, sending fifteen to twenty 82mm mortar rounds into their perimeter which wounded thirteen more soldiers.

The following day Regional Force (RF) and Popular Force (PF) soldiers, working a targeted RDA, came under heavy fire near Nha Hoa, halfway between Quang Ngai and Pinkville. Artillery was called in by a forward air controller flying above, and the PF's claimed thirty VC killed. But the price to "win hearts and minds" was high. Five civilians were killed in the artillery fire and ten wounded with five houses destroyed and twenty more damaged. The remaining VC withdrew closer to Pinkville.

On May 27, Charlie was released from the 1st/52nd and returned to LZ Gator. Delta patrolled northeast of the Batangan Peninsula along Route 523. As it left its night position at 8:15AM it came under small arms fire from a squad of VC which seriously wounded an RTO. One squad was pinned down behind a small wall in a sub-hamlet to which it had been sent to check out. The remainder of the company was pinned down in a ditch nearby.

The battalion's Chaplain, Captain Jim Cosner was with the troops on the ground, something he frequently did to lend moral support to the men. While under intense fire, the pistol-packing Chaplain rushed out to the wounded soldier and assisted in treating him by holding a pressure bandage over his stomach wound while exposed to enemy fire. When the dustoff arrived, Cosner helped carry the soldier to the Huey across open terrain while bullets were flying about. He remained with the soldier to comfort him on his life-saving trip to the hospital. This act would earn him his second Bronze Star for valor as Chaplain of the 5th/46th.

FNG's, "Fucking New Guys", watched the seriously wounded soldier lying in agony on a poncho before Cosner could get him on the dustoff. The scene brought a reality check to the company's newest soldiers that they were in a kill or be killed situation. This was the only positive thing to come out of the tragedies of their daily war and it gave some small hope to the sergeants and lieutenants that the message of "paying attention" would sink in to the FNG's.

Delta moved out of the immediate area and called for air strikes, which were prompt in coming. The ordnance was dropped about four hundred and fifty yards to the north, where the enemy was expected to retreat. This was a "danger close" mission for the grunts as they popped smoke to mark their position, trying to give a clear indication where they were for the F-4 Phantoms dropping their loads. The 1st platoon had been closest to the firefight and now was closest to the air strike. They hunkered to the ground and watched the F-4's swoop over them dropping their bombs, the exploding shrapnel fluttering back with a feathery sound over their position, with several hot chunks landing near the platoon. Three soldiers were slightly wounded, the price paid for buying some covering fire to move out of the area.

By 7:00PM, Delta had moved one and one-half miles farther north near Phu Nhieu (1) when it came under sniper fire. One soldier hit a mine which peppered him with shrapnel in both legs, a thigh and abdomen. During Delta's challenges, Alpha continued to screen the southern rocket pocket and Bravo Company defended LZ Gator.

On May 28, elements of the 2nd/6th ARVN Regiment were picked up by Hueys on LZ Dottie and air assaulted to the area being cordoned by Delta. Within two hours after landing they requested engineers to blow ten to fifteen tunnels they found in Phu Nhieu (1). Cobra Gunships from F Troop- 8th Cav ("Blue Ghost") screened the area east of Binh Son and killed two Vietcong. A Blue Ghost Light Observation

Helicopter (LOH or "Loach") searched the ground at low levels for the gunships and dropped a white phosphorous grenade on a hooch. The pilots watched twenty to thirty VC with AK-47's scramble out, running in all directions, firing at the LOH as they ran. This flying was dangerous duty, up close and personal for a Loach pilot and his crew chief. The prior day a LOH was shot down three miles farther east, and the two-man crew was killed.

On May 29 the ARVN, working near Delta, got an early wake-up call at 5:50AM. They were hit with six-60mm mortar rounds inside their perimeter. The explosions killed one ARVN and wounded two. As the combined ARVN/Delta Company force worked northwest of the Batangan, Alpha Company air-assaulted out to the base of Hill 294, six miles west of Gator, to seize the hill and operate in conjunction with elements of the 3rd/6th and 4th/6th ARVN to conduct search and sweep operations. Alpha's 81mm mortar platoon was lifted out to the former LZ Chippewa for fire support, with a platoon from Charlie Company for security. Two tubes of 4.2-inch mortars from Echo Company were lifted off Hill 26 to add to the firepower on Chippewa. Echo's Recon Platoon continued to supply security for Delta and the 26th Engineers as they built a major New Life Hamlet and refugee village in An Ky, the small peninsula anchored by Hill 26.

Through the remainder of the month Delta continued its work with the ARVN, finding a mile-long tunnel large enough to stand in, between the hamlets of An Thinh (1) and An Thinh (2). Engineers were called to demolish the tunnel. Their ARVN counterparts, operating one-half mile southeast of An Thinh (3) found a small cache of grenades, medical supplies, a gas mask and a VC suspect. On June 1, as they swept south, the ARVN killed four more VC.

On the afternoon of June 2, Charlie and Alpha Company's returned to LZ Gator to prepare for a one-day operation to secure the Tra Bong Road (also known as the Cinnamon Road) that led from Binh Son moving west to the Tra Bong Special Forces camp in the mountains. The road was reportedly heavily mined and had to be cleared to allow a convoy of engineers to return from the Special Forces camp, where they had improved its defenses. Charlie Company would control the operation, with the first and second platoons of Alpha in support. All platoons would have engineers attached to them to sweep their portions of the road for mines.

On June 3 at 6:30AM, Hueys picked up Charlie's 1st and 2nd Platoons and air assaulted to the Cinnamon Road at a point six miles west of Binh Son and ten miles east of the Tra Bong camp. The 1st platoon started pushing west to hook-up with Alpha's 2nd Platoon which was moving east after landing four miles from the camp. Charlie's 2nd platoon pushed east sweeping for mines, destined to link up with Alpha's 1st platoon, which landed two and one-half miles west of Binh Son and was moving west. The plan was simple enough, sweep the road of mines, allow the engineer convoy to traverse the road back to Highway One, and then return to LZ Gator in time for evening chow.

In a war that taught the troops to "expect the unexpected", the simple operation would soon turn into a nightmare. 1LT David Taylor's 2nd Platoon of Charlie Company moved east but was continually slowed due to buried mines in the road which required the attached engineers to blow in place. South of the road sat an open expanse of dry rice paddy interspersed with low scrub brush, which ran for approximately 300 yards to a wood line. Beyond the wood line was the abandoned hamlet of Thach An Dong (1).

After moving only a half-mile, because of three mines which had to be destroyed, the patrol came under sniper fire from the wood line south of the road. This hampered their movement even more and link-up times were in jeopardy. Charlie's Commander, Captain Dan Porter, flew overhead concerned about the slow progress the platoon was making. His helicopter door gunners fired into the wood line which allowed the platoon to move again. More mines and more sniper fire kept the platoon's movement to a crawl.

A Blue Ghost "White" team (small team of one light observation helicopter (LOH) and one gunship) monitored Taylor's radio traffic and came to have a look. Taylor sent them south to the wood line where the snipers resided. On the way, the LOH spotted two uniformed NVA jumping into a tunnel. The bird dropped a smoke grenade to mark the location for Taylor's grunts. The smoke plumed up not more than one hundred yards from the road yet the enemy was completely hidden. The LOH flew over the wood line to the abandoned hamlet and the pilot saw NVA uniforms hanging out to dry. Going in to take a closer look, the LOH was hit by an RPG round. 1LT Taylor on the road heard a loud explosion and saw a large billow of black smoke as the LOH fell to the ground, pitching in on its side. The gunship above the LOH fired its mini-guns to rake the area around the downed craft, screaming on Taylor's radio frequency, "Bird is down, bird is down!"

It was now 12:05PM and LTC Wagner's Command and Control (C&C) Huey landed on the road with Captain Porter on board. Wagner directed Taylor to get a rescue team on his bird to fly into the area to secure the downed LOH and its crew. Porter had argued against it. "Colonel, once the team is dropped into the area we've lost all control". Part of the road clearing patrol moving west from Binh Son were tracks from the 2nd Platoon, H Troop, 17th Cav. Porter argued, "Let me get the armored personnel carriers and go in on land." Porter was overruled. Unknown to Wagner, division intelligence had radio intercepts from the area, not passed to Charlie Company prior to the operation, that indicated a regimental-sized headquarters of the NVA was near. The ARVN also had intelligence that a battalion of the 21st NVA Regiment had been reported two miles due south of the road. None of this was known to the platoon leaders conducting the road clearing operation.

Taylor hurriedly selected one of his M-60 machine gunner's, Harry Italiano and his assistant gunner, Mitchell Sandman. He picked one squad leader, Sgt. Michael Scherf and Taylor's new RTO, PFC Robert Zimmerman, who was spending his first day in the field. Zimmerman was an intellect, who was a dissertation shy of getting his PhD in Chemistry when he was drafted. Taylor thought he would make a good RTO with a clear head and decided to try him out on this "simple" one day road clearing operation. In a few short minutes Zimmerman would be fighting for his life. As they ran to get on the Huey another squad leader, Sergeant Randy Backovich, ran up to ask "Do you need more help?" Taylor, puzzled that someone would volunteer replied "Sure, get on the bird!" Backovich joined them. It was a decision that would save the platoon leader's life.

The Huey lifted off with the six man rescue team and the Cobra gunship followed the Huey in. As they dropped into the area the C&C pilot hoped to hover while the rescue team picked up the downed crew and then fly out. But the bird came under heavy fire, wounding the pilot in the leg. After dropping the team over a ditch, he was forced to leave them before his own bird was shot down on top of them.

Taylor was first out the door and ran to the LOH, the gunship behind him firing its 40mm grenade rounds across the area for protection. Backovich, Scherf and Zimmerman jumped into the ditch. Italiano and Sandman exited out the other side with the M-60 and were cut down by enemy fire. Taylor found the pilot and crew chief dead and burned from the crash. He turned to leave for the ditch but saw another soldier who had been on board, a rifleman, who was wounded severely, unable to move.

Taylor examined the soldier as AK-47 rounds pierced through the air. The grunt had been shot in the stomach and across the neck. Taylor thought he was dead and turned to leave when he saw the soldiers hand slowly make a fist, clenching his fingers in and out. He was signaling he was still alive but was too weak or scared to move. More fire came at them and Taylor returned fire, emptying his M-16 magazine across the brush in front of him.

At the same time Sergeant Backovich, realizing he needed the M-60 machinegun for firepower, leaped out of the ditch to grab it. As he reached it an NVA soldier appeared out of the brush with the same intention. Backovich was quicker on the draw and shot him with his M-16, grabbed the M-60 and ran back to the ditch.

Taylor was now reloading his second magazine, trying to suppress the fire coming at him. The pause to reload gave the enemy an opening and he was shot in the left side, the round ripping open a hole eight inches long. Realizing he was outgunned and completely exposed, he ran back to the ditch with Sergeants Backovich and Michael Scherf providing covering fire. Just as he reached the ditch he was shot a second time, the round entering the left side of his lower right leg and exiting the right side, shattering his tibia and fibula. Both shattered bones protruded through his leg, the trauma causing the lower leg to shake like Jell-O.

Scherf crawled to Taylor and tied both his legs together with a boot lace to stabilize the throbbing right leg. Scherf assured his leader "They would get out of this mess" but had lifted his head just above the wall of the ditch. In an instant he was shot in the face in his right cheek, slowly placed his hand on his head as if having a headache, slumped forward on Taylor's legs and died. Backovich and Zimmerman were just few feet away at the other end of the ditch. With Taylor immobilized the remaining two defended the ditch.

By this time jet fighter bombers from Chu Lai were overhead asking Backovich where to drop their ordnance. Backovich was to the point, "They're everywhere, just drop it". The ditch had been marked by smoke from the gunship so the five hundred-pound bombs could be dropped everywhere else. With each explosion the pilots saw small groups of NVA running in all directions. At the same time a NVA soldier tossed a grenade into the ditch, but Backovich threw it out before it exploded.

The Armored Personnel Carriers Captain Porter wanted to use for the initial rescue effort also received orders to move into the area to rescue the LOH crew. They were unaware Taylor's group was also trapped. As they approached, the NVA began retreating to avoid the pounding from the air. The tracks, partially protected from RPG fire by thick elephant grass, were not challenged except by small arms fire. They arrived on the scene surprised to find the rescue crew was there and trapped as well.

While still under some AK-47 fire, the Cav soldiers picked up the dead and wounded and retreated to the Tra Bong road where a Medevac was waiting. Taylor and the dead were placed on the same bird and arrived at the 312th Evacuation Hospital at 1:40PM. Backovich and the RTO, PFC Zimmerman, returned to their platoon on the road. Taylor, Backovich and Scherf were awarded Silver Stars. PFC Zimmerman, the first day RTO was awarded a Bronze Star. The machinegun crew, SP/4 Harry Italiano and PFC Mitchell Sandman were awarded posthumous Bronze Stars for valor.

SP/4 Harry Italiano was age twenty-one and single from Suitland, Maryland. His assistant gunner, PFC Mitchell Sandman, was also single and age twenty, from Syosset, New York. Sergeant Michael Scherf, was age twenty and single from Golden, Colorado.

Shortly after the rescue crew was brought out the engineer convoy which had been moving east from the Special Forces camp protected by other Charlie Company troops, reached the area where the remainder of Taylor's platoon was on the road. The NVA, hiding in tunnels south of the road, opened up on the convoy with RPG and small arms fire. Sergeant Ron Bentley of Charlie Company was riding on a two and one-half ton truck, unaware his best friend, Sergeant Scherf, had just been killed. Someone on the truck had pulled out a small pint of Southern Comfort and passed it around, each taking just a sip, thinking the road mission was about over.

As Bentley was handed the bottle his truck was hit by an RPG round which tore the tail gate off. The troops off-loaded rapidly to return fire when a second RPG hit the truck. Bentley was the last to get off and jumped out just as a third RPG round hit the trucks' gas tank and exploded, which sent him flying through the air, landing thirty feet away.

Bentley saw an engineer sitting on a bulldozer drivers' seat, bleeding in the face. He ran and pulled the driver down behind the dozers blade to protect him from AK-47 fire hitting the blade. Bentley's thought: "Some son-of-bitch is really trying to kill us!"

More helicopter gunships which had arrived to support the rescue team extraction flew up the road to suppress the RPG fire. Fifteen minutes later another truck two hundred yards farther east in the convoy (fourth from the front) hit a command-detonated mine, catapulting its occupants from the truck, but none were seriously injured. It appeared the mine was non-metallic and was not detected by the engineers sweeping the road. The damaged truck was quickly hooked up to another vehicle and the convoy lumbered back to Binh Son and Highway One.

June 3, 1969 also claimed another death for the battalion. PFC Tomas Gomez-Robles, a member of Bravo Company who was wounded by shrapnel in the chest from a booby-trapped mortar round when his team attempted to fill canteens at a small stream on April 28, succumbed to his wounds. Robles was single and age twenty-one from Caguas, Puerto Rico.

On June 4, Alpha Company replaced Bravo on the bunker line at LZ Gator as Bravo prepared to move to LZ Dottie and conduct saturation patrols and ambushes in the area. Charlie split its platoons to screen for VC in the southern sector of the rocket pocket. Delta continued its operations in support of the ARVN on and near the Batangan Peninsula. Echo's heavy 4.2-inch mortars remained on Hill 26 overlooking the Batangan in support of Delta and the ARVN. Its Recon Platoon provided added security on the hill.

Alpha was glad to be back on Gator having pushed itself in the field for some time. For field soldiers, LZ Gator bunker duty was better than walking on mines in the Batangan. The showers, mess hall, beer and occasional weed for those who wanted it, provided "Hotel accommodations" although no longer with the same sense of security, since the attack on Gator in early May. The only thing better was a stand-down on the Chu Lai beach and, for those who lasted long enough to earn it, a Rest & Recuperation (R&R) out of country, or, as some termed it, an "I&I", (Intercourse & intoxication).

As Alpha took over the bunker line its 3rd Platoon settled into its assigned area. The break from mines and bobby-traps offered an opportunity for a different level of camaraderie. The platoon had a country boy from Georgia, red haired and freckled, who talked like the television character of the time, Gomer Pyle. Hence, his name became "Gomer". Gomer received regular packages from home, homemade cookies, and the unwritten law of grunts specified some generous sharing with your buddies.

Gomer's idea of sharing was to give one cookie to each buddy. His squad mates (Bob Wolf, Rick Massey, Jim Barker and Dave Barney) decided to teach him the meaning of "Sharing" and, finding his stash in a bunker, ate all of the homemade cookies. The next morning Gomer was furious, stomping around and yelling in a high-pitched, squeaky voice, "You people are nothing but a bunch of buddyfuckers! That's all you are! A bunch of buddyfuckers! Do you hear me? You're nothing but a bunch of buddyfuckers!"

Had Gomer used the word once it probably would have been ignored, but Gomer used it three times and the name was sealed in the platoon's lexicon. Massey looked at Wolf and asked, "Yeah, buddyfucker Wolf, why did you take his care package?" Wolf replied, "Hey buddyfucker Rick, you helped. And so did buddyfucker Barker and buddyfucker Barney." Grunts, having no use for long titles, shortened their names to BuddyWolf, BuddyBarney, etc; no hyphen and not two words, just one word as decided at the moment by those who were there. And the names remained. Thirty-five years after the war, one soldier in Wolf's squad finally located him and called on the phone. The first words out of his mouth were, "BuddyWolf, how have you been?"

LZ Gator always had its own opportunities for tense moments. The entrance to the mess hall had a 55-gallon drum, cut in half and filled with sand. Soldiers on Gator had to carry a weapon with them at all times. For safety, before entering the mess hall the ammunition clip was removed from the weapon, cycling the action, then pointing the weapon into the drum and pulling the trigger. Slinging an M-16 on one's shoulder while carrying a tray of food became a juggling act so soldiers often exchanged a .45-caliber pistol to take to dinner. One FNG borrowed a .45 to go to chow and did not follow the prescribed procedure of clearing his weapon. Pointing the pistol into the drum he pulled the trigger and the pistol went off, creating a resounding "BANG" in the tin-roofed mess hall. The soldiers hit the floor and mess trays went flying in every direction. What happened to the FNG after that is unknown to this day.

On June 8, elements of the 1st/52nd Infantry Battalion captured several documents two miles southeast of Thach An Dong (1), the site of the LOH crash and rescue attempt on June 3. The documents confirmed an element of the 21st NVA Regiment was operating in the area, preparing for major attacks on Binh Son prior to June 10. The air strikes in support of the trapped rescue team had inflicted casualties and equipment losses on some of this force, but to what extent were unknown. The documents revealed the Vietcong were also storing fish and rice to support the NVA and a cache had been established just north of the Tra Bong River in the vicinity where Taylor's platoon had been sweeping the Cinnamon Road.

Early on the morning of June 8, LZ Gator came under small arms and mortar fire, but the heavily reinforced bunker line was not penetrated. This was a diversion for an attack on Nuoc Mau, the village intersecting the LZ Gator road and Highway One, which was hit by a sapper platoon. The attackers killed three Vietnamese, wounded three more and destroyed or damaged eighteen hooch's in the ville. Binh Son, their refugee camp and CAP teams near it were also hit by heavy mortar and small arms fire.

By late morning, Delta was bearing the pain once again of prolonged duty on the Batangan Peninsula where the odds always went against you. At 10:55AM, PFC Robert Martin was wounded by a bobby-trapped 105mm Howitzer artillery round, suffering a broken arm and amputation of his lower right leg. Forty minutes later SFC Richard Countermarsh hit a mine which took both his legs, one above the knee and one below. Both were dusted off to the 27th Surgical Hospital in Chu Lai. ARVN working in the area killed eight NVA and captured three. The captives revealed they had been in the area for only one month. They had trained in Hanoi, the capitol of North Vietnam for three months and then made the three-month journey down the Ho Chi Minh trail to infiltrate onto the Batangan. Two ARVN had been killed in the clash and eight wounded. At 1:20PM west of Gator, Charlie's 2nd platoon killed one VC and captured another in the southern portion of the rocket pocket.

The increased Vietnamization of operations under Operation Geneva Park was met with frustration by the battalion's soldiers. The 5th/46th Battalion was expected to work hand-in-hand with the Vietnamese forces. LTC Wagner received word the PF Company protecting LZ Minuteman would not step off the firebase to support Delta Company without orders from the District Chief in Binh Son. The District Chief had told the PF Group Commander two days prior to make it happen and the Group Commander had given the orders on June 7 but the PF Company Commander on LZ Minuteman claimed he never received the order and was not moving.

Support from the Vietnamese regular army (ARVN) was markedly better during this period of time than the militias of the PF and RF. The militias generally refused to leave LZ Minuteman to secure the immediate area around its perimeter, making Delta's task that much harder in the extremely dangerous terrain. Only when militias came under the supervision of American advisors, such as the Marine squads in the CAP's or advisors from Quang Ngai City or Binh Son, could the militias be counted upon to perform.

June 11 saw Bravo Company in support of the 1st/52nd Battalion as a blocking force northeast of Quang Ngai City. Bravo anchored its headquarters on a small hill astride Highway One, five and one-half miles north of Quang Ngai to work its blocking mission by sending out hunter-killer teams. The 1st squad of its 1st platoon was situated one and one-quarter miles southwest of the headquarters element when at 8:20AM it hit a Bouncing Betty mine. Normally, a Bouncing Betty mine could injure or kill one or two soldiers in close proximity to it, but the team was bunched up and, with LTC Barnes no longer commanding the battalion, had been wearing soft headgear, "Booney Caps", for more comfort, stealth and better hearing. The well-placed mine took its toll:

PFC Tommy Smith, fragment wounds shoulder, arm, back & head
PFC Jay O'Conner, fragment wounds right hand, arm, chest
SP/4 Walter Yeargin, fragment wounds shoulder, face, possible brain & eye damage
PFC Francis Meli, fragment wounds face, head, right arm and chest
SP/4 William Gallager, fragment wounds head. Left arm, thigh, possible eye or brain damage
SP/4 Victor Justiano, fragment wounds head, left arm, right hand, possible eye or brain damage
SGT Robert Page, fragment wounds head, left leg, possible eye or brain damage

By 9:21AM, the wounded had been evacuated and LTC Wagner's C&C picked up the remaining grunts. Hunter-Killer team 1/1/B was out of action.

Bravo was released from operational control of the 1st/52nd Battalion and its commander, Captain Steven Schopp sent out six more hunter-killer teams working off LZ Dottie. Charlie continued its work in the rocket pocket but extended its reach by having the artillery on LZ Gator fire harassment & interdiction (H&I) fires during the night on trail networks it could not cover with ambushes.

At 7:00PM on June 12, Delta spotted fifteen Vietcong fishing in a stream one-half mile west of Phu Nhieu (2). When a Huey flew over, the VC ran for cover as they fired their AK-47's at the low-flying bird. Artillery was called with two "fire-cracker" rounds exploding in the air, sending shrapnel over several hundred square yards of turf. In the declining daylight two VC were seen being carried away. An additional twenty-five to thirty VC were spotted one-half mile farther south. Artillery was again thrown at them, the VC being too far away to engage with small arms fire. A sweep of the area at first light revealed nothing.

On the evening of June 13, Division and 198th Brigade intelligence advised the 5th/46th Battalion the period of June 13-20 would be crucial, characterized by a significant increase in enemy activity with mortar and sapper attacks aimed at LZ Stinson and Quang Ngai City. LZ Stinson had been the former LZ Buff, the firebase for the 1st/52nd Infantry Battalion but was renamed when their battalion commander, LTC William Stinson, was killed in a helicopter crash on March 3, 1969.

Bravo continued to push out Hunter-Killer teams north & south of LZ Dottie. In the early morning hours of June 14, a team from the 1st platoon working an ambush two miles southwest of Dottie froze in place as two hundred NVA moved past their position in the thinly lit night, walking west to east. The NVA wore full uniforms with packs. The ambush team also counted six recoilless rifles and three-82mm mortars being carried in the formation. A short time later about fifty VC walked by on the same path. Artillery was called on the suspected location of the formation once it had passed the ambush and gunships also worked the area over guided by flares.

LTC Wagner and the battalion's staff were enraged the small team had failed to take this opportunity to kill the NVA. But the small hunter-killer would have been quickly annihilated had they opened fire and they were happy to see the morning sun. Their company commander, Captain Schopp, supported their decision. At first light they swept the immediate area and found an RPD machinegun.

By 1:00PM, an air strike was placed on the hamlet of An Thinh (1) where Delta and the ARVN had seen continuous movement of NVA and VC. Twenty-three hooch's in the hamlet were destroyed and nine VC bodies were counted from the air. Delta had also transitioned from platoon-size patrols to the smaller hunter-killer teams which could better saturate the area on and near the Batangan. Like other hunter-killer operations, unless the VC or NVA were within range of M-16's or machinegun fire, artillery was called in. Preferring to keep their locations secure, no sweeps were made after the artillery concentrations were fired.

The early morning hours of June 16 saw Bravo air assault west of Binh Son in conjunction with Vietnamese Provincial Unit (PRU) assets, to sweep the area after intelligence reported an increase in enemy activity.

Later that evening at 9:00PM, Delta's 2nd Platoon suffered four wounded, two with serious head wounds and one with shrapnel in the back. Another soldier, SP/4 Dennis Curtis was killed. Curtis was age twenty and single from Greece, New York.

Lieutenant Robert Wight had his Delta platoon positioned with the company headquarters section at CAP 142 on the coast. The 2nd Platoon had reported its night ambush position allegedly north of Chau Me (2) on the southern edge of a large lake.

Wight and the company command group heard and observed several explosions, and Delta's commander was immediately on the radio calling his 2nd Platoon for a situation report. The 2nd Platoon leader replied he had been mortared and Wight could hear his voice shaking on the radio. The platoon leader called in his position but this did not match with the position he called in earlier for his ambush. The site of the explosions was much closer to the sea.

After dustoff's removed the wounded, the platoon leader was ordered to move the remainder of his men to the beach for more security with their backs to the sea. At that point SP/4 Curtis' body was discovered and, because the dustoff's had departed, his comrades carried the body with them to the beach. The platoon leader also left two weapons behind but retrieved them the next morning when he returned to the area.

It was apparent to Lieutenant Wight that the 2nd Platoon leader's "ambush" position was not mortared but hit by enemy grenades at close range. A lack of security and/or too many solders sleeping could only account for the enemy's ability to get that close, within grenade range of its position. There was no heavy rain or heavy foliage to be used as an alibi. One of the platoon's soldiers later discovered a partially destroyed plastic spool from a Claymore wire roll, which appeared to have been a homemade grenade stuffed with C4 explosive on the inner layer with nails on the outer layer, all taped together.

An investigation was conducted the morning of June 17 and the 2nd Platoon leader insisted at that time his platoon had been spread out in four ambushes close together and probably had fired on each other. Lt. Wight wasn't buying it and felt the platoon leader's likely falsification of his ambush position and failure to maintain security led to the disaster. Wight felt a court-martial would have been in order, but it was not his decision to make. The sordid affair was an example of a small unit leader falsifying information to take a perceived "easier way", either out of boredom or fear of the enemy. This lack of leadership cost some serious casualties and a soldier's life. It has haunted Wight ever since.

The 1st Squad of Delta's 1st Platoon had been providing security for an engineer unit in the refugee village of An Ky, on the north side of Hill 26, in the area of CAP team 144. Late morning on June 17, a Combat Engineer Vehicle (CEV) left for CAP 143 without asking Delta's troops to provide security. The CEV detonated a mine which killed four engineers and wounded three more. The mine was a 105mm Howitzer round that was command detonated. One dead engineer was found by Delta's soldiers forty-five minutes later. He had been stripped of his clothes and shot four times. The soldiers found signs he had been dragged a short distance before being executed.

As the battalion's soldiers and ARVN continued their coordinated operations under Operation Geneva Park, life for the Marine CAP teams remained the same, a day by day contest for control of their assigned slice of Vietnamese real estate and the security of the hamlet the Vietnamese entrusted to them. At 2:30AM June 18, CAP 137's small squad was hit with a barrage of B-40 rockets, 82mm and 60mm mortar rounds followed by a ground attack by an estimated fifty VC/NVA, using satchel charges, Bangalore Torpedoes and grenades. The Marines and their PF's answered the attack with M-16 and M-79 small-arms fire. Illumination rounds and Cobra gunships also supported the CAP defenders. When it was over one PF soldier was killed and three wounded. The Marines suffered three wounded while capturing an enemy machinegun, hand grenades and recovering two VC bodies. At

3:20AM CAP 136 spotted three more VC, opened fire and killed all three, capturing a new M-16 rifle, cartridge belt, medical bag and documents.

The 198th Light Infantry Brigade renewed its coordination of a "Herbicide" (Agent Orange) mission to be run on June 19, covering a corridor five and one-half miles west to east of LZ Gator, and one-half mile north to south, which would end on the western rim of the southern rocket pocket. Charlie Company's patrols in the area were advised to be only one-quarter mile north or south of the corridor "as a matter of precaution".

Despite the occasional aggressiveness of the Vietnamese Popular Force (PF) and Regional Force (RF) soldiers in their defense of hamlets, "Vietnamization" in the battalion's area of operations brought mixed and conflicting results. At 1:00AM the morning of June 19, CAP 137 Marines and its PF's by Binh Son, spotted a light in their assigned hamlet. Upon approaching it they spotted AK-47 weapons and then some Vietcong which prompted a short firefight in which one Marine was shot in the back three times by a PF soldier, allegedly an accident. He died before reaching the hospital.

Soldiers on LZ Dottie were warned that some PF and RF soldiers were turning their US-issued weapons over to children to turn in as part of the Volunteer Informant Program (VIP) to collect money. Yet in other hamlets PF's, RF's and PRU's continued to die in small shoot-outs against the enemy each and every day. On June 22, two PF and RF company-size sweeps killed thirty VC and NVA in the Binh Son District. They also captured one NVA along with a machinegun, recoilless rifle and explosives.

"Snatch Missions" were intensified in which scouts from air cavalry units flew low over suspected concentrations of VC and NVA. If one or two VC or NVA soldiers were isolated the birds pursued them. If they turned to fire they were cut down. If they chose to run, the birds landed almost on top of them to snatch them up for questioning. Intelligence collected from these "snatched" insurgents continued to point to the 21st NVA Regiment planning a major attack on Binh Son, the New Life Hamlets, and the Marine CAP teams throughout the 5th/46th Battalions AO.

The work of the "Snatch Teams" was arduous and full of surprises. Flying low some four and one-quarter miles west of LZ Minuteman on June 24, an air-scout team found a guerilla too fleet of foot to catch, and so he was cut down. The team then flew northeast to

Phu Nhieu (1). As it approached at low level the team surprised a group of Vietcong seated for a propaganda lecture. The VC promptly reached for their Ak-47's to fire on the Huey. Gunships worked over the hamlet with unknown results.

On the morning of June 21, 1969 Echo's Recon Platoon suffered a severe loss without a shot being fired at the enemy. Four of its soldiers were graduating from the Americal Combat Center's Recon School on the Chu Lai beach. As they waited for the graduation ceremony to begin, a 122mm Soviet rocket slammed into a building next to where they stood. Recon's platoon sergeant, SSG John Forshag and platoon leader 1LT Jim Daniels flew to Chu Lai to identify their men from some other soldiers who were also killed in the rocket attack. Forshag did not see the gaping wounds on the dead they were accustomed to seeing in the field. He remembered, "There was very little evidence of injury that I could see. There were some small marks on them but not what I would have thought to be enough to kill someone." The two leaders thought they had done the men a favor by sending them to Chu Lai for two weeks of training, coupled with some free time and a chance to have some fun on the beach.

Echo's Recon soldiers who answered their final roll call that day were, PFC Danny Endicott, age twenty and single from Columbus, Ohio; PFC Andrew Kokesh, age twenty-three and married from Aitkin, Minnesota; PFC William Malone, age twenty and married from Afton, Tennessee and PFC Robert Nozewski, also twenty and single from Dearborn, Michigan. Recon's PFC Richard McConnell was hit by fragments in the chest, arms and legs, but would live.

Alpha Company also had soldiers in the class and two were killed. SP/4 Robert Bittle, age twenty-four from Arkansas, Kansas had only been in-country for one month. Also killed was PFC Gordon McMillan, age eighteen and single from East Meadow, New York. Another Alpha grunt, PFC Thomas Bahner, suffered fragment wounds in the buttocks, back and legs but he survived.

Charlie's 2nd Platoon air assaulted into the area where Chu Lai's radar plotted a back azimuth to the rocket launch site. They shot at one Vietcong who dropped a bag of rice and some sandals and jumped into a tunnel. The platoon found no air holes nearby and threw some CS gas canisters into the tunnel opening. One hour later the VC had not surfaced. They surmised he was killed and moved on. Nothing else was found.

On the afternoon of June 22, the Americal Division headquarters informed the battalion another defoliation mission would be flown on June 25, one-half mile south of the track of the mission flown on June 19, also following the same west to east pattern.

The early morning of June 23 presented some hope the battalion would bag a large group of VC reported to be in Binh Yen (2), three and one-half miles southwest of Gator. Bravo, which was still working west of Binh Son with PRU soldiers, moved further west to set up three blocking positions in an arc south of the targeted hamlet. Charlie Company, north of Binh Yen in the southern rocket area, made a night move the evening before to occupy positions northwest of the hamlet (2nd and 3rd Platoons) and northeast (1st Platoon). At first light Charlie's soldiers moved in with Vietnamese National Police to search and clear the hamlet. Only three peasants were questioned and released, a disappointing result for a long nights march.

Delta's troops continued to work in conjunction with ARVN on the Batangan as well as provide security for the combat engineers sweeping for mines just south of LZ Minuteman. While on a sweep, the mine team missed a mine and the third man behind the sweeper hit it, wounding seven engineers and three of Delta's troops who were providing flank security. Delta's grunts were treated and remained in the field as "walking wounded."

On the morning of June 24, the battalion was alerted for yet another defoliation mission, to take place June 27, covering a five and one-half mile west to east corridor between the defoliation missions flown on the 19th and 22nd. Charlie Company continued its mission in the rocket pocket on the periphery of the defoliated area, being assured the one-quarter mile distance from the spray would be sufficient. In just six days, three defoliation missions were flown west of LZ Gator, with the periphery of the spray missions ending only two and three-quarter miles west of the LZ. The winds from the mountains undoubtedly carried the toxic fumes farther east over Gator, the results of which are still impacting its soldiers forty years later.

At noon Delta's 1st Platoon, commanded by 1LT Robert Wight, working on the neck of land leading to the Batangan about one-quarter mile north of Chau Me (1), spotted ten to fifteen Vietcong. As they moved to contact the point man's M-79 malfunctioned and the VC moved into a series of bunkers concealed in thick vegetation next to the Chau Me Dong River. The platoon called for an air strike which a forward air controller flying nearby was happy to oblige, then finished with artillery rounds as they approached the area. No bodies were found from the air strike but the walk turned up numerous command-detonated mines and punji pits, deep holes with sharp bamboo stakes pointed upward to pierce the unlucky soul who fell into them. The next day, walking through an abandoned hamlet the platoon found some pressure-release mines, two two-foot by three-foot punji pits and blood inside a bunker. Fresh foot prints indicated wounded VC had passed through quickly.

Several days later Wight's platoon established several observation posts (OP's) spread out on sand dunes on the coast. One OP spotted a Vietnamese male in black pajamas carrying two wicker baskets. They decided not to yell "Dung Lai" ("Stop") as the individual had too much distance from them and would escape. Although he carried no weapon, there was no doubt he was VC, for all "civilians" were ensconced in New Life Hamlets in the area, unable to walk the countryside.

The OP opened fire with two M-79 grenade rounds landing at his feet, good shooting at a fleeing enemy, which brought him down. The OP rushed forward to find the man bleeding from wounds to his arms and legs. A search of the baskets uncovered medical supplies, cloth bandages, penicillin, sulfa tablets and the like. A chopper came in to pick him up for interrogation but not before one grunt cold-cocked him with his fist as a farewell gesture. In the daily battle with the Vietcong, sometimes successes came in small measures. The squad was happy to take an enemy medic with supplies out of the field, and hoped that the intended recipients, perhaps from the recent air strike a few days prior, would suffer more for not having them.

On June 25, the 198th Brigade advised the battalion that yet another defoliation mission would be flown on the 28th, this time five miles southwest of Gator, covering a four-mile long corridor from the western edge of the Annamite Mountain Chain moving east. To insure proper coverage, the Brigade advised "There will be two sweeps from the air". Bravo and Charlie companies had begun making a sweep parallel to each other, to search and clear the area north of the Tra Bong River in CAP 138's zone. On the morning of the 26th, Bravo was air assaulted south of Phu Long (1) on the coastal peninsula while Charlie air assaulted east of the hamlet to set up a search and destroy mission against, what intelligence reports indicated, was the 95A Sapper

Company. The Marines and PF's of CAP 133 also participated in the operation.

By mid-morning Bravo's second platoon found a cache of clothes and food in a sub-hamlet south of Phu Long. The clothes, food and hamlet were burned. Sporadic automatic weapons fire wounded one grunt. Charlie detained a VC female suspect, who was flown to LZ Bayonet. At 10:00AM, Charlie came under small arms fire and requested some artillery from a Forward Air Controller (FAC) flying overhead. At the same time CAP 133 came under fire and called the FAC for support. The FAC looked at both requests and concluded Charlie Company and the CAP were firing at each other. Neither element took casualties.

To The Mountains Again

Little did Bravo and Delta know that a larger mission was just around the corner, one that would test their mental mettle and physical stamina beyond what they had experienced on the coastal plain. Delta's commander, Captain John Goorley, was ordered to move his company to LZ Minuteman by noon, get resupplied at Minuteman and to say nothing to the ARVN other than, "We are leaving for a while." B-52 bombers were dropping heavy payloads of bombs ("Arc Light Strike") in the Nui Hoi Mountains ten miles southwest of Binh Son. Bravo, Charlie and Delta were tasked to air assault into the rugged mountains early the next morning to exploit the B-52 strike, conduct a battle damage assessment (BDA) and hit the NVA wherever they found them.

Early on the morning of June 27, LZ Stinson was established as a forward Tactical Operations Center for LTC Wagner to monitor the operation. Bravo, Charlie and Delta landed nine miles further west, deep into the mountains to seize and search three separate company objectives. Bravo landed first to secure the LZ for the others. When all had landed, Bravo immediately pushed one-quarter mile eastward where they engaged two NVA, killing both and capturing uniforms, steel helmets and two AK-47's. Delta moved due south from the LZ and Charlie pushed slightly north.

The mountain terrain was the most treacherous the battalion's soldiers had encountered in many months. The small landing zone was on the bank of a river, peppered by large boulders and surrounded by towering ridges which sandwiched the soldiers into a narrow valley. The steep sides of the valley were covered with dense vegetation at the lower elevations and a combination of scrub brush and trees at the higher elevations. On each side of the river were well-worn trails that led to "nowhere". The grunts off-loading the birds instinctively knew the trails belonged to the NVA.

The grunts were loaded down with extra ammo in case they met main-force NVA and moved slowly through the heavy undergrowth and steep ridges. Each soldier knew the obvious without saying it, the sound of the landing birds had alerted the NVA and they would be soon coming out to meet them. Bravo led the assault, landing in Hueys to secure the LZ. Delta and Charlie arrived in larger Chinooks, a riskier gamble with such large and cumbersome aircraft landing in a narrow valley, but the move was designed to get more troops on the ground quicker. The NVA were not present and the gamble paid off. Each company labored hard to get out of the narrow landing zone and to make the relative safety of the thick vegetation, even though movement was difficult and the heat overpowering.

At 1:25PM, Delta called a dustoff for three heat casualties. By noon Bravo had started a slow climb up a high hill following a preplanned route to reach their objective, Hill 270. At 4:23PM, a "Minuteman" Huey (175th Assault Helicopter Company) was shot down by .50 caliber heavy machine gun fire on the same hill. The crew made it to the river bed and was picked up by another bird. Captain Schopp, Commander of Bravo, sent two platoons to secure the M-60 machines guns, an M-79 grenade launcher and a M-16 rifle left on the Huey. The bird was set on fire and then an air strike was placed on it for good measure.

The dense undergrowth required the soldiers to cut a trail whenever they moved, making movement very slow and exhausting. Machetes were not up to the task, becoming dull quickly and exhausting the men who used them, but it was all they had. Captain Schopp sent one of Bravo's platoons forward to cut a trail, changing the lead element every half-hour then allowing them to move to the back of the file for rear security. When the column came upon an old bomb crater where they planned to accept resupply, it proved too small for a landing site. Moving on they found another crater which again, proved too small. The third crater they found was large enough to allow a helicopter to hover and drop supplies. With machetes his men cleared the area, their resupply was dropped, and they moved out.

The 4th/6th ARVN Battalion was also lifted to the mountains and conducted operations north of the 5th/46th on a parallel course. At 10:30AM on June 28, Charlie Company found a hooch just north of the Landing Zone, which contained one ton of salt. The salt and hooch were promptly destroyed. Charlie found six more hooch's at 1:00PM and they were also burned. Delta, fifteen minutes later, captured one NVA soldier just west of the battalion's landing zone, who admitted to being part of the 21st NVA Regiment and reported there were three hundred and fifty Vietcong one mile southwest of their location.

AT 6:40PM, Bravo was still making slow progress eastward, coming down off a ridge to a stretch of flat land. The 1st Platoon reported finding some bunkers and beyond them hearing Vietnamese voices. Schopp caught up with his 1st Platoon and they started moving west, back past the bunkers, looking for the enemy in the direction of the voices. After hitting a solid wall of brush by a dried streambed, Schopp sent the 2nd Platoon upstream and the 1st Platoon downstream, looking for the NVA. He returned to his headquarters element and his 3rd Platoon to secure his CP and prepare for whatever may come.

The 2nd Platoon started upstream and killed one NVA, capturing a pack while one of their men was wounded in the shoulder. The first platoon found a trail leading south up a hill and ran into .50 caliber machine gun and small arms fire, but suffered no casualties. At this time Schopp with the 3rd Platoon was hit from three directions, the NVA close enough to throw some grenades downhill at their position. One soldier was hit in the leg, one in the back and another, running straight towards Schopp, was hit with fragments in his buttocks. The soldier went down and rolled over, where Schopp could see his right cheek hanging out his pants. He looked at Schopp and yelled, "I'm hit". Schopp laughed out loud, not believing what he was seeing, "I know."

The ARVN, who's Fire Coordination Line was just one-quarter mile farther north, coordinated artillery fire against the NVA encountered by Bravo. Blue Ghost helicopter gunships came on station at 7:30PM to provide more pinpoint fire support and the artillery was placed on "check fire" to allow the gunships to work the area. At 8:00PM Bravo started blowing trees with C-4 to prepare an LZ to lift out their wounded. The dustoff came in with its lights off in the dark, turning on its landing lights just as it descended to keep from hitting trees. The NVA opened up on the bird and it quickly pulled away without landing, returning to Chu Lai to assess its damage. Bravo's troops worked on improving their defenses. An hour later another dustoff came over only to be driven away again by ground fire.

At 11:00PM another dustoff made a try, coming under automatic weapons fire at tree top level, but landed anyway. As it lifted back up to tree top level, the NVA raked it again with heavy fire, wounding the medic on board just as the bird pulled away. The pilot radioed he was losing oil pressure and couldn't fly much longer. He limped three miles east to get out of the mountains, and then set down on a dry river bed.

Lieutenant Colonel Wagner had his own Command & Control chopper, already low on fuel, pick up the dustoff crew and the wounded. This made his C&C Huey overloaded and Wagner decided to stay on the riverbed with his radio operators to give his pilot a chance to make it back with the wounded. His pilot refused to leave him there in NVA country so Wagner's team climbed back on the Huey.

There were now seventeen soldiers inside or on the Huey's struts outside the door. The battalion commander was one of those standing on the struts, hanging on for dear life, to make room for the wounded inside the bird. The UH-1H Huey managed to make it to the hospital at Chu Lai and ran out of fuel while touching down at the hospital's landing pad. The bird had to be towed by truck across the Chu Lai base for refueling.

At 9:30PM, the ARVN north of Bravo found ten NVA killed by the B-52 strike. The gunships which had come to support Bravo moved one mile northeast, to support the ARVN who also came under enemy fire. At 11:00PM while Bravo was getting their wounded out, the gunships, firing in support of the ARVN, killed one ARVN soldier and wounded eight more, in a friendly fire screw up, hitting part of the ARVN Battalions CP. By 11:30PM, the NVA finally broke contact.

Although tasked with multiple missions in rapid succession, and now with three of its companies strung out in the mountains, the 5th/46th Infantry Battalion had the advantage of good strength in numbers compared to previous operations it undertook, such as Task Force Cooksey. Many of its troops were seasoned in the field, but this experience made the grunts more cautious and in the minds of some company commanders, too cautious.

The newest company commander to the battalion took over Alpha Company from Captain Ben Anderson, who finished his time in the field and was assigned as the battalions S-4. Anderson had built up the morale and expertise of Alpha after the previous commander was relieved for incompetence. The new commander replacing him was to bring the company down again, to a new low.

On June 28, with the battalion's total assigned strength of eight hundred and seventy-five, Wagner had seven hundred and eighty-six present for duty. A better ratio of strength than LTC Lyon had in the late summer of 1968, when the battalion was strung out in the high hills west of Tam Ky. On the 28th another twenty enlisted soldiers, FNG's, were processed into the battalion. Alpha's new commander got his feet wet with his company manning the bunker line on LZ Gator but once they returned to the field the unit would begin to unravel.

By mid-morning on June 29, Bravo sent two platoons back up the streambed to check it out. After forty-five minutes they had not traveled far, the terrain being dense and the troops being cautious, Schopp thought too cautious. Schopp, concerned at the slow pace, went to check them out. The 2nd Platoon was in the streambed, afraid to move up. The 1st Platoon was on their left at the bottom of a steep hill. Schopp took a soldier from 2nd Platoon to move with him and reached a small trail to the left which led up the hill. He yelled to his first platoon to move up the hill in tandem with him. As they moved uphill they saw hooch's and some people in them. Because of the prior night's fight with the NVA who tried to destroy the dustoffs coming in for their wounded, there would be no hesitation in this assault and no mercy, the gloves came off.

Both platoons assaulted through the complex, hosing the area with their M-16's and M-79's and taking no chances for return fire, shooting everything in sight as they moved through the complex of thatched huts. When the sweep through the camp was over, Bravo had killed fourteen NVA and captured four. The "camp" turned out to be an NVA hospital. They found six hooch's, each twenty feet by twenty feet with fifty litters inside, serving as the hospital wards. Nine other hooch's ten square feet in size were used for cooking and as quarters for hospital staff. Dead littered the area, patients who were too ill to escape into the hills. Bravo's troops found a stack of documents which Schopp secured in his rucksack and, as small compensation for the evening before, found an NVA Officers belt which he kept.

Artillery was called in just beyond the area that was searched, to prevent a counter attack or ambush. After the search of the hooch's was completed, Bravo burned them down. Bravo's troops also found a communication wire that led into the heavy brush. Reluctant to follow the wire, they cut it wherever they found a line.

Aware of a big find, Wagner told Delta and Charlie Company to pack up and move to Bravo's location quickly, in case of a major counterattack. One of Bravo's prisoners told Schopp that one doctor and nine nurses had been at the hospital the night before and fled when the artillery fire began. Bravo was now in the 4th/6th ARVN Battalion area, having crossed the fire coordination line. The ARVN, unnerved by the friendly fire incident the previous night, were reluctant to call in the artillery requested by Bravo to keep any approaching NVA at bay. Bravo came under small arms and machinegun fire from an estimated squad of NVA in bunkers nearby. Schopp called for an air strike and this time the ARVN obliged. Jet fighters overhead dropped five-hundred pound bombs and napalm. Although hunkered down, one soldier caught a piece of shrapnel in the neck which cut an artery; a stray bullet hit another man in the thigh. A dustoff was called for the two wounded soldiers and four captured NVA patients. An interrogation team in Chu Lai eagerly awaited the NVA.

That afternoon a resupply ship came in with food, ammunition and replacements. It came under heavy enemy fire which wounded three Bravo replacements on board who remained on the bird to be dusted off. The bird was only able to kick out four cases of C-rations (forty-eight meals) and two boxes of M-16 ammunition before the ground fire got too hot. The resupply birds then aborted the mission and departed with most of the C-rations and replacements. The continued enemy fire throughout the area gave Bravo's troops vindication for their blazing sweep through the hospital.

The find of the NVA hospital became the division's attraction for the day. At 10:15AM, the Americal Division Commander, Major General Lloyd B. Ramsey, was briefed by LTC Wagner on LZ Stinson. At 2:35AM, Brigadier General Clement, Assistant Division Commander arrived at LZ Stinson and was briefed by the battalions S-3, Major James Krause. Twenty-five minutes later Colonel Jere Whittington, new commander of the 198th Light Infantry Brigade was also briefed at Stinson.

Three hours after the four NVA prisoners were dusted off the results of the interrogation came back to Wagner. The camp Bravo had discovered was an area-wide hospital for Vietcong and North Vietnamese Army (NVA) regulars, manned by a provisional unit which sent forty walking wounded farther west into the mountains as Bravo closed in to the camp. One hundred other patients were reported to be in the area, too ill to walk far, but strong enough to get out of the hospital complex before being swept by Bravo. One prisoner was from the 16th NVA Recoilless Rifle Company, which had made contact with the 1st/52nd Infantry Battalion and a Marine CAP team ten days prior.

Another NVA was a cook from the 3rd NVA Division who was blind, and had been at the hospital since April. He mentioned that each of the three companies in his battalion had two .51 caliber anti-aircraft guns. A third prisoner was a rifleman/sapper who had been in the hospital since May 30. He told his captors the hospital staff moved west on June 25. The fourth prisoner was a rifleman/sapper with the 526th Local Force Sapper Battalion. The strength of his company was thirty men. He arrived at the hospital on June 25, two days before the battalion air assaulted into the mountains.

The prisoner Delta captured shortly after landing in the mountains was interrogated on LZ Bayonet by the intelligence section of the 6th ARVN Regiment. This NVA had been wearing a green uniform and the classic "Ho Chi Minh Sandals", made of rubber tire treads. He had infiltrated from North Vietnam three months prior but came down with malaria. He had been in the same hospital swept later by Bravo to recover, but was on his way to rejoin his unit just when the 5th/46th landed in the mountains. The 5th Battalion of the 21st NVA Regiment was, by his description, a "two hours walk west and one and one-half hour walk to the north" from his spot of capture.

As night closed in on June 29, the 1st Battalion of the 6th ARVN Regiment moved in to support the 4th ARVN Battalion, turning east and northeast to search for NVA while the 4th Battalion remained in place. The ARVN were no more than three-quarters mile north of Bravo's position, but in this operation as most joint efforts under Operation Geneva Park, the US and Vietnamese did not make physical contact.

Bravo, Charlie and Delta were also tasked to move east in tandem with the ARVN, but Charlie and Delta, moving slowly in the dense vegetation and up steep ridgelines, had still not reached Bravo's location. Schopp was not willing to move Bravo alone with more NVA lurking in the mountains while he was low on ammunition, food and was weighed down with eight extra rucksacks of his evacuated wounded. He elected to stay near the hospital and strengthen his position. This was Schopp's second combat tour in Vietnam. With virtually no resupply for days and dwindling ammunition, he was angry that his commander "left us dangling out there way too long."

By the morning of June 30, the 4th/6th ARVN reported finding twenty-one more NVA bodies from the B-52 strike. They wanted the 5th/46th to move east with them in case they flushed out a large group of NVA but Bravo was still waiting for the slow moving Charlie and Delta, and had more of the hospital complex to check out. At 12:40PM, Bravo found sixteen old graves and thirty feet away, another thirty freshly dug graves. It reported its find to the forward Command Post on Stinson only to hear the command group order the soldiers to dig the graves and confirm the body count.

At 1:10PM, a much-needed resupply Huey came in with an escort of gunships but came under heavy ground fire, despite the gunships prepping the area, and the ship had to abort. Three more Bravo soldiers were aboard the ship to come in as new replacements. All three soldiers were wounded by ground fire as the bird hovered to find an opening to drop supplies. The Huey took them to a Chu Lai hospital along with the supplies it could not drop. On the bird PFC Ronald Gingros was hit with fragment wounds on the left side of the head, SP/4 Steven Anderson a head wound with a possible loss of his left eye and Sgt. James Eklund, fragments wounds in his right hand.

Air-Scout Snatch Teams flew missions five miles southeast of Bravos location, where the mountains ended and the Piedmont began, just north of the Tra Khuc River and eight miles west of Quang Ngai. The snatching part of the mission was difficult but the killing part was easy. At 3:20PM, in the span of ten minutes five Vietcong evading in uniforms were killed. At 5:00PM, Bravo reported they had dug up four of the "fresh" graves at random and estimated these individuals had been killed within the past twenty-four to forty-eight hours. They would do no more digging. With little food, ammunition or water, Bravo chose to stay near the hospital complex a third night until Charlie and Delta, now only one-quarter mile away, could link up with them the next morning.

Charlie and Delta made slow but steady progress moving east, trying to link up with Bravo. In the words of one grunt, the area was "spooky". The soldiers could sense the enemy was nearby, and there were a lot of them, always in the shadows. As they moved cautiously they could hear noises ahead of them, the breaking of the underbrush and the sound of metal rubbing against bodies as enemy hospital patients tried to evade the grunts.

Delta's LT Wight noticed a solitary grave on the north edge of a speed trail. It was man-sized, with a foot of rock and dirt covering the length of the body. A bamboo cross shaped into a circle with a star woven on the inside was positioned at the foot of the grave. Wight found the grave a lonely existence for this dead soldier with only the rain drops, leaches and falling leaves of the season to decorate his grave. How did he die? By sickness or shrapnel? The hardened platoon leader felt sympathy, knowing his men could face the same fate. Death was the only common link they had with the enemy.

The battalion's soldiers were unable to get resupplied, the resupply birds claiming the weather was getting too bad and the cloud ceiling too low to fly in the mountainous terrain. Most soldiers had little or no rations. They found water in bomb craters made by the B-52's. Some of the "seasoned" grunts had not yet experienced mountain movement, having cut their teeth with the enemy on the coastal plains or the rolling hills of the Piedmont. This terrain challenged their very souls.

The undergrowth was thick, the terrain was steep, the triple canopy jungle almost impenetrable, with water slowly dripping from the leaves. Occasionally some daylight appeared where the B-52 bombs had ripped through the canopy to create a hole to the jungle floor. In night positions discipline was strict, no poncho shelters, no noise, lights, cigarettes or lighting small blocks of C-4 explosive to heat what few C-rations were left. Each night they prepared to expect a massive attack. Many had bouts of dysentery. But, in the memory of one grunt, "the mountains bent us over but we did not break."

By late morning of July 1, Charlie and Delta descended the north side of Hill 270 and approached a dry streambed. In this movement into the NVA base camp discovered by Bravo, the companies did not have a close feel for each others position. They were tired, hungry and mesmerized by what they found. Freshly dug graves were on one side of a small footpath while bunkers were on the other. Lt. Wight of Delta placed his men by the graves for security, the salmon-colored dirt giving evidence of their recent construction. Wight figured they came from the B-52 Arc Light strikes, and were hastily buried before the hospital staff left the area with their walking wounded.

The platoon leader and his point man, Dan Chaffin, followed a trail moving west which revealed several more bunkers, each constructed with layers of logs and mud. They passed a small fresh water stream, ideal for an encampment. Soon the vegetation covered over the trail and the two went to ground crawling forward. Suddenly the point man came face-to-face with a claymore mine just off the trail and a trip wire attached to a flare. Wight recognized this ordnance as G.I. They pulled back and Wight radioed Captain Goorley for the location of Charlie and Bravo. It was then they realized they had almost walked into a defensive position of Bravo.

Another platoon of Delta walked into the enemy complex on a trail, walking single file and sullen. They passed by a dead female NVA nurse off the side of the trial. Each soldier fired one round into her lifeless body as they walked by. There was no emotion or hesitation. When the platoon leader reached the body it was a puddle of blood. He looked at her body and his men stared at him. The Lieutenant shot her again and walked on, thinking "How did I and my men get like this?" In a few days he would see how the enemy could turn his comrades in Lieutenant Wight's platoon into a puddle of blood, and he became more emotionless and stoic like the others.

Charlie Company made a small perimeter southeast and east of the hospital area, Delta moved across a stream which flowed through the camp to the northeast sector, and Bravo kept their position a short distance away to the northwest, along a ridge line.

Before the arrival of Charlie and Delta, Bravo spotted a Vietcong sitting on a rock and killed him at 8:00AM. Once Charlie and Delta were in place Captain Schopp climbed a small tree and asked the new arrivals to pop smoke, to insure they were where he wanted them to be, having had the best feel for the terrain in the area. But they were not where he wanted them to be in case of attack, and so he grabbed a machete and hacked his way to redirect their positions. This was at 12:55PM.

Realizing he was walking around the area alone, Schopp had one of his soldiers accompany him back to his crudely arranged landing zone. On the way they spotted another Vietcong stalking them in the area, possibly a wounded patient hiding nearby. Schopp borrowed the other soldiers M-16 and, when the VC raised his head from the brush, shot him twice in the head. The other soldier said, "There's another one, it's my turn, let me get him." Schopp gave him the M-16 and the second VC was killed. Weapons were not found, but documents were, which were sent back on the resupply bird which came in shortly after. The resupply boosted the morale of the soldiers greatly, with C-rations, soft drink and mail.

As Charlie settled in on their part of the hospital complex for a noon meal they saw bodies everywhere as a result of the previous artillery and napalm strike and Bravo's subsequent assault through the complex. Sergeant Ron Bentley, who one month prior had been blown off a truck on the Tra Bong Road from RPG fire, set down to eat some food. He was having a bout of dysentery and needed to eat to keep his strength up. Two dead female NVA laid nearby, nurses he thought, who had been incinerated from the napalm, their eye sockets hollowed with smoke coming out of them. Numbed by the trek through the mountains and now intense hunger, he kept on eating, thinking "this is cold but I must eat".

A short distance away was another dead patient, lying on the ground and partially covered with leaves, next to a cot. He had one bullet hole in the head, his eyes wide open, staring at Charlie's grunts as he must have stared at the soldier who shot him. Each walked over to look at him. After their noon meal Bravo moved a short distance to set up on a ridgeline in some abandoned NVA bunkers. They found a wood-carved Chinook helicopter, some wooden Chicom practice grenades and a cardboard tank cutout.

At 2:00PM, a resupply ship came in with gunships for protection. The gunships spotted two suspected .51 caliber anti-aircraft gun locations one-half mile northeast of Bravo's position and laid down rocket fire while the resupply ship offloaded its cargo. In its haste to drop its load and run, two water bladders broke, leaving the grunts without safe water. Charlie's grunts filled their canteens from the stream running through the hospital complex, not sure what bacteria may be picked up in the stream from the dead bodies lying in the camp. They dropped their iodine tabs in the water and hoped for the best.

At 2:20PM, Bravo found four more graves and a quick dig found bodies in each. As night fell requests were made for more air strikes at first light, in the easterly direction the three infantry companies were ordered to go. At 9:28PM, Bravo reported finding nine more graves, each with a decomposed body. The bodies had white t-shirts and black shorts. Charlie Company discovered fifty-seven graves with bodies in all. A quick dig revealed ten of the graves were fresh, and five of them contained bodies in NVA uniforms. Forty seven graves were older, with bodies already decomposed. During the evening some of Delta's soldiers heard the cry of a wounded NVA soldier hiding close by. His groans of agony continued throughout the night and ended early in the morning.

The next morning (July 2) ended the grave digging activity and the three rifle company's set out to move in an easterly direction to cover the west to east corridor of the Arc Light (B-52) strike that preceded their arrival into the mountains. Each company was tasked to hack their own separate trail but keep on a parallel course, staying close together, with visual contact if at all possible, in case of attack.

Delta formed the north column; Bravo was in the center and Charlie to the south, all trekking eastward. Deltas Commander, Captain John Goorley had date of rank so he was appointed Commander of the three-company movement. Lt Wights platoon took up the task of pointing Delta Company and started cutting a path through the dense foliage to ascend the terrain, moving east. In short order the point element passed a stream in which Wight detected communications wire running the length of the stream. The four in the point element, LT Wight, SSG Melvin Fujita, PFC Larry Bryan and PFC Dennis Mobley hacked on and came to a deep gorge through which ran a swift-moving steam. Once they reached the stream the point element filled their canteens and was joined by the rest of Wights first platoon who did the same.

Wight saw the way forward as being extremely tough. To proceed down the riverbed would take them through physically hazardous terrain. He wanted to turn northwest but thick vegetation would require immense hacking to get through. He radioed Goorley to suggest that another platoon that was behind and above him find a better route but Goorley said to push on.

With the platoon waiting in the riverbed, Bryan and Mobley on point started cutting away at the dense vegetation, with Fujita and Wight behind them. As they moved to the top of a small rise a burst of fire cut into the two hackers and both went down, Bryan with a body wound and Mobley with a bullet across his wrist. The enemy fire was intense. Wight yelled to Mobley, to pull Bryan back, but with both wearing full rucksacks and pinned down, it was impossible.

Mobley managed to crawl free from the direct fire and crawled down a few short feet to Wight and Fujita, calling for a medic. Staff sergeant Fujita and Lieutenant Wight poured fire into the suspected enemy position. Then Wight heard a "peck", the familiar sound whenever the pin flew off a hand grenade and yelled "Grenade!" The grenade exploded as it rolled down the small path, but the foliage and slightly lower position they were in shielded them, as two more grenades exploded and shrapnel sailed over their heads.

Wight radioed Goorley to have soldiers from the main company element move to the flank and put down fire to get the pressure off their backs. One team of soldiers tried to do just that, and two, PFC Timothy Nunnally and SP/4 Kenneth Mahl who lead the charge, were cut down. Mahl was hit with a bullet to the head, guaranteeing him a quick death. Several others were wounded.

Bryan still lay wounded in the front, yelling to Fujita, "Fuj, don't leave me!" Fujita looked at Wight and without saying a word threw off his rucksack and started crawling towards Bryan. After crawling just two body lengths, Fujita lifted his head to get oriented and caught a round in his right temple, throwing him back. Wight then saw Bryan rise up to look for Fujita, Bryan caught a burst of fire in the chest and blood gushed from his mouth. Wight's medic Ronald Selle rushed forward from the safety of the riverbed and crawled forward to Fujita, confirming he was dead. Wight and Selle then crawled back behind a boulder. Air strikes were called and the three infantry company's popped smoke to mark their locations, fearful of friendly fire. The strikes, of necessity, would not be able to hit the NVA ambush position because it was too close to Delta's men, but would hit any other NVA positions in the direction the soldiers were headed.

After a half-hour of air strikes, Goorley ordered Wight's platoon to retrieve the bodies. Wight knew this was a task he must do himself. He reached Fujita's body while his platoon poured fire into the brush above him and pulled Fujita's body back down the path, with the help of Sergeant Amann, a squad leader. Wight noted that the wires to the claymore on Fujita's rucksack had been chopped up by the NVA's grazing fire. His rucksack, two M-16's, Fujita's ammo belt and Bowie Knife had already been taken by the NVA. Wight moved forward again and grabbed Bryan's body and dragged it back down the path as Bryan's blood mixed into the dirt of the land that claimed his life. Both bodies were wrapped in double ponchos.

SP/4 Leo Pillow and his squad from the third platoon, who had originally been designated to take the point that morning, volunteered to carry their dead comrades back to the dustoff site. They carried all four, the hackers Bryan and Fujita and the flankers, Nunnally and Mahl, three with gunshot wounds to the head and one with a bullet hole in the neck. Three more, one from the point element and two on the flanking attack were wounded, one seriously, with the possibility of losing a leg. As the volunteers brought the dead and wounded up the hill, the flanking survivors told of their sudden ambush, almost on top of the enemy under heavy fire. After the devastating burst of fire, the NVA walked out of the bush and the wounded flankers played dead as they felt their watches being taken from their wrists.

Pillow and nine others from the 3rd platoon made two trips to carry the dead, which required four soldiers to carry one body in the rough terrain. On each trip Pillow watched brain matter from his comrades' heads ooze onto his shirt, aware that only fate had allowed him to live. His comrades helped pass the ponchos up the narrow trail, the blood and brain matter continuing to leak out the ends of the ponchos. Pillows 3rd platoon was the same that fired rounds into the dead female NVA nurse by the NVA hospital. This action completed the cycle and left them with no further empathy for life or death. Delta's relatively new 3rd Platoon leader felt fear grow inside him and his seasoned men could see it in his eyes, but after a couple more days he began to settle down and became de-sensitized like everyone else.

Delta's troops had to blow trees with C4 explosive to clear a small opening for the dustoff to land. The tree stumps would only allow one bird to hover at a time, so each casualty had to be lifted up into the hovering ship.

The first attempt came at 10:05AM, but heavy machinegun fire came from a ridge one-quarter mile further north which hit the ship several times. It limped back to Chu Lai. The FAC called in an air strike on the suspected gun emplacement and at 11:15AM another dustoff was back on station, bringing in supplies for Delta and picking up the dead and wounded.

Those answering Delta's final roll call on July 2, 1969 were PFC Larry Bryan, age twenty and single from Highland, Michigan; SSG Melvin Fujita, age twenty-five and single, from Honolulu, Hawaii; PFC Kenneth Mahl, age twenty and single from New Orleans, Louisiana and PFC Timothy Nunnally, age twenty-one and single from Pico Rivera, California. Wight, Selle and Amann would receive Bronze Stars for valor for their actions at the deadly point of the ambush.

By 1:00PM, the three rifle companies were on the move again in an easterly direction towards the Piedmont, this time with Bravo in the lead, Delta slightly to the north and Charlie slightly to the south, in a modified wedge formation. A total of five air strikes were dropped in front of the moving formation, to the sides and behind the slow-moving column. As night approached the three rifle companies set up a defensive perimeter in a tall stand of elephant grass which greeted them when they started breaking out of the mountains. The next day, July 3, the three infantry companies continued their move east. Charlie was scheduled to be picked up on the 4th. At 7:05PM, a Charlie grunt was wounded by a sniper and was picked up by dustoff as the column continued to trek eastward.

By 3:50PM on the July 4, Independence Day, the 5th/46th was clear of the mountains and five Hueys came in for the first of three lifts to pick up the eighty-nine men of Charlie Company. Delta was now at a strength of only fifty-eight soldiers, with one of its squads still providing security at Tri Binh (1). Bravo's strength was at eighty-seven. After Charlie's extraction, Bravo and Delta moved one-half mile farther east and set up defensive positions for the night. At 6:20PM, Delta detained twenty-seven females and thirty-five children in the area, and placed them within their perimeter for the night. Sniper fire greeted the soldiers during the night.

The next morning LTC Wagner landed his C&C with an interrogation team to question the female villagers, who were subsequently released. Both remaining rifle companies and the interrogation team were lifted to LZ Stinson and then by larger Chinooks to LZ Gator. Artillery fire swept the area around the pick-up zone (PZ) to keep any lingering NVA at bay. By 2:55PM, Wagner's forward tactical operations center on Stinson was closed and all were "home" on LZ Gator.

Charlie, manning the bunker line on Gator set out an ambush team at dusk, one-quarter mile southwest of the bunker line. During the ambush they spotted movement and with enough light left, swept the area to find one of their claymore mines had been turned around to face their position.

Alpha departed Gator in the afternoon and moved by air back to the Batangan Peninsula. One platoon was placed in support of CAP 143. Another platoon plus mortars and the headquarters element would reside with CAP 142. The last platoon was charged with dividing itself to conduct two ambushes west of CAP 142. Alpha's overall mission was to interdict the continuing infiltration of Vietcong and NVA back onto the peninsula.

At mid-morning on July 6 Delta, along with a Provisional Reconnaissance Unit (PRU) and some Vietnamese National Police, air assaulted to one-half mile west of Tri Binh (4), to cordon and search a sub-hamlet suspected of harboring a sapper squad. Alpha of the 1st/6th

Infantry Battalion which had patrolled the area while the 5th/46th trekked through the mountains, served as a blocking force.

The PRU's found a tunnel with a closed door, just south of the landing zone. A PRU soldier opened the door with a stick and received a burst of AK-47 fire. The PRU returned the fire whereupon a Vietcong promptly closed the door. Five minutes later the VC attempted to escape through a rear exit but Wagner's C&C flying overhead took him in its sights and cut him down. A search of the tunnel revealed four hammocks, a transistor radio and some documents.

Delta set out to screen the southern rocket pocket area. The 4th Squad of its 2nd Platoon continued to assist the PF's in Tri Binh (1), where the squad had maintained a presence since early May and thus missed out on Delta's trek through the mountains. At 11:55AM on July 7, Bravo was lifted off Gator to LZ Fat City, three and one-half miles northeast of the northern boundary of the base at Chu Lai, to come under control of the 1st/6th Battalion in conjunction with operations in the northern rocket pocket.

Alpha on the Batangan found more bunkers and tunnels despite the saturation of the area during Russell Beach in January and February, the continued operations of Delta with the ARVN through June, and the establishment of additional Marine CAP teams on the peninsula as part of the extensive pacification effort. The six and one-half square mile peninsula never disappointed the soldiers and continued to cough up discoveries despite the heavy concentration of military forces.

One mission required Alpha Company to move down a grassy hillside to search some small hamlets. The ARVN were to accompany them but the ARVN sat for an hour and no one moved. Sergeant Raymond "Duke" Moriarty was anxious to move his squad and asked his platoon sergeant, Staff Sergeant "Birkie" Birkholtz, "What the hell is holding us up?" The platoon sergeant replied the ARVN were reluctant to move. Moriarty noticed a small circle of ARVN and Alpha Company officers talking, the body language of the ARVN indicating they weren't going anywhere near the hamlets. Birkholtz told his platoon the ARVN were flying a couple Kit Carson Scouts out to lead the way. The KC Scouts arrived, went into a pow wow with the ARVN and decided they too weren't moving down the hill. Both the ARVN and Scouts were chattering and waving their arms in excited debate.

Alpha Company was getting edgy. They were sitting on the hillside too long and becoming exposed to an attack. Another bird arrived and two Vietnamese soldiers jumped out, "Tiger Scouts", "Rangers", "The best of the best." With a cocky swagger they walked over to the group of ARVN officers, their tiger fatigues reminding Moriarty of strutting peacocks. Five minutes later Birkholtz came back and told his men, "The Tigers aren't walking down there either!"

Moriarty, not known for having much patience, replied, "We don't need those chicken shit little bastards to lead us anywhere!" He ordered his squad up, he took the point and the company started moving down the hill. Birkholtz warned, "Go ahead but keep your eyes open and watch your step."

Moriarty held his breath, waiting for the whole hill to open up on him. Behind him was Griffin, "Griff" a private who had been designated the squad leader before Moriarty had arrived and taught him a lot. Griff was from South Carolina and, as Moriarty fondly remembered, "A real country boy with a lot of common sense and experience in the bush. I would rather have two of his type of 'hillbillies' than a dozen of those city boys."

Behind Griff was "Jackson", a cautious, hyper and talkative black soldier regretting the position he found himself in. Moriarty reached a tree line and when his right foot lifted up to take a step, he heard a muffled "click". There was no time to run, no time to think about his wife, his little girl or his family. A second later he heard a loud thump and Griffin's voice behind him, "Shit!" A Bouncing Betty mine had sprung up between Moriarty and Griffin but it failed to explode.

Jackson, third from the front, starting jumping in small circles, "Fuck! Mother Fucker! Fuck! Fuck!" Moriarty regained his senses and yelled at Jackson to stop jumping up and down or he'd set off another mine. Griffin asked, "Now what?" Moriarty, "Well I guess we move on, we don't want to look like a bunch of pussies to the company do we?" Jackson spoke up, "Boss, fuck it. Let those Tiger gooks go first!" Moriarty continued with the point and Alpha reached their destination.

Later that evening "Birkie" walked over to Moriarty. "I thought I told you to watch your step?" They both laughed and Moriarty replied, "Yeah, I think you put the damn 'Moe Joe' on me, Birkie". Jackson sitting next to his squad leader wasn't laughing. "Boss, you know you a lucky Mother Fucker man! You could have been a dead Mother Fucker right now! Only reason your ass is still here is your number ain't up. If your number comes up, ain't a fucking thing you can do about it." Moriarty finished the conversation, "Well, I guess your number and Griff's number didn't come up either, now did it?"

Five Chieu Hoi's turned themselves in to CAP 143 on July 7, four males and one female. The males gave themselves up because of the constant pounding from air strikes in their assigned area one and one-half mile west of Highway One. They walked the eleven miles further east to the peninsula to see their families and then give up. The female was a VC cook in a tunnel system just east of Tan Duc where she said twenty VC were located in two large tunnels. An air strike was scheduled for the location.

Working at CAP 142 on the northern coast of the Batangan could be an idyllic situation when not dodging mines outside the refugee camp. The large refugee settlement protected by the CAP team lay astride an expansive sandy white beach capped by the blue waters of the South China Sea. At 10:00AM on July 8, Alpha Company's SP/4 Bob "Pete" Peterson decided to accompany some villagers to help them fish offshore. Peterson was tall and considered a practical joker. He was well liked and had just returned from an R&R in Hawaii where he spent time with his family and fiancée.

Peterson and two others pulled the pins on their hand grenades, waited two seconds, and then threw them into the water. This allowed the four second-delay fuse to explode just below the waters surface, stunning the fish which floated to the top for the Vietnamese to collect. But one of Peterson's grenades malfunctioned and exploded in his hand, killing him instantly and wounding two other soldiers and the Vietnamese with them in the boat. It was a tough and needless loss, owing to carelessness in the war zone. Peterson was twenty-one and single, from Jacksonville, Florida.

As idyllic as the beachside refugee camp was, it did not always compensate for frayed nerves and the death that waited the soldiers beyond the sand dunes. One Alpha patrol came back to the tin-roofed refugee camp after an arduous patrol around mine fields. They were tired and emotionally spent. Children greeted the grunts as they walked in with the usual banter, "Hey GI, you want fuck pictures?" "Hey GI you want back rub, you want soda, you want M-16 cleaned?" It was fifty cents for anything and everything except prostitutes, which cost five dollars.

Alpha's erratic but brave platoon leader had led the patrol around the mine fields and was in no mood for fifteen kids in his way. He yelled, "De De Mau" ("Get the hell away") several times but the children did not leave. He screamed at them, no response. The Lieutenant turned to the machine gunner next to him, grabbed his M-60 and proceeded to spray the kids with automatic weapons fire but as soon as he pulled the trigger the firing pin broke; an act of God for the children. No bullets exited the barrel. He threw the gun back into the chest of his gunner and walked away.

At 1:40PM a Charlie Company roving patrol, protecting engineers on Highway One just outside LZ Dottie, was approached by a group of Vietnamese with a "turn-in" under the VIP program. The Vietnamese unloaded nine 82mm and twenty-three 60mm mortar rounds, ten M-14 mines, seventy-seven Chicom grenades, fifty-two M70 grenade rounds, fifteen 105mm and one 155mm Howitzer artillery rounds, a satchel charge and two sticks of dynamite. The patrol summoned the battalions S-5, who paid the Vietnamese fourteen thousand Piasters, about one hundred and sixty-five American dollars

Daily activity on Gator's bunker line offered occasional sniper fire and the fleeting glance of VC too far away to engage with small arms and too insignificant to call fire missions. Numerous Vietnamese walked below the perimeter during the day, their eyes never looking forward, always up the hill to the bunkers. One Vietnamese boy was herding some cattle but was observed examining the several rows of concertina wire which encircled LZ Gator.

On the morning of July 12, a roving patrol just south of the bunker line saw a female with a weapon coming out of the bushes and she was promptly shot. When the soldiers approached the body the weapon turned out to be a metal sickle for cutting rice stalks.

The soldier who shot the young girl (the girl found to be eighteen years of age) was a FNG who, upon arriving at the battalion a few days before, claimed he may be a conscientious objector. The battalions Executive Officer told him to file paperwork if he was serious about his claim, but that he would be assigned to Charlie Company which wisely placed him in a good squad. During the morning patrol the conscientious objector (CO) saw the "insurgent" raise up three feet from his squad leader with a "knife in her hands" and he blasted her with eighteen rounds from his M-16. The soldiers CO claim was never filed.

On July 13 at 7:55AM, Alpha's 2nd Platoon patrolled in CAP 143's area, in the hamlet of Tan Duc, "inspecting" some freshly-dug tunnels by throwing in grenades. Sergeant John Martin stepped across a small gully but dragged his feet in doing so and set off an 81mm mortar round triggered by a pressure release device. Martin lost his left foot and right leg and suffered fragment wounds to his face. His wounds were too massive for life support and he did not survive the day. Martin was age twenty-four and single, from Lamesa, Texas.

Delta also found a tunnel in the rocket pocket but spotted booby-trapped wires across the entrance and exit holes. The tunnels were blown in place as best as they could with C-4 explosive. On the 14th at 10:20AM, Alpha's troops in CAP 143 were introduced to a Chieu Hoi, age seventeen, who told of a tunnel complex with weapons and mines. He also mentioned the VC in the area carried mines with them at all times, as they were considered more useful than AK-47 assault rifles. When the enemy saw US soldiers approaching, they hurriedly planted them in the soldier's likely route of travel.

Alpha called for an air strike on the tunnels, and then its 3rd Platoon took the Chieu Hoi to investigate. They found one thousand pounds of rice, eating utensils, two Bouncing Betty mines (which the Chieu Hoi dug up), bloody bandages (including female sanitary napkins) and a booby-trapped two hundred and fifty pound bomb. As an added bonus one NVA soldier was found dead from the air strike. By the end of the day two more Chieu Hoi's surrendered, one a VC nurse.

Another Chieu Hoi gave up at 9:00AM near CAP 142 and was interrogated. He was forty-four years of age and claimed there were one thousand VC five miles northwest of the Batangan, preparing for a major attack on LZ Minuteman and the Marine CAP locations, "very soon." Alpha requested air strikes on the supposed enemy location. While highly implausible that one thousand VC and or NVA would mass for such an attack, the continued infiltration of VC and NVA back onto the Batangan and the greater coastal area, was of concern to the American advisors and ARVN in Quang Ngai City and the Americal Division.

The "Extensive Pacification" phase under Operation Russell Beach was still being hotly contested by the enemy. Operation Geneva Park had given both the 5th/46th Infantry Battalion and ARVN the opportunity to work in concert using fire coordination and phasing lines, but not without coordination difficulties that resulted in some friendly fire incidents.

But the experience helped the two forces work closer together and, for the 5th/46th Battalion, it helped to insure that the ARVN battalions were getting more involved in securing their own territory.

Coordination with the ARVN and 5th/46th Battalion was deemed to be working well enough that the Americal Division headquarters was resolved to begin another joint operation with the ARVN called "Nantucket Beach" that would secure the coastal population "once and for all".

11 – NANTUCKET BEACH

Mid-July 1969 saw the Americal Army Division continuing combat operations to destroy the enemy units in its division area of operations but with an increased emphasis on supporting the Accelerated Pacification Program of 1969, spearheaded by operations such as Russell Beach.

Throughout South Vietnam, the Vietnamese Army (ARVN) and U.S. forces sensed the tide of war shifting on two levels. First, main force units of the NVA and VC were increasingly more difficult to engage in large formations where American firepower could be brought to bear. The B-52 strike in the Nui Hoi Mountains west of Binh Son in late June was a case in point.

It destroyed a well-developed base camp with an established hospital complex and forced the survivors to flee farther west. Some of the patients undoubtedly succumbed to their wounds because of the hasty march they were required to make. The enemy rearguard dogged the battalion's three-company sweep, but was not substantial enough in number to stop the soldiers from accomplishing their mission of assessing the B-52 strike. The close air support killed more of the enemy as the battalion was leaving the mountains. The many graves found by the soldiers also testified to the heavy price the enemy was paying in Quang Ngai Province.

On the second level of this shifting tide, the South Vietnamese Governments military forces were forced to step up the tempo of their operations. They were expected to exert more control over operational areas as America looked at a gradual exodus from Vietnam under President Nixon's "Vietnamization" doctrine.

For the 5th/46th Infantry Battalion, the combined ARVN and American operation of Russell Beach in early 1969, set the groundwork for the transition of forces that would take place over the next two years. Operation Geneva Park and the establishment of Operational Zones (OZ) to replace Tactical Areas of Responsibility (TAOR), coupled with Revolutionary Development Areas (RDA), Fire Control Areas (FCA) and Controlled Fire Zones (CFZ), were all part of the "Vietnamization" of the Vietnam War in the 5th/46th area of operations.

The biggest challenge to operational control in the 198th Brigade's area of responsibility remained the large coastal area bounded by Chu Lai and the South China Sea, Highway One and Quang Ngai City. The most contentious area in that large coastal plain continued to be the My Lai and My Khe hamlets, Pinkville and the greater Binh Duc Cape – the infamous Batangan Peninsula. The enemy's mines and booby-traps were exacting a heavy toll for control of that landscape.

To further accelerate the pace of pacification in this area, the 198th Infantry Brigade issued Operational Order 8-69, "Nantucket Beach", to begin in mid-July 1969. The mission was to combine the forces of the 198th Brigade and the 6th ARVN Regiment and use them to initiate combat operations between the Batangan Peninsula and Quang Ngai City to "Destroy the Vietcong main force (MF) and local force (LF) units and eliminate the Vietcong Infrastructure (VCI) and the political apparatus that supported them".

Operation Nantucket Beach consisted of four phases. In Phase I, two battalions of the 6th ARVN Regiment and one company of the 5th/46th under operational control of the ARVN's, would initiate road clearing and security operations along the Quang Ngai – Batangan Road, known as Route 521. This would take approximately three days to complete.

Phase II was to take approximately thirty days, and required the 5th/46th to commit three rifle companies north of the 6th ARVN in a combined sweep east. A US Marine Shore Landing Force (SLF) would also arrive from the sea to operate northeast of Binh Son, which expanded the scope of the operation.

Phase III was estimated to take sixty days and would further expand the operational area for the 5th/46th and the ARVN by replacing the Marines after they swept their assigned area.

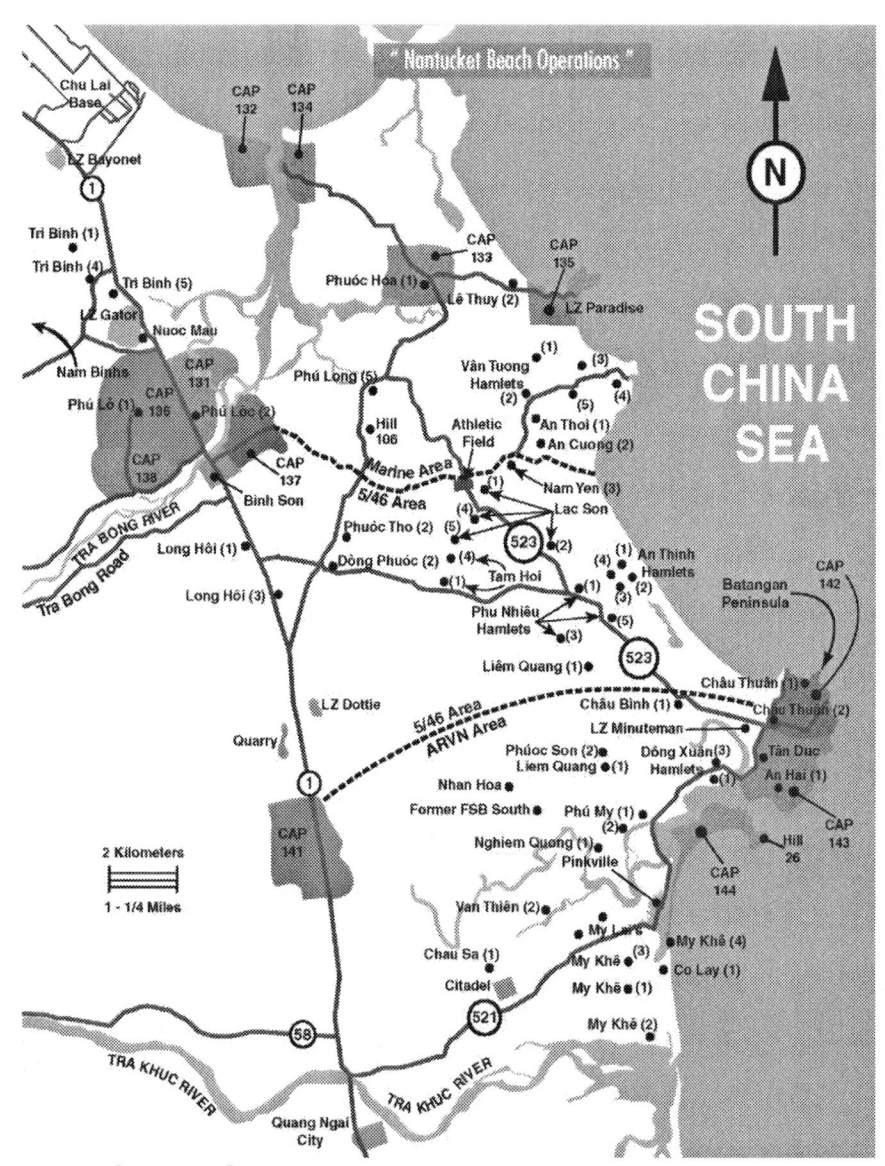

Nantucket Beach

Finally, Phase IV would consist of consolidation and security operations which required the grunts of the 5th/46th to camp inside targeted settlements of the Pacification Development Program (New Life Hamlets) and upgrade the effectiveness of local security forces. The largest of these settlements was in CAP 142's area, in the large New Life Hamlet on the coast of the Batangan.

The enemy in the target area consisted of the 48th VC Local Force (LF) Battalion, supported by the 95th LF Vietcong (VC) Sapper Company, C-31 LF VC Company, T-20 LF VC Company, and K-51 LF VC Weapons Company. Their support came from Vietnamese civilians in the hamlets who made up the Vietcong infrastructure. The 48th LF Battalion was estimated to have as many as two hundred and fifty guerillas, with approximately twenty percent of its ranks filled by NVA regulars, who had infiltrated into the area from the mountains.

Some brief history is necessary to further understand the tenaciousness of the 48th LF VC Battalion. The 48th local force Battalion had strengthened its grip on the Batangan back in July of 1968 by improving its fighting positions and storing caches of food and ammunition as it regained its strength after its massive losses in the 1968 TET offensive.

Enemy contacts made by the 5th/46th around Pinkville in early July of 1968 had engaged some of these forces, but the bulk of the 48th remained on the Batangan during the fight. The battalion was pulled from the Pinkville fight because they were deployed to the north to take part in Task Force Cooksey "Burlington Trail" operations near Tam Ky. In August 1968 while the battalion operated near Tam Ky the 48th VC Battalion combined its forces with elements of the 107th VC Anti-Aircraft Battalion, to attack the Tra Khuc River Bridge in Quang Ngai City. The 48th sustained heavy losses in its attack on the bridge and regrouped on the Batangan during September.

From October 1968 to January 1969, the 48th Battalion continued to operate on the Batangan Peninsula with the 38th LF Battalion, to train for a future attack on Quang Ngai. Operation Russell Beach in January-February 1969 upset those plans and kept the 38th and 48th Battalions on the defensive. Although there were VC losses in both men and supplies during the operation, the interrogation of Chieu Hoi's, VC prisoners and hamlet guerillas revealed that many elements escaped the cordon of American and ARVN forces. Some escaped down the coast of the South China Sea, avoiding the swift boats patrolling the coastline, or ex-filtrated west overland in small groups though the cordon.

By late February and early March 1969, with the American ground phase of Russell Beach terminated, the 48th VC Battalion regrouped once again in preparation for a late March - April offensive which consisted of a mortar attack on LZ Minuteman, a ground attack on the CAP 143 compound and two attacks on the Combined Holding and Interrogation Center (CHIC) northwest of Quang Ngai in Son Tinh.

After recovering from those attacks two companies of the 48th attacked the Tra Khuc River Bridge on June 8 but were beaten back. By July 1969, as Operation Nantucket Beach was being planned, intelligence estimated the battalion was heavily fortified in the My Khe hamlets southwest of Pinkville only one-quarter mile south of Route 521.

Intelligence gained through the questioning of Chieu Hoi's determined that the morale of the 48th VC LF Battalion was at a low ebb due to the continuous separation from family as a result of Operation Russell Beach, lack of food, equipment and medical supplies, fear of certain death if found, and the need to be continuously "on the move" because of US/ARVN operations in the area.

But the enemy constantly adapted its forces to accomplish its new missions. The 95th VC Sapper Company split its ranks in June 1968 into 95A (operating in the eastern Binh Son District) and 95B (operating in western Binh Son). By July 1969 its main strength was estimated to be near the Lac Son and Nam Yen hamlets, in an area known as the "Athletic Field", a flat and open piece of terrain with low cut grass. One squad of the 95th had penetrated the perimeter of LZ Bayonet nine miles further northwest, resulting in one sapper killed and one captured.

The P-31 and K-51 Local Vietcong Company's operated in support of the sappers. Another, the T-20 VC LF Company specialized in operations east and southeast of Quang Ngai. By July 1969, the T-20 LF Company was thought to be in close proximity to the 48th LF Battalion near Pinkville and the My Khe hamlets where the 5th/46th now aimed its Alpha Company.

Command Incompetence

Alpha Company's new commander came from the 2nd Infantry Division in Korea and he had not yet served in Vietnam. He was now a senior Captain awaiting promotion to the rank of Major in the fall. The opening phase of Nantucket Beach would be his first opportunity to lead troops in actual combat.

Alpha's new commander faced one major drawback; his combat-experienced men didn't trust him. When Alpha moved to the Batangan and CAP 142 on July 5, Alpha's platoons operated fairly independently of each other but they soon realized their new commander didn't understand combat operations. He gave his platoon leaders reckless orders on where and how to move, which placed his company in needless jeopardy. To Alpha's field-savvy vets, their commander "commanded" with reckless abandon.

Alpha's situation was a classic example of experienced field soldiers and small unit leaders making a realistic evaluation of the capabilities of their company commander. Unrealistic orders given in a combat environment was costing this company commander the trust and confidence of his platoon leaders and the infantrymen he commanded. To make matters worse, he was rather rotund and carried a pipe in his mouth, trying to look authoritative. The final stroke against him was that he was replacing a respected warrior, Captain Ben Anderson.

On the morning of July 15, Alpha left LZ Minuteman on Hueys and combat air assaulted (CA) into the My Khe hamlets to begin Operation Nantucket Beach with a "search and clear" mission. Elements of H Troop, 17th Armored Cavalry drove their tracks to meet them along with a Vietnamese Provincial Recon Unit (PRU) a popular force platoon (PF) and national police (NPFF) from Son Tinh.

At 9:30AM, a track hit an antipersonnel mine near My Khe (3) but continued south and linked up with Alpha. Alpha discovered homemade mines and a newly made brick hooch, in a "cleared" sub-hamlet, supposedly devoid of any civilians. Clothes were hanging outside the building and fresh manure littered the cattle pen but the occupants had disappeared. The grunts marveled at the hooch's construction and cleanliness.

At 3:15PM, a soldier stepped on a Bouncing Betty mine which failed to detonate. Alpha's soldiers, weaned on mines on the Batangan, carefully poked around, trying to avoid the mines they knew the VC had set out for them. They entered another sub-hamlet full of women and children. Alpha's commander had them herded into an adjacent dry paddy and the tracks formed a circle for a night position. He hoped the

VC would not attack them because they held their families inside the perimeter.

The following morning Alpha and its attached tracks began their assigned sweep to move north through My Khe (1), continuing through My Khe (3), then turning west on Route 521 to the Vietnamese PF garrison called the "Citadel". At 8:00AM, they blew an empty VC bunker but in the process wounded an elderly woman hiding inside whom was undetected. She suffered a concussion from the blast, requiring a dustoff. Medics patched her up as she screamed, her blood sticking to her hair. There was nothing else they could do.

The medics left her alone on a small open patch of ground serving as an LZ then ran for cover from some sniper fire. As the dustoff approached she began crawling back to her bunker. The medics ran out once again to load their patient on the bird, knowing her only hope to survive was to get to a hospital. She whimpered a death cry as she was gently placed on board and died on the flight to Chu Lai. Two hours later two Alpha soldiers were wounded by another Bouncing Betty mine.

The small task force of armored personnel carriers and Alpha soldiers approached My Khe (1) in two columns of tracks moving abreast. Alpha's grunts rode on the tracks to avoid booby traps and the almost impossible foot movement through swollen rice paddies, which resembled a large marsh with mud up to a mans thighs. The constricting terrain forced the tracks into a bottle neck as the two columns approached the hamlet.

At 10:00AM, the tracks were hit with a heavy volume of small arms fire and five RPG rounds from the hamlet. The cavalry soldiers screamed at the grunts to get off the tracks, to enable them to fire their 50 Caliber and M-60 machineguns. Alpha's grunts did just that, jumping off the sides and rear, and immediately got mired in the muck, barely able to move.

At that point things went from bad to worse. To get out of the range of the RPG's being fired at them the tracks went into reverse at full speed, the "Immediate Action" tactic for armored personnel carriers when faced with heavy fire. The tracks rapidly reversed distance between themselves and the enemy fire, and maneuvered into a straight line from left to right, to maximize their firepower.

Alpha's soldiers stuck in the muck could barely move as the tracks repositioned themselves. They were helpless. One track ran over PFC Roger McElhaney who, short in stature, deep in the muck, and carrying a radio, could not move. He was promptly smothered and crushed to death. PFC Irving Paige jumped off his track but his foot got caught inside the moving treads, cutting his foot off at the boot top as he was spun into the water. 1LT Frederick Loop, although hit with RPG fragments in the back of his head, gamely slogged through the muck to pull Paige out. PFC Edward Ortiz was luckier. His right foot was cushioned by the muck when a track's pads ran over it, fracturing his foot but not severing it.

This was the first operation in the field for Sergeant Chuck Barbo, a squad leader. He was riding on the lead track in the right column when the attack began. He heard a distinct "pop" sound, and watched an RPG round fall short, landing in front of his track, hitting the water which cushioned the explosion. He was in the vertex of an "L-shaped ambush", with enemy fire coming directly from his front and down his right flank.

The driver saw the RPG round explode to his front and placed his track in reverse as his crew screamed to the grunts to jump off but Barbo could not move. He was stuck with his legs pinned under the barrel of an M-60 machinegun that was firing away. Barbo turned his face to avoid the heat and flash from the muzzle, and saw four men struggling in the marsh trying to get on line to return fire. When the M-60 finally jammed, Barbo took his queue and jumped off the track.

Alpha's grunts moved back to a paddy dike, some without weapons or equipment, to form a skirmish line. The attack had caused a complete rout. Weapons and gear were left in the marsh-like paddy while other equipment was still on the tracks, strapped to rucksacks which hung over the sides. It was then discovered that McElhaney, the RTO, was missing, but Alpha's commander did not want to go back to find him.

The tracks formed a line in the paddy alongside the grunts and the first air strike came in at 10:36AM. The second strike was dropped at 11:10AM and the third at 11:25AM. The jets were also taking some fire from the coast, just south of Coy Lay (1) as they dived to drop their bomb loads. Dustoff's were also called to pull out twelve of the seriously wounded, nine being sent to the 91st Evacuation Hospital and three to the 27th Surgical Hospital. Six, with smaller fragment wounds were treated in the field.

With the air strikes completed, the tracks moved out on a straight line looking for McElhaney, with Alpha's soldiers slogging through the marsh-like paddy between and behind the tracks. No one wanted to be the one to find his body, but someone drew the short straw and found him face up in two feet of water, his radio was still strapped to his back, completely submerged in the mud under him. PFC Roger McElhaney was age twenty and single from Jamestown, Pennsylvania.

During this debacle bravery displayed itself amidst chaos. PFC John Haas exposed himself to hostile fire repeatedly while operating a portable mine detector, locating five anti-personnel mines; SP/4 Joseph Palmeri and PFC Scott Schuelke, both RTO's, were wounded but ignored their injuries and directed in dustoffs while under fire. PFC Jim Pudlas, a medic, was also wounded but moved across the swollen rice paddy to treat the casualties while under heavy fire. They and others were awarded Bronze Stars for valor.

As the soldiers continued looking for their equipment and weapons dropped in the water, Alpha's commander ordered Barbo to take his squad with some PF scouts to the tree line on their right flank and maneuver behind the enemy position. Halfway to the tree line a PF scout, second to last in the group, stepped on a mine which wounded two Alpha grunts and killed two PF's. Barbo's group was then called back. Alpha's Commander and the track commander argued about what to do next. They had been arguing since they were "married up" the previous day. The track commander, sensing the inexperience of Alpha's CO, was not willing to risk his men and tracks doing something that was not tactically sound. The same feelings were shared by many of Alpha's soldiers, except they had no veto power.

The enemy repositioned itself while there was indecisiveness on the American side. The tracks wanted the grunts to walk in front, using their portable mine detectors, to detect possible 105mm Howitzer mines that would destroy the tracks and everyone on them. Alpha's commander wanted his men to ride on the tracks, as they did before the ambush and complete the sweep. Moreover his platoon leaders would not agree to walk in front of the tracks, fearful that the few minesweepers they had would not be enough to detect the mines and more men would be killed.

More arguing ensued and Alpha's commander was starting to lose it, on the verge of tears, asking "What are we going to do?" Someone pointed to the direction they had come from and pleaded, "What the hell is the matter with going back that way?" A compromise was reached with the track commander. The grunts could ride on the tracks but they would take a wide berth around the remaining My Khe's, return to the road (Route 521) and leave the area. LTC Wagner was made aware of the debacle that had happened and ordered Hueys to pick up Alpha on the road and return them to CAP's 142 and 143.

New Objectives – Same War

July 17 saw Bravo Company under operational control (OPCON) of the 1st/6th Infantry Battalion near Tam Ky, and Charlie Company defending the bunker line at LZ Gator while performing ancillary tasks, such as guarding bridges on Highway One and conducting local patrols. Delta screened the rocket pocket with six patrols of two squads each, trying to cover a wide area. Most of Alpha, back on the Batangan, resided at CAP 142 while one platoon settled in with CAP 143. The armored cavalry tracks from H Troop were released and made their way back to LZ Bayonet.

Delta's mission in the rocket pocket was typical of the duty the battalion's soldiers increasingly found themselves engaged in. With less chance that main force VC or NVA units would be encountered, American units in Vietnam were directed to search in smaller squad-size patrols, unless intelligence reports indicated larger enemy formation was nearby. This direction came straight from the commander of the Military Advisory Command Vietnam (MACV), General Creighton Abrams, who had replaced General William Westmoreland. Abrams continued to push his divisions to "own the night" and insisted on roving night ambushes. Small ambush teams were to move from one ambush location to another during the night hours. Delta's tactic called for each platoon to push out two ambushes each night at dusk, with each ambush team moving again at approximately 2:00AM to a second ambush site. Therefore on paper at least, each platoon conducted four night ambushes.

How much Abrams directive was followed by infantry platoons in the field was problematic. Much depended on the leadership of the platoon, the experience of the men and the type of terrain to be covered. Night patrols were also expected on the mine-infested Batangan Peninsula but movement at night on the Batangan was largely ignored. Most platoons placed out listening posts (LP's) and/or ambushes close to the perimeter. There was no willingness to risk more casualties from mines at night and increase the bloodshed trying to dustoff the wounded in the dark.

Delta's platoons patrolled their assigned areas of the rocket pocket, generally operating two and one-half miles apart. In comparison to the stress of the Batangan these were "restful" operations. The platoons moved from sub-hamlet to sub-hamlet, the Nam Binh's, Tri Binh's and Phuoc Binh Tay's. Some offered an oasis of comfort with fresh running water and friendly, or at least neutral peasants, and few mines to worry about. Other sub-hamlets were partially or completely abandoned with fallow rice paddies and stagnant wells. In each case the villagers were checked for identification and questioned about any VC presence in the immediate area. Local militia and PRU soldiers often accompanied Delta's patrols.

While operating in the southern rocket pocket, Delta's 1st Platoon found a hamlet that was pleasant enough, with cattle and plenty of rice. The peasants were accommodating, even taking up a collection from the GI's so some girls could ride their bikes down the narrow trails and dirt roads to Nuoc Mau, to purchase Coke and ice. The route was two miles each way in scorching heat but worth the effort for the tip the children received. C-rations were also shared with the peasants, those the grunts did not want, and the soldiers settled into empty hooch's.

Some females became more than friendly, sensing the soldiers' needs for more comfort than shade and cool streams. In the relatively secure hamlets of the rocket pocket, the young women, thin and small in stature, were quite attractive for soldiers away from home and commanded a good price for sex in a "sellers market". The extent to which this occurred depended largely on the culture of each platoon, the platoon leaders' outlook, the personal desires of each grunt and the perceived security of the local area.

Delta experienced the usual challenges of war in a guerilla environment. While checking peasant identification's one peasant girl peddling into the hamlet on her bike, saw the Americans and quickly turned around and peddled off, prompting fire from the grunts. Another female got in the way and was hit in the hip, prompting a dustoff. Delta cordoned Nam Binh (7) and detained seven young males who had no identification. They turned out to be South Vietnamese draft dodgers.

Delta's 3rd Platoon was supplied beer from LZ Gator while at the hamlet. Most grunts didn't want it, aware they'd be moving out shortly during the heat of the day. But the platoon sergeant decided that left more beer for him and started drinking them quickly. As the platoon moved out their drunken sergeant started breaking pottery in the hamlet. While on the march, the sergeant fired some rounds into a dirt bank and the platoon leader took his weapon from him. The NCO grabbed another soldier's weapon.

A squad leader, Sergeant James Briscoe, tried to take the M-16 away and in the struggle was shot in the foot. The platoon sergeant was taken back to LZ Gator on the battalion commanders C&C helicopter, accompanied by Deltas company commander. He was put up for courts-martial but was ultimately acquitted, the shooting having been ruled an "accident". His good field record saved the Staff Sergeant from punishment but he was transferred to another company. There was no love lost for the sergeant from the men of Delta's 3rd Platoon, many who felt the acquittal was an injustice.

On July 18, Delta lost a soldier who had already left Vietnam. PFC William Proctor was wounded in May when Delta was under operational control of the 1st/52nd Battalion and operated off of LZ Stinson (formerly LZ Buff). During a firefight several Delta soldiers were wounded, including Proctor. Proctor had been sent to an Army hospital in Japan where he finally succumbed to his wounds. William C. Proctor Jr. was age twenty-three and married from Burbank, California.

On July 19, Bravo was released from its commitment to the 1st/6th Battalion and joined the ARVN 2nd/6th Battalion in support of Operation Nantucket Beach. The next morning they air-assaulted to Chau Sa (1), just north of the Citadel which was garrisoned by PF soldiers. The Citadel was located two miles west of My Khe (1), the scene of Alpha's debacle. By 11:00AM, Bravo Company started receiving small arms fire from Vietcong evading the area.

On July 21, Echo Recon on Hill 26 which overlooked the Batangan, finally was released from perimeter duty where it had been stuck for two months, protecting the 4.2-inch heavy mortars. The duty had been relaxing at first, but recon troops like to recon and this valuable asset had been wasted for far too long. The mortars were relocated back to LZ Minuteman and fifty PF soldiers took over the hilltop. Echo's Recon Platoon moved to the pine tree covered sand dunes of CAP 142 for a screening mission.

The movement of Echo Recon off Hill 26 marked the official end of Operation Russell Beach, which began in early January. In the interim, operation Geneva Park and now, Nantucket Beach, had taken hold, each with slightly different objectives to build on what was accomplished in Russell Beach.

But, except for staff officers whose duties required planning and staffing grand stratagems on paper, no one from company commanders on down knew or cared much about the bigger picture. Each day their focus was the same, killing the enemy while staying alive and keeping morale up among seasoned troops who were becoming increasingly disenchanted covering the same ground time and time again, with little progress to show for it. As one platoon leader recalled, "It became a vicious circle. We chased the enemy during the day and they harassed us at night."

By the morning of July 22, Phase II of Nantucket Beach was set to go. This required a multi-company cordon and search operation north of the ARVN's fire coordination area (FCA) which started roughly north of Pinkville, moving west and passing north of the My Lai's. Everything south of the FCA was for the ARVN's and everything north for seven miles was the responsibility of the 5th/46th Battalion. The 2nd/26th Marine Shore Landing Force (SLF) swept the area north of the 5th/46th Battalion's boundary line, with particular emphasis on searching the area around the Athletic Field.

LTC Wagner had his battalion's rifle companies stripped of their 4th Platoons, which controlled the company 81mm mortars and placed them instead under the control of Echo Company, forming "Light mortar sections" along with Echo's organic 4.2-inch heavy mortars. The 81mm "Light Teams" were placed on LZ Gator, LZ Minuteman and CAP 142. "Snatch" missions were also increased in the Nantucket Beach area with helicopters from Blue Ghosts' scout platoon (F Troop, 8th Air Cav) sweeping low and fast to catch the enemy moving in small groups of one to three insurgents, hoping to take prisoners who would offer "real-time" intelligence.

At first light on the 22nd, Alpha (from the Batangan) and Delta (from the rocket pocket) combat air assaulted to Tam Hoi (1), a large hamlet situated between Highway One and the coast for a cordon and search mission. Delta's 3rd Platoon landed on the western edge of the hamlet and came under small arms fire. The other platoons were dropped farther out and had to hump through the heat to get to the action.

Wagner ordered F-4 Jets to drop napalm and two hundred and fifty-pound bombs on the hamlet to soften it up. Alpha landed east of the hamlet to serve as a blocking force. Their grunts immediately detained five females who were in direct support of the VC K-51 weapons company, which had scampered out of Tam Hoi just as the air assault was coming in to land. The women said the departing Vietcong carried 60mm mortars. Additional intelligence pointed to a large multi-level tunnel complex, able to accommodate three hundred enemy soldiers, just north of Phu Nhieu (3) two and one-half miles southeast of Alpha and Delta. Wagner called for an air strike on that location which resulted in a sustained series of secondary explosions, a sure indication a cache of enemy ammunition was hit.

Additional questioning revealed the Vietcong frequently moved in and out of Tam Hoi (1) but the two-company cordon didn't capture any. The VC remained like phantoms, firing a few rounds then fleeing, too fast to engage with rifle fire and too evasive for the gunships to find in the dense foliage.

National Police Field Force (NPFF) accompanied the battalion's soldiers as well, to question the peasants. One NPFF found an old wrinkled-skin woman who was nearly blind. She had been in a bunker inside her hooch when the air strikes began but survived the napalm and the bombs. Although she could walk slowly without assistance, Delta's acting commander, 1LT Robert Wight, thought she should be medevaced to a refugee area. She refused. The NPFF gave her a can of water and led her back to her hooch, there to die unless the VC could get back to take care of her.

With no VC at Tam Hoi, Delta and Alpha received word they would be picked up for another CA in the morning. Alpha's commander, still shaken by his performance at My Khe (1) asked 1LT Wight commanding Delta, his junior in seniority, to coordinate the tactical effort for the evening. Wight felt they should have stayed another full day in Tam Hoi to insure they checked everything in the expansive hamlet as there had not been enough time to properly clear it. But he didn't contest LTC Wagner's order to move out the following morning. Wight chose to leave the hamlet that night since it had not been thoroughly cleared and he didn't want the enemy to come out of tunnels under his feet. Delta and Alpha carefully moved their way through the thick hedgerows to set in for the night closer to the pick-up zone established for the next morning.

That same day Chieu Hoi's began appearing at CAP locations throughout the large coastal area, reporting that the Vietcong's 95A Sapper, K51 Weapons and C31 Infantry companies were moving north and east of Alpha and Delta. The Chieu Hoi's indicated more of their comrades wanted to give themselves up but were afraid of being cut down by ARVN or American firepower as they attempted to come in.

At first light on July 23, Alpha and Delta were picked up in Hueys and air assaulted to Phu Nhieu (3) on the southern border of the air strike. This time Alpha had the sweep mission starting east of the hamlet while Delta landed on the west to act as a blocking force.

One-half mile south of them laid the contentious hamlet of Liem Quang (1). Bravo Company landed on that hamlets south side and prepared to move north as a blocking force to support Alpha and Delta. PRU's and NPFF accompanied the soldiers, along with loud-speaker teams from hovering Hueys.

In Phu Nhieu the soldiers found about forty women and children, their black pajama clothes soiled with dirt, evidence they had been hiding in tunnels. The PRU and NPFF knew instantly they were the wives and children of Vietcong. Three males were detained who gave Delta's soldiers the "hard look", the deep stares of hate the GI's had become accustomed to when cordoning hamlets on the coastal plains. They were detained as suspects.

Delta's soldiers found several tunnels in a dirt embankment behind some hooch's. One of Delta's platoons searched the northwest sector and saw Vietnamese running away. They gave chase but were called back, ordered instead to move south to Liem Quang and Bravo Company, where a firefight had just started.

When Bravo landed in Liem Quang, their attached PRU went to work on the villagers, who quickly acknowledged forty VC were on the western edge of the hamlet, ready to fight. Delta, now moving in that direction, drew small arms fire. Alpha also came under fire on the east side of Phu Nhieu (3). LTC Wagner had them picked up in Hueys so the entire hamlet, absent Alpha and Delta, could be rocketed by gunships, with artillery salvos for good measure.

Delta's 3rd platoon found three enemy dead at 8:30AM. Bravo's interrogations of peasants revealed the VC had a 60mm mortar, two 30-caliber machineguns, and one heavy machinegun in the vicinity.

Alpha, moved by Huey from Phu Nhieu to the western edge of Liem Quang, immediately came under heavy small arms fire when they landed which wounded six of their soldiers. The headquarters element followed the company commander into a little gully while under relentless fire.

The commander's RTO, SP/4 Tim O'Brien radioed a command and control helicopter flying overhead to get a quick evacuation for the seriously wounded, which included a platoon leader and PFC Myron K. Renne. By his call sign, O'Brien realized the Huey above was the 198th Brigade Commander, who refused to land, citing he was "directing the battle" and "was not in the medevac business". O'Brien knew the fire fight was the battalion commander's (Wagner's) responsibility, not the brigade commander. He pleaded then argued, but to no avail.

The firefight under Alpha's uncertain commander once again became pure chaos. Renne was finally evacuated to Chu Lai but died at the 27th Surgical Hospital. Myron Renne was age twenty and single from Glasgow, Missouri.

Delta continued its sweep south through the northern edge of Liem Quang and found thirty-three tunnels but the hooch's in their section of the hamlet were deserted. At the southern edge Bravo gathered up eighty detainees, keeping two for questioning. As Alpha moved through its portion of the hamlet they found one NVA soldier and two Vietcong who were killed by gunship fire, along with medical kits and notebooks, which were sent to LZ Gator.

By nightfall Bravo established night positions on the eastern portion of Liem Quang (1) with Delta placing its positions northwest and Alpha placing positions southwest of the hamlet. Just past midnight Bravo was hit with enemy mortar fire which wounded six soldiers. Artillery fire was placed on the suspected mortar location but two hours later more rounds fell on Bravo from the same location.

At first light on July 24, the Aero Scout team for F Troop, 8th Cav (Blue Ghost) snatched three insurgents three-quarters of a mile southwest of Liem Quang. The pilot reported seeing a large group of women and children heading further south. A lone male was spotted as he attempted to evade into the brush and was cut down by M-60 fire from the bird. At 10:00AM, while engineers were blowing some demolitions, always a dangerous undertaking, one of Alpha's soldiers, PFC Brauberger, suffered a fractured skull from a flying block of wood sent airborne from the explosion. He was evacuated to the 91st Evacuation hospital but died shortly after arriving. PFC Everett W. Brauberger, age twenty and single, was from Soda Springs, Idaho.

Throughout the day, the battalion's soldiers, supported by engineers, demolished over forty small tunnels while under continuous sniper fire. The Liem Quang (1) search and cordon was the "hot ticket" for the day and the battalion had no shortage of jet fighter-bombers, gunships and artillery support. At 1:20PM, Bravo's 2nd Platoon spotted thirty VC fleeing north of the hamlet with weapons and field gear. The VC were too far away for effective small arms fire and too fleet of foot for gunships to corner. A search of the area they departed uncovered more discarded equipment. By days end the battalion prepared for another night, still not able to engage the VC in a firefight but undoubtedly killing or wounding many with their heavy fire support. For the grunts however, there were too few enemy bodies to look at and justify their effort. Seven more of their own had been taken from the effort around Liem Quang.

Early on the morning of July 25, the three infantry companies air-assaulted farther north, into the sub-hamlets of Tam Hoi (1) and (4) and Lac Son (4) and (5), where the Vietcong had reportedly fled after the air assault into Liem Quang (1).

Delta began detaining military-aged males near its three LZ's one-half mile east of Lac Son (5). Alpha landed one-half mile east of Tam Hoi (1) with gunships providing covering fire. This time the LZ was cold but two children and their mother were wounded by the gunships supporting Alpha's insertion and were evacuated to Chu Lai. Bravo was inserted to the northwest border of Lac Son (4) at 6:36AM.

One hour later Bravo's Sp/4 Albert Vick Jr. detonated a mine, which sheared off both his legs and wounded another soldier. Vick's wounds were too severe despite the gallant work of medics to try to keep him alive and he was pronounced dead on arrival at the 91st Evacuation Hospital. Albert Vick was twenty years of age and single from Goldsboro, North Carolina.

Nantucket Beach operations were to be characterized by the constant shuffling of forces by helicopter over short stretches of ground based on "URI" (Usually Reliable Information) reports.

The battalions Tactical Operations Center (TOC) on LZ Gator had received these daily intelligence reports from the 198th Brigade TOC at LZ Bayonet. With so much to do, the 5th/46th Battalion's S-2 and S-3 initially filed them with other reports and no action was taken. The battalion's operations officer (S-3), Major James Krause, was then questioned by brigade headquarters concerning why they were not followed-up. His response was "Why should we, we have lots of things to do".

The brigade then revealed to him what was not known to the battalion before, that the "URI's" were based on secret radio intercepts from the few radios the 48th LF VC Battalion had in their possession. Krause then developed a concept called "Chasing URI's". The battalion was limited to four Huey helicopters each day, one for the battalion commander (his command and control bird) and three for supply missions. In response to URI reports, the limited Hueys available were used to ferry soldiers short distances to cordon hamlets based on the timely intelligence.

At this point Phase II of Nantucket Beach was in full swing. The Marine's Shore Landing Force (SLF) operating north of the 5th/46th in the Nam Yen and Van Tuong hamlets was also finding and killing the enemy in small numbers and recovering equipment. LTC Wagner and MAJ Krause flew to the Marines operational base on the coast for a briefing.

The Marines always operated "lean" with few support staffs, as 5th/46th Battalion officers had seen on operation Russell Beach. The Marine S-3 Operations Officer gave the briefing but Krause and Wagner observed he was tired and worn-out, talking zombie-like as he gave his report.

Wagner and Krause were asked to fly to the assault carrier off-shore for a tour and another briefing in the ships "Ward Room". When they arrived they were surrounded by polished silver, wood and glass cabinets which held the ships serving dishes and unit memorabilia. They observed starched linens and clean uniforms. Krause and Wagner were in awe, were they stateside? The ship was alien territory.

The Marine SLF had come ashore in full field gear, flak jackets and very heavy rucksacks. In short order many started dropping from heat exhaustion. They carried too much weight which caused slow movement and many heat casualties. The 5th/46th Battalions' staff officers saw little concern from Marine officers for their men's plight. Similar to the Russell Beach operation, it was apparent the Marines received little support in supplies from their off-shore ships.

The Navy also demanded to be part of "fighting the battle" and its destroyers cruised up and down the coast looking for action against a nimble Vietcong that grunts on the ground had a hard time pining down, let alone the big guns of destroyers. The Navy's guns fired high-velocity, low trajectory shells. Wagner and Krause had to carefully insure no friendly troops or civilians were anywhere in target areas when giving fire missions, in this operation to pacify and "win hearts and minds". The shells often skipped in the rice paddies and ended up farther downrange, past their intended targets.

While the Navy insisted on firing their large guns to be part of the operation, none of the Navy's fire missions actually supported real-time operations. The battalion carefully picked targets for them that were trails and locations the Vietcong might use but that were away from populated hamlets, whether they contained Vietcong or not.

The ARVN working south of the 5th/46th were catching large pockets of Vietcong and their supporters. With no language barriers and a deep antagonism for the Vietcong and NVA, the ARVN needed no lengthy interrogations to decide who, in their minds, were friendly and who were not. Their discernment on this issue did not always afford much compassion for the civilians caught in the cross-hairs of the VC and the ARVN. But the ARVN did gain "real-time" intelligence with their detainees who indicated a substantial number of Vietcong were moving north into the 5th/46th area of responsibility.

To block this enemy move, Lieutenant Colonel Wagner had his infantry companies picked up by Hueys once again and air-assaulted to an area west of Liem Quang (1). Alpha Company landed two and one-half miles west of the hamlet, Bravo landed in the middle one mile further east, and Delta inserted between Bravo and the hamlet of Liem Quang.

The ARVN obtained another Chieu Hoi defector who was a platoon leader in the 48th Battalion. He said the 48th had been preparing for another attack on the Tra Khuc Bridge in Quang Ngai City when the current ARVN/American operation began. At this point the Vietcong were moving in small groups of twenty to thirty insurgents, trying to keep ahead of the ARVN and the 5th/46th Battalion.

Alpha's position was on some rough and hilly terrain on which stood a Buddhist monastery. The Buddhist monks indicated the VC were two miles southeast, having passed by on the southern edge of their enclave earlier in the day. The GI's were warned to be careful, as the hills were heavily mined in the vicinity of the monastery. After providing some fruit to the soldiers, the monks returned to their prayers.

First Lieutenant Dan Martin moved his platoon up the hilly terrain covered by hedgerows when he stepped on a "Toe Popper" mine made from a C-ration can. The blasting cap went off but not the explosive and his foot was spared. Martin's RTO, Jack Hass, would never forget the look on Martin's face. These incidents required soldiers to push the "what if" to the back of their minds and continue with the mission. Reflections of field duty would come later and the "what if's" would have a haunting effect.

While the multi-company cordon and search operation took place, Echo's recon platoon was still dodging mines in its sweeps on the Batangan Peninsula in support of CAP 142. On July 25, while setting up a position on a sloping, pine tree covered hill, a sergeant stepped on a beer can "Toe-Popper" mine which did not detonate. Looking around, the Recon grunts saw numerous C-Ration spoons sticking up from the ground, each with a "Toe-Popper" next to it. As the troops gingerly tried to move out of the immediate area another soldier stepped into a hole containing a booby-trapped 105mm Howitzer round. With the protection of unseen angels, his foot plunged down between the edge of the hole and the round, just missing the detonation device.

After clearing the immediate area, the recon soldiers rigged a grenade with an electrical cap, strung some wire from a claymore mine, and blew the artillery round. The explosion created a deep crater which sheared off a tree limb twelve feet off the ground. But for the luck of unseen angels, the mine could have wiped out half the platoon.

Moving farther from the hill they found a sleeve to a C-Ration case which had Vietnamese writing on it, warning local peasants to stay away from the low hill because it was mined. The soldier who escaped the 105mm booby-trapped artillery round did not get a free pass for the day. That night he was bitten on the ear by a snake while sleeping and was medevaced to Chu Lai.

Delta Company was assigned the mission to secure an LZ for Alpha which was scheduled to fly to Chu Lai for a stand-down the next morning. The slow, cumbersome Chinooks ("Hooks") helicopters were tasked for the pickup. Demolition work and increased security around the landing zone was required. Not all company commanders were satisfied with the support given them by engineers from LZ Bayonet for demolitions. Some engineers seemed to hurry to get out of the field, too eager to use up their demo in a haphazard way in order to return as quickly as possible to their base at Bayonet.

Delta was fortunate in that they had their own demo man, Sergeant Carey, who at age twenty-six was married and mature and confident, loved his special responsibility and never lost his enthusiasm. In a war where special skill-sets were many times learned with "on-the-job-training", Carey was a bonus, he received some schooling in the Army for demolition work and was a metal-trades worker in civilian life.

As Delta prepared the LZ for Alpha, they found booby-trapped 105mm and 155mm Howitzer rounds hidden in leaves on the eastern edge of the LZ. Carey set to work to blow them. Vietnamese in the area were evacuated, as one of their hooch's stood next to a tunnel which had to be blown as well. Some soldiers chopped down young banana trees in the area to deny food to the VC, which also resulted in denying food to the peasants in the area. These acts were performed with regret. The soldiers were supposed to help shift the villagers to New Life Hamlets where food was readily available, but the grunts could clearly see the hamlet was more important to the peasants than anything else.

With soldiers and civilians moved out of the area, Carey blew the charges. The explosion threw large clumps of dirt everywhere. One of the charges did not blow and Carey returned to it to blow it with another fuse. The fuse was shorter than specified which nearly killed Carey but everything worked out. With the mission completed, the small group caught up with the rest of the company and returned to patrolling.

The daily courage and devotion of soldiers in the battalion such as Sergeant Carey was often overlooked, but routinely took place. Carey received an Army Commendation Medal for his hazardous work, the same medal clerks in the rear received for pushing paper. But Carey would also receive something the clerks would not get, the coveted Combat Infantryman's Badge and the satisfaction of making a difference for his fellow grunts in the field.

Bravo set about looking for a large cache of rice that was possibly located on the southeast portion of the hill on which they had landed. Delta searched a hamlet (Nhan Hoa) on the southern edge of their hilltop LZ then swung northeast to move back through Liem Quang (1). At 9:50AM, they found two hundred pounds of rice, four hundred pounds of potatoes and twenty-five pounds of salt. Empty sandbags were sent to the field to collect the food and air-lift it to Binh Son.

At 12:45PM, Bravo called for a dustoff for a Vietnamese mother in labor, who was taken to the district hospital in Binh Son. At 11:30AM Bravo, having called some H&I (Harassment & Interdiction) fires the previous night on "cleared" areas where VC might be on the move, spotted four women carrying a man who had been hit by artillery fire. The VC suspect was dusted-off with his daughter to the 27th Surgical

Hospital while the three other women were sent to Binh Son for questioning.

With so many areas now being searched by the ARVN, Marines and the 5th/46th, the VC were kept constantly on the move, staying out of their tunnels and ahead of their pursuers. CAP 144 spotted ten VC on the move, called in an air strike which was on target with the first salvo, killing five of the enemy.

The morning of July 28 saw another air assault with Bravo landing on three LZ's on the north side of Provincial Route 523 to block and screen north of the hamlet of Phu Nhieu (1). Delta humped north to search out the hamlet from the southwest. While sweeping the area they found a twelve year-old girl and seven year-old boy killed by the gunships which had prepped the LZ's for Bravo. Two other boys were wounded. A dozen dead cattle were also casualties.

This was another cost of war and a moral dilemma. The soldiers always appreciated gunship support preceding their insertion as it gave them the margin of safety they needed to get on the ground safely. The VC were certainly in the area but this time chose not to fight. The appearance of dead children left the battalions soldiers frustrated and remorseful. These emotional burdens of counter-guerilla warfare would stay with them forever. One-quarter mile farther north a gunship cut down several VC evading from the same hamlet.

Delta found trails west of the hamlet that were covered by brush for concealment and lined with rocks on either side, to facilitate the enemy's night movement. The grunts also found five tunnels and five hundred pounds of potatoes.

Further south the ARVN received a Chieu Hoi who was a VC Assistant Platoon Leader. He told the ARVN the heavy fighting around Liem Quang on July 23 killed or wounded fifteen VC of the 48th Battalion, which was now down to one hundred and fifty guerillas. Their weapons included one-82mm mortar, one-57mm Recoilless Rifle, three-M79 Grenade Launchers, two radios, several rockets, and an unlimited supply of mines.

At 11:45AM, Bravo found a young boy and girl, each about the age of five, killed west of Phu Nhieu, in the same area Delta discovered the other dead children. The hardened grunts turned quiet, tears flowing down some faces, with some wondering what the sense of it all was.

An hour later, Bravo's 2nd Platoon spotted two escaping VC who left an SKS Rifle. Shortly thereafter, the 3rd Platoon observed five Chieu

Hoi's surrender, three males and two females. The three males turned out to be hard core VC who had had enough of the Americans fire power. Delta found fifteen caves and bunkers around the expansive hamlet and set about destroying them with demolitions.

On July 29 Alpha Company, rested and refitted, came to the field to replace Bravo, whose turn had come for a stand-down in Chu Lai. The enemy was under constant pressure but was striking back. They entered one of the most secure New Life Hamlets in CAP 144's area and severely beat the pro-government hamlet chief, breaking his arm and two wrists, as well as beating his face to a bloody pulp for all the villagers to see.

Further north on the coastal area of CAP 142, one VC was killed and six captured while fishing for food. Alpha and Delta moved southeast to continue their cordon and searches in the Phu Nhieu hamlets. Alpha's company commander, still unsteady, deferred to Delta's commander whenever possible while Alpha's platoon leaders tried to make the best of his poor leadership. In their searches of hamlets they found more tunnels and fighting-type bunkers. Their questioning of the peasants revealed that Phu Nhieu (1) had been under VC control for five years.

One peasant admitted being forced to be a guerilla but was armed with only a grenade. Twenty-three VC lived in the hamlet and were armed with only six carbines, seven hundred and twenty rounds of ammunition and forty grenades. Their mission was to harass the American's or ARVN's that came near the hamlet. If their enemy attacked they were to evade to the Lac Son hamlets. If attacked there, they were instructed to move back to the Phu Nhieu hamlets, taking advantage that neither the Americans nor the ARVN's were able to field enough soldiers to control the terrain in both hamlet areas at the same time, with so many other missions to occupy them.

Night illumination by moonlight was nearly one hundred percent in late July which prompted more nighttime movement by both the enemy and the battalion's soldiers. But night movements also raised the possibility of friendly fire incidents. On July 26, Delta's 1st platoon moved into a night ambush. Another platoon, along with Delta's company command section made a night move to another position but passed through the kill zone of the 1st platoon. The heavy noise of movement gave the 1st platoon reason to pause, Vietcong didn't make that much noise, and they watched their fellow grunts pass by in silence.

Early the morning of July 31, before first light, Alpha and Delta moved independently to cordon another hamlet. Delta spotted two VC and opened fire. The soldier's fire crossed into Alpha's terrain, wounding two of its soldiers. The enemy escaped.

As July faded into August, continuing cordons and searches by the battalion collected VC suspects and cached rice and potatoes, with Delta Company locating two thousand pounds of rice on July 31. Aeroscout teams were kept busy snatching lone males wandering in the bush, many with fake or no identification. Their bodies were dirty and bruised from hiding in tunnels and moving over rough terrain.

Interrogations of VC suspects confirmed the accuracy of the 5th/46th's intelligence as to the locations and dispositions of the VC in the battalion's AO. One prisoner near Tam Hoi (5) told of a coordinated attack being planned by the 95th Sapper Company in Phuoc Hoa (CAP 133 area). Villagers told of Vietcong in Tam Hoi (1) moving to attack Alpha Company. Tactically the enemy walked in groups of four to five to avoid detection, wearing green uniforms and carrying bandoleers of rice around their necks.

CAP 142 received fifteen Chieu Hoi's the morning of August 1. One Chieu Hoi was a main force Vietcong soldier with the 31 LF VC Company. The other fourteen Chieu Hoi's were laborers for the VC. This group of fifteen had left their unit ten days prior when it was located ten miles west of CAP 142, and made their way slowly to the Batangan, avoiding ARVN and American gunfire as well as retribution from the Vietcong until they reached the protection of the CAP camp. At the time they defected, their VC Company had about sixty men armed with thirty AK-47's and two hundred and fifty rounds for each rifle. They also had two RPG Rocket Launchers with twelve rounds each, one M60 machinegun with one thousand rounds and twenty-five SKS rifles with one hundred and twenty rounds for each.

Alpha and Delta continued to find villagers in the isolated hamlets who were promptly questioned by the Vietnamese PRU and NPFF. In one hamlet a small girl showed Delta's soldiers where a VC was buried the night before, having been killed by helicopter gunships. Alpha detained fifteen civilians and two were classified as VCI. The detainees ranged from two years to sixty-five years of age, all women and children. Other insurgents were turning themselves in to local hamlet chiefs as their tunnels and bunkers in hamlet areas were being demolished. PF

Platoons also moved into targeted hamlets to take up residence to deny the hamlets being used as rest areas or way stations for the VC.

Another VC Chieu Hoi said he heard that thirty VC from the 48th Battalion had been killed in a tunnel complex from air strikes just north of Phu Nhieu (3) on July 22. Armored Calvary tracks from C Troop, 1st/1st Cav and the 3rd Platoon of B Troop were brought down from the Tam Ky area and added to strengthen the efforts of Alpha and Delta. Bravo returned to the field after its stand-down on August 1st to continue the three-company sweep by the battalion and attached one of its platoons in support of the cavalry troops.

At 2:55PM on August 3, Bravo's 3rd platoon was hit by sniper fire and grenades at close range near Nam Yen (3), wounding five. Delta was extracted on the 4th to take its turn at a stand-down in Chu Lai and then returned to Gator on the 5th to take over bunker line duty from Charlie Company. At the same time the Marine shore landing force began its withdrawal from Nantucket Beach operations after making a solid contribution in its sector north of the Athletic Field.

August 6 saw Charlie move to Chu Lai for a short stand-down. Bravo received its platoon back from the Cav and searched an area three-quarter of a mile southeast of Lac Son (1). A lone VC sniper shot PFC Jim Talbott in the head. There was little the medics could do and the soldier died before the dustoff arrived. PFC James Franklin Talbott was age twenty-one and single, from Kewanna, Indiana.

C Troop of the Cav found ten 82mm mortar rounds and two hundred pounds of rice on the southeast corner of Tam Hoi (4). A close inspection of the rice and ammunition revealed they were booby-trapped and they were blown in place.

Alpha Company was not as fortunate. That night Alpha set up a perimeter on the north side of Lac Son (2) near Provincial Road 523. The grunts could hear a lot of activity and talking in the enemy-controlled hamlet. This was something they were not used to observing and it made no sense. The next morning Alpha's Company Commander ordered a patrol to be sent into the village. The men weren't buying it. Their instincts told them it was a trap due to the unusual level of noise which the enemy simply did not make unless it had an ulterior motive. The commander overruled his soldier's field instincts.

Sergeant Moriarty's squad was tasked to go by their acting platoon leader, Staff Sergeant Birkholtz. Moriarty responded, "Bullshit Birkie, doesn't that asshole know you never go back through a place you just came from?" Brikholtz replied, "Yeah, I know. I'm just relaying the order. He wants a patrol to go."

Sergeant Ronny Dunn offered his squad to make the patrol. Moriarty told Dunn, "You don't have to do this, its bullshit" Dunn replied, "I know, but I kinda owe you guys one for taking the ambush duty for us the other night." Dunn's squad was composed of mostly FNG's, PFC Charles Reefer, Roosevelt Abraham, Ralph Greer, Freddy "Shorty" Eason, and Sergeant Dunn. Abraham didn't want to go, he had told his friend Stephen Rudy he wasn't coming back and asked him to mail a letter home. Rudy told him not to worry, that he'd be back, but he took the letter anyway. Rudy was also in the same squad but Dunn left him behind because of a serious cough he was plagued with. Dunn didn't want the patrol compromised with his coughing.

As the patrol crossed a trail just north of the hamlet, Rudy and the others at the company command post heard a large explosion and saw a huge cloud of black smoke rise to the sky. The company commander tried to radio the patrol but received no answer.

PFC Abraham, carrying the radio, had tripped a booby-trapped 105mm Howitzer round which sent him flying into the air. Both of his legs were amputated from the blast. He was killed instantly. Reefer, next to Abraham, was wounded seriously and only lived a couple of minutes. Dunn and Eason, although both badly wounded, established some security in case the enemy tried to attack their position. Greer made his way back to the command post to go for some help because the radio carried by Abraham had been destroyed.

Rudy, back at the company perimeter, went forward to check on his buddy telling his fellow grunts he was going out and not to shoot him "If all hell breaks loose." He encountered Greer coming the other way for help, covered with blood from head to toe. His fatigues were soaked with blood, wet blood, more blood than Rudy thought imaginable. He was helped back to the perimeter as more grunts moved down to the decimated patrol. Moriarty arrived and found Dunn bent over, holding his stomach, hit with shrapnel in the stomach and upper legs.

An RTO called the battalion commander flying nearby to pick up the critically wounded. The RTO was told the bird couldn't land because of enemy fire from the nearby hamlets. The grunts on the ground neither saw nor heard enemy fire. Wagner's Command and Control bird kept circling above but would not land. One soldier, incensed, screamed "If they want small arms fire they'll get it!" He fired a magazine of ammunition at the Huey as it passed overhead.

LTC Wagner's command and control helicopter made another pass and landed to take the dead and wounded back to a hospital, unaware one of his own men fired at his bird. Answering their last roll call from the mine explosion were PFC Roosevelt Abraham, twenty-two years of age and single from Wilmington, North Carolina and PFC Charles Reefer, age twenty-one and single from Jamestown, Pennsylvania. Reefer had also been hit with fragmentation wounds from the friendly fire incident on July 31. This tragedy caused Alpha's commander to remain unglued. Morale in the company was now at an all-time low.

August 7 also claimed another Alpha soldier in an attack that was to prove that no one was safe in South Vietnam. PFC Leo Joe Adakai had been wounded earlier and was recovering from his wounds at the Sixth Army Hospital at the huge coastal base at Cam Ranh Bay. On the evening of August 7 Communist sappers set off some thirty satchel charges in the hospital compound killing two patients and wounding ninety-eight others. On of the fatalities was Adakai. Leo Joe Adakai, American Indian, was twenty-five years of age and married from Blackfoot, Idaho.

Blue Ghosts' Aero-scout team was kept busy snatching VC who were evading the area. They spotted a middle-aged man in a grey uniform near Lac Son (2) who attempted to evade and he was cut down before he could disappear in the thick foliage. They had better luck at grabbing a prisoner on the south edge of Lac Son (1), when Blue Ghost snatched a forty year-old man with no identification. The detainee was taken to LZ Bayonet for questioning by Vietnamese interrogators. The Aero-scouts also spotted bunkers and trenches near Nam Yen (3). They and the myriad of helicopters flying over the Nantucket Beach area kept watch for movements of evading VC or general movements of women and children in the area.

The Huey crews flying resupply or troop carrying missions also volunteered as dustoffs to quickly pull out wounded soldiers, and saw combat up front and personal, even though they did not walk the ground. Enemy ground fire which hit the choppers as they attempted to land caused numerous casualties among helicopter crews. The blood and gore which soiled their floors and seats during these missions left the chopper crews with a hardened attitude towards the enemy.

Sgt Moriarty of Alpha briefly worked off LZ Minuteman in early July. One Huey resupply bird came in and Moriarty walked over to see if any beer had come in. One of his squad members and his best friend, "Griff", walked over with him.

As they approached the Huey, Moriarty noticed another squad member, "Ironhorse" walk over. "Ironhorse" is a pseudonym. He was a large six foot tall American Indian with a barrel chest and the strength of an ox, always walking with a scowl on his face. Ironhorse was tough, brave and ruthless when provoked. He was not afraid of any situation or any individual; the kind of soldier most men wanted by their side in a firefight.

There was no beer on the bird but when the chopper was being unloaded one of the pilots told Moriarty they were fired on when flying over a nearby hamlet bringing in the supplies. "You guys wanna jump in and take ride, we'll go buzz down there?" Moriarty and his comrades were bored so they jumped on with their weapons for the short hop to the hamlet.

The Huey circled the small hamlet containing a dozen or so hooch's, and saw a few villagers in the middle of the hamlet but drew no fire. The bird then flew to the south side of the hamlet which held a hedgerow and a small, dry rice paddy. As the Huey banked to the right the pilot spotted three peasants who appeared to be carrying weapons. The bird landed and the pilot suggested Moriarty check it out.

Moriarty and his two comrades, Ironhorse and Griff, jumped out with no radio to call for help if they ran into trouble. It was the kind of stupid decision Moriarty would muse over from many years. Trouble began immediately as the insurgents, two men and a woman, placed automatic weapons fire on them and then took off running. The insurgents ran to an opening in the hedgerow but Moriarty's team with longer legs quickly gained on them.

The three insurgents lost traction and time as they tried to climb a small, muddy and slippery bank through the hedgerow. Ironhorse shot one male insurgent attempting to pull himself up, hitting him in the right side of the head. The insurgent dropped his weapon. Moriarty and Griff continued after the other two insurgents, who had climbed the bank but dropped their weapons. The bank was slippery for the grunts as well but Ironhorse bounded up with no difficulty and took the lead. When they reached some hooch's on the edge of the hamlet the two insurgents disappeared. Then Griff lifted a large bamboo cover over a spider hole, let out a shout and the two insurgents raised their hands in surrender.

Moriarty was happy to have two prisoners and captured weapons. He wanted to take the head-wounded insurgent in as well. Ironhorse wanted to kill all three and Griff opted to let the wounded solder die and take the other two. Moriarty, the squad leader, won the argument.

All three prisoners were taken back to the paddy and the Huey, which had been circling above observing the chase, landed again. Ironhorse held the women prisoner by the back of her neck with his giant left hand and the male prisoner with his other. Moriarty and Griff gamely carried the wounded prisoner. The bird landed at LZ Minuteman and disgorged the prisoners. The pilot told his three new "Friends", "Maybe you can go on another ride with us sometime?" Griff yelled, "Bullshit". Ironhorse, miffed he was shot at, told the pilot "Fuck you!"

A crowd developed around the three prisoners on Minuteman. Moriarty had his platoon's medic see what he could do for the prisoner with the head wound who occasionally let out a low moan or a slight twitch with his hands or feet. A Lieutenant came over and Moriarty briefed him on what happened. The officer called for a Huey to take the prisoners back for questioning. The platoon medic, "Mario", continued to work on his patient with the head wound, now heavily bandaged with an IV in his left arm and another in his foot at the ankle. Mario was ready to administer another needle. Moriarty asked, "God dam doc, what the hell are you doing to that poor bastard?" Doc injected the needle and relied, "Practicin medicin", which received laughter from the crowd.

One soldier, in admiration for the medical skills he was witnessing said, "You're a crazy fucker Mario!" A black soldier from another squad came up to see what was going on and eyed the patient with the bandages on his head soaked in blood. "What happened to him?" Someone answered, "Ironhorse popped him." The soldier's eyes and mouth rolled wide open, "Damn Ironhorse, you bout made this Mother Fucker lose his mind." More laughter in the group.

Ironhorse stayed with his two prisoners. The male insurgent, small in stature, stared at his goliath enemy with an evil eye, showing no fear, just hate. Ironhorse yelled at him, "Your gook ass is lucky it's still alive and if it were up to me you'd be dead!" The prisoner showed no emotion, just stared at Ironhorse as if he were saying, "Fuck you, I ain't scared of your big ass!" Ironhorse read his mind and was pissed. He stomped his boot on the prisoners bare foot, grinding his boot heal back and forth on the insurgent's foot. The enemy soldier did not flinch. Moriarty thought to himself, "If all these little bastards are this tough, we're in big trouble."

The Lieutenant returned and ordered Ironhorse to leave the prisoner alone. Shortly after, a Huey landed. It was not a dustoff or Medevac. The crew chief yelled over the "Whoop", Whoop" of the rotary blades, "We're supposed to pick up some gooks for questioning." The prisoners were loaded on, the two uninjured insurgents with hands tied behind their backs, the head-wounded insurgent incapable of moving. Moriarty watched the Huey head south, and then bank east and north, heading for Chu Lai. He turned to walk away when someone yelled, "Holy shit! They're jumping out!" as the soldier pointed a nervous finger to the bird in the sky. Moriarty saw two bodies falling to the earth then a third exited the aircraft. There was disbelief.

Disbelief; the soldiers were at a loss to explain it. "What the fuck is going on?" Another, "Do you believe this shit?" Still another, "Did those crazy bastards really jump out?" The disbelief, like most other imponderables in war was expressed by grim humor. "Doc, I gotta say you know your shit. I swear that guy was dead but you practiced on him and five minutes later he's jumping out of helicopters."

Later that night while on guard duty Moriarty heard Ironhorse approach him in a hushed voice, "Are you sleeping?" Moriarty replied, "Hell no Ironhorse, I'm on guard duty." "Good answer" replied Ironhorse, who was known to hit soldiers who were asleep on guard duty, regardless of rank. Ironhorse sat with his squad leader and for a moment stared straight ahead, not saying anything. Then a hushed question, "Hey, do you think those gooks really jumped out?" "I don't know" was the hushed reply from Moriarty who added, "That one little bastard was pretty tough don't you think?" Ironhorse then stood up to walk away and turned to his squad leader, "Yeah, he was."

On the morning of August 10, Bravo relinquished control of its 2nd Platoon to Alpha. Bravo was tasked to assist in the screening of the western edge of the Batangan Peninsula, while Alpha worked the Tam Hoi area with tracks from A troop, 1st/1st Cav. Bravo set up blocking positions south of An Thinh (1) while Charlie, now back from its stand-down, entered from the north to sweep the hamlet.

Although the VC were on the run, intelligence indicated the VC would attack in a campaign dubbed "Autumn of Gallantry" to hit key towns in Quang Ngai Province. The enemy planned to infiltrate the towns by posing as civilians looking for work or seeking relatives. Weapons were to be concealed in fruit such as bananas and melons. Explosives were to be planted in restaurants, hospitals, and government facilities in advance of the attacks.

At 8:00AM on August 10, Alpha's Company Commander was finally relieved of command and replaced by Captain Paul Longgrear, the battalions acting Executive Officer, who had been waiting for a company command to open up. Longgrear was the consummate warrior, having spent a tour in Vietnam as a Special Forces "Mike Force" commander in 1967, leading one hundred and sixty mercenaries along with five Special Forces sergeants, in long range patrols across the Laotian border. He survived the battle of Lang Vei, an isolated Special Forces outpost that was overrun by Soviet tanks which had been moved down the Ho Chi Minh trail for the battle. That action earned him the Silver Star. Longgrear wanted a command with a conventional unit, as Special Forces Captains did not command Infantry Company's in the SF. This was his chance to do so, and it was Alpha's fortune to get him.

LTC Wagner wanted the relief to occur quickly. Alpha's erratic commander was on the list to be promoted to Major and if he stayed in the field much longer, Wagner would have to write a bad efficiency report which may mean no promotion. Of such thinking were some officers promoted to a higher level of incompetency in the Army. It was a failure of leadership by the battalion commander that he waited so long to relive him. Since the debacle on July 16 when PFC McElhaney was crushed by the armored personnel carrier, others in Alpha were needlessly killed.

Longgrear landed in the field and told Alpha's commander, "The old man wants to see you". Alpha's commander knew he was losing his command and was relieved about it. He was appointed as the Echo Company Commander, a position which did not require him to leave LZ Gator.

Each rifle company in the battalion's war periodically received new commanders and the dynamic of the unit changed for better or for worse. If a company was strong and received a competent commander, the most ideal situation, the commander and the soldiers learned from each other. But if a strong company received a weak commander which had occurred in Alpha, morale disintegrated and casualties needlessly occurred. If a weak company received a strong commander, old lessons had to be relearned again, sometimes at the expense of soldiers who could not accommodate change and were relieved.

Longgrear told Alpha's First Sergeant and Executive Officer on LZ Gator, and a number of other soldiers to pack their bags for the field. Nine soldiers were authorized to be in a rear company headquarters (Americal Division policy), Alpha had twenty-two. The day before he took over Alpha, there had been only sixty-four men in the field.

Longgrear was not enamored with the "ticket-punching" of senior officers in Vietnam. Most could not relate to the conditions on the ground their men faced over which they made life and death decisions. But as the Battalion Executive Officer he shared quarters with LTC Wagner on LZ Gator and felt Wagner's nine month experience advising a South Korean Army Brigade gave him enough understanding of the ground war to be effective. Wagner had extended his tour in Vietnam to get command of the 5th/46th.

At 12:45PM on August 10, Alpha's grunts made a sweep through an area from which they had received mortar fire the night before, three-quarter of a mile southwest of Tam Hoi (1). Longgrear observed two Hispanic soldiers walking side-by-side, conversing in Spanish. Walking nearby was a Sergeant First Class (SFC), the only one in Alpha, who ignored the soldiers bunching-up. Longgrear called for him to walk to him, a distance of ten yards, and told the senior sergeant to get his men spread out. The sergeant turned to move closer to his men and at that moment PFC Rodriguez-Guzman detonated a mine, the explosion slicing into several soldiers bunched together. The explosion wounded five soldiers and killed PFC Abelardo Rodriguez-Guzman, age twenty and single from Hato Rey, Puerto Rico.

Sergeant Chuck Barbo was wounded along with four others. Barbo recalled the grizzly scene as the medics worked on the wounded, "Martinez tripped the mine and was torn up pretty bad in his forearms, hips, upper shoulders; Jim "The Kid" Rhode was hit in the right temple with a large piece of metal; Rodriquez had a small hole in his chest and that's what got him. Hector was hit in several places, his eye brows were gone where a piece of shrapnel cut through them across his forehead. A piece went through the front of his shin bone, another piece through his wrist and another through his cheeks. I had small fragments in the right side of my back and above the knee of my right leg."

When the dustoff arrived, a fifth "wounded soldier" appeared to be the senior sergeant who failed to keep his men spread out. He walked over to get on the bird and Longgrear called him over to ask what he was doing. The Senior Sergeant pointed to a small puncture wound in his upper arm, saying he was going in to get it treated. Longgrear saw a "performance-threatening" fear in his eyes and said, "OK, but don't come back!" The battalion commander asked him why he relieved a senior sergeant in the field. Longgrear's response was "I'd rather have 'Shake and Bake' Sergeants. At least they are trainable!"

It was the last time Captain Longgrear would lose a soldier killed in action in Alpha until the last day of his command, January 4, 1970, when an Alpha soldier was killed during an attack on LZ Gator. One squad leader years later would reflect, "Longgrear was a man of his word. When he promised you something, you knew he would deliver. He didn't put the lives of his men in danger unnecessarily; he was gung-ho and he liked men who were gung-ho but he wasn't a risk-taker. He didn't waste time on small talk, yet he was approachable. The men followed him because they trusted him".

Captain Longgrear soon found out he had good platoon leaders and Alpha's problems with its high casualty rates was the result of their former commander. The men literally hated him. During a platoon leaders meeting the day after Rodriguez-Guzman's death, one Lieutenant pointed out white adhesive tape wrapped around one soldiers hand grenade. The grenade had the former commander's name on it. Longgrear was livid. He called for a company formation in the middle of the rice paddy. The First Sergeant was aghast because they were in a combat zone. Longgrear chewed out his company and had the white tape removed from all grenades, telling them if he saw a taped grenade again he would consider that a threat that would be handled harshly. Alpha Company was about to be morphed into "Alpha's Raiders" and become highly effective again.

Meanwhile, Charlie and Bravo working in An Thinh (1) were finding more tunnels and small caches. To further the effort at "turning" civilians and VC to the South Vietnamese Government, the 5th/46th Battalion began employing Special Action Pacification (SAP) teams which included a Vietnamese intelligence officer from Binh Son, some former VC who had turned pro-government (Hoi Chanh's), National Police, loudspeaker teams, and medical treatment teams. Three hundred and twenty-five villagers were detained in An Thinh with eight selected for further questioning. The remainder received food, water and medical care. Of those, one hundred and fifty were treated in one day.

The "Accelerated Pacification" effort was designed to demonstrate who controlled the area, who had the resources to help the peasants, and who had the most firepower to kill at will. To further "Accelerate the pacification" some of the Marine CAP teams in crucial areas around Binh Son were expanded with more popular force militia to increase their control.

The following day, August 11, Bravo and Charlie moved southwest to search out Phu Nhieu (1) while Alpha remained in the Tam Hoi area. Bravo drew first blood killing a VC who was carrying six-M79 rounds. Five other Vietcong escaped.

By 4:50PM, Charlie Company had detained one hundred and twenty civilians, twenty-one of whom were sent to Binh Son for questioning. One detainee revealed that fifteen guerillas had left Phu Nhieu in small group's just minutes before the grunts arrived. The insurgent that Bravo killed was in one of those groups. These VC moved to hilly and dense terrain one and one-half miles southwest of the hamlet, following the same pattern as other VC, playing a shell game, seeking a safe haven in nearby dense terrain or in hamlets which had been vacated by their pursuers. The game of hide and seek continued to frustrate LTC Wagner and his maneuver companies from killing more of the enemy.

At 3:00AM on August 12, the enemy "Autumn of Gallantry" campaign made its debut with a mortar and small-arms attack on LZ Minuteman, now exclusively defended by ARVN, RF and PF soldiers with mortar support from the 5th/46th. No casualties were sustained from the attack. Binh Son was hit at 3:30AM with mortars, followed by a sapper attack. One home was destroyed and six civilians wounded. CAP 138's compound, guarding the western edge of Binh Son was hit and three Marines were killed.

A few mortar rounds and small arms fire also hit LZ Gator. An early morning sweep of the perimeter beyond bunker #9 uncovered one dead VC apparently killed by a malfunctioning grenade. A Bangalore Torpedo was also found along with several blood trails, some leading to the village of Nuoc Mau at the eastern edge of Gator on Highway One.

Nuoc Mau was hit at 11:45AM by VC and NVA firing B-40 Rockets and automatic weapons. The Village Chiefs' home was destroyed and three civilians killed with another three wounded. One Vietcong was killed. Binh Son was hit again at 1:00PM by thirty VC, who killed four civilians and wounded twelve. The attack was directed at the headquarters of the Popular Force militia in Binh Son. Echo's Recon platoon, having returned from its stand-down in Chu Lai, began establishing ambushes around Nuoc Mau in conjunction with some PRU to avert further attacks.

By 7:50AM Alpha, Bravo and Charlie were on the move again. Alpha Company air assaulted south of Liem Quang (1) while Bravo landed at two LZ's north of the hamlet. Charlie Company simultaneously landed by Hueys southwest and west of the hamlet, also in the vicinity of Nhan Hoa (2).

To some grunts in the battalion the constant shuffling from hamlet to hamlet appeared as though the battalion was grasping at straws, with no clear cut goals. But the constant air assaults required to "chase URI's" were making a difference. The simple, short hops from hamlet to hamlet, in response to the most actionable intelligence on enemy locations reportedly kept the enemy on the run. A Troop of the 1st/1st Cav also provided more screening capability for the grunts. Throughout the day, the three infantry companies found tunnels, uncovered small caches of food, and culled out suspected VCI from seventy-five peasants they detained for questioning.

The next morning at 1:50AM the An KY refugee camps in CAP 144's area, which included Hill 26, were hit by an estimated company-sized force from the 48th Local Force Battalion. The attack was begun by forty to fifty mortar rounds and B-40 rockets. The CAP Marines and their PF's counterattacked at night to engage them. When it was over, two Marines and three PF's were killed, nine civilians killed and ten wounded. On Hill 26, two civilians were killed and four PF's wounded. Vietcong atrocities of civilians continued throughout the coastal plain in an effort to demoralize and thereby control the populace.

Charlie Company, operating one-quarter mile north of Phuoc Son (2) found two 105mm Howitzer rounds, an anti-tank mine, three thousand and one hundred pounds of rice and a hooch that served as a fabricating shop to make booby-traps. The enemy's tools and explosives had been hastily abandoned.

To further achieve the pacification objectives of Nantucket Beach the battalion began working much closer with the CAP teams throughout the large coastal area. For example, Alpha combined with Marine CAP 137 and PF Platoon 13 (Later the 21st Platoon) to bolster daytime patrols and night ambushes. They hoped to stop VC infiltration into Binh Son. Alpha's 1st Platoon joined up with A Troop, 1st/1st Cav, dubbed

"Team Trooper" to conduct mobile reconnaissance around the Tam Hoi hamlets.

Bravo Company worked the area one and one-half miles northeast of the An Ky/Hill 26 peninsula which was recovering from its recent attack. Bravo's 1st Platoon found seven hundred pounds of salt in Dong Xuan (3) along with enemy fighting bunkers. Fresh sandal tracks indicated the Vietcong made a rapid exit. The seven hundred pounds of salt would prove to be the tip of a "Salt Iceberg", and would gain Bravo some fame throughout South Vietnam. Bravo's move into the hamlet was not welcomed and they were continually harassed by sporadic small arms fire as they searched the area.

Charlie occupied Phu My (2) approximately one mile further southwest of Bravo. They detained one hundred and thirty-five civilians and called in a medical team to treat one hundred of them who had various ailments. Their efforts were rewarded two hours later with small arms fire from west of the hamlet.

The following morning on August 16, Bravo's 1st Platoon found another seven hundred pounds of salt as it finished blowing the bunkers it found two days prior. Bravo's 2nd Platoon killed two VC and one NVA in Dong Xuan (1), with several other enemy soldiers escaping. At 2:00PM another two thousand pounds of salt was discovered. Salt was vital to the enemy to preserve food in hidden caches, particularly meat and fish. But of more concern to Captain Schopp, Bravo's commander, was the constant harassing fire they received day and night, and a near-miss of friendly fire from the 4.2-inch mortars on LZ Minuteman. Schopp wanted his 81mm mortar platoon back under his control rather than have his company mortar platoon under the control of the battalions weapons company (Echo), as directed by Wagner. Schopp got his way and his 81mm mortars were sent back to him.

At 7:00PM, Bravo received more automatic weapons fire. A sweep of the area the next morning found no enemy, but uncovered another six to eight tons of salt covered by straw mats.

Charlie Company kept busy with a shoot and run contest with the VC, killing one. They found concrete fighting bunkers measuring four feet in height and six feet in width and depth. Punji pits were also discovered by their scout dogs. The An Ky hamlets continued to be a priority target for the enemy so Charlie's 2nd platoon was airlifted to that location to neutralize the enemy pressure in the area.

For many weeks Delta's 4th Squad of its 2nd Platoon remained in Tri Binh (1) one and one-quarter mile north of LZ Gator, working with the popular militia to defend that largely pro-government hamlet. Its success spoke volumes for the concept of integrating small teams with local forces, like the CAP teams had done since the Marine's arrival in Vietnam. Becoming familiar with the people and the local terrain established the basis for successful countermeasures against the enemy. The squad's nighttime ambushes and daytime patrols were having an effect. On August 17 the squad wounded a VC and captured his AK-47. Interrogation revealed an attack was planned against the hamlet in order to undermine the growing confidence of the populace.

Bravo exerted more control over the Dong Xuan area. In the dark of night at 11:30PM a squad entered an abandoned hooch only to see two VC escape through the back door.

Early the next morning Alpha leapfrogged by Huey to Phu Long (5) and found a Vietcong supply base. The attached Kit Carson Scout (former VC turned recon specialist) estimated the VC had vacated the premises one hour prior.

Charlie Company was lifted to the An Ky Hamlets (CAP 144) to join its second platoon, and place more assets in that area to counter the increased enemy activity. In the joint operation spirit of Nantucket Beach, Popular Force (PF) Platoons 58, 48, 46, and 66 were added to work with Charlie Company along with loudspeaker teams and medical treatment (MEDCAP) teams. Swift boats were tasked to conduct nightly sweeps on the south and east coasts of the An Ky Peninsula.

By the close of August 19, Bravo's growing salt cache of eleven thousand pounds bagged at this point was sent to LZ Gator, Binh Son and five refugee camps. MEDCAPS had treated four hundred civilians in the An Ky area.

LZ Gator received a reminder that work in the war zone, regardless of location or duty, could never be assumed as "secure". At 1:00AM on August 21, three of Charlie's grunts manning Gator's bunker line were wounded by a hand grenade which accidentally exploded. Two were dusted off that night. One had a chest wound and the other, PFC Brown, suffered massive fragmentation wounds. He was pronounced dead on arrival in Chu Lai. James Henry Brown Jr. was age twenty and single from McClellanville, South Carolina.

That same morning Alpha air assaulted to An Thoi (1) near the infamous Van Tuong Hamlets. Detainees revealed there were thirty VC in the hamlet the day before who knew the soldiers were coming. Prior to the air assault the VC fled to hide in small groups until the soldiers left. Small caches of corn and rice were found throughout the hamlet. The soldiers were surprised the villagers showed no emotion when the supplies were found. This was an indication to the grunts that much more was nearby. Alpha then moved north to Van Tuong (2), detained one hundred civilians, and found another two thousand pounds of rice and corn.

By August 22, Charlie Company joined Bravo to assist in its salt-bagging operation with neither company being enthralled with the heavy labor required to bag salt under the hot sun. By this time eighty tons of salt had been found and Bravo's Commander, CPT Schopp, was dubbed "The Salt King" by Americal Division headquarters. The division was pleased by the press they were getting while sitting in their air-conditioned offices at Chu Lai.

Alpha was continually plagued by small arms fire and snipers around the Van Tuong, An Thoi (1) and An Cuong (2) hamlets as the Communists' "Autumn of Gallantry" operation continued.

First Lieutenant Dan Martin led a small patrol among the enemy hamlets to check the area before setting up a night defensive position (NDP). His patrol took a hail of small arms fire and it returned fire, knowing it had hit some insurgents. Martin returned to the remainder of his platoon and brought them back to the scene, finding many blood trails and drag marks, two AK-47's and some 82mm mortar rounds. The next morning the platoon found more equipment and documents and four Chieu Hoi's who came out of the brush to surrender. They indicated Martin's small patrol had wounded eight Vietcong and killed two the day before. For his bravery Martin was awarded an Army Commendation Medal for valor.

Intelligence reports indicated the 427th NVA Battalion (strength estimated at three hundred and fifty) was moving east from the Tra Bong area to attack either Binh Son or Quang Ngai. Echo's Recon Platoon, now screening the western flank of the Batangan encountered more fleeing Vietcong near Chau Binh (1).

The battalion's patrols, sweeps, cordons and searches continued, keeping the enemy on the run while discovering caches of food, equipment, documents, weapons, tunnels and an occasional Chieu Hoi. Alpha's 3rd Platoon supported H Troop, 17th Cav in sweep operations while Bravo Troop, 1st/1st Cav operated in support of the ARVN.

Alpha's company operations were particularly contentious. Each night the Vietcong fired into their small patrol perimeters, throwing grenades or occasionally launching mortar fire. Alpha responded with its own firepower, afterward not finding many bodies but plenty of blood trails. The PF's, working with the three rifle companies of the battalion were starting to pull their load. On August 25 alone, nine PF's were wounded and dusted off while working with Alpha.

In another effort to kill a large group of the enemy, Charlie Company lifted off in Hueys early on the morning of August 26 to assault three locations north of Phu My (2) ("Objective A") while Bravo moved to the eastern edge of Nghiem Quong (1) ("Objective B"). The ARVN screened the west and south of both objectives as a blocking force. At 8:30AM Bravo's 1st Platoon saw ten VC running from a hooch and they killed two, one male and one female carrying equipment, but no weapons. One hour later, they found a 105mm Howitzer round hanging from a tree, waiting to be detonated by Charlie's grunts who were approaching from the north. Charlie' soldiers killed another female VC at 9:30AM. Both Bravo and Charlie were squeezing the noose and the VC were desperately trying to escape it.

Bravo's 3rd Platoon leader, 1LT Gary L. Byler, had been keeping the pressure on the enemy while under repeated automatic weapons fire as they evaded. At 11:30AM, the platoon was in pursuit of more fleeing Vietcong when Byler stepped on a 155mm Howitzer round triggered with a pressure release device. The explosion sheared off his right arm and leg.

Captain Schopp and his headquarters element were nearby with a resupply helicopter offloading its cargo. Schopp jumped on board and kicked out the remaining supplies and stayed in the bird to pick up Byler. In short order the Huey was on its way to a hospital, all the time with Schopp by his lieutenant's side, encouraging him, talking to him, offering any words of comfort to keep him from going into shock. Byler stayed conscious all the way. The lieutenant would later receive the Silver Star for his aggressive actions that day.

The next day Alpha killed a Vietcong in Van Tuong (2) and captured another who was reportedly the head of the Vietcong in Binh Son Province. Another VC female was found with her leg blown off from Alpha's defensive artillery fires the night before. They also captured a carbine, radio, medical kit, and Chicom grenades.

Back on LZ Minuteman Echo's mortar platoon was told to instruct the ARVN on the use of the heavy mortars as part of the "Vietnamization" effort. Later the classes were to extend to the 81mm and 60mm mortars as well. Echo's mortar men wisely chose "Maintenance and Ammunition Storage" as the first subject, and gave the ARVN "practical experience" by having them clean up Echo's mortar pits. The grunts were pleased with the arrangement.

ARVN soldiers sweeping near the Phu My hamlets were attacked by Vietcong the previous night. In the ensuing battle seventeen VC were killed with a loss of one ARVN soldier. By 10:45PM that evening, the PF's operating with Alpha spotted twenty VC in the open. Artillery was called and the PF's swept the area, finding many blood trails and several Chicom grenades left behind.

Just before dawn on August 28, many VC were seen moving in and out of the shadows in front of the bunker line at LZ Gator as the darkness transitioned to first light. Aware of the enemies "Autumn of Gallantry" campaign, Gator was on high alert.

At 6:50AM out in the field, Alpha's 1st Platoon spotted three VC, killed one and wounded another. Warlord gunships and LOH's flew the skies east of CAP 133's area, killing five Vietcong and landed to capture two more.

Charlie Company's 1st Platoon was hit with small arms fire, M-79 grenade rounds and 60mm mortars. The VC were so close, artillery could not be used. Two grunts were wounded with shrapnel in their arms and legs. Gunships raked the area, but the grunts found nothing.

The next day Alpha hit another mine in Van Tuong (4). They were moving to a new location when a patrol file of nine men unknowingly stepped over a booby-trap. The first eight soldiers stepped over a concealed M14-type mine but the ninth soldier, PFC Robert Smith, detonated it and lost his right foot. PFC Hollis Watts next to him was hit in the face and body with shrapnel.

Echo's Recon Platoon kept busy screening the western flank of the Batangan. They spotted twelve VC fleeing near Chau Binh (1) and later found explosives for mines: Two M79 rounds, one 155mm Howitzer artillery round, one 105mm Howitzer round, two bunkers, rice and medical supplies.

On August 30, Bravo Company finally began to see the end of its salt excavation project. By months-end the salt discovery amounted to over two hundred and thirty-eight tons, making headlines in the Military's newspapers throughout South Vietnam.

But by this time, Bravo's commander regretted his troops had ever found the stuff. The bagging operation required his men to stay in the same small area far too long, allowing the enemy to set mines and booby traps which made movement for Bravo's soldiers more dangerous each additional day they stayed. Captain Schopp would learn later as the battalions Civil Affairs Officer that the province chief, rather than distributing the salt to the people, used it as graft, making sure all his government officials got a part of the action.

The month closed on August 31 with Alpha Company working in CAP 135's area along with two PF Platoons and the tracks from B Troop, 1st/1st Cav.

Bravo was packed up and ready to move by Chinook ("Hook") back to Gator, with Delta in place to finish what little salt extraction remained. As they waited for the big "Hook" to take them back, LTC Wagner flew over and called Captain Schopp, telling him he could see a shovel where a salt pile had been and to send someone to get it. Schopp advised Wagner he had a full accounting of all shovels and each salt pile had been "Policed up" before it was abandoned.

Schopp suggested the battalion commander fly lower to have a better look. Wagner refused and directed Schopp to send out men to retrieve the shovel. Schopp told Lieutenant William Kaseberg to send a group but Kaseberg reminded him the site had been closed the day before and it had not been secured overnight and might be mined. Wagner insisted that what he thought was a shovel needed to be retrieved.

SP/4 Lawrence Millett's squad was sent with a rope and a hook, in the unlikely event there was a shovel, to not approach the tool but throw the rope and drag back the shovel. He was told not to get near the former salt pile. But on the way Millett stopped his squad and walked ahead on his own contrary to instructions, perhaps to protect his squad, and stepped on a booby-trapped explosive (heavy mortar or artillery round). He was killed instantly. Both his legs were sheared off; the explosion cauterizing the wounds and left no blood. One of the battalion commander's rules was to have a dog tag attached to a boot lace. Millett's legs and boots were gone and his comrades tagged his body as best as they could.

Captain Schopp called the battalion headquarters to explain why there would be no dog tags or other identification to what was left of the body, but it was surely Millett. The headquarters disregarded his explanation and chastised Schopp for sending in a dead body without proper identification. SP/4 Lawrence Arthur Millett died at the age of twenty-four, leaving behind a wife and young daughter, trying to retrieve a phantom shovel. He was from Norway, Maine. Another grunt, PFC Robert Gregory, who was closest to Millett when the mine exploded, was hit by shrapnel in the head, neck and abdomen, but survived.

Later on LZ Gator LTC Wagner stopped Lieutenant Kaseberg in the mess hall and angrily demanded to know why there was no dog tag sent in with the body. Kaseberg responded with, "Did you ever find a shovel there sir?" Wagner glared back at the Lieutenant and walked away.

President Lyndon Johnson reviews 5th/46th Infantry Battalion at Fort Hood, Texas, December 12, 1967. Standing in jeep left to right: Lieutenant General G.R. Mather, Lieutenant Colonel David Lyon, President Johnson
(U.S. Army photo courtesy of David Lyon)

Lieutenant Colonel David Lyon, Commander, 5th/46th Infantry Battalion (left) reviews troops with Major General Samuel Koster (right), Commanding General, Americal Division, upon the battalions arrival in Chu Lai
(U.S. Army photo courtesy of David Lyon)

LZ Gator facing east toward Artillery Hill. Beyond the hill are Nuoc Mau and Highway One. To right of photo is main entrance to LZ Gator
(Courtesy Steven Schopp)

LZ Gator facing west toward the tactical operations center, radio unit, etc. To left of photo is VIP landing pad and farther left is main landing pad
(Courtesy Steven Schopp)

VIP landing pad and briefing shack on LZ Gator (foreground). Main landing pad is in the background *(Courtesy John Forshag)*

Huey's pull pitch off main landing pad at LZ Gator for another combat air-assault *(Courtesy Everett "Doc" Rowles)*

Bunker on LZ Chippewa facing west to the Annamite Mountains
(Courtesy Bob Mioducki)

Riverboat South (CAP 134) at headwaters of Tra Bong River. Boulder area in foreground was used by villagers as their latrine area *(Courtesy Lee Gunton)*

"Field Expedient" fresh water shower on LZ Paradise. Refugee village on beach in the background *(Courtesy Bob Mioducki)*

Aerial view of Vietnam countryside in 5th/46th Battalion coastal area. Coast is in the background *(Courtesy Michael Esslinger)*

Typical hamlet structure as seen in a Huey fly-over *(Courtesy Michael Esslinger)*

Typical "Hooch" in Vietnamese countryside *(Courtesy John Arruda)*

Lieutenant Colonel Alfred Barnes, Commander, 5th/46th Infantry Battalion March 15, 1969 – May 12, 1969, killed in action during a sapper attack on LZ Gator in the early hours of May 12th *(US Army photo)*

Lieutenant Colonel David K. Lyon, first commander of the 5th/46th Infantry Battalion after reactivated (October 2, 1967-October 11, 1968)
(U.S. Army photo courtesy David Lyon)

Lieutenant Colonel Ronald K. Richardson, Commander, 5th/46th Infantry Battalion, October 11, 1968 – March 15, 1969
(U.S. Army Military History Institute photo)

Lieutenant Colonel Julian F. Wagner, Commander, 5th/46th Infantry Battalion, May 20, 1969 – November 17, 1969 *(U.S. Army photo)*

Lieutenant Colonel Melvin C. Snyder, Commander, 5th/46th Infantry Battalion November 17, 1969 – May 9, 1970 *(Courtesy Steven Schopp)*

Lieutenant Colonel Wereszynski, Commander, 5th/46th Infantry Battalion May 10, 1970 – September 8, 1970 *(U.S. Army photo)*

Lieutenant Colonel James R. Henry, Commander, 5th/46th Infantry Battalion September 9, 1970 – December 18, 1970 *(U.S. Army photo)*

Lieutenant Colonel Edwin E. Passmore, Commander, 5th/46th Infantry Battalion, December 19, 1970 - May 21, 1971 *(Courtesy Edwin W. Passmore)*

A battalion short range recon patrol (SRP) also known as a "Hunter Killer Team", 1st Platoon, Alpha Company *(Courtesy L. D. Loftis)*

A captured Vietcong given an empty M-16 rifle and flak vest to pose with members of 1st Platoon, Alpha Company *(Courtesy L.D. Loftis)*

Armored Personnel Carrier (APC) hit by enemy rifle-propelled grenade (RPG) (note hole on side of APC), during operation Russell Beach, January-February 1969 *(Courtesy L.D. Loftis)*

Four of the enemy dead from attack on Alpha Company during Operation Russell Beach, January-February 1969 *(Courtesy L.D. Loftis)*

Alpha Company soldier attends to captured Vietcong during Operation Russell Beach, January-February 1969 *(Courtesy L.D. Loftis)*

Popular Force (PF) militia on Batangan Peninsula *(Courtesy L.D. Loftis)*

Marine Combined Action Platoon (CAP) 142 and refugee camp on coast of the Batangan Peninsula *(Courtesy Robert Wight)*

Making new friends in war: Alpha Company soldier with children in a refugee village on coastal plain (weapons not loaded). *(Courtesy Bob Mioducki)*

Thanksgiving 1969 in a pacified hamlet in Delta Company's "Area of Operation Serene" *(Courtesy Robert Wight)*

Irregular Defense Force peasant with son in a pacified hamlet on the coastal plain *(Courtesy Robert Wight)*

Soldier with captured AK-47 Assault Rifle, the main weapon of the enemy
(Courtesy Michael Esslinger)

Chieu Hoi (NVA Deserter) Kit Carson Scout with enemy Rifle Propelled Grenade (RPG) *(Courtesy Michael Esslinger)*

Chinese Communist (Chicom) hand grenade *(Courtesy Michael Esslinger)*

The battalion's small arms weapons (left to right): M-16 rifle, Light Anti-tank Weapon (LAW) and M-79 Grenade Launcher *(Courtesy Michael Esslinger)*

Artillery round which did not detonate (used by the enemy for mines) *(Courtesy Michael Esslinger)*

Quad-50 caliber machineguns on back of a 2-1/2-ton truck - "Deuce and a Half" *(Courtesy Jim Klebau)*

Medevac directed by Captain Steven Schopp, Bravo Company *(Courtesy Steven Schopp)*

Close-in fire support *(Courtesy John Arruda)*

Light Observation Helicopter (LOH) *(Courtesy Michael Esslinger)*

Scout Dogs were used frequently on patrols of the battalion
(Courtesy Michael Esslinger)

Aerial view of My Lai (4), scene of infamous massacre. Note two APC's to the left of briefing tent. The line above between the hamlet and rice paddies is Provincial Route 521 from Quang Ngai City (father right of photo) leading to "Pinkville" (My Lai 1) farther left of photo *(Courtesy of John Forshag)*

Briefing tent at My Lai (4), one of several erected during investigation of My Lai massacre *(Courtesy of John Forshag)*

Bunker #2 on LZ Gator perimeter, destroyed during sapper attack January 4, 1970 *(Courtesy Jim Klebau)*

Some of the sappers killed during attack on LZ Gator, January 4, 1970. After the numerous sapper attacks on LZ Gator while the battalion was there, the enemy dead were loaded on trucks and taken off the hill to the village of Nuoc Mau, as evidence of the price paid by the enemy for the attack. The insurgents would retrieve the bodies for burial *(Courtesy of Jim Klebau)*

Charlie Company patrolling in mountain stream near LZ Lizard, April 1970 *(Courtesy Ken Teglia)*

Huey's land on LZ Lizard during search and destroy operation deep in Annamite Mountains, April 1970 *(Courtesy Ken Teglia)*

May 4, 1970: Soldiers of Charlie Company place captured Soviet 122MM rockets on Huey's to destroy back in Chu Lai, after using up all explosives in the field. Over 50 rockets were found by Charlie's soldiers just prior to being fired by the enemy into the Chu Lai base *(U.S. Army photo – National Archives)*

Combat Air Assault of soldiers of the 5th/46th Infantry Battalion into the Ky Tra / Dragon Valley area, Fall of 1970 *(U.S. Army Photo – National Archives)*

Soldiers of the 5th/46th Infantry Battalion patrol in Dragon Valley near Ky Tra during the monsoon season of the fall, 1970 *(U.S. Army Photo – National Archives)*

Ky Tra Outpost as seen from the air, both upper and lower portions
(Courtesy David Pace)

Regional Force militia in formation at Ky Tra Outpost *(Courtesy David Pace)*

12 – CLEAR, HOLD AND PACIFY

Pacify – With Body Counts

On September 1, 1969 Bravo Company returned to LZ Gator to take responsibility for its perimeter security. Delta, with a new company commander, Captain Donald F. Duncan, flew from Gator to take over where Bravo had left off in bagging salt, including working with Charlie Company which was recovering more salt as it pacified the area just north of Delta's position.

The next day a Delta patrol spotted a possible booby-trap near a bunker next to a salt pile. Duncan fired into the booby trap at short range and was greeted with a large explosion which wounded four men, including himself. FNG's, both officers and enlisted soldiers, were dangerous in the field, especially the first one to two months. The wounded were dusted off and Delta's Executive Officer, 1LT Robert Wight returned to the field to take command of the company. In was an inglorious start for Captain Duncan, but he would turn out to be a solid leader.

The battalions VIP program was still paying dividends as civilians turned in munitions found throughout the area. These munitions were also brought in to Regional Force (RF) and Popular Force (PF) militias and ARVN soldiers in addition to standard turn-in points such as LZ Dottie. The cash incentive for the impoverished villagers led them to take dangerous chances. Civilians brought in an unexploded 155mm Howitzer round to Alpha Company which was blown just where the Vietnamese left it.

Although the peasants were taking great risks for the money, the battalion's soldiers saw each turn-in as improving their chances for survival. More Chieu Hoi's were also coming in and surrendering. Their casualties from constant air strikes and artillery fire were proving to be too much. A few of the enemy, however, surrendered to use the program for a respite, to get food and have wounds taken care of. Then they escaped back to their strongholds.

The static nature of the pacification mission which the battalion was increasingly shifting its attention to, allowed the enemy to more effectively plant mines since the battalion's soldiers were required to remain in the same areas for longer periods of time. On September 3, Delta's troops stepped on another booby-trapped mortar round which wounded three. Alpha Company also continued to find M-14 mines while working in the Van Tuong – CAP 135 area.

The Americal Division's pacification effort required the RF's and PF's to begin assuming the primary responsibility for protecting the hamlets undergoing pacification. By early 1969 South Vietnam's Civil Operations and Revolutionary Development Support (CORDS) Directorate, supported heavily by the USA, estimated that eighty-four percent of South Vietnam's RF Company's and seventy-nine percent of the PF Platoons possessed firepower equal to or better than the Vietcong units they faced. Most of this firepower came from newly-issued M-16's supplemented by M-79 grenade launchers and M-60 machineguns.

Total RF/PF strength in South Vietnam was raised to four hundred and seventy-five thousand by the end of 1969, twenty percent higher than their strength the end of 1968. It was not unusual for the 5th/46th Battalion soldiers to encounter RF and PF militia with newer M-16's than they had. The challenge for the battalion was to get the militias to effectively use those weapons. It wouldn't be easy.

Adding to the new challenges the RF's and PF's were given, was that they often defended hostile peasants in resettlement camps after the peasants were forced from their ancestral hamlets. The PF's and RF's were despised by their own countrymen as enforcing policies against their cultural values.

On September 3, 1969, Ho Chi Minh, the ninety-seven year-old Communist leader in Hanoi died from a heart attack. The Communists declared a three-day truce to mourn his death. This allowed the battalion's soldiers to mostly enjoy a well-earned rest and they were grateful to "Uncle Ho" for making it happen. No artillery fire missions were to be called except for illumination at night. Security patrols were also limited to no more than two hundred yards beyond night defensive perimeters. But Alpha Company wasn't buying the static defense and patrolled vigorously around Van Tuong (1), capturing six Vietcong that same day.

The Communist truce was short-lived and followed by a nation-wide attack on September 6 to celebrate Ho Chi Minh's life. The Marine base at Danang was hit with fifty-two rockets, causing extensive damage and knocking out seventy-five percent of that city's electrical power. The Danang barrage was followed by sapper attacks which killed three Marines and wounded over forty more.

These phony cease-fires increasingly frustrated the battalion's soldiers and led to their doubts of the competence of the generals who ordered them. The field experienced veterans knew only too well that cease-fires simply gave the enemy a chance to reorganize and reequip its forces and it was the field soldier who always paid the price for that.

The battalions focus on pacification worked reasonably well but only with "clear and hold" operations working with it. But brigade and division staffs would not ignore tactical opportunities to fight the enemy head on to claim higher body counts. This periodically sidelined the pacification mission.

September 7 marked the high tide of the salt recovery operation with a total of two hundred and seventy-two tons evacuated.

Early that morning, Charlie Company combat air-assaulted to the south of Pinkville in the vicinity of the Co Lay hamlets where a large group of VC were believed to be residing. Their mission was to sweep the area while the Marines of CAP's 145 and 146 and their assigned PF Militia served as a blocking force. Charlie served as the "sweepers" to move the enemy and it paid off. Shortly after landing the grunts spotted twelve VC who were out of small arms range and artillery fire was requested. Later they killed one insurgent and captured another attempting to escape. Working one-quarter mile northeast of Co Lay (2), Charlie's mine-sniffing dog discovered five mines, one, a large anti-tank mine and four anti-personnel mines.

While Charlie swept through their area the CAP blocking force detained thirty VC suspects evading by boat, another fifteen evading on land and captured three VC with weapons. The South Vietnamese Navy captured eighteen VC suspects evading the dragnet at the mouth of the Tra Khuc River south of My Khe (2).

Two days later the 198th Brigade commander visited LZ Minuteman, not to check on its progress, but prepare for the Division commanders visit. Feeling there was inadequate security for the 4.2-inch mortars there, he ordered a squad of Echo's recon platoon to return from their screening mission for guard duty. He then turned to shaves and haircuts as another priority. Charlie Company, successfully pursuing the VC, was brought back by Huey to CAP 142. Its 1st Platoon was sent to LZ Minuteman to beef up security for the general's visit.

The next day Charlie had to needlessly walk across the mine-strewn Batangan from CAP 142 to LZ Minuteman to join its 1st Platoon to impress the visiting general how secure Minuteman was, even though an RF Company had taken over that duty and was doing well. Brigade commanders don't like to be second-guessed by generals.

Delta was lifted by Huey to backfill Charlie on the coast. Both companies were now back in the cross-hairs of the mines and booby-traps on the Batangan. The assignment once again reduced the aggressiveness of the soldiers ordered to serve there.

Delta was required to execute a patrol eastward to search for a tunnel complex. After leaving one platoon behind as a reaction force, First Lieutenant Robert Wight set his troops in two parallel columns, walking within close supporting distance. A mine-sniffing scout dog headed one column while a soldier with a portable mine detector led the other. In short order the dog proved its worth and detected a mine. Scout dogs could smell powder or hear the vibrations of trip wires which were present in most mines or booby-traps. Handlers and soldiers accepted the dog's instinct as almost one-hundred percent fool-proof. The problem was scout dogs tired quickly from the heat. Wight wanted a mine detector to provide additional insurance. The patrol returned successfully but the assigned dog, although worn down from the heat, was immediately pulled out for another mission.

On September 11, Delta's 1st Platoon departed CAP 142's coastal complex to set out for a night ambush. Dogs could not accompany the night ambushes and a mine detector could not be tied up for that length of time. The patrol set out solo, walking north on the beach for several hundred yards before turning inland, cutting across the sand dunes to the interior.

As they moved from the beach to a grassy area a soldier detonated a Bouncing Betty mine which wounded seven men. A resupply Huey flying nearby landed to pick up the seriously wounded and a dustoff arrived later to pick up the remainder. Two soldiers close to the mine would not recover. PFC Thomas Glenn Cornwell, age twenty and single from Port Huron, Michigan died on September 13 and PFC Robert Lee Person, also twenty and married from Richmond, Indiana died a day later.

Another Delta patrol was tasked to gain intelligence "about the terrain in the area". A mine-sniffing dog and mine detector were used, and three mines were detected by the canine and blown in place. As the patrol continued its mission the dog tired and missed a mine that was picked up by the detector. That was enough risk. Wight ordered the patrol to return. The danger was simply too great for the small amount of intelligence to be gained.

The Ho Chi Minh remembrance attacks offered more reasons for the division's military planners to set pacification aside and turn again to body counts. The next morning Alpha, Bravo and Charlie moved by combat air assault to follow through on a B-52 "Arc-Light" strike against a suspected NVA complex deep in the mountains, sixteen miles west of the Tra Bong Special Forces Camp. Charlie Company from the 1st/52nd Battalion also joined the operation to secure LZ Boxer, a support base north of the Tra Bong Camp. This new battalion operation, known as "Operation Searchlight" had been in the planning since mid-August.

While on the Batangan Peninsula, Delta Company received late word they would replace Alpha on LZ Gator's bunker line during the searchlight operation and that the birds were already in-bound to pick them up. Caught unaware, they rapidly humped the one-quarter mile in scorching heat to make their pick-up time on the coast. Their designated pick-up site was on the beach on the north side of CAP 142's resettlement camp, the area which the refugees used as their sandy outhouse. This practice allowed the evening tides to flush out their feces to the sea. As the Hueys arrived their rotary blades created a sandstorm on the beach, blowing the shit out of the sand and onto the grunts as they hurried to get on the Hueys. It was a fitting departure from the deadly area.

On September 16 Bravo Company, deep in the mountains, found the first evidence of an NVA presence by locating a series of hooch's with cellars, each about fifteen by twenty feet. NVA green uniforms, rucksacks, grenades and ammunition had been abandoned by the enemy.

The following day Charlie Company, with an attached CIDG platoon from the Tra Bong Special Forces camp, found weapons caches in various bunkers under hooch's. Included were eight 122mm rocket launchers with tripods, sights and field telephones.

Bravo found fifteen more hooch's destroyed by the B-52 strike on the 19th, along with thirty-seven freshly dug graves, about one week old. The terrain was rugged and similar to the terrain the battalion had trekked in the Nui Hoi Mountains in late June. The soldiers were dogged by sporadic small arms fire as they continued their search. Given Bravo's previous experience with locating graves, LTC Wagner pressed them into grave-digging duties again, to verify bodies were in the graves and not buried ammunition.

By September 20 the short mission was over. It ended just in time as the monsoon rains were growing in intensity and the full monsoon was expected in early October. The monsoon's heavy winds and cooler temperatures would make a mountain trek virtually untenable. Pacification had to be attended to as well, as the VC continued efforts to control the coastal plains. Binh Son was hit at 11:20AM by a barrage of forty to fifty rounds of 81mm mortars, followed by sappers using satchel charges. Eighty-seven houses were destroyed, ten civilians killed, and nine wounded.

During the short mountain excursion, Delta remained alert on Gator's bunker line for a possible attack. One attentive grunt with an M-79 grenade launcher killed a VC sapper during a night attack in front of bunker #9, which evidently caused the rest of the sapper team to turn tail. A sweep in the morning revealed an undetonated Bangalore Torpedo under the concertina wire. Also found were Chi-Com grenades and a satchel charge wrapped in burlap which weighed thirty pounds. The grunts cringed at the thought of the devastation it would have caused had it reached them.

Alpha, Bravo and Charlie returned to LZ Gator to receive new assignments. Alpha drew bunker line duty at Gator. Their company commander, Captain Longgrear, was asked to accompany his brother-in-laws body home after he was killed in action elsewhere in South Vietnam. Bravo would move to CAP 135 on the coast near the Van Tuongs, Charlie to LZ Minuteman and Delta back to the Batangan Cape near the An Phuoc hamlets. Echo Recon continued its mission of screening the western edge of the Batangan with patrols and ambushes.

On the morning of September 22, Delta's 2nd Platoon made contact with five VC on the northern edge of An Phouc (2). One VC was wounded and captured with grenades, rucksacks and documents placing him with the Vietcong K-51 LF Company. Newly dug tunnels surrounded the area that had just been searched and cleared by the battalion's soldiers just the previous month.

A few minutes later Delta received small arms fire while searching the hamlet. PFC James I. Yates sustained a chest wound and died. He was twenty years of age and single from Mount Eden, Kentucky.

Charlie's third platoon had also moved into the area to assist Delta. In the same action that killed Yates, Charlie Company's PFC Eric A. Lord was killed instantly from a head wound. Lord was twenty-one years of age and single from Philadelphia, Pennsylvania.

Loudspeaker teams and PF soldiers accompanied the grunts in the pacification effort. Twenty-six villagers were treated for various medical ailments but, after losing two of their own, the grunts felt pacification was coming at a steep price. Intelligence reports identified various Vietcong meetings throughout the Binh Son and Son Tinh Districts to plan harassment of secured hamlets to demonstrate that U.S. and South Vietnamese Government efforts in the area would not be capable of protecting the population. Through force and intimidation the VC hoped to persuade refugees to return to their ancestral hamlets where the Communists promised political and economic support.

Captain John Swek was now the battalion's S-2 (Intelligence) staff officer. Prior to his assignment he served in Binh Son in support of the Phoenix Program, the CIA-conceived program whereby Vietnamese Provincial Recon Units (PRU) set out to neutralize the Vietcong infrastructure (VCI) which was deeply embedded in hamlets and villages. But the nation-wide Phoenix program was turned over to the South Vietnamese government in 1968 and by July 1969, American support of Phoenix shifted from the CIA to the Military Advisory Command (MACV).

Under South Vietnamese government control, the PRU increasingly became "Bag Men" for Provincial and District officials and they conducted fewer VCI neutralization programs. Swek thought the District Chief in Binh Son was more interested in what stereo sound system he could get for himself, and that attitude filtered down to the PRU.

The brunt of this intimidation fell on the Popular Force (PF) and Regional Force (RF) soldiers who carried the burden of protecting hamlets that had not yet been relocated to resettlement areas. At noon on September 23, two RF Company's were hit by mortars and machine gun fire near Dong Le (7), north of CAP 133 which required their extraction by Swift Boats. CAP 133 personnel also came under heavy attack while serving as a blocking force for the RF in this action, and was forced to withdraw to their fortified compound with the loss of one Marine killed and two PF's wounded. Another PF platoon five miles due west of Pinkville had been overrun on the September 14.

Major Robert C.G. Disney, the battalion's new operations officer flew a Visual Reconnaissance (VR) mission along the coast of the Batangan, just south of CAP 142's refugee camp. He spotted five VC next to the water. Flying slow and low the bird opened up with its M-60 machine gun. A squad of soldiers was flown in from LZ Minuteman to search the coastal terrain. The grunts found fishing nets, diving masks, and soap but no additional enemy.

Delta in An Phouc (1) found mortar positions, fighting positions and a number of graves, all recently prepared. It appeared the NVA and VC had been preparing a training camp with bunkers to defend it. Delta moved south to their NDP between Lac Son (2) and An Thinh (4), finding communications wire strung in trees that led to some nearby high ground. These stone-fortified fighting positions and large hooch's that had been used recently as sleeping quarters, guaranteed the grunts a restless night.

On the morning of September 24, Charlie moved from Minuteman to the coastline north of Delta, near An Thinh (4), with its 2nd Platoon farther south in the area of Chau Binh (2). Four hours later a Charlie grunt, SP/4 Thomas Lawler detonated a home-made mine, losing one leg from the explosion and the other leg remained barely attached. He also suffered fragmentation wounds over most of his body. He was dusted off to the 27th Surgical Hospital but the medics, doctors and nurses lost the battle to keep him alive. He died eight hours later. Lawler was age nineteen and single, from Tampa, Florida.

Interrogation teams accompanying both Charlie and Delta found no VC in the hamlets being searched. But there was reluctance on the part of the villagers to be anywhere near the Americans. It was apparent from the recently-constructed defensive positions prepared by the departing VC and NVA that the villagers were caught, once again, in a no-

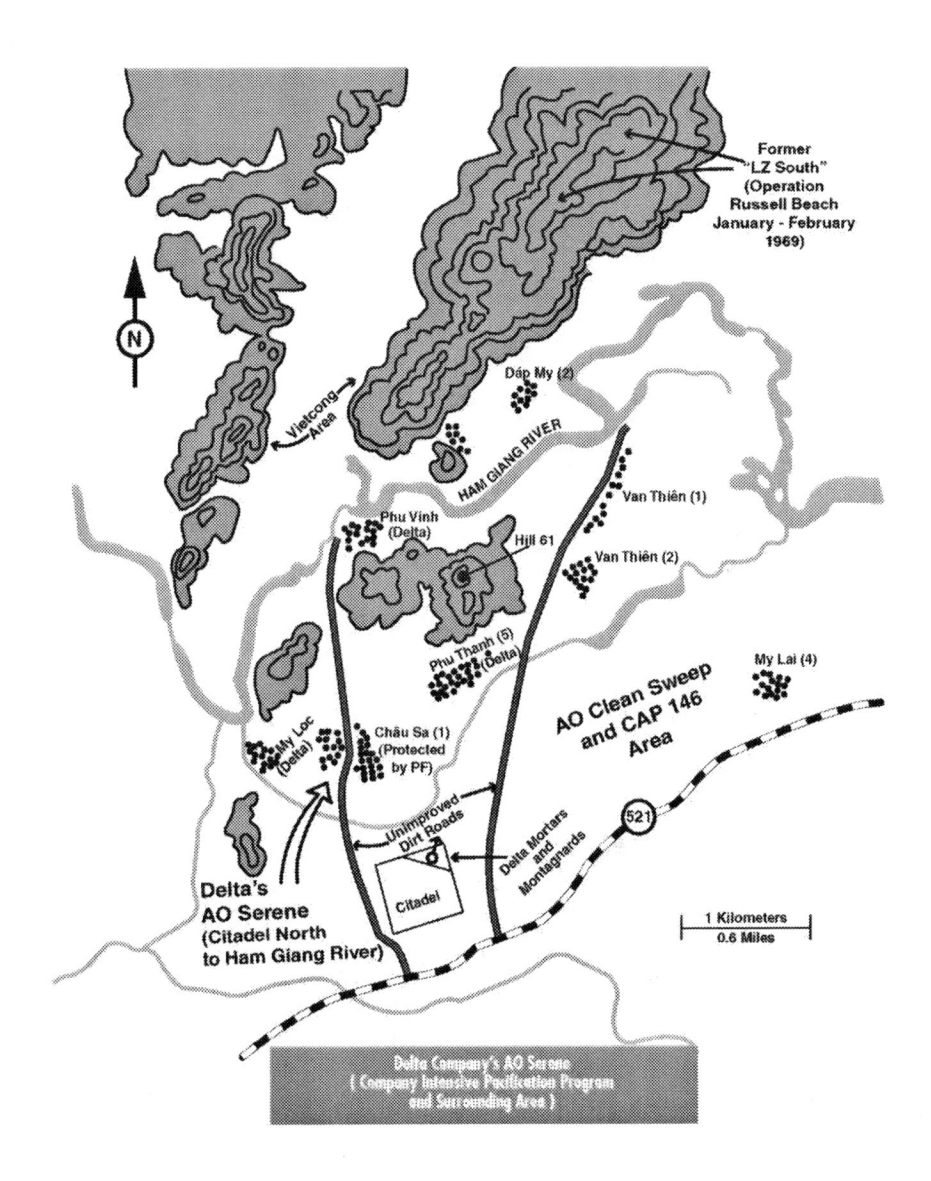

Delta AO Serene

win situation. While the enemy was not able to control territory they did control a significant number of "hearts and minds" through terror.

Many villagers did not embrace the Communists or the government, as neither could provide security or consistent control. The Vietcong Infrastructure, present in many hamlets, contained "Deep" agents unknown to the villagers, who marked peasants for retribution if they cooperated with the "Puppet Forces", the National Police Field Force (NPFF), ARVN, PF's and RF's.

On the 20th Charlie and Delta moved back to the Batangan to more thoroughly search the coastline where Major Disney reported seeing five Vietcong. Charlie Company discovered numerous tunnels on the sides of cliffs leading to the South China Sea, most having two foot by three foot openings that led to eight to twelve foot-length chambers. Medicine and clothes were found and in one tunnel there was an active cooking fire with fish that was half eaten.

The tunnels were demolished. One tunnel blew with a large secondary explosion, indicating a hidden arms cache missed by the grunts. A Navy diving team searched cave entrances below the water and found a pair of dog tags that belonged to a dead Marine along with rice, fish, salt, medical supplies, vitamins, small bandages, a hypodermic needle and a vial of penicillin.

The game of "hide and seek" continued as Charlie and Delta found fifteen more tunnels on September 27, the same day the Communists proclaimed "South Vietnam Resistance Day." To "celebrate" the occasion the enemy attacked CAP's 145 and 146 with heavy fire from all directions. The peasants moved out as the enemy attacked, to escape the artillery and air strikes that were sure to follow. September moved into October and "Accelerated Pacification" continued.

The beginning of October saw the battalion strung out, as usual, on a variety of missions. Alpha Company defended LZ Gator. Bravo's first platoon provided security in CAP 142's area while the balance of the company worked at CAP 135. Charlie rested and refitted at a stand-down in Chu Lai, but one squad was positioned with the local militia in Tri Binh (1) replacing the Delta squad which had successfully worked there for several months.

Echo's Recon Platoon was lifted back to LZ Gator to conduct patrols and ambushes in the surrounding area in conjunction with a PRU team from Binh Son. Echo Company's 4.2-inch mortars remained on LZ Minuteman along with a "light" 81mm mortar section. Another 81mm mortar section was positioned on Gator, while a third section was sent to Chu Lai for some rest.

Consolidate and Secure

At this point the battalion's operations were firmly committed to Phase IV of Operation Nantucket Beach, which required "Consolidation and Security Operations". Delta Company was to be located close to the New Life Hamlets, the settlements under pacification, to upgrade the effectiveness of local security forces.

Delta moved by convoy to the Citadel, an abandoned French fort from its colonial occupation northeast of Quang Ngai City. They then moved to the hamlets further north at Chau Sa (1) and (2). Delta's mission was to assist PF (Popular Force) and RD (Rural Development) cadre in the pacification of that area. Their assignment was part of the Infantry Company Intensive Pacification Program (ICIPP), being initiated throughout South Vietnam to support the gradual withdrawal of US forces. ICIPP required those infantry companies designated for the mission to move from cordon and search missions to protecting pacified hamlets.

Delta settled into the area around the Citadel. Vast quantities of food, ammunition and defensive materials such as concertina wire were moved into the area. Three major hamlets would be protected by Delta and PF/RF units from the Citadel moving north to the Ham Giang River, a distance of one and one-half miles. An RF Company of Montagnard tribesman moved in to provide additional security at the Citadel. They set up a base in the northeast corner of the abandoned fort and brought their families with them, as was their custom. Delta's 81mm mortar platoon was also placed with them to provide area fire support.

Delta's first task was to fortify their assigned hamlets' defenses against attack and organize and train the local forces to defend their homes. Delta was given six months to get it done. One hamlet was one-quarter mile northwest of the Citadel, designated Chau Sa (2) on maps, and re-designated My Loc for pacification purposes. One platoon of Delta was assigned to build its defenses and protect it. Another platoon took up the same task at a hamlet one-half mile due north of the Citadel, designated as Phu Thanh. A third platoon with Delta's headquarters settled in a hamlet just south of the Ham Giang River, near An Thinh (3), the hamlet now designated Phu Vinh.

Delta's officers in Phu Vinh looked around at the "Defense Force" they had to work with. There were young children, a few Chieu Hoi's and old men and women with rusty weapons. One platoon of Montagnard's moved from the Citadel to Hill 61 which overlooked the area. Delta kept one soldier on Hill 61 to coordinate mortar fire from the Citadel if needed.

Language was a major barrier in fulfilling this new mission. To contact their soldier assigned to Hill 61, Delta radioed the Montagnard RTO on the hill and yelled "Waki, Waki" ("American, American") and the RTO handed the radio to Delta's grunt. It was one of the easier language problems to resolve.

It was rare to find Montagnards (French for "Mountain People") operating in the lowlands because of their cultural identity with a "slash and burn" food existence in the hill country. Their presence near Quang Ngai was also rare because the Montagnard people did not co-exist well with the Vietnamese who viewed them in much the same way frontier settlers viewed the American Indians in the 1800's. But the Montagnards or "Yards" were tough and loyal and Delta Company was happy to have them.

Unlike the ARVN who were notorious for stealing from the American's (and to a lesser extent the RF, PF and NPFF), the Montagnards were completely trustworthy. Delta's Executive Officer, 1LT Wight, befriended the Montagnard RF Platoon Commander, an aspiring Lieutenant, who carefully wrote down a request for medicines by describing the ailment's in broken English. One such request read: "Good morning Lieutenant. Sir, please souvenir my company some: cough, abdomen pain, diarrhea, catch cold, headache and typhoid-fever. Thank you very much, Aspirant Nguyen Duong."

Delta provided much of the support for the RF Montagnard Company but gave little support to the Vietnamese units when requested. The ARVN and some PF and RF units sold some of their supplies on the black market. Delta's troops embraced the "Yards" because they were effective and kept them well supplied.

Phu Vinh, the "Headquarters" Hamlet, was situated on low, marshy ground where footpaths were generally muddy throughout the year. The area was made much worse now that the monsoon rains were a daily occurrence. The soldiers clearly felt their presence took away the cultural privacy of hamlet life. But the headquarters group and its rifle platoon could not set up outside the hamlet and properly secure it.

Looking for a hooch to use as their headquarters was done with caution, to insure the chosen structure was not needed by the villagers. They initially chose an abandoned and partially destroyed hooch on the southwest corner of the ville but the marshy muck and high water table made it impossible to dig defensive positions around. The headquarters element moved into a large five-room house which was occupied by a family. They used the one room which was empty. But it was the room reserved for worshiping the family ancestors. It was the only site available and it was occupied with some apprehension.

The Vietnamese landlord did not seem upset at his new occupants but Wight always wondered if cultural sensibilities prevented them from expressing their true feelings. "Rent" was paid each day by offering the family a complete C-Ration meal.

The family unit consisted of a middle-aged Mamasan (Mother), Papasan (Father) a young married daughter with a baby son, a teenage girl and a young boy. The soldiers surmised the married daughter probably had a husband who was VC. This young mother would drown in the Ham Giang River later in the year and the younger teenage girl took up the child-caring chores.

The soldiers were reminded when it was house-cleaning time when the Mamasan periodically poked her head in the door and gave the "evil eye" at the mess of C-ration boxes, bags and equipment that cluttered the floor. Occasionally PF, RF and NPFF cadre passed through the hamlet as well, stringing their hammocks in the hamlets hooch's for the night. Delta's grunts kept close tabs on their equipment until their "Allies" moved on.

Early on October 4, Bravo Company air-assaulted into Dop My (2), one and three-quarters of a mile north of the Citadel on the north side of the Ham Giang River, to search and clear an area in conjunction with two PF platoons and four NPFF policemen. This was to be a four day operation prior to Bravo's scheduled stand-down in Chu Lai. Their commander, Captain Steven Schopp, was nearing the end of his command tour and wanted his platoon leaders and platoon sergeants to take on more decision-making responsibility. Schopp, a two-tour veteran, could not be sure what kind of commander his platoon leaders would receive after he left. Letting go of his "close-hold" style required letting them work out their movements themselves and he would critique them later. This sometimes left the platoons with what they perceived as nebulous instructions.

By noon the NPFF with Bravo detained four Vietcong Suspects (VCS). A medical team was brought in to attend to the sick in the hamlet. Sniper fire accompanied Bravo throughout the afternoon as they searched and cleared the area. Bravo detained a number of VC suspects, all male except one female. The chopper that was supposed to pick them up couldn't make it in so the troops were stuck with their detainees for the night. The males were placid but the female detainee continued to curse and threaten Bravo's troops. Nothing Bravo's soldiers could say would shut her up and the male detainees became concerned her actions would cause them retribution.

Bravo's 2nd Platoon RTO suggested giving her the "PB Treatment." They loaded up two cans of C-Ration peanut butter into one big glob on a plastic spoon, forced her mouth open and put it all in. It immediately stuck to the roof of her mouth, her teeth and tongue. She couldn't spit it out, swallow it or even open her mouth for about twenty minutes. As the platoon leader, 2LT William "Bill" Kaseberg remembered, "Her silence was bliss. Even the other VC suspects nodded their appreciation." After her saliva worked her mouth free of the peanut butter she became pensive, then started to rant again and the soldiers reached for the peanut butter, which immediately silenced her. More small arms fire plagued Bravo Company the following morning as the NPFF picked up more VCS in a thinly populated hamlet nearby.

By late afternoon on the 5th, Bravo settled into its night defensive position (NDP) one-quarter mile south of Dop My (2). They had covered a lot of ground in and around the hamlet and were ahead of schedule in searching their ground objectives. The area wasn't ideal for an NDP. It was indefensible terrain with many hedgerows and marshland, made worst by the continuous rains of the monsoons and the moonless and foggy nights. Schopp mused they had been in far worst NDP's in the mountains. This NDP, however, would prove to be the costliest night for Bravo's commander.

The platoon leaders took charge of defensive preparations. Schopp kept his hands off to give them the responsibility they desired. No listening posts were placed beyond the perimeter because, with no moonlight and heavy rains, movement back to the perimeter would be chancy if the enemy approached and friendly fire deaths would be likely. SOP's for trip flares were followed and they were placed in the marshy terrain. Given the dark and heavy rain, the troops remained close to each other with ponchos covering their prone positions.

And then it began. At 11:30PM, Bravo's perimeter was hit from the east, southeast and southwest with heavy small arms fire and, what appeared to be fifteen to twenty mortar rounds. The "Mortars" turned out to be RPG rounds fired at close range. Even more devastating was the heavy barrage of grenades thrown into the perimeter. The VC were able to close on Bravo's position by taking advantage of the driving rain. Bravo's troops couldn't see in front of their faces and they couldn't hear.

In ten short minutes the attack was over. Four Bravo soldiers were killed and twenty-one wounded. Fourteen were dusted off that night and the remainder treated in the field. Illumination rounds were called throughout the night to aid in defensive fires, one grunt recalling the dark night had become so bright the birds started chirping, believing it was morning.

In anguish over the costliest attack on his company, Captain Schopp stood alone with a strobe light between his legs, directing the dustoff's while under sniper fire. With the morning light twenty-six unexploded hand grenades were found on the defensive perimeter and the soldiers could clearly see the blast areas where twenty-three more had gone off. Only then did they realize they'd been hit by sappers.

LTC Wagner, Major Disney and the battalions Chaplain arrived at first light to review the situation and pick up the dead. Schopp, as the commander, took the blame for his losses but his soldiers stuck with him. After many months in the field under his command, it was only the second or third time they had been hit by fire at night and the first time by a ground attack.

Answering their final roll call that night were: PFC Larry Gene Burkholder, age twenty and single from Portland, Indiana; PFC Shelby Gene Foster, age twenty-one and single, from Ohley, West Virginia; SP/4 Robert Marion Haynes Jr. age twenty-two and single from Amarillo, Texas and PFC Ralph Ernest Piano Jr. age twenty-one and single from Madison, New Jersey.

That same day fifteen new soldiers, "Fucking New Guys" or "FNG's", were processed into the 5th/46th Infantry Battalion and eight were sent to Bravo Company. The list of the wounded from the night attack brought home the devastating effectiveness of sappers:

FW= Fragment Wounds
MFW = Multiple Fragment Wounds

Dusted Off to Chu Lai:
Sgt. William Sprinkle, FW left leg
SP4 David Saal, MFW to back
PFC Stephen Donley, FW right leg
PFC Steven Fenhrenbach, FW to back
SFC Lazu Esquilin, FW both legs
PFC Randal Cagie, MFW legs, arms, right side
PFC John Kirk, FW left arm, left side of face
Sgt. Dale Murdock, FW left buttock
PFC Michael Kashuba, MFW in back
SGT. Acie Hodge, FW to head, left arm
PFC Robert Gregory, FW left arm
PFC James Klebau, FE to head

Treated in the Field:
PFC William Shields, FW to right foot
SP4 Murphy Parkhurst, FW to face
Sgt. Ronald Rodriguez, FW to right leg
SP4 Thomas Welsh, FW to face
PFC Tommie Murphy, FE to back
PFC Bernard Bush, FW to hand
PFC Merrill Doyle, FW to buttock and left flank
PFC Claude Riggs, MFW right shoulder
PFC Thomas DeLorenzo, FW right foot

    The next day Bravo moved southeast to continue its search and clear mission around Van Thien (2), one and one-half miles north of the Citadel. They detained seven VC suspects who were sent to Binh Son. Delta searched the area farther west and south near the hamlets of An Thinh (3) and Chau Sa (1).
    On the morning of October 7, Delta captured four Vietcong females near its own headquarters hamlet of Phu Vinh. The four were the wives of a VC hamlet chief, the VC Chief of the Farmers Association, a VC Chief of Security and a VC Guerilla Chief. The females were whisked off to the Son Tinh Interrogation Center. Two hours later the results of their questioning revealed the 20th VC Company of the 48th LF Battalion

was located two and one-half miles farther northeast near Nghiem Quong (1) with a mission to harass Delta's New Life Hamlets and mortar the PF outposts in the area.

In the late afternoon, Delta was hit with two mortar rounds and small arms fire south of An Thinh (3). Artillery and gunships failed to bag the VC doing the shooting. As Bravo and Delta settled into their positions that night, LTC Wagner's directions were succinct: First, dig deep and second, don't fire into occupied hamlets unless targets are confirmed. There was a clear concern the VC were trying to draw fire into neutralized hamlets to produce civilian casualties, believing the battalion's soldiers would be trigger-happy after the night attack on Bravo.

On October 8, Alpha Company moved from Chu Lai by truck down Highway One to Son Tinh, and then was airlifted to LZ's near An Thinh (1) and Dop My (2). Bravo was moved out in reverse order to Chu Lai for its stand-down. Charlie Company continued to secure LZ Gator as Delta pursued its stability operations with Popular Force (PF) and Rural Development (RD) cadre north of the Citadel. Both Alpha and Delta were now charged with covering a three and one-quarter square mile area in their accelerated pacification efforts.

Marine CAP 145 with its RF Company was attacked at 8:00AM on October 9, on the southern edge of Pinkville. The RF stood their ground and killed eleven VC while suffering four killed and twenty wounded. Delta's 1st Platoon captured three VC with rucksacks and documents near An Thinh (1). After questioning by the NPFF, the prisoners revealed the location of five mortar tubes located north of the abandoned hamlet. Alpha was tasked to check it out. In short order they found one and one-half tons of rice cached for VC use, which was sent to Delta's Phu Vinh hamlet. A PF outpost northwest of Delta encountered four Chieu Hoi's who walked into their position, choosing to surrender rather than confronting the Americans.

The ongoing presence of GI's in this pacification area gave the Vietcong ample opportunity to plant mines to be used against the soldiers who now had fewer choices on their entry and exit routes when leaving their assigned hamlets for security patrols. Dog teams were crucial to even the odds but the team assigned to Delta was of little use. The dog handler arrived in the field with no equipment and was promptly sent back to LZ Gator to get some gear. He refused to return to the field, citing he had only four days left in Vietnam.

The Vietcong were determined to maintain a presence in the area against the overwhelming force of the 5th/46th Infantry Battalion, ARVN, RF, PF and CAP teams. Forward Air Controllers (FAC's) spotted thirty to forty enemy fighting positions, mortar pits and bunkers on October 10 in and around Trung Son (1) two miles northwest of Pinkville. Air Strikes were called to level the area. Reports from government agents revealed the 48th VC Battalion was now in Trung Son (1) with a company of Vietcong near Nghiem Quong (1).

Alpha, working on the southern side of the Ham Giang River, detained four more Vietcong Suspects (VCS) when they moved into its night positions. The next day interrogation reports revealed one was a VC platoon leader from An Thinh (5) and another, a member of the VCI in the same hamlet. These two also confirmed the 48th VC Battalion was in the Truong Son (1) area. The 48th's mission was to conscript healthy laborers in the area to serve as ammo bearers for operations that would take place over the next two months. Due to combat losses the 48th Battalion strength was now forty-five percent NVA regulars. Two other detainees who were not talking were sent in to the Vietnamese National Police.

Intelligence reports also indicated a build-up of Vietcong in the Nam Truong, Tam Phuoc and Binh Yen hamlets three and one-half miles southeast of LZ Gator with a mission to attack LZ Gator, Nuoc Mau and Binh Son in the time frame of October 11-15. At 9:22PM on the 10th, soldiers on LZ Gators perimeter spotted four VC crawling just beyond bunker 16. Small arms fire and the Quad-50 machine gun raked the area. No bodies were found.

Two days later CAP 135 came under heavy attack from automatic weapons fire, RPG's, grenades and satchel charges. One Marine was killed and four wounded. Seven of their PF's were killed and fifteen were wounded. At 3:30AM, a platoon from Charlie Company was moved by Huey from LZ Gator to the CAP compound as a relief force. They found six VC/NVA bodies on the CAP's perimeter with numerous blood trails leading away. With the help of illumination rounds, Charlie's grunts swept the area, finding enemy body parts, arms and legs from the artillery barrage on the attackers. They returned to Gator at 9:30AM for chow and some sleep.

That evening CAP 146 was also hit by fifteen to twenty Vietcong who attacked their command post. Three Marines and two PF's were wounded. As flare ships flew above, the Marines spotted fifteen VC carrying their wounded to the south. The Marines were surprised to see the enemy wearing pith helmets and boots, leaving no doubt the NVA were now buttressing the ranks of the depleted Vietcong.

At 10:00AM on October 13, Bravo, now back from its stand-down, patrolled the area around Phu My (2) where a Vietcong buildup was reported. They found a long tunnel which increased in size as it steadily descended below ground. It was well built, constructed with wood beams which supported the ceiling every sixteen feet. Branches of the tunnel extended in all directions. But this time the monsoon rains were on the side of the Americans and the tunnel system was completely flooded.

Chieu Hoi's continued to turn themselves in because of their uncertain future and, according to one who surrendered, fear of being killed and not properly buried. They too confirmed the growing presence of NVA regulars brought in from the mountains to fill the depleted ranks of VC. Those surrendering worked with the 21st VC sapper unit, which was now sixty-six percent NVA, and Company A sappers of the 48th Battalion. Company A was composed of all NVA.

On October 16, Bravo Company moved by air to CAP 134, while Alpha moved back to the Van Tuong hamlets and CAP 135 (LZ Paradise). The next day Alpha combat air assaulted to the northern tip of the large coastal plain located just six miles southwest of the Chu Lai base. Bravo also air-assaulted to join them after intelligence revealed a concentration of NVA and VC were preparing to launch attacks against the sparsely defended hamlets in the area. Their area of operation was designated, "AO Diamond Head."

Delta continued its pacification effort in the three assigned hamlets near the Citadel, their pacification area now designated as "AO Serene" but the hazards of deadly force were always present. Sgt Jason Woody placed three of his squad, all new men, on his night perimeter with instructions to fire their claymore mines if the trip flare attached to it ignited. At 2:00AM, a flare ignited but the claymore stayed silent. Woody walked over to check the position. When he arrived the trip flare finally ignited the Claymore and Woody caught the back-blast of the Claymore, losing three teeth and suffering shrapnel wounds to his legs. He was dusted off, two weeks before his DEROS date (end of tour in Vietnam).

Delta's 2nd Platoon spotted ten VC near An Thinh (3). A firefight ensued but the VC melted away. Night-time activity increased as the enemy took advantage of minimum moonlight in the middle of October, no more than thirty-five percent. This occurred each month.

With growing confidence in Delta's pacification efforts, more VC were seeking to Chieu Hoi. Twenty-four VC, sixteen males and eight females, in the hamlet of An Thinh on the north side of the Ham Giang River, wanted to cross to Delta's location at Phu Vinh, but were afraid to make the journey for fear of VC retaliation. A Rural Development (RD) Propaganda Team and some National Police Field Force (NPFF) cadre took on the task and requested soldiers from Delta to come along for security.

At 2:15PM on October 19, the group crossed over on two boats, the villagers clearly visible on the opposite bank. Vietcong hid in the bamboo thicket and opened fire; killing two RD's who fell into the swollen river, and wounding two more who also dropped into the water. SP/4 Frank Davis Jr. jumped into the river to rescue one of the RD's while under fire from the VC, but other Delta soldiers reached the drowning man first. Davis turned his attention to the second RD who was flailing away, trying to keep afloat in the fast moving river. Before Davis could reach him, the RD disappeared under the water, and then Davis, struggling against the currents, also disappeared.

Delta brought in more soldiers and crossed the river on two flimsy bridges, one a wooden dam-like structure and the other, a single strand bamboo bridge designed for the lighter Vietnamese. When they reached the other side the Vietcong fled. Navy frogmen were brought in to search for the drowned men and recovered both, as well as the two men killed outright by the Vietcong. SP/4 Davis was nineteen years of age and single from Logansport, Louisiana. He was posthumously awarded a Silver Star and the ARVN awarded him the Vietnamese Cross of Gallantry for his actions.

Davis was well-liked by his comrades. He and Mike Stachowiak often talked about the first thing they would do when they got home. Davis told him, "I'm gonna sneak into my mother's kitchen and say 'Mama, I'm hungry'. The only one you can always count on is your mother" Stachowiak would always ponder if his mother knew just how much his friend loved her.

One of the male villager's who had waited to cross the river, had been shot through the head in the initial burst of fire from the VC. Delta's grunts watched a fellow villager stroll over to the body and collect the loose brains scattered on the river bank, and place them in the conical hat the man had worn. The peasant carried the man's body away to be buried. The nonchalant way in which it was handled left Delta's grunts wondering if the deprivation, death and destruction accompanying hamlet life in the war had hardened most peasants beyond the point of grieving.

Delta did their best in the melee. 2Lt Donald Reigles, PFC Steven Ahern and PFC Richard Camacho were awarded Army Commendation medals for valor for assisting the NPFF while under fire.

Progress in building protective shields around Delta's New Life Hamlets was slow. Construction of defensive positions and the concertina wire in front of them required local help to erect the tons of single strand barbed wire, concertina wire, engineering stakes, culverts of all sizes, sandbags, and timber that was supplied. It would take three months before it was all completed. Delta's grunts worked in the wet paddies each day, feet never dry, then staked out perimeters or ambushes each night. The much needed labor from the Vietnamese was spotty and always inadequate. The Rural Development cadre solicited support from the hamlet chiefs. Sometimes the entire hamlet population would show up to work. At other times there were very few. Communications and cultural barriers left Delta's officers at a severe disadvantage.

The VC continued to apply pressure to reverse the growing effects of the serious pacification effort to keep the populace under government control. An increasing number of villagers were seeking haven in the New Life Hamlets as well as low-level VC. CAP 138, which guarded the western corridor into Binh Son, came under heavy attack in an effort to open up the district city to a main force NVA assault. Alpha kept its 2nd Platoon in the CAP 135 area and sent the others to CAP 138 to lend support to the Marines.

Intelligence reports indicated that part of the 48th VC Battalion was in Con Chieu (1) on the north side of the Cho Moi River opposite the Son Hai Refugee camp on the An Ky Peninsula. The Vietcong P31 Local Force Company was located further north in Chau Binh (1).

Early on the morning of the 19th at 1:20AM, thirty VC crossed the river in boats and entered the Son Hai camp. The PF's guarding it fled. After securing a large amount of rice the VC returned to the north side of the river. Bravo combat air assaulted at first light to look for them. ARVN and PF units also screened the area northwest of the Batangan in an effort to trap small groups of evading VC/NVA.

Clear, Hold and Pacify

Three days later during an ARVN sweep, one soldier from the 3rd/6th ARVN Battalion stepped on a booby-trapped 155mm Howitzer Round in Liem Quang (1) which killed three ARVN and wounded sixteen others.

A Troop of the 1st/1st Cavalry (Armored Personnel Carriers) screened to the east of the Citadel for a "Reconnaissance in Force" mission to discourage any attack on Delta's refugee camps. Although they were restricted in their movements in the field, they carried substantial "pushing power" with their numerous 50 caliber machineguns. On the 22nd, the cavalry soldiers observed three VC running into an abandoned hooch in Nghiem Quong (1). The 50 calibers which had a longer reach and larger shell than M-60's, opened up and reduced the hooch to rubble. As the Cav moved on they saw what appeared to be peasants rush to the hooch and drag three bodies away. Later they barely discerned forty NVA in uniform on the north side of the hamlet, out of range for effective fire. Artillery was called and two NVA bodies were found near several blood trails.

As October moved into its final week, moonlight illumination was back at ninety-eight percent, which gave the friendly forces a nighttime advantage against the enemy.

October 22 saw Charlie Company leave perimeter duty on LZ Gator and exchange positions with Bravo. Alpha returned to the Diamond Head AO to continue searching for enemy in the area. On October 24 villagers from the Van Tuong hamlets moved north to Alpha's location, claiming they were forced from their hamlets by members of the 31st VC Company and 95th Sapper Company.

Charlie Company moved to the vicinity of old LZ South to search and clear hamlets and move some remaining peasants to Delta's protected hamlets. Charlie moved north of the Ham Giang River opposite Delta's Phu Vinh hamlet and found eight tons of rice cached in large baskets and in sixty-five gallon drums. They also found some hooch's set up as factories to make booby-traps and some tunnels which were recently used but were now flooded. Military-aged males were rounded up and sent to Delta's locations for processing.

Delta continued to strengthen defenses in its refugee camps and worked with the NPFF to detain Vietcong suspects. Echo's Recon Platoon moved from LZ Gator to assist Alpha work in the Diamond Head area. The growing allied presence inspired the VC to plant more mines. One villager stepped on a mine rigged to a 155mm Howitzer round, killing three civilians and one Marine. Two Echo soldiers and one PF were wounded.

BATTLES FOR HEARTS AND MINDS

Accelerated Pacification continued to yield results as the months of October 1969 crossed into November. More low-level Vietcong sought to Chieu Hoi rather than remain on the run from the battalion's soldiers, Marines, ARVN's, RF's and PF's and the constant surveillance by helicopters and forward air controllers (FAC's). But the ability of the battalion's soldiers to maintain their pacification roles became more problematic.

The Americal's Assistant Division Commander for Operations, Brigadier General Howard Cooksey informed his battalions that main force NVA and VC units were avoiding major contact to prepare for a forthcoming offensive. To thwart those preparations, Cooksey directed that daily intelligence reports obtained from Chieu Hoi's, visual reconnaissance flights, and interrogations must "Be followed up by ground exploitation". Engagement of suspected enemy positions by artillery and air strikes alone "Will not yield desired results" (body counts).

To respond more rapidly to intelligence reports, division policy required one platoon in each Americal Division battalion tasked to serve as a rapid reaction force, deployable in thirty minutes. Further, a full company would be ready to deploy within one hour of notification.

Each day numerous intelligence reports flowed in to the 5th/46th Battalion, marked as "Usually reliable information" (URI). The challenge for the 5th/46th was to balance the requirement to "Chase URI's" while also supporting the increased pacification efforts that would ultimately determine the stability of the area before the battalion departed. Several "URI's" pointed to a major attack on LZ Gator between October 31 and November 10.

Much of the enemy's pressure can be explained in a captured enemy document dated October 27, 1969. The enemy's major political and military tasks to be accomplished in November were in response to (according to the document) *"The deceitful speech which should be delivered by President Nixon on 3 November 69, and in support of the upcoming struggle of the American people to support our cause for peace in Vietnam and the withdrawal of US troops from Vietnam, we (VC) are to launch intensive attacks in all respects on the enemy (South Vietnamese and US Forces) on 14 and 15 November. In the military field we (VC) are to carry out annihilation attacks on the South Vietnamese self-defense, Popular and Regional Forces to accelerate the annihilation of tyrants."*

Limited attacks from the enemy increased in early November in the CAP areas protected by the Marines and in the refugee settlements guarded by PF militia. Those attacks were designed to create instability. Small arms fire, mortars and RPG's were most often used to test defenses and foster a sense of insecurity in the minds of Vietnamese civilians in the protected areas. The battalion kept up the pressure with daytime patrols and nighttime ambushes. Aerial visual reconnaissance and timely fire support were used against enemy sightings.

At noon on November 1, the 4.2-inch heavy mortars on LZ Minuteman fired in support of CAP 145 after which the PF Platoon with Marines swept the area and found three dead VC. At 12:40PM helicopters flying over the old FSB South spotted two VC evading and cut them down. And so it went, the Americans and South Vietnamese locating and killing insurgents in small numbers while pacification continued.

Alpha Company in the Diamond Head AO north of LZ Paradise and CAP 133, found more bunkers, small caches of food and abandoned equipment as the VC tried to keep one step ahead of Alpha's soldiers.

Delta was becoming more familiar with the terrain surrounding the three refugee settlements they were assigned to protect. One night the 2nd Squad of the 2nd Platoon moved out to their night ambush at 11:10PM and spotted two VC. Rather than open fire, they followed the insurgents to a river bank where the insurgents were joined by three more VC. Using a Starlight Scope which provided night vision, the squad watched the five VC walk to a wood line where ten more VC joined them. With just one hundred and fifty yards separating them, the grunts opened fire with their M-16's and then pulled back to call in artillery fire. It was useless to search the area at night and draw needless casualties as the grunts knew the bodies would be gone by morning. But satisfaction came from showing the enemy the night hours were no longer their exclusive domain.

Charlie Company assisted Delta with the construction of defenses for the refugee camps but on the morning of November 3 Charlie air-assaulted to Van Thien (1), where, according to a "URI", a group of VC were hiding. The hamlet had been cleared of villagers. Sergeant David Napier led his squad as it searched a large hut and stepped on a pressure plate connected to a mine. He realized instantly his foot had touched the plate and froze in place, not picking his foot back up which would cause a detonation.

Napier ordered his men away from the hooch then attempted to place some other weight on the plate to hold it down. His effort failed and a 105mm Howitzer round detonated, killing the squad leader and wounding another soldier. Napier's heroism in dealing with the mine himself, in his private moment of hell, saved the lives of his squad. He was posthumously awarded a Silver Star. Sergeant David Napier was age twenty and single from Glen Allen, Virginia.

Charlie was tasked to buttress security for various CAP teams through patrols and ambushes. Its 1st Platoon, with thirty-one soldiers, worked with CAP 142; the 2nd Platoon with twenty-eight soldiers went to CAP 146 south of My Lai (4) and Route 521, in the shadow of Hill 85. The 3rd Platoon with a strength of thirty-two worked with CAP 144.

Delta continued rounding up VC suspects from within its pacified area in "AO Serene" with help from the NPFF. It was a never-ending task. Chieu Hoi's drifted in while Delta's patrols killed one VC and wounded another in Van Thien (2). Both VC were confirmed to be on a NPFF "Black List" of Vietcong infrastructure. With some luck Delta also discovered a trip wire in front of a hooch that was rigged to a 105mm Howitzer round. It was blown in place. Maximum emphasis was now being placed on night operations.

Alpha continued to find more caches of salt and rice. One thousand pounds of rice were hidden in ten graves. It was promptly redistributed to the villagers in the protected hamlets. Three days later Alpha grunts captured two Vietcong, a male and a female who were carrying a pouch of documents. Some of the documents were valor awards to Vietcong for killing the enemy.

At 10:30AM on November 4, Bravo Troop of the 1st/1st Cav watched a FAC's aircraft, which was supporting them, go into a dive to mark an enemy position with a phosphorous round. The aircraft never came out of the dive and crashed, killing two. No enemy fire was observed. Charlie Company was lifted to the scene and destroyed fourteen high explosive rockets and four white phosphorous rounds from the wreckage used for marking targets, before the VC could get to them for booby-traps.

Another tragedy struck at 9:30PM on the evening of November 8, when an 81mm fire mission went badly from the mortars on LZ Minuteman. The mission was to hit a group of enemy on the Batangan coast, one-quarter mile south of CAP 142. The deflection and elevation used on the mortar tubes were miscalculated and five rounds fell inside the camp, killing twenty refugees and wounding another twenty-nine who required evacuation. Another seven wounded were treated in the camp.

Major Roman, the battalions Executive Officer commandeered a Huey and set out at 1:20AM to Minuteman, taking with him the artillery liaison officer, battalion surgeon, headquarters First Sergeant, a medic and a RTO. The bird they secured was piloted by two new aviators who were new in-country and had not flown night missions. After a brief time on Minuteman they took off to fly to the refugee camp. The controls on the Huey went stiff and the bird rolled on its side and crashed. The medic and artillery officer suffered multiple lacerations and were dusted off to the 91st Evacuation Hospital in Chu Lai.

The chief of the refugee camp now had a dilemma on his hands. He had to keep his peasants' confidence in their American protectors or he would loose their morale to the enemy. He therefore told his refugees the mortar fire came from the Vietcong.

1LT John Shelk, the battalions S-5 in charge of civil affairs at the time, took the parents of one of the dead, a young girl, to the hospital in Chu Lai. The parents, thinking she was recovering, found their daughter dead from a small piece of shrapnel in the head. Shelk recalled that "The wailing over the loss of the young life filled the hospital ward". Shelk returned to the camp to pay Solatium (compensation) funds to those who lost family members. It was no easy task in trying to sort out who was related to whom. The payments were miniscule, but for the Vietnamese peasants they represented a sizable amount. Shelk arranged for twenty sheets of plywood to be airlifted to CAP 142 for the construction of coffins and another seventy sheets to rebuild refugee structures.

Shortly after, Shelk returned a second time to make more payments and spent some time with the Marine CAP's responsible for the camp. While surveying the landscape, Shelk saw something shiny on a small conical hill in the middle of a rice paddy. Then he saw several NVA walking up a path. He turned to call in an air strike but was rebuffed by the Marines. They retorted "If we call in fire we'll get retribution later.

It's live and let live with these guys." Several nights later the CAP's were hit anyway. Shelk pondered the senselessness of it all and wondered if the Marines on CAP's were losing their sense of mission. Shortly there after on November 16, his tour as S-5 ended and Captain Steven Schopp, Bravo's Commander took over the S-5 duties.

On November 10, Bravo Company left LZ Gator to exchange missions with Charlie Company. Bravo's 1st Platoon went to CAP 142, 2nd Platoon to CAP 146 and the 3rd to CAP 144. Its headquarters element settled in at the Son Hai refugee camp on the An Ky Peninsula (CAP 144). While the battalion's soldiers focused on pacification the ARVN continued their sweep and clear operations. As they swept the area near Liem Quang (1) an ARVN soldier stepped on a pressure plate rigged to a 155mm Howitzer round which killed eight ARVN soldiers and wounded three more.

During these pacification efforts senior officers from the I Corps Command in Danang, the Military Advisory Group Vietnam (MACV) from Saigon and the Pacific Command (PACOM) in Hawaii began short visits to Delta's AO Serene to witness the progress of a "textbook" intensified pacification effort.

The battalion's soldiers drew assignments to protect the visiting brass, which interrupted their own operations. While enemy action was largely limited to shoot and run harassment by the VC, intelligence reports continued to point to another enemy offensive designed to stem the tide of the accelerated pacification which was beginning to make its mark. Each day more Chieu Hoi's walked into protected hamlets. Some were deep-cover VC agents, trying to establish themselves in the refugee camps for future operations. But most were low-level VC support personnel whose lives on the run from American firepower had reached its breaking point.

Bravo's 2nd Platoon quickly set out to build their defensive positions on the north side of CAP 146, which sat in the shadow of Hill 85, on the south side of Provincial Route 521. Directly across the north side of the road was My Lai (4). CAP 146 and the refugee settlement camp it protected consisted of about one hundred sheet metal-roofed shanties crammed in narrow rows perpendicular to, and abutted against the northern face of Hill 85. It was on the top of Hill 85 that enemy mortars reigned down on Bravo Company during the Pinkville battle on July 7, 1968. Now the area was under the firm control of the Americans and South Vietnamese.

The CAP team of about seven Marines and an interpreter were entrenched in a small bunkered compound halfway up the northeast face of Hill 85. The camp was protected on the remaining three sides by a stockade fence of narrow logs and sticks. The entire camp covered about five acres. There was one large opening in the fence near the northeast corner, close to the east-west dirt road, Route 521. In addition to the seven CAP Marines, Bravo's 2nd Platoon only numbered about twenty-two soldiers. One of their squads still protected Tri Binh (1) north of LZ Gator, and other soldiers were recovering from wounds or taking their R&R outside Vietnam.

At 2:30AM on November 14, CAP 146 came under heavy small arms fire from the northeast and then a ground attack through the main gate by about thirty attackers. Bravo's soldiers were ready and took the brunt of the attack. About twenty Chicom grenades and eight satchel charges were thrown at the undermanned platoon. Bravo's soldiers repelled the attackers with small arms fire from its rain-swollen night defensive positions.

Lt. Kaseberg called for mortar fire from the Montagnard position two miles east at the Citadel. At first the fire mission was not granted political clearance by the Vietnamese province chief. Kaseberg, incensed, turned his radio frequency to operations at the division headquarters, not a wise move for young lieutenants, and the division got the permission for fire support. Heavy mortar fire reigned down on the anticipated areas of enemy withdrawal. By 3:00AM the attack was over and helicopter gunships arrived on station to work over the area of the retreating enemy. Intelligence reports later indicated the enemy took heavy loses, not only of the attackers on CAP 146 but other enemy formations on the move in the surrounding area.

At this time, there were other developments relating to the My Lai hamlets, and particularly My Lai (4), now unoccupied. On the morning of November 16 two Hueys carrying "VIP's" and escorted by the Division's Provost Marshall, the chief military justice officer of the Americal Division, landed on Route 521 near My Lai (4). Two hours later a helicopter carrying reporters descended on the same location.

Bravo's 2nd Platoon nearby at CAP 146 was detailed to secure an LZ then provide security for these VIP's and the media. The official reason given was that "This VIP visit is an investigation of certain incidents taking place in the area; this visit doesn't concern any activities related to the 5th/46th. The battalion's only function is LZ security."

A report had surfaced in the US press that a massacre had taken place in the My Lai area, specifically My Lai (4). The "Incident" occurred on March 16, 1968, the same day LTC David Lyon, the first commander of the 5th/46th, arrived at the division's headquarters in Chu Lai with an advance party of ten soldiers. The battalion did not become operational on LZ Gator until the end of March. In the period between that eventful date and the accelerated pacification program, the 5th/46th had suffered one hundred and sixteen deaths and hundreds of wounded casualties, including many multiple amputations. The mines, booby-traps and heavy fighting in the My Lai's, Pinkville and the adjoining Batangan Peninsula were responsible for many of the casualties. Some soldiers in the security detail wondered, "Exactly what did happen on March 16, 1968?"

Alpha continued to assert its presence in the Diamond Head AO working with CAP's 133 and 134. On November 16 an Alpha patrol was ambushed and one PF was wounded. Gunship support came on station and six VC were killed. Villagers later saw additional bodies being carried away from the area.

The next day a Chieu Hoi (VC medic) surrendered. He had been caught in an Alpha ambush the previous week but escaped. He told Alpha's soldiers that another wounded Vietcong who escaped was a VC doctor and said there was a VC hospital near Phu Nhieu (1), farther south along the coast. More Chieu Hoi's appeared near Dong Le (4). One was a doctor's aide and another, the "Chief of Supply Lines" for the area. Four more VC were caught trying to cut through the wire surrounding the perimeter of CAP 133. Alpha Company was having a profound effect on the enemy. Since October 23 they collected fourteen Chieu Hoi's, detained seventeen Vietcong suspects in addition to numerous VC killed and weapons captured.

Adding to the worries of the VC and NVA on the large coastal plain were the "Blues", an aerial scout platoon which supported the Cobra gunships and light observation helicopters (LOH's) working the area. Usually operating in squad size, the Blues frequently landed after air strikes to search for survivors or fleeing enemy to question. The Blues performed "Snatch missions", landing hurriedly to grab isolated enemy soldiers.

The Marine CAP locations continued receiving more Chieu Hoi's and attempted to screen them to prevent infiltration by VC agents. Chieu Hoi's throughout the area painted a picture of dire conditions for the 48th Vietcong Local Force Battalion. One Chieu Hoi, a fourteen year old boy, appeared at CAP 143, carrying a .30 caliber machinegun. He had been a squad leader with the 48th Battalion for two years and said that the VC battalion was now composed of eighty percent NVA. He also confirmed other VC were posing as villagers in order to provide information about 5th/46th Battalion's movements.

In the midst of these continuing operations it was time, once gain, to change battalion commanders for the sake of career advancement of senior officers. LTC Julian Wagner's six month tenure as commander had ended and, on November 17, 1969, the new commander, Lieutenant Colonel Melvin C. Snyder took over the reigns of leadership. Snyder was a graduate of the US Military Academy. His career was marked by extensive staff assignments in research and development duties including three years with the Defense Atomic Support Agency, three years in France and two years with the Army's Office of the Chief of Research and Development. His assignment to command a battalion at war was needed if he had a chance to be promoted to the rank of Colonel.

Snyder realized his absence from troop command and tactical training was a deficit that had to be upgraded. He relied heavily on his Company Commanders, most particularly Captain Longgrear commanding Alpha and a few staff officers whose decision-making he trusted.

In Captain Swek's (Battalion S-2 Officer) opinion, both LTC Wagner and LTC Snyder were effective in their own way. Although Wagner was constantly in his command and control Huey, "He was involved, although scattered at times." LTC Snyder on the other hand was "very intelligent but reserved, asking very direct questions and very focused. He knew how to cut through the bullshit."

Other staff officers and some company commanders had seen Wagner as a "cowboy who could not connect with people". One officer remembered, "When having a beer with his staff in the evening on LZ Gator, we found it hard to hold a conversation with him".

On the other hand some officers in the battalion saw LTC Snyder as "someone who was completely out of his league." Often the view of the company commander depended if his personality matched that of his battalion commander. One company commander felt LTC Snyder "didn't know a gun from a molecule."

As the Intelligence Officer, Captain Swek's task was the same under both commanders, deciding how to sort out the reams of intelligence reports that flowed in each day from the brigade and division headquarters, and sort out what was pertinent for the S-3 Operations Officer and the battalion commander.

The Montagnard RF Company at the Citadel sprung an ambush on a VC platoon early the morning of November 18 just one-quarter mile east of the Citadel killing two and capturing one. Captain Duncan, Delta's Company Commander flew a visual reconnaissance north of the Ham Giang River and found new hooch's being built in a VC-controlled area that had been previously burned by his troops. He requested an air strike on the new construction. Delta's 2nd Platoon followed up after the strike with a patrol, finding a five hundred pound bomb from the air strike which had failed to detonate and various blood trails in the area. The bomb was destroyed.

On November 21, Alpha Company shifted its operation eastward to cover a larger area, now dubbed "AO Eagle", which included the areas of CAP 134 and 132. Bravo Company air assaulted to the southeast coast of the Batangan Peninsula to follow-up on a "URI" report about VC activity. They found some arms, ammunition, rice, corn, booby-traps, fishing nets and eight tunnels dug into the rocky coastline, but no VC. The corn offered an opportunity for Lieutenants Bill Kaseberg and Larry Betts to roast some ears of corn during the day; a small pleasure to remind them of home, but it would be Bett's last pleasure.

At 5:00PM Bravo's Vietnamese scout, "Tommy" tripped a wire attached to a Chicom grenade. Bett's was standing next to him with his flak jacket open and one small piece of grenade shrapnel made a tiny puncture wound at the base of his sternum. It was a small wound and drew little blood but hit a vital area. Tommy was hit in the head and two other soldiers suffered minor wounds.

Bravo's medic froze at the prospect of more booby-traps and the seriousness of Betts wound. LT Kaseberg worked on Betts chest wound, trying hard to keep his comrade from going into shock. Betts said he was sleepy and Kaseberg screamed and slapped him to keep him focused. Betts stopped breathing and Kaseberg gave him mouth-to-mouth resuscitation. Betts threw up in Kaseberg mouth but he started breathing again. Kaseberg cleaned him up but, as he remembers, "When the dustoff arrived Bett's was as pale as paper and cool and couldn't keep his eyes open. I hoped they'd have someone on the chopper that would bring him out of it, but I guess they didn't". He died during the flight to the hospital. Larry Leroy Betts was twenty-three years of age and married, from Eagle River, Alaska.

Bravo's extended mission in the area was to sweep the Batangan coastline with night patrols and ambushes to interdict VC movement. The lush coastline and magnificent scenery overlooking the South China Sea lent itself to Bravo's new AO designation, "AO Millionaire".

The armored personnel carriers ("Tracks") of H Troop of the 17th Cavalry moved into the area of the Nam Yen Hamlets with an RF platoon, in response to reports of increased enemy activity. On November 25 they found newly constructed hooch's and bunkers that were not present when the battalion swept the area in August. The enemy moved another five hundred pound bomb that had not detonated into the area to be used as a mine. One dwelling appeared to be a mine assembly station.

The enemy was trying to establish a hamlet with occupants who could provide the food and logistics support needed to sustain them. The soldiers destroyed the hooch's, the bunkers and the bomb, and detained seventy-eight peasants, thirty-three of whom the RF platoon suspected as being VC. All were sent to Binh Son.

Questioning of these detainees revealed that elements of an NVA battalion and a sapper unit had passed through the area five days prior and were moving south. It was apparent from their interrogation in Binh Son that many of the detainees, mostly women, were wives of VC in the area. One was the wife of a top VC leader. Another air strike was placed on An Thoi (1) one-half mile north of the Nam Yen's, in an area previously cleared of villagers and designated a free fire zone. But after the strike twenty-five women, children and old men were found and sent to Binh Son. Their newly constructed hooch's and livestock were destroyed.

Echo's Recon Platoon joined the Cav troops on November 27 to lend support to their sweep operations in an area now designated, "AO Patton." It was Thanksgiving and the armored personnel carriers went into a "wagon wheel perimeter" as a Huey arrived to provide a hot turkey dinner.

Refreshed, the Cav troops pulled out to recon an area between Nam Yen (6) and (5). At 6:30PM they spotted two VC and opened fire with their 50 caliber machineguns, followed by some artillery. The Cav then established a night position and circled their tracks with the recon soldiers filling in the gaps between the tracks and individual fighting positions.

One of the recon soldiers was PFC Craig Frye, only two weeks in the battalion and his first time in the field. As they set up for the night they were hit with automatic weapons fire from several directions. Frye watched a fellow soldier who was beyond the perimeter laying out his claymore mine, low crawl back to the tracks at a record breaking speed. Frye had an M-79 grenade launcher and poured out fire, depleting his ammo quickly. He returned to a track to get more ammo when an enemy recoilless rocket round sailed across the perimeter's opposite side, hitting his track. Three cavalry troopers, one PF soldier and Frye were wounded. Frye suffered multiple shrapnel wounds from his ankles up to his face. The track was rendered inoperable. The wounded were dusted off and Frye was evacuated home, his Vietnam tour of two weeks ended.

On the 26th Delta's 1st Squad of its 2nd Platoon patrolled the area near Chau Sa (4). PFC David Ritz, an FNG was on point. Having little field experience he kicked a small stick protruding from the ground which detonated a 105mm Howitzer round. The explosion sheared off both his legs and wounded the man behind him, SP/4 Jimmie Shepler, with multiple fragment wounds to both his legs. Both were dusted off to Chu Lai but Ritz died on the Huey. PFC David G. Ritz was nineteen years of age and single, from Croghan, New York.

The battalions shift to "Vietnamization", placing more responsibility on the ARVN, was not without its challenges. Vietcong attacked the hamlet of Phu Qui on the Batangan coast, an area controlled by the ARVN's, on the evening of November 29. The PF's defending the ville called for fire support from LZ Minuteman's mortars. It took four hours to receive political clearance through the provincial chain of command just to fire some illumination rounds.

H Troop, 17th Cav, with Echo's recon platoon moved into the Tam Hoi area on November 30 and encountered the same dilemma with detainees they found in the Nam Yen's and Van Tuong's. In an area supposedly cleared of all civilians, eighty-nine women and children were found and evacuated to Binh Son.

In early December H Troop, 17th Cav left the operational control of the battalion and was replaced by C Troop, 1st/1st Cav. Alpha and Charlie were given opportunities for brief stand-downs in Chu Lai in late November. Alpha returned to its AO Eagle operations while Bravo took up the defense of LZ Gator, and Charlie moved in to replace Delta in its refugee protection mission to allow Delta a short rest in Chu Lai.

Alpha's first platoon returned to its hunting grounds near Van Tuong (1) and, true to form, found a previously destroyed hamlet being rebuilt. Twelve detainees were rounded up, three of whom were VC suspects. CAP Marines and their PF's continued to interdict and eliminate small groups of VC.

A typical action occurred at CAP 146 on December 5, when five VC were spotted one-quarter mile north of My Lai (4). CAP 146 was responsible for the area north and south of Route 521 around the My Lai's. The five enemy they spotted were too far away to engage with small arms so they called in an artillery fire mission. The area was then swept and a separated hand, foot and other body parts were found along a blood trail. Thirty minutes later the same patrol was hit by small arms fire one-quarter mile farther east. Again artillery was called and a sweep revealed two more blood trails.

One of the ironies of the dire situation of the insurgents was the lack of medical care for their wounded. This forced more than a few insurgents to walk into battalion or CAP positions, claiming they were civilians who were wounded by mines or dud ammunition while working in the fields. In a few cases they came in as Chieu Hoi's. It was their only hope for medical care or they would face eventual death. In many cases they carried no identification and were questioned while being treated.

Charlie Company had such a case the same day CAP 146 engaged the Vietcong one and one-half miles further east. A "farmer", thirty-five years of age, said he was hit in the legs and back from shrapnel from a dud M-79 round which detonated while he was working in the field. Charlie's VC-turned-pro-government Kit Carson scout recognized him as a Vietcong.

The contentious enemy continued to pressure the refugee hamlets, hitting the Son Hai camp (CAP 144) at 3:00AM December 6, with sixty rounds of 82mm mortar fire, killing two PF's and wounding four. Charlie's night positions also received fire. Intelligence reports pointed to a new buildup of enemy personnel for purposes of attacking the resettlement areas. Weapons and ammunition were being moved by bicycles from the mountains to the coastal areas. During the day Charlie's 1st Platoon interpreter, a boy of fourteen, stepped on a booby-trapped 60mm mortar round and lost a leg. This was in Van Thien (1), the same hamlet SGT Napier lost his life on November 3.

Delta moved back to AO Serene which freed up Charlie Company to sweep the area east of Delta, "AO Clean Sweep", to keep the enemy from launching attacks on the New Life Hamlets. Its mission would be a costly one. Charlie was hit by a mortar barrage which seriously wounded three, including a dog handler. The uninjured but crucial mine-sniffing dog was placed on the dustoff with his handler, as he would not be effective without him.

As the 1st Platoon moved out of its night position, Sergeant Russell Gedeon stepped on a pressure-release fuse hooked to an 81mm mortar round. The explosion sheared off both his legs and wounded three other soldiers and an RF militiaman with metal fragments slashing their faces and midsections. Gedeon's traumatic amputation was too much for the young soldier and he died in the field. He was age twenty-three and single from River Grove, Illinois.

In the early afternoon of December 7, Charlie was lifted back to the Citadel in Delta's AO Serene to sweep an area where VC were reportedly gathering. Delta's mission of pacification involved three tasks: building defenses, keeping the VC from moving refugees back into VC controlled areas, and weeding out the Vietcong in the refugee population. It was a never-ending challenge.

Delta detained six women and fifteen children who were avoiding Charlie's sweep. The women carried provisions including gasoline hidden inside baskets of rice. Delta's 2nd Platoon in Phu Vinh detained a boy aged nine who stole M-60 ammo from the soldiers. The NPFF questioned his brother, age fifteen, and mother age fifty-two. They were identified as VC and sent to LZ Bayonet. This same scenario took place throughout the larger battalion operational area.

Cavalry troops with the Echo recon platoon swept through An Phuoc (2) in "AO Custer". The hamlet was supposedly abandoned but they found sixty-five civilians who asked to be evacuated. They were sent to Binh Son.

Intelligence from a variety of sources continued to point to a build-up of the enemy for a major attack in December or January to blunt the pacification effort. Two battalions of the NVA's 21st Regiment had reportedly crossed the north side of the Tra Bong River to stage a strike on Binh Son. For this reason Charlie was lifted to Binh Son on December

8 to be a blocking force in Binh Son's western flank, now dubbed "AO Safeguard".

C Troop of the 1st/1st Cav moved down from AO Custer to backfill Charlie in AO Clean Sweep, keeping the pressure on the enemy to prevent attacks on Delta's pacified hamlets.

Additional intelligence identified a group of one hundred Vietcong which had moved into the rocket pocket northwest of Gator on December 6. Charlie Company was repositioned to hunt for them. Three zones were established: "AO Florida", west and northwest of Gator to shield the southern perimeter of LZ Bayonet and the western approach to Gator; "AO Razorback", north of Gator to cover the Tri Binh hamlets and "AO Texas", northeast of Gator across Highway One, to extend to the southern perimeter of the Chu Lai base. Charlie established day patrols and night ambushes in AO Florida while Echo's recon platoon took up the same tasks in AO Texas.

The recon platoon from the 1st/6th Battalion operated west of AO Florida and captured a VC from the 409th Sapper Battalion on December 12. The prisoner confirmed a major attack was coming prior to Christmas, most likely on LZ Bayonet. This would be followed by attacks on smaller bases in the days that followed.

Snatch missions were increased in an attempt to gather more intelligence. On December 13, one snatch team spotted a VC burning papers near Co Lay (1) south of Pinkville. As the LOH swooped in to make the snatch it was greeted by AK-47 fire. Gunships opened up, killing an NVA soldier in uniform. The LOH made another try and was hit again by enemy fire. Artillery fire was called and an Aero Scout platoon inserted. While sweeping the area the scout platoon spotted a company of NVA in uniforms spread out in groups of three to five. The scouts opened up with the support of their gunships and killed thirty-four NVA at a cost of three wounded. Weapons, homemade bombs and documents were also captured.

Not to be outdone, C Troop of the 1st/1st Cav in its "clean sweep" mission engaged NVA near My Lai (6) one-quarter mile west of Pinkville. They hit the enemy hard and killed eighteen, capturing medical supplies and documents. The Cav captured eleven more enemy, four of whom were females and three were dusted off with wounds. Later, near My Khe (4) they located four Vietcong hiding in a tunnel. The insurgents did not respond to requests to come out. Grenades were tossed in, killing two. The other two surrendered. Twenty Chicom grenades, a light anti-tank weapon (LAW), and a carbine were retrieved.

The next day Bravo's 2nd Squad of its 2nd Platoon swept Highway One outside Tri Binh (1), finding numerous papers on the road held down by bricks, which read, "All Vietnamese remember Ho Chi Minh." The field-wise grunts didn't touch the bricks and, upon close inspection, found them booby-trapped. They were detonated with M79 rounds.

It was apparent the large coastal plain from Chu Lai to Quang Ngai City had come alive with increased NVA infiltration from the mountains to thwart the growing success of the accelerated pacification effort. A CAP 142 patrol near Chau Me (2) was ambushed, but three of the enemy were captured with weapons, two were aged twelve and one aged ten. The Vietcong increasingly drafted children for lack of older males who were dead or captured.

CAP 135 had a similar engagement, killing three VC and recovering hand grenades and documents. CAP 134 forces at the headwaters of the Tra Bong wounded two VC and captured two more but two others escaped. Alpha Company nearby captured the two insurgents who escaped. A medical team from Chu Lai performed a MEDCAP in CAP 134's area. In one hamlet a Navy doctor noticed fresh graves. The hamlet chief told him no one had died; the graves were being prepared by Vietcong as storage areas for an upcoming offensive.

Clearing the area was tedious work. In one hamlet Alpha's explosive charge set to destroy an enemy bunker did not detonate. PFC Denton Terrell volunteered to disarm the device, taking a chance it could explode at any moment, then resetting it. He had no demolition training, but getting trained engineers to do this kind of work was a luxury for the field troops. After rearming, the bunker was destroyed. Terrell was awarded an Army Commendation medal for valor.

The ARVN went on the offensive to mitigate the gathering NVA threat to the region. The ARVN 4th Cavalry Troop moved out of Quang Ngai City to sweep the area north of Pinkville. One company of the ARVN's 1st/6th Battalion combat air assaulted to the same area. The balance of the battalion moved in by land. Their recon element, which had moved into the area earlier, killed four VC and captured one, along with weapons and ammunition.

Four Regional Force (RF) Companies were also moved to the "clean sweep" AO, south of the ARVN, to support C Troop, 1st/1st Cav.

Delta's pacification area around the Citadel was becoming the "shining example" of accelerated pacification and the Americal Division could not afford to have it fall under a major attack.

Echo Recon, operating in AO Texas, found eighteen freshly dug graves, believed to be possible storage areas. They dug into four graves and found bodies in advanced stages of decomposition. This ended the grave digging exercise.

Morale in the battalions reconnaissance platoon had been on the decline for weeks. Many of its men had been with the platoon for a long time with little rest from the field. They were also "short" but no rear jobs had opened up for them on LZ Gator. And to compound matters, their new platoon leader did not command much respect from most of the men. The experienced soldiers became lackadaisical and some carried hard liquor in their rucksacks and drank frequently. Newly assigned men to the platoon could do nothing. They were afraid to question the actions of soldiers who were more experienced than they. What happened next would result in a shake-up of the entire platoon.

On December 15 the recon platoon moved into the area next to My Hue (1) by the western shore of the headwaters of the Tra Bong River. A small contingent of Popular Force (PF) militia was in the hamlet, commanded by a "Honcho" who was a former Vietcong who turned himself in as a Chieu Hoi. The honcho carried two pearl-handled pistols in western style holsters and his word was law with the PF's.

Arthur Castillo was a newly assigned medic to the recon platoon. As the recon platoon walked into the hamlet he could sense from the faces of the peasants they were hated. No American soldiers had been in this area for months and the PF's assigned there were the hamlet's only "protection". The field-savvy grunts sensed the PF's may have been working both sides of the war to maintain control for themselves.

Late in the day the recon platoon left the hamlet to develop a night ambush. The weather was overcast with periodic downpours. The PF honcho insisted his group accompany the recon platoon and, at the ambush site when it was dark, that they line up behind recon's soldiers. Sp/4 Darryl Wayne Patrick, the platoon s RTO, vehemently insisted the PF's get on line with his soldiers. The PF's refused. Patrick made a call on the radio to get a higher authority. While he talked a shot rang out and he was hit in the left clavicle. Castillo checked the wound with a small flashlight and knew Patrick was in bad shape.

More shots rang out from in front of the ambush. Gunships were called from the Chu Lai Base just three miles north of the hamlet. A Medevac was also called for Patrick who was dying. Even though illumination rounds were fired above the ambush site the heavy monsoon squalls made it difficult for the gunships to see the ground and look for the enemy. A dustoff left from the Chu Lai base but, before it could clear the southern edge of the Chu Lai perimeter, it developed mechanical problems, went into a steep dive and crashed, killing all on board.

Moments later Patrick succumbed to his wounds. SP/4 Darryl Wayne Patrick was age twenty-one and single from Murdock, Kansas. When daylight arrived the recon platoon was lifted out of the field and brought back to LZ Gator. The platoon leader and disgruntled soldiers were removed from the platoon and replaced with new soldiers, some of whom were sergeants from the "Shake and Bake" NCO Course at Fort Benning and were Ranger qualified. From that point on the battalions recon platoon carried more sergeants than it was authorized, in recognition of the higher level of performance required for the recon mission. The new platoon leader, First Lieutenant Richard Decker, was Airborne, Ranger and Special Forces (Green Beret) trained.

The debacle at My Hue (1) and the strong suspicion the PF unit was responsible for Patrick's death, reached the Marine CAP Command in Chu Lai, which was responsible for the CAP areas throughout the coastal plain. My Hue (1) was part of the CAP's responsibility.

The morning after the night ambush saw a lone jeep with a US Marine driver and a Vietnamese (ARVN) officer drive down the dirt roads from Chu Lai into the My Hue hamlet. The Vietnamese officer took out his .45 caliber pistol and walked into the hooch where the PF commander was sitting. The officer told the PF leader to take off his holsters and come with him. Instead the PF went to draw one of his pistols and was shot dead. The Marine driver told some recon grunts later, "That ARVN officer was highly decorated by the US Army, and he has shot a lot more men for a lot less reason than that PF!" December 18 saw the reconstituted recon platoon sent back to the Batangan Peninsula to patrol near CAP 142 and LZ Minuteman.

On December 20, Charlie's headquarters and 3rd Platoon were lifted from AO Falcon to the coast of the Batangan, near the An Hai (1) area to exploit intelligence given by a Chieu Hoi that VC were reoccupying coastal tunnels by the sea. The soldiers found twenty-one small tunnels which were searched, but yielded little. Six newly constructed hoochs with bunkers underneath and eleven separate fighting bunkers were also found and destroyed. One hooch was bobby-trapped. A grenade tossed inside it yielded a secondary explosion of stored ammunition and wounded one soldier who was dusted off. After several days of searching the area, Charlie was hurriedly returned to AO Falcon because reports indicated a unit of fifty-five NVA was now in the area.

In CAP 144's area a patrol of Marines and PF's spotted twenty-nine VC in small boats, fishing in the Cho Moi River. The patrol opened fire and killed three, wounding three more and capturing twenty-three. The captives were sent to Son Tinh for interrogation.

At CAP 143 children entered its headquarters hamlet claiming their Vietcong parents were wounded by an air strike. The PF's picked up the parents who pointed to an additional four VC who had been wounded and were hiding with another sixteen uninjured VC in the area. Another air strike was called, killing four more VC. Later a Chieu Hoi brought in a wounded female from the same strike. A sweep of the area located five hundred pounds of corn and rice, tunnels, bunkers, and blood trails.

Delta's work in AO Serene continued to gather an increasing number of peasants who were resettled within the protected hamlets. By late December the three New Life Hamlets sheltered over eighteen hundred Vietnamese:

Pacified Hamlets

Delta Unit	Phu Vinh	My Loc	Phu Than
	HQ & 2nd Platoon	1st Platoon	3rd Platoon
PF Soldiers	16	17	27
RD cadre	5	16	20
Villagers	389	235	421
Refugees	435	128	221

On December 24 offensive operations, including patrols and ambushes, were to be halted at 6:00PM for Christmas. Officers from the divisions command group were tasked to go to the "field" in small groups and visit each battalion in the division. The 5th/46th received Brigadier General McDonald and two Lieutenant Colonels who visited

LZ's Gator and Minuteman. Troops in the bush were hunkered down in defensive positions, happy to have one night of relative peace. Bob Hope gave a show at the massive base in Chu Lai which only a few field grunts were able to attend. Moonlight illumination for Christmas Eve was at one hundred percent and ninety-eight percent for Christmas night, an added bonus for security.

The lull in activity created some tension between the allied forces. Charlie's 1st Platoon operated near Truong An (1) in AO Texas with a PF platoon one-quarter mile to the east in Truong An (4). The PF's continually wandered over seeking handouts, their eyes surveying the supplies that lay around the platoon's encampment. The platoon had no trust in the Vietnamese and no one could relax as long as the PF's walked around. They were told to leave. Ten minutes later the grunts received about twenty rounds of M-16 fire from the PF location.

By 9:25PM on Christmas Day the short truce was over and CAP teams throughout the area received small arms and mortar fire. The next day Alpha Company was airlifted to LZ Gator for perimeter duty while Bravo exchanged missions and headed out to AO Eagle. Charlie moved by truck to LZ Gator. Without cavalry troops to do sweeps of AO Custer, enemy activity picked up to fill the void. This included the 95A Local Force (LF) Sapper Company, the P31 LF Company and the K51 Weapons Company, operating in the Phu Long hamlets.

With hopes of bagging a larger enemy unit than the customary groups of three to four insurgents, Charlie air assaulted to Nam Yen (4) on December 27 while Bravo air assaulted to An Quong (2). Their operational area was designated "AO California".

In short order the two companies sweep detained one hundred and thirteen men, women and children. Moving further north to the Van Tuong's, the sweep pivoted to the east at 6:00AM on December 29, with the objective of reaching the Phu Long hamlets one and one-half miles away. Marines and their PF's from CAPS 131, 133 and 134 provided blocking forces to the north and west. Snatch teams flew above supported by Cobra Gunships as well as a FAC to coordinate air strikes.

The sweep was effective but costly for Charlie Company. At 8:20AM on the 29th, SP/4 Michael Dinda was shot in the right thigh which hit an artery. Before the bleeding could be stopped, he died. Dinda was nineteen years old and single from Kensington, Connecticut. The enemy set out their mines in advance of the soldiers' line of march. One RF soldier stepped on a soda can mine which wounded two. A Charlie

3rd Platoon grunt detonated a small pressure-release mine which took off some of his toes. Thirty minutes later five more 3rd Platoon soldiers were wounded from a 105mm Howitzer round rigged to a pressure-release device.

Small arms fire greeted Bravo and Charlie Company's as they moved westward, one-quarter mile apart. As this two column sweep swept the bushes, CAP 134 spotted fourteen VC and killed one while directing artillery fire on the others. The Aero Scout platoon snatched five VC as prisoners and killed another. An air strike was dropped on Phu Long (4), which caused secondary explosions punctuated by white smoke, a sure sign an ammo cache was hit. By 2:30PM Charlie Company collected seventy-one detainees from Phu Long (2) who were evacuated to Binh Son. One hour later they collected another fifty-five Vietnamese.

On December 30 at 1:15PM, PFC Kenneth Lawson of Bravo's 3rd Squad, 1st Platoon stepped on a M-14 anti-personnel mine near the hamlet of Phu Long (1). He suffered multiple fragmentation wounds and his right heel was amputated. Lawson was the last wounded casualty for the battalion in 1969.

Late in the afternoon, Charlie was picked up to return to LZ Gator while Bravo was tasked to remain in the Phu Longs to saturate the area with night patrols and ambushes. Charlie was also told they'd be returning to My Lai (4). The brief November investigation of an alleged massacre in the area was now moving into its next phase, which required a thorough on-the-ground investigation to include the questioning of nearby villagers who were present at the massacre. This investigation was to proceed even though the war was still being fought around the hamlets.

Two miles to the west of My Lai (4) sat AO Serene and Delta's protected hamlets. Enemy activity continued nightly in hopes of destabilizing the camps. Four miles northeast of My Lai along the Batangan coast (CAP 142), a PF platoon in an ambush position observed a large group of NVA walk past them, but was afraid to fire because the enemy unit was so large. Intelligence reported the NVA were gathering to hit CAP's 142, 143 and LZ Minuteman on the Batangan.

This increased enemy threat developed as the My Lai massacre investigation was being set into motion. Charlie Company, the H Troop of the 17th Cav and a host of other support units were organized under the command of the battalions Executive Officer, Major Richard Roman, and designated "Task Force Roman". The plan to secure the My Lai (4) site for the investigation was designated "Operation Hammurabi". Part of the 5th/46th Infantry Battalion was now tasked to secure the investigation site of the most infamous incident of the Vietnam War.

13 – RETRIBUTION

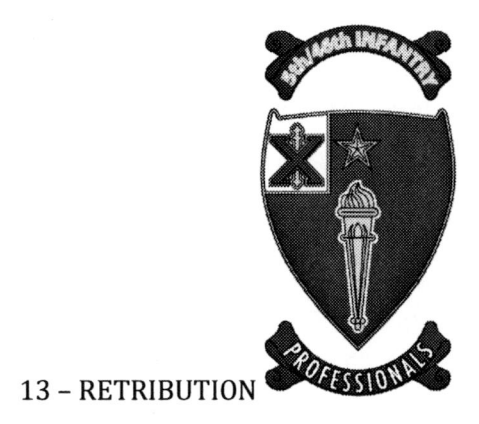

Pacify but Investigate

Task Force Roman was given the task to secure the abandoned hamlet of My Lai (4) before a full war crimes investigation could begin. The hamlets' old men, women and children who had survived the alleged atrocity had been moved to one of several protected camps in the area. Just a few dwellings were still standing in My Lai (4) but aerial surveillance on December 28 revealed enemy activity near the hamlet. Fighting bunkers and numerous footprints were spotted just three-quarters of a mile north of the hamlet. An air strike was called on December 29 to demolish the bunkers and anyone in them.

That same day armored personnel carriers of H Troop, 17th Cavalry traveled up Route 521 to sweep the area prior to the delivery of the construction materials needed to build a secure investigation site. The tracks established a night defensive perimeter on the road just one-half mile west of the My Lai hamlet. That night the Cav's trip flares were triggered outside their perimeter and fifteen insurgents were counted running through the shadows as the Cav soldiers blasted the area with their machineguns. But a morning sweep revealed only discarded NVA uniforms and four enemy fighting positions near the Cav's perimeter.

A snatch team flew over My Lai (4) and picked up two males hiding in the bushes. Later that evening, ten individuals were spotted moving in and out of the deserted hamlet. During the day Charlie Company landed by Hueys on Route 521 adjacent to the hamlet and laid claim to the area. Their mission was to secure the construction of the investigation site and provide security during the investigation itself.

Bulldozers were brought in on Route 521 with tons of construction equipment to build shelters. These were used in the questioning of the My Lai peasants who were returned to the site. To prevent an attack, security sweeps were made by Marines from CAP's 144,145 and 146 with their Popular Force (PF) platoons, along with four Regional Force (RF) Companies and Delta's troops west of My Lai in AO Serene. Delta's 2nd Platoon found seven freshly dug graves and six abandoned bunkers. Uncertain if the graves contained bodies or enemy ammunition, they were unearthed and they revealed partially decomposed adult bodies killed by artillery strikes several days prior.

In the meantime, progress at Delta's "pacified" hamlets two miles west of the My Lai site continued at a slow pace. Getting assistance from the villagers to work on defensive positions and other hamlet projects was problematic at best, and yet, it was peasant involvement that would ultimately determine the success or failure of the program. The villager's requirement to work in the rice fields and perform other chores, sometimes real and sometimes contrived, took time away from improving the hamlet defenses.

The Vietnamese interpreters provided to Delta Company by provincial authorities were mostly inept and corrupt, which added to the communications barriers the soldiers encountered. Although certified as "trained", most interpreters barely spoke English but used their positions of authority to bribe villagers. They also became scarce when needed by Delta's soldiers for local patrols.

Delta's platoon leaders subsequently turned to some teenage boys who had befriended the Americans. They were too young to be drafted in the Vietnamese Army but savvy enough to be of service to Delta's soldiers. One translator, "Bobby", was from Tri Binh (1) north of LZ Gator. He spoke excellent English and, as a teenager, fit right in with Delta's soldiers, many who were barely out of their teens themselves. Bobby's favorite expression was "Me Cherry Boy" but he was often seen with an attractive village girl who sold cokes in Phu Vinh. Several others like Bobby were adopted by the platoons, and paid by Delta's officers. Their interpretative skills and immediate attention to Delta's requests endeared them to Delta's soldiers, who would readily fight to protect their lives.

Cultural differences were a unique challenge to "winning the hearts and minds" of the peasants in Delta's care. Living accommodations were less than ideal. Out of necessity some peasant homes had to be shared with their American protectors. Soldiers used whatever rooms were vacant, which were, in some cases, rooms reserved for ancestor worship, which became the predicament of the company headquarters.

In Phu Vinh the old "Papasan" of the house quartering Delta's headquarters element requested from time to time that sweet-scented punks be lighted in a shrine to honor an ancestor. The shrine was positioned above the headquarters' radio equipment in a small room.

The lack of sanitary conditions was an additional problem. Delta's Executive Officer, 1LT Wight, was content to have his soldier's dig a slit trench in the ground as a toilet, and then cover it up. But the battalion's surgeon required "Shit Houses" (outhouses) be built similar to the specifications as constructed on LZ Gator. The shit houses were nothing more than sawed-off 55-gallon drums positioned under crudely constructed toilet seats. The American's outhouses left the Vietnamese a bit dumbfounded, since the rice paddy's had served the same purpose for centuries. Gas had to be flown in periodically to burn the shit, the same procedure required on LZ Gator, which added another supply requirement. Lime and insecticides also had to be ordered to control the flies.

Delta's platoon medics were responsible for shit-burning details until they found village kids willing to do it in exchange for C-rations. But solutions in pacification are never simple. In Phu Vinh, after lime was spread around the outhouse for fly control, six young ducklings being raised by a refugee family ingested some of the lime and died within hours. The "Mamasan" of the family angrily held her ducklings in front of 1LT Wight, pouring water down their throats to try to revive them, screaming this was an "atrocity" by the Americans. Wight compensated her with the only thing he had available, C-Rations. Days later she asked him for a pass to send someone to Quang Ngai City to sell the rations on the open market to acquire funds to buy more ducks.

The Rural Development (RD) and PF soldiers who assisted Delta's platoons became more of a hindrance than help. Theft of Delta's personal equipment was rampant in the protected hamlets. All of the grunt's personal equipment, camera's, radios, ponchos, etc. were fair game and had to be watched or secured. The villagers were trustworthy but the Vietnamese authorities, the PF's and RD sought to steal everything not secured by the Americans.

On one occasion as Lieutenant Wight slept, a case of C-rations was taken from a pile of cases stacked by him. The C-ration cases were then wired together to prevent further theft but another case was stolen in the middle of the night. Immediately after this theft a Delta Sergeant pursued the thieves to a hooch that the RD's shared with a family. When he arrived the food cans had already been hidden in all parts of the hooch and in the RD's clothing. The sergeant recovered the rations and in the process, caused the RD leader to lose face.

Similar problems existed with National Police Field Force (NPFF) personnel who resided in the hamlets. Their presence was necessary to maintain some semblance of Vietnamese control. Delta's 3rd Platoon turned in five peasant girls to the NPFF. They were selling marijuana to Delta's soldiers in an effort to weaken the field readiness of the unit. Nothing happened to them.

The Vietnamese militia, mostly PF's, also failed to cooperate on joint patrols and ambushes. When they learned a patrol was in the planning, PF leaders quickly reduced the size of their force, allowing some to go on errands to Quang Ngai City or on leave, without Delta's knowledge. The PF leader would then plead he had too few men for the mission.

Delta's patrol requirements, together with the complaints about rampant thefts, led to frequent showdowns between Delta's leaders and the PF leader, backed up by a few of his "Toughs". The PF's threatened to leave the hamlets if the pressure was not relaxed.

PFC Michael Stachowiak, like other Delta soldiers, did his best to work with the PF's. He recalled, "Some of the PF's were old men we were suppose to train to shoot and patrol, conduct ambushes, etc. They had brand new M-16's, not the beat-up weapon that I had. I remember trying to teach an old PF to shoot properly, but he would literally close his eyes and turn his head away before pulling the trigger. It was hopeless. The younger PF would steal anything that was available, but not munitions, because they knew that would be least tolerated. We were forced to take them out on our night ambushes which they didn't want to do. When they sprung an ambush over nothing we caught hell. I believe they did this to get back to their dry hooch. For them it sure beat sitting in the rain and dark all night."

This failure in cooperation made it hard for Delta's soldiers to pursue their mission with any crusaders zeal. The possible lost of an arm, a leg or a life protecting those who did not want to defend their own territory, sapped soldier morale. But Delta's fighting spirit was sustained if for no other reason than they looked out for each other.

To add to Delta's burdens, the increased visibility of the My Lai investigation nearby brought more visitors to Delta's pacified hamlets which required briefings on the "success" of the pacification program. Delta's officers knew what was expected and produced the numbers that showed progress; the amount of concertina wire laid, the number of defensive positions added, the number of refugees added from Delta's patrols, etc.

But behind the numbers were many reasons why the program could fail, not the least of which was the genuine support of the local militias. The critical questions were never asked, and Wight and others sensed that the visitors did not want any comments that would require a curtailment of the battalion's withdrawal schedule.

While Delta continued its mission in AO Serene, Bravo Company conducted its search and sweep operations eleven miles further north in the Phu Long hamlets just south of AO Falcon, where the VC increasingly relied on mine warfare to replace their depleted ranks.

The 4th/6th ARVN battalion took up the same sweep, three miles further south, in the area of the Lac Son hamlets. At 6:30PM on December 30, one ARVN tripped a Bouncing Betty killing him and wounding six others. When the dustoff arrived it received heavy automatic weapons and mortar fire, which drove it away, leaving the wounded to wait. A firefight ensued that lasted throughout the night, requiring cobra gunships, artillery and C-130 - "Puff the Magic Dragon" Gunship support. By early morning fourteen ARVN were dead and thirty-nine wounded from the fight. The bodies of twenty-one VC were found in the area.

Construction of the My Lai (4) investigation site continued but not without the difficulties which was to be expected when operating in the home of the enemy. An armored personnel carrier (APC) threw a track about thirty feet from the briefing tent being built for visiting VIP's. As the soldiers repaired their vehicle, another track bypassed it by pushing into some bamboo which caused the detonation of an anti-personnel mine. The mine wounded the soldiers who were repairing the other track.

Helicopters landing with supplies quickly unloaded to take off as soon as possible to avoid enemy mortar fire. All personnel leaving aboard choppers were searched to ensure nothing was taken from the investigation site. Road blocks were established on Route 521 to prevent Vietnamese soldiers and political officials from entering the area from Quang Ngai, unless specifically authorized.

The investigation site became an elaborate base with a briefing tent, tent for questioning peasants, investigation office, mess hall and aid station. A pathfinder team from Chu Lai controlled all air traffic coming from Chu Lai or Quang Ngai. Three helipads were constructed with night landing lights, something the soldiers from Charlie Company marveled at. Such a luxury in the middle of Indian Country was something to behold. A four hundred and fifty-gallon potable water trailer was delivered every day along with hot food for all. Thirty sets of flak jackets and steel helmets were at the ready for visitors and dignitaries.

At one point Echo's Recon Platoon sergeant, John Forshag, was tasked to fly slow and low over the My Lai site in a light observation helicopter, to make a map of the trails and hooch's inside the investigation area, for briefing the VIP's. After several passes and some sniper fire, Forshag convinced those in charge that "the task is beyond my capabilities" and his map exercise was cancelled.

January 1, 1970 saw Alpha Company defending LZ Gator's bunker line, as Bravo Company continued sweeping the Phu Long Hamlets six miles further east in conjunction with C Troop, 1st/1st Cav. Charlie Company continued its security mission in and around the My Lai investigation site while Delta labored in its pacification role in AO Serene. Echo's Recon Platoon screened the area around My Lai (4) as part of Task Force Roman. The Task Force, operating under Operation Hammurabi now established a security zone extending a half mile in all directions from the investigation site. This zone was designated "AO Babylon". Marine CAP 146 and its PF forces added to the AO's security.

Intelligence reports indicated the 48th VC Battalion had gathered approximately three hundred VC and NVA soldiers north and northeast of Pinkville, for planned attacks on the New Life Hamlets in the Marine CAP 142, 143 and 144 areas.

With the attention on the My Lai investigation and possible VC attacks on the CAP hamlets near it, the enemy chose again to make its presence felt on LZ Gator. At 1:30AM on January 4, the LZ was hit with a mortar attack, with thirty rounds hitting the eastern portion of Gator overlooking Nuoc Mau and Highway One. A sapper attack followed, which hit Bunkers #2 and #3, manned by Alpha's grunts.

Sergeant Thomas Blanks had just posted his relief and was sleeping in one of the bunkers. A soldier on guard outside his bunker decided to take a pee by his position. He saw bushes moving toward him and threw grenades at the bushes just as the sappers rushed forward. A satchel charge was thrown into the aperture of the bunker Blanks was in, collapsing the bunker and killing him instantly.

Another soldier named Hatfield was hit by a satchel charge thrown behind him, which took off the top of his skull, but did not instantly kill him. Miraculously, he survived. Gunships arrived at 2:15AM and the night sky became fully illuminated. Those defending bunker #4 spotted four VC and killed them. Other sappers were spotted near bunkers #20 and #21 moving in and out of the shadows of aerial illumination, on the western side of Gator.

David Schrier, an Alpha medic was sitting in a jeep with his platoon leader, Lieutenant John Fedorek, near the battalion's landing pad, as part of a night reaction force in the event of attack. Enemy mortar rounds slammed onto the pad which detonated a pile of ammunition stacked there for an early morning resupply mission. One enemy round blew open a box of 4.2-inch mortar rounds stacked on the pile, sending an unexploded shell flying one hundred yards through the air, landing in Schrier's jeep. One end of the shell hit Schrier in the ankle while the other end smashed against LT. Fedorek's spine.

By 3:40AM, control was restored on LZ Gator. The grunts swept in front of bunker #21, finding numerous blood trails and one wounded Vietcong who had already applied a splint to an injury suffered early in the attack. He was shot on the spot.

The sweep uncovered six Chicom grenades, a B-40 Rocket and an AK-47 rifle. Four unexploded satchel charges were found in front of Bunkers #21 and #22. Fifteen feet inside the perimeter more Chicom grenades were found. Gators mess hall, the control hooch on the main helicopter pad and several other small shacks were damaged.

Alpha's sweep in front of Bunkers #2 and #3 found the body of a Vietcong women, estimated to be age 50. Seven soldiers on Gator were wounded (three from the artillery battery on the eastern high point of Gator) with Sergeant Thomas Blanks the lone KIA. Blank's was age twenty-one and married from Riverdale, Georgia. A total of six Vietcong bodies were found along with numerous blood trails of others who were dragged away.

Staff Sergeant Robert Hopper, Bravo's Supply Sergeant and two others from Bravo, SP/4 Joe Gniadek and SP/4 Jim Klebau, followed a blood trail off Gator for two hundred yards beyond the perimeter. They found another wounded sapper and killed him as well.

During the day Bravo moved back to Gator to help strengthen its defenses. More attacks were expected because moonlight illumination was set to fall to twelve percent the night of January 5, five percent on the following night and down to only one percent on the 7th. Bravo's stay on Gator was short-lived however, and they were air-lifted to the Batangan and An Ky Peninsulas the morning of the 5th, to counter a reported buildup of the 48th VC Battalion. Bravo's 1st Platoon and headquarters moved to CAP 144, its 2nd Platoon to CAP 142 and 3rd Platoon to CAP 143.

While a major attack in the area was a distinct possibility, the My Lai (4) investigation site, although a tempting target with so many Americans bunched up in such a small area, was not attacked. The investigation undoubtedly served the enemies propaganda interests to a far greater degree than attacking the site. The investigation went on with VIP's shuttling in and out by helicopter, including a seventeen-man map-making team. January 5 saw a large contingent of Vietnamese and American Colonels, Majors and Captains arrive; part of a defense team and trial counsel designated for a junior officer by the name of Lieutenant William Calley.

Just past midnight on January 6, LZ Minuteman was hit with ten RPG rounds, four 60mm mortar rounds, and small arms fire. The barrage was concentrated over the span of a few minutes but Minuteman's perimeter was not penetrated. SP/4 Earl William Marlin Jr., one of Echo Company's mortar men, received shrapnel wounds in the chest, neck and shoulder, causing a sucking chest wound. A dustoff was completed at 1:50AM, but he died enroute to the 27th Surgical Hospital in Chu Lai. Marlin was age nineteen and single from Keokuk, Iowa. All enemy fire broke at 2:00AM. A dud satchel charge was found just inside LZ Minuteman's perimeter with the dead Vietcong who threw it tangled in the concertina wire, his body riddled with bullet holes.

When Minuteman was hit, CAP's 142 and 143 also came under RPG, mortar and small arms fire. Flare ships illuminated the night sky, giving the defenders the advantage of superior fire power. Artillery pounded Vietcong positions. The attack lasted one and one-half hours but most casualties were suffered in the initial assault. When it was over, four Vietnamese civilians in the camps were killed and fifteen wounded, along with three Marines wounded.

Despite the risks posed by combat in the area which surrounded My Lai (4), the press now sensed blood of a different kind and demanded access to the My Lai investigation site. They were restricted to a one-hour visit on January 7, and two one-hour visits each day on January 8 and 9, but only when the investigation personnel were not present. Task Force Roman was now burdened with press briefings and reporter security, along with VIP visits which were increasing in frequency.

The ARVN's were still clearing the center sector of the large coastal plain from Chu Lai to Quang Ngai, after the heavy fighting on the evening of December 30. The 4th/6th and 2nd/6th ARVN Battalions, operating from LZ Dottie, set out to sweep the area from Dottie moving east to the coast, looking for pockets of VC and NVA. On January 7, H Troop and Echo Company's Recon Platoon were sent north from the My Lai area to assist them.

These battalion operations of "search and clear" and "Intense Pacification" in early 1970 were continued under the umbrella of Operation Nantucket Beach which was begun in July 1969. The operation was now in its 4th phase, "Accelerated Pacification" in preparation for the battalion's eventual withdrawal to the division's base in Chu Lai, and handover of the war to the Vietnamese. Chieu Hoi's continued to report that the 48th VC Battalion's main objective was to loosen the hold of the Marine CAP teams on the Batangan, and Delta Company's hold over the resettlement camps in the Pinkville area.

The enemy's strategy to achieve that objective was one of retribution to the peasants for the substantial gains made by the Americans and Vietnamese government forces. Improvements in pacification were gradually occurring despite the less than enthusiastic support from RF and PF in any cooperative offensive actions.

Bravo's presence in support of the CAP teams reduced the possibility of VC attacks and forced the enemy to move farther north and west, away from the CAP areas. Bravo was ordered to keep the pressure on, and on January 11 they air assaulted to the western edge of the former LZ South in reaction to reports of an enemy buildup in that area.

That same day Task Force Roman was deactivated as the My Lai site investigation had run its course and Charlie Company was moved to back-fill Bravo Company in securing the CAP locations.

Echo's Recon Platoon was relocated to Bravo's AO to support their search and clear operations. In so doing, numerous small groups of women and children, in areas supposedly cleared, were detected. The recon soldiers found two military-aged males hiding in a tunnel that refused to come out. Persuasion was achieved by tossing in a hand grenade which exploded and wounded one. Both were later classified as ARVN deserters and sent to LZ Bayonet.

The hunt for the elusive Vietcong became as risky as ever due to mines. RF's patrolling near Chau Me (2), three-quarters of a mile north of LZ Minuteman, hit a 105mm pressure-released artillery round on January 12, killing two PF's and wounding two more. That same day an NVA soldier surrendered to Bravo's troops. He confirmed that the enemy's strength was greatly reduced in the area because of many casualties, which precluded any credible offensive action. Until more NVA reinforcements could be infiltrated from the mountains, mines and booby-traps were emphasized to remove their enemy from the battlefield.

This prisoner had departed North Vietnam in late October 1969 as part of "Group 360", with approximately eleven hundred men. They infiltrated into South Vietnam in groups of one to three hundred. This soldier's group of approximately one hundred entered into the western edge of Quang Ngai Province on December 3 and trained briefly in the mountains while waiting for another three hundred from the original eleven hundred of the main force.

His group of one hundred was then assigned to the Quang Ngai city area and departed the mountains on December 15. They broke down into smaller groups (Twenty-four soldiers in his group) as they infiltrated into government-controlled areas just east of Highway One on January 4.

He finally reached the coastal plain and the 48th VC Battalion, but on the morning of January 11 their VC guide observed helicopters approaching. They took evasive action and hid in nearby bunkers. As they continued on another helicopter was sighted which further scattered their small group. Isolated, in unfamiliar territory, and worn down from his long journey from the north, he surrendered when he saw Bravo's soldiers on January 12.

The 2nd Platoon of H Troop, 17th Cav was released on the 13th from its support of the ARVN to aid Bravo Company's search and clear operation in the Con Chieu (2) area two miles west of the Batangan

Peninsula. Bravo found tunnels and bunkers, some of which were booby-trapped. On January 14 they detained ten males, seventy-five females and one hundred and ninety children in an area supposedly cleared of all civilian peasants.

Search, Clear and Kill

Charlie Company kept busy patrolling the Marine CAP areas on the Batangan and An Ky Peninsulas. Early on the afternoon of January 14, the 3rd Platoon discovered a hooch near Tan Duc. Its occupants had hurriedly left, leaving a cooking fire with rice and corn. Inside was a sleeping area and, below that, a tunnel entrance which led to a large room where gunpowder was stored. While waiting for explosives to destroy the tunnel, 2LT Martin Schiller Jr. stepped on a booby-trapped howitzer round, which killed him instantly and wounded seven others. The wounded had been wearing flak jackets, which probably saved their lives. Martin Schiller was twenty-three years of age and single from Memphis, Tennessee.

Delta was to fare no better that day. At 3:15PM, as a patrol spotted some VC, PFC Gilbert "Frenchy" Benaim stepped on another booby-trapped 105mm howitzer round which severely wounded him and eight comrades. Joseph Ach and others were wounded but struggled to keep Frenchy alive. One of Benaim's legs was attached only by skin from the knee to his boot. His stomach was blown wide open and his comrades stuffed a shirt into the open cavity to hold his intestines inside. Ach had been carrying a radio and, despite it being riddled with shrapnel, was able to call in a dustoff. They were picked up and flown to Chu Lai.

Benaim survived the chopper ride but died in the hospital hallway as they wheeled him to surgery. His loss of blood was too much despite the efforts of his wounded comrades to keep him alive. Gilbert Benaim was age twenty-two and single from New Orleans, Louisiana.

Ach and SP/4 Dickey Cooley suffered fragmentation wounds with shards of metal penetrating Cooley's stomach. For days they were attended to in the 91st Evacuation Hospital, both in critical condition. But Cooley's determination to live waned and he gave up, dying two weeks later on February 19. Cooley was twenty years of age and single from Galex, Georgia. Ach left the hospital the day after, transferring to

Japan and then home, his war having ended after seven months with the battalion.

The following day Ronald Mackie, a new arrival, was assigned to Delta Company and was given Benaim's equipment. As he recalled, "The helmet was dented but serviceable. Benaim's M-16 was destroyed with the rounds in the magazine exposed from the blast. I was given his flak-jacket which was coated in dry blood. Welcome to Vietnam!"

Charlie Company discovered another large mine hidden on a path near Chau Me (1). It was covered with twigs and leaves. A trip wire was connected to a smoke grenade firing device which was, in turn connected to a .50 caliber machine gun round leading to the mine. The ingenuity of the enemy to create death knew no bounds. The soldiers blew the mine in place with C-4 explosive and the explosion created a three foot by four foot-wide crater.

Vietcong were spotted in small groups of two to three but never close enough to engage with small arms, and the enemy disappeared into the bush before accurate artillery fire could be called. The enemy continually exposed themselves at a distance out of small arms range, trying to draw the soldiers in their direction, and to more mines.

At 4:15AM on January 16, CAP 142's compound on the north coast of the Batangan Peninsula was hit with nine to twelve 82mm mortar rounds and intense small arms fire from an estimated thirty Vietcong. Charlie Company's 1st Platoon was in its defense along with the Marine CAP squad and the PF militia. The CAP compound overlooked the refugee camp, sprawled on the sandy slope leading to the beach. Charlie's platoon sergeant, Staff Sergeant Clyde Murray, had sent five men into the camp as a listening post (LP). But the Vietcong had slipped into the camp with support from some of the refugees who were secretly Vietcong. They brought a 30 caliber machinegun with them.

When the mortar rounds began landing on the CAP compound the enemy machinegun in the camp opened up on the CAP perimeter. The CAP defenders were in a dilemma. The My Lai investigation had influenced the rules of engagement throughout the Americal Division and soldiers were told never to fire into a hamlet or, in this case, a refugee camp. The CAP defenders endured the deadly fire because retaliating could injure innocent refugees.

The five man LP was trapped with the refugees and watched the VC darting in and out of the shadows. Murray ordered the LP back because the CAP perimeter had been breached by sappers. The five soldiers ran through heavy enemy fire from the camp up the small hill and through the CAP perimeters' concertina wire.

SP/4 Carlton F. McCagg, nicknamed "Chicken Man" was next to Murray when enemy machinegun fire raked their position during the attack. McCagg had only thirty days left to serve in Vietnam. He suddenly slumped over into Murray's lap. Murray was pre-occupied with the fight and talking on the radio and it took a few moments for him to realize McCagg was dead. McCagg had caught a .30 caliber round through the helmet. He was age twenty-two and single from Chatham, New York.

One other soldier was wounded in the attack along with thirteen refugees. One PF soldier and eight refugees in the camp were killed. The retreating attackers were spotted near the beach and artillery fire and gunships raked the area. Second Lieutenant Kenneth Teglia had just joined Charlie Company as its artillery forward observer and the attack on CAP 142 was his first enemy contact. He called for and adjusted about one hundred and forty artillery rounds from two different batteries in an effort to cut off the enemy's likely escape routes but later, only three Vietcong bodies were found.

All the wounded Vietnamese were dusted off and taken to the 91st Evacuation Hospital. Thirteen refugee homes were destroyed. This was Teglia's baptism by fire. The death and destruction he saw and the thought of what he may have caused by calling in fire support made an indelible impression on him. When it was over he sat in a bunker and wrote on an envelope his first impressions of combat:

Shot over!
Shot Out!
Blood Over!
Blood out!
A body count to boost morale,
Does it matter if we all burn in hell?
To err is human
But to kill becomes
That truth is witnessed by the thunderous guns.
But this need not be wrong.
It's that thing in man that loves a dirge
Which is the doorway through which emerge
All the pain and suffering of war
Which is the cancer, not the sore.

At 8:00AM, Alpha Company lifted off LZ Gator and air assaulted to Phuoc Hoa (1), the headquarters hamlet of CAP 133, seven miles southeast of the Chu Lai base's perimeter. This was in response to reports of increased enemy activity in the area. Charlie Company returned to LZ Gator for bunker line duty but their artillery forward observer, 2LT Teglia, remained one more day to work with the Marines at CAP 142.

Teglia at CAP 142 showed the Marines how they could plan defensive targets with the Army's artillery located on LZ Dottie, to quickly thwart future attacks. He taught them how to ring their compound with preplanned fires on likely avenues of attack. For example, a "Battery Four" could place four high explosive artillery rounds on six different targets in quick order and he taught the Marines how to call in the fires without his help. The Marines were astounded and replied, "We like that". Bravo was lifted to the Batangan to backfill Charlie Company at CAP's 142 and 143.

By noon, Alpha drew its first casualty when a soldier stepped on an underwater mine, losing his right foot. His platoon leader, LT Greene, walking behind him, was also wounded. The battalion commander, LTC Melvin Snyder, flew over Alpha's area in support of his soldiers and his bird was hit with small arms fire. Gunships saturated the area with fire and Alpha's first platoon swept the area. The point man spotted six VC and the platoon engaged them, killing two and capturing a French-made machinegun and an American M-14 rifle.

At CAP's 142 and 143 Bravo was alerted that a battalion-size element of Vietcong was moving in their direction for another possible attack in a couple days. Bravo's 2nd Platoon conducted a sweep west of the Batangan with the tracks of the 3rd Platoon, H Troop, 17th Cav. On the 17th they detained sixteen females and fourteen children in Chau Binh (1), another area supposedly cleared of all civilians. The peasants were escorted to CAP 142.

On January 19, Delta Company likewise encountered more civilians; three hundred children, one hundred and seventy-five females and thirty-seven males one-quarter mile northeast of their pacified hamlet of Phu Thanh (5). The group was escorted to the hamlet.

Bravo Company was air lifted to assist Delta by conducting a search and clear operation in the northeast sector of Delta's assigned area. At 4:30PM they were hit with small arms fire which wounded a soldier. As they swept the terrain, the savvy soldiers took every precaution, wearing their flak jackets, staying off the trails, walking on rocky ground, and walking through thick hedgerows while avoiding the natural openings. It was not enough. One soldier stepped on a mine after three soldiers in front of him missed it. The explosion blew off his right foot and shrapnel tore into his left leg and right arm.

The next day Alpha and Delta continued to receive sporadic fire, and spotted small groups of uniformed NVA and Vietcong moving hurriedly through the area. Enemy equipment was found here and there but no bodies. The ARVN were having a rough go of it as well. The 3rd Battalion, 6th ARVN Regiment swept the area three miles north of Bravo and at 8:05PM hit a 155mm howitzer round (trip-wire type), killing two of their soldiers and wounding nine. Earlier the ARVN had captured a Vietcong who disclosed that approximately one hundred and eighty soldiers of the 48th VC Battalion were located in the area of Alpha's troops. The Vietcong forced thirty civilians from the Batangan to work as laborers for an upcoming attack at CAP 142.

January 21 saw Alpha combat air assault into two landing zones to act as a blocking force for the 3rd/6th ARVN who were sweeping south from the western side of former LZ South, just north of AO Serene. Bravo Company's 2nd Platoon was lifted by helicopters to search the area northeast of the Batangan and landed in An Thinh (1), close to the coast.

At 10:30AM, the enemy hit Bravo's 2nd Platoon with a burst of fire. The enemy was situated in some small spider holes spread throughout the area, almost on top of the platoon. The platoon leader, Second Lieutenant Michael Foutz, had wandered a short distance away from his men and was hit in the chest. The company's headquarters element listened to the anguished voice of the patrols radio telephone operator (RTO) as his comrades desperately tried to keep their platoon leader alive while the enemy continued its gunfire as it evaded the area. Artillery could not be used because the enemy was simply too close to the soldiers. 2LT Foutz was dying quickly from a sucking chest wound. The RTO's anguished voice soon turned to despair as he told his headquarters their well-liked platoon leader's life had slipped away. Michael George Foutz was age 20 and single from Roseburg, Oregon.

Bravo's 2nd and 3rd Platoons were quickly air lifted to the area. Continuous fighting around the hamlet resulted in three Vietcong killed in a bunker. An SKS rifle, 57mm Recoilless Rifle and documents were recovered. Gunships then came on station and Bravo pulled back to let them have their way from the air. The birds pulverized the area with rockets and 40mm grenade fire followed by a Navy F-4 air strike of napalm.

Bravo then approached the ville a second time and was hit from the same bunker. This time they destroyed it using light anti-tank weapons (LAWS) and a flame thrower. They found the bodies of six Vietcong with two rifles. One Vietcong was still alive but his body was completely burned from the napalm strike, yet he managed to raise an arm in defiance. Someone walked up and shot him in the head.

The heavy enemy contact faced by Bravo called for valor and the challenge was met. PFC Reilly Bryan was a machine-gunner who reacted immediately to the enemy fire on Bravo. He assaulted enemy positions with machinegun fire but was seriously wounded and knocked to the ground. Bryan rose to his feet and continued the assault until he was wounded a second time. Still he continued until being wounded a third time and his machinegun was damaged beyond repair. He was awarded the Silver Star.

Staff Sergeant Carl Bauer was Foutz's platoon sergeant who took over the platoon when Foutz went down, exposing himself continuously to enemy fire to keep his platoon organized and placing effective fire on the enemy. Staff Sergeant James Breedlove from another platoon led his men to the opposite side of the hamlet and attacked the hamlets rear guard bunkers. It was Breedlove who directed the use of the LAW's. Bauer and Breedlove were awarded Bronze Stars for Valor.

By mid-afternoon, Bravo detained six females and five males in the area, all military age, and sent them to the 198th Brigade Headquarters at LZ Bayonet for questioning along with five children. By 4:40PM the company was extracted by Chinook helicopters and sent back to CAP's 142, 143 and 144.

The remaining days of January saw Alpha conducting night ambushes and day patrols in AO Eagle which was the area of responsibility for CAP teams 133-134-135. Bravo patrolled the Batangan to beef-up the CAP's defense on the peninsula. On the 29th Bravo returned to LZ Gator for bunker line duty, and Charlie Company once again took up responsibilities on the Batangan.

Delta continued to secure its pacified hamlets in AO Serene using aggressive patrolling to keep the VC on the defensive. The Vietcong were in no condition to overwhelm the protected hamlets because a Delta platoon protected each, but periodic attacks in the surrounding area were a stark reminder to the refugees that their protection from the government was tenuous. Small pockets of enemy were engaged causing short but intense firefights. Delta's grunts found themselves killing as many female Vietcong as males. One captured and very pregnant female was carrying detonation fuses and blasting caps used for mines.

With the battalion's soldiers fully committed on the large coastal plain east of Highway one, the area west of Highway One became open to enemy movement. Elements of the 1st/6th Battalion were moved south from the northern rocket pocket, to screen LZ Gator's western flank and fill this void.

Intelligence reports pointed to an enemy build-up for attacks during the Tet Lunar New Year in February. Charlie Company on the Batangan noticed an up-tick in Chieu Hoi's who were surrendering rather than be part of the upcoming fighting. One defector was a nurse for the 48th VC Battalion who brought her medical supplies with her. She had served with the VC for four years and told interpreters that, five days before, her battalion was located near An Thinh (2), only two and one-half miles north of LZ Minuteman. Half the 48th Battalion's strength of approximately two hundred soldiers were NVA reinforcements.

Another defector led Charlie's 1st Squad, 1st Platoon to a mine located one-eighth mile east of LZ Minuteman. The mine was an expended illumination round filled with metal fragments and gun powder with a trip wire hooked to a smoke grenade fuse. After blowing the mine the squad received small arms fire from a nearby hooch. They returned fire killing one VC and wounding another while securing two SKS rifles and two carbines. Eleven mines in total were blown in place. Nearby they discovered a large tunnel which led to a room fifteen feet square and eight feet high. It was also destroyed.

The opening of the TET holiday on February 1 began at 1:30AM with a heavy barrage of enemy mortar fire on the district town of Binh Son. An hour later Alpha's 1st Platoon was hit with enemy mortar fire in CAP 144's hamlet, along with small arms fire and satchel charges thrown by attackers. Twelve hooch's were damaged in the attack and six wounded civilians were dusted off that night. Regional Force (RF) Company 933, the Montagnards guarding the Citadel in Delta's AO Serene, conducted a night raid one-quarter mile north of their position and killed five Vietcong while capturing two AK-47 assault rifles.

The Chieu Hoi's kept flowing in, preferring surrender to facing the heavy firepower of the 5th/46th Infantry Battalion in the TET attack.

They divulged locations of arms caches and mines. One guerilla took a Charlie patrol to a rough dirt road one-quarter mile south of Tan Duc on the Batangan. He pointed to a mine-field of buried 155mm Howitzer rounds waiting for armored personnel carriers the next time they swept through the area. Anti-personnel mines were also found nearby.

At 7:45AM on February 5, six male Chieu Hoi's surrendered at Delta's headquarters in Phu Vinh. They told Delta's commander that of the two Vietcong killed by Delta the week before, one was actually a NVA commander. Word was received by the battalion a TET 24-hour cease fire would take place starting 6:00PM that day. Three VC were killed by a CAP 144 patrol at 3:00PM, as more mines were discovered by Charlie and Delta soldiers.

The following day, just twenty-five minutes after the TET cease fire ended, Delta killed one VC and captured two. CAP 144, suspecting a gathering of VC nearby, called for mortar fire from the heavy 4.2-inch mortars on LZ Minuteman. The fire mission was on target. One hour later the Marines noticed more VC in the target area and called for mortar fire once again. This time one of the mortar tubes misfired, its deadly rounds landing in a hamlet nearby, killing two villagers and wounding nine others.

The next day five Chieu Hoi's, four males and one female, surrendered to Alpha's 1st Platoon in AO Eagle. On February 8, a female VC turned herself in to the Marines at CAP 142 on the Batangan coast. She had participated indirectly in the heavy attack on January 16, the night Carlton McCagg was killed. She told the Marines the Vietcong had actually lost fifteen killed and twenty-five wounded in the attack, many from the artillery fire directed by 2LT Teglia. In addition, three companies of the 48th VC Battalion, the 3rd, 4th and 5th, were just five miles due west of the Batangan forming for another attack. They had a total strength of eighty-two of which only twenty were Vietcong and the remainder were NVA regulars.

The deserter also divulged that one week after the attack of January 16 the 48th Battalion lost nineteen men in An Thinh (1). This was the fire fight that Bravo fought on January 21st, which killed Lieutenant Foutz, after which they found only six enemy bodies.

The increased influx of deserters provided the battalion confirmation of enemy casualties that could not be proven after firefights due to the enemy's strict doctrine of removing its dead after an engagement. On February 9, for example, a Vietnamese part-time guerilla told Alpha Company the VC suffered four killed and three wounded when a routine patrol by Alpha's 1st Platoon on February 3 called in artillery on some fleeing VC.

Helicopter reconnaissance detected newly dug graves that were one to two weeks old. Charlie Company's 1st Squad of the 1st Platoon made contact with six Vietcong at noon. Rapid artillery support and a quick sweep of the area located a male and female Vietcong, both dead. Mines were lying at their sides. Nearby were a group of twenty camouflaged hooch's containing one hundred bags of rice, three hundred bags of corn, and about a ton of potatoes. The abandoned camp also yielded freshly dug graves.

With the guerilla strength of the 48th Vietcong Battalion greatly depleted, infiltration of NVA regulars continued. Intelligence from Binh Son indicated the NVA were infiltrating in groups of fifteen to eighty, following the north side of the Tra Bong River while moving east towards the coast, to link up with dispersed elements of the 48th Battalion east of Highway One.

Alpha's platoon leaders were enjoying their independence with small unit patrolling. They had recently acquired a new company commander to replace the capable Captain Longgrear whose time in the field had ended. But Alpha was to be cursed again with another bad company commander. The new commander was a First Lieutenant soon to be promoted to Captain who, unlike his predecessor, did not have a previous tour in Vietnam. His German-sounding name and comedic appearance did not endear him to his men.

On his first day in the field the new commander called for gunships to fire on movement to his left flank which happened to be his 2nd Platoon. Spotter aircraft shot white phosphorous marking rounds into the platoon's formation. The soldiers knew they were marked for death and only the detonation of many smoke grenades gave the approaching gunships some pause, averting a disaster.

On another occasion the commander's ill-planned mortar fire mission caused his 3rd Platoon to be mortared by friendly fire, but fortunately friendly casualties were avoided. Alpha's 2nd Platoon leader, Lieutenant Bill Wolski convinced the company commander to consolidate his platoons "for more strength". Wolski's real reasoning was to prevent another friendly fire incident by keeping everyone together. Saddled with an incompetent commander, Alpha's effectiveness began to wane and its morale plunged once again. Platoon leaders and soldiers made comments behind their commanders back, calling him a "dufus" and "asshole."

To disrupt the enemy's TET attack plans, multiple air assaults were conducted on February 11. They were designed to be a one to two day search and clear operation to confuse and unnerve the enemy, causing him to expose himself. An additional mission was launched to locate unexploded five hundred-pound bombs that had been dropped in support of soldiers on the ground. More dud rounds from the increased number of air strikes gave the Vietcong a ready source of materials for its mine warfare.

Alpha Company combat assaulted from the three CAP areas it was sweeping in AO Eagle into three locations among the Lac Son and Nam Yen hamlets. Bravo left LZ Gator to air assault into a small valley three miles north of Delta's AO Serene. Charlie Company was picked up on the Batangan and landed at three locations south of the Phu Nhieu hamlets, about three miles southeast of Alpha to thoroughly cover the area assigned. Each platoon of each company patrolled in a three-leafed cloverleaf fashion. Each platoon patrolled its loop of the larger company loop which formed the cloverleaf, then moved into adjacent terrain to do it again.

For just a short one-day operation each company was to hit some pay-dirt, locating recently used tunnels, detaining Vietcong suspects and engaging some small pockets of fleeing enemy soldiers. But Alpha Company's intrusion into their area, five miles south of AO Eagle, yielded the biggest payoff.

Alpha's 2nd Platoon found a cave. Their Kit Carson scout "Chot" yelled into the cave that he would throw in a grenade if the occupants did not surrender. A thin high-pitched female voice pleaded for mercy and emerged with several children and four elderly men.

Chot was not satisfied. He fired a few rounds into the cave as a warning and Chot's shout of "Chieu Hoi!" brought out three Vietcong males. A search of the cave revealed large flat baskets overflowing with rice, several sets of black pajamas, and a large roll of Vietnamese Piasters. Through Chots interrogation of the VC, Alpha learned there were a large number of NVA in the area. Other Alpha platoons detained eight Vietcong and NVA posing as peasants, killed two others and retrieved two SKS rifles. One of the dead was identified as a NVA officer based on the identification card found on his body.

In the afternoon Alpha's three platoons were directed to a designated pick-up zone (PZ) for helicopters to return them to their CAP areas. The 2nd Platoon walked in single file paralleling a rice paddy dike as they moved to the PZ. To their right was a large dry paddy with woods at the far side. The platoon leader, LT Bill Wolski, glanced to his right and couldn't believe his eyes; three NVA soldiers in blue uniforms were walking towards the shelter of the wood line, their weapons clutched in their hands, just hanging at their sides, oblivious to the American's presence nearby. The grunts opened fire with the initial volley dropping all three enemy but two crawled to the wood line. Several soldiers moved forward to the wood line and threw grenades where the enemy disappeared. An additional body was found riddled with shrapnel, and a blood trail indicated the remaining NVA had gotten away, no doubt to face a slow death. They recovered two SKS rifles.

A light observation helicopter (LOH) heard Wolksi's call to his company commander and flew over with two cobra gunships in trail. The LOH pilot hovered over the trees and told Wolksi to lead his men away from the tree line and "sit back and watch the show." The cobras came in with mini-guns and rockets blasting the wooded area and then flew away.

Moving on, the platoon found a five hundred-pound bomb lying in the open. Wolski crawled up to it himself and saw it was an empty casing, the Vietcong having already removed the explosive from inside. Wolski's commander pressed him to move faster to get to the PZ on time. A short distance away they found another five hundred-pound bomb. This one was still live. A cache of rice was found in a hay stack indicating the enemy was near. Wolski called for a demolition team to destroy the bomb as he had no C4 explosive to do it himself. Alpha's commander nixed the request and told him to keep moving to the PZ. The bomb was left in place to kill and maim.

Alpha's commander identified a suitable spot for their pick-up, a large field through which an irrigation ditch flowed. As each platoon arrived they were directed to man a section of the perimeter for security and prepare for an orderly pick-up. The order for extraction back to the CAP areas was the 1st, the 2nd, and then the 3rd Platoon, each being pulled out on a lift of four Hueys. As Wolski's 2nd Platoon entered the field a soldier from another platoon directed them to their side of the perimeter. Wolski was unaware his first three soldiers, Sergeant Wayne Cherryholmes, PFC Paul Curtis and SP/4 Michael Glenn were directed by the company commander to move beyond Wolski's position to another section of the perimeter to serve as a listening post. The company commander told Wolski he changed the order of extraction since his platoon was "late", and they would be the last to leave.

At 5:15PM, the radios cracked with the message the first lift of Hueys was inbound. There was a rush of activity. The company of soldiers gathered their belongings, hastily-shoved their half-eaten rations into their pockets and jerked heavy rucksacks onto their weary shoulders for the ride back. The soldiers felt relief knowing they would depart for the more familiar grounds around their CAP areas. At the same time, like all soldiers, they experienced the usual anxiety surrounding the crucial few moments of lift off, which made them vulnerable to enemy fire. Would the enemy let them depart without incident?

The radios brought the news the birds were in-bound and a yellow smoke grenade was thrown to guide the choppers into the center of the perimeter. Soon the whop, whop, whop of the rotor blades could be heard, and four choppers were seen coming across the tree line, slowly descending in single file. The 1st Platoon's soldiers moved hurriedly to their assigned Hueys, conscious of their vulnerability as the helicopters "Hung in the air" before landing.

The first men jumped on the Hueys and turned to assist their comrades. Just as the birds lifted off with their human cargo the heavy whoomp of an incoming mortar round was heard near the tail section of the last helicopter. The blast sent shards of hot metal through the bird's fuselage. The pilots strained to pull pitch and climb as fast as possible with their heavy loads, as door gunners fired into the foliage beyond the perimeter.

The soldiers remaining on the ground opened up, sending fire into the surrounding woods in the direction of the mortar fire. Each soldier tried to find shelter from the enemy fire behind the one foot-high rice paddy dikes that surrounded their field. Lieutenant Wolski then heard the slow, cyclic rate of a .30 caliber enemy machinegun firing on them a short distance away.

In fifteen minutes the sound of rotor blades announced the birds had returned for the second lift. As they descended, the door gunners, now alerted, opened up with their M-60 machineguns hanging on each door of the Hueys, firing beyond the perimeter, acutely conscious of the mortar fire received previously. This time the enemy did not open up.

When the birds landed, the door gunners ceased fire so as not to hit Alpha's troops, but one door gunner would not stop firing.

When the birds touched ground to pick up the second lift, Sargent Wayne Cherryholmes, just beyond the perimeter at his listening post, saw the door-gunner continuing to fire in his general direction and thought, "He's either a new guy who is too scared, or a short-timer who is taking no chances." Then Cherryholmes watched the door-gunner swing his gun and shoot at him. The squad leader started running for the irrigation ditch inside the company's perimeter with PFC Paul A. Curtis running by his side. The helicopters lifted off and the birds' flight path paralleled the two men running to the ditch. The lone door-gunner was still firing. Cherryholmes was hit in the left thigh and left hand. Curtis caught an M-60 round in his left arm.

LT Wolski called for a dustoff for his wounded men. The Hueys returned for the final pick-up before the dustoff's arrival. Wolski remained on the ground with his medic, the two wounded, and two other soldiers under darkening skies. The dustoff arrived for Wolski's small group and Cherryholmes and Curtis were taken to the 27th Surgical Hospital in Chu Lai. Wolski and the others were returned to CAP 135. It was at this time that Wolski learned the rest of his platoon had been taken to the wrong CAP area. The company commander had not bothered to tell the birds he had changed the order of extraction.

A count was taken of Alpha's soldiers on CAP's 133, 134 and 135, and it was discovered one soldier was missing, PFC Michael Glenn, the third soldier manning the listening post with Cherryholmes and Curtis. It was then Wolski learned these three men had been separated from his platoon on their arrival at the PZ without his approval and sent beyond the perimeter as a listening post. Wolski and five soldiers were airlifted to H Troop, 17th Cavalry's field position, which was just west of Alpha's earlier PZ. With the tracks they began their movement back to the pick-up zone. One lift helicopter, two gunships and one flare ship provided on-call support for the unit.

During their movement back to the PZ the search party received heavy small arms fire from a hedgerow. The tracks immediately went into attack formation, on line side by side, charging towards the enemy fire with their .50 caliber machineguns blasting the enemy position. A Huey gunship made its approach from the north and its mini-guns also blasted the enemy in the bushes. The bird then made a second pass from the opposite direction. In short order the gunship and tracks finished off all opposition.

Wolksi's small group and the cavalrymen on the tracks, aided by flares from above, found thirteen bodies of NVA regulars. One NVA survived and surrendered. Another wounded NVA was captured while attempting to crawl away from the site. Interrogation revealed Wolski's search party had come across an NVA meeting. The enemy, upon hearing the armored personnel carriers approaching, chose to stay in place and fight rather than evade, thinking the aerial flares fired in support of the rescue effort would have made their attempt to escape more hazardous.

At first light the group reached their former PZ perimeter but a group from Charlie Company had landed just minutes before and discovered Glenn's body. They found him with his rifle by his side still at the LP, lying face down. Two of Charlie's soldiers examined the body but did not touch it, for fear it was bobby-trapped. Assured he was dead they tied a cord to his legs and pulled him away from the LP position. No explosion occurred so they rolled him on his back and carried him away.

Glenn had been hit in the back of the neck by an M-60 machinegun round fired by the erratic door gunner. This probably happened just as his two comrades, Cherryholmes and Curtis, had started running for cover. Michael Glenn was age twenty-one and single from Smyrna, Georgia. Alpha's company commander failed to control the early evening extraction and showed little interest in recovering his missing soldier. Soon after the unfortunate incident he was relieved of command.

Mid-February saw Alpha Company defending LZ Gator while Bravo, after a rest and refit in Chu Lai, air assaulted to two miles northwest of Pinkville where intelligence reported groups of VC were forming. Delta was lifted to Chu Lai for its turn at resting and refitting and part of Charlie Company took over Delta's pacification role in AO Serene. The local Popular Force soldiers were now expected to pick up more of the slack in defense of the hamlets. It was a slow process but they started to respond with the sure knowledge the Americans would soon be leaving. Part of Charlie patrolled the hamlets north and northeast of Serene, and ran into small groups of VC. They killed some and captured others with weapons and grenades. But in the closing weeks prior to handing over the entire area to South Vietnamese soldiers and local defense forces, the battalion continued to take casualties.

One of Bravo's 2nd Platoon soldiers stepped on a booby-trapped 105mm Howitzer Round and lost both legs from the explosion. Another soldier lost a leg and arm from the same exlosion. Both were wearing flak jackets and maintaining an interval of twelve feet between each other while walking, but the large artillery explosion negated these usually sound precautions.

By this time the enemy's ranks in the area were clearly decimated and they were unable to launch any major TET attacks as they had done in previous years. Even many of the NVA replacements from the mountains were killed or wounded shortly after arriving in the coastal area. The enemy's primary offensive tactics continued to be stand-off attacks by mortar fire, harassing fire and small scale sapper attacks against carefully chosen targets.

Mines and booby-traps remained the enemy's primary defensive measures and the cause of most of the casualties for the 5th/46th Infantry Battalion. At 3:00AM on February 16, sappers attacked a hamlet northeast of Binh Son, destroying two schools and damaging twenty-three dwellings. The enemy's lack of explosives forced them to try to damage the dwellings using bayonets. Local Popular Force soldiers killed four Vietcong and captured two B-40 rockets. They watched the enemy flee carrying five of their dead with them.

The enemy's failure to gain control over the Southern Chu Lai Tactical Zone, from Chu Lai to Quang Ngai City, was due in large measure to the nimbleness and perseverance of the 5th/46th Infantry Battalion. Intelligence reports were received concerning another major attack on LZ Gator, which was the command and control source of the enemy's frustration in its failure to achieve dominance in the area. On February 19 it was reported that an NVA unit of one hundred and fifty soldiers were poised west of Gator, with 82mm mortars, recoilless rifles and elements of the 95B Sapper Unit, to "attack LZ Gator at some unknown time."

Casualties continued in the battalion despite minimal enemy contact. Two Delta soldiers were wounded by a pressure release booby-trapped grenade on February 19. The next day another Delta soldier tripped a booby-trapped 81mm mortar round just north of the Ham Giang River. The blast caused a traumatic amputation of both legs. More mines were located nearby. One was an antipersonnel mine consisting of gunpowder and metal inside a Coke can. When it was destroyed, the explosion caused a secondary explosion of a larger mine buried next to it.

The following day Delta's PFC Michael Stachowiak triggered a pressure-release mine near Van Thien (1). His squad had been on a day ambush the previous day, then a night patrol led by their squad leader, Dave Morton. Stachowiak, wearing a flak jacket, volunteered to walk point the next day because he had been in the area before. He followed the imprinted marks made by the treads of an armored personnel carrier. Morton walked behind him. Suddenly a giant blast threw Stachowiak ten feet to the left and threw Morton to the ground. Morton, covered with dirt and the smell of explosives, slowly got on his feet and gingerly moved to his point man. The blast had thrown Stachowiak on a blue cactus. Both his legs were sheared off above the knees, and his right arm was coal black, just attached to his body by a chunk of flesh. Shrapnel covered his entire body and his right eye was gone.

Morton called for a dustoff, but after seeing a resupply Huey flying nearby he called the bird to pick up his comrade. Time was critical. Morton noticed the explosion had cauterized both of Stachowiak's legs which provided some relief from the impossible task he faced. Any bleeding would have been impossible to stop and he would have had to watch his comrade bleed to death. Stachowiak was loaded on the resupply chopper, his lifeless arm folded over his body. The blast at the soldier's feet created a crater three feet across and two and one-half feet deep. Stachowiak survived. SP/4 Oscar Connell was also dusted off with serious injuries.

On February 23, Delta's 1st Platoon found three well-constructed tunnels only three-quarters of a mile west of Delta's company headquarters at Phu Vinh, but north of the Ham Giang River which was the boundary line for AO Serene. One tunnel measured two and one-half feet high and wide, and contained at its terminus a five foot by five foot room reinforced with sheet metal and bamboo. The tunnels were destroyed. Helicopters providing aerial reconnaissance spotted newly-constructed tunnels throughout the large coastal plain from Chu Lai to Quang Ngai, a sign of recently prepared positions for fresh troops to infiltrate into the area. Intelligence reports indicated the K-51 VC Local Force Company (strength of forty-two) had moved into the area near CAP 133 to join the 95A Sapper Company (now estimated at thirty-five Vietcong) and P31 Local Force Company (estimated at thirty-four Vietcong) who were positioned farther south of CAP 133.

At noon on February 24, Alpha and Bravo Company air assaulted to assigned sectors three to five miles north of Delta's assigned area of operations to search and clear this area of any enemy. The platoon-sized air assaults to different locations once again paid dividends. Two hours after landing, Bravo found six-60mm mortar shells attached to a pole for transporting, the ammo's two transporters having fled shortly before. At 3:30PM, Alpha's 3rd Platoon saw twenty-five Vietcong evading but out of range for their M-16 rifles. Artillery and gunships were called. A helicopter observed one female evading and flew in to snatch her as she threw an object into a tree line. She was taken to Alpha's 3rd Platoon location. A second female was snatched twenty minutes later by the same bird, after which the chopper spotted four hastily abandoned military packs.

The following day Bravo found some camouflaged hooch's containing stretchers and medical supplies. Alpha was kept busy finding mines made with mortar shells rigged to detonation devices. Intelligence reports indicated that eighty Vietcong and NVA were now in the same area being searched by Alpha and Bravo. They were coordinating an attack on the Van Tuong hamlets south of CAP 135.

On February 26, Bravo's 3rd Platoon discovered three hooch's in densely-covered low-lying hills two miles southeast of Tam Hoi (1). Two dwellings were twenty feet by forty feet in size and contained beds. A third hooch, measuring twenty feet by ten feet, contained benches, chairs and a stage. The discovery sent chills into the hardened bodies of the soldiers. Clearly another buildup of the enemy was underway. Alpha's 3rd Platoon shot one evading Vietcong who was carrying Ak-47 ammunition. A diary found on his body was sent to LZ Gator for translation.

As Charlie Company continued efforts to improve the bunker line at LZ Gator more intelligence reports indicated an impending attack on Gator was certain. Three elements were forming for a ground assault. One company (estimated size of forty soldiers) from the VC 406th Battalion was forming two miles northwest of Gator. Another battalion of one hundred and fifty was located two miles southeast of the LZ and a third element of sappers was located four miles south of Gator on the north side of the Tra Bong River.

At noon on February 27, Bravo Company was lifted out by chopper and deposited near Van Thien (2) in Delta Company's zone to assist in the accelerated pacification efforts by creating another pacified hamlet. That evening the enemy welcomed Bravo to the area with mortar fire which wounded three soldiers. Bravo built an extensive bunker system around their hamlet in just a few days.

It was clear to Bravo's soldiers that Delta's AO Serene was anything but "serene". Its 3rd Platoon discovered a mine and destroyed it, the blast leaving a crater three feet by two feet wide. It was at least one mine that would not rob a Bravo soldier of arms and legs. Later in the afternoon Bravo was hit with six 82mm mortar rounds and small arms fire, but luckily suffered no casualties. Delta spotted five VC fleeing in their zone, and killed one while capturing some documents.

Alpha continued its search and clear operations farther north in the area of the Lac Son hamlets, spotting fleeing NVA who were out of range of their M-16's. On March 1, Alpha found and destroyed a 105mm Howitzer round booby trapped near Lac Son (1). Tell tale signs told of an increased enemy presence. The 3rd Platoon found a carefully prepared .51 caliber machinegun position near what appeared to be an animal pen. They detained military-age males and females nearby with no identification. One of the captives divulged her husband had been a Vietcong for sixteen years and had walked to North Vietnam for specialized training. She remained in the area to support the local VC.

Charlie Company strengthened the bunker line on Gator. One squad was dispatched to Tri Binh (1) north of Gator to assist the local PF's in the hamlet's defense. At 9:00PM the hamlet was hit with small arms fire and grenades and the soldiers called for support from Gator's 81mm Mortars. Two soldiers were wounded but the squad kept the attackers at bay. A sweep of the area the next day revealed four blood-trails leading west. A day later they found a detailed map with a plan of attack on the hamlet. The Popular Force militia working with Charlie's grunts insisted another attack would come to the hamlet on March 3 to correspond to a simultaneous attack on LZ Gator.

The same night Tri Binh (1) was hit at 2:20AM, Bravo received incoming mortar fire on their night position which wounded six soldiers who were dusted off in the dark. At first light Alpha's 1st Platoon near the Lac Son hamlets swept an area believed to be a enemy mortar position and found bunkers and six "Molotov Cocktails". They were constructed from glass jars with a flammable liquid and a rag fuse. Later they captured three Vietcong, one of whom was wounded.

At first light on March 2, Alpha Company air assaulted to the area around Nghiem Quong (1), approximately two miles north of

Pinkville. The company landed its three rifle platoons at separate locations surrounding the hamlet, with the mission to search and clear the area. One of the birds observed three of the enemy fleeing into the ville. Another lift bird received small arms fire as it offloaded its troops south of the hamlet. Alpha's 2nd Platoon moved in to block the north side of the ville and engage any enemy that tried to escape.

PFC Richard Gould was a "Fucking New Guy" (FNG), but a soldier who picked things up quickly, took the point as they moved in to block exit routes. The file of soldiers moved forward cautiously to a junction where three trails met in a small opening at the hamlets edge. The quiet was suddenly broken by a large blast. The point element saw Gould go down as the blasts' concussion stunned everyone nearby. The soldiers froze as the scream for "Medic!" filled the air. PFC Earl "Doc" Brannon, the platoon's medic moved up the file to attend to Gould. Someone said, "Be careful Doc" to which he merely replied, "Sure". A minute later another large blast filled the air and Brannon went down. Sergeant Jim Pene, a squad leader, moved forward on his own, shouting at the others to remain in place. He then realized that they were in a mine field.

Pene found Brannon covered with dirt and shrapnel. His right leg was gone above the knee and his left leg ended just below the knee with a jagged bone protruding out like a dagger. Attached to the bone was a strip of flesh that ran to a booted foot lying on its side near the edge of the trail. In dire condition, Doc held up his right hand to say something. His index and middle fingers flopped backward over the top of his wrist. He looked at Pene and nodded his head towards Gould, "Help him". Gould was also covered with dirt but appeared to Pene to be less critical.

Pene, who had substantial first aid training as a civilian, went to work. He ordered the nearest soldiers to move out of the mined area, not sure where other mines were, and to get more bandages. Pene assumed the chore of bandaging the two soldiers himself. There was no adequate way to carry their shattered bodies so he ordered his men to stay in place and guard the wounded while he backed out to find poles to use as improvised litters with their flak jackets.

Once the crude litters were ready he guided his men back in to pick up the wounded. Lieutenant Colonel Snyder's Command and Control helicopter hovered nearby. As they picked up Brannon to carry him to the hastily arranged LZ, Brannon let out a scream about his foot. The strip of flesh running from above his knee to the top of his boot was stretched out about a yard and the boot was dragging on the ground. The foot was placed between the remaining parts of his legs. Pene looked at Gould on his litter and saw the leg that had been covered with dirt was now exposed. Bare bone was exposed from the hip down. His foot was gone.

The battalion commander's bird settled to the ground to pick up the casualties. The Executive Officer (XO), a Major, was also on board. Brannon was lifted up first. Because they needed more space for Gould, the XO moved Brannon's litter over. Doc's lone foot, still in the boot, didn't move with the litter. It rolled off to the middle of the floor. The Major bent to move it then hesitated, and growled at Pene, "Get in here and move that!"

Pene was filled with anger over the Major's reluctance to help but jumped in and moved the foot. He looked at Brannon's face, whose eyes started rolling in their sockets with his hands raised up and twitching. Pene slapped him in the face, "Doc! Don't do that! Don't go to sleep! Stay awake until you get to the rear!" Brannon weakly replied with one word, "Okay".

Brannon and Gould made it to the Chu Lai hospital and survived their wounds. Once the Huey lifted off to take them to the hospital, Pene looked at his own situation. He was covered in blood, and his flak jacket was pitted with shrapnel. He had been carrying a Light Anti-Tank Weapon (LAW) on his back. It too was pitted with shrapnel from the mines but the LAW had not exploded. After returning to the grassy hill where they landed previously, Pene dropped his pants for his buddy to see if he had any wounds in "critical areas". His buddy slapped him on his back, "No, no man you're Okay!" and walked away. For his valor Sergeant Jim Pene was awarded the Silver Star.

Later, Alpha's 1st Platoon found and destroyed a buried 105mm Howitzer round set to explode by trip wire. Shortly after, they received small arms fire from a small group of Vietcong. The 1st Platoon of H Troop, 17th Cavalry, operating close by, was called to link up with them for added fire power. At noon on March 3 a platoon leader, Second Lieutenant Russell Becker, stepped on a booby-trapped M79 grenade that was inside his small field perimeter, wounding himself and three others near Phu My (2).

Alpha's 3rd Platoon patrolled one mile west of Becker's platoon, in the eastern shadow of the same hilltop that served as LZ South during Operation Russell Beach in January 1969. The abandoned hamlet of Truong Son (1) was still at the base of the hill. During the Russell Beach

Operation enemy fire from the hamlet hit the soldiers on the LZ. A truck with Quad 50's (four synchronized 50 caliber machineguns) had backed up to the edge of the hilltop and leveled the village with thousands of rounds. Now Alpha's 3rd Platoon was back patrolling the same area.

Periodically the patrol halted, with each squad walking in a loop, searching an assigned portion of a larger platoon cloverleaf pattern, then returning to their starting point. One squad of thirteen soldiers was halfway through its section of the cloverleaf when they walked into a L-shaped ambush. Heavy fire from a nearby hedgerow drove the men to the ground. The enemy's bullets sought out their prone bodies, kicking dirt into the eyes of the grunts and offered death to anyone who moved an inch. Immediately three men were wounded but no one dared to move.

The armored personnel carriers of the 2nd Platoon, H-Troop were alerted and moved quickly over barren rice paddies on line, side by side in attack formation. They understood the enemy's capability to disable their tracks with rocket propelled grenades (RPG's) and the attack formation was their only chance to offer more death than the enemy could deliver. Their M-60 and 50 caliber machineguns blasted away at the hedgerow as they moved in, but the movement of the tracks made it difficult to keep their firepower directed on the hedgerow and not on Alpha's soldiers. With Alpha's soldiers barely separated from the hedgerow, friendly fire would be the price for their rescue. One round from the tracks hit SP/4 Daniel Aguilera in the chest, killing him instantly. SP/4 Aguilera was 20 and single, from Cutler, California. The rest of the squad was rescued. It was a costly day for Alpha, seven wounded and one killed in action.

The next day, March 4, Charlie Company air assaulted to the An Thinh and Phu Nhieu hamlets, two and one-half miles up the coast from the Batangan, where enemy activity had been reported. That night CAP 144 on the An Ky Peninsula was attacked, forcing Charlie to move back to the Batangan, near Dong Xuan (3). When Charlie arrived, the soldiers encountered small pockets of fleeing Vietcong. They also found salt caches and enemy tunnels.

Alpha Company, its ranks depleted from numerous firefights and mines, moved to LZ Gator to take up its defense on the bunker line. At 5:10AM the field-savvy grunts heard movement and the sound of wire being cut on the north side of Gator's perimeter. They opened fire and

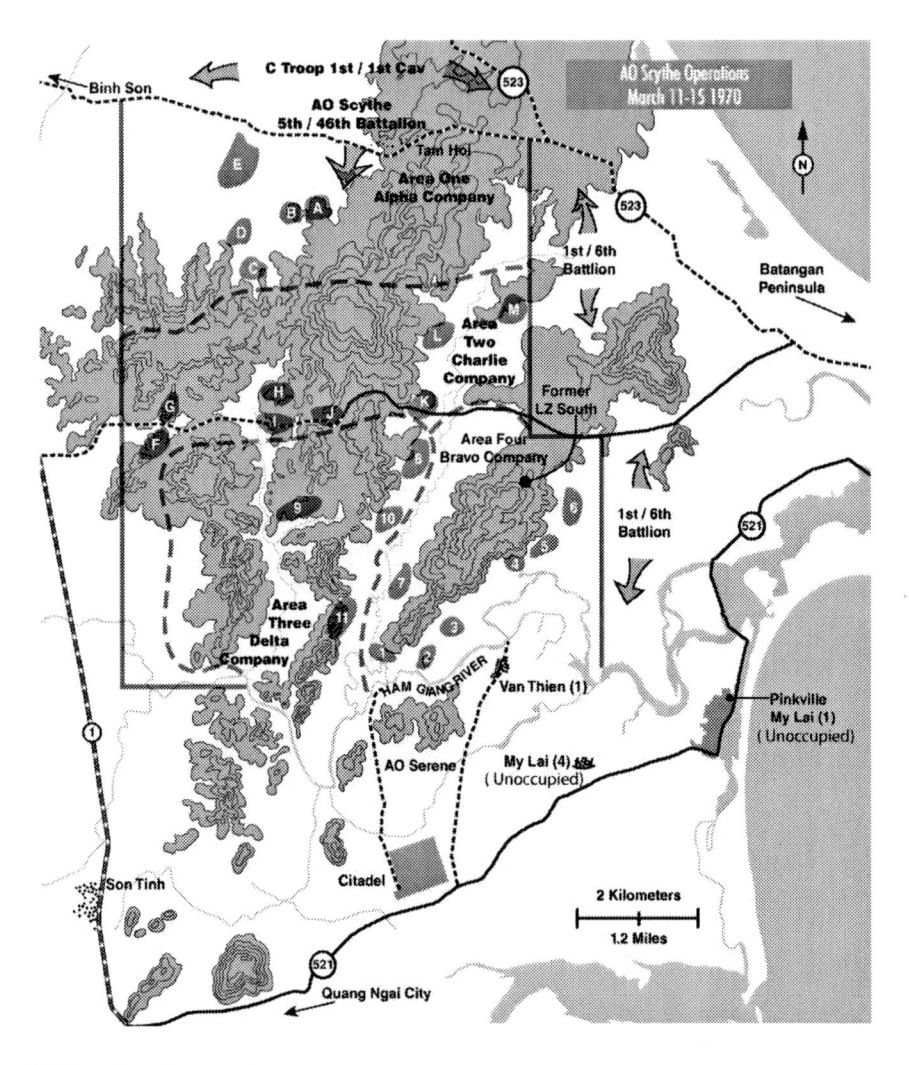

AO Scythe Operations

observed two Vietcong slipping away. A patrol at first light revealed three strands of concertina wire had been cut. The enemy was making advance preparations for a sapper attack.

By March 7 Charlie's platoons expanded their patrol area beyond Dong Xuan (3) and found caches of rice, corn, and potatoes and detained women, children and twenty-two military-aged males, all of whom were sent to the district town of Binh Son. In addition to enemy mines and ambushes, Charlie's grunts encountered another attack, this time by a villager's water buffalo that resented the soldier's intrusion onto his field. The cow charged the patrol head-on but the grunts were too laden with heavy packs to get out of the way of the attacking animal and shot it in self-defense. The battalion's civil affairs officer reimbursed the peasant for his loss.

Intelligence reports continued to point to a buildup of forces in the battalion's area of operations east and west of Highway One. What lent additional credence to the reports was the increase of Chieu Hoi's, both Vietcong and some NVA, who voluntarily surrendered from a "life on the run" rather than face American firepower in the coming attacks. By this point the 48th Vietcong Local Force Battalion was largely finished as a fighting force using insurgents from the area, but the unit was kept in tact through the continued reinforcement of NVA from the mountains.

The Battalion's Last Coastal Sweep

To keep the enemy off balance the 198th Infantry Brigade issued a Fragmentary Order ("Frag Order") #5-70 to Operation Nantucket Beach, to be effective March 11. It called for all four rifle companies of the 5th/46th Infantry Battalion to converge on an area designated as "AO Scythe". This rough terrain had been nominally swept by the ARVN in January, but intelligence continued to point to enemy activity in the area.

AO Scythe's northern boundary was the district road running west to east just south of the Tam Hoi hamlets. C Troop, 1st/1st Cav would screen the area north of the boundary line, with help from the battalion's recon platoon. The eastern boundary was a north to south line approximately four miles west of the Batangan. Elements of the 1st/6th Infantry Battalion were tasked to patrol east of this boundary to halt enemy movement to the coast. The southern boundary was the Ham Giang River, south of which was Delta's Company's AO Serene. The western boundary was a north to south line (Longitude 64 on tactical maps) roughly one mile east of Highway One.

Alpha Company moved from LZ Gator to search and clear the northern sector of AO Scythe, designated "Area One" with five specific search objectives (A thru E) based on intelligence reports of likely enemy positions.

Charlie Company was to cover "Area Two", the center sector, to sweep eight objectives (F thru M) with particular emphasis on searching the area around the remote Buddhist Monastery.

Delta left one squad in each of its pacified hamlets and crossed the Ham Giang River to search out the rough terrain in "Area Three" where Vietcong moved with impunity while planning attacks on the pacified areas. Delta had four objectives (8 thru 11), most of which were in densely wooded areas.

Bravo Company left one platoon in Van Thien (1) as bulldozers continued clearing the area to create a pacified hamlet. The rest of the company moved north across the Ham Giang River. Its mission was to move on two axes and sweep through seven objectives (1 thru 7).

On March 11 Bravo Company encountered harassing small arms fire near Objective 4 throughout the day. They located a mine near Objective 5. Delta's foray north of the Ham Giang River uncovered five tunnels near objective 11. Further north near Objective 10, six Vietcong were spotted with AK-47's. The distance to the enemy targets was too far for Delta's weapons, and artillery fire was called. No bodies were found but a Delta soldier later shot a Vietcong with his M-14 sniper rifle.

Charlie Company likewise discovered seven tunnels by Objective J. Two of the tunnel entrances were booby-trapped. The tunnels led to underground bunkers measuring six feet in height and five feet in length and width. One bunker was steel reinforced as a defense against air strikes. Nearby were five concealed hooch's with temporary sleeping quarters prepared for enemy soldiers on the move.

The following day Charlie's 4th Squad, 2nd Platoon, ambushed a group of ten VC at Objective I in the pre-dawn hours. One Vietcong was found dead with blood trails leading away. Other Charlie Company soldiers found two empty tunnels near Objective M that contained ten-foot long corridors.

Alpha Company found three military-aged males walking with no identification and located two artillery rounds: a 155mm Howitzer round set for command detonation and a 105mm Howitzer round set to detonate by a pressure release device. Both mines were located near Objective E, cleverly planted under the imprints of tracks made by armored personnel carriers that had recently passed through. An unexploded 8-inch artillery round was found nearby. It apparently had not yet been found by the enemy or was considered too dangerous to handle.

Bravo Company was hit by small arms fire from two or three Vietcong just north of the Ham Giang River. It was a small skirmish but enough to cause irreparable harm. Two soldiers, PFC's Ozzie Moheit and Richard Durant were wounded but Durant did not survive his wounds. He was age twenty and married from Vernon, New York. Small arms fire continued to plague the soldiers throughout the day.

March 13 saw Alpha Company locate another unexploded 105mm artillery round near the district road leading from Binh Son. Alpha's 1st Platoon spotted six VC with field packs one and one-quarter mile away along the eastern boundary of AO Scythe and called in artillery fire. A sweep of the area yielded two boys, aged fifteen and eighteen. Two others managed to escape. The young enemy solders were carrying blasting caps, one pound of C-4 explosive and an empty casing from a 105mm Howitzer round. The platoon later found a tunnel and opened fire on three fleeing Vietcong. A homemade backpack was found near two blood trails.

Delta Company detained seven females, aged fifteen to twenty-four, who had been forced to carry rice for the Vietcong. They were evacuated to LZ Bayonet. Charlie Company located and destroyed four tunnels and found a Vietnamese male who claimed he was shot by a helicopter gunship. He was evacuated to a hospital. While moving to a night ambush, Charlie's 1st Platoon fired on four fleeing VC, killing one and retrieving his backpack.

The next day yielded more of the same. Alpha encountered small groups of Vietnamese who quickly evaded their small arms fire. Sweeps of the area revealed dropped equipment, such as backpacks, medical kits and clothing. Bravo detained Vietnamese males with no identification and sent them in for interrogation. Delta spotted two females in the distance who chose to run after Delta's Kit Carson Scout told them to stop. Delta opened fire and wounded both and they were evacuated to Chu Lai.

Two Chieu Hoi's walked into CAP 142 and one, worn down from his daily escapes from death, became very talkative. He told the Marines that one hundred NVA had passed though Liem Quang (1) with a mission to attack the New Life Hamlets which were protected by the Marine CAP's, once the moonlight was reduced to near zero. He added the NVA habitually split into smaller groups and headed for hilly and dense high ground whenever the soldiers of the 5th/46th swept through their area. The talkative Vietcong had been tasked to carry rice and collect taxes. He had a wife and four small children. Two older children, a son and daughter, worked with the 48th Vietcong Battalion. He had not seen them since July 1969 and did not now if they were alive or dead.

Charlie Company finished its sweep and clear mission and walked back to LZ Dottie near Highway One to be picked up and sent back to LZ Gator for bunker line duty. By late afternoon Bravo Company moved back to the Van Thien pacification area but with its 3rd Platoon assigned to Phu Vinh. Along the way Bravo's soldiers found a dud 155mm Howitzer round stripped of its contents for the enemy to make another mine. North of AO Scythe's boundary the Marines in CAP 133 noticed increased sightings of enemy soldiers driven out from the battalion's search and sweep area. One group of VC was setting up a mortar position. The Marines called in artillery fire and swept the area. Their concise radio report back to LZ Gator noted, "Swept the area, found one hand, one leg, one arm and a multitude of intestines. Estimate two VC KIA."

The sweep of AO Scythe was largely concluded on March 15, but Delta Company continued to search the southern sector of the AO, covering areas three and four, with help from the battalion's recon platoon which searched an area northwest of Delta near the former LZ South. Alpha continued its sweep in the northern half of AO Scythe, capturing a Vietcong Nurse, age thirty-five, who was laden with medical supplies. Alpha was finally picked up by Hueys on March 17 and air-assaulted to the Phu Long Hamlets south of CAP 133.

Thirty minutes after midnight on the morning of March 17, a Delta ambush received small arms from two to three Vietcong. Although it was a small and brief skirmish the enemy took blood, shooting PFC Robert Wayne Culver in the head, killing him instantly. Culver was twenty-one years of age and married from Eureka, Louisiana.

Bravo Company's 2nd Platoon found a pressure release booby-trapped 81mm mortar round one-eight mile from the Van Thien hamlet it were protecting. The enemy continued to respond to the establishment of this pacified hamlet by Bravo Company. That night six B-40 rounds were fired into Bravo's night perimeter but no one was injured.

Farther north near CAP 133 two Popular Force (PF) soldiers from PF Company 197, operating near Alpha Company, hit a booby-trapped 81mm mortar round, seriously wounding both. Vietnamese villagers nearby took some Alpha soldiers to a hooch where the Vietcong had dropped off one of its own soldiers, a female, who had a high fever. The soldiers had her evacuated to the 91st Evacuation Hospital in Chu Lai.

March 18 yielded much of the same shoot and run activity from a dispersed enemy. Vietnamese irregular forces such as PF's and RF's were favorite targets for this enemy on the run. Regional Force (RF) Company 933, the company of Montagnards quartered on the northeast corner of the Citadel, was attacked by a company from the 48th VC Battalion (mostly filled by NVA). The attack began as always with a heavy barrage of forty-81mm mortar rounds, followed up with a ground assault. One RF was killed along with two Montagnard babies, the tribesmen having brought their families with them into their base camp, as was their custom. Ten RF's were wounded. Rapid artillery defensive fire was brought to bear which quickly broke up the attack, killing six enemy with many blood trails marking their escape routes.

Amidst this activity the battalion's soldiers were quickly approaching their final days on the large coastal plain from Chu Lai to Quang Ngai. The clear and sweep operation in AO Scythe marked the last major operation it would undertake in the mine-infested coastal area, an area that had severely tested the battalion since it's arrival at LZ Gator in March 1968, two years earlier.

Responsibility for this area was to be shifted to the 1st/6th Infantry Battalion and the ARVN. The 5th/46th Battalion's officers were told informally on LZ Gator their mission had been accomplished on the coastal plain. It was now time for the ARVN to take over the sweeps under the plans of Operation Nantucket Beach and the PF's and RF's to assume responsibility for protecting the New Life Hamlets. The 1st/6th would also sweep the area but had primary responsibility to secure a major land-clearing project by engineers to deprive the enemy of much of its cover and concealment.

LZ Gator was being dismantled and the 5th/46th Battalion was to relocate its headquarters to Chu Lai. The 5th/46th was ordered to shift its operations north and west of LZ Bayonet and Chu Lai, to protect the Americal Division's base from attack, and accelerate the areas pacification, and to transfer the security of hamlets to the RF and PF militias. The pacification mission would be accomplished largely by search and sweeps in an increasingly larger area moving west from Chu Lai, with RF and PF militia's protecting the pacified hamlets in their wake.

A rumor also floated among the battalion's staff that the 1st/6th Battalion, whose area the 5th/46th was taking over, had some problems and was being relocated to the coastal plain to work out its "issues". The critical Chu Lai defense mission was now in the hands of the 5th/46th Battalion. In short order the battalion would learn that the 1st/6th Battalion Commander had located his first command post on the beach north of CAP 142, a well-known heavily mined area, and that they took many casualties. The 5th/46th Battalions officers collectively wondered, "Didn't they learn anything from us?"

Bravo Company was lifted out of its pacification area and returned to LZ Gator while Charlie left Gator to briefly replace Bravo in AO Serene. Echo Company's Recon Platoon, operating near the former LZ South, was plagued by fleeing VC it couldn't engage because they were fast on their feet by dropping equipment to lighten their loads. The Recon soldiers managed to capture one Vietcong with his backpack. That evening a recon soldier triggered an enemy trip flare, which invited two mortar rounds to be fired on its position, but it drew no casualties.

The next day Lieutenant General Hoang Manh Dang, the South Vietnamese Army (ARVN) Commander for I Corps, reported the day had been designated by the Communists as National Anti-American day. Major attacks were to be focused on ARVN units who were "puppets" of the Americans.

Alpha Company ended its sweep and clear operations near CAP 133 and moved to LZ Dottie on March 20. The next day it air assaulted west of Binh Son, into the area controlled by CAP 138, where NVA were reportedly preparing for an attack on the district town. In short order the 4th Squad of Alpha's 2nd Platoon spotted four NVA in uniform and one Vietcong at a distance of four hundred yards and opened fire. The

NVA evaded but the VC soldier, a female, was captured. She was a member of the 48th VC Battalion tasked to escort NVA soldiers moving in small groups back into the mountains; the pressure from the 5th/46th on the coast had drawn too many casualties.

Delta was also pulled out of its search and clear mission, returned to LZ Dottie and on March 22 moved by vehicle to LZ Fat City, just north of Chu Lai for a search and clear mission in the northern rocket pocket. Its challenging pacification mission in AO Serene was over. The Popular Force militia was now to operate by themselves and complete the hamlet protection mission with primary support from the ARVN.

Delta had performed its accelerated pacification mission well considering the many constraints it faced, not the least was the hurried time frame for completion, brought about by the generals and their planners from the MAVC in Saigon down to the Americal Division, who waited far too long to seriously pursue the pacification strategy in the contentious coastal area.

Further west, Alpha was kept busy with gunfights against pockets of NVA west of Binh Son. In one brief episode, Alpha's 1st Platoon spotted four NVA carrying a .30 caliber machinegun and three Ak-47 assault rifles. The enemy got off the first shots with one round hitting a hand grenade carried by the Alpha point man. It did not explode. The enemy melted away.

When Delta pulled out to LZ Dottie, Charlie Company was also pulled out from AO Serene and its pacification duties and moved north to Hill 76, a low-lying hill seven miles due west of the massive base at Chu Lai. Its mission was the same as Delta's, to search and clear its portion of the northern rocket pocket to prevent enemy infiltration towards Chu Lai and to keep enemy rockets from being fired on the base. An NVA battalion was also reported to be in the area.

One platoon from Bravo Company was pulled off LZ Gator and sent to LZ Fat City to help in its defense to free up more of Delta's soldiers to patrol the terrain around it. Echo's Recon Platoon was tasked to insert by helicopter seven miles west of Chu Lai, into the mountains, to search for rocket caches and evidence of the NVA battalion.

By March 26, 1970 the 5th/46th Infantry Battalion had officially decoupled itself from pacification duties in AO Serene and the search and sweep operations throughout the large coastal plain from Chu Lai south to Quang Ngai City, including the notorious Batangan Peninsula.

The battalion re-established its headquarters on "LZ Beach" on March 23, inside the massive Chu Lai base approximately one and one-half miles south of the Americal Divisions headquarters. The move to relocate the battalion from LZ Gator to Chu Lai was almost complete. LZ Gator was to be turned over to the ARVN, if they wanted it.

Charlie Company, searching its sector of the northern rocket pocket discovered some rockets, but found its share of mines and booby-traps as well. On March 27, it located an 81mm Vietcong mortar round and a 155mm Howitzer round; both were rigged with pressure release devices. One soldier stepped on an anti-personnel mine. Charlie's 3rd Platoon found two Army combat boots near a crater from a previous mine explosion. The crater sat alongside an unimproved dirt road which served as Provincial Route 532.

Alpha Company had moved north from the Binh Son/CAP 138 area to search and clear an area seven miles west of LZ Gator. One day later it moved another two miles farther west into the mountains. The battalion's recon platoon was positioned farther west of Alpha, both units intent on locating the NVA who were reportedly gathering for an attack on LZ Gator. In the dense mountainous terrain Alpha found three 55-gallon drums of CS (riot control) gas, sitting under a tree.

On March 29, Alpha Company moved east into the southern rocket pocket and found an unexploded 105mm Howitzer round. The month ended with Bravo Company splitting its forces, continuing its security mission to hold what remained of LZ Gator and protecting LZ Fat City. Charlie Company patrolled its slice of the northern rocket pocket in the vicinity of Hill 76, while Delta conducted patrols near Hill 54. The battalion recon platoon continued its security patrols to the south and west of Alpha.

The 48th Local Force Vietcong Battalion, beaten down in men and material, had been kept on a lifeline with NVA replacements and supplies flowing through the Annamite Mountains into Quang Ngai Province. That infiltration also included the resources to attack LZ Gator from time to time. But the coastal sweeps of the 5th/46th Infantry Battalion and the ARVN from September 1969 to late March 1970 severely weakened the VC and the NVA who were sent to support them. As the battalions mission shifted to an area farther north and west of

Chu Lai, it would be tasked one more time to seek out the source of the NVA's infiltration to the coast. The battalion was to be sent, once again, deep into the Annamite Mountains to look for the NVA.

14 – DEATH AND DESTRUCTION

RETURN TO THE MOUNTAINS

The 5th/46th Infantry Battalion's eight month "Accelerated Pacification" on the coastal plains drew attention and resources away from another tactical challenge, the activities of the North Vietnamese Army (NVA) in the dense Annamite Mountains west of LZ Gator. The mountains provided sanctuary for enemy bases to support its infiltration into Quang Ngai Province.

The Americal Division's Headquarters and the 198th Light Infantry Brigade monitored worrisome reports of enemy activity in the mountainous region twenty miles due west of LZ Gator. In November 1969 intelligence reports indicated an enemy buildup in the mountains. Agents reported the 2nd NVA Division may have established itself there in addition to a Vietcong (VC) controlled POW camp and a VC transportation unit in the same area.

December's intelligence reports indicated a large food cache had also been established. Aerial reconnaissance flights spotted well-used trails. Some of the reconnaissance aircraft were fired on by heavy machineguns. Other aircraft spotted suspension bridges over ravines with large hooch's that were barely discernible under double canopy foliage.

In January 1970, an intelligence report indicated the presence of a NVA battalion of four hundred men with thirty laborers in the same mountainous area. By March, agents were reporting a cache of rockets had been brought down the Ho Chi Minh trail from North Vietnam as well as an additional NVA regiment which was assigned for an upcoming summer campaign in Quang Ngai Province.

With the Battalion now off the coastal plains, it was given the mission to air assault into the mountains on a three company sweep to find the enemy and destroy it. The operation was scheduled to begin the morning of April 1st at first light.

The battalion developed "Frag Order 6-70" to Operation Geneva Park as its Operations Plan, tasking Alpha, Charlie and Delta companies along with its Echo Reconnaissance Platoon for the mission. Geneva Park was established by the 198th Brigade in March 1969 to establish a common area of operations with the 6th ARVN Regiment which was tasked to eventually replace the 198th Brigade. The mission of Geneva Park included locating and destroying enemy forces attempting to attack Chu Lai or Quang Ngai City. During the current brigade push towards intensive pacification, it was the only operational order still on the books that had a "search and destroy" mission. Each rifle company would be picked up from its current patrol locations in the field and flown directly to the mountains.

Bravo Company continued its security operations with its 1st Platoon on FSB Fat City, 2nd Platoon at LZ Bayonet and the remainder securing the perimeter on LZ Gator. Although the battalion had displaced its headquarters and company areas to Chu Lai at LZ Beach, Gator was to be defended until the ARVN could take possession of the LZ.

LZ Gator always required a full rifle company on its extensive perimeter to insure reasonable protection from an attack, but the number of Bravo's soldiers sent there was much too lean for the job. Most of the original perimeter was abandoned and a smaller perimeter was established on the high point of Gator where the TOC, communications bunker and helicopter landing pads existed. Armored personnel carriers of the 1st Platoon, C Troop, 1st/1st Cav with some tanks were directed to Gator to help with its defense.

Bravo's grunts on LZ Gator were proud of what the battalion had accomplished using Gator as the base of operations for the past two years. Bravo's Mike Laughlin recalled, "We were made aware of an intelligence report that said the 5th/46th Infantry Battalion had pretty much neutralized the enemy in its area of operations on the coast. For this reason, we all felt the Dinks would try to make a statement and hit us one more time before we abandoned Gator".

The sacrifice that had been required to neutralize the enemy was made clear again on March 31 when SP/4 Oscar Connell of Delta Company succumbed to his wounds in a Chu Lai hospital. Connell had been seriously wounded from a mine in AO Serene on February 21. Oscar Allen Connell was age twenty-two and married from Montevallo, Alabama.

Control of the mountain operation now underway was placed under the battalion's Executive Officer and the forces going to the mountains were designated "Task Force Lizard." Alpha Company was assigned to air assault to some mountainous high ground designated as "LZ Hustler" and, along with engineers, a scout dog platoon and a pathfinder team, clear space to form a forward tactical operations center. Four 105mm Howitzers from Battery C, 1st/14th Artillery Battalion would be flown out to Hustler to provide direct fire support for the mission. Alpha's air assault to Hustler would be preceded by artillery fires from the large 8-inch Howitzers of Battery A, 3rd/18th Artillery Battalion located at the Tra Bong Special Forces camp some nine miles southeast of the targeted mountaintop.

Once LZ Hustler was secured, Alpha was to search the steep ridgelines around it, moving one-half mile in each direction to search for enemy movement and then secure the area. Their tactical zone was designated AO Custer. Charlie and Delta Companies with the recon platoon were tasked to air assault into "LZ Creek", a mountainous streambed two and one-half miles southwest of Hustler. Charlie and Delta were each supplemented with two scout dog teams. Once their LZ was secured they would initially search the area in two directions, Delta moving southwest about one mile (Route Red) and back to the LZ; Charlie would move northeast on Route Blue.

The enemy, of course, had other plans in mind. As the mountain operation was set in motion the enemy planned to attack pro-government hamlets near the coast because of upcoming elections in pacified areas. An added incentive for the enemy was the almost zero nighttime illumination from the moon, making night attacks ideal. The first attack came on March 31 against Tri Binh (1) north of LZ Gator. But the Regional Force (RF) platoon defending the hamlet gave as good as they got, suffering three wounded but killing two Vietcong and driving off the attack.

Operations of April-June, 1970

The artillery battery on Fire Support Base (FSB) Fat City was hit with small arms fire and hand grenades along the perimeter. Bravo's 1st Platoon responded to the attack and suffered four wounded. They later found one VC killed and another wounded. Then at 2:00AM on April 1, LZ Gator was hit by mortar fire and B-40 rockets as sappers hit selected portions of the down-sized perimeter, throwing Chinese Communist (Chicom) hand grenades into bunkers which included some gas grenades. Nine soldiers and one Vietnamese interpreter were wounded, but none seriously and the perimeter was not penetrated. It was searched at dawn. Two dead VC were found along with sixty Chicom grenades and three rocket propelled grenades (RPG's).

Despite these attacks, the three-company air assault to the mountains took place as scheduled at dawn on April 1 and by 8:14AM Alpha Company, near LZ Hustler, found an enemy training camp with mock-ups of mortar tubes and a Huey helicopter, along with Chicom grenades.

Charlie Company was inserted in the wrong spot. Adding to its quandary was the double and triple canopy jungle above them, making it almost impossible to get its bearings. Charlie's artillery forward observer (FO), Second Lieutenant Ken Teglia ordered two white phosphorus artillery rounds to be fired at fifty feet height, at different coordinates. He then "resectioned" from the exploding rounds to determine Charlie's exact position. Getting a firm fix on its beginning location would pay dividends later for close artillery support. And setting down at the wrong location would also prove fortuitous for Charlie Company. It would place them in a direction of movement leading to an NVA hospital. No enemy contact was made by any of the companies on the first day.

Just past midnight LZ Gator was hit again on the southwest portion of the perimeter with small arms fire and RPG's. One tank from the 1st/1st Cav was in the sector of the bunker line that was attacked first. Helicopters immediately lit up the sky with searchlights and the tank fired one canister round in the direction of enemy fire, a position two hundred yards away. The canister contained 1,281 spherical steel balls designed for just such an occasion. The round hit its mark and the enemy fire promptly ended. Three of the Cav's soldiers were wounded by RPG fire as enemy automatic weapons fire opened up on other sectors of the perimeter. The defenders spared no expense on munitions which prompted a nighttime emergency resupply of ammunition by helicopter. A helicopter flare ship spotted two VC in a drainage ditch by the dirt access road leading from Gator to Nuoc Mau. They were promptly eliminated.

By 2:15AM the attack was over. The soldiers on the perimeter at the point of the attack recovered seven RPG rounds, two B-40 rockets and hundreds of small arms rounds. Intelligence reports later revealed that Gator was hit by two platoons of the 95B Sapper Company which suffered three killed and four wounded. Villagers around the area said the wounded enemy attackers were carried in the night eight miles west to the hamlet of Ting Trung, nestled deep in the mountains.

Task Force Lizard continued to search for NVA in the dense mountains, encountering heavy foliage and little flat terrain. From the outset it rained every day, bringing out thousands of leeches which hung on the wet leaves and branches, dropping on the heavily laden grunts as they passed by. Their uniforms were soaked from rain and caked with mud. The steep and dense terrain offered no paths. The soldiers clawed their way up and down the mountain sides, each soldier helping the man behind him take a few steps up, before climbing the next few steps himself. Tree roots which protruded from rocky crevices were the only help the terrain offered.

Charlie Company climbed up a treacherous mountainside, made all the worse by a thin waterfall flowing down on the rocks, creating an ice-like surface. One soldier slipped and plunged ten feet, slamming onto a huge boulder. But luckily his heavy rucksack cushioned his fall. He stood up, shook it off, and gamely started the climb again.

Periodically the dense terrain opened up, making foot movement easier for a short time. But open terrain created frayed nerves because the easier movement increased the risk of being spotted and ambushed. Charlie Company was forced to take risks in this manner when tasked to be at a certain location by a certain time. On one movement Charlie walked single-file down the center of a shallow river, completely exposed and feeling it was ripe for a slaughter but the company was not attacked.

The nights were coal black. Any moonlight was completely shielded by double-canopy jungle. The jungles' inhabitants opened up in a nightly chorus; animals, birds and even insects combined into a constant high-pitched opera. Listening for enemy movement was impossible. Some nights the sky also joined in the chorus, sending a torrential downpour of rain onto the weary soldiers wrapped in their ponchos. It became worse if the infantry company could not find a relatively flat ridge to hunker down for the night. The prospect of sliding down a mountainside kept many solders awake all night. Some awoke in the morning to find their tired bodies had slid ten feet from their night position.

On its third day, Charlie moved in single file along a trail up a steep slope. Near the top, the point squad came upon five NVA soldiers and immediately fired on them. The contact brought Charlie's commander running to the front with members of his command element, including the artillery FO team. The only reward to be gained by working in such harsh terrain was killing the enemy and Charlie wanted to reward itself. Two of the NVA were cut down and four enemy field packs were discarded. The enemy soldiers were loaded with enough provisions for ten soldiers, which included bags of soybeans with the wrappers marked, "Donated by the People of America". Charlie's grunts also found a dwelling alongside a well traveled trail, an apparent enemy way station for soldiers on the move.

Sensing something important awaited them at the top of the high ground in front of them, the company moved into an attack formation and advanced side by side. One part of the advancing line spotted another NVA soldier, arriving almost on top of him before the NVA noticed their approach. Hoping to take a prisoner they shouted "Dung Lai!" ("stop!") The lone enemy bolted into the bushes, and rifle fire plunged into the bushes behind him. The soldiers cautiously approached and found him dying in the brush, shuffling around for what few minutes of life remained. They searched his body and found an ID card and a photo of his family. It appeared they had just killed an NVA doctor.

Moving farther in the direction the doctor had run, they came upon a base camp, silent and eerie, with a well-developed layout of thatched hooch's and one large dwelling measuring thirty feet long by fifteen feet wide. As Charlie's soldiers moved cautiously about the area, some decided it was a good a time to relieve themselves while they had a chance. As one soldier's urine splattered on the ground at his feet, the pee-soaked soil started to move and a camouflaged tunnel door began to open. Two soldiers next to him quickly emptied their M-16's into the tunnel entrance, and then followed up with fragmentation grenades.

A larger dwelling nearby was searched; it was an operating room. Most of the building was below ground level but extended five feet above ground for air circulation. The small hospital contained an operating room table, IV equipment, surgical tools, bandages, penicillin, syringes, litters and rubber gloves. Documents and signs described the camp as a battalion headquarters with field hospital.

Charlie Company took up their night defensive positions in the enemy camp and stayed on full alert. The terrain around them was simply too dense to create good fields of fire for defense. Charlie's commander knew if the enemy wanted to attack they could be on top of his soldiers before they knew what hit them. His only defense was accurate and timely artillery fire. He ordered his FO to register defensive artillery fires just beyond Charlie's defensive position. LT. Teglia was sure of his location but the 105mm battery on LZ Hustler refused to fire where he wanted it – citing it was just too close to Charlie's troops.

This was a life or death decision and Charlie's commander was incensed. It was just that kind of close fire support that was needed if they were attacked in the dense terrain at night. Grabbing the radio handset from his RTO, Charlie's commander raised hell with the battery, demanding they fire the mission. After giving his initials to identify himself and take full responsibility for friendly fire, the battery fired. Charlie's grunts put their heads down and sought what little cover they could find. The rounds hit where they were designed, with shrapnel whizzing over the heads of Charlie's soldiers in what the artillery calls, "Danger Close Fire."

Teglia glanced at his fellow soldiers and felt great relief with pride. Here they were, deep in the mountains where no other Americans had gone and positioned in an enemy base camp. They were ready to punish their adversaries with artillery fire to their immediate front should the enemy dare attack. These were ordinary infantry, not specially trained mountain troops. He admired their toughness and ability to adapt. This moment was a source of pride that would stay with the artillery lieutenant the rest of his life.

In the morning the camp was set on fire as the company exited, but the soldiers had no way of knowing how many of the enemy still hid underground. The tunnel network was simply too large for the weary grunts to handle. Once away from the camp Teglia called for high explosive, delayed-fuse rounds to be placed on the camp behind them. The artillery shells penetrated through the jungle canopy and hit the ground before exploding. It was Charlie Company's farewell to the enemy.

The following afternoon more evidence of the enemy's hasty departure was found. Charlie's 1st Platoon found more hooch's and tunnels with signs of recent use. Delta, one mile away, found a small base camp with twelve fighting positions and eight-foot square storage areas.

A day later at noon Charlie's point element, the 3rd Squad of the 3rd Platoon, dubbed "The Power Squad" came upon three NVA washing by the side of a steam. Before the startled enemy could run they were cut down by a heavy burst of M-16 fire. Moving closer, the soldiers found one female among the dead and surmised she may have been a nurse. The impact of fire had flung her on her back, sprawling her out with her legs apart and one knee crooked. Her left foot was completely shot off. Another burst of fire had blown her head off. The grunts glanced at her brains oozing out of her skull as they picked up her AK-47 rifle. Since she carried an assault rifle there was no remorse. They also collected two AK-47 rifles from her dead comrades.

That night Charlie set out trip flares around the bodies and established three listening posts (LP's), believing the enemy would come back for their comrades. They did. During the night the trip flares were set off and one of Charlie's LP's opened fire. But the enemy was able to escape. No bodies or blood trails were found in the morning.

Just past midnight on April 4, Alpha, defending LZ Hustler, was probed by enemy fire. At 9:00AM one Alpha soldier stepped on a Bouncing Betty mine, wounding himself and Alpha's Kit Carson Scout. An hour later Alpha was hit with six-60mm mortar rounds.

The next day Delta discovered a large thatched hooch hidden from view, with a pot of meat, enough to feed sixty men, still warm. Its occupants scattered just as the grunts approached. Outside the hooch under some straw was a pool of blood where a large animal, likely a water buffalo, had been butchered.

Charlie continued to move through its assigned area, electing on occasion to have artillery fire placed forward of its direction of movement to break up possible ambushes. One round caused a secondary explosion, giving evidence of an anti-personnel mine. The telltale signs of enemy activity kept everyone on edge. As Charlie's FO would later recall, "If you weren't scared, you weren't paying attention." That night LZ Hustler was hit with one well-placed 82mm mortar round which wounded three of Alpha's soldiers.

The 198th Brigade's perimeter at LZ Bayonet continued to be probed each night. At 1:00AM on April 6, some Bravo soldiers augmenting Bayonets defense line were manning two listening posts (LP's) when artillery was fired in front of their positions on suspected enemy movement. The guns were off their mark and five soldiers were wounded. Back in the mountains Charlie and Delta searched through the dense terrain finding few enemy but ample evidence of their presence. Hooch's and bunkers were found in small clusters and destroyed.

On April 7 Delta arrived at an area five miles southwest of LZ Hustler. Spirits were high because it was the first day of clear weather since arriving on the mountain mission. At 9:30AM, the Kit Carson Scout in the point element accompanied by three other soldiers spotted two Vietcong washing themselves. They wounded one before both scattered into the dense brush. The soldiers followed the blood trail, picking up some discarded rice, a poncho and canteen.

One hour later the same point platoon came to a streambed. Sergeant Clayton Whitcher and PFC John Kucenic had moved from the center of the platoon to the point element to keep the momentum going. They took the lead and started moving up a streambed but paused to take a breather from the intense heat and humidity. Kucenic straddled a log lying across the stream while Whitcher sat below him. The log reminded Kucenic of younger, more pleasant times when he rode horses as a youth. He asked Whitcher, "Did you ever ride a horse?" As the question left his lips a .30 caliber machinegun round slammed into his left side, knocking him into the streambed. The gunner adjusted and poured a burst of five rounds into Whitcher's chest, killing him instantly. Whitcher was twenty-two years old and single from Cuyahoga Falls, Ohio.

The enemy gun crew quickly faded into the brush as other Delta soldiers moved the short distance to pursue the enemy. Delta recovered its two comrades and evacuated them downstream for a dustoff. Artillery fire from the Howitzers on Hustler pummeled the surrounding area. Kucenic recovered from his wound and was back in the field in two weeks.

Delta's soldiers estimated they were hit by three to four NVA at that machinegun position. A search of the area further upstream revealed six bunkers which they destroyed. Later that afternoon, a helicopter searching the area was hit by ground fire which wounded the pilot and both door-gunners. It was forced to land on LZ Hustler.

On April 11 Charlie Company killed another NVA soldier and searched his backpack which contained clothes and documents. One hour later Charlie found four more backpacks hastily discarded, which contained three to four hundred bottles of penicillin, glucose, vitamins, blood expander, quinine tablets, IV sets, alcohol, sutures, peroxide, streptomycin and medical handbooks. Charlie's previous incursion into the hospital complex had caused the enemy's hospital staff to hide in the mountains with what they could carry until the Americans left. The hospital complex was destroyed along with many medical supplies. One hundred pounds of salt, corn and rice were also found and destroyed.

Smelling more pay-dirt, Charlie Company continued on. By late afternoon they found a bloody bandage thrown alongside the trail. The trail was followed, prompting an NVA soldier to jump up and evade. He bounded through the jungle while bullets seeking his body tore through the foliage. Nearby a tree had the letter "H" affixed to its trunk with an arrow pointing down the trail. Some soldiers thought they heard movement. With darkness approaching, the company decided it had advanced far enough and prepared its night position. They called for artillery fire on suspected enemy positions. That night, as in every night since their combat assault, the soldiers felt the presence of the enemy, watching and waiting for the right time to attack. Charlie Company reduced its vulnerability by a fire mission on its planned defensive targets, serving notice to the NVA the heavy price it would pay for a night attack.

The mountain mission was wearing down the soldiers. The next day Alpha evacuated nine of its soldiers on LZ Hustler with heat stroke. Alpha then moved southeast off the LZ to search and clear an area that had not been patrolled. Delta Company was picked up by Huey and dropped at LZ Hustler to defend the mountaintop while Alpha moved east. There was a threat of another enemy attack on FSB Fat City, and Echo Company's Reconnaissance Platoon was redeployed to help secure the firebase.

The following morning Charlie moved cautiously down the trail previously marked by the enemy, and engaged three evading Vietcong who left an AK-47 behind. The trail led to another small camp of seven hooch's with bunkers under each, measuring eight feet-square.

That day, April 12, saw the end of Bravo Company's bunker line duty on LZ Gator. Gator was abandoned; there would be no American presence for the rest of the war. The firebase had been offered to the ARVN, PF's and RF's if they wanted to maintain a presence there. But the site was simply too large and required too much manpower to be of use for any unit other than an American battalion. What was not taken to Chu Lai by the battalion in terms of lumber, corrugated metal, etc, was promptly stripped by the local militia.

Bravo Company was transferred nine miles west of Chu Lai into the Ky Thanh area, composed of the Phuoc Khach and Thon Hoi hamlets, in a valley surrounded by mountainous terrain. Its mission was to search and clear the area to prevent a build-up of enemy forces trying to reach the pacified hamlets further east in the Ly Tin District. The rest of the battalion remained with Task Force Lizard.

Out on LZ Hustler, duty on the mountaintop was still not without risk. Delta's PFC Thomas Olsen stepped on an M-14 mine which blew off his left foot. The next day the Delta defenders received three enemy mortar rounds which landed inside the perimeter. The enemy probed the perimeter at night, setting off trip flares but escaped into the dark. Artillery fire was called beyond the perimeter on pre-selected defensive targets. The following morning Delta's troops found one dead NVA soldier beyond the perimeter with documents linking him to the 14th Company of the 3rd Battalion, 3rd NVA Regiment, which arrived in South Vietnam in December 1968.

The mountain search and clear operation did not yield more discoveries, just harassing fire from an elusive enemy. So, late in the afternoon of April 14, Alpha was picked up and flown to the northern rocket pocket near Thanh My Trung (2), three miles west of Chu Lai. The 2nd Platoon of H Troop, 17th Cav was sent to support them. Alpha's 2nd Platoon was sent to Thanh Tra (3), three miles west of the abandoned LZ Gator where enemy activity was reported.

The following day Alpha moved to Chu Lai to rest and refit (standdown). Delta, still harassed by enemy fire on LZ Hustler, received three 60mm mortar rounds which exploded inside their perimeter that night, wounding three soldiers. The perimeter opened fire to blunt a ground attack which usually followed the enemy's mortar fire. Delta also called in artillery fire from the large 8-inch Howitzers at the Tra Bong Special Forces camp. The first round was on target, so a second round was requested. But a hydraulic hose broke on the trail of the gun, causing the tube to elevate and overshoot its target, hitting Delta's Sergeant William Brill with shrapnel to his back. Brill was dusted off from the mountaintop perimeter. An early morning sweep beyond Hustlers perimeter revealed NVA equipment, documents and numerous blood trails leading to the north.

The Vietcong continued to exert pressure on the pacified hamlets near Chu Lai. The PF platoon at Tri Binh (1) engaged an enemy force while on patrol just west of the hamlet. After an exchange of intense small arms fire seven Vietcong bodies were found with an M-60 machinegun.

The morning of April 18 saw Charlie Company finally lifted out of the mountain operation and sent to Chu Lai for a standdown. Echo's Recon platoon was sent to Chu Lai for the same purpose. Alpha's 1st Platoon took over security duties on Fire Support Base (FSB) Fat City with the balance of Alpha searching and clearing the area one and one-half miles west of that LZ. Bravo searched and cleared the mountainous area six miles west of the base while Delta remained on LZ Hustler, enduring nightly probes from the shadowy enemy as the artillery position was slowly dismantled.

The enemy was intent on attacking the coastal plains to obtain rice from the April harvest and disrupt local elections. One intelligence report from the I Corps, which was passed to the battalion, indicated the VC were having problems obtaining enough rice to feed main force NVA units hiding in Laos and Cambodia. The Vietcong in the hamlet infrastructure's were ordered to infiltrate rice storage centers in pacified areas and move the rice to intermediate storage stations, termed by the enemy as "Economic Financial Installations". The rice would then be transported by night to the mountains.

On April 20 Delta was lifted off LZ Hustler, the mountain operation now officially concluded, and given the mission to search and clear for enemy around FSB Fat City after resting and refitting in Chu Lai. Bravo Company continued its search and clear operations in a two and one-half mile square area located in a valley bounded by hilly terrain which overlooked the Ky Thanh area. Included in this area were the hamlets of Phuoc Khach, Thon Hai (1) and (2) and Trung Tin, nestled among a network of dirt roads nine miles northwest of Chu Lai. The valley marked the western boundary of the battalion's area of operation, the "Chu Lai Defense Area".

Bravo had numerous "shoot and run" enemy contacts with both NVA and Vietcong, but no major contact was made. One such contact on April 21 occurred near a streambed one-half mile west of Phuoc Khach. SSG Carl Bauer was on the point of his patrol when he was hit in the head by a burst of fire which killed him instantly. His patrol reacted immediately but the enemy melted away. The patrol returned his body to Bravo's main perimeter to wait for a dustoff, and they covered him in a poncho liner. He lay with his comrades for several hours before a Medevac could pick him up. Medevac priority had to be given to soldiers more seriously injured, but alive, rather than to the deceased. By the time the Medevac arrived the blood from his head wound had soaked through the liner. Bauer's comrades gave him homage with silence and reflection. Carl Bauer was twenty-three years of age and single from Rock Island, Illinois.

After a rest and refitting in Chu Lai, Charlie Company was sent eight miles south to an area west of CAP 138, which served as the enemy's western "Avenue of Approach" to attacking Binh Son. One of the Vietcong's "Economic Financial Installations" was reported to be in the area. This was an underground tunnel system, reportedly defended by one hundred and fifty Vietcong.

Echo Company's Reconnaissance Platoon finished its rest in Chu Lai and was sent to search and clear the southern rocket pocket. Delta also completed its refitting in Chu Lai and was sent to secure a line of observation posts (OP's) on the perimeter of LZ Bayonet. Delta's 2nd Platoon and Alpha's 1st and 3rd Platoons were sent in support of the 1st/1st Armored Cavalry in their sweep operations.

Bravo Company came into Chu Lai for rest and refitting on April 24. The standdowns in Chu Lai were much needed periods of rest. The first order of business was always to turn in all weapons. But each unit's standdown in Chu Lai was often met with altercations with rear echelon (REMF) groups of black soldiers. For example, on this standdown Mike Laughlin was attacked on the beach by several black REMF's, after returning from the NCO Club. He was also "whacked in the head" with a board during fighting after a group of blacks attacked one of his comrades.

Black soldiers from the field were often placed in a difficult situation while on standdown's. They confided with their brother field grunts they could not be seen with them while in Chu Lai, or they would be beaten by their fellow black soldiers in the rear.

On April 27, Bravo Company combat air assaulted to the northern rocket pocket. The next day two of its soldiers received wounds from a homemade mine, an old smoke canister filled with explosives. On April 30 a recon platoon soldier also hit a mine and lost his right foot.

New Mission – New Terrain

The beginning of May, 1970 saw the 5th/46th Infantry Battalion spread out in various search and clear missions to protect Chu Lai and the pacified and heavily populated hamlets in Ly Tin District near Highway One. Alpha's headquarters remained on FSB Fat City while its 1st and 3rd Platoons guarded key bridges and road junctions near populated areas northwest of Chu Lai. Alpha's 2nd Platoon took up positions in the Ky Xuan village area just north of Chu Lai. Bravo continued to patrol the northern rocket pocket while Charlie patrolled the southern rocket pocket. Delta remained on and near LZ Bayonet providing security. The battalion's recon platoon was sent into the mountains on the west of the southern rocket pocket to search for enemy base camps.

On May 3, Charlie moved to Chu Lai for a rest and refit. Delta was loaded on Hueys to continue the southern rocket pocket search and clear mission. The next morning at 6:00AM Chu Lai was hit by eight to ten 122mm Soviet-made rockets. The 1st/14th Artillery radar section in Chu Lai quickly picked up the "Signature" of the launch location in the southern rocket pocket.

Delta was not close enough to quickly move to the location so Charlie's 3rd Platoon was alerted and ordered to "saddle up" to chopper out and find the launch site. This was on the platoons second day of a three-day standdown in Chu Lai. The night before they had already had their first beer fest and life was good. To the field weary grunts, the rockets had not come near them or their beer, which begged the question, "What was the big deal?" The enemy, they mused, would be long gone before they got to the launch site. But orders were orders and the platoon took off on the Hueys.

As the Hueys approached the rocket pocket the scenery below the birds was green and lush, flat and open terrain, with some knee-high vegetation scattered about. A tree line marked the point where low-lying hills began the ascent to the mountains in the west. As the Hueys descended to their selected landing zone they came under heavy fire from the tree line which forced the birds to move one-quarter mile away where they landed unencumbered.

The enemy fire was a major gift to Charlie Company. After some sporadic enemy fire at the second LZ, the platoon moved on line through a hedgerow. The first soldier breaking through the thick row of bushes let out a shout, "Oh my God, look at this!" Sitting in front of the platoon were fifty rockets lined up on tripods, ready to be fired. Another forty lay on the ground next to their firing positions. Nearby a pig was roasting on an open fire.

Charlie's grunts searched the area, radioed their find to higher headquarters, posted security and proceeded to continue their standdown by eating the pig. The soldiers disarmed the rockets by shorting out the wires connecting them to the firing devices. Engineers were flown in to destroy most of the rockets. When the explosives were expended the remaining rockets were loaded onto Hueys to be returned to Chu Lai and destroyed.

Later in the morning Charlie's soldiers fired on four fleeing Vietcong. In their haste to retreat the enemy left behind four combat packs containing documents, a large supply of batteries used to fire the rockets, a hand generator used as a firing device and a rocket testing device.

Later in the afternoon Delta, which arrived in the area, discovered shipping plugs for the rockets and fifty aiming stakes. Scattered nearby were over one hundred burn marks in the ground made from previous launches. Some aiming stakes were still in place and they pointed directly to Chu Lai. Echo's Recon Platoon had also moved into the rocket area and killed one NVA soldier, capturing documents, three Chicom grenades and a rocket aiming device.

This major rocket discovery drew attention from the high commands throughout South Vietnam. It also drew the attention of helicopter gunships which promptly searched the area for more targets. One bird spotted a Vietcong fleeing the area and promptly killed him with rocket fire that set off a secondary explosion of enemy cached ammunition.

As the area was searched, enemy fire from a ridgeline to the west harassed Charlie's soldiers. A Jet aircraft approached and Charlie's grunts watched a large canister drop from its belly, tumbling end over end as it bounced on the ridge, disgorging a long sheet of fiery napalm on their nemesis. That ended the harassing fire. It was an impressive sight, and one much appreciated by Charlie's troops. Delta Company drew the only casualties in the hunt for rockets. Two men suffered multiple shrapnel wounds from a mine detonated with a trip wire device.

The 122mm rockets that were recovered were designed for area targets such as the Americal Divisions sprawling base at Chu Lai. The Russian-produced rockets were fin-stabilized with a length of 6.2 feet, weighing one hundred and one pounds and offered a maximum range of approximately two and one-half miles when fired at an elevation of ten degrees. The warheads carried fifteen pounds of explosives and used instantaneous or delay fuses. The launchers designed for the rockets were 8.1 feet in length and weighed fifty-five pounds. As such, the launchers were a logistical burden that were rarely used. Instead the enemy preferred improvised launching devices, such as tripods made of bamboo poles or carefully prepared dirt mounds.

At 7:00AM on May 5, Alpha's headquarters and the artillery battery on FSB Fat City were hit by more rockets. Two soldiers from the battery were wounded. Fat City's defenders could see the flashes of the rockets being launched from just one-half mile south of their hilltop, near Ky Sanh (2). Mortars on Hills 270 and 76 were fired on the launch site. A search revealed tunnels, rocket pits, detonation cord and clothing. Bamboo aiming stakes were also found, each stake was marked with black lines to guide the enemy in setting the correct elevation, based on the launch location and its relationship to its target.

The same morning that Fat City was hit, Charlie Company combat air assaulted by Huey from the rocket pocket to a point on Provincial Road 532, nine miles due west of LZ Bayonet, between the hamlets of Dong Co and Tu Chanh. The mission was the same as always, search and clear an area based on intelligence reports of enemy activity.

Search and clear missions continued for the battalion, and Charlie Company was brought to LZ Bayonet as a brigade reaction force on May 7. Bravo Company patrolled the northern rocket pocket but one platoon was sent to assist Echo's Reconnaissance Platoon that was pinned down by fire. When they finally hooked up with Echo the enemy contact was over. Having completed their mission, the platoon was ordered to move quickly to a pickup point for Hueys to collect them and bring them back. The grunts had to be on time at the pickup zone, the Hueys had other missions to fly.

A hurried decision was made by a Sergeant First Class, a career NCO, who had been forced to go to the field just a few days before. He ordered the patrol to walk on a recently used tank trail. The tread tracks of a tank were still visible in the soil so the trail looked undisturbed. The fifteen members of the platoon walked in a file in silence, each soldier hating each step he had to take, knowing in his gut they were tempting fate. The movement was rapid as the imprints of the tank treads were clearly visible, undisturbed. But they were rolling the dice by trading speed for security, and each man knew it.

SP/4 Shelton Ashworth walked in the center of the platoon file, with Sergeant Ronald Dills next to him. Hedgerows lined both sides of the tank trail. It happened in an instant. The ground erupted with a vengeance, just under Dill's feet. The explosion threw Ashworth into the air, flailing him over the hedgerow and landing him forty-feet away, screaming in pain. His comrades rushed to help him.

Mike Laughlin was just ahead of Ashworth and the explosion smacked him to the ground, face down. When he rolled over he saw something fall out of the sky. It was Dills body. Laughlin moved over to his body but did not recognize him. His lower body was missing from the rib cage down and he was burned. The mine was a 105mm Howitzer round, cleverly planted by digging from the side of the trail to not disturb the tank tracks. Moreover this artillery round was not high explosive but a "Bee Hive" round, containing thousands of metal razors designed to stop enemy assaults on artillery positions. These rounds were always fired at "Barrels Level", into the teeth of the enemy, with deadly effect. Sergeant Ronald Eugene Dills was twenty-one years of age and single from Valparaiso, Indiana.

Echo's Recon Platoon heard the blast and came to their aid. When all the dustoff's had departed, it was near dark so the recon soldiers set up a perimeter with Bravo's traumatized patrol inside. The recon grunts made sure they were fed. Laughlin remembered, "We cried throughout the night."

Ashworth and three others were laced with shrapnel, but Ashworth was the worst since he was hit next to Dills. Multiple shrapnel wounds ripped open his body and his right arm and right leg were shredded. He would end up losing both. His comrades worked fast to keep from him from dying and he and the others were placed on a dustoff and brought to Chu Lai.

Ashworth had lost consciousness on the bird when it arrived at the hospital. Because of the severity of his wounds the waiting medics thought he was dead. The receiving team on the pad pulled on his hair to drag him out, not wanting to touch his bloody body. They pulled some of his hair out of his skull which awoke Ashworth and he screamed, "Hey, I'm still alive!" One and one-half years later after extensive medical care he would be returned to civilian life.

The next day a Delta soldier was killed by another buried 105mm Howitzer round. Part of Delta was on the old LZ Chippewa to provide security for some Howitzers which supported search and clear operations in the area. PFC Larry Foster walked to a toilet area on the hilltop to relieve himself and stepped on a buried mine, losing both legs and part of his left side. He was picked up by a Huey but did not survive the flight to Chu Lai. Foster was age twenty and married from Gastonia, North Carolina.

Out near Fat City on May 9 an element of Alpha Company came under sniper fire, wounding a squad leader. As the medic attended to his wounds, enemy bullets rained down on the two soldiers who were exposed in the open. PFC Eugene Nolan, a quiet country boy from Louisiana and the platoon's machine gunner, jumped up and placed himself between the medic and the snipers, becoming a target himself while he poured machine gun fire on the insurgents. He squelched the enemy fire and returned to his protected position.

When the dustoff came in to lift out the wounded man, more enemy fire opened up from a hedgerow, attempting to bring the Huey down. Nolan would have none of it. He left his sheltered position again and placed himself in front of the hovering helicopter, ignoring the bullets whizzing past him. He approached the nearby hedgerow with his machinegun blazing. The dustoff made it out and the enemy fled. For his actions Nolan was awarded the Silver Star.

The battalion continued its aggressive patrolling west of Chu Lai where intelligence reports indicated enemy movement. Day patrols and night ambushes marked the soldier's daily routine. The area was also saturated with aerial reconnaissance flights from fixed-wing aircraft and helicopters. Small enemy base camps were spotted on the eastern border of the Annamite Mountains, camps which provided food and comfort for an enemy on the move. Helicopter gunships, artillery fire and jet aircraft destroyed the camps when they found them.

In the midst of these search and clear operations another change in battalion commanders was made. LTC Snyder's command tenure had ended and another officer was to get his chance to command a battalion at war. On May 10 LTC Melvin Snyder, the battalion's commander since November 17, 1969, departed and LTC Henry J. Wereszynski took command. Snyder, the West Point graduate with considerable experience in research and development assignments was replaced by an Officer Candidate School graduate who was Special Forces qualified.

Henry Wereszynski, like Snyder, saw infantry duty in the Korean War as a platoon leader. Schooling and subsequent assignments included Special Forces duty at Fort Bragg, North Carolina and in Germany. His first Vietnam tour was with the First Infantry Division in 1965-1966. After a tour in the Pentagon he rejoined the First Infantry in Vietnam, then the 198th Brigade as its Executive Officer until his opportunity to command the 5th/46th opened up.

Fleeting encounters with the enemy became routine but it was the curse of mines and booby-traps that would continue to inflict the most casualties on the 5th/46th Infantry Battalion. Alpha Company patrolled the area near the valley hamlet of Phouc Khach, four and one-quarter miles due west of FSB Fat City. Morale was slipping in Alpha from constant snipers and booby-traps, and reduced enemy sightings did not compensate Alpha for its labors. Alpha used some high ground one-quarter mile northeast of the valley for their base camp. And they stayed too long.

On May 12, at first light, the company moved off its hill to more level ground to receive supplies, taking everyone with them for the task. They were gone for three hours; enough time for the enemy to move into their abandoned camp before it was reoccupied. It was a tactical blunder.

Lieutenant David Bright was ordered to take his men back up to resecure the hill. Immediately after arriving on top, Sergeant Robert "Corkie" Huddleston detonated a booby-trapped 105mm Howitzer round. Both legs were torn to shreds, with only threads of skin holding them to the bone. SP/4 Timothy Pfalzer was near Huddleston with some bushes separating the two. The blast picked him up and tossed him through the air, blasting shrapnel into his body. Two shards of metal flashed into his upper right thigh, two more into his right side, one lacerated his liver and two more into his right arm and elbow. SP/4 Jim Renze was also hit with multiple fragment wounds in his left thigh. Nine total were wounded. Only three were able to remain in the field and the rest were evacuated to Chu Lai.

SP/4 Renze was next to Huddleston in the hospital as they prepped Huddleston for surgery. He saw Huddleston come out of semi-unconsciousness on the operating table to look at his shredded legs "To see what was going on." He died at that moment. Sergeant Huddleston was twenty-one years old and single from Lafollette, Tennessee.

Renze recovered after three weeks but suffered hearing loss and was given a hearing device for his ear. He spent his remaining time in-country assigned to security duties in Danang. Pfalzer was judged to be stabilized when asked for his name, rank and serial number in the hospital, but he then felt excruciating pain. His stomach was promptly opened up and the wound to the liver was discovered. They kept his wounds open in case of infection until he reached the intermediate hospital in Japan, where they were closed up. Pfalzer was sent to the Valley Forge Hospital in Pennsylvania until discharged, then transferred to Fort Lewis, Washington to a mechanized infantry unit, where seventy percent of the unit were like him, wounded vets from Vietnam, finishing their service time.

The next day, May 13, "Saber 77", a light visual reconnaissance aircraft spotted several dispersed camps in dense mountains north of My Son (1). The low-flying pilot could see camouflaged hooch's with tables and even the eating utensils placed on them. Trails led to the valley below, which would soon be identified by the battalion's grunts as "Dragon Valley". Close by were clotheslines with uniforms flowing in the soft mountain breeze. Artillery was used to destroy the small camps as they were simply too numerous for the battalion's over-extended troops to recon.

Air reconnaissance spotted potential rocket launching sites in the mountainous terrain west of the Southern Rocket Pocket. Delta's 1st Platoon air assaulted to the area at 2:45PM, hoping to land a big catch like Charlie Company's find on May 4. Delta's 3rd Platoon was also sent on the hunt but not before Private William Carmichael stepped on an anti-personnel mine losing his right foot. Launch sites were found with wooden bipods and electrical wire, but no rockets.

Throughout the Americal Division's area of operations enemy activity was characterized by rocket and sapper attacks and ground probes against CAP teams and Vietnamese militia. Pacified hamlets were also hit. These were relatively "soft" targets for a weakened enemy. The enemy attacks were expected to reach a high point by May 19, the birthdays of Buddha and Ho Chi Minh.

Organized attacks against American forces were largely avoided for two reasons. First, there were not enough enemy soldiers to launch effective attacks or even defend their own base camps in dense terrain, hence they faded away in advance of approaching American forces. Second, the enemy's attacks against Vietnamese militias defending pacified hamlets could shake the confidence villagers had in government forces and would test the mettle of those whose job was to defend them in the absence of American soldiers. This was to be the enemy strategy to buy time until the American withdrawal from the Chu Lai area was complete.

Charlie Company pushed out from LZ Bayonet to patrol the southern rocket pocket one and one-half mile west of the now abandoned LZ Gator. On the morning of May 14 SP/4 Terry Duncan stepped on a mine and lost his right foot. Shortly after Charlie's Kit Carson Scout stepped on another mine, losing his foot. To round out the day a Delta soldier, Sergeant Thomas Polak stepped on a mine and suffered a serious stomach wound.

On May 16, Delta's 3rd Platoon found one hundred and sixty rocket launch sites with aiming stakes and electrical wire. The next day Delta's 1st Platoon hit a booby trap, a claymore mine detonated by a trip wire. Four soldiers were wounded with shrapnel to the head and body. They were dusted off but one soldier, Sergeant Guy Stokes, succumbed to his wounds. Stokes was twenty-three and single from Commerce, Georgia.

That same day Charlie Company was lifted out of the rocket pocket and air assaulted to the area known as Dragon Valley to search and clear the valley floor, beginning on a mountaintop at the southern end of the valley. This is where intelligence reports indicated a large enemy base camp was situated. Dragon Valley sat five miles farther west of the Ky Thanh area, and the battalion was now pushing far west, out of the Chu Lai Defensive Zone, to expand its control. Echo's Recon Platoon was air-lifted from Chu Lai to the mountainous area one mile west of the valley, in support of Charlie.

Soon after landing on their LZ, Charlie's 1st Platoon received automatic weapons fire from a ridgeline linked to the mountain they were to search. Gunships came on station and strafed the area as the grunts started the climb up. They were again hit with hand grenades and small arms fire but the soldiers persisted, driving off the enemy and eventually reaching the summit. Their climb was rewarded with the discovery of an NVA camp which contained ten hooch's, each measuring fifteen feet in width and twenty feet in length. Each hooch contained a fighting bunker.

The camp was hastily abandoned judging by the contents left behind: a medical bag, syringes and thermometers, two transistor radios, a 9mm pistol, camera, two hundred pounds of rice, maps, 25 hammocks, clothes, ten hand grenades, five hundred blasting caps, three flashlights, a sewing machine, five claymore mines, five pair of American jungle boots and twenty-five fighting positions around the camp.

The next day the battalion recon platoon moved out early to search its portion of mountainous terrain west of Dragon Valley. At 11:20AM they engaged two NVA and killed one. "Warlord 8" helicopter gunships came on station and fired rockets in the direction of the fleeing NVA soldier. The Warlords light observation helicopter (LOH) flew low looking for more targets, and its pilot was hit in the elbow by ground fire, prompting the firing of additional rockets into the dense undergrowth.

The recon soldiers moved warily, they were a small platoon of men, never at full strength and now swallowed up in foreboding terrain. Recon soldiers were supposed to be used for reconnaissance, but the platoon was too often used for search and sweep missions, like the other platoons of the battalion. At full strength the platoon should have had about forty-five soldiers, but usually it could only muster fifteen to twenty-five, sometimes as few as twelve men.

The recon grunts stopped at noon for a quick rest and lunch, the best time to eat because there was no concern about light discipline when heating their rations over small squares of C-4. The point squad advanced fifty yards farther for security before stopping. The remaining soldiers formed a tight circle in silence, as they had done many times before. After lunch the platoon moved out.

Sergeant Lewis Coate, the platoon's tunnel rat, was the last man in line. He hurried to heave his heavy ruck sack on his back as he watched the tail of his platoon departing twenty yards in front of him. In an instant he heard a noise behind him and his gut told him the enemy was near. Just as the thought entered his mind an enemy bullet entered his right shoulder, puncturing his lung, hitting his spine and stopping behind his left shoulder blade. Coate was slammed to the ground with severe pain. Then a grenade exploded between his legs. Coate thought his left leg was gone but it was still intact, although the shrapnel severed his femoral vein. The sergeant waited for the final bullet that would end it all.

"Well here I come Lord" he thought.

Coate decided to defend himself until a final bullet finished him off. He pulled out his 45 caliber pistol and fired in the direction of the enemy, unloading all five magazines, about thirty-six rounds. By then Coate was caught in a cross fire, the enemy to his right and the platoon to his left pouring out devastating fire at each other. The initial burst of fire that hit him also slammed into the rest of his platoon, prompting their response which caught Coate in the middle. Coate wasn't sure if the grenade that hit him came from a fellow grunts M-79 or the enemy but he was sure the quick reaction from his comrades saved him from a coup de grace.

Coate was now in shock and losing blood. The exchange of fire lasted less than a minute, the enemy evaded and the platoon's medic began treating the Sergeant. Coate could only see shadows because of his shock but knew from the medic's shaky voice he was in trouble. His comrades hacked a small opening in the dense terrain. A helicopter came over, a basket was lowered through the hole and Coate was lifted out.

Sergeant Lewis Coate was dusted off and survived. When his platoon leader saw him in the hospital, he was sure Coate had been hit by friendly fire but the sergeant told him about the initial fire from the rear. The Lieutenant responded, "I wondered why you had your gun out pointing away from the platoon with all those discharged 45 shells on your chest". Coate, happy to be alive, replied in humor, "If the platoon had shot me I would have been shooting back at you!" Two years later the Army removed the slug from behind his left shoulder blade. It was an AK-47 round.

Later that day Charlie's 3rd Platoon found a small way-station with two hooch's off the southwest summit from the larger NVA camp they previously discovered. The way-station was burned. Nearby the 1st Platoon killed one NVA soldier and retained his AK-47 rifle. Later Charlie Company discovered more hooch's in the mountains, some of which were built to contain livestock. Those dwellings were also torched. The 1st Platoon killed another NVA and wounded some others in a brief skirmish. They followed the blood trail which led from the site of contact. The blood trail dried up and disappeared, allowing the enemy to escape in the dense terrain, but most likely to die slow deaths from their wounds.

The terrain was just as treacherous as the mountains Charlie Company had traversed twenty miles west of LZ Gator as part of Task Force Lizard. Sergeant John Arruda, a 3rd Platoon squad leader plunged twenty feet down a cliff. His rucksack broke his fall. He suffered an ankle sprain that made it difficult to walk. Another squad leader, Sgt. Olsen, had developed a fever of one hundred and four degrees and both were medevaced.

The Medevac helicopter was an official Medevac that included a red cross on each side of the bird, the international sign of neutrality. As such, it had no door gunners. As the Huey flew to Chu Lai it stopped at a Marine CAP team to pick up two wounded Marines, a Lieutenant and a Sergeant. The Medevac lifted off again for the final leg to Chu Lai but it received heavy small arms fire as it pulled pitch from the CAP compound. Arruda, Olsen and the Marine officer promptly poured out M-16 fire towards the insurgents. The medic on board frantically pulled at their legs shouting, "No, No, Stop! We're a Medevac, we can't shoot!" The Lieutenant sarcastically responded, "Ah … they're shooting at us!"

The Recon grunts located another small NVA camp one and one-quarter mile northwest of Charlie. Their silent approach surprised a NVA soldier, who was shot dead. They entered the camp cautiously, realizing their vulnerability as a small group. Any sizable enemy element could annihilate them, and the enemy had a significant advantage over them with its knowledge of the local terrain. The Americans had superior firepower at their disposal, but it required survival in a quick, violent life and death struggle before artillery could be obtained.

At first the enemy camp appeared empty. The recon soldiers searched enemy bunkers carefully, using hand grenades before entering them. In one bunker two Vietcong were found who refused to come out. They were eliminated and their dead bodies pulled out for inspection. There were no weapons. They appeared to be the camp's cooks or other support personnel; they were not fighters.

The battalion commander flew over in his helicopter, asking the recon troops to pop smoke so he could identify their location. The platoon refused. There was no need to tell the enemy for miles around, with smoke billowing upward, where their small and vulnerable platoon was positioned. What they could do was offer to LTC Werezynski to signal their location with a mirror. The battalion commander reprimanded them at their next standdown in Chu Lai for their failure to give him their position but the brigade commander got wind of the argument and supported the troops. In the words of one recon grunt, "common sense prevailed." The camp yielded ten thatched hooch's and some medical supplies. The camp was torched and the grunts moved swiftly away.

In the midst of searching out the enemy, the battalion received a message from the Americal Division headquarters on the morning of May 18, 1970: "All units will temporarily cease aggressive operations from 12:00 noon on May 18 to noon on May 19 in honor of Buddha's birthday. US Forces will not make aggressive contact during this period." The directive was largely ignored by the grunts in the field. And that included Alpha Company.

At 9:20AM Alpha's 1st Platoon, operating in hilly terrain, found and destroyed a camouflaged canvas hooch one mile southwest of Fat City. The dwelling contained a GI air mattress, pots and pans, fifty pounds of rice, small bags of salt and sugar, peanuts, canned milk, a mosquito net and assorted enemy uniforms.

The platoon remained in the hill country looking for more signs of the enemy. At 3:30PM, their resupply Huey spotted a small group of Vietcong on the other side of the hill and alerted the platoon. Sergeant Tony Hernandez was detailed to take his squad to snag the enemy. Hernandez found some old dirt impressions of tracks from an armored personnel carrier and elected to stay on the tracks as his squad sprinted toward the enemy. It was a costly error. He tripped a pressure-release mine planted underneath the tread marks.

The explosion ripped off both of the sergeants legs below his knees and wounded two other soldiers. The mine left a two foot-deep hole in the ground. Another Huey was already inbound to bring a replacement to the platoon, a "Fucking New Guy" (FNG) when the crew was told there was an urgent need to lift out a casualty. The new replacement stepped off the bird just as the legless Hernandez was placed on the Huey's floor, his former legs now stumps, covered with bloody bandages. Shortly after, another Huey was called to pick up SP/4 Michael Esslinger, the RTO who was with Hernandez squad. The platoon discovered shrapnel wounds to his back. After he climbed aboard the Huey, the bird pulled pitch to lift off when suddenly the FNG jumped on board, completely unnerved by his first glimpse of war. He refused to get off the bird and was never seen again.

Blue Ghost cobra gunships from F Troop, 8th Air Cavalry conducted aerial reconnaissance flights over the southern and northern rocket pockets in support of the battalion. Their lead observation helicopter flew low at tree top level, finding camouflaged hooch's that were promptly destroyed by rocket fire.

No respite was given to the enemy as pacification efforts by the South Vietnamese Government grew in the populated hamlets. National elections were held and the rice harvest began.

To add to the battalion's unrelenting pressure, Ground Surveillance Radar (GSR) placed on hilltops scoured the countryside for enemy movement. When GSR detected small groups of enemy moving at night, mortars, artillery fire or gunships smashed them. Three AN/PPS-5 GSR Sets were tactically positioned, one each on Hill 76, Hill 270 and LZ Chippewa. The AN/PPS-5 set was a lightweight ground-to-ground surveillance unit that could detect soldiers walking as far as three and one-half miles away with its line-of-sight radar antenna. Most often the battalions 81mm mortars positioned with the radar sets provided the quickest response to enemy movement.

When the "Buddha Ceasefire" ended on noon, May 19, the enemy welcomed Charlie Company with small arms fire and 60mm mortar rounds. The next day enemy fire continued to plague the soldiers as they moved out of the northern reaches of Dragon Valley through a series of elevated terraced rice paddies, each separated by a dike. The landscape was marked by beauty everywhere. There was lush green foliage, terraced floors of carefully cultivated land with a view of the scenic valley floor below. The enemy enjoyed the view as well, as it waited for the approaching soldiers.

Small arms fire greeted the 2nd Platoon which led the company's upward climb. They were hit with small arms and .30 caliber machinegun fire. PFC James Nichols was hit in the stomach and left arm and SP/4 Clyde Jones was hit in the shoulder. Another official Medevac with Red Cross symbols and no door gunners came in to pick up the wounded. As it lifted off it was hit by machinegun fire. One bullet caused the hydraulic system to malfunction. The bird came down fast on autorotation and set down hard between Charlie's position and the enemy. It was immediately raked with enemy fire.

Nichols, although severely wounded, grabbed one of the M-16's on board and put down a base of fire towards the enemy. As enemy bullets tore into the thin skin of the downed helicopter the two pilots were having difficulty un-strapping themselves from their seats. Their slowness meant it was just a matter of time before enemy bullets would find them. Nichols exposed himself to the enemy fire and helped the two pilots exit the bird. He then placed suppressive fire on the enemy. For his actions that day he was awarded the Silver Star. Another Huey came on station and landed to pick up the wounded and the Medevac crew. By this time SP/4 Kenneth Bruck joined the wounded with shrapnel in his temple above his right eye. The second dustoff made it out.

The company spent the morning of May 21 protecting the downed Medevac while enduring sporadic enemy fire. A resupply of ammo was sent in via "High Speed Delivery", Hueys flying fast and low, the crews kicking out their loads as the birds flew over the grunts. Artillery fire was adjusted on likely enemy locations and Cobra gunships prowled the area looking for targets.

The enemy didn't let up. At 10:22AM, a NVA sniper hit SP/4 Bruce Nichols (no relation to James Nichols) in the chest, killing him instantly. Nichols was twenty years of age and single from Lower Burrell, Pennsylvania. The grunts swept the area with gunship support from above. After returning to their positions they were hit again with small arms fire which slightly wounded another soldier. In the early afternoon the 2nd Platoon took the lead to move the company one-half mile farther up and out of what became known to Charlie as "The Hellhole" to a hilltop that dominated the valley below. As they ascended the terrain, enemy fire wounded two more soldiers who were dusted off.

SP/4 Jacob Spaid was on the point of 2nd Platoon, still leading the company file, when it approached its night defensive position (NDP). SP/4 Somers followed Spaid, and Sgt Carl Kannapel was third in line. They were making steady progress when the lights went out on Kannapel from an enemy mine. He woke up sitting on his rear, his fatigues completely soaked with blood from the waist down, including his socks and jungle boots. He was in shock. Shell fragments had lacerated his skin and muscle before coming to rest in his left thigh.

Spaid was in worst shape, losing most of his left leg and the use of his left arm. He also lost his left eye. Medics rapidly worked on them until they were dusted off under enemy fire. Forty years later Kannapel visited his comrade Jacob Spaid, living in Florida. They made a "show and tell" trip to Spaid's doctor to review some recent X-rays that showed all the shrapnel remaining in the left side of Spaid's head, his left shoulder, arm, chest, hips and upper left leg. It was still there because it was too risky to remove.

The day of horrors did not end there. At 6:55PM as they prepared their NDP a platoon leader, First Lieutenant Gary Mower tripped a bobby-trapped 81mm mortar round which blew off both his legs. Another platoon leader standing next to him, 1LT Michael Mesich, was hit by shrapnel in the right eye and right side. Six other soldiers were wounded with shrapnel in their legs and chests. They were all dusted off and made it to Chu Lai but Lieutenant Mesich died shortly after. Lieutenant Mower made it through surgery but he died the next day. First Lieutenant Michael Mesich was twenty-three and single from Milwaukee, Wisconsin. First Lieutenant Gary Mower was twenty-six and married from Fairview, Utah.

That same day Delta continued its mission of providing security on LZ Chippewa and conducting patrols and ambushes two miles out in all directions from the hilltop. At 3:00AM, the 3rd Platoons 4th Squad lying in ambush, spotted flashes near Phuoc Binh Tay (1), one and one-half miles southeast of Chippewa. Eight rockets were launched which slammed into Chu Lai. The heavy 4.2-inch mortars on Chippewa returned fire on the rocket site; followed by forty-six 105mm Howitzer rounds which systematically blanketed a half-mile area around the rockets launch location.

The next day on May 22 Charlie Company and the battalion's recon platoon were picked up by Huey and sent to Chu Lai for a forty-eight hour standdown. Intelligence reports at the 198th Brigade headquarters indicated the enemy was stepping up its efforts to place mines and booby-traps in the battalion's area of operations because of its aggressive operations. One report noted thirty anti-personnel and vehicle mines had recently been planted near Phuoc Binh Tay (1), the rocket launch area now patrolled by Delta.

Two days later the recon platoon left Chu Lai and air assaulted far south to the edge of the mountains near Phuoc Lam (1), eight miles west of the district town of Binh Son. Intelligence reports pointed to an enemy hospital on the eastern slopes of the mountains that was built to support Vietcong attacks on the heavily pacified area around Binh Son. The next day Alpha Company moved off FSB Fat City with a mission to search and clear the hilly terrain west and south of the northern rocket pocket. Charlie Company moved to Fat City to replace Alpha and continue base security operations and nightly ambushes in the area. Bravo continued its search and clear operations in the hilly and dense terrain that separated the northern and southern rocket pockets while Delta secured LZ Chippewa and patrolled the southern rocket pocket and the rugged terrain west of it.

Gaining Control – At A Price

The end of May saw Bravo manning OP's at LZ Bayonet with its 1st Platoon at Fat City to bolster it's defenses. Charlie saturated the area with patrols and ambushes northwest of Fat City and between Hill's 76 and 270. Charlie's 1st Platoon hit two Vietcong who sprinted away on May 30, leaving a trail of blood. The next morning they swept the area and found one dead Vietcong with his AK-47 at his side.

While the pacification momentum was on the side of the ARVN and American soldiers, "soft" targets were always susceptible to attack by the enemy. The ville of Nuoc Mau, next to the abandoned LZ Gator, was hit in the early morning hours of June 1. Popular Force Platoon 27 stood its ground against B-40 rockets and small arms fire and suffered two killed and three wounded. The lesser trained and armed self-defense forces working with them panicked and ran. The PF's saw about fifteen of them run off with the attacking Vietcong. On June 3 PF Platoon 239 ambushed two VC platoons near Dong Binh (2), three-quarters mile south of the Chu Lai base near Highway One. Four Vietcong were killed.

The Popular Force (PF) and Regional Force (RF) militias continued to take over security for the hamlet areas near Highway One, including the heavily populated Ly Tin District just north of Chu Lai. There was little American presence in these populated hamlets and the militias, perhaps more than the ARVN, came to understand their days of reliance on American hamlet defense were coming to an end. The earlier inactivity of RF and PF units (during the battalion's pacification effort) now forced a more active role, if for no other reason than their own defense.

The battalion's mission was to screen farther west of the populated areas to insure that no large scale attack could be developed from the mountains. This involved seeking out logistical bases as was accomplished in mid-May in the mountains west of Dragon Valley, and preventing small pockets of VC or the NVA from moving east to carry out rocket attacks or obtain supplies for its beleaguered forces. It was clear that tactically the enemy was on the ropes because of the destruction of enemy base camps, the constant pressure of radar surveillance, visual air reconnaissance, daytime clear and sweeps, and night ambushes by the 5th/46th Battalion. But for the soldiers themselves, the necessity to patrol the far-reaching terrain kept them in deadly contact with an enemy still willing to fight.

On June 4, Delta's 3rd Platoon in the southern rocket pocket found pieces of a 122mm rocket next to an artillery crater. An artillery round that was fired in response to a radar signature that indicated the enemy was preparing to launch the rocket, had hit the site dead-on. Bits of flesh lay in the area. The grunts were well satisfied. Radar on LZ Chippewa was making night movement for the enemy extremely hazardous. Each night when movement was detected, usually by small groups of two-three insurgents, it was greeted by artillery or mortar fire.

The battalion commander, LTC Wereszynski, now believed his soldiers owned the night and that enemy contact at night in the more open areas around FSB Fat City should be followed up immediately, not "at first light" as before. Artillery or mortar illumination rounds would guide his soldiers to their prey after making contact.

At 3:50AM on June 7, B-52 bombers made an "Arc Light" strike in Dragon Valley. At 7:15AM Alpha Company and the recon platoon air-assaulted into the area to assess the damage. Spotter planes reported sighting destroyed tunnels and bunkers. For the next several days the soldiers found remnants of base camp areas but they were judged to be older camps which had not been occupied for some time.

But three days later a POW captured by a Marine CAP team indicated Alpha had just missed encountering the Vietcong's V20 Company which evaded into the mountains. The company had a strength of forty-eight of which eighteen were NVA regulars. This prisoner had sold soda to US soldiers in the Chu Lai area before being conscripted by the Vietcong. He escaped to return home after a month under VC control but was forced back into the mountains by the enemy. The B-52 strike, he said, "Just missed the V20 Local Force Company". The VC commander, however, was later killed by a helicopter gunship during a visual reconnaissance.

The POW had two uncles working for the Regional Force Militia and he wanted to become a Kit Carson Scout for the Americans. Working with the Americans in the field was the best security he could find for his life. He was ready to lead them to a cache of weapons. Battalion records do not record what happened to this peasant who was caught in the middle of a no-win struggle.

Delta continued to patrol and ambush in the southern rocket pocket and the hilly terrain west of it. On June 8, one of its soldiers tripped a booby-trap on a trail junction near Phuoc Binh Tay (2), losing his left heel with the shrapnel shredding his left leg. The crater left by the small anti-personnel mine was eight inches across and three inches deep. That night radar picked up a group of insurgents one and one-half miles farther west. Twenty-two 4.2-inch and sixteen 81mm mortar rounds were fired from LZ Chippewa. To add coverage, twenty-four 105mm Howitzer rounds also pummeled the terrain. A sweep of the area revealed blood trails and an insurgent's leg.

Charlie Company continued its search and clear work in the area of Hill's 270, 76 and FSB Fat City. Day patrols and squad-size night ambushes were conducted near suspected rocket launch sites. Emphasis was now placed on relying more heavily on "Mechanical Ambushes" (MA) to increase the battalion's killing capacity and control of its terrain. MA's were unsupervised booby-traps which allowed a rifle squad or platoon to increase its effectiveness in its assigned area. The MA's were bobby-trapped Claymore Mines set up in a "Daisy Chain" of several claymores to expand a lethal kill zone near suspected areas of enemy movement. The MA was detonated by a trip wire.

The field savvy soldiers needed no special supplies to set-up mechanical ambushes. A small hole was placed in the handle of a plastic C-ration spoon and a trip wire was attached through the hole. The wire was strung cross a likely enemy avenue of movement. The plastic spoon was placed between the jaws of a wooden clothes pin. Each jaw contained an embedded thumbtack on the end to complete the electrical circuit which detonated the claymore mines. The electrical cord from a claymore mine was split and attached to each jaw. The claymore mines were placed in an overlapping pattern; the more claymores the better, to increase the kill zone.

The set-up was simple enough. The wire across the trail is tripped by the insurgent, dislodging the spoon which allows the thumbtacks to make contact and complete an electrical circuit, detonating the mines. During rainy weather a large banana leaf was placed over the clothespin to prevent water from closing the circuit.

Mechanical ambushes were established to complement a "live ambush" of soldiers nearby. Mechanical ambushes killed any variety of "prey", from Vietcong to NVA regulars, dogs and wild pigs. But sometimes the hunters themselves became the prey and the enemy exacted a deadly price on July 30.

By mid-1970 the war waged by the 5th/46th Infantry Battalion had largely morphed into a squad leader's war. The platoons broke into squads as often as possible, if not during the day then certainly at night. The exception was the battalion's recon platoon which often operated far from any other troop support and when the company platoons operated in more dense and hilly terrain.

On June 9 Charlie Company's 3rd Squad, 3rd Platoon, set out to patrol its assigned area for two days. The squad took a break in the late afternoon and then set out on a night patrol which ended with an ambush position emplaced at 9:30PM. The enemy continued to use the same general areas for night movement and rocket launches, which required the infantry squads to patrol the same area themselves. This resulted in deadly consequences.

Sergeant John Arruda, 3rd Squad leader, selected a position that was used by his platoon a few days prior, but he reasoned it offered the best protection and concealment in the area. It was set in an old, dried rice paddy surrounded by a two to three foot high dirt berm near Ky Sahn (1). His small group of men formed the defensive perimeter as before, in a quasi-circle, each man facing outward while lying down, their feet touching each other, like the spokes on a wheel.

The humid Vietnam night remained quiet until 2:30AM when Sgt. Arruda changed his watch with his medic, "Doc" Castillo. As they switched positions so Castillo could be close to the radio, each heard the ping of a pin being removed from a hand grenade and in seconds heard the thump of the grenade landing in their midst. Arruda slapped the man's helmet next to him, SP/4 David Concepcion-Nieves, yelling "Incoming!" and jumped to the opposite side of the berm for cover. As he made his leap the grenade exploded behind Arruda, sending shrapnel into Arruda's right leg. Concepcion, in the prone position caught the full impact of the blast. He never had a chance and was killed immediately. A native of Arecibo, Puerto Rico, Concepcion-Nieves was twenty years of age and married.

More explosions raked the ambush site. The squad was now the target of an attack by twenty to twenty-five NVA and VC. Grenades flew into the squad's position and some small arms fire reached out to the enemy. The squad's claymore mines were clicked to activate but did not detonate. The small perimeter quickly disintegrated, torn apart by the incoming grenades.

Arruda, who had jumped outside the small perimeter to escape the first grenade, now jumped back in and found one soldier moving around, PFC Geary, and pushed him outside of the kill zone. He found another unconscious soldier, Gary Stotterboom, and carried him out just as another grenade exploded behind him. The concussion threw both of them over the berm. Realizing he had no weapon, Arruda crawled back inside the perimeter and found an M16 with a bandoleer of ammunition. He turned to go to back to Stotterboom when another grenade exploded. The concussion threw him onto his back, blowing the hand guards off the M16 and sending his bandoleer flying into the air. This time the shrapnel missed his body but hit his watch and froze it in time, forever, to the time of the attack.

Grenades continued to explode as some small arms fire sputtered out to the attacking enemy. Life itself would be the only prize that determined who won and who lost the encounter. Arruda was with the two men he pushed outside the perimeter and prepared to return to retrieve additional men. Suddenly the gunfire and grenades stopped. He and his two companions could hear the enemy talking, coming closer.

PFC Geary yelled, "I can see them coming!"

Arruda yelled to those still inside the small perimeter, "Who else has a weapon?" No Reply.

Arruda looked at his damaged M16 and prayed it would still function. He then saw the enemy walk out of some tall grass toward the perimeter; six enemy soldiers, some in black pajamas and some in NVA uniforms. He took aim at the enemy closest to the tall grass, hoping to draw them away from the ambush position. He waited as they came closer, closer, closer. Arruda fired a single shot and a darkly silhouetted body slammed to the ground. The dead soldiers' comrades moved into an open area, their eyes still fixed on the small perimeter and Arruda continued to fire. Two more insurgents went down. The remaining enemy continued firing into the small defensive perimeter as they withdrew still ignoring Arruda and his comrades who were lying in the open, only twelve feet away.

Arruda jumped back into the ambush perimeter and found the M-60 machinegun. He opened fire, sweeping the area in front of him and emptied the box of ammo attached to the gun. By now another rifle squad arrived at the site and Arruda went back to treating Stotterboom's head wound and others along with their medic, "Doc" Castillo. Mortar fire was called on the surrounding area. The attack had been intense but brief, lasting no more than eight minutes. Gunships came on station with a flare ship and were met with ground fire from the retreating enemy moving to the northwest and northeast.

The dustoff arrived at 3:15AM and the entire squad was extracted on the same bird with wounded soldiers lying on other wounded. The battalions Daily Staff Journal listed the casualties as a mere footnote to another day of "Accelerated Pacification":

Concepcion – Killed in Action (KIA)
Kramer – Wounded in action (WIA), gunshot wound to the head
Whidden – WIA, fragment wounds to buttocks
Castillo – WIA, fragment wounds to left foot, buttocks and chin.
Geary – WIA, fragment wounds to left leg, right leg and stomach.
Stotterboom – WIA, head and face wounds.
Sullivan – WIA, fragment wounds to arm
Arruda - WIA, fragment wounds to left leg.

The squad that rescued Arruda's group surveyed the ambush site. The one trip flare that was placed in the direction of the enemy, which would have given them the early warning needed, had malfunctioned. The wires to the claymore mines had then been cut by sappers. Ground radar units on the surrounding hills had detected over fifty movements around the ambush site just prior to the attack but there was no system to communicate with Arruda's squad.

Late that day Echo's Recon Platoon, led by a Chieu Hoi, found a large weapons cache in Dragon Valley which included thirty-one 60mm mortar rounds, large shape charges for anti-tank mines, a machinegun and nine AK-47's. Bravo's 3rd Platoon, operating in the northern edge of the valley, found a rice cache, RPG rounds and bomb-making materials. Everything was destroyed.

Up by Fat City Sergeant Stephen Krajewski from Charlie's 1st Platoon accidentally tripped one of its mechanical ambushes at first light on June 12. He took the full blast of the deadly claymore mines intended for the enemy. He was dusted off at 6:17AM but was dead on arrival at Chu Lai. Krajewski was twenty-four years of age and single from

Groveland, Massachusetts. It was unclear whether Krajewski tripped the MA or the heavy rain at the time shorted the circuit and caused the claymores to detonate prematurely. Charlie Company suspended the use of MA's during conditions of heavy rain.

Alpha and Bravo Companies patrolled the rugged terrain around Dragon Valley, locating small caches of enemy equipment, food and weapons. The terrain was made more difficult for the grunts by the daily rain and cold nights at these higher elevations. Enemy contact was sporadic. It was the typical shoot and run tactics offered by a dispersed and depleted enemy.

Enemy mines and booby-traps continued to be a threat. On one occasion, Alpha's SP/4 Tracy Austin from Birmingham, Alabama and his comrades settled into a night defensive position, hoping for a quiet night. Austin, an RTO, pulled radio watch from 12:00PM until 1:00AM. After his watch, he lay down to sleep and felt something hard under his head. He reached back to move it and felt three prongs of a booby-trapped pressure release device. Austin recalled, "It scared me half to death" Alphas commander called for their Kit Carson Scout "Chot", an expert at mines and booby-traps to disarm it. Chot dug it up and found the device was attached to an artillery round. It was also discovered that one of the prongs was bent by Austin's head but the full weight of his head had not set on all the prongs. By an act of divine providence the mine had not exploded.

June 14 was another miserable day in the bush for Alpha Company. The day temperature was in the high 90's but torrents of rain moved in and out of the area, making it impossible to stay dry. At twilight the dark clouds brought more rain which rapidly dropped the temperature some thirty degrees, causing the night to become bone-chilling cold. The night chill was made worst by the water the troops had slogged through during the day while searching for the enemy and trying to avoid mines or ambushes. The grunts feet were wet and clammy white, some infected with fungus, difficult to heal with the absence of sunlight.

Alpha's night perimeter was set up in a small flooded rice paddy. Its position was surrounded by thickly foliaged hills, terrain that would take a rifle company a whole day to hack though with machetes just to cover a half-mile. Earlier that day Bravo Company required a dustoff for two soldiers with machete wounds to the legs and feet while cutting through the same type of terrain. But their morale was up, they had not made enemy contact for five days and the next day the rain-soaked and mud-covered grunts were scheduled to be pulled out for a rest in Chu Lai.

More rain pummeled Alpha's soldiers as they huddled under their ponchos while taking small drags on their cigarettes, careful not to expose the lighted ends to the driving rain or the enemy. Sergeant Donald Ehlke worked with other squad leaders in his platoon to improve their defensive positions. Ehlke was in his tenth month of field duty and looked forward to soon getting a job in the rear. A new soldier, an FNG, committed an unconscionable sin by burning a C-ration box to warm himself. Ehlke rose to his feet to have the FNG extinguish the fire. By so doing, he was silhouetted in the dark and shot by a sniper some sixty feet away. The bullet tore through his intestines and grazed his spine.

Other enemy soldiers positioned near the crest of a surrounding hill began to pour fire on the company. The plunging bullets of AK-47 assault rifles sent streams of water and mud into the air. After a few seconds, Alpha's machineguns opened up on its attackers, their carefully-spaced tracer rounds guiding the machinegun fire as it moved up the hillside, ripping apart trees and brush. M-79 grenade launchers plopped explosive rounds closer in, to blunt any grenade attacks by the enemy. The shrapnel of the "Clunkers" could be heard zinging over everyone's heads.

Ehlke laid in the water and mud, seriously wounded. He was pulled onto a muddy dike and dressings were applied to cover his wounds as the radio cracked with an urgent call for a dustoff. The enemy fire ceased but the monsoon rains continued as the medic stayed by Ehlke and watched him go into shock. After twenty minutes flying through the "Soup" of low visibility a bird came in, guided to Ehlke by a battery operated strobe light held by one of his fellow grunts. He would survive. Twenty-six years later his wound would require the insertion of a metal rod in his back.

The next day Bravo Company found a large potato field carved out of dense terrain to support the NVA. It was too big for the patrol to handle so artillery was called in to destroy it. More encampments were found with hooch's and fighting bunkers and small gardens. Everything was destroyed. Bravo's night positions were often hit with sporadic small arms fire but that night Bravo's soldiers were hit by six 82mm mortar rounds. The first four rounds landed north of its perimeter by thirty yards. The enemy adjusted with two more rounds which overshot its perimeter by fifteen yards. Firing ceased because the enemy ran out of ammunition before it could adjust on Bravo's position.

By mid-June 1970 the enemy remained dispersed and weakened. The enemy's sole objective was to conserve what was left of its fighting ability and target limited attacks against South Vietnamese government pacification efforts when conditions were favorable to them. The enemy "Order of Battle" faced by the 5th/46th Infantry Battalion had a diminished capacity to fight but was still potent:

1. NVA 409th Sapper Battalion, estimated strength of 150, located far west of Tam Ky but with a capability to rapidly infiltrate the Chu Lai Defense Area for a coordinated attack.
2. NVA 78th Rocket Battalion, estimated strength of 150, located five miles west of LZ Chippewa in the rugged Annamite Mountains.
3. NVA 402nd Sapper Battalion, estimated strength of 160, located in the southern sector of Dragon Valley.
4. Vietcong V14 Local Force Company, estimated strength of 65, located in the northern sector of Dragon Valley.
5. Vietcong V20 Local Force Company, estimated strength of 60, now located three miles west of FSB Fat City.
6. Vietcong 95B Sapper Company, estimated strength of 60, located 2-1/2 miles southwest of the abandoned LZ Gator.
7. Vietcong 125th Battalion, estimated strength of 150, located in the heavy terrain just south of Dragon Valley, five miles due west of Hill 76.

Bravo Company continued to search and clear the rugged terrain north of Dragon Valley, finding more small camps used by a widely dispersed enemy. A typical enemy camp was located on June 16. A large hooch contained pots and pans, bottles of medicine, corn, rice, scattered weapons and ammunition, some occasional mortar rounds, animal traps and fishing nets. Nearby were two camouflaged eight-foot long bridges over a deep stream. Everything was destroyed.

On June 17, Delta moved to search and clear the area southwest of LZ Gator. As one of its patrols moved into a night position, PFC Francis Haubner stepped on a mine that blew off his right foot and shredded both legs with shrapnel. Haubners face was facing downward when he tripped the mine and he became blinded by the dirt and shrapnel that was blown into his face. His medic went to work on him, offering encouragement that he got his ticket to go home, the so-called "Million Dollar Wound." The medic had just received by mail special T-shirts he ordered for his platoon which read, "Fuck Vietnam." He stuffed one into Haubners fatigue jacket just before he was dusted off. It would be the only personal belonging Haubner brought back from Vietnam.

Haubner was still blind at a hospital in Japan when a fellow grunt in the bed next to him offered to light a cigarette and they both discovered they only lived ten miles from each other in Massachusetts; Soon after Frank Haubner regained his sight. Each year since then on June 17 Haubner has worn his "Fuck Vietnam" shirt, happy to be alive and grateful to his medic for saving him.

One rifle company rotated in and out of Chu Lai for rest and refitting while the others took up security operations either west in Dragon Valley, closer to Chu Lai near FSB Fat City, or the southern sector of the Chu Lai Defense Command (CLDC) near LZ Gator and the southern rocket pocket. The "rest and refit" company in Chu Lai became the CLDC reaction force.

Mines and booby-traps continued to be the main threat for the grunts in their CLDC mission. The mines were also affecting the pacified civilians who were drawn to the government as security improved. On June 20, a Delta patrol southwest of Gator saw distraught villagers bring in a female from the Binh Yen hamlets, who had lost her left foot to a mine. She was promptly dusted off.

The following day Charlie Company hooked out on Chinooks to LZ Young to provide road security for a convoy traveling from Tam Ky to Tien Phouc. LZ Young sat seven miles northwest of the upper reaches of Dragon Valley. The day was concluded at 8:55PM when Delta's 3rd Platoons' mechanized ambush detonated near Thanh Tra (2). A sweep revealed one Vietcong chicken killed in action.

Delta's search and clear operations southwest of Gator denied any sanctuary for the enemy in that area. On June 22, their soldiers discovered one ton of rice in one hooch, stored in thirty-six large cement jars. The next day five more tons of rice were found, along with trip wire, medical supplies and NVA clothing. The rice was moved by helicopter to Binh Son.

Intelligence reports which flowed into the 198th Brigade Headquarters pointed to planned attacks from Vietcong and NVA units against Popular Force and Regional Force installations. The targeted areas were Nuoc Mau village by the abandoned LZ Gator and Highway

One, continuing north through the Ly Tin District east of Fat City. Hills 76 and 270 were to be mortared by the enemy to provide cover for units infiltrating from the mountains for the attacks. The enemy objective was two-fold: Create instability among the pacified hamlets and secure much needed rice for the enemy hiding in the mountains. The enemy was reportedly gathering its strength for the attacks, in the Dragon Valley/Ky Tra area twelve miles west of Chu Lai.

To spoil the enemy's attack plans the battalion was saddled up once again. The morning of June 25 saw Bravo Company air assault into the northern boundary of Dragon Valley. Its arrival was met by small arms fire. Later Bravo received more small arms fire near My Dong (1) but the enemy evaded. Bravo's pursuit yielded ten NVA uniforms and documents. A booby-trap hit one soldier with shrapnel wounds to his arms and legs. In the span of that first day, Bravo found and destroyed twenty-two enemy fighting bunkers. Alpha Company air-assaulted to the southern end of the valley by the Quan River and began search and clear patrols.

Delta's 3rd Platoon landed one and one-quarter mile west of Bravo near Duc Phu (3), a Popular Force outpost in Ky Tra. The Ky Tra PF outpost was to serve as the battalion command post for the operation. The remainder of Delta moved to Fat City to secure the surrounding area. Echo's recon platoon was tasked to search the dense terrain west of LZ Bayonet for any enemy activity.

On the morning of June 26, Charlie Company was relieved from convoy protection duties and also air-assaulted to the center and western edge of Dragon Valley near Thuan Yen (3). Three companies, Alpha, Bravo and Charlie were now in place to scour the valley area and search for enemy activity. Bravo's second day in the northern sector yielded another small camp with potatoes, NVA backpacks, training manuals and sixty-nine glossy prints of Ho Chi Minh's funeral.

Alpha pushed west into the mountains one and one-half mile from the valley floor. Sergeant Kenneth Schanke led the 2nd Platoon through the dense terrain while looking for a suitable night defensive position (NDP). He by-passed some double-canopy jungle which was too dense for movement and chose to follow a streambed which curved around a blind corner. The enemy had made the same choice as it approached Alpha from the opposite direction.

Schanke came face to face with the NVA's point man and for a split second they stared into each others eyes. Schanke then poured a burst of M16 fire into his chest. Schanke's M60 machine gunner was just behind him and stepped up to pour devastating fire up the streambed as the NVA quickly scattered. Schanke's souvenirs for the encounter were an AK-47 assault rifle, ammunition, pistol belt with strap, belt with silver buckle, wallet and a pack of Winston cigarettes.

Alphas soldiers moved upstream in the direction of the fleeing NVA and found a cache of equipment and food, dumped in the steam by the fleeing enemy. The battalion commander, LTC Werezynski, landed to survey the fight and picked up the captured AK-47 to take back for "Intelligence Value", promising Schanke he'd get it back. When Schanke finally made it back to Chu Lai for a standdown he inquired about his captured AK-47 and received the response, "What AK-47?"

Shoot-and-run tactics continued against the battalion's soldiers as they searched and cleared the Dragon Valley/Ky Tra region. Small groups of VC or NVA were encountered but they evaded quickly. Periodically the enemy used 60mm mortar fire against its pursuers but rarely fired more than two or three rounds for lack of ammunition. Isolated hooch's were found containing hastily abandoned food and equipment.

The radar sets on LZ Chippewa and Hill 270 continued to pick up nightly movement of small groups of insurgents and quickly rewarded the enemy's daring with mortar and artillery fire. Visual reconnaissance by helicopter gunships made the daytime equally hazardous for the enemy. Closer to Highway One and the populated hamlets, Vietnamese forces exerted their control with sweeps of their own, designed to pick up infiltrating Vietcong and in the process, often discovering some of their own soldiers who were deserters or draft dodgers.

At 9:10PM on June 30, Popular Force (PF) Platoons 202 and 84 engaged an estimated company of Vietcong at close range near Ky Sanh (1) one and one-half miles south of FSB Fat City. They slugged it out in a short but intense firefight as the VC fired B40 rockets and threw hand grenades within twenty feet of the PF's. Seven VC were killed before the enemy fled at the cost of two PF's killed and two wounded. Numerous weapons were captured as artillery fire punished the fleeing enemy.

By the end of June 1970, the Vietnamese government control and stability of the Chu Lai/Ly Tin area was such that all U.S. Marine CAP teams in the area were withdrawn.

15 – TACTICAL HEGEMONY

A WAR OF MINES AND AMBUSHES

On July 1, 1970, Alpha Company in the northern sector of Dragon Valley continued its search and clear operations in conjunction with Bravo Company. Alpha received orders to search Thuan An Tuy (1) where intelligence reports indicated an NVA unit of unknown size was quartered. Alpha's commander divided the company into two elements and moved into the hamlet from opposite sides. The same time they approached the hamlet a platoon of NVA walked in from another direction which prompted a sharp firefight. Alpha's M60 machineguns, M79 grenade launchers and M16's quickly took control of the situation. The NVA split into two groups and evaded to the east and south, leaving behind five dead and four wounded. To Alpha's surprise the enemy seemed well armed and equipped; some were wearing steel helmets and carrying back-packs with sacks of Chicom grenades.

That night at 2:35AM, Bravo's night defensive position (NDP) was hit by ten to fifteen sappers near Thuan Yen (2), one and one-half miles west of Alpha. The fighting was close-in and two soldiers were wounded with multiple fragment wounds requiring a dustoff. The RTO for Bravo's Forward Observer was severely wounded, losing his left leg to a satchel charge. Seven other soldiers were slightly wounded and remained in the field. The sappers disappeared as quickly as they came.

Alpha and Bravo continued to be harassed by small arms fire and 60mm mortars as they patrolled the area. The next evening Bravo was once again hit by small arms fire and Chicom grenades while in their NDP. Preplanned artillery fires were called on the attackers. A morning sweep revealed bloody clothing and a severed arm. Ten more Bravo soldiers were slightly wounded from the nighttime encounter but they remained in the field.

At first light Bravo's 1st Platoon was moved to the battalion's forward command post at the Ky Tra Regional Forces outpost to help secure the perimeter. The remainder of the company was sent to FSB Fat City to replace Delta, which was moved to Chu Lai for a standdown.

Early on the morning of July 4 Echo's Recon Platoon air assaulted into the southern end of Dragon Valley to reconnoiter suspected enemy positions. Its mission was to clear its assigned area, then be picked up and air-assault four miles farther south to search for other enemy camps. Charlie Company patrolled two miles farther west into the mountains overlooking the middle sector of Dragon Valley and found some small way stations used by the enemy. The grunts called for artillery fire to destroy the dwellings but the targets were out of range for the guns. The soldiers destroyed the small camps as best they could with C-4 explosive in the bunkers and by burning the hooch's.

At 5:30PM, Alpha spotted six NVA soldiers just west of Thuan Yen (2) in the northern reaches of the valley. They opened up with small arms fire until artillery fire could be brought to bear on the enemy. The 2nd Platoon swept the area and spotted a booby-trapped 105mm Howitzer shell attached to a trip wire. Sergeant Steve Hall sent two men forward to examine the mine. As they moved forward Hall spotted an NVA slipping through the brush preparing to throw a grenade at his comrades. Hall quickly charged into the wood line and emptied a full magazine of M16 rounds into the insurgent. His quick action earned him a Bronze Star. Gunfire erupted as three more NVA bolted out of the bushes and ran to the west. The platoon's rifle fire hastened their departure. The terrain was too dense for pursuit and the sky was getting dark so the soldiers settled into a night defensive position.

Regional Force (RF) Company 931 at the Ky Tra outpost also contributed to clearing the valley in conjunction with the battalion's efforts by aggressively patrolling the area north of its outpost. The 5th/46th assisted the RF's by air-dropping 10,000 Chieu Hoi leaflets in the Ky Tra area.

The next day Alpha joined forces with the RF company in a combined sweep and, at 7:10AM bumped into a platoon of both VC and NVA near Thuan Yen (1). Alpha and the RF's briefly slugged it out with small arms fire before the enemy fled west, leaving behind five of their

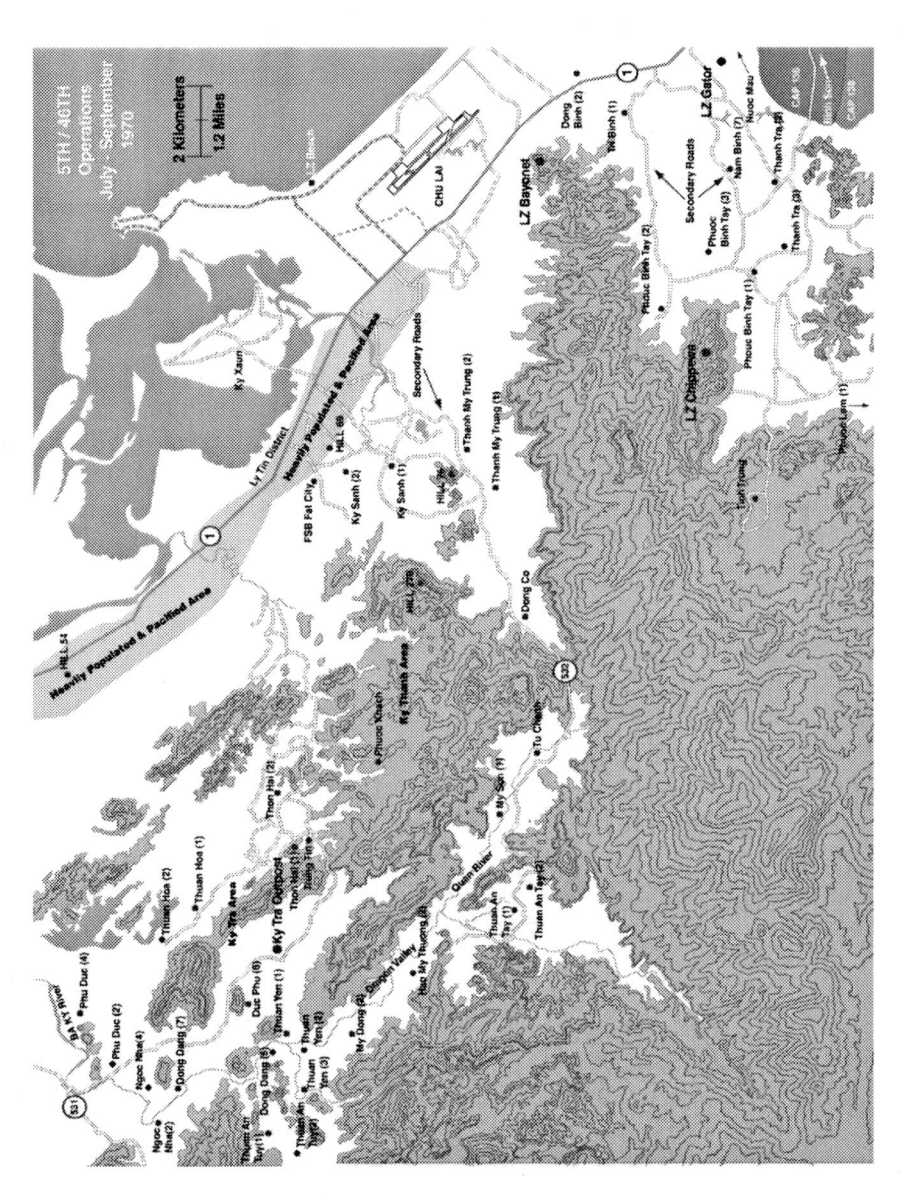

5th/46th Operations, July-September, 1970

dead comrades. Two hours later Alpha's 2nd Platoon found another dead NVA in a shallow tunnel. He had escaped the firefight but died of his wounds while hiding.

Two days later on July 7, the RF's hit some more VC in a midnight ambush just southwest of their Ky Tra command post, killing two Vietcong. Later they received intelligence from civilians in the area that a platoon of Vietcong was hiding near Duc Phu (6), one and one-half miles northwest of their base camp. LTC Werezynski planned an air-assault on the hamlet for early the next morning on July 8 that would take the RF's in by helicopter for a sweep of the area in conjunction with Alpha, which was already close to the target. The battalion's recon platoon was also to be choppered in to serve as a blocking force, but before this operation, enemy action would abort recon's part of the plan. Alpha Company starting moving into their sector the night of July 7 and set up live and mechanical ambushes. Early the morning of July 8 it moved out to make contact with the enemy. On their way Alpha found one NVA killed from one of their MA's. Blood trails led away from the ambush site.

Two miles further south on July 6, the recon platoon patrolled the western edge of Dragon Valley near Hao My Thuong (3). To its east lay the valley floor which contained an old banana plantation in open terrain that was interspersed with banana trees. To the valley's west, where it now patrolled, there was mountainous jungle.

Recon had been in a deadly cat and mouse game with a larger enemy force that had been stalking them ever since they arrived in Dragon Valley. The thick jungle was marked with numerous "speed trails" used by the enemy. These trails were pathways wide enough for rapid movement for large groups of insurgents hoping to avoid artillery fire.

The recon platoon tried to get resupplied at twilight in a small open area that was just off a speed trail, but the weather was too overcast and the LZ too small to make the drop. Only a few supplies were pushed out of the Huey in hopes of helping the grunts get through the night, then the bird returned to Chu Lai with most of its cargo.

The recon grunts moved four hundred yards off the speed trail and settled in for the night on a steep ridgeline. It rained all night. Nighttime illumination was only six percent and the rain made it worst, darkening the skies further. Sergeant Mark Edwins could not see his hand in front of his face during his night watch. The heavy rain made it extremely difficult to listen for enemy movement, with torrents of rain beating down on the thick foliage, but he knew the enemy was near. The field savvy grunt could smell them because they had a distinct odor, "like a wet dog", that he would never forget.

On the morning of the 7th, the platoon moved back to the speed trail and cautiously approached their drop zone to make another attempt at resupply. Sergeant Edwins took the point. Behind him were SGT David McClellan, then Sgt. Tom Brissey followed by the RTO, SP/4 Harry Kulchinsky and then SP/4 Michael O'Neil.

They had moved only two hundred yards. Brissey's mind was contemplating the supply of drinking water that the Huey would deliver when he was suddenly hit by a bright flash of light. The entire point element was shattered by a command-detonated mine which propelled their bodies to the ground, ripping their flesh with shards of shrapnel. It was a textbook ambush, the enemy waited until the center of the patrol reached the mine before detonating it. No sooner had the blast occurred than the scream for "medic!" rang out and the staccato clacking of AK-47's filled the air.

Brissey unloaded two clips of M16 fire toward the sound of the AK's. Edwins was stunned like the others but attempted to pour out fire until he looked at his midsection. Blood covered his whole body. He opened his fatigue pants to find his body torn apart by shrapnel. His apprehensive eyes caught the source of his misery, a tree stump just off the trail, which had held the mine. The wire that triggered the detonation led away into denser foliage. O'Neil reached him and took Edwin's M16 to blast the area around him, keeping the enemy at bay as other comrades arrived and called for a dustoff.

The enemy's careful stalking of the elusive recon soldiers had paid off. Edwins had twenty shrapnel wounds to his body; McClellan suffered shrapnel to his arms and legs. His right leg and left arm were broken. Brissey suffered shrapnel to his neck and head. Kulchinsky, carrying the radio, took shrapnel to the neck and legs. McNeil was the least wounded but suffered a painful wound to his left leg.

The recon platoon completed the move to the small resupply clearing but this time to receive a dustoff. The dustoff was hit with enemy fire as it approached the clearing so it promptly pulled pitch to escape the enemy bullets and did not land. Gunships appeared behind the dustoff and raked the area with rocket and machinegun fire. The dustoff returned again and picked up the wounded recon soldiers the undermanned platoon could ill-afford to lose. Three of them, Edwins,

McClellan and Kulchinsky were severe enough to warrant a trip home. Brissey and O'Neil would eventually return to the platoon.

Air strikes continued to pound the terrain in and around Dragon Valley whenever enemy movement or evidence of enemy base camps was spotted by low-flying spotter planes. A small enemy camp was sighted on a mountain hilltop two miles southeast of the southern end of Dragon Valley and the site was promptly hit with eight - five hundred-pound bombs followed by canisters of napalm. The valley was a distant twelve miles west of Chu Lai but still contained hamlets that were targeted for pacification in an ever-expanding reach of population control. The battalion's mission was no longer coastal pacification, but securing small populations in remote mountain hamlets which were once the secure enclave of the enemy.

On the afternoon of July 9, Alpha's 3rd Platoon spotted several NVA who chose to flee. The soldiers were too far from the enemy to be effective with their organic weapons so an artillery fire mission was laid on. Later a sweep of the bombed area found NVA uniforms, helmets, an AK-47 assault rifle and an SKS rifle along with some rice. Blood trails led away from the site.

The next day at twilight seven more NVA were spotted and Alpha called on the 81mm mortars from the Ky Tra outpost as well as 105mm artillery fire. The enemy was not pursued after the artillery pulverized the area because another dark, near-moonless night was approaching. Unlike night sweeps around FSB Fat City, where the terrain was more open and the enemy less likely to be operating in larger units, the Dragon Valley area, with its dense terrain and the possibility of encountering a large NVA element, precluded nighttime sweeps. But the battalion continued to saturate the area with nightly live and mechanical ambushes.

While the 5th/46th Infantry Battalion worked in the mountains to expand pacification and deny solace to the enemy, the Vietnamese militias also expanded their control beyond the Chu Lai area. Popular Force (PF) Platoon 175, operating three-quarters of a mile west of FSB Fat City, hit a Vietcong platoon on the move. 81mm mortars on Fat City illuminated the sky while the PF's slugged it out at close range in a brief but intense fire fight, the enemy using B40 rockets and hand grenades. One PF was killed and another wounded. Six Vietcong were killed. An examination of the dead bodies revealed no shoes, or shirts and only short pants. The PF's had caught a sapper platoon on the move.

The morning of July 11 saw Charlie Company operating near Hill 54, seven miles up Highway One from Chu Lai, in conjunction with RF Company 196. Delta was moved to the center of Dragon Valley to support Alpha after it had rested and refitted in Chu Lai. Alpha continued to push out beyond the northern sector of the valley floor, moving into mountainous and dense terrain. Bravo assigned its 1st Platoon to help secure the Ky Tra outpost which was still a forward command post for the battalion's operations, while the balance of the company secured FSB Fat City.

Delta's 3rd Platoon made its first enemy contact in the valley at 11:10AM near My Dong (2). Five NVA were spotted at close range. All wore green uniforms. They bolted into the bush as M16 fire plunged after them. The platoon pursued the enemy and came upon a small abandoned camp. Left behind was a pistol belt with a Chicom grenade, loaded AK-47 magazines, documents, canteens, NVA medical kits, ponchos, assorted bags of food and, most importantly, a roster listing the names of villagers in the surrounding hamlets who were supporting the enemy.

Air surveillance continued in support of the battalion's soldiers. Spotter planes often located isolated hooch's with remote but cultivated potato and corn fields and signs of recent enemy activity. Some of the camps were ingeniously camouflaged but the pilots spotted green NVA uniforms hanging out to dry. The camps were destroyed with air strikes.

Alpha had the last kill for July 11 when a mechanical ambush killed an NVA soldier at 7:05PM near Thuan Yen (1). The dead enemy soldier was well-equipped. He carried one AK-47, two thirty-round clips of ammunition, a pistol belt with three Chicom grenades, knapsack, hammock, two bandages, documents concerning his units' personnel, a ball point pen, can of milk, bag of candy, deck of cards, poncho and flashlight. In the typical mode of an insurgent on the move, he was dressed in black pajamas to fit in with the local populace if forced to quickly flee from Alpha's troops. His NVA uniform was tucked into his knapsack.

The next evening two of Alpha's mechanical ambushes exploded in the dark night which was now at almost zero moonlight illumination. The soldiers, hearing the sound of muffled explosions in the distance, could only wonder what their handiwork had accomplished.

At first light the soldiers set out to examine their sites. At one mechanical ambush a dead NVA was found with two Chicom grenades at his side and blood trails leading away. One quarter of a mile farther north the second site revealed three Chicom hand grenades lying in a pool of blood. Several blood trails, made by dragged bodies, led off into the brush. In the enemy's wake were a pith helmet, ponchos, hammocks, first aid packs, rucksacks and a woman's wallet with documents. Nearby the grunts found an improvised sapper training area with the type of concertina wire used on the bunker line at the Ky Tra command post.

Delta found and destroyed three storage structures ten feet by fifteen feet and six fighting bunkers nearby. It also uncovered two fresh graves, one a female and one a male, who were judged to be the insurgents they had shot on July 11 near My Dong (2). The next day the battalion recon platoon was sent to support Delta, back to the valley's center sector, the area where they were previously ambushed.

On the afternoon of July 14, Charlie Company air assaulted from Hill 54 to a location five miles farther west and landed just north of Phu Duc (4) to search and clear the hamlet and surrounding area. RF Company 931 was also inserted by Huey farther south of the hamlet to set up a blocking position.

Charlie came in on two lifts of Hueys. As the first lift departed the landing zone it received small arms fire from a bunker just west of the hamlet. Gunships came on station and poured rocket fire into the fortified position which caused a large secondary explosion of cached ammunition.

Charlie then found two more fortified bunkers complete with a twelve foot-deep well that yielded potable water. Speed trails ran north and west from the well. The Hueys that brought in Charlie picked up Alpha from the bushes and moved them to FSB Fat City to continue security operations in the area in place of Charlie Company.

Delta and the recon platoon patrolled the center of Dragon Valley as the shadowy enemy continued its evasive tactics. Two and one-half miles farther west, aerial surveillance identified an enemy camp with some NVA soldiers in a small area that covered only four hundred square yards. The Air Force had lots of bombs and few opportunities to use them, so an immediate air strike dropped over fifty - two hundred and fifty-pound bombs, obliterating the camp and the terrain around it. That night Delta spotted small lights one-half mile from its patrol base and called in artillery. The first rounds landed directly on the target. The lights went out.

In the morning Delta's 2nd Platoon approached the area of the night lamps and found one dead Vietcong killed by the artillery. Nearby another VC body was found in a freshly dug grave. The body's partially decayed state indicated it was killed the previous week as a result of another fire mission called by Delta.

Delta and the recon soldiers patrolled west of the Quan River which ran north to south through the valley. At 11:15AM they received sporadic small arms fire and staccato bursts from a 30-caliber machinegun on the east side of the river, approximately two hundred yards away. The machinegun fire was seen coming from a bunker.

The enemy made a poor decision to fire on Delta. Fire support was readily available to the battalion at all levels of destruction, from Howitzers to mortars and gunships to air strikes and each support group was eager for some work. Delta started with its 81mm mortars from its patrol base followed by 105mm artillery fire as it maneuvered toward the enemy. Gunships appeared and pulverized the area, followed by a spotter plane which had a jet aircraft on call. The air strike took place just as the grunts crossed the river.

Once again the enemy fled. Delta's soldiers found twenty-two enemy structures measuring eight feet by twelve feet with a bunker under each. Nearby, Delta's 3rd Platoon found an unexploded rocket from a gunship, propped up on its end and booby-trapped with a grenade.

The enemy's retreat was not surprising. The battalion did not lack for fire support and major firefight's were generally a thing of the past for the Americal Divisions soldiers. The enemy in the area usually sought to launch sapper attacks on pacified hamlets (considered more soft of a target) manned by RF/PF militia. The enemy's tactics for the 5th/46th Battalion was to continue to take as many American casualties as possible with mines and booby-traps.

Alpha Company's 1st Platoon at FSB Fat City was nudged into another VIP program through the initiative of seven Vietnamese children who brought them enemy hand grenades. The platoon leader thanked them and paid them in Vietnamese Piasters. The following day the children returned with more grenades, fuses for mines and ammunition.

At 11:50AM on July 17, Delta discovered three more graves containing NVA soldiers in green uniforms. Their bodies were buried the day before, and were attributed to the assault on the bunkers across the

Quan River. Three hours later two additional fresh graves were discovered containing more NVA in uniform.

Charlie Company was hit at 6:45PM with nine rounds of mortar fire near Phu Duc (2). Two of the enemy rounds were white phosphorous but there were no casualties. The following afternoon the 3rd Platoon's point element which include a scout dog and handler, hit a booby-trapped grenade which tore off the dogs left front leg. Its handler took shrapnel in the eye. PFC Stephen Dant, the soldier providing point security, was in front of the dog when the explosion went off underneath and behind him, lifting him into the air. Dant took most of the concussion while the dog took most of the shrapnel, but Dant also took shrapnel to his back, right arm and left leg.

This was an avoidable incident that sometimes happened when the instincts of the point element were disregarded. Dant saw that his patrol was heading into the middle of an open field with the grass about knee high. He wanted to maneuver along the tree line, still heading in the same direction, but with some cover and concealment. Dant halted the patrol to walk back to his squad leader, a new sergeant who had been transferred from the 4th Infantry Division which was departing Vietnam. The discussion developed into a heated argument and the Sergeant pulled rank, ordering Dant to "Move it right down on the line you're on!"

Charlie Company was picked up by Huey the morning of July 19 from the Duc Phu hamlets north of the Ky Tra outpost and air assaulted four miles farther south, deep into the mountains two miles west of My Dong (2) to search for a suspected enemy base camp.

That night PF Company 931 raided a church near their Ky Tra outpost that reportedly was the gathering place for Vietcong and the exchange of supplies. The PF's killed four VC and captured four more, along with eighty pounds of rice that was taken back to their outpost. The militia's aggressiveness cost them casualties the following day when four of the militia were wounded from a booby-trapped 105mm Howitzer round. Later two more were wounded from a booby-trapped grenade.

RF Company 196 killed two VC and captured four suspects one and one-half miles west of Ky Tra. The RF Company moved farther south to support the grunts of Charlie Company in its search and clear operations. Sniper fire and bursts of small arms fire were a constant menace for the RF's and Charlie's grunts in the dense terrain.

At 7:30AM July 22, Alpha returned to Dragon Valley to replace Delta in the center sector of the valley. Delta hooked out by Chinook to Chu Lai for rest and refitting. Farther northwest RF 196 was providing security for villagers to harvest crops when a patrol hit a group of insurgents near Duc Phu (6), killing four Vietcong and capturing Chicom grenades, an AK-47 and some documents. Four hours later they killed two more VC.

Another 198th Brigade-sponsored defoliation mission was set into motion. On July 23 the 198th Brigade Chemical Officer accompanied an aircraft flying a defoliation mission near Charlie's search and clear area. The aircraft, flying slow and low, was fired on and the aircraft commander wounded. Gunships were dispatched to neutralize the suspected areas of enemy fire and Charlie Company was tasked to sweep the area where the defoliant had just been dispersed.

Having not discovered any enemy camps, Charlie was lifted out of the mountains two days later and moved to Chu Lai for a rest and refitting. Its partner militia, the RF 196 Company returned to Hill 54 for some rest as well.

Delta combat air assaulted from Chu Lai to an uninhabited stretch of hilly terrain three miles northeast of the Ky Tra compound to search and clear while Bravo Company controlled the Fat City area and Alpha continued its operations in the middle of Dragon Valley. The battalion's recon platoon was tasked to operate with Delta.

Alpha's 1st Platoon spotted five Vietcong, three of them carrying AK-47's, walking only one hundred yards away. Alpha opened fire, killing one insurgent and wounding the others who fled. The dead insurgent wore a rucksack filled with rice, salt, eating utensils and documents. At noon on July 27, Alpha's 3rd Platoon was hit by small arms fire and called in artillery. One NVA body was found afterward.

Hostile activity was expected to remain low the rest of July as the enemy resupplied itself in preparation for the dark-moon phase at the end of August, when night attacks offered a higher chance of success. The enemy's main focus became stealing and caching food prior to the upcoming monsoon season.

On July 28, Delta lost its valuable Kit Carson Scout in an avoidable tragedy resulting from a simple miscalculation. As Delta's 3rd Platoon was returning to its patrol base in the mid-afternoon, they encountered a fork in the trail. The lead element followed the turn to the right because it knew the path to the left led to one of its own mechanical ambushes, which was composed of three claymore mines daisy-chained together with a trip wire. The last man in the patrol file was the Kit Carson Scout. He chose the path to the left as a shorter return route and detonated the claymores. He was killed instantly, absorbing hundreds of steel pellets from the hidden claymores. One other Delta soldier was wounded from the blast, which blew shrapnel across the low-lying brush onto the other trail.

During the early morning hours of July 29, Charlie Company once again packed up and was air assaulted back to the field, this time some three miles northwest of the Ky Tra outpost near Ngoc Nha (4). By mid-morning it had just finished setting up a mechanical ambush when it spotted three NVA soldiers walking into the kill zone and detonate the claymores. One NVA was killed and one wounded. The wounded soldier and his unscathed comrade promptly evaded into the bush, leaving behind a trail of blood. The dead NVA turned out to be an officer who was carrying maps, documents and a 9mm pistol.

Alpha Company's 3rd Platoon also caught the enemy in a mechanical ambush later that day. One North Vietnamese Soldier was killed and another wounded who was taken prisoner. The next day, July 30, Alpha's grunts checked another mechanical ambush site and found yet another NVA killed near Thuan Yen (1).

It was becoming routine. Like frontier trappers, the battalion's soldiers placed their traps with precision then returned the next morning. The catch was not furry creatures offering pelts, but enemy dead, or the blood of the dead removed by comrades, perhaps themselves wounded and destined to face a slower death. But in Vietnam the enemy was not helpless and they too could set traps, for a deadly effect.

What happened next on July 30 would tear at the seams of Charlie Company's morale for a long time. The battalion had been granted an extension of its operating area to pursue the enemy farther northwest from Dragon Valley into an area controlled by the 196th Light Infantry Brigade.

Charlie Company was tasked to push in that direction. In the late afternoon the company set up its patrol base and night position on a high ridge in dense terrain, a short mile and a quarter southeast of LZ Bowman. It was a textbook position for a night defensive position and patrol base. The high ground commanded a panoramic view of the valley floor to the east, and resupply would be easy. What the company commander did not know is that the terrain was so ideal it had been used many times before by units of the 196th Brigade. This reality was not fully understood ... except by the enemy.

At 5:00PM, as they prepared their defensive positions, a grenade with a trip wire was detonated and three soldiers were wounded who needed to be dusted off. Twenty minutes later a resupply bird came in. As the supplies were being off-loaded Private Ernie Hopkins, part of the forward observer team, reached his designated position on the perimeter. Dropping his heavy rucksack to the ground he watched as a rifle platoon slowly walked past him, on its way to their assigned sector on the NDP. The Huey completed its resupply mission and pulled pitch to move up and out, with the whooshing of its rotor blades parting the grass as it left the ground.

Charlie's Kit Carson Scout saw something appear on the ground that was revealed by the rotor-whipped grass and walked over to investigate. Hopkins watched the Huey lifting off as the riflemen walked pass him. He was satisfied he had reached his personal patch of dirt on the ridge where he would spend the night. One of the soldiers passing him suddenly stopped and stared at Hopkins, his face just one foot away. It was a black soldier, Private Jesse Hill from Tennessee who Hopkins did not know. It was a three second stare, no words exchanged, during which the Kit Carson Scout approached the object he saw on the ground. At that precise moment Hill mysteriously ended his stare and turned to face the other direction, with his back to Hopkins.

The scout took another step and triggered a daisy chain of mines, made up of old 81mm mortar canisters carefully placed to sweep the entire defensive position. The shrapnel shredded the scout who was killed instantly along with a Vietnamese interpreter at his side. Four Charlie soldiers were killed outright and seventeen others were shredded with shrapnel including Private Jesse Hill.

Hill's body took the shrapnel blasting across the perimeter destined to reach Hopkins. Hopkins quickly examined the gravely wounded black soldier and found nine holes in his body. There were too many severely-hemorrhaging entry wounds, not enough bandages and many additional screams for help emanating from the wounded across the hilltop. Sixteen other soldiers were down with wounds. Hopkins did the only rational thing he could think of at this critical moment. He placed nine of his fingers into the nine holes of his black comrade's body to stop the bleeding. Some makeshift bandages were found and Hill was moved to an arriving dustoff. Hopkins watched him depart, not sure if he would live or not.

The carnage was complete. Sergeant First Class (SFC) Donald Auten, the field first sergeant who the men affectionately called "A Lifer" led his men in death. He was from Cramerton, North Carolina, age 25 and married; PFC Jerold Franklin died on the hill at age 21. He was single from Greenville, Mississippi; Staff Sergeant (SSG) Dale Sathoff, single and 25 from St. Louis, Missouri and PFC Edward Whitten, single and 25 from Gaston, Oregon also died on the hill.

Seventeen other soldiers were wounded and dusted off, including PFC Donald Dean Layton who died on August 4. Layton was 21 and married from Aberdeen, South Dakota. Another soldier, PFC Robert Hart succumbed to his wounds on August 17. Hart was 22 and single from Chicago, Illinois. The "search and clear missions" in Dragon Valley and the Ky Tra area had come hard for Charlie Company. Every one of the ten battalion soldiers killed in action since May 21 were Charlie grunts and many more in the company had been wounded.

Alpha Company's presence in Dragon Valley continued to hamper the enemy's movement. Another mechanical ambush killed a uniformed NVA soldier near Thuan Yen (1) on July 31. But one Alpha soldier accidentally detonated a trip flare near Dong Dang (5) resulting in a traumatic amputation of his right foot. Small arms fire plagued Alpha's patrols and another Alpha grunt was dusted off for a gunshot wound to his right arm near the hamlet.

Charlie Company was added to operate in conjunction with Alpha, its ranks decimated and demoralized from the tragedy on the hill. On August 9 twenty-nine new replacements to the battalion would all be assigned to Charlie Company. Also on July 30 Alpha's mechanical ambush killed another NVA near Thuan Yen (1). When an Alpha patrol reached the site, the soldiers' body had already been stripped of clothing and equipment.

Bravo Company was kept busy providing security for the FSB Fat City area by saturating the area with squad-size ambushes, supplemented by mechanical ambushes to deny the enemy easy movement. On August 1 they were moved by truck to Chu Lai for a rest and refitting.

Taking Control

The Americal's pressure on the enemy was unrelenting. Visual air reconnaissance constantly searched for any signs of enemy movement, construction of enemy way stations or small camps. On August 2 alone, four - five hundred-pound bombs were dropped on a suspected enemy position three miles southwest of Hill 76. Another air strike dropped nine - five hundred-pound bombs on Phuoc Khach, halfway between Fat City and Dragon Valley. And twelve - five hundred-pound bombs were dropped on a target one-half mile east of Phuoc Khach in dense terrain. Helicopter gunships flew low and fast through the narrow valleys and over dense mountainous terrain looking for "lucrative targets", which, at this point of the war could even be one enemy soldier.

All three battalions of the 198th Light Infantry Brigade continued to conduct operations that denied food to the enemy from the summer harvest. They interdicted known and suspected routes of supply and communications, and worked with Vietnamese Provincial (RF's) and District (PF's) forces to strengthen South Vietnamese government pacification efforts.

Early in 1970 the 5th/46th Battalion had been frustrated in its efforts to get the militias to take control of pacified hamlets in the AO Serene area near the My Lai's. The PF's, even though they were provided with new M-16's, preferred to sit back and let the Americans do the heavy lifting. Now the reality of American withdrawal sunk in. Under pressure from the Vietnamese provincial governments in Quang Ngai and Tam Ky, the militias were functioning more effectively, especially RF Company 931 at Ky Tra and PF Platoon 174 near Fat City. The Vietnamese also formed a special reconnaissance platoon made up exclusively of former NVA soldiers who were becoming quite effective.

When the Ky Tra outpost received enemy mortar fire it promptly returned its own mortar fire while American gunships sped to the area to find targets. As long as these irregular forces had a modicum of combat air support for routine fire support missions, and ARVN or 5th/46th Battalion ground support if a larger enemy force appeared, it maintained control over the northern reaches of Dragon Valley without the battalion's soldiers.

The battalion kept expanding its reach even farther to the west, looking to confront larger enemy elements. Bravo air assaulted to the LZ

Bowman area on August 4. The next day Bravo's patrols found small camps containing tunnels and storage pens for chickens. One Vietcong was killed by the 1st Platoon and his carbine captured. Bravo's 2nd Platoon also found a small camp with bunkers and pens for livestock. It was burned.

The battalion's and rifle companies in the 198th Infantry Brigade were often shifted to other battalions when intelligence indicated larger enemy movements may exist in a particular area. In this vein the 5th/46th sent a company to aid the 1st/52nd Battalion's operations, which were now working in the LZ Chippewa area. Likewise Charlie Company of the 1st/52nd Battalion had been inserted onto the Ky Thanh area one mile north of Phuoc Khach to search for enemy movement after the areas' previous pounding by air strikes. The 1st/52nd soldiers soon experienced the enemy's deadliness that was all too familiar to the soldiers of the 5th/46th. One soldier tripped a booby trap of two claymore mines, killing two soldiers and wounding eight others.

Delta of the 5th/46th Battalion, now operating two and one-half miles north of the Ky Tra outpost, found one dead VC by a mechanical ambush, with several blood trails leading away. During this transition to the Vietnamese, coordination of artillery fires became more crucial as the 2nd ARVN Division took more responsibility for field operations, extending from its headquarters in Quang Ngai City to Tam Ky City, north of Chu Lai. It was a hopeful sign because the 2nd Division was known to be much less aggressive than the 1st ARVN Division which operated farther north near Danang.

At 4:45AM the morning of August 5, 1970, nine rounds of 155mm artillery fire landed in the Ky Tra fire control zone, exploding in the hamlet at the base of the Ky Tra outpost, decimating the hamlet and almost hitting the outpost itself. This prompted a quick debate whether it was ARVN or US friendly fire, but the battalion's officers at Ky Tra quickly realized the ARVN artillery at Tam Ky fired the mission with poorly registered guns. Many peasants were killed or wounded. Those wounded were dusted off to Chu Lai. The incident was buried in official communications, better to bury the tragedy than to question the momentum of an ARVN takeover from US Forces.

At the same time the special "Chieu Hoi Recon Platoon" made up of NVA deserters engaged a group of Vietcong three miles north of LZ Bowman, killing nine of the enemy. A Delta patrol found another of its mechanical ambushes had detonated and found scraps of flesh and bones in its wake. Two blood trails led off into the bush. One body was found nearby.

Bravo Company continued operating deep in the mountains two miles south of LZ Bowman. Its 1st Platoon found a small camp and killed one Vietcong. Its 2nd Platoon found another small VC base camp near Don Qua (1) that contained bunkers, chickens and a blacksmith shop with tools. The camp was destroyed. Charlie Company of the 1st/52nd Battalion continued its operations in the center of Dragon Valley patrolling east and west of the valley floor. Its 1st Platoon patrolled one-quarter mile west of Dong Dang (5) when, at 8:50AM, the patrols point man tripped a flare which alerted a hidden enemy soldier to detonate two claymore mines. Two soldiers were killed outright and eight soldiers were wounded. Another 1st/52nd Battalion soldier died aboard the dustoff while flying to a Chu Lai hospital.

The following day a PF Platoon was sent from Tam Ky to look for a weapons cache one and one-quarter miles north of Bravo's location. Bravo's 1st Platoon moved north to assist in the search and found ten RPG rounds and a highly-prized starlight scope for an M16 rifle. Enemy contact in Dragon Valley accounted for five more casualties for Charlie of the 1st/52nd. Artillery, helicopter gunships and an air strike of napalm assisted the grunts overcome the enemy.

Because the enemy could not mass their forces for a major attack, it elected to launch limited attacks to make its presence known. In the dark of night at 3:40AM on August 7, it fired twenty to twenty-five mortar rounds and eight to ten rifle-propelled grenades at close range on the perimeter of Fire Support Base Fat City. A sapper attack followed but with limited success. Four satchel charges and nine grenades were found along the perimeter. One Vietcong was found dead. One American was wounded and dusted off while two others were treated and remained on Fat City. One five ton truck was destroyed after receiving a direct hit from a mortar round.

Charlie Company of the 1st/52nd under operational control of the 5th/46th, continued to take casualties in Dragon Valley. More of their men were wounded by booby-traps and small arms fire on August 7. Two days later they were withdrawn from their Dragon Valley mission.

The 5th/45th Infantry Battalion continued its work under Operation Geneva Park in support of the South Vietnamese Accelerated Pacification Program. Its tactical operations were focused on food denial operations and the interdiction of known and suspected routes of enemy resupply and communications. But increasingly the Vietnamese district and provincial forces were taking on a bigger role in the battalion's area of operations.

Mid-August saw Alpha Company operating off FSB Fat City, saturating the area with live and mechanical ambushes. Bravo conducted search and clear operations in mountains one and one-half miles southwest of LZ Bowman extending to an area four miles farther southeast of Bowman. Delta conducted operations in the southern boundaries of Bravo's area. Charlie Company was lifted out to Chu Lai for a rest and refitting along with the battalion's recon platoon.

Each opportunity at "rest and refitting" was an occasion for the battalion's soldiers to unwind on the Chu Lai beach. The goal was to rotate each company every two to three weeks back to Chu Lai for several days of rest, depending on the tactical situation in the field. When a company arrived back at the battalion's base camp - LZ Beach - it was met by the First Sergeant and Company Armorer. Immediately weapons, ammunition, hand grenades, Claymore mines, smoke grenades etc. were turned in and secured before the "resting" could begin. The arms and ammunition were returned only when the soldiers climbed on trucks to be sent back out to the field.

For most soldiers rest involved beer, more beer and nightly BBQ on the beach. Pot (marijuana) was available on the huge Chu Lai base for those who wanted to smoke joints to wind down. Others sought out liquor at the base exchange, to supplement their beer with bourbon, tequila or rum. The choice a soldier made to forget about the war usually came down to being a "Juicer" (booze) or a "Head" (drugs).

Soldiers found relaxation by swimming in the ocean, playing beach volley ball, or listening to their favorite music which most frequently was either country or Motown. To be sure, not all soldiers embraced alcohol or drugs, but beer remained the most popular choice to "loosen up." The music, booze and/or pot were a quick way to bring a soldier's mind back to his hometown and the relationships he left behind.

Relationships were important and sometimes the bonds between soldiers were stronger than their families. As the war's unpopularity reached a fever pitch in 1970, some letters to the battalion's grunts from family members were critical of their duty in Vietnam. The 5th/46th

Battalion's chaplain increasingly counseled soldiers whose mothers put them down for being in the war.

Even the chaplain's own mother criticized him for going to Vietnam, (an assignment the chaplain volunteered for), and "Dying for nothing". The chaplain reminded his mother "My orders stated, 'Proceed to Vietnam' they didn't state, 'Proceed to die in Vietnam." It was a personal rift that would never heal between the Episcopal Priest and his mother, to the day she died.

The Black Power movement was ever present on the large Chu Lai base and grew, largely fomented by those in rear echelon jobs who were commonly know as "Rear Echelon Mother Fuckers" or "REMF's". When the battalion's black soldiers returned from the field for a rest and refitting with their comrades, intense efforts were made by Black Power REMF's to convince their "black brothers" not to fight a "white mans war."

On a few occasions black soldiers within the battalion refused to go back to the field. As one white soldier noted, "The back power thing got into their heads and there was not much that could be done". When Charlie Company returned to the field after their heavy losses on July 30, three black soldiers refused to go on patrol and were court martialed. This type of refusal, however, was rare for the battalion.

On one standdown Charlie's soldiers eagerly entered the enlisted club in Chu Lai, ready for cold beer served by Vietnamese women who worked on the base (the Vietnamese females with French blood were especially attractive). Entertainment included a floor show, this time by two blond female Australian singers, dressed in tight, glittering gold costumes.

It was time for the field soldiers to fall in love again. As the show progressed with the band singing, "We Gotta Get Out of This Place" the grunts heard jeers and cat calls coming from behind them. They turned to see a large group of twenty to thirty "soul brothers" jeering at the Aussie band.

As one soldier recalled, "These guys had the 'Look', dark wire-rimmed sun glasses, bracelets made from bootlaces, bush hats pulled down over their eyes and facial sneers designed to intimidate us 'white boys'. The problem was we had faced far worse in the field and the beer made us tougher than usual".

Charlie's soldiers could sense the blacks wanted to take their racial tensions out on the field grunts. One of Charlie's soldiers, a biker from Seattle who stood over six feet tall, stood up to take care of business. Charlie's company commander told him to sit down. But the incessant cat calls and jeers from the group of blacks spoiled the pleasure from the music and singing and accomplished what was intended, to agitate the soldiers.

The black REMF's approached the whites who were still sitting in their chairs. A black hand holding a smoldering cigarette hovered over a soldiers half-filled can of Pabst beer. The cigarette was dropped into the can which had the effect, as one soldier recalled, "Of a starter's pistol going off to start a race." The fight was on.

Charlie's black field soldiers made it out of the club quickly. Tables were overturned and chairs flew through the air. In a few short minutes everyone started leaving or being dragged out by buddies after someone shouted, "The MP's are on the way!" As was usually the case, the field grunts were confined to their company area for the rest of the standdown for fighting, while the REMF's waited until they could do it again to the next field unit on standdown.

Nighttime in Chu Lai could be dangerous for soldiers from the field if they wandered alone too far from the battalion area. On several occasions white soldiers were beaten by small groups of black REMF's. The potential for small riots on the large base lifted its ugly head from time to time, but was usually mitigated by Military Police or security contingents in each unit. Most riots were squelched but anger over the war and "white injustice" continued to boil and would only stop when the division withdrew from Vietnam.

Alpha's assigned area around Fat City required it to walk a tightrope to interdict Vietcong in a populated and increasingly pacified area. Early on the morning of August 15, some children detonated a mechanical ambush, which killed one and wounded three.

Delta's 2nd Platoon air assaulted to a river bed by Danh Son (1), surprising four Vietcong who quickly tried to evade. One was killed. A sweep of the area revealed twenty new NVA uniforms tucked inside four knapsacks. Bravo's 2nd Platoon shot an NVA soldier one mile due south of LZ Bowman and tried to keep him alive for questioning, but he succumbed to his wound. RF Group 132 killed four more Vietcong at 9:00PM, capturing two AK-47 assault rifles, eight pounds of TNT and ten hand grenades near Dong Dang (7).

Adding to the pressure exerted on the enemy by the 5th/46th Infantry Battalion and the RF and PF forces which supported them, were specialized sniper teams inserted into areas of known enemy movement not being covered by ground troops.

The deadly business of hunting and trapping the enemy continued. Delta found a dead NVA soldier by one of its mechanical ambushes on August 15 in dense terrain south of LZ Bowman. The soldiers hoped the dead soldiers' comrades would return for his body so they left him there and set up another mechanical ambush. The following day they returned to find the dead body still in place but the claymores had been detonated, and blood trails led off into the bushes.

On another occasion in Dragon Valley, a Charlie Company platoon was on patrol with its Vietnamese Scout, "Bo" walking point. Bo saw a trip wire on the trail in front of him. The patrol set up a mechanical ambush about ten feet up the trail, then purposely set off the booby-trap (a Russian grenade) hoping the enemy would come to check out the explosion.

The patrol left the immediate area for about thirty minutes when they heard their claymores go off. Returning they found three enemy insurgents, two whose lower half of their bodies were gone and a third full of shrapnel but still alive. As one soldier remembered, "The look of shock and surprise was cemented on their faces." Bo, the Vietnamese scout looked at the insurgent still alive but barely breathing and said, "I kill you now", then put him out of his misery with an AK-47 round.

On August 16, RF Group 132 (Company's 196 and 104) returned to the control of the Ly Tin Provincial District on Hill 54. Enemy activity remained low as the full moon favored night movements for battalion soldiers and the South Vietnamese militias. The night of August 17 presented one hundred percent illumination and the following night ninety-nine percent illumination. On August 18, Alpha was moved from the Fat City area to Chu Lai for a rest and refitting. Bravo continued its operations from LZ Bowman south to the northern reaches of Dragon Valley. Charlie moved by trucks from Chu Lai to the Hill 54 area then moved by foot southward to conduct day patrols and night ambushes. The battalion's recon platoon operated close by.

In addition to poor race relations and drugs in the rear, the problem of Venereal Disease (VD) grew in scope during the months of the American's withdrawal, the 5th/46th and other battalions in the war. The absence of enemy activity around large populated areas and bases, such as Fire Support Base Fat City, and the pacification of those populations, brought about looser control between soldiers and Vietnamese "Boom-Boom Girls" (Prostitutes).

Not only did soldiers contract VD through carelessness in Vietnam, but some soldiers returning from rest and recuperation (R&R) from abroad also came down with the disease. One example in the battalion reflected one of the many ways the war broke the human heart. A married soldier remained chaste while in Vietnam but after returning from an R&R in Hawaii where he was reunited with his wife, he was diagnosed with VD. The experienced field grunt wrote his wife "the marriage is over". He returned to the field to the only companionships he still valued.

Still, love can help compensate for many things. Another battalion soldier returned from R&R in Australia where he met "The love of my life, the most wonderful girl, Ellen." The battalion surgeon diagnosed him with VD which he contracted from Ellen while on R&R. The soldier wrote to her, "Get cleaned up because I'm coming back after my tour." The battalion's surgeon, bemused by the whole thing, found this soldiers love-smitten situation to warrant special merit and called a formal formation with his medical staff and the soldier, to present him a special citation (next page):

Delta continued its operations in the rugged terrain south of Bravo. On August 19, a soldier tripped a wire connected to a Chinese Communist grenade near Long Son (2), which ingeniously hung ten feet in the air to cause maximum damage. Two soldiers were dusted off with multiple fragment wounds.

Bravo's 1st Platoon bumped into a VC on a trail near Phuoc Loi (4). Their Kit Carson Scout tried to talk the VC into surrendering but he turned to run and was promptly cut down by M16 fire. He was carrying a bag that contained a NVA uniform. Close by, the patrol found a ten foot by ten foot hooch that contained more uniforms, GI entrenching tools and rice. Later tunnels were found that contained documents which were sent in for examination.

DEPARTMENT OF THE ARMY
Headquarters Company,
5th Battalion 46th Infantry
198th Infantry Brigade, Americal Division
APO San Francisco 96219

ACVD-FNG-69-MD   15 AUGUST 1970

SPECIAL ORDERS #69

1. Specialist ___, EN___, is awarded the Purple Heart with "VD" device for wounds suffered in combined operations with Australian forces.

2. Specialist ___ did during the period 22 July 1970 to 28 July 1970, while on attached status with Her Majesty's Australian Forces suffer injury of a serious and painful nature.

3. The aforementioned injury occurred while the individual was taking part in a cordon and search operation in the area around LZ Ellen, near Sidney, Australia.

4. After assessing the situation Specialist ___ did take action to preclude such injury occurring again.

5. By his ability to respond to duty despite great personal injury, and his display of clear thinking and initiative in taking action to preclude such injury in the future, Specialist ___ has shown extraordinary devotion to the ideals of life, liberty and (especially) the pursuit of happiness. In so doing he reflects great honor upon himself, his unit, and the United States Army (foreign and domestic).

FOR THE COMMANDER:

                    Beauregard Q. Dickhurtz Jr.
                    Major, VD, Agitator General

Three days later Delta troops discovered three potato fields ready for harvest near Dan Thuong Dong (1). Animal traps had been planted in the fields. The potatoes were dug up and a call for fuel was made to burn them. Three and one-half miles further east Delta's 2nd Platoon found that one of their mechanical ambushes rigged with two claymore mines had killed four enemy soldiers near Thuan An Tuy (2). Their ages ranged from eighteen to twenty-two. An M-16 rifle, two AK-47 assault rifles, one SKS rifle and six hand grenades were retrieved.

The following day Delta found two military structures loaded with NVA equipment, documents and ammunition near Dan Thuong Dong (4). Everything except the documents was destroyed. Nighttime illumination was now declining to about fifty percent but the battalion continued to exert pressure on the evading enemy.

Whenever intelligence reports pointed to possible movement of the Vietcong or NVA to hit pacified hamlets, spoiling attacks were launched in the form of "eagle flights". The flights were composed of several Hueys carrying a platoon of grunts, ready to land and engage the enemy where small groups of VC or NVA could be spotted.

On August 24, another group of RF Companies from Tam Ky was placed under the operational control of the 5th/46th Battalion. In addition, an ARVN mobile battalion from Tam Ky (#102) was scheduled to join the battalion from late August to early September. The timing coincided with the likelihood of small scale attacks with the declining night illumination. Election Day was also scheduled for August 30 and Vietnamese Independence Day was to be observed on September 2.

Division sniper teams were inserted when intelligence pointed to high value targets in areas not patrolled by the battalion. In addition, the Americal Divisions Long Range Reconnaissance Patrols (LRRP's) were also inserted into the battalion's large operational area to assist in detecting enemy movements. The small LRRP teams rarely made their presence known, opting to watch small groups of NVA and call for artillery or air strikes. Napalm continued to be dropped on small fields in the mountainous terrain when it appeared crops were being cultivated to feed the enemy.

The battalion's tactics and the support given to its soldiers allowed it to control an area that began deep in the rugged Annamite Mountains a full twenty miles west from Chu Lai, stretching east through the Piedmont of rolling hills to the coastal plains and the Americal's headquarters.

In the Americal Division's zeal to strengthen its hand in pacification and domination of the enemy, chemical defoliation missions, Agent Orange, continued to be flown in this large expanse of territory. The defoliation would have lasting effects on the soldiers who served there and the many Vietnamese who lived in the region, long after the armed struggle ended.

Delta Company continued to patrol a large area south and southwest of LZ Bowman, searching for signs of enemy activity. At noon on August 24, the 3rd Squad of the 2nd Platoon found and destroyed two NVA hooch's with bunkers that had been recently used near Thuan An Tuy (1), four miles southeast of Bowman. The next day the squad wounded and captured a Vietcong near the hamlet who was sixteen years old. The teenager wore NVA-type clothing and carried an AK-47, three magazines of ammo and two Chicom grenades. He was dusted off for questioning.

Another Delta patrol two miles farther west heard voices from within a thatched hooch in an area frequented by the NVA near Long Son (1). A hand grenade was tossed in the hooch before the grunts entered. They found a twenty-six year old female wounded in the head from the shrapnel. A young boy was by her side. Both were dusted off to a hospital.

RF Company 931 operated on the eastern edge of the high ground where Charlie Company was decimated on July 30. The RF's were now sharing the risks of field duty that the 5th/46th had become all too familiar with. One RF soldier stepped on a mine near Don Qua (2), suffering an amputation of his right leg. He was dusted off to the 23rd Surgical Hospital in Chu Lai.

On August 26, the Americal Division sent out a "Flash Message" to all its battalions to maximize its presence in the field against expected attacks the end of the month. Delta's soldiers near LZ Bowman were directed to pay special attention to any enemy attempting to infiltrate across its area in an attempt to attack the provincial city of Tam Ky. RF and PF units were designated to secure all bridges.

Bravo Company was moved to the southern rocket pocket in anticipation of another rocket attack on Chu Lai and Alpha moved from the Fat City area closer to Ly Tin, placing its night defensive position on Hill 69. Ambushes saturated the area bordering the heavily populated hamlets near Highway One. The battalion's recon platoon was placed on the eastern boundary of the densely covered mountains that overlooked

Hill's 76 and 69, to be a "Trip Wire" for enemy movement. The high ground it patrolled extended as close as two and one-half miles to Highway One. The enemy favored the area because the terrain provided cover and concealment for movement to launch an attack on FSB Fat City, Hill 69 or the Ly Tin District.

A Delta patrol encountered three Vietcong near Phuoc Lai (1). In response, a Vietcong promptly threw a grenade which wounded one Delta soldier with shrapnel. The outcome of the brief fight yielded one dead VC female in her forties while a male of the same age was captured. A Third VC in his twenties was wounded but escaped. His body was discovered a short distance away by a tracker dog assigned to the patrol. The heat was oppressive and, after making his find, the dog could go no farther. It was pulled out of the field with its handler as the dog was at risk of dying with a high body temperature.

Delta continued to make its presence known to the enemy. On August 29 at noon, another mechanical ambush killed two Vietcong near Long Son (1). The following day a small military camp was discovered near Phuoc Lai (1), containing three - six foot by eight foot dwellings constructed with stone walls. Each building contained a bunker and the dwellings were connected to one another by fighting trenches. Pots and pans were found inside. This time Delta's grunts did not destroy the camp but set up mechanical ambushes for its occupants, should they decide to return.

The deadly game of cat and mouse continued to work both ways. The following day a soldier tripped a booby-trapped grenade that wounded two, requiring a dustoff. That night at 8:00PM, Delta's night perimeter near Phouc Lai (2) spotted some movement. A patrol swept the area and received AK-47 fire which was answered in turn with M-16 fire. One hundred yards farther north the patrol found their nemeses, a dead Vietcong in a green uniform.

Alpha and Charlie Companies, operating in the Ly Tin area by Highway One, expanded their reach with eagle flights that transported them back to Dragon Valley. An Alpha Company eagle flight passed over the center of the valley near My Dong (1) on September 1. The Hueys spotted some military structures and promptly landed the grunts. Five - eight foot by ten foot buildings were searched and destroyed along with the NVA uniforms inside them. After completing their house cleaning, the grunts were fired on from a ridgeline one-quarter mile southwest of their position. Gunships snuffed out the enemy fire. Twenty minutes later the soldiers spotted three NVA one-hundred and fifty yards away, trying to return to their now destroyed camp. They were greeted with M16 fire and quickly evaded.

Charlie Company's eagle flights were sent two miles north of the Ky Tra outpost. Occasionally enemy soldiers were spotted, usually one soldier at a time, who quickly evaded into thick brush nearby. Sometimes Charlie's grunts elected to remain in the area for the night, placing out mechanical ambushes as well as squad-size live ambushes. The monsoon rains had begun which made movement for the enemy tougher and the field conditions for the battalion's soldiers more miserable.

Near Hill 69 and Fat City another Alpha ambush was unleashed on a group of twelve Vietcong at 9:30PM, but only one claymore mine found its mark. A sweep of the area the morning of September 2 found one dead VC whose body was dragged sixty yards from the ambush site to be buried later. The Vietnamese militia also contributed to the security of the Ly Tin area. PF Platoon 73, along with some RF's from Hill 54 ambushed a group of Vietcong near Tam Ky killing, among others, the deputy commander of the Viet Cong V/20 Light Force Company.

The area south of LZ Bowman, where Delta expanded its patrols into a larger area, also drew more attention from visual reconnaissance flights. Intelligence reports indicated the possible presence of the 72nd Sapper Battalion, located on a densely-covered mountain three miles south of Bowman. An air strike was brought down on the mountain which obliterated the terrain. The battalion strength was stretched so thin in people, no troops were available to assess the damage. Camouflaged structures were discovered in other parts of the region by helicopter gunships, which promptly destroyed them by rocket fire.

September 2 presented zero moonlight and the next night illumination would only improve by four percent. These were ideal conditions for enemy attacks on pacified areas or small hilltop defensive positions, but none ever came. The intensive pressure by the 5th/46th Infantry Battalion in conjunction with the area's popular force and regional force militias, and continuous air reconnaissance, gave little opportunity for the enemy to exert itself.

Delta's presence in the LZ Bowman area continued to yield enemy casualties, even if only one enemy soldier at a time. While setting up a patrol base at noon on September 3 near Don Qua (1), two NVA in uniform were spotted thirty feet away. Gunfire erupted killing one NVA and the other escaped. Aerial reconnaissance spotted small fields of cultivated gardens and freshly dug fighting positions around them. Gunships destroyed the positions wherever they were found. Two days later another camp was spotted on a densely-covered ridgeline only one and one-quarter mile southwest of Bowman. Twenty-five freshly dug fighting positions surrounded the camp. Several enemy soldiers were spotted running for cover as rocket fire from Cobra Gunships poured into the enemy position.

Another small enemy camp was spotted on a densely-covered ridgeline sitting on the western edge of Dragon Valley, overlooking My Dong (2) on the valley floor. This time jet aircraft were available and a strike mission of twenty - five hundred-pound bombs pummeled the camp and immediate area.

On September 6, Bravo returned from its operation in the rocket pocket. National Elections and the first anniversary of Ho Chi Minh's death had passed without incident and no rocket attacks were launched on Chu Lai. Bravo then air-assaulted out to the LZ Bowman area to replace Delta, which was sent to Chu Lai for a rest and refitting.

Pressure on the enemy from the Vietnamese militia continued as well. RF Group 132 was inserted to search and clear a sixteen square mile area running west to east and north to south of LZ Bowman. RF Group 118 air assaulted to the vicinity of Don Qua (1) one and one-half miles south of Bowman with a mission to sweep five square miles west and south of Bowman. The ARVN Mobile Assault Battalion out of Tam Ky was inserted five and one-half miles due south of Bowman by the Bong Mieu River to begin a long sweep that would cover twenty-one square miles of dense terrain, searching for main force enemy units.

Bravo's 3 Platoon found a small unoccupied enemy camp containing food and clothing three miles southeast of LZ Bowman. The grunts did not have the explosives to destroy the camp so they prepared a mechanical ambush to welcome any of the enemy that wished to return. Bravo's 1st Platoon found another small camp one-quarter mile farther southeast and it too was unoccupied but held three chickens, rice, fifty pounds of potatoes, pots and pans and a cooking fire still burning. East of Bowman the RF militia discovered sixteen Vietcong mines which it destroyed while sweeping the area.

Aerial reconnaissance spotted NVA soldiers four miles north of the Ky Tra Outpost which prompted the air-lift of Delta's 2nd Platoon to the area from its rest in Chu Lai. Upon Delta's arrival a firefight broke out which resulted in two NVA killed and one grunt wounded in the leg from rifle fire.

At 2:00PM on September 7, RF militia discovered seventeen more anti-personnel mines which were destroyed. Their afternoon work was concluded with killing two NVA regulars and the retrieval of two bags of documents. In the evening at 8:05PM, the RF's engaged more enemy in a short firefight which resulted in three green-uniformed Vietcong being killed, their equipment confiscated and numerous blood trails leading off from the site of the contact.

At 5:25AM on September 9, the Vietcong managed to launch an offensive action by firing eight rockets into Chu Lai from the southern rocket pocket. The rockets smashed onto the 198th Brigade stand-down area on the Chu Lai beach. The outpost on LZ Chippewa saw the flashes of light as the rockets were launched and counter-battery fires were immediately poured into the launch site from artillery in Chu Lai.

Intelligence reports on enemy activity from pacified villagers greatly increased in the fall of 1970 as security improved and a more competent Vietnamese militia exerted itself. But it was the villagers who were caught in the vise of a war that would not permit the normal hamlet life they desperately sought, and often they were the ones who suffered the most. At 7:00PM a hamlet chief in Ky Sahn Village was assassinated by two Vietcong dressed in militia fatigue uniforms and carrying M-16 rifles.

The pressure on the enemy continued. The next day at 6:30AM, RF Company 500 raided some enemy positions two miles west of Hill 54 where two squads of Vietcong were sleeping. Five VC were killed, their weapons captured, and artillery fire was called on those that fled. Later RF Company 931 killed three VC during a sweep in Dragon Valley near Thuan Yen (1). Its presence in the valley would come at a cost. On September 11 at 3:30PM, one of the RF's stepped on a homemade pressure-release type mine, killing him and wounding two comrades. Close by another patrol from the same company engaged twelve Vietcong, killing three of the enemy before the remainder fled.

That same morning Delta Company combat air assaulted from Chu Lai back to Dragon Valley, landing separate elements in the My Dong (2) and Thuan An Tuy (2) areas. Bravo Company was also air-assaulted to the Phuoc Loi (1) and Don Qua (2) hamlet areas south of LZ Bowman. A few hours later Bravo's artillery forward observer, 1LT Erdman, was hit by a booby-trapped claymore mine that seriously wounded him in the right arm and both legs.

Alpha Company continued its daylight observation and nighttime ambushes in the Hill 76, Hill 270 and Fat City area along with Echo Company's Recon Platoon. Charlie Company was withdrawn from the field for a rest and refitting at Chu Lai.

On September 12 two Vietnamese children, ages thirteen to fourteen brought munitions to Alpha's 2nd Platoon two miles northwest of Fat City. Six – 60mm mortar rounds and one 105mm Howitzer round were turned in for payment in Vietnamese Piasters. Delta, out in Dragon Valley, shook the bushes and made contact with seven VC just south of My Dong (2), killing two and capturing an AK-47 with some Chicom grenades while the remainder of the enemy fled to the southwest. A sweep found two dead VC close by without their weapons. One body yielded pictures of the insurgent's family and two documents. The bodies were still warm to the touch but their war was over, having been ended by Alpha minutes before.

September 12 was expected to be the "High Point" of any enemy offensive that could be launched after the anniversary of Ho Chi Minh's death on September 3. Small groups of NVA and Vietcong attempted to destabilize the region but without success. Many of the battalion's ambushes were down to squad size elements, although they kept close to other squads for mutual support. A typical enemy encounter occurred at 6:00PM when Delta's 3rd Squad of its 2nd Platoon spotted four Vietcong, one-quarter mile away. Artillery was called on the insurgents who broke and ran as seven rounds of 105mm high explosives landed near them. The enemy was seen running into a bunker. The artillery adjusted fires and the second volley scored a direct hit. The following day while sweeping the area, Delta's grunts found four fresh graves.

Tactical Dominance

The 5th/46th Infantry Battalion, supported by artillery and helicopter gunships and the Vietnamese militia, now controlled an area that reached well beyond the original assigned boundaries of the Chu Lai Defense Command (CLDC). That "reach" stretched from Chu Lai north to the southern boundaries of Tam Ky; to sixteen-twenty miles west into the mountainous terrain beyond LZ Bowman and south to the southern rocket pocket and the Nam Binh hamlets west of the now abandoned LZ

Gator. The battalion could and would appear at any time on any terrain where intelligence revealed possible enemy movement.

The battalion's plans for September 13-19, 1970 reflected the operational flexibility it had gained. Alpha Company was tasked to conduct spoiling attacks, eagle flights and aerial reconnaissance to hunt for VC/NVA in "known and suspected locations." It would also work with the Vietnamese militia in the Ly Tin District during the rice harvest to interdict the enemy's attempts to secure rice for the monsoon season. Its assigned area covered eight square miles of terrain that included Hills 270, 76 and FSB Fat City. Alpha was slated to return to Chu Lai on September 14 for a rest and re-training and then be reinserted back onto the field on September 17 in "An area to be determined by the tactical situation."

Bravo Company conducted platoon-size and squad-size patrols and saturation ambushes in a dense area covering three square miles south of LZ Bowman. Maximum emphasis was placed on manned and mechanical ambushes which reinforced its control over this contentious area. Bravo was scheduled to return to Chu Lai for a rest and re-training on September 17.

Charlie Company finished its rest in Chu Lai and prepared to be reinserted into a five square mile area north of the Ky Tra Outpost which remained the battalion's forward command post. Delta continued its operations in a nine square mile quadrant that encompassed the center of Dragon Valley and the rugged terrain north, east and west.

Electronic sensors were used to aid the battalion in detecting enemy movement. The battalion recon platoon was tasked with the setup of these sensors in the bush and the replacement of batteries when needed. The recon platoon was also sent to Chu Lai for a rest and preparation for reinsertion into the field on September 17.

Throughout the summer and fall of 1970 the battalion's mortars were tactically placed to offer offensive fire against enemy infiltration into pacified areas. "Light" teams of 81mm mortars and "Heavy" teams of 4.2-inch mortars were placed on Hill 270 and Fire Support Base Fat City, along with ground surveillance (AN/PP5-5) radar. Sniper teams continued to be inserted to fill gaps of coverage where enemy movement was reported. The Americal Division's Long Range Reconnaissance Patrols (LRRP's) also continued in the battalion's tactical area of responsibility (TAOR) to watch for enemy movement. Finally, intelligence reports continued to flow in from a Vietnamese population that increasingly grew more confident in their government's ability to protect them.

Bravo's 2nd Platoon on September 14 found a bunker with cooking utensils, documents and a small assembly operation designed to make enemy hand grenades near Don Qua (2). Close by Bravo also located a small military structure with cooking utensils and two – forty foot-long tunnels, each four feet in diameter. Nearby was a booby-trapped Chicom grenade.

Charlie Company found a booby-trapped 105mm Howitzer round near Thanh Hoa (1). The following day two - eight foot by seven foot bunkers were discovered which yielded fifty pounds of potatoes, seventy-five pounds of rice, tea, fishing nets and rice harvesting equipment. Two fifteen foot by twenty foot cornfields were located nearby with two US canteens clearly seen lying in the open. Each one was booby-trapped. Ak-47 fire harassed the grunts as they went about their chores destroying the bunkers and corn fields.

The pressure continued. Popular Force Platoon 75 ambushed a small group of Vietcong near Fat City at 3:40AM on September 16. The VC responded with AK-47 fire and B-40 rockets before evading. Two Vietcong were killed with no friendly casualties. An early morning air strike was called on the high ground west of Phuoc Khach in the Ky Thanh region. Eight five-hundred pound bombs struck a suspected enemy position.

Bravo's 2nd Platoon was hit by six rounds of 60mm mortar fire and small arms fire while it retrieved one of its mechanical ambushes. The enemy fire came from a small group of insurgents positioned one-eighth mile away. PFC Donald Lee Percy received a direct hit from one of the enemy rounds and was killed by the blast. He was nineteen years of age and single from Devers, Texas.

Another soldier, Sergeant James Brown Jr. was hit in the head and shoulders by shrapnel and dusted off but was pronounced dead on arrival in Chu Lai. Brown was twenty-three years of age and single from Port Allen, Louisiana. A third wounded soldier, Ralph Stogsdill, survived. Mortar, artillery and gunship fire was directed on the insurgents.

On September 17, Bravo Company lifted out of the LZ Bowman area and returned to Chu Lai for a rest and retraining. Taking its place in the region was RF Battalion 102 which lost no time in engaging the enemy. That same day the RF's made enemy contact in several locations east and north of Bowman, killing five Vietcong and capturing ten 82mm mortar rounds, a large cache of rocket warheads and four AK-47's.

Further north RF Company 928 killed two Vietcong while RF Company 195 engaged a company of Vietcong in a heavy fire fight. One RF soldier and thirteen Vietcong were killed while five AK-47's, a B-40 rocket launcher and numerous Chicom grenades were retrieved.

At noon on the same day, Alpha Company air assaulted by Huey deep into the mountains, two and one-half miles south of the center of Dragon Valley. Its mission was to sweep a thirteen square mile area bounded by Provincial Road 532 by the Thuan An Toy hamlets in the southeast and north to the center of Dragon Valley, stretching west two and one-half miles from the valley floor.

Charlie Company found evidence that the enemy was attempting to establish a presence north of the Ky Tra Outpost near Thanh Hoa (2). Charlie's 3rd Platoon located eleven freshly dug tunnels along with two structures above ground and six bunkers below ground. Inside the small structures were uniforms with blood stains, hand grenades, pottery and bags of corn and potatoes. Charlie's 1st Platoon near Thanh Hoa (4) was hit with 60mm mortar fire while positioned in an ambush at 7:30PM. It answered the mortars with seven rounds of 105mm Howitzer fire, which promptly silenced the enemy.

Delta continued its day patrols and night ambushes in the Dragon Valley area, finding the enemy in brief encounters. On the morning of September 19, the grunts found a dead Vietcong who was no older than seventeen, killed from a mechanical ambush. He wore a green uniform which yielded three Chicom grenades and one knife. Delta's 2nd Platoon two hours later engaged three VC wearing green uniforms and killed one, wounded and captured another while the third escaped. Nearby they found a 122mm rocket. A search of the area revealed two concrete-reinforced bunkers which required three forty-pound crater charges to destroy them.

Helicopter gunships from "Blue Ghost" (F Troop, 8th Air Cav) continued its support of the battalion as it had for the many months since the 5th/46th assumed its new duties west of Chu Lai. Almost every mission it flew guaranteed small arms fire as its light observation helicopters (LOH) flew close to the ground looking for enemy positions or remote gardens. Each time fire was received from the enemy, the Cobra gunships flying in support promptly responded with rocket fire.

The radar sets on Hill 270 and Fire Support Base (FSB) Fat City continued to make night movement hazardous for the enemy. The reports sent in early on September 20 were typical:

 #620 Target Mission Force String 11, 16 Paks (Enemy Soldiers) moving east to west, metal detected, Time detected 0551, location BT 422060 (These were dense hills 1-1/4 mile southeast of FSB Fat City). Expended 36-105mm rounds.

 #630 Target Mission Force, string 7, 12 Paks, moving west to east. Metal detected, time detected 0622, located BT 422060 (This was the same location as above, as they enemy fled from their objective). Expended 5 – 4.2-inch mortar rounds. Will fire again."

The air strikes continued. "Helix 01" a forward air controller, flew over the mountainous terrain in his small, single engine plane looking for enemy targets. For the helix pilots it was a daily routine. The pilot found newly constructed structures and bunkers near My Dong (1) and he called for his "Back-up support". A jet fighter dropped four - seven hundred and fifty-pound napalm canisters which caused some secondary fires in a plowed field, a sign of cached enemy ammunition.

The elusive enemy continued to be tracked down, one soldier at a time. The battalion's recon platoon, now operating southeast of Bowman, killed a VC in uniform. They searched him and found a first aid kit, a poncho and a letter from his sister. Nearby was a bunker made of cement blocks, a small hooch and small garden. Everything was destroyed.

Although the enemy was diminished in its strength and capabilities, its potential to exert itself continued to give the battalion's soldiers a daily, 24-hour challenge.

At 8:30PM, Delta Company spotted four Vietcong only one hundred and fifty yards southeast of their NDP, near My Dong (3). Three more VC were spotted seven hundred yards northwest of their position. The grunts opened up with M-16, M-79 and M-60 machineguns while 81mm mortar and artillery fire missions were called.

The initial burst of fire from Deltas soldiers prompted fire from another group of enemy that had not been seen. A platoon of Vietcong was hidden in a tree line only two hundred yards east of Delta's perimeter. In an instant the firefight escalated into an intense exchange of firepower, brought on by the savagery of an enemy that had suffered too much, and now wanted retribution at close range.

After just ten minutes the first dustoff was called for two casualties. One Delta soldier was hit in the shoulder with multiple shards of metal shrapnel. The other casualty spoke of another type of injury, one not witnessed often by the battalion. The intense exchange of fire between the two antagonists proved too much for one soldier and he went berserk, suffering a nervous breakdown in the middle of the fight. Five minutes later one of Delta's medics attending to the injured, SP/4 Gary Lee Abrahamson, was shot in the chest. It only got worst.

The dustoff arrived at 9:20PM, but crashed into Delta's perimeter after hitting some treetops as it glided to the intended LZ. The crew members were extracted quickly from the bird. Four suffered minor injuries and the main pilot suffered a broken leg. Two of Delta's soldiers near the crash site were also injured. Another dustoff was called, this time to pick up nine wounded. The downed aircraft began burning and exploding, from ammunition left on the bird that started "Cooking off". A new location had to be established for the next dustoff.

Delta's grunts moved one hundred yards northeast of the burning craft while under fire to set up another landing area. The next dustoff arrived at 10:30PM and picked up seven of the injured followed by another bird which picked up the remaining two. But the birds were too late for the medic, Abrahamson, who died of his chest wound. Gary Lee Abrahamson was age nineteen and married from Albia, Iowa.

Illumination rounds from the artillery kept the night skies light enough for Delta's soldiers to see beyond their patrol perimeter. The grunts spotted two dead Vietcong they had killed with small arms fire. A Blue Ghost gunship flying overhead spotted more evading VC and another enemy body by the perimeter.

The hunt for the enemy continued throughout the night. At 1:35AM one gunship spotted a Vietcong moving just inside a tree line where the enemy platoon had attacked with so much firepower. Rocket fire from the Cobra promptly eliminated him. Another enemy soldier was spotted crawling away and he was eliminated. One hour later Delta's troops spotted another Vietcong south of their NDP and killed him with a well-aimed M-79 round that landed on top of him.

Continuous illumination kept the dark sky bright throughout the night. Gunships remained on station, one bird trading space with another when it came time to return to Chu Lai and refuel. At 6:45AM

September 21, one gunship received .30-caliber machinegun fire from three enemy positions one-half mile north of Delta's night defensive position. The gunship was not hit and retaliated by pouring rocket fire on the enemy. As it left to refuel still another gunship came on station to continue the task. One light observation helicopter was forced to land with mechanical problems just south of Delta's NDP and soldiers were dispatched to secure the aircraft and protect the crew.

Elsewhere Charlie Company enjoyed a "calmer" night north of the Ky Tra Outpost near Thanh Hoa (1). During the night they heard one of their mechanical ambushes detonate in the distance. In the morning a patrol swept the area and found a blood trail. They requested a dog tracker team which arrived at 9:10AM. In short order the dog found part of a left leg separated from the knee cap and a right foot severed at the ankle. Three Chicom grenades were also found.

The night attack on Delta prompted speculation the enemy may be trying to re-assert itself in Dragon Valley. At 10:30AM Bravo Company, rested from its standdown at Chu Lai, air assaulted to the valley, landing just south of Delta's position. RF Company 722 was brought in by Huey to join them. At 11:15AM, one-half mile southeast of My Dong (2), they found a cache of fifteen rifle-propelled grenade (RPG) rounds still in their shipping canisters which contained Russian markings. Bravo's 1st Squad of its 2nd Platoon found what appeared to be a training camp nearby, with food still cooking on the fire, the enemy having just fled.

The battalion's recon platoon operated in the area north of Dragon Valley from the Ky Tra Outpost and northwest to the mountainous terrain by LZ Bowman. It too found evidence of enemy movement, and located sleeping quarters in what appeared to be a rest station for enemy soldiers, on a mountainous ridgeline overlooking the hamlet area of Ngoc Nha (3).

Blue Ghost gunships also surveyed the same area from the air, flying just north of the recon soldiers. Their backup were the "Blues", the infantry platoon assigned to the F Troop, 8th Cavalry for protecting Blue Ghost aircraft when shot down, performing snatch missions on evading enemy and now, checking out enemy positions that were spotted from the air. On September 22, they were kept busy working in tandem with their gunship support. The discoveries in the Ngoc Nha hamlet area gave ample evidence of an enemy trying to re-establish itself around LZ Bowman.

One location yielded an enemy hooch with a poncho liner inside. It was destroyed. Another position was a rest area used in the last twenty-four to twenty-eight hours that contained ten pounds of charcoal for cooking. It was destroyed. Another camouflaged hooch was found nearby that had been used for sleeping quarters. It too was destroyed. Alongside a well-used trail the Blues found a Vietcong letter and farm tools for harvesting rice. More sleeping quarters were found along with bunkers with rice, cooking materials, two mines, eleven hand grenades, eleven 60mm mortar rounds and two RPG rounds. The enemy had evaded south. Everything was destroyed.

Checking these small enemy camps was hazardous. Charlie Company found similar dwellings while searching an area five miles north of the Ky Tra Outpost. One soldier stepped on a homemade pressure-release mine that blew off his lower left leg.

The RF Group 132 that worked with the battalion near Phu Duc (2), three miles east of LZ Bowman, had better luck. They engaged three Vietcong near the hamlet, killing two and wounding the other, who was evacuated to the provincial hospital in Tam Ky for questioning. But the next day, on September 23, the RF's had their hands full. One of their militia was wounded by a mine and three Vietnamese villagers were wounded by another mine. Shortly after, the RF's came under enemy fire and five more militia were wounded with shrapnel from a B-40 rocket round. The villagers and militia were dusted off to the Tam Ky hospital.

Charlie Company's 1st Platoon, operating north of the militia, spotted two Vietcong carrying a third man on a liter. After radioing the RF's to insure this wasn't part of their group, the grunts opened fire, which prompted the liter bearers to drop their comrade and evade into the bush. Upon reaching the wounded soldier the grunts saw he had lost his left leg and speculated his injury was from one of their mechanical ambushes the night before. He was dusted off to the 91st Evacuation Hospital in Chu Lai for medical care and questioning.

Shortly after, the battalion received a report about Charlie's prisoner. He was a North Vietnamese soldier, a private that had only been in South Vietnam for two months. He had walked down the Ho Chi Minh Trail with Infiltration Group 111 composed of two hundred and fifty men. He was assigned to the Viet Cong V/20 Local Force Company, whose strength was now down to twenty men. They were armed with eight Ak-47's and three SKS rifles. Their mission was to secure food, and it was while trying to find supplies of rice that he was wounded.

The prisoner did not know much more about his unit because he had contracted malaria upon his arrival in the south. The doctors in Chu Lai confirmed he still had it. His company headquarters was a "Two hour walk east" of where he was captured. Their commanding officer was a Vietcong aged twenty-seven and the chief political officer was age thirty. Both carried pistols. V/20 operated as a "Production and Infantry Force" although it had not seen combat since he arrived.

The heat remained unbearable for those who were tasked to seek out the enemy in the dense forested terrain or rolling hills which offered little shelter from the sun. Every few days at least one soldier was dusted off for heat exhaustion or malaria. On September 23 Charlie Company dusted off a soldier with a temperature of one hundred and four degrees; an Americal sergeant who was an advisor to RF Group 132 was dusted off as a heat casualty, and two RF militia soldiers in the same group were dusted off with suspected cases of cholera. One of them was in a coma.

The battalion's food denial and interdiction operations continued. On September 24 Sniper team "Crockett" engaged four Vietcong at a distance of six hundred yards two and one-half miles west of Hill 76. Two VC were killed. The following day Charlie Company was lifted out to rest and refit in Chu Lai. Bravo Company, still working in Dragon Valley near the My Dong hamlets, found a uniformed NVA soldier killed by one of its mechanical ambushes.

Delta Company moved into the Nam Binh hamlet area west of the abandoned LZ Gator after a rest in Chu Lai. In short order they engaged three Vietcong, killing one, capturing another and obtaining two assault rifles. The prisoner was later identified as an NVA corporal assigned to the 409th Sapper Battalion as a transportation worker in the headquarters company, located in the mountains "one day's walk west" of his point of capture. The corporal walked to the Nam Binh's with a small group looking for food which he admitted "was very difficult to get for the battalion", which now numbered three hundred and ten soldiers.

On the evening of September 26, one of Delta's mechanical ambushes killed two more NVA near Nam Binh (7). Delta's soldiers captured two assault rifles, rice and military papers.

Two days later Bravo Company's 4th Squad of its 2nd Platoon, returning from a day ambush found one dead Vietcong at a location it had called for mortar fire two days prior.

Delta was wary of the Nam Binh area, which had seen so much enemy activity when the battalion worked off LZ Gator. Delta searched an old night defensive position near Phuoc Binh Tay (3) and found numerous anti-personnel mines waiting for the battalion's soldiers. The mines were marked by three small stones in a circle or by vines twisted in knots. The mines were neutralized.

On the afternoon of September 28, Alpha Company lifted out of the mountainous terrain south of Dragon Valley to return to Chu Lai, while the RF's that worked with them returned to Tam Ky. Charlie Company, in turn, departed Chu Lai to the Dong Dang hamlets one and one-half miles northwest of the Ky Tra outpost.

Blue Ghost gunships continued to hunt in the battalion's area of operation with their platoon of infantry, "The Blues", as their backup for action on the ground. The next day at 11:44AM Blue Ghost 21 spotted four camouflaged hooch's two and one-half miles north of the Ky Tra outpost near Thuan Hoa (1). The standard Blue Ghost one-two punch was applied: The dwellings were rocketed as the Blues were landed to search the area for enemy soldiers, equipment or supplies. The Blues received small arms fire which wounded one of their own but they captured an enemy soldier. The gunships spotted a concealed bunker nearby, just as enemy fire poured from its aperture directed towards the Blues on the ground. Gunships poured massive amounts of rockets onto the bunker and the soldiers moved in, finding two dead Vietcong.

The following day on September 30, interrogation of the prisoner captured by the Blues revealed another profile of the enemy in the 5th/46th Battalion area of operation. The prisoner was a North Vietnamese soldier named Pham Van Hung, a private with the 5th squad, 2nd platoon of the 2nd Company, B52 Battalion of the 30th NVA Regiment. He was nineteen years of age.

Hung left his home province in North Vietnam on July 29, 1970 and traveled by truck with five hundred other freshly trained soldiers along Highway 9 to a liaison station on the border with Laos. From there he started his trek down the Ho Chi Minh Trail, arriving in Quang Nam Province, (Tam Ky was the Provincial Capital), on approximately August 29.

Since arriving in Quang Nam Province his small group was engaged by "unidentified aircraft" on six occasions, resulting in six of his comrades being wounded and ten others deserting. Hung's company was last located near the Thinh Phuoc hamlets six miles west of LZ Bowman.

His company had forty-six soldiers each armed with an AK-47, one hundred rounds of ammunition and two Chicom grenades. The four officers in the company each carried pistols.

The private had not received any further training since arriving in South Vietnam and did not know the tactics his unit would employ. Food was adequate but medicine was in short supply. Morale in his company was good because "they had not seen combat."

The final day of September 1970 brought a report at 4:30AM that two platoons of Vietcong planned to attack the pro-government hamlet of Tri Binh (1). Delta, still patrolling the Nam Binh's south of the Tri Binh's were told to dismantle their mechanical ambushes and, at first light walk north and sweep through the Tri Binh's on its way out to Highway One and a pickup to return to Chu Lai.

Alpha Company finished its last day of rest at Chu Lai and prepared to air assault back to the field on October 1. Bravo Company spent its last night in Dragon Valley before it too would be returned to Chu Lai some time the next day for a rest and refitting.

But on the 30th of September tragedy would once again fall on Charlie Company, the company that had lost thirteen of the last fifteen soldiers killed in the battalion since mid-May. Charlie's Command Post (CP) was located near Dong Dang (1) three miles north of the Ky Tra outpost. Its 3rd Platoon, however, operated four miles farther west, in mountainous terrain one-half mile southwest of Phuoc Loi (2) and two and one-half miles southwest of LZ Bowman.

At ten minutes past midnight the morning of September 30, PFC Jerome Frilling finished his watch on the 3rd Platoon's patrol perimeter and woke Tong, the platoon interpreter, a Chieu Hoi who was a former Vietcong. It was Tong's turn to stand watch. The monsoon rains and dense terrain meant another miserable night in the bush. No one could see their hands in front of them. Even without the rain and heavy clouds, moonlight illumination was at zero during this time of the month.

Frilling had been with the platoon since July 19 and was a seasoned grunt. No so with another PFC lying nearby who was concluding his first day in the field. The men were uncomfortable getting saddled with him thinking, "Why them? Why here deep in the mountains?" No one wanted a Fucking New Guy, an "FNG", with so much at stake.

With Tong now awake, PFC Frilling moved to his sleeping position but he realized he forgot to give Tong "the watch." The platoon used the same time piece for all soldiers on watch at night to insure continuity for the time each relief spent awake. Frilling walked gingerly the short distance to Tong in the dark night to hand him the watch. The FNG spotted some movement he didn't understand and shouted "Chieu Hoi!" No one bothered to respond because everyone instinctively knew what was taking place. Two shots rang out and Frilling was hit by M-16 fire in the lower and upper back. He was killed instantly.

PFC Al Fultz, the platoons RTO tried desperately to reach the Company CP but to no avail. The terrain was too dense, the weather too foul and the distance too great. Finally in the morning, communication was established, but the heavy rain and low cloud cover that descended over the mountains made bringing in a dustoff too hazardous. It would remain that way for three days and Frilling's body stayed with the platoon.

The body remained in the mountainous patrol base along with the FNG who killed him. The FNG isolated himself inside the small perimeter which was now, for him, a mountainous hell. No one spoke to him and he said nothing to anyone else. Mentally he was no longer there. As Fultz recalled, "He was whacked out."

After three days a bird was able to reach their site and extract the dead soldier along with the soldier who killed him. The FNG was now equally dead in spirit although still breathing. He was never seen again. James Raymond Frilling was age 20 and single from Sidney, Ohio.

16 – BEGINNING OF THE END

Punishing the Enemy

October 1, 1970 saw Bravo Company completing its Dragon Valley interdiction mission so it could rotate to Chu Lai for a rest. At 4:40PM the grunts had to cross a section of the Quan River near Thuan Yen (2), which had become treacherous due to the heavy monsoon rainfall. Sergeant Larry Berkholtz led the way but lost his footing and drowned in the swollen River. Berkholtz was twenty-one years of age and single from Sullivan, Wisconsin.

That evening near its night defensive position (NDP), two Vietnamese were spotted by Bravo's Kit Carson Scout walking across a rice paddy. The scout yelled "Chieu Hoi!" The two Vietnamese walked directly towards him with their hands up. One was twenty-five years of age and the other was twelve. The older man was married with a small child and fifteen-day old baby. The VC was surrendering because his baby was badly burned and needed medical care. The young man had tried to Chieu Hoi before but the Vietcong stopped him and took away his AK-47. Bravo's soldiers accompanied the VC to a hooch near Dong Dang (5) and recovered the wife, two children and the man's weapon.

The next day at 10:45AM, the battalion's recon platoon moved into the hilly terrain one and one-quarter mile southwest of FSB Fat City to replace the dead batteries in motion sensors that were planted in the terrain west of the fire base. As it approached, the hidden sensors recon spotted two Vietcong sleeping in hammocks and promptly shot them. The area around the sensors contained fifteen small shelters made from ponchos and was a resting station for enemy on the move, undetected because of the dead batteries. The recon soldiers moved through the small camp, firing their M-16's and M-79's in front of them as they walked through. This spooked six more VC who were awakened by the intrusion and promptly evaded in their shorts, leaving behind their equipment.

Ten Chicom grenades, medicine and other equipment were found in the wake of the startled enemy, along with khaki-type uniforms usually worn by the NVA. Two AK-47 assault rifles were taken off the two dead Vietcong.

After replacing batteries the recon soldiers began the walk back to Fat City carrying enemy equipment which contained serial numbers and which could be of intelligence value. Once they cleared the enemy camp, 4.2-inch mortars from FSB Fat City and Hill 270 dropped eighteen high explosive and white phosphorous rounds on the camp. On their way back they discovered two freshly dug graves. Standard procedure required the graves be dug up to insure there was no hidden ammunition. But the grave digging quickly ended when the smell of decomposing bodies overwhelmed the soldiers.

On the morning of October 3 Alpha Company, which had been resting in Chu Lai, was tasked to move to LZ Baldy to come under "Task Force Saint" and conduct cordon operations in that area. Charlie Company kept busy in interdiction operations between the Ky Tra outpost and LZ Bowman. At 11:20AM, one patrol encountered three fleeing VC and found in their wake three military structures one mile west of Dong Dang (1). The dwellings were destroyed.

Farther north, another Charlie patrol fired on three Vietcong who darted away from a camouflaged hooch just off a trail. PFC Phillip Tatom and Sergeant Frank Coughenour remained behind when the rest of the patrol pursued the enemy. This was Tatom's first mission in the field.

Coughenour moved to cover the trail leading to the hooch while Tatom remained near a clump of undergrowth in front of the hooch. After a few minutes Tatom was shocked to see a woman carrying a baby emerge from the undergrowth waving her arms in a sign of surrender. She was pointing her fingers to her mouth in a sign of hunger. Tatom called for Coughenour and then saw a man also appear out of the undergrowth in a sign of surrender. The male was aged thirty and the female age twenty-five, with a baby three years of age.

The two soldiers took them into the hooch and gave them their C-rations and covered them with their poncho liners. Although these peasants worked with the VC they decided to surrender for lack of food. While they ate the father told the grunts the hooch was his but they had been forced to farm for the Vietcong, with little time to provide for his family. By now the rest of the patrol had returned and the soldiers contributed more food to the family. The father pointed out the locations of other hooch's in the area which the VC used. A quick search yielded five structures, each twenty feet by twenty feet. Under each was a well-constructed bunker. The dampness of constant monsoon rains made it impossible for the grunts to burn the hamlet-turned VC camp. It was left in place. The destitute family was dusted off to Chu Lai.

In the afternoon Bravo was lifted out of Dragon Valley and returned to Chu Lai for a rest and refitting. Delta Company exchanged lifts on the same birds and was sent back to Dragon Valley. The next day Delta patrols found enemy structures near the area of Danh Son (2). Each had a fortified bunker, with some containing cooking equipment and rice. Nearby more dispersed camps were found. Rather than destroy the camps, mechanical ambushes were put in place in case the enemy chose to return and reclaim their food.

Both sides of this war of insurgency west of Chu Lai tried to complete their missions with depleted strength. The enemy's strength was especially low and now, even the NVA had a difficult time reinforcing the Vietcong as they had been able to do with the 48th VC Battalion on the Batangan Peninsula. Charlie Company, for example, saw its platoon strength decrease to as few as fifteen soldiers in each platoon. Mines, malaria, other illnesses and some "shamming" in the rear, all accounted for the loss of soldiers in the field in all companies. Some soldiers refused to take their malaria pills, preferring malaria to the harsh conditions in the field and dealing with mines. The medics made sure the soldiers were given their daily malaria pills but could not be sure they swallowed them.

On October 4, forty new personnel were brought into the battalion and most of them were assigned to the rifle companies. The American withdrawal from Vietnam was well on its way and the battalion was able to pick up replacements from units which were departing from Vietnam because these soldiers still had time to serve in-country. Most of the battalion's replacements in the fall of 1970 came from the 4th and 25th Infantry Divisions.

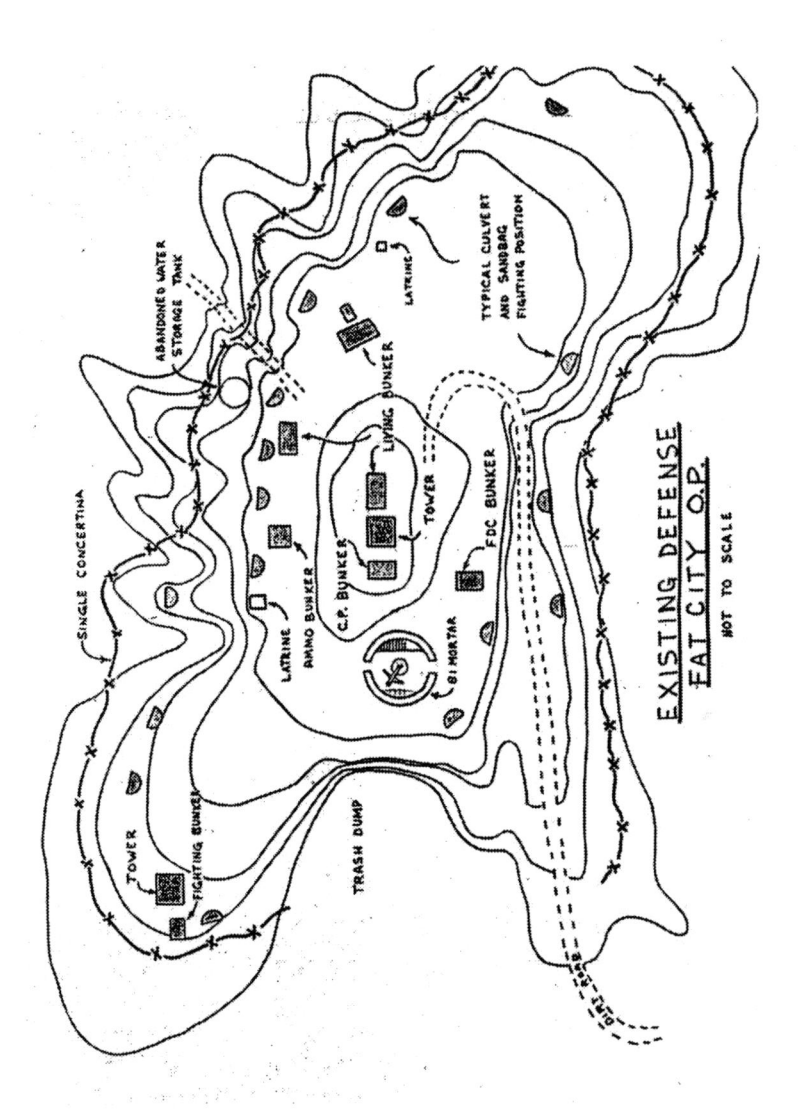

Fire Support Base "Fat City"

Charlie Company, operating north of Delta on October 6, found small enemy camps near Dong Dang (7), two and one-half miles northwest of the Ky Tra Outpost. One small camp was a sapper training site. It held two hooch's that measured fifteen by twenty feet used as living quarters and a ten foot by ten foot hooch used as a classroom. Concertina wire was laid out on the ground nearby, in a manner replicating a bunker line. Five other hooch's with bunkers were nearby.

At 6:15PM, Warlord Cobra Gunships spotted a similar training camp one and one-half miles further northeast at Phu Duc (1). Enemy soldiers were seen darting in and out of bunkers as the Warlord's Light Observation Helicopter (LOH) swooped low over the camp. Rocket fire was placed on the complex. Helix 25, a forward air controller in a small plane flew over to get in on the action. He directed air strikes from jet aircraft looking for work, which dropped six - five hundred-pound bombs of high explosives and six canisters of napalm.

More high explosive and napalm were dropped on a wider area where suspected bunkers were emplaced, and this additional measure was rewarded with a secondary explosion from hitting an ammunition cache. After the two air strikes the Warlords tried to insert their infantry platoon, the "Blues", but the Hueys were fired on by .30 caliber machineguns which prompted more rocket fire from the Gunships.

The Blues then landed and found six enemy dead, one with a satchel charge around his body which confirmed a sapper training site had been destroyed. Charlie's 1st Platoon was also brought into the area to assist the Blues but received machinegun fire as the Hueys attempted to land. The birds took the grunts one-half mile farther north and inserted them at Phu Duc (4).

As Delta's 3rd Platoon patrolled the valley near Dong Dang (5) they spotted three NVA soldiers. Using a Vietnamese Psychological Operations Speaker Team working with them, they tried to encourage the enemy to Chieu Hoi. But the enemy chose to flee and were cut down by small arms fire.

Enemy activity near Phu Duc (1) prompted an operational plan to be set into motion for October 7 where Charlie Company would form blocking positions west, north and east of Phu Duc (4) and Bravo would land south of Phu Duc (1) and sweep north through both hamlets, picking up any enemy in the area.

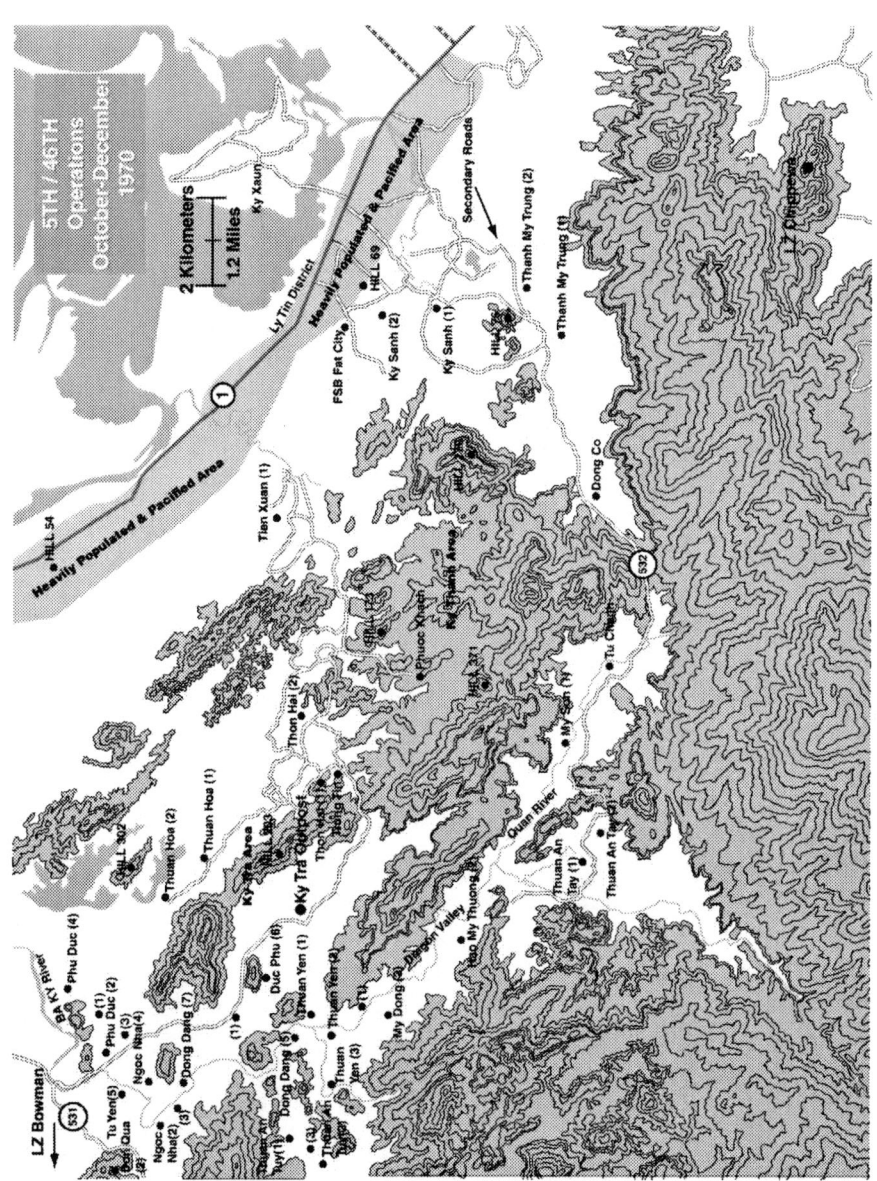

5th/46th Operations October-December, 1970

October 7 began with Alpha moving out to examine a mechanical ambush that had detonated the night before, one-half mile east of My Dong (2). They found a dead NVA soldier in uniform along with equipment, official-looking papers and a twenty-five pound sack of potatoes.

Bravo flew from Chu Lai and landed at its designated landing zones just before 8:00AM for the sweep operation. Charlie's 3rd Platoon, while enroute to its blocking position, discovered some small structures which showed signs of recent use. Found inside were claymore mines, American-made sandbags, documents and sacks of potatoes and tomatoes. The documents were evacuated to Chu Lai. Everything else was destroyed.

Bravo Company started its sweep north at Phu Duc (1) and quickly began picking up the litter of an enemy on the run. Around the hamlet area they found eight chickens, six Chicom grenades, NVA uniforms, an Ak-47 assault rifle, first aid kits, hammocks and documents. Six bunkers were found along with seven above-ground dwellings used as living and training structures. All the structures were destroyed. The search also revealed a head, an arm and a recently dug grave containing a soldier's body.

Delta's search in Dragon Valley yielded a family of six. The parents were reluctant VC who chose to Chieu Hoi. The father was age fifty, mother forty-five and two sons were aged ten and five. There were also two small girls in the family aged thirteen and eight.

The father approached Delta's grunts carrying French land deeds, family history deeds and some extra clothes. The NVA in the area had continually harassed them to support their operations. The extra labor for the NVA left no time for the father to support his family. They had intended to Chieu Hoi the day before when they heard the loudspeaker imploring the three NVA to surrender (those who ran and were shot), but the family could not reach the Delta patrol in time. The father said he saw a heavily armed NVA platoon with a mortar tube the previous day but did not know which direction it was headed.

Bravo's sweep into Charlie's blocking positions was methodical but not without cost. At 3:55PM, Charlie's soldiers just south of Phu Duc (4) hit a mine detonated with a trip wire. The mine sent shrapnel into eight grunts, two of whom were severely wounded. The detonated mine formed a hole six inches deep and one foot wide. The soldiers were promptly dusted off and all survived. Max Nelson, an RTO, was severely injured but radioed for a dustoff. When he reached the hospital he was asked where he was wounded. Nelson responded, "The only place I am not hit is my left testicle!"

The following day Delta also tripped a Chicom grenade booby-trapped with a pressure-release device which wounded three grunts and its Vietnamese interpreter. Delta's 3rd Platoon, upon moving out from its NDP found signs on a hill near Thuan Yen (3), that the hill was mined. Delta's 2nd squad of its 2nd Platoon, operating one and one-quarter mile farther northwest also found evidence of an evading enemy inside a small camouflaged structure, which contained uniforms and medical manuals.

Blue Ghost and Warlord gunships remained busy throughout the early days of October finding evidence of small enemy camps that had been recently occupied. Blue Ghost 29, searching over the Tu Yen and Phu Duc hamlet area on October 8, spotted seventeen camouflaged enemy structures which they destroyed with Cobra rocket fire. A platoon of its infantry, the Blues, was inserted between Phu Duc (2) and Phu Duc (3). The Blues promptly encountered three enemy soldiers, wounding all three. The Blues then followed a blood trail which led to a small base camp large enough for thirty to forty men. Cooking utensils, rice, small animals, documents and six NVA rucksacks were found.

Charlie Company and Echo Recon were lifted out of the field on October 8 and returned to Chu Lai for rest and refitting. The next day Bravo Company moved to the high ground west of Fire Support Base Fat City. Alpha Company continued its operations in the southern sector of Dragon Valley while Delta cleared the area in the northern sector.

On October 10 at 11:00AM, Alpha's 1st Squad of its 1st Platoon patrolled the area by the Quan River, near the hamlet of Hoa My Thuong (2). The foliage was dense. Too dense to see the 105mm Howitzer round hanging above ground on the side of the trail the patrol was following. PFC Thomas Charles Schiess tripped a wire across the trial that detonated the mine which killed him instantly. Another soldier next to him, but separated enough to avoid the same fate, was sprayed with fragment wounds. He was dusted off and survived his wounds. The dustoff had to lower a "Jungle Penetrator", a metal litter, through the densely canopied foliage to lift out both men. Schiess died at twenty years of age. He was single from Edgewater, New Jersey.

The next morning the battalion's recon platoon was inserted back into the Thanh Hoa and Phu Duc region to conduct daytime observation and nighttime ambushes. The platoon, as it did on occasion, landed at several false landing zones, the birds touching down to pretend troops were dropping off but then flew off with the troops still on board. This served it was hoped, to confuse the enemy watching from a distance, as to where the small group would be. As they landed on their real LZ, one Vietcong evaded the area. A quick sweep found a small potato patch he had been cultivating.

Part of Delta's 3rd Platoon patrolled the area near Thuan An Tuy (3) when a tracker dog tripped a wire across a trail, detonating a Chicom grenade. The dog, low to the ground, was not injured but its handler was shredded with shrapnel to his legs and abdomen. Both the dog and tracker were dusted off. One quarter mile southwest of the mine incident another squad of the 3rd Platoon engaged two NVA in uniforms with small arms fire. The enemy quickly evaded and artillery was called in on their escape route.

Regardless of their locations in the field, the mission of the battalion's rifle companies remained the same, food denial to the enemy and interdicting enemy movement along known and suspected routes of supply and communications. This continued to be done in conjunction with South Vietnamese district and provincial militia who, in seven short months, would be on their own.

On October 12, Charlie Company and the recon platoon left Chu Lai and air assaulted back into the Phu Duc area. Echo's recon platoon discovered a trench system with tunnels near Thanh Hoa (1) two miles southeast of Charlie. The battalion's forward command post remained at the Ky Tra Outpost and the battalion continued its daily coordination with the Tam Ky provincial headquarters, and Ly Tin district headquarters just north of the Chu Lai base by Highway One.

The American withdrawal from Vietnam continued, primarily in the southern portion of South Vietnam. On October 11-12, the 199th Light Infantry Brigade (Separate) left Vietnam with its four infantry battalions. Four of the 9th Infantry Division's battalions departed. The departures served notice to the South Vietnamese military that the time was approaching for them to assume the total ground responsibility of the war.

The withdrawals also provided propaganda for the enemy, even in the northern regions where the 5th/46th operated. The few enemy soldiers able to work their way into the pacified hamlets told of the many thousands of American soldiers departing the country and that it was just a matter of time before the American forces in Chu Lai departed as well.

Field patrols, while drawing few casualties, continued to test the mettle of its soldiers. Each day at least one soldier was medevaced from the field for physical ailments, most often malaria. Malaria was suspected when a grunts body temperature quickly spiked to one hundred and four degrees. Without medical attention a further rise in temperature could be fatal. The constant wet and cold monsoon rains, interspersed with periods of hot sun and high temperatures worked havoc on the bodies of the battalion's soldiers. In Mid-October 1970 another weather challenge came into the picture, the heavy winds and rains of a major typhoon.

Monsoon Misery

The climate of northern Quang Ngai and southern Quang Tin provinces, the area the battalion now operated in was monsoonal in nature and was divided into two major seasons. The wet season began abruptly in September and continued through . The dry season began in March and continued through late August.

On October 15, the 198th Brigade issued a warning for Typhoon Joan which was off the coast of Danang and headed south to Chu Lai. Heavy rain and winds of ninety nautical miles per hour were expected by midnight on the 15th, to last until October 17. Each unit in the field took stock of its location and searched for higher ground. The storm, although several hundred nautical miles off the coast, kept all Americal Division aircraft from flying on October 16.

The Americal Division's headquarters on the sandy beaches of Chu Lai was in a precarious position due to its location. So too was the headquarters of the 5th/46th Infantry Battalion, located at LZ Beach along the South China Sea, a short distance south of the Division's Headquarters.

Plans were made to evacuate all documents and classified records of company-level units at the Chu Lai base, to the higher ground at LZ Bayonet on the western side of Highway One. Each company headquarters on the huge base was ordered to have a jeep with trailer ready, to quickly load its administrative records and take them to Bayonet if needed.

At 5:50PM on the 16, Bravo Company requested a dustoff for two soldiers with one hundred and four degree temperatures. A dustoff helicopter flew through the stormy weather to pick them up and rush them to the 27th Surgical Hospital.

The next morning Delta Company, which had been prevented from returning to Chu Lai for a scheduled rest period due to the approaching typhoon, found two dead Vietcong by one of their mechanical ambushes. By noon, they were able to be picked up and returned to Chu Lai for rest and refitting. The typhoon passed the coast of Chu Lai one hundred and fifty nautical miles out, but left heavy rain and moderate winds in its wake. Damage to the Chu Lai base was minimal. One year later the Chu Lai base would not fair as well, and be virtually wiped out by another typhoon.

That evening Bravo's platoons found it necessary to return from their separate ambush positions to the company command post two miles west of Hill 76. An illness had hit the company and many soldiers were weak with diarrhea and low fevers. That night an urgent dustoff was called for a soldier whose body temperature had reached one hundred and six degrees. The Huey picked up its patient but as it pulled pitch to climb up, the bird lost power and crashed onto Bravo's night defensive position. No soldiers were injured. The dustoff crew and its patient were picked up by another bird.

Problems at Bravo's jinxed landing zone continued. The next morning at 7:55AM, while soldier's unloaded supplies from a hovering Huey, the supply bird developed mechanical difficulties and pitched down on its side, badly damaging its rotor blades. Three soldiers were seriously injured, one with head injuries (he was unconscious), another with back injuries and a third with a broken leg. They were promptly dusted off. Bravo's command post now had two damaged helicopters on its hands. Both were recovered during the day by heavy Chinooks, one bird at 11:00AM and the other at 5:00PM.

Charlie Company continued to find evidence of small enemy encampments in the Phu Duc and Thanh Hoa hamlet areas. Typical of the recently abandoned camps was what Charlie's 1st Platoon found on the north side of a lake, north of Thanh Hoa (2). Two camouflaged structures, each ten feet by fifteen feet with underground bunkers, contained two rifles, five Chicom grenades, NVA uniforms, one hundred pounds of rice and twenty-five pounds of potatoes, along with two live chickens. Everything was destroyed.

At this stage of the war the enemy's priority was to save its dwindling forces in the field, even if it meant abandoning its equipment. South of Thanh Hoa (2) Charlie's 2nd Platoon received sniper fire but the enemy quickly evaded. Alpha Company, while crossing the Quan River by My Dong (1) also received sniper fire which wounded one grunt.

Popular Force (PF) Militia saturated the Ky Sanh Valley area southwest of Hill 76 to locate enemy fleeing from the constant air strikes leveled on known and suspected enemy camps in the dense hills. Intelligence reports indicated an enemy build-up could be occurring in the hills to prepare for an attack on Hill 76. The security of the hill was now in PF hands.

But the PF's were not without US help. One and one-quarter mile north of the hamlet of My Son (1), nestled in the Ky Sanh Valley, was a dense hill mass three hundred and seventy-one meters high (Hill 371) that intelligence reports indicated may be the site of a enemy build-up. This hill mass was six miles due west of Hill 76.

On October 20 at 7:00AM, five one-hundred pound delayed-fuse bombs were dropped to penetrate the ground and destroy any bunkers on the hilltop. Forty minutes later six more one-hundred pound bombs were dropped followed by two "Daisy Cutters", technically known as "Bomb Live Unit 82/B" (BLU 82/B). The BLU 82/B was a fifteen-thousand pound thin-walled tank (1/4-inch steel plates) with a twelve thousand pound "slurry" explosive mixture inside the tank.

Daisy Cutters were used to clear vegetation to create landing zones for helicopters. They detonated three feet above the ground without creating a crater, keeping the surface fairly level for landing helicopters. The cleared areas averaged 260 feet in diameter. Because of its size, the BLU 82/B could only be dropped from C-130 cargo planes, and the bomb, attached to a small platform, was dropped by parachute. Delta Company air assaulted onto the newly created landing zone on Hill 371 at 9:00AM and set out looking for the enemy.

North of the Ky Sanh air strikes was another suspected enemy camp in the Ky Thanh region, three-quarters of a mile northeast of Phuoc Khach on a densely-covered hill, 137 meters in elevation (Hill 137). At 8:40AM the same procedure was followed. Five - one hundred pound delayed fuse bombs were dropped, followed by five more at 9:00AM, and then two BLU 82/B Daisy Cutters pulverized the hilltop. Bravo Company air assaulted to the LZ created by the massive bombs and by late morning started its search of the area.

As the PF militia patrolled the Ky Sanh Valley, Regional Force (RF) Group 132, working off the Ky Tra Outpost five miles further northwest, conducted a 2:00AM raid on October 20 on a suspected enemy camp near My Dong(2), killing five Vietcong. Later in the day they retained six more NVA/VC suspects, who carried VC propaganda bulletins, hand grenades and NVA money.

Gunships joined the battalion's sweep operations during the day and at 6:10PM, some fortified enemy bunkers in the process of being rebuilt were spotted three-quarters of a mile due west of Delta near Hill 371. Rockets and mini-gun fire were poured into the area by Cobra gunships. The heavy bombing and sweeps by Delta and Bravo forced the enemy to evade north, towards Charlie Company. At 4:40PM Charlie's 1st Platoon encountered Vietcong heading northeast. Unfortunately the VC were out of small arms range so artillery fire was called to reach the fleeing enemy.

During the morning when Charlie Company moved to its blocking positions, RF Company 931 moved into the Thanh Hoa area which was vacated by Charlie. They killed three Vietcong while capturing five Chicom grenades in a bunker. In the afternoon they killed four more VC and captured several more weapons. As darkness began to close-out the busy day, Charlie Company received three-60mm mortar rounds, but the closest round landed thirty-five yards outside its night defensive position. There were no casualties.

Delta Company, operating near Hill 371 found evidence of enemy activity. At 7:30AM on October 21, Delta's 2nd Platoon heard a mechanical ambush detonate two hundred yards from their live ambush. They found a dead soldier wearing a green NVA shirt and black shorts, an AK-47, three full magazines of ammo, three Chicom grenades, a bag of clothes, one bag of rice and a letter from his son.

RF Group 132 kept busy that afternoon north of the Ky Tra Outpost by killing two VC and capturing four (two males and two females). Later another Vietcong was hit, receiving a chest wound. He and fifteen other detainees were medevaced to Tam Ky for questioning. The prisoner with the chest wound divulged the location of a Vietcong hospital in the hills overlooking Dragon Valley east of My Dong (2). The following day RF Group 132 killed another VC and four NVA and captured twenty Chicom grenades with assorted equipment.

Echo's Recon Platoon searched the area south of Hill 137, about three-quarters of a mile east of Phuoc Khach, near a rain-swollen stream.

It found a small camp with a boat dock made of bamboo, which rose one foot above the water. Three "spider holes" along the shoreline provided cover and concealment from aircraft overhead. The recon soldiers then heard movement of enemy soldiers evading to the south. In their wake they found five well-built hooch's, each fifteen by forty feet in size, with ten-foot square bunkers underneath, each four-feet deep. One of the hooch's appeared to be a "Mess Hall" with pots and pans, some of which were still hot. Also found were forty pounds of rice, twenty pounds of potatoes, ten pounds of corn, two well-used latrines, clothing, Chicom grenades and a few medical supplies. Everything was destroyed.

Southwest of the recon platoon, Bravo's 3rd Platoon heard voices in the lowlands at a point where the hilly terrain opened up leading to Phuoc Khach. It alerted Bravos 2nd Platoon nearby to join forces and use 81mm mortar fire to serve as a "Blocking Force." But the night arrived too quickly to complete the sweep and mechanical ambushes were set in place.

As the enemy continued to evade the battalion and its Vietnamese allies in small groups, replacements for the 5th/46th Infantry Battalion continued to arrive. On October 21, the battalion received seventeen new soldiers and the next day another twenty-six. Out of this influx of soldiers Alpha Company was assigned eighteen "Fucking New Guys" (FNG's), Bravo four FNG's, Charlie three and Delta sixteen. Two FNG's went to the battalion's headquarters. Most of the new soldiers already had some combat experience from their previous units, which were now departing Vietnam, but the battalion's grunts generally looked at them as FNG's until they could prove themselves in the field.

On the afternoon of October 23, Alpha air assaulted to the Hill 137 area while Bravo back-lifted on the same birds to return to Chu Lai for a rest and refitting. Echo's recon platoon also returned to Chu Lai. Alpha had not been on its new mission for more than one hour when a soldier was dusted off with a fever of one hundred and four degrees.

At 10:00PM, the battalion was alerted for the possibility of another typhoon, Typhoon Kate, located six hundred miles off the coast of Chu Lai ("Condition 3") and headed in their direction. The next day all division-wide air movements were cancelled at 9:00AM. Typhoon Kate was now located three hundred and forty nautical miles north/northeast of Chu Lai and headed south/southeast to the base under "Condition 2".

While the division prepared for the high winds and heavy rains, RF Group 132 was busy with other matters. At 7:00AM, the RF's engaged a large force of NVA/VC on the ridges of the western side of Dragon Valley, three-quarters of a mile southwest of My Dong (2). Warlord gunships came on station to assist the RF's and, when low on fuel, Firebird gunships took up the task, placing heavy rocket fire and cannon fire on the enemy in connection with the RF's engaging them on the ground. The fight was ended before the aircraft had to be grounded because of the approaching typhoon. Thirty-two NVA and VC were killed, with twenty-seven of the enemy dead credited to the RF's and five to the gunships.

By 3:00PM, Typhoon Kate was elevated to a "Condition 1" Typhoon, with the storm expected to hit Chu Lai at 3:00AM the next day. The center of mass for the storm was thirty-five miles north of Chu Lai but the Americal base was expected to receive four to eight inches of rain with winds of thirty-five to fifty-five knots. The high country where the grunts were deployed would receive eight to twelve inches of rain over a five hour period.

Typhoon Kate hit Chu Lai on the morning of October 25 but a reduction in wind speed downgraded Kate to a tropical storm. Damage to the battalions Chu Lai headquarters area on LZ Beach was limited to some damaged latrines. In the midst of the storm eighteen more FNG's were processed into the battalion.

In the field, Delta found several enemy structures with bunkers underneath them one-half mile northwest of Phouc Khach. Several enemy soldiers fired at the grunts as they evaded. By the close of the day the battalion's recon platoon moved from Chu Lai to Fat City to help secure the area.

Small enemy way stations continued to be found by the battalion's soldiers who conducted small-unit patrols (squad and platoon size) in their assigned areas. The enemy continued to offer only limited resistance with harassing small arms fire from a distance. Delta's 2nd Platoon was hit by enemy fire at 10:00AM on October 26 resulting in three soldiers being wounded by AK-47 fire in the hilly terrain one mile west of Phouc Khach. The next day Delta's 2nd Platoon was hit with two enemy grenades thrown at close range, which wounded their Kit Carson Scout.

Bravo in Chu Lai returned to the field from its rest and was assigned the Hill 76 area to conduct day patrols and ambushes at night. Its 3rd Platoon found a dilapidated hooch with two bodies inside, estimated to have been dead for four to eight months. Various items such as pistol belts and clothing were also found in the dwelling.

The battalion's soldiers continued to search their assigned areas, finding indications of a dispersed and evading enemy even as rain and winds continued to make conditions miserable in the aftermath of the tropical storms. By late afternoon on October 29, travel between Chu Lai and Quang Ngai City on Highway One was next to impossible. The road was under water in most areas and the bridge just north of Binh Son was flooded over with eighteen inches of water by the rising Tra Bong River.

The rain and wind from Typhoon Kate continued for the remainder of October bringing havoc to the villagers in small hamlets nestled in lowlands throughout the battalion's area of operation. October 30 brought five more inches of rain followed by four more inches on October 31. Bravo, operating west of Hill 76 found forty homes flooded in a hamlet area. They helped approximately three hundred villager's move to higher ground. Some were, no doubt, Vietcong Infrastructure (VCI). The villagers were provided three days of food.

Charlie Company, making its way back to the Ky Tra area on foot, was hit by small arms fire the afternoon of October 30, wounding one soldier in the upper left arm. He chose to continue walking with the company.

The heavy rains caused a shift in operations due to the difficulty of foot movement and the lack of flying time because of the weather. Emphasis shifted to lifesaving operations for the villagers in flooded areas, and re-supplying the troops in the field when helicopters could fly. The battalion used more eagle flights when weather permitted, to search for the enemy in elevated terrain as it sought to avoid the flood waters.

Most helicopter aircraft available to the 198th brigade were used for flood relief and evacuation of soldiers and civilians endangered by floods. A special effort was made to screen groups of refugees for VC and VCI attempting to escape the flooded conditions and the lack of food in their hidden camps.

Delta Company in the Phouc Khach hamlet area near Hill 371 continued to be harassed by small arms fire with both Delta and the enemy now preferring the high ground.

Early afternoon on November 2, Delta's 1st Platoon found an enemy camp on a ridgeline north of the hilltop. The camp contained three fortified structures measuring fifteen feet wide by thirty feet in length and fifteen feet in height. Each structure held a well-constructed bunker underneath. The platoon backed out and called in artillery fire to destroy the buildings since the area was so wet that the usual fires set by Zippo cigarette lighters would not work. The platoon moved back into the camp and found pots and pans along with twenty NVA uniforms, socks, ponchos, rucksacks, six hammocks and nineteen Chicom grenades. The camp showed evidence of recent use by four to six insurgents.

As the platoon swept the area they saw two enemy soldiers who were evading. The platoon's snipers took up the challenge and fired well-aimed shots. One insurgent went down. When the platoon approached his location, he had crawled away to face a slow and agonizing death.

Alpha Company, working north of Fat City in the Tien Thuan hamlet area, began an impromptu VIP program when, on November 2, two teenaged Vietnamese boys brought in two-60mm mortar high explosive (HE) rounds. The next day they returned with other children bringing in two more 60mm HE rounds, two-60mm White Phosphorus rounds, one 105mm Howitzer artillery round, seven M-70 HE rounds and one anti-tank mine. For their efforts the grunts paid them two thousand Vietnamese Piasters (approximately seventeen dollars), furnished from the Vietnamese District Headquarters at Ly Tin.

As the floods subsided enemy activity began to increase. The Ky Tra Outpost was hit by five-60mm mortar rounds fired from the enemy on a nearby ridgeline. The enemy fire was promptly answered with 60mm and 81mm mortar fire from the outpost. More fire was requested from American artillery batteries which were eager for the fire missions, with little else to do. Seventy-three 155mm Howitzer rounds and sixty 105mm Howitzer rounds blanketed a one mile area of dense ridgeline northwest of the outpost. In a subsequent patrol two destroyed enemy structures were found. While the response from the artillery was massive and effective, it was another example of an RF Company that was being weaned on American firepower that would not last.

At noon, November 4, Charlie Company was lifted out of the field for a rest and refit in Chu Lai. Replacements continued to pour into the battalion, with eleven new infantrymen arriving on November 3, twenty-one on November 4 and eleven more on November 5. Most were from the 25th Infantry Division scheduled to depart Vietnam with four of its organic infantry battalions on December 8.

On the morning of the 5th, Delta lifted out of the Hill 371 area and air assaulted back up to the Phu Duc hamlets three miles east of LZ

Bowman. By 11:00AM three Vietcong, one male and two females, were killed by Delta's gunship support one-quarter of a mile southwest of Phu Duc (4). A search of the insurgents' bodies revealed one female was pregnant. No weapons or equipment were found, only documents which were sent to Chu Lai. Later Delta's 2nd Squad of its 1st Platoon found a booby-trapped 105mm Howitzer round with a trip wire across the trail. It was destroyed in place.

Brigade headquarters informed the battalion that another tropical storm ("Marge") was moving towards Danang and Chu Lai with landfall expected on November 7. Rain was expected to reach eight to twelve inches where the grunts were operating but the following day the storm mercifully dissipated to only three knots per hour when it was still one hundred and twenty miles off the coast. But daily rain squalls still plagued the soldiers, Vietnamese civilians and the enemy.

Alpha's headquarters element continued to receive munitions from Vietnamese children in the Tien Xuan hamlet area northwest of Fat City. On November 6, teenagers brought in hand grenades, two 4.2-inch mortar rounds, one 105mm Howitzer round and three 155mm Howitzer rounds. The continuing turn-in of the types of heavy explosives commonly used by the enemy for mines, caused Alpha Company to run out of repatriation money. They issued I.O.U.'s for Vietnamese Piasters until more funds could be obtained.

That same day, Alpha's three rifle platoons were engaged in eagle flights six miles farther south, in the dense hills overlooking Provincial Road 532 and the Trau River. In just one day, the platoons landed at seven locations, searched their assigned terrain and then were picked up by helicopters to go elsewhere. No enemy was found.

The following morning Charlie Company left Chu Lai and air assaulted out to Dragon Valley in the Thuan Yen and My Dong areas, landing once again on the dense ridges on the western edge of the valley.

At 1:40PM, Charlie's 3rd Platoon detained seven VC/VCI near Thuan Yen (3). Included were one male, seven females, two girls and one boy. The male was caught making hand grenades when captured. Charlie's 2nd Platoon found an old bunker complex one-quarter mile west of My Dong (1) and Charlie's 1st Platoon sighted a male Caucasian with blond hair, dressed in Vietnamese clothes, by the Quan River one-half mile southeast of My Dong (2). The grunts took off in pursuit of the blond-haired enemy and, along the way, destroyed a pressure-release toe popper mine.

More discoveries slowed the pursuit of the mysterious "Blond-haired Vietnamese", including encountering a bunker complex. While they maneuvered toward the bunkers they engaged seven VC with small arms fire. Two VC males were killed and two captured. One female was captured along with her baby. Another baby was wounded from a grenade blast and was flown to a Chu Lai hospital for care, along with the first group of detainees that had been captured at 1:40PM. Another helicopter picked up the second group of captured VC to be interrogated. In the midst of it all, the Caucasian "Vietnamese" slipped away.

On the morning of November 8, Charlie's soldiers found a hidden dwelling and tunnel complex on some dense ridges west of My Dong (2). The twelve by twenty-foot enemy structure contained a booby-trap at its entrance which the grunts detonated with a hand grenade. Inside were Vietcong clothing, medicine and bags of food. Outside were fresh footprints of a hastily departed enemy. A tunnel under the floor of the dwelling led off in three directions. One of Charlie's tunnel rats went down under, finding some cutting tools and a poncho. The tunnel was destroyed. Nearby the grunts found a burnt-out Huey Helicopter that appeared to have been abandoned for some time, its metal frame now rusted and buried by the dense foliage that would ultimately claim everything in the war-torn land, long after the war ended.

Further north near Thuan Yen (3) Charlie's 3rd Platoon found a small military structure with two bunkers near it and a tunnel system connecting them. Recently used cooking utensils and an American field jacket were left behind when the enemy fled.

Intelligence reports from the 196th Light Infantry Brigade, whose operational boundaries began at the LZ Bowman area and extended north and west, including east to Tam Ky, provided an opportunity to bag a large group of the enemy. The V/16 Local Force Sapper Battalion, estimated at a strength of one hundred and eighty men, was reportedly near the hamlet of Ngoc Giap (1), one and one-half mile southeast of LZ Young and three miles southwest of LZ Bowman. Gunships spotted thirty NVA in the area the morning of November 4 and other sightings continued, with the birds spotting small groups of enemy and numerous bunker complexes.

The 1st/46th Infantry Battalion of the 196th Light Infantry Brigade dispatched its Charlie Company along with its assigned RF and PF companies to air assault into the area and engage the enemy. Help was needed to establish blocking positions south of the area and Alpha of the 5th/46th received the mission.

Delta's 2nd Platoon was kept busy south of the Phu Duc area and discovered enemy hooch's and bunkers near Thuan An Yen (2). At 6:00PM on November 8, the new enemy situation prompted a change of mission. Delta was picked up by Huey and flown to Fat City while the birds in turn, picked up Alpha and combat air assaulted to the western edge of the 198th Brigade boundaries, in support of the large sweep being made by the 1st/46th. They were deposited on Provincial Road 531 near Ngoc Nha (3), south of LZ Bowman.

That same afternoon the battalion's recon platoon was assigned to patrol the hill area west of Hill 76 in response to reports of enemy movement. It engaged a group of Vietcong one-quarter mile northwest of Hill 127 at 3:10PM. The recon grunts heard one of its mechanical ambushes detonate in the near distance and moved in to check it out. They spotted four enemy soldiers two hundred yards away and a sharp exchange of small arms fire began. The recon grunts called for mortar and artillery fire to block the enemies expected retreat route. Moving forward they found one dead soldier with his Ak-47. As they closed in on the ambush site they found five more dead enemy soldiers with indications that three more had been wounded and slipped away. Hammocks, rucksacks, food, clothing and hand grenades were found in the area, along with one opium pill. An emergency resupply of ammo was called in as they sifted through the enemy's equipment.

The morning of November 9 saw Alpha's 2nd Platoon, moving out of its night position at 6:45AM when it discovered two enemy bear traps near Don Qua (2). At 8:30AM Alpha's 1st Platoon hit a tripwire attached to a hand grenade which wounded three soldiers who were dusted off. At 9:00AM, Alpha's grunts found one - two hundred and fifty-pound bomb and one 155mm Howitzer round. The munitions were too delicate to try to destroy so an Explosive Ordnance Demotion (EOD) team was called to take care of them. This held up the grunts from moving elsewhere. The platoon also found ample evidence of an enemy presence in the area, with US Army mess hall utensils such as pots and pans, along with NVA mess kits, clothing and firing mechanisms in small shelters.

Bravo Company was extracted from the Hill 76 area at 7:30AM and combat air assaulted to four separate landing zones (LZ's) south of Alpha's location, to set up blocking positions south and east of Alpha's operation. Bravo's 3rd Platoon landed in the dense hill country one mile due south of Alpha. The company headquarters and mortar section landed in an open area near Phu Duc (3). The 2nd Platoon was positioned on a third LZ near Ngoc Nha (4) and the 1st Platoon also landed near Phu Duc (3).

At 1:15PM, Alpha's 3rd Platoon found another abandoned enemy camp in the Don Qua (2) area with several bunkers, tunnels and fighting positions. The camp had been hastily abandoned. There were fish on plates ready to eat, AK-47 ammunition and hundreds of pounds of rice nearby.

Also at 1:00PM, Bravo's 2nd Platoon spotted four Vietcong at close range by the Ba Ky River near Ngoc Nha (4) and opened fire, killing one VC. The remainder quickly fled south without returning fire. The grunts pursued the enemy while calling in artillery in the direction they fled. The artillery fire prompted seven more of the enemy to bolt out of the bush wearing helmets and rucksacks and they too evaded to the south, with Alpha's small arms fire helping them along. Two blood trails were discovered in the path of the feeling enemy.

At 3:20PM, Bravo's 2nd Platoon received three Chieu Hoi's, a mother, girl and boy, who walked up to their patrol. They reported seeing twenty NVA and twenty to thirty VC in Ngoc Nha (2). At the same time Bravo's 3rd Platoon, while crossing a stream on a dense ridge, spotted three VC, killing one and capturing his weapon, which was an American M-16. In the wake of the retreating enemy they found two hundred pounds of rice with pots and pans. Later one of the platoon's soldiers was wounded when sniper fire hit rocks next to him which sent debris into his legs. He was dusted off along with another soldier who came down with a high fever.

The day ended with Alpha conducting a reconnaissance in force in the extreme western boundaries of the 198th Brigade's area of operation around LZ Bowman. Bravo provided a blocking force southeast of Bowman while Charlie Company continued to search and clear the dense ridges on the western edge of Dragon Valley. Delta had moved from Fat City to Chu Lai for rest and refit while the battalion's recon platoon continued to sweep the area west of Hill 76. The recon grunts were continually beset with shoot and run activity from the enemy, and it was apparent their presence disrupted the enemy's plans to gather for an attack on Hill 76.

Tightening the Screws

On November 10, Delta Company of the 1st/46th Infantry Battalion pursued a group of NVA, killing three in the Phuoc Loi (2) hamlet area south of Bowman. The company was placed under the operational control of the 5th/46th.

The enemy increasingly sought to intermingle within the populated hamlets, leaving their military clothing in the small camps to avoid American firepower. As such, several artillery fire missions were cancelled because the evading enemy had reached groups of civilians.

Artillery from LZ Young and Ky Tra was fired on a suspected enemy position north of Phuoc Loy (1), causing a secondary explosion from cached enemy ammunition. LTC Henry, the battalion's new commander flew over the area in his Light Observation Helicopter (LOH) and received fire from a .51 caliber machinegun near Long Son (8), one mile northeast of the Bowman hilltop.

The next day was a costly one. Enemy contact was made by Bravo's 3rd Platoon at 8:20AM near Nhoc Nha (5). While moving into a blocking position, the point element was ambushed by four Vietcong firing AK-47's and throwing Chicom grenades at close range. The platoon returned fire as did Alpha's 3rd Platoon which was nearby. The enemy quickly evaded but three of Bravo's soldiers were wounded with shrapnel from the grenades. A fourth soldier, SP/4 John Joseph Farnsworth was killed in the brief exchange of fire. Farnsworth was age 19 and single from Frackville, Pennsylvania.

Later at 5:05PM, the same platoon spotted two NVA wearing grey uniforms and carrying rucksacks with helmets, in the same area of the morning encounter. But the enemy was too far away to be effectively engaged with small arms fire. Alpha's mortar platoon nearby fired twenty-eight rounds of 81mm mortars on the enemy, adjusting and firing as the enemy fled.

That same day at 1:00PM, Charlie Company found a group of enemy structures with bunkers and fighting positions at a recently abandoned camp on the dense ridgelines one-half mile west of My Dong (2). While destroying the bunkers with C-4 explosives, a secondary explosion occurred, indicating a buried cache of ammunition the grunts had missed.

Alpha Company placed its headquarters and mortar platoon just north of Provincial Road 531 near Don Qua (2). As it prepared its night position, the enemy fired twelve 60mm enemy mortar rounds that crashed into its perimeter at 6:30PM. The company's 81mm mortars returned fire at the enemy mortar position to the southwest. Artillery from the Ky Tra Outpost was also directed at the enemy. The heavy return fire silenced the enemy mortars but the insurgents drew blood. Six Alpha soldiers were wounded and quickly dusted off to Chu Lai. One soldier, SP/4 Monroe Alan Powers was pronounced dead on arrival. Powers was age 21 and single from Newport News, Virginia.

Delta Company was now back in the field in the area around Tien Xuan (1), two miles northeast of Fat City. The battalion's recon platoon along with a sniper team continued to search for enemy movement two miles west of Hill 76, in the immediate area around Hill 270. The remainder of the battalion operated fifteen miles west of Chu Lai in the LZ Bowman and Ky Tra area, and the Dragon Valley south of Ky Tra.

While the battalion's fire support of artillery and mortars undoubtedly accounted for enemy casualties, November 13 had ended with nine soldiers wounded and two dead, and only one enemy body found. It was not an exchange the soldiers wanted to make for a war which was, for them, drawing to an end.

The next morning at 8:25AM two more of Alpha's soldiers hit a small mine, wounding both with multiple fragment wounds. Two hours later Charlie Company's 2nd Squad of its 1st Platoon found two Vietcong, a male and female who had been killed by artillery near the Quan River and My Dong (2).

That evening at 9:30PM Bravo's 2nd Platoon, working with an RF Intelligence Platoon, approached a suspected enemy position located in dense terrain southwest of Thanh Hoa (4). The PF Platoon took the lead while Bravo's troops followed as backup. The RF's walked into an ambush but reacted quickly with small arms fire. Bravo's platoon maneuvered to hit the enemy and suppress their fire. The fighting was too close for artillery support but the guns at Ky Tra fired illumination rounds which took away the enemy's night advantage.

After one hour the intense fight was over. The RF's swept the area and found ten dead Vietcong, two AK-47 assault rifles, a B-40 rocket with rocket launcher, and some Chicom grenades. The victory did not come cheap. One RF was killed and ten wounded. They were dusted off in the night to Chu Lai. Bravo and the remaining RF's pulled out of the immediate area to allow artillery to be fired throughout the night in the direction of the evading enemy.

That same night the battalion's sniper team west of Hill 76 had separated itself from the recon soldiers to establish a more secure sniper position. In the darkness close to its position, the small team heard Vietcong talking and then throwing rocks, trying to draw out the snipers location. This continued, but by 2:00AM, the snipers had had enough of the harassment. They detonated their two claymore mines and prepared to be attacked. Instead there was silence. In the morning they found footprints and drag marks on the ground as the wounded enemy limped away.

On the morning of November 15, Delta left the Fat City area by chopper and landed in Alpha's area to relieve them so Alpha could return to Chu Lai for a rest and refit. Two of Delta's platoons landed farther south on the dense ridgelines that had been the source of the 60mm mortar fire on Alpha. Their mission was to sweep north while Delta's headquarters and another platoon worked as a blocking force.

That afternoon Bravo Company called an urgent dustoff for one of its grunts and a Kit Carson Scout who had tripped a booby-trapped mine one quarter mile east of Phu Duc (3). The soldier suffered a concussion and the scout took shrapnel to his hips.

The day ended with RF Group 132 engaging a group of Vietcong in the hilly and dense terrain south of Thanh Hoa (4). The RF's swept the area as the enemy evaded and found seven bunkers with a large mess hall and a water piping system that led to the dining area. Four dead VC were found along with two AK-47 rifles, uniforms and four B-40 Rockets.

Moving through the camp they encountered ten more insurgents and eight were killed. The RF's captured three AK-47 rifles along with two Vietcong flags and one Soviet flag. Their successful day ended on a bad note however. At 8:30PM, another part of RF Group 132, operating just north of Thanh Hoa (4), detonated a mine within its night defensive position. Five soldiers were wounded and evacuated to Chu Lai.

The morning of November 18 saw Alpha Company finish its rest and refit and move back to the Phu Duc hamlets to conduct squad-size patrols and night ambushes. Bravo was picked up south of LZ Bowman and returned to Chu Lai for a rest. Charlie Company continued its blocking operation in conjunction with Delta Company by working in the northern sector of Dragon Valley while Delta operated farther north near the Song Ba River.

Echo Company's Recon Platoon combat air assaulted into the mountainous Ky Sanh area one–half mile north of Tu Chanh and

Provincial Road 532. Intelligence indicated there was enemy movement in the area. Echo Company's heavy 4.2-inch mortars were relocated with two tubes on Hill 270 and two tubes on Fire Support Base Fat City. Each mortar site also included an 81mm mortar.

That afternoon Delta's 1st and 2nd Platoons found six bunkers in the densely foliaged ridges southwest of Don Qua (3). As it moved about to search the bunkers they made contact with six Vietcong who quickly fled. Two were killed, a male and female. The grunts captured two AK-47 rifles, two RPG rounds, six Chicom grenades and a claymore mine. Blood trails led out of the enemy camp. As the two platoons left the area to establish night defensive positions, they found a small cave with five 60mm white phosphorus mortar rounds. The cave and munitions were destroyed before they continued on.

The weather in the battalion's area of operations from the Chu Lai coast to seventeen miles west into the Annamite Mountains continued to be plagued with rain, high winds and chilly temperatures. The battalion's slice of Vietnam normally saw temperatures in the ninety-degree range, but with tropical storm-like weather, temperatures reached only into the mid-seventy degree range during the day. In the mountains, nighttime temperatures were much cooler which presented miserable conditions for night ambushes and defensive positions.

The flooded terrain offered little dry ground for movement and the dry ground that was available was a prime candidate for enemy mines. With the constant daytime patrols and nighttime ambushes, little opportunity existed for soldiers to stay warm and dry. On the morning of November 19, Bravo Company was forced to dustoff six of its soldiers whose feet had deteriorated from the marshy terrain of daytime patrols and the dampness at night.

There was no end in sight for the miserable weather conditions the occupants of the Southern I Corps of South Vietnam had to endure. Another typhoon ("Patsy") was sighted near the Philippine Islands and was expected to be two hundred nautical miles off the coast of Chu Lai by November 21.

The battalion's soldiers continued to find small camps with abandoned equipment which was too burdensome for the fleeing enemy to carry. Charlie found a small camp near Dong Dang (5) that contained corn, fish nets, eating utensils and enemy uniforms. Delta's 2nd Platoon spotted two NVA near Ngoc Nha (1), killing one and capturing his weapon. The other managed to slip away in the dense foliage.

Although it was just a few months to go before the battalion would cease operations and exit Vietnam, the soldiers did not know when, but could sense the end was coming as new replacements from other departing units reinforced that reality.

By late 1970 battalion casualties were low, both in terms of dead and wounded, compared to duty on the coastal plain. Moreover the enemy could not establish a foothold in the vast area assigned to the 5th/46th Infantry Battalion and the regional and provincial militia in the area.

The battalion's main obstacles became complacency due to the lack of enemy contact and a lack of aggressiveness by some; soldiers did not want to risk death or lost limbs in a war their country would not be ending on its own terms. It was up to the leadership at the company and battalion level to keep their soldiers focused on their mission of accelerated pacification, food denial and denying the enemy sanctuary in the vast area assigned to the battalion.

Despite the emphasis placed on pacification throughout South Vietnam, and the realization the Vietnamese military had to assume the burden of fighting the enemy, the commander of the 198th Light Infantry Brigade still looked for enemy body counts, and he pushed his battalions to get them. This translated to expectations at the platoon level for soldiers to take risks many were unwilling to take. Increasingly the field-savvy soldiers took on their assigned missions with a resolve to complete them, but in a manner of their own choosing.

The combination of small-unit daytime patrols and nighttime ambushes (both manned and "mechanical" ambushes), prevented the enemy from massing its forces even for limited attacks on populated areas. Nighttime mechanical ambushes became a scourge for the enemy who increasingly chose to use flashlights for night movements, to avoid the deadly trip wires. This was deemed less risky than having the battalion's soldier's call in mortar and artillery fires on the moving lights.

The constant influx of new replacements to the battalion continued. Between November 16 and 19, sixty-five new soldiers were processed into the battalion.

Bravo's 2nd Platoon heard one of their mechanical ambushes detonate at 2:30AM on November 20. They checked the ambush site at first light and found one dead eighteen year-old VC male, wearing a green uniform. Later in the day Alpha's 3rd Platoon hit a booby-trap one-half mile west of Tien Xuan (1) which wounded seven soldiers.

The day ended with Charlie's 1st Platoon spotting three VC with weapons on the far side of the Quan River. One was fishing while the other's kept guard. At four hundred yards distance, the platoon was unlikely to kill any with its M-16's so mortar fire was called on the fishing site. That sent the enemy scurrying as the mortar fire was adjusted to follow their departure. The rivers high water line kept the grunts from pursuing the insurgents.

Typhoon Patsy was now forecasted to hit land between Danang and Chu Lai the morning of November 23, bringing eight to twelve inches of rain in the mountains with wind gusts up to forty-five nautical miles per hour.

The battalion's patrols continued as the weather worsened. Delta's 4th Squad of its 2nd Platoon found an abandoned structure with bunkers near Ngoc Nha (3). Two fresh graves were nearby and the grunts, as usual, were required to dig them up to insure there were no caches of ammunition or to gain intelligence from dead bodies.

The first grave revealed a young male soldier in a NVA uniform, aged eighteen to twenty, who had been dead for one to two days. He was killed by small arms fire to the chest and stomach. The second grave yielded a soldier in his thirties, wearing a cleaned and pressed NVA uniform with pistol belt and compass case. His body was covered with shrapnel, indicating he had been killed by a mechanical ambush (MA). The grunts set up another MA and left the immediate area.

Delta's 2nd Platoon killed another NVA soldier in the same area on November 22, capturing his AK-50 assault rifle with a backpack and canteen. A search of his body revealed a wallet which contained names, dates and receipts of villagers who sold rice to the VC and NVA. Militia of RF Group 132 operating in the rain squalls of the approaching typhoon engaged a group of Vietcong north of Delta near the Ba Ky River and killed four VC, capturing an AK-47 rifle and various documents.

Typhoon Patsy hit landfall at 5:00AM on November 23 in the Phu Bai area near Danang, north of Chu Lai. Although Chu Lai was spared a direct hit, the typhoon brought heavy rains and wind to the Americal Division's area of operations but the battalion's grunts continued their missions in the field.

Delta Company took a Vietcong prisoner after wounding him in the stomach. He was dusted off at 10:45AM and taken to the 91st Evacuation Hospital in Chu Lai for treatment and questioning.

Despite the foul weather, the Hueys could still fly most of the time and the war was pursued. Bravo Company, which had been in Chu Lai for a brief rest under rainy skies, was picked up by late morning and combat air assaulted near Hill's 302 and 203 to conduct a sweep of the area in conjunction with RF Group 132. The dense terrain around the two hill masses, which had offered enemy activity in the past, now appeared to be reoccupied again. The RF's moved to the western edge of Hill 302 to act as a blocking force for Bravo.

Bravo's headquarters and mortar section landed near the hamlet of Than Hoa (1). The 2nd Platoon landed two miles farther southward on the southern edge of Hill 203's dense terrain. The 1st and 3rd Platoons were placed on the eastern edge of the hill mass between the 2nd Platoon and the company headquarters.

As Bravo began its search and sweep, Delta continued its operations near the Ngoc Nha hamlets and the Ba Ky River. Its 3rd Platoon bumped into a group of three VC and killed one, capturing his weapon and equipment, before the others scampered off into the brush. Three hours later they found two dead NVA in uniforms, which had been killed by small arms fire. It appeared they had been shot the day before by Delta's 2nd Platoon and escaped into the brush to face a private death.

The next day Charlie Company was notified they would be picked up in the field and flown to Fat City, then trucked to Chu Lai for a rest and refit. The company's separated elements walked to a designated pick-up zone (PZ).

The 1st Platoon, led by First Lieutenant Michael Petrashune arrived at the PZ at 10:10AM. The platoon's single file (patrol file) of soldiers walked towards its position on the PZ but the machine gunner in front of Petrashune slipped off the muddy trail. Petrashune and his RTO, PFC Thomas Van Meter walked past as the gunner got to his feet, which place the platoon leader closer to the point.

Someone tripped a booby-trapped hand grenade that was hanging in a tree. It was thought a trip wire strung across the footpath detonated the grenade but no one was sure. The vegetation appeared to be hanging lower than normal and quite possibly when someone pushed through the trail the low branches acted as a trigger. Petrashune caught shrapnel in the chest and head with a shard of metal traveling inside his skull to the back of his brain. Van Meter was laced with shrapnel to his arms and legs.

The dustoff bird came in quickly. Petrashune, in bad shape, flashed the "V" sign with his fingers to his platoon, as he was being loaded on the Huey. He was a well-liked and competent leader. The shrapnel in his brain was difficult for the doctors in Chu Lai to handle and a neurologist at the hospital in Camp Zama, Japan was called to fly down and evaluate him. But pneumonia set in and on December 11 First Lieutenant Michael John Petrashune succumbed to his wounds. He was twenty-three and single from Lyon Mountain, New York.

At 3:30PM the same day, November 24, Delta's SP/4 Robert Gottier from the 4th Squad of the 3rd Platoon tripped a mechanical ambush that had been set by his own company on an earlier patrol near Ngoc Nha (1). Gottier was dusted off but pronounced dead on arrival in Chu Lai. Robert Carl Gottier was age 21 and single from East Stroudsburg, Pennsylvania.

Gottier's death should not have happened and resulted from a breakdown in fundamental tactical procedures. Gottier was the point man in the squad's patrol. As was typical of some squad-size patrols, white phosphorous rounds fired from an 81mm mortar were fired in front of the patrol at various check points to aid the patrol in moving in a pre-arranged pattern. These rounds were called "Road-Runners," but the mortar started firing off course which caused the patrol to be off course. Realizing he was losing control, the patrol leader passed the word to Gottier to stop on a small road, as they were getting close to some mechanical ambushes (MA) the company had set out. Gottier reached the road but continued to walk onto a small trail where he detonated the MA.

The brigade commander ordered an investigation which revealed a breakdown in tactical procedures. First, the patrol was off course and did not have a good fix on their position. Second, the patrol did not adequately report its concerns that it was moving in the wrong direction and was lost. Third, SP/4 Gottier did not follow the instructions of the patrol leader and fourth, the patrols' check points were plotted too close to previously rigged mechanical ambushes by the company.

Finally, the company had not followed the standard policy of checking each MA site early in the morning and removing them, to avoid the type of tragedy that occurred. The MA's should also have been removed as there was a likelihood Vietnamese militia and civilians would use the trails in their daytime activities.

Bravo Company continued its search of the Hill 203 area, finding abandoned bunker complexes with mines and booby-traps. Scout dogs were requested to aid them in their mission.

On November 27, Charlie Company returned to the field and was tasked to air assault onto Hill 410, four miles due west of Hill 76, to search and clear the dense ridges in the area. The battalion's recon platoon, which also had a chance to rest and refit, was inserted by Huey in the Ky Tra area around the Than Hoa hamlets for daytime reconnaissance and nighttime ambushes. The battalion's sniper team was sent to Fat City to help provide night security.

November passed into December and the rains continued. Another storm front was predicted to move into the battalion's area of operations on December 1, with heavy rains and potential flooding in the lowlands.

Bravo Company, after scouring the Hill 203 area moved north to Hill 302. The battalion's recon platoon was tasked to serve as a blocking force for Bravo and patrol the northern area of the hill mass. Signs of recent activity were found, but no sightings of enemy soldiers. The enemy did make its presence known in Chu Lai which was hit by a rocket attack, something it had not experienced for over two months. The deadly rockets landed in the headquarters area of H Troop, 1st/1st Cavalry, killing seven of its soldiers.

On December 3, Delta Company on patrol near the hamlet of Thuan Yen (3) hit a pressure release mine which left a small crater three feet in diameter and one foot deep. One soldier was dusted off.

Alpha Company working northwest of Fat City was plagued with sniper fire but had to be very cautious since its assigned area was heavily populated and pacified. One soldier was wounded by a sniper, who positioned himself close to a group of innocent villagers. The grunts had no choice but seek him out at close range and use their M-79 grenade launches which offered a small impact zone rather than M-16's whose bullets traveled a greater distance.

That afternoon Bravo's 4th Platoon spotted five Vietcong, four males and one female with AK-47's and packs on the north side of the Ba Ky River near Ngoc Nha (4). The grunts opened fire and saw one insurgent go down while the rest quickly scampered off. The river was too swollen to cross over in pursuit so artillery was called on the enemy's avenue of escape.

One hour later another eight VC were spotted again on the north side of the river. All carried Ak-47's except one who shouldered a 60mm mortar tube. Again small arms fire was poured on the insurgents while artillery was called. This time the enemy was seen jumping into small spider holes, an ideal situation to fix the enemy in place and pour on the artillery. Seventeen rounds of 105mm High Explosive (HE) fell on the enemy and, for good measure, another eight rounds of eight-inch HE Howitzer fire added to the pummeling. For added measure Blue Ghost helicopter gunships came over and expended their rockets on suspected enemy positions.

The following day at noon Bravo's troops found freshly dug graves containing two males in their twenty's. The torn bodies gave evidence the artillery fire mission had killed them the day before. Undoubtedly more graves were in the area. The grunts later found two military structures with abandoned NVA uniforms.

Alpha was provided enough birds to make eagle flights over the Ky Tra area during the day which was far more preferable for the soldiers than slogging through knee-deep water and mud. At the end of the day they were returned to Chu Lai for a rest and refit.

December 6 found Bravo conducting small unit operations in the Phu Duc and Ngoc Nha hamlet areas north of the Ky Tra Outpost. Charlie Company conducted small unit patrols in the Ky Sanh region of dense ridgelines from Phuoc Khach moving south to provincial Road 532. Delta continued its operations in the northern sector of Dragon Valley while the battalion's recon platoon operated north of the Ky Tra Outpost.

At 7:15AM on December 7, Bravo's 2nd Platoon found two NVA soldiers sleeping in a small hooch near Ngoc Nha (4). The grunts killed a NVA sergeant and captured a junior officer. Their souvenirs included an Ak-50 rifle, 9mm pistol, Chicom grenades and documents which were sent to Chu Lai.

Charlie Company was provided the air assets to conduct eagle flights over the battalion's assigned terrain and landed on ten separate landing zones throughout the day to search and clear suspected enemy positions. With the advantage of rapid movement some of the birds took Charlie's troops far north into the Ky Tra/Phu Duc area where intelligence reports suggested the enemy was lurking. Charlie's 3rd Platoon landed near Phu Duc (4) just south of the river, and detained six suspected Vietcong: four females and two males with documents and military equipment.

December 7 saw the 4th Infantry Division depart from Vietnam taking three of its infantry battalions with it. On December 8, two more battalions of the 4th Division departed. The same day the 25th Infantry Division and five of its infantry battalions departed Vietnam.

The wet and chilly weather, mines, booby-traps, snipers, malaria and rugged terrain challenged each infantryman on a daily basis. Their fortitude and dedication will never be fully understood except by the grunts that were there. On rare occasions a man would break.

At midnight on December 9, one soldier from Charlie Company in a night position two and one-half miles west from Hill 76, woke up with hallucinations. He stayed awake for two hours then lapsed back to sleep. He woke up again at 3:00AM hallucinating and vomiting blood. Night security and foul weather prevented his comrades from dusting him off. The soldier went back to sleep and at daylight woke up babbling incoherently and vomiting again. The cause of his behavior was unknown, anything from parasites to combat stress. He was dusted off and never seen again.

Alpha left Chu Lai on December 11 and air-assaulted to the intersection of Provincial Roads 531 and 532 by the Ba Ky River, four and one-quarter miles north of the Ky Tra Outpost. Its mission was to move southeast for three miles, conduct small unit patrols, then move south and west and swing back up to the Phu Duc (3) area.

Charlie's capture of VC suspects on December 7 gave hope that Alpha could encounter some insurgents along its patrol route. When Alpha landed in the field, the Hueys picked up Bravo on its return trip to Chu Lai for a scheduled rest and refit.

Charlie returned to ground patrols in the Ky Sanh area west and southwest of Hill 76. Delta Company, in the high ridgelines overlooking Dragon Valley, avoided some of the flooding from the lowlands, but suffered from the steady rains and cooler temperatures of the higher elevations.

The next day Alpha's 2nd Platoon hit a booby-trapped grenade north of Phu Duc (2). The grenade was hung eighteen inches above ground and was detonated by a trip wire across a path. The platoon Leader was hit with shrapnel to his legs, left side and upper arms and dusted off. It was the first of many booby-traps Alpha would encounter in its search area. All booby-traps were blown in place.

Delta was picked up in the afternoon to take its turn at eagle flights and landed at nine LZ's in the dense terrain northwest of Dragon

Valley and the Ky Tra Outpost. Delta went back to ground patrols on December 13 when its 3rd Platoon wounded a Vietcong near Dong Dang (5). Although the insurgent managed to escape, the wound usually meant a death sentence for the enemy, carried out slowly over a period of several days.

Charlie Company participated in eagle flights throughout the day, landing at eight separate LZ's in the high ground south of Hill 76 and west of LZ Bayonet, searching for suspected enemy positions.

The following day, December 14, near Dong Dang (5) Delta's 4th Squad of its 3rd platoon found a six foot by eight foot hooch with a well-prepared bunker next to it. Inside the bunker were potatoes, rice and corn.

Three hours later as the squad crossed a small stream, the second man in the patrol file tripped a pressure-release mine embedded in the side of the stream bank. The patrols point man, PFC Dennis Ralph Moreno was hit with shrapnel to his face and upper body. He was dusted off in less than twenty minutes but was dead on arrival in Chu Lai. The exploding mine created a hole in the stream bank six inches deep and two feet in diameter. Moreno was only nineteen years of age but married from Bay Springs, Nebraska.

Later in the day more eagle flights took Charlie Company's three rifle platoons to search the dense high ground west of LZ Bayonet. Delta's 2nd Platoon saw a group of enemy on the north side of the Quan River and crossed it using one Huey for three trips to get all across, one-half mile east of My Dong (2). The first lift received small arms fire and a base of fire was placed on the enemy to allow the remaining two lifts to land. By then the enemy had evaded.

On December 15 it was Bravo's time to re-enter the fray and they did so by air assaulting from Chu Lai to the area south and southeast of LZ Bowman. In standard fashion the returning birds, after each lift taking Bravo to the field, picked up Charlie Company to return to Chu Lai for a scheduled rest.

That afternoon Bravo found small way stations used by the evading enemy, the hooch's typically containing pots and pans, small bags of rice or corn, with NVA uniforms. The enemy continued its practice of trying to survive by discarding its uniforms and blending in with villagers in the area.

The next morning the scout dog being used by Bravo's 1st Platoon detonated a pressure release mine on the south side of

Provincial Road 531, southeast of Don Qua (2). The dog was killed and three soldiers wounded. When the dustoff arrived, it received small arms fire from one hundred yards distance as the wounded were being loaded on the bird. The bird promptly pulled out, leaving one of the wounded behind. Gunships came on station to rocket the area as Bravo's soldiers positioned themselves to go after the insurgents. Then another three soldiers were wounded by another mine. A second dustoff landed and pulled out the four remaining wounded.

Alpha's 4th Squad of the 2nd Platoon found one enemy structure one-half mile west of Thanh Hoa (4). After destroying the structure they killed a Vietcong in uniform who was lurking nearby and captured his Ak-47. Delta's 1st Platoon bumped into a VC in uniform on the low-lying ridges west of Dragon Valley near Danh Son (1). He was only thirty-five feet from the grunts when spotted but attempted to run and was promptly cut down. He carried a 9mm pistol and a backpack which contained three Chicom grenades and ten pounds of rice.

The enemy tried to continue its efforts to destabilize the battalion's largely pacified area and create an uncertainty among the Vietnamese that their security would be threatened once the Americans left. To this end a credible intelligence report indicated a group of female sappers had been created among women who worked at the Chu Lai base. Their mission was to smuggle explosives onto the massive complex beginning on December 15 and lasting through the early part of 1971, to support an attack on Chu Lai.

In the field Bravo's 2nd Platoon was alerted by its scout dog of an approaching enemy soldier. The platoon's pointman quickly hid until the VC was within fifty feet, then the insurgent was cut down. The enemy soldier carried a resupply list for his unit but no weapon. As the day ended Bravo's 4th Platoon began setting up its night mechanical ambushes (MA) on a trail near Ngoc Nha (3) when another VC came into view on the same trail. He was promptly eliminated.

The next morning Delta's 3rd Platoon heard talking and singing in a heavy stand of bushes along an isolated riverbed one-quarter mile north of Thuan An Tuy (1). The platoon opened up with a burst of M-60 machinegun fire and moved in. They found a group of fifteen Vietnamese, six males, four females and five children. Two other males were killed by the gunfire. The adults were wearing uniforms not seen previously and were carrying Vietcong identification. They were evacuated for questioning. One of the dead males was identified as an NVA medic whose back-pack contained medical equipment.

Bravo's 2nd Platoon dog handler tripped a booby-trap north of Tu Yen (5) near the Ba Ky River. The dog, low to the ground, was not injured but its handler was seriously wounded with metal fragments to his head, chest and legs. Another grunt next to him was also hit in the arms and legs. Both were dusted off, along with the dog, which was useless without its handler.

The battalion's soldiers continued to find small camps that were recently used, containing abandoned food, eating utensils and equipment. This intense patrolling came at a price. A Delta patrol tripped another booby-trap on December 18, while filling their canteens in a stream. A concealed hand grenade wounded three soldiers, one with the amputation of both legs. They were promptly dusted off.

Amidst the continuing search and clear operations at the platoon and squad level, the 5th/46th Infantry Battalion exchanged battalion commanders for one last time. Lieutenant Colonel James R. Henry, a West Point graduate, had taken command on September 9 but his command tenure was being cut short. The rumor among the battalion's officers was that Henry was not considered aggressive enough by the brigade commander and was replaced. Henry understood the hardships and realities of his grunts in covering large amounts of terrain to go after the enemy body counts desired by the brigade commander. But it left the soldiers too tired for aggressive night actions and Henry tried to reconcile the demands of the brigade commander with the realities faced by his troops. The brigade commander was not satisfied.

On his last day of command Henry's helicopter spotted a fleeing Vietcong and he ordered his bird to land in front if the enemy, with all guns onboard aimed at the fleeing soldier. Henry walked out and escorted the Vietcong back onto his ship to be questioned at Tam Ky. The VC later took a PF patrol back to where he hid his assault rifle.

The following day, December 19, Lieutenant Colonel Edwin Passmore took command of the 5th/46th Infantry Battalion. He would remain in command until the battalion left Vietnam five months later.

By mid-afternoon on the 19th Charlie Company finished its rest in Chu Lai and air assaulted back to the field while the same Hueys picked up Delta Company for a rest and refit in Chu Lai. Charlie Company was moved farther west than ever before, five miles west of Dragon Valley into the Bong Mieu River Valley three miles southeast of LZ

Professional. It was the first time since 1968 the battalion worked in the LZ Professional area.

Throughout the battalion's area the enemy kept appearing in small numbers, trying to survive in the same terrain the 5th/46th and Vietnamese militia controlled. Alpha's 1st Platoon, while laying out its night mechanical ambushes late in the afternoon, spotted four uniformed NVA soldiers near Tam Son (1) and Provincial Road 231. Each carried an AK-47 rifle with a rucksack. The lead man also carried three RPG rounds across his chest. The distance to the enemy was not ideal for small arms fire, but Alpha opened up with their M-16's and wounded the point man. By the time they reached the enemy's position, all that remained were drag marks and blood trails leading into the dense bushes.

Bravo's 1st Platoon killed a NVA soldier on December 20 near Ngoc Nha (3). Charlie Company was kept busy in its new assigned area, finding and destroying military structures and the tunnel systems below them, in dense terrain by the Bong Mieu River. The river was bracketed by steep ridgelines on each side, which placed the soldiers in a vulnerable position.

Alpha's 1st Platoon patrolled near Dan Thuong Dong (4). In a rare instant of luck, a soldier detonated a crude booby-trap that caused no injuries. The trip wire was a poncho string that connected to a smoke-grenade fuse and C-ration can that was filled with C-4 explosive. The can was positioned six inches above the ground close to a trail, but was positioned incorrectly. When the improvised mine detonated the blast blew away from the trail. It could have been deadly. The mine left a crater ten inches deep and eight inches wide.

Each day darkness came early in the dense terrain occupied by most of the battalion's soldiers. At 6:30PM, Alpha's 3rd Platoon was already laying in its night defensive position (NDP) when it heard one of its MA's detonate approximately seven hundred and fifty yards from its NDP. A patrol swept the area and found a dead Vietcong with papers on him.

As the battalion pushed farther west in its operations, the PF and RF militia continued the pressure in the Ky Tra and Dragon Valley area. At 9:00PM, a Popular Force (PF) ambush killed three Vietcong and captured three weapons by Phu Duc (4) and the Ba Ky River.

The next day Charlie's 3rd Platoon found another enemy structure on a ridgeline. This time it contained a sleeping NVA soldier who was captured with his equipment. Nearby the 1st Platoon found a stone structure recently occupied, measuring twenty feet squared. Inside were four pounds of tobacco and twenty pounds of marijuana, all of which were destroyed by burning. Several grunts remembered as the tall mound of marijuana went up in smoke, "It smelled real good."

Alpha continued to be plagued by mines and booby-traps, the crude kind first encountered by the battalion in April 1968. Its 2nd Platoon found several booby-traps made from discarded C-ration cans and C-4 explosive which were destroyed.

Bravo Company continued its operations in the Ngoc Nha and Dong Dang hamlet area along the lower reaches of the Ba Ky River. It too found abandoned military structures with the discarded equipment of an enemy who constantly avoided contact. What hampered Bravo in the area was the rapidly-flowing river which was fifteen feet deep. It was impossible to cross and pursue the enemy soldiers who were sighted on the other side. Helicopter support was too scarce and the waiting time too long to be of any tactical value. Bravo's Commander, Captain Roger Templar, called for some rubber rafts to be flown out.

The following day, December 23, six men from Echo Company, 26th Engineers were flown out by helicopter with two inflatable rafts. Artillery fire was on standby from the Ky Tra Outpost to cover the river crossing. The rafts were placed into the river for a "Swing Line" crossing where the rafts would be guided by a line tethered across the river. But the first raft had two holes in it and was discarded. The second raft was inflated but had several holes as well. Patchwork on the holes began, but the raft was too wet for regular patches so wooden pegs were plugged in with glue.

SP/4 Daryl Hart began to swim the river with one end of the Swing Line attached to the near side and the other end held by him, to be attached to a tree on the far side. But the rivers currents were too strong and the soldier was swept downstream as he clung to the life preserver tied to the end of the rope.

Hart was pulled ashore and PFC Walter Colon stripped down to try to make the swim across the river. This time he succeeded and tied the other end of the rope to a tree. The raft, which held ten men, moved across the river. Ten trips were required to move the company across and the enemy long since had left the area when the crossing was completed. Bravo continued the search on the far side, without having to wait for helicopter assets.

That same day, Delta finished its rest in Chu Lai and participated in eagle flights in the morning, landing at suspected enemy camps to sweep the terrain. In the early afternoon the company command element and 1st and 2nd Platoons were lifted by Huey to the rugged terrain by the Phuoc Lai hamlet three miles south of LZ Bowman to search and clear the area. Delta's 3rd and 4th Platoons were used for more eagle flights. Alpha Company returned to Chu Lai for its rest and refit.

The next day, December 24, Delta's 3rd Platoon continued eagle flights west of LZ Bayonet while the battalion's recon platoon operated near the Ky Tra Outpost, finding recently abandoned military structures but no enemy.

With Alpha in Chu Lai taking its rest but standing by as the brigades reaction force, Christmas Eve saw Bravo Company settled in its NDP near Ngoc Nha (3). Charlie Company saturated the Bong Mieu River Valley with small patrols near the Dan Thuong and Tam Song hamlet areas, east of LZ Professional with six squad and platoon-sized ambush sites. They laid-out numerous mechanical ambushes (MA's) as well.

Charlie's ranks were depleted of soldiers despite the influx from other units departing Vietnam, and the MA's now became more defensive in nature to protect them against a night attack by the NVA. Their reasoning was sound; the heavy thickets around them would betray an approaching enemy and the MA's would offer additional early warning on nearby trails.

Delta established its night positions three miles south of LZ Bowman by Phuoc Loi (2). Its 3rd Platoon landed two miles west of LZ Bayonet from an eagle flight and set in to monitor any enemy movement threatening to attack Bayonet. The battalion's recon platoon remained near Thuan Yen (1) just northwest of Ky Tra while the battalion's mortars remained on Fat City and Hill 270.

Christmas Day brought some relief for those in the mountainous terrain with the temperatures climbing to eighty-one degrees, a light wind and no rain. Nighttime illumination from the moon was down to only fourteen percent which kept everyone watchful. But the day was serene and a supposed Christmas "Cease Fire" had been agreed to.

Charlie's 1st and 2nd Platoons were able to rendezvous for a "Christmas Party" which included a brief appearance of "Donut Dollies" from Chu Lai, Red Cross workers who brought out treats. Charlie's 3rd

Platoon did not make the party as they were continuously shadowed by the NVA and chose to stay in a reasonably strong defensive position.

There was little activity by the battalion's soldiers until 6:00PM when preparation began for the usual night activities, mechanical ambushes (MA), live ambushes and defensive positions. That evening Bravo spotted a "moving light" walking down a trail near Ngoc Nha (4), a sure sign the enemy was on the move, using a flashlight to spot trip wires connected to MA's. Bravo fired its 81mm mortars on the light.

The next day while sweeping the area Bravo spotted another Vietcong, who was five hundred yards away and too far for their M-16's. Mortar fire was called on the insurgent.

On December 27, Bravo was lifted to Chu Lai for rest while Alpha took off from the Chu Lai base on eagle flights over the Ky Tra area near the Thon Hai and Than Hoa hamlets two and one-half miles east of the Ky Tra Outpost.

Alpha's 3rd Platoon was inserted near Trung Tin, just south of Than Hai (1). After moving five hundred yards it spotted two military structures with two VC inside, who were promptly killed. Each insurgent was in peasant garb, the typical black pajamas, but NVA equipment was next to them. No weapons were found. Alpha's 3rd Platoon received small arms fire when touching down at its landing zone. The platoon swept the area but found nothing.

Three hours later the 3rd Platoon was hit with more enemy fire. Gunships came on station as Alpha's 1st Platoon spotted Vietcong near the 3rd Platoon. Both platoons swept the area, moving west in the direction of the enemy when they were hit by an estimated squad of VC who were dug in. The patrol's point man was hit in the neck by AK-47 fire. The VC threw some Chicom grenades at close range which wounded another soldier, sending shrapnel into his legs.

Both platoons put down a base of fire while gunships poured down fire as close to the grunts as possible. Darkness was approaching and the enemy evaded into the thick terrain. After dusting off their wounded the platoons prepared their positions for the night.

The next day a patrol returned to the site of the ambush and received more small arms fire. Artillery was called to allow the grunts to disengage. They moved in again after the artillery fire mission but found nothing.

Mid-morning on December 30, Bravo and Charlie Company's were picked up in the field and returned to Fire Support Base Fat City.

Bravo subsequently moved to the Ky Sahn high ground north of Provincial Road 532 and the Quan River, west of Hill 270. Charlie Company moved by truck back to Chu Lai for a rest and refit.

The final day of 1970 saw much of the same activity that had preoccupied the battalion's soldiers in the field for months. There were occasional discoveries of small, abandoned military structures and shoot and run activity from a diminished enemy seeking to maintain a presence until Americans eventually withdrew from the area.

The year had cost the battalion another forty soldiers killed in action. One hundred and sixty-one lives had been lost carrying out the battalion's missions since it arrived in Vietnam in March of 1968. Many hundreds more were wounded, and many with multiple amputations. The price of war would claim another thirteen soldiers in the few remaining months the battalion had, before its Vietnam journey would end.

On December 31, 1970, approximately three hundred and fifty thousand U.S. personnel remained in the Southeast Asia Theater. Army strength was at two hundred and fifty-five thousand and Marines at twenty-five thousand, four hundred. Nearly two hundred thousand troops had already departed Vietnam. American losses in South Vietnam for the year were four thousand, two hundred and four killed in action; Vietnamese losses (ARVN, PF/RF Militia, etc) at twenty thousand, nine hundred and fourteen.

The South Vietnamese (ARVN) losses were about to climb much higher on February 8 1971, in a major strike into Laos called Lam Son 719. Much of the Americal's 196th Brigade, whose AO lay north and west of the 5th/46th Battalion, would be moved north in January to help pave the way for the ARVN operation. That required someone to help secure the terrain the 196th was relinquishing. That task would fall to the 5th/46th Infantry Battalion.

17 – END OF THE TUNNEL

By the end of 1970 many more Americans were questioning whether the sacrifices being made by their sons were worth the uncertain outcome in Vietnam. General William Westmoreland had spoken optimistically before the National Press Club in Washington in November 1967 about the coming year. "With 1968" he said, "A new phase is starting, we have reached an important point where the end begins to come into view". And Westmoreland used the phrase "Light at the end of the tunnel" to describe the improved situation on the ground in Vietnam. Three months later the country was hit with massive attacks during TET 1968.

Now, three years later after the TET attack, the "End of the tunnel" for the 5th/46th Battalion's soldiers was not the end of the war, but their departure from Vietnam. The final outcome would depend on the South Vietnamese military because it was very clear the Americans would be going home.

A supposed ceasefire was arranged for New Years Day, January 1, 1971, among the American, South Vietnamese and the enemy, although communication of a ceasefire to a scattered enemy west of Chu Lai was highly problematic.

At first light on the first day of the New Year 1971, Alpha's 1st Platoon spotted five Vietcong nine hundred yards from its positions near Thon Hoi (1), two and one-half miles east of the Ky Tra Outpost. Artillery fire was not called on the enemy due to the ceasefire. But the ceasefire was ignored by the enemy when Alpha's 2nd Platoon received six enemy 60mm mortar rounds fired at their defensive perimeter. Fortunately, the rounds were off target and exploded one hundred yards outside their perimeter. The platoon responded with an artillery barrage on the mortar location but no sweep was made on "Ceasefire Day".

On January 2, Charlie Company's headquarters and its 2nd and 3rd Platoons moved by Huey to Hill 76 and then fanned out on patrols in conjunction with the Popular Force (PF) militia. The 1st Platoon was lifted by air to Ky Xuan Island just north of the Chu Lai base, to search and clear the island in conjunction with PF platoons 80 & 173. The PF's believed the Vietcong, who had been hiding in deep tunnel systems on the island, had been forced out of their hiding places due to flooding from heavy rains and were now living with their families in two hamlets. The PF's were to search the hamlets with Charlie's 1st Platoon as a reaction force.

Casualties were taken before Charlie Company ever left Chu Lai. While loading their gear in the company headquarters area, one of PFC Tatom's grenades dropped from his equipment when the safety pin broke off. The grenade exploded and wounded Tatom and two others who were rushed by truck to the hospital. Tatom took the blunt of the blast and was shredded with metal fragments to his back, which lacerated his spinal cord, permanently paralyzing him.

The 5th/46th Battalion was then notified not to patrol near heavily populated areas on January 3-4 because of expected Buddhist demonstrations. Use of military vehicles on Highway One would also be curtailed, unless absolutely necessary. The Buddhists were reportedly trying to create an incident with American forces.

Delta returned to Chu Lai on January 4 for a rest and refit and the battalions recon platoon air assaulted to the Ky Tra Outpost to patrol the area in conjunction with RF Group 931. Alpha conducted small unit operations among the Thon Hoi hamlets in the Ky Thanh area while Bravo Company worked the same mission in the dense terrain south of Alpha Company.

At 11:25AM on January 4, Alpha's 3rd Platoon leader, Lieutenant Westerlund, stepped on a pressure-release mine on Hill 203, causing severe wounds to his arms and legs. The dense terrain required a jungle penetrator, a metal object which resembled a vertical torpedo, with two fold-out seats and handles for the wounded to latch onto. Westerlund was lifted out and flown to Chu Lai.

Alpha's 1st Platoon spotted three Vietcong just as the enemy spotted them north of Thon Hoi (1). The enemy took advantage of the thick terrain and quickly bolted without returning fire. Alpha poured small arms fire on the fleeing enemy anyway, because wounding an escaping insurgent was usually a death sentence, given the enemy's lack of medical resources.

KILLING AND DYING

Killing the enemy with small arms fire was highly problematic at this stage of the war. Grunts were wary of being drawn into an ambush or booby-trap from an evading enemy. Then too, enemy fire was sometimes used as a ploy to draw the grunts away from hidden base camps in the area. The probability of hitting an enemy soldier with M-16 fire at more than fifty feet in the three to ten seconds the insurgent needed to find cover was low. "Charley", the Vietcong, was uncanny. The general view of the battalion's grunts was "You can take what Charley gives you but you must be willing to pay the price." In other words, aggressively pursuing the enemy to kill a few of them would most likely result in friendly casualties from mines and booby-traps.

Bad weather continued to plague the soldiers in the field. On the afternoon of January 5, Bravo tried to get a priority dustoff for one of its soldiers who had a 104 degree fever but the birds were grounded due to the weather.

The next day Alpha received a change in its mission and was tasked to gradually move its patrols north into the Ky Chanh area, two miles southeast of Hill 54. Bravo was tasked to move north into Alpha's area around the Thon Hoi hamlets. Both moves were directed by the brigade commander who believed soldiers should move rapidly like chess pawns over dense and hilly terrain, with heavy rucksacks. The expectation of a brigade commander, four levels of command above the common soldier, did not reflect the realities of mines, booby-traps, worn-down soldiers and an enemy light on its feet, that could rapidly cover great distances with little food.

Before Alpha Company could begin its trek northward, the 4th Squad of the 3rd Platoon found an enemy cache of three Browning Automatic Rifles (BAR), one AK-50 Assault Rifle, three cases of AK ammunition (with two hundred rounds in each case), a Soviet 7.62 Light machinegun with six hundred rounds, three rifle-propelled grenades (RPG's), seven 60mm mortar rounds and eighteen Chicom grenades. Alpha's 4th Squad of its 1st Platoon was not as fortunate. As the patrol exited from some thick vegetation on the southern rim of Hill 203 to

End of the Tunnel

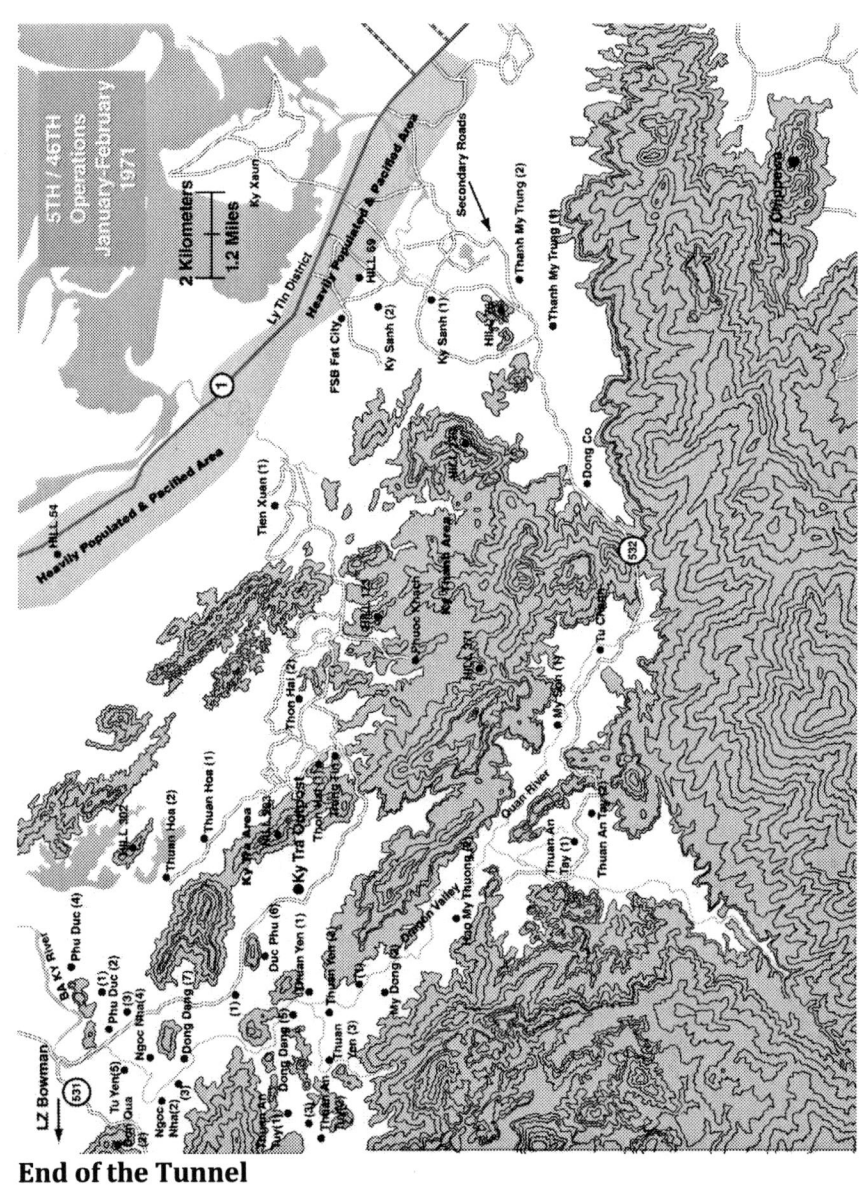

cross over a trail, one soldier stepped on a pressure-release booby-trap. He was seriously wounded with fragments to his legs and head.

Alpha Company finally shifted to the northeast which placed it in a position to eventually walk out of the field to Highway One on January 10. Alpha was trucked to Chu Lai for a standdown.

Helicopter support for the battalion's operations for air assaults, eagle flights, and troop airlifts from the field would be spotty throughout January. Unknown to the grunts at the time, a larger operation was launched far north near the Demilitarized Zone (DMZ) which separated North and South Vietnam. Operation "Dewey Canyon II" was taking place on the "Red Devil Road", Route 9, leading to the Laotian border in Quang Tri Province. Two battalions of the Americal's 196th Brigade, which normally operated north of the 5th/46th Battalion area, the 2nd/1st and 4th/3rd, were now being flown far north to assist in clearing Route 9 toward Khe Sanh to prepare for the South Vietnamese Army's (ARVN) incursion into Laos beginning February 8. This movement required much of the Americal's aviation assets for a short period.

The ARVN attack into Laos, which would last until April 6, was designated "Lam Son 719". Casualties in the operation were significant, with 215 US Soldiers killed, 1,149 wounded and 42 missing. The South Vietnamese suffered 1,483 killed, 5,420 wounded and 691 missing. Enemy dead was estimated at 13,636 with 69 prisoners. The costly operation would take its toll on American aviation assets. One hundred and eight helicopters were destroyed and six hundred others damaged in the operation.

On the morning of January 6 before Bravo Company began its move into Alpha's area, its 2nd Platoon spotted four NVA in uniform in the dense terrain one-quarter mile east of Hill 371. The terrain again provided the enemy an advantage for quick evasion but helicopter gunships quickly came on station and fired their rockets into the terrain where the enemy fled. Bravo's search revealed a dead NVA in khaki shirt, shorts and a pith helmet. By his side was a AK-50 rifle, sixty rounds of ammunition, two Chicom grenades, twenty pounds of rice, assorted cooking equipment, a poncho, mosquito net, papers and photos. If the gunship killed one target it was hoped that others were wounded and would therefore suffer a longer but sure death sentence.

As the soldiers continued to sweep the area they spotted two Vietcong wearing ponchos and carrying AK-47's while dragging a body. The soldiers opened fire but the enemy escaped.

Bravo's 2nd Platoon spotted four enemy soldiers in green uniforms near a streambed south of Phouc Khach. It opened fire just as the enemy fled, killing one insurgent. Papers found on his person identified him as a member of the 402nd Sapper Battalion. The platoon moved farther west onto dense ridges where it encountered two VC in uniforms with Ak-47's. The enemy quickly fled down a narrow trail as Bravo's gunfire hurried them along with small arms fire. The grunts warily followed the enemy but came to a fork in the trail where the blood trail ended.

The enemy increased its efforts to plant mines and exact a price in blood for the battalion's control over the large amount of terrain it was assigned. On January 7 Bravo's 1st Platoon, patrolling just north of Phuoc Khach, located another booby-trap on a small trail. The trip wire was placed three inches above the ground and led to a 60mm mortar round planted on the side of the trail. The mine was blown in place with C-4 explosive.

Charlie's 2nd and 3rd Platoons, along with a platoon of "Blues", the infantry assigned to Cobra Gunship units, spent that afternoon on eagle flights, landing in eight separate locations to search the immediate area for enemy soldiers or small base camps. The grunts detained some women and children near Phu Duc (4), an area that was off-limits for civilians, and took them to a detention point. After intense questioning, one woman admitted she was a member of a VC hamlet in the Ky Tra area where four guerillas were living. She related that during the first week of December thirty-five to forty Vietcong had passed though the hamlet in small groups, moving west to the mountains. She revealed the enemy had dug small foxholes on the sides of isolated trails they used for day movement, so they could quickly hide when helicopters flew overhead.

Another eagle flight found two camouflaged hooch's and three 81mm mortar rounds which were set up as booby-traps alongside a trail, north of Thanh Hoa (2). They were destroyed. A break in the weather and the short term availability of some Hueys gave the battalion an opportunity to shuffle its soldiers around by rapid air movement, to try to make contact with the elusive and scattered enemy.

On January 8, Delta left Chu Lai to Combat Air Assault to north of Hill 302. Its mission was to patrol farther north to the Ba Ky River, then swing south to the Phu Duc's and the VC hamlets that were mentioned by the woman who had been detained with her children. Intelligence reports pointed to recently constructed tunnel systems and enemy camps in the area.

Charlie's three platoons were inserted into the Thanh Hoa hamlet area with the same mission. Charlie's 4th Squad of its 2nd Platoon found fresh tracks and some cultivated fields on the ridges south of Thanh Hoa (1). An enemy structure was being rebuilt which contained NVA equipment such as canteens, belts and cooking utensils. The enemy had also started to dig a tunnel into a soil bank. It was late in the afternoon so the grunts set up a mechanical ambush with plans to revisit the site the next morning.

That same day Bravo's 3rd Platoon air assaulted into the Trung Tin hamlet area to confirm reports of enemy sightings. It took some enemy fire when landing and promptly moved out to sweep the area. The platoon moved cautiously to avoid mines and booby-traps. PFC Cecil Olsen was the point man, breaking brush in front of him to avoid walking on trails. Avoiding trails meant avoiding mines but moving through thick brush was a sure way of announcing your movement to the enemy. At 3:55PM, he was suddenly hit with a burst of AK-47 fire by a lone insurgent and was killed instantly. The platoon quickly swept the area but the insurgent melted away. Cecil Chancey Olsen had been in Vietnam for only three months. He was single and twenty-one years of age, from Rowley, Iowa.

Alpha's 3rd Platoon sighted eight VC in black pajamas carrying weapons northeast of Thon Hoi (2). The enemy was out of range for M-16's so an artillery fire mission was called. Permission was not given because friendly villagers were in the area. As the enemy moved farther west they walked into the area being patrolled by Charlie's 1st Platoon. Charlie opened fire on the VC then swept the area finding two military structures with bunkers. Inside one dwelling was an M-79 grenade launcher.

On January 9 Bravo's 3rd Platoon, still in the Trung Tin area, received small arms fire from a group of Vietcong only one hundred yards away. Two soldiers were hit, one with gunshot wounds to the back and shoulder and another with a wound to the arm. A third soldier, a dog handler, stepped into a punji trap, a hole with sharpened bamboo stakes facing up and covered with excrement. All three were dusted off. Punji traps were a crude way for the Vietcong to eliminate grunts from the field and were rare in this stage of the war. It was possible the enemy was finding it difficult to obtain materials in that area for more deadly mines and booby-traps.

The increased enemy contacts made by Bravo led the battalion's intelligence officer to surmise that the Trung Tin area was either a base camp for the V-20 Vietcong Local Force Company or that a large supply cache was in the area. Bravo's other platoons were tasked to move into the area and increase the search effort.

Charlie Company's 2nd Platoon was also engaged in enemy shoot and run activity just south of Thanh Hoa (1). After receiving fire, it swept the area and discovered a small base camp of five structures, each hooch measuring twenty feet in length and ten feet in width, built next to a cultivated field. A small tunnel yielded batteries, radios and assorted equipment. When the grunts destroyed the complex with fire and C-4 explosives, secondary explosions erupted indicating a small stash of ammunition had been missed. Close by were bunkers and fighting positions littered with the refuge of a hastily abandoned camp; canteens, AK-47 ammunition and two live chickens.

Another part of Charlie Company patrolled the ridges between Thanh Hoa (1) and Hill 203 when, at 1:30PM, a patrol detonated another booby-trap which wounded four grunts. Three were promptly dusted off, one with shrapnel wounds to the face, another wounded in the arm and a third with shrapnel in the legs. The fourth soldier was treated in the field.

The battalion's recon platoon now moved into the dense terrain south of Provincial Road 532 one mile southeast of Trung Tin. At 10:25AM, they heard voices from approximately five insurgents who fled as the grunts moved in. They found only footprints. Farther northwest some PF's claimed they spotted a group of one hundred VC near Ngoc Nha (2). Artillery from Ky Tra was fired on the site and Delta Company, up in the Phu Duc area, was tasked to sweep the hamlet.

January 10 began with Delta's 1st Platoon hearing enemy movement beyond its night perimeter one-half mile east of Phu Duc (1). It called in artillery fire and swept the area at first light, finding no enemy. RF Group 931 stepped up its efforts to deny the enemy movement in the Ky Tra area by planting numerous mines and booby-traps on frequently-used enemy trails. Enemy mines, and now "friendly" mines increased the danger of operating in the Ky Tra area. The 5th/46th Battalion provided map overlay's to all the battalions in the

198th Brigade for coordination if future operations required other platoons, companies or battalions to operate in the Ky Tra area.

Charlie's 2nd Platoon continued to receive sporadic enemy fire in the vicinity of the base camp it had discovered near Thanh Hoa (1). The terrain was very thick, raising the possibility of enemy ambushes. The grunts decided to call in artillery fire as a substitute for a ground patrol. Four white phosphorous rounds and eight high explosive rounds fell in the area of the harassing enemy fire.

Three-quarters mile farther northeast, near Thanh Hoa (3), Charlie's 3rd Platoon found a well-cultivated potato field and animal traps, with fresh sandal prints of a quickly departed enemy. The platoon's 4th Squad came upon a burned-out hooch and four bunkers with clothing strewn inside one of them. A search of the immediate area drew enemy fire. The squad fired and maneuvered through the terrain, spotting four Vietcong on the run carrying AK-47's. One female VC could not escape fast enough with her children and was captured with a two year old boy and six year old girl. The girl was wounded by the gunfire and they were all dusted off to Chu Lai.

Gunships ("Musket 24") supporting Bravo Company were diverted to Charlie in search of the fleeing enemy. The squad which located the mother and children also found a dead male Vietcong nearby, believed to have been killed the prior day by artillery fire. The tracker dog with Charlie's 3rd Platoon alerted the soldiers of enemy movement as it moved up a ridgeline. Seconds later the enemy opened up on the soldiers with AK-47 fire and one Chicom grenade, then evaded alongside the hill.

At approximately the same time that Charlie was hit, Bravo's 2nd Platoon, east of Charlie, observed five to six Vietcong five hundred yards away to its east (west of Trung Tin) and another group of nine VC much closer to its west. All wore green uniforms, bush hats and carried AK-47's. Bravo engaged the second group with heavy fire at close range and the enemy responded by throwing Chicom grenades. Bravo swept the area but found no enemy. The encounter cost them three wounded soldiers however, including their platoon leader, LT. Fisher, who was critical with wounds to the head and body. The head wound was unusual because Fisher was one of the few battalion soldiers who still wore a steel helmet in this stage of the war. Later the platoon found a freshly dug grave which contained the body of an enemy soldier in a green uniform.

Delta's 2nd Platoon located ten hooch's one half mile southwest of Thanh Hoa (4) near the Phu Duc hamlets. The deserted camp was surrounded by punji stakes and it appeared the PF's from Ky Tra had burned the camp earlier. It was growing late. The platoon began setting up a mechanical ambush (MA) on a ridge trail south of Thanh Hoa (4) that was believed to be used by the enemy. Their hunch was proven correct when three Vietcong approached their position as they set up the MA. The grunts opened fire, killed one and wounded another while the third insurgent escaped.

The morning of January 11, 1971 did not begin well for the battalion and the day would only get worse. Delta's 2nd Platoon moved out of its night position at first light to walk to a nearby LZ site to receive supplies. PFC Edward Wayne Bethards was the last to move out and lagged far enough behind that he lost momentary sight of the man in front of him. It was a critical moment. The patrol reached a fork on the trail and walked on a safe trail, knowing the other one led to one of its mechanical ambushes set out the night before. Bethards came to the same junction and made the wrong turn. After walking a few feet he detonated the MA and was killed instantly. Bethards was twenty years of age and single from Novato, California.

Bravo's 2nd Platoon's contact with the NVA the prior day and the 3rd platoon's contact on January 9, raised a red flag with the battalion commander that main force NVA, perhaps in a large number, were in Bravo's area. Bravo, like the other companies, operated with platoons dispersed, each assigned a different sector, sometimes several miles apart. LTC Passmore flew in to accompany Bravo company as things developed.

Bravo's 1st Platoon commanded by 1LT Larry Kenney was down to only twenty-two grunts. They were two miles from the headquarters element on January 9, when they spotted a small squad of four to five NVA moving north, crossing an old rice paddy, all carrying weapons. Kenney's platoon fired, killing one and wounding some others who evaded. The enemy fled in the same direction Kenney was ordered to go, towards the rest of the company in order to consolidate Bravo's strength because of growing enemy contacts.

It was obvious to Kenney and his men that this area was "Home Sweet Home" to some hard core NVA who didn't like them very much. There were lots of indications of recent activity such as well-worn paths and cleared trails, fresh footprints, etc. Kenney's men did not like the order to close with the rest of the company in a rapid move, knowing that the NVA was in a "kick ass" frame of mind.

Kenney's platoon moved all night on January 10-11, walking through flooded rice paddies, a risky move walking in the open, but its only choice to avoid the mined trails. By early in the morning on the 11th they could see the company's defensive position. The company command post (CP) was situated on a thin finger of high ground jutting out into a wet paddy with steep sides and heavy brush. Kenney's platoon hid in some vegetation. The platoon leader decided the best way to approach the company position was to walk up a saddle that connected the finger to a ridgeline. Other approaches required crossing too much open paddy and then cutting though thick brush, exposing them too long with the NVA threat around them.

All of a sudden ten to twelve enemy soldiers, one with an M-60 machinegun and bandoleers of ammunition, came out of nowhere and walked within ten yards of Kenney's platoon. They came from the direction of the saddle Kenney wanted to approach and walked pass the hidden grunts, never seeing them. The platoon kept silent, Kenney reasoned he was there to relieve the rest of the company and not get his men killed from a quick assault by the enemy.

When they were certain the NVA had passed, the platoon bounded across a paddy to the saddle in groups of seven to eight men, running all the way. The first group was about two-thirds across the paddy when all hell broke loose. In front of them on the saddle, were fifteen to twenty evading NVA, shooting at Kenney's approaching grunts. The platoon finally reached the CP and Kenney briefed Bravo's commander, Captain Roger Templar.

Bravo's 3rd Platoon patrolled some trails and a ridgeline nearby where it spotted other groups of enemy the day before. The battalion commander was with them. The trail network appeared to be an east to west corridor for enemy movement. Bravo's 2nd Platoon remained in place at the CP for security. Kenney's 1st Platoon grunts, newly arrived at the CP, were drying off their feet which were soaked from the wet paddies of the prior night's march.

Captain Templar wanted the 1st platoon to search the saddle that connected its position to the larger ridgeline and, looking at Kenney's feet, insisted he would lead the patrol himself. The platoon took its assigned scout dog while the 2nd Platoon's mine-sniffing dog remained at the patrol base. It was a fateful choice.

The scout dog led the patrol file to the saddle which was just north of Provincial Road 532, west of Trung Tin. This was the same area the NVA had been, that fired at Kenney's platoon earlier. All the signs were there, there was no reason not to expect an ambush or at least a well-placed booby-trap. The NVA could read the terrain as well as the grunts. The saddle was the only practical and semi-secure way to come or go from the company's command post.

Templar, the company commander, was fourth from the front of the patrol. His medic, Nolan Borel was just behind him. Borel could hear Vietnamese "Yacking" and he could smell them nearby. It seemed they were trying to draw the grunts to them. He warned Templar not to go any farther. The point element continued and walked into a small clearing.

Then it happened. A command-detonated 105mm Howitzer round was exploded under Templar, sending a deafening blast throughout the area. The 3rd platoon received a call from the 1st Platoon shouting they needed medevacs for six to nine soldiers. 3rd Platoon moved quickly to the scene on a trail that led in that direction, its mine-sniffing dog alerting to mines and booby-traps all the way. The grunts jumped over several booby-traps with each man pointing them out to the man behind him and then kept running. They arrived at the 1st Platoon position in ten minutes.

The devastation was horrendous. Lying around a crater fifteen feet in diameter were a dead scout dog alongside his dead handler and eight severely wounded soldiers, including Templar who lost both legs in the blast. A resupply Huey (Minuteman 11) heard the call for an emergency dustoff and promptly kicked out its mermite cans carrying hot food to another unit and rapidly flew to the scene of carnage. Despite Templar's critical wounds he remained on the radio and directed the dustoffs, at times having his RTO hold the radio receiver to his head as he directed the relief.

Minuteman 11 picked up two of the most critically wounded and departed. Shortly after, Dustoff 88 came in, picking up four more wounded grunts. Another Huey, Hornet 42 completed the dustoffs with three more grunts, including the company commander.

Three of Bravo's grunts did not survive their injuries. Dying shortly after the blast were PFC Lee William Clore who was nineteen years of age and single from Westchester, New York and SP/4 Rex Alan Vogelpohl, age twenty-one and single was from Butler, Indiana.

Vogelpohl was the dog handler assigned to Bravo from the 57th Scout Dog Platoon and not an assigned member of the battalion. PFC Dennis Ray Easter succumbed to his wounds two days later on January 13. He was twenty years of age and married from Brownville, Pennsylvania.

Elsewhere that afternoon Charlie's 2nd Squad of its 3rd Platoon, its 4th Platoon and company headquarters element were picked up by Huey and dropped onto the ridges east of Duc Phu (1) in response to intelligence reports of enemy activity. Before long they found enemy structures, tunnels, bunkers, scattered clothing and pens for chickens and pigs. None of it could be destroyed due to the lack of explosives. By now Charlie and Bravo were both patrolling in close proximity to each other.

Bravo's 1st platoon, after moving off the CP, discovered a bunker used for making homemade mines. American steel helmets were used to melt the wax to hold bomb materials in place. The trails leading to and from the site were all booby-trapped with trip wires. Engineers were requested to send a demolition team and a mine sweeping team to clear the area. There were simply too many mines for the soldiers to safely handle.

The following morning, January 12, Charlie's 2nd Platoon was hit with small arms fire near Hill 203 east of Duc Phu (2). One soldier received a gunshot wound to the arm and another was shot in the leg. Gunships came on station at the same time the grunts spotted some movement in the brush. The gunships raked the area with 40mm grenade fire while the platoon called for artillery to be placed on the enemy's expected areas of retreat. But a sweep of the area found no enemy.

The next day the battalion's rifle companies shifted locations again to try to intercept the elusive enemy. Delta Company was air assaulted into the Trung Tin area. Alpha was moved from Chu Lai to Fat City, then air assaulted back into Dragon Valley on the western side of the Quan River near My Dong (1). Bravo was lifted out, its strength greatly depleted, and moved to Chu Lai for a rest and refit. Charlie Company remained in the Hill 203 and Duc Phu hamlet area, still finding small enemy way stations which were increasingly protected by mines and booby-traps.

Three booby-traps were blown by C-4 explosives but the heavy saturation of mines took its toll. Soldiers in Charlie's 2nd Platoon hit a mine, a pressure-release type with a shape charge which seriously wounded four soldiers. The mine crater measured three feet by five feet and eighteen inches deep. The dense terrain required a jungle penetrater to be lowered to extract the wounded.

Delta's 4th Squad of its 2nd Platoon found enemy foot prints, mines and booby-traps on the ridges west of Thon Hoi (1). One booby-trapped Chicom grenade had been tripped before the grunts arrived and the trip wire lay limp across the trail. Apparently an animal tripped the wire and experienced a lucky day. The grenade had failed to detonate and was blown in place.

The next morning, January 15, the squad was plagued by sniper fire. A squad-size patrol in Delta's 1st Platoon also received forty rounds of harassing fire just to the east of Trung Tin. One soldier was shot in the back. The grunts popped purple smoke to guide the dustoff in to pick him up, and they noticed a red smoke was popped at the enemy location. The dustoff pilot spotted both smokes but taxied to the correct location.

January 16 saw Alpha Company in Dragon Valley with a sweep and clear mission, requiring it to move south from the vicinity of Dong Dang (1), sweeping the western side of the Quan River for one mile, and then swinging west into the dense high ground to search for enemy camps.

Bravo Company finished its rest and refit in Chu Lai and also air assaulted back to Dragon Valley, to the eastern side of the Quan River near Dong Dang (1). Its mission was to move south, sweeping the eastern edge of the river valley then move farther east into the high ground to search for enemy camps.

Charlie Company was sent back to Chu Lai for a rest and refit while Delta Company was tasked to sweep south from the Thon Hoi and Trung Tin area to Phuoc Khach then swing west into the dense high ground to search for evidence of enemy movement. The battalion's reconnaissance platoon worked south of Delta in the Ky Sanh region, covering the dense terrain from My Son (1), moving east to Dong Co, along the ridges north of Provincial Road 532.

The following day Alpha's 1st Platoon spotted three Vietcong wearing green uniforms west of Dong Dang (1). The enemy was two hundred yards away and quickly evaded into the dense terrain. Alpha's 4th Squad of its 3rd Platoon detonated a booby-trapped Chicom grenade one mile west of the valley floor. Three soldiers were wounded and dusted off.

Bravo Company, on the eastern side of the Quan River found a 60mm mortar with a base plate just south of Dong Dang (1). Its 4th Platoon on the ridges north of the hamlet found two hooch's that had been recently used. They decided to leave the dwelling intact and plant some mechanical ambushes to see what the enemy's nighttime activity might yield.

Delta's sweep of its assigned area continued with only sporadic enemy contact. Each encounter demonstrated the enemy's advantage of shooting and rapidly evading. At noon on January 18, the 3rd Squad of Delta's 2nd Platoon was hit by enemy small arms fire while crossing a rice paddy west of Trung Tin, wounding two soldiers. It was a price that was to be paid time and time again for the battalion's control of its assigned terrain. But squad and platoon-sized ambushes, augmented by mechanical ambushes nearby, continued to challenge the enemy's movement in the night.

At 8:25PM, Alpha's 1st Platoon spotted "moving flashlights" used by enemy patrols at night to avoid the mechanical ambushes. The MA's had become a scourge to the enemy much the same way its mines and booby-traps were a scourge to the battalion's soldiers. The MA's were usually placed one quarter mile or more away from the grunts night positions, to give the enemy a feeling of free movement. This time artillery fire was called on the moving lights. Eighteen high explosive rounds pummeled the area topped off with two white phosphorus rounds for good measure.

Bravo's 2nd Platoon heard an MA explode at 8:00PM. A patrol found a dead female approximately forty-five to fifty years of age, by My Dong (2) along the Quan River. She wore khaki shorts, a brown sweater and was carrying a 25-pound bag of rice. She had no weapon. It gave the grunts no comfort to find a dead woman without a weapon but there was no remorse. The deadly rules of Vietnam operations had been established for years. "Civilians" did not travel or wander outside their hamlets in the dark. Night movement was reserved for the protagonists and antagonists in the unrelenting war to kill or be killed. The only conclusion available to the grunts was that she was Vietcong, possibly carrying food to an enemy way station.

The next day another Alpha Company MA detonated at 4:30PM near My Dong (2). This MA was set out earlier than usual but in terrain where no civilians were present. A patrol found a blood trail with more blood than usual splattered among the foliage leading off into the dense brush. Scattered about was a hand grenade, black pajamas, a sandbag and a partially opened C-ration can. Three sets of footprints led to the southwest and the patrol took up the hunt with 81mm mortar fire directed in front of its route. After one-quarter mile of careful stalking, the search was called off due to darkness and the grunts returned to their patrol base.

The following day, January 20, Alpha's 3rd Platoon had better luck nailing a Vietcong using a mechanical ambush in the dense ridges overlooking the western edge of My Dong (2). That afternoon Delta was extracted from the field and sent to Fat City while Charlie Company, finished with its standdown in Chu Lai, was trucked to Fat City and picked up by the same birds that returned Delta.

Delta trucked to Chu Lai for a rest where the weary grunts were greeted once again with ammunition "Shake-Downs" as they climbed off the trucks. This helped insure no weapons or ammunition were kept by the soldiers while resting in the increasingly volatile atmosphere in Chu Lai.

Drug use and Black Power incidents continued to present problems on the massive Chu Lai base; problems not uncommon on bases throughout Vietnam during the drawdown of forces from Vietnam. There was constant friction between the soldiers returning from the field after enduring mines, booby-traps and enemy fire, and those permanently assigned to rear duties in Chu Lai.

Even within the 5th/46th Battalion hard drug use became an occasional problem. One soldier, hooked on heroin, was sent to the Ky Tra Outpost to work with the battalion's forward operations center. This was a transfer meant to isolate him from drugs. But he couldn't cope without them and approached the battalion's operations officer on Ky Tra, Major Donald Van Eynde, with a grenade in his hand, the pin pulled, demanding to be lifted off the outpost and returned to Chu Lai.

A resupply Huey was in-bound and Van Eynde radioed the pilot he would "have a passenger with a grenade in his hands" to go back to Chu Lai. The pilot refused to land. Van Eynde told the soldier, "The only way you'll get on that chopper is to put the pin back in the grenade." The soldier complied and was taken back to Chu Lai where military police took him into custody. He was taken to the Long Binh Jail ("LBJ") outside of Saigon.

Charlie Company was flown out to the Ky Thanh area around the Thon Hoi and Trung Tin hamlets. After a short time on the ground the grunts found camouflaged military structures with bunkers and small garden plots. The next day they received harassing fire near Thon Hoi (1) where more enemy bunkers and fighting positions were located. CS (riot gas) grenades were used to clear the bunkers. Later Charlie's 4th Squad of its 3rd Platoon found a booby-trapped 60mm mortar round attached to a trip wire. It was blown in place.

Alpha, in Dragon Valley, was not as lucky. Its 4th Squad of the 1st Platoon drew casualties when its pointman, SP/4 Joseph Stone, hit a trip wire on a trail, which detonated a bomb, shredding Stone's legs and the Kit Carson scout next to him. Both were promptly dusted off but Stone eventually succumbed to his wounds, dying on February 3, 1971. Joseph Lamar Stone was age twenty-four from Desert Hot Springs, California.

Constant daytime patrolling, sometimes down to the squad level, left the grunts extremely fatigued by nightfall. Live ambushes at night were at a minimum, to allow the grunts the chance for more sleep, despite pressures from the brigade commander to stay active both day and night. Night offensive activity was mostly in the form of mechanical ambushes, set in place to kill roving enemy at night and for early warning of approaching enemy soldiers coming towards night defensive positions.

Units of Bravo Company were engaged in eagle flights the afternoon of January 22. When Bravo's 1st Platoon was picked up by Hueys after searching a site three miles west of the Ky Tra Outpost, a nervous door gunner fired too soon, and shot a Bravo soldier in the back with his M60 machinegun. The grunt was sent to the 91st Evacuation Hospital and survived.

January 23 brought more of the same activity for the battalion's soldiers. Mechanical ambushes could be heard exploding in the night and were checked at first light. More often than not the sites revealed blood trails, footprints and drag marks, but no bodies. The enemy continued to reoccupy small way stations that had been previously destroyed by the battalion. Much of what Charlie found near the Thon Hoi hamlets had been rebuilt just a few weeks after another unit in the battalion had destroyed the same sites.

Alpha's 2nd Platoon, operating south of My Dong (2) near the Quan River, discovered a small base camp of three structures which had been previously destroyed. Like a Phoenix rising from the ashes, the three dwellings had been rebuilt, complete with a mess hall containing pots and pans. Animal traps were found in one bunker, an important tool for the enemy to supplement its meager rice rations. Animal hair was found in one fire pit, indicating the enemy did have some trapping success.

Gunships and spotter planes continued to patrol the skies over the battalion's large area of operation, looking for "Targets of Opportunity" which were usually in the form of concealed hooch's, small garden plots or one to two insurgents on the move. "Saber 78", a light observation helicopter (LOH) flew low along a tributary of the Ba Ky River near Duc Phu (6), one and one-quarters mile west of the Ky Tra Outpost. The LOH spotted what looked like muzzle flashes from Ak-47's and saw five Vietcong hiding under a bush. One insurgent moved farther into the dense brush while the other four elected to cross the river. It was a bad idea. The LOH opened up with machinegun fire and the insurgents were cut down.

Several hours later it was learned the "insurgents" were Popular Force (PF) militia and civilians. Two PF's and two civilians had been killed crossing the river and another PF was wounded. Clearance for the LOH to fire had been given by two PF Lieutenant's at the Ky Tra Outpost. The dead PF's had left the camp without permission.

Farther south in Dragon Valley, Alpha's 2nd Platoon located six more enemy hooch's. Each had a deep bunker which contained hollowed-out logs with gunpowder, M-2 fuses, and internal trip wires that suggested the site was used for improvising booby-traps.

On the morning of January 25, Alpha's 2nd Platoon inspected one of its MA sites that had detonated the previous night. One dead boy, approximately fourteen years of age was found wearing black pajamas but no weapon or pack. The body was found on a dense ridge west of the Quan River. Nearby were three small shelters, measuring five feet by four feet, each with a fighting position. Outside one shelter a shallow grave was found which the grunts estimated was one week old.

Despite the stench of decaying flesh, the grunts had to dig it up to confirm its contents. The grave revealed a young male approximately twenty-five years old whose legs were torn apart by shrapnel. The location of the corpse made sense. A week earlier another MA had detonated nearby and the blood trail led to the present grave location.

The continued threat of rocket attacks on Chu Lai caused Delta Company to place a hunter killer team in the rocket pocket west of LZ Gator. Other Delta soldiers were tasked to begin night patrols in the relatively open terrain between Hill 76 and the Chu Lai base where night movement was easier and illumination more readily available should enemy contact be made.

Despite the supposed transition of the combat responsibility to the South Vietnamese military, pressure continued on the battalion's soldiers to "find and fix" the enemy. The soldiers were pushed by the demands of an aggressive brigade commander to cover larger areas of terrain in smaller squad-size patrols. The demands of distance and time over difficult terrain forced the grunts to use more trails, which increased the possibility of injury and death to mines and booby-traps.

A good example was a Charlie Company patrol that found a 60mm mortar round hanging upside down from a tree, three feet above the ground. A trip wire was strung across a trail and attached to the round. Close by a 105mm Howitzer round was found alongside a shallow hole. The hole looked inviting to tired grunts seeking to rest by the trail, because it kept them below the ground surface in case of enemy fire. But a pressure-release plate lay buried in the bottom of the hole, guaranteeing instant destruction for those using it. Both mines were destroyed. Close by the soldiers found a small tunnel.

January 27 saw Alpha Company in Chu Lai for rest & retraining. Bravo was tasked to sweep Provincial Road 532 beginning four miles northwest of the Ky Tra Outpost then move south to Duc Phu (6), then move west three miles into dense terrain that had not been cleared for some time.

Charlie Company continued its operations in the Ky Thanh area while, closer to Chu Lai, Delta covered a wide stretch of terrain from south of Hill 76 moving five miles south into the rocket pocket west of LZ Gator, then moving east into the hilly terrain west of LZ Bayonet.

On a brigade commander's map all these missions looked doable, but the large distances tasked to the grunts were more suitable for mechanized infantry. The difference between the mission and the reality of what was accomplished was now determined by the field-savvy grunts operating at the "tip of the spear"; the platoons and squads exposed to mines and ambushes. It was the platoons and squads that ultimately determined the pace of their movements in the waning weeks of a war that would be concluded several years after the battalion's departure from Vietnam. Everyone sensed the battalion would end its operations in a matter of a few months.

The battalion's reconnaissance platoon continued its patrols, as it had for many weeks, in the Hill 270 and Hill 76 area. Hill 76 continued to be a strategic high point for control of the rolling Piedmont terrain from the Ky Thanh hills to the populated area by Highway One, Chu Lai and the Ly Tin District.

Operations in the more densely-populated Piedmont presented special challenges to the battalion's soldiers. The My Lai Massacre which occurred when the battalion first arrived in Vietnam influenced the Americal Division's engagement policies. The murder trail of Lieutenant William Calley began on November 17, 1970, and was featured in the American news media each night. This was an event not lost on the enemy. Calley was convicted of premeditated murder on March 29, 1971. The pro-Communist hamlet dwellers knew of the increased sensitivities the division felt when dealing with peasants who lived as farmers by day and insurgents by night. The enemy leveraged this sensitivity to its advantage.

Shoot and run harassment from insurgents continued to dominate the battalion's enemy contact. At this point, Charlie Company in the Ky Thanh area was having more contact than the other companies. A typical contact was made by Charlie's 1st Platoon the afternoon of January 29. The patrol received about ten rounds of AK-47 sniper fire near Trung Tin. Rather than engage the enemy in a helter-skelter foot race after one or two insurgents and be drawn into an ambush, four 105mm white phosphorous rounds were called down on the enemy position followed by fifteen high explosive rounds to cover a wider area in case more insurgents lurked nearby.

A search of the area afterward revealed a fresh grave that was several days old. It was dug up and revealed a dead Vietcong soldier wrapped in a blue hammock and covered with a Vietnamese-made poncho. Charlie's 2nd Platoon, while moving to a night defensive position, found a small stash of American ammunition. There were eight hundred rounds of M60 machinegun ammunition and two American rucksacks. It was obviously left by a previous patrol in the area. Such carelessness would have been unheard of in 1968 or 1969. The battalion headquarters searched its reports to see what unit had been in the area previously.

Bravo's 2nd Platoon also found a grave estimated to be two weeks old near Phu Duc (3). Lying on top of the ground next to the grave was another Vietnamese body clad in a khaki uniform, dead for several days. His body was riddled by small arms fire.

On January 30, 1971, Alpha finished its standdown and combat air assaulted back to Dragon Valley. The birds picked up Bravo Company on its back haul to return Bravo to Chu Lai. One Huey lift ship coming into Bravo's pick-up zone spotted five enemy soldiers wearing blue uniforms with packs and weapons near two hooch's. Gunships which escorted the birds poured rocket fire on the site. But the helicopters were on a short leash for time and were required to fly another mission, so Bravos grunts were not sent in to check the area.

At 7:00PM some Alpha grunts, while on a night ambush, spotted seven NVA crossing a rice paddy six hundred yards away. Two wore green uniforms and carried weapons while five others carried heavy packs. The grunts opened up with small arms fire while directing their own 81mm mortar and artillery fire from Ky Tra. The approaching night offered only thirteen percent moonlight illumination so the soldiers remained in their position rather than search the area.

Later that evening the defenders of Hill 270 watched a red light to their northeast slowly approach their hilltop. It appeared the enemy was preparing to attack and was guided by the light to avoid mechanical ambushes. Four 81mm mortar rounds were fired and the light went out. The perimeter went on full alert. The battalion's recon platoon on Hill 76, one and one-quarter mile to the east, was also alerted.

Mission versus Survival

The next day, January 31, the battalion's grunts continued their work at clearing terrain, neutralizing the evading enemy and interdicting its known supply routes. Charlie's 1st Platoon found another mortar round hanging from a tree but with no trip wire. It appeared the patrol had interrupted the insurgents work in setting up the booby-trap.

Alpha's 3rd Platoon found several hooch's in Dragon Valley containing papers and notes arranged in a systematic order, believed to be propaganda documents. Cooking utensils and fresh potatoes were an indication the occupants had recently fled. It was getting late in the day so the site was not destroyed. A live ambush was set up nearby and a mechanical ambush was set up farther out from the site. At 7:00PM, the MA detonated and a patrol immediately checked it out, finding a dead NVA soldier in a green uniform who wore a pistol belt but no weapon. He had been carrying a load of firewood.

Staff Sargent Tim Woodville of the recon platoon on Hill 76, took a new soldier, "Max", who had transferred from a battalion of the 25th Division, to do some early morning hunting near the hamlet at the base of the hill. Returning back they passed through the hamlet while the villagers were celebrating the lunar New Year. Woodville talked to an elderly lady (Mamasan) he had routinely purchased Pepsi from, when a young boy asked him, "How much longer GI stay on hill?" Woodville told him it was "None of your fucking business."

The Mamasan, seeing Woodville was irritated tried to divert his attention but the boy responded, "GI stay on hill one more night." Woodville pondered how he knew that information when the Mamasan replied, "No listen to kid. He knows nothing." Woodville decided to not act on his instincts and thought nothing about it.

That same afternoon another recon soldier walked the zigzag path through the concertina wire from the top of Hill 76 towards the hamlet when a PF soldier passed him, quietly saying out of the corner of his mouth, "VC come tonight." The evening before, the recon grunt had seen a PF officer on the perimeter looking out beyond the wire, a view the PF's never cared about before. Seeing the grunt looking at him, the PF made the motions as though he was going to pee. The grunt discussed both incidents with his fellow soldiers and their newly assigned platoon leader but nothing was made of it. The fact that their field instincts were not acted upon would soon have devastating results.

The battalion's weekly intelligence report remained consistent with previous reports. Part of the NVA 402nd Sapper Battalion, which had a total estimated strength of two hundred and ten soldiers, was located in mountainous terrain three miles southwest of Hill 76. The NVA 409th Sapper Battalion, with an estimated strength of two hundred and sixty-nine was reportedly located in dense terrain eleven miles west of Hill 76. The NVA 78th Rocket Battalion, responsible for supplying rockets for attacks on Chu Lai, was at a strength of some one hundred and fifty rocketeers and laborers and located in the Ky Sanh area south of Provincial Route 532, two miles southeast of the valley hamlet of Tu Chanh.

The Vietcong were organized around two Local Force (LF) Company's. The V-14 LF Company, with an estimated strength of sixty insurgents was estimated to be in the dense hills east of the Thanh Hoa hamlets about two miles northeast of the Ky Tra Outpost. The other VC unit, the 74th LF Company (V-20), with an estimated strength of fifty insurgents, operated near the Thon Hoi and Trung Tin hamlets.

As midnight slipped into February 1, 1971, Echo's Recon Platoon was positioned on the top of Hill 76 for this final night to provide security to a small group of PF's. Hill 76 had five bunkers on its small hilltop perimeter with fighting holes next to each bunker. In the center was a tower. When one looked west from the tower the mountains seemed to sweep down with ridges from the north and south, and Hill 76 was at the convergence of those ridges. The forward slopes of the hill were strewn with concertina wire, trip flares and Claymores. At the bottom of the hill on the southwest side sat a small hamlet and close to it was a maze-like barb-wire entrance that opened to a path leading to the hilltop. The path entrance was close to the hamlet and it was reasoned its location would offer an early warning in the event of an attack.

At 2:20AM, Staff Sergeant Tim Woodville was in the tower with some others and heard mortars landing on his hilltop. His first thought was that they were friendly mortars firing erroneously and that someone should get on the radio and redirect their fire. The thought lasted only a few seconds when he realized the mortars were coming from the enemy. Woodville groped for his CAR 15, a shortened version of the M-16, as his best friend, Staff Sergeant Joe Casino quickly scampered down the tower steps. Casino and Woodville had gone through NCO School together, then Airborne and Ranger Schools, each earning the coveted Ranger tab which earned them a promotion from Sergeant to Staff Sergeant.

Woodville heard a long burst of automatic weapons fire and then a moan and instinctively knew Casino was dead, killed by friendly fire. Woodville yelled to those below the tower, "Which one of you shot Joe?" There was a reply, "Not us!" Then he realized that "Gooks were already inside the hilltop perimeter".

The mortar rounds were now replaced by satchel charges and grenades, being tossed about by an enemy that had gained easy access inside the hilltop position. Unknown to Woodville, an enemy sapper waited at the base of the tower to shoot soldiers coming out. Casino was killed instantly as he was the first one to leave the tower. Woodville swelled with revenge, his best friend had just been killed. Casino was not supposed to die, not like that; not after all that training and experience in the field.

Woodville found his CAR-15 and moved to get out of the tower and avenge his friend. His friend "Max" headed out first and was hit by a burst of automatic weapons fire from the same sapper. He turned to Woodville, quietly and calmly telling him he was hit in the back. Woodville crouched and told him, "I'm sorry man." Woodville carried his comrade out of the tower, the sapper having moved on.

Crouching at the base of the tower he asked the group around him if anyone was hurt. No sooner were the words out of his mouth than his whole world was turned upside down. His ears rang and he struggled to breathe, choking from explosive dust while his left leg was in terrible pain. Reaching down he felt a warm sticky goo. His leg was practically severed above the knee. His buddy Max whom Woodville brought out of the tower yelled that his pants were torn off and he couldn't work his legs. Both had been hit by a satchel charge.

Woodville yelled out for a medic. A voice from a bunker pleaded that it was too hot with the attackers all over and for them to come to the bunkers. Woodville told Max to crawl in front of him to the nearest bunker believing that Woodville could catch up to him and help him along if he didn't make it all the way. Once he started moving he didn't want to turn around and crawl back to get his friend.

By this time illumination rounds were being fired over the hilltop from Hill 270, creating shadows in between flickering patches of light on Hill 76. In those shadows Woodville saw the face of an attacker running in front of him and stopping. He watched the enemy pull the pin on a Chicom grenade and throw it on him. Woodville covered his face with his arms as the grenade exploded on top of his right leg. This explosion brought more excruciating pain and his right leg was shattered below the knee. Had Woodville been up on his knees while moving the grenade would have killed him outright, but the blast came downward, obliterating his leg but not his torso.

The two made it to the nearest bunker where their comrades pulled them in. Woodville's left foot was attached by only a thin strand of sinew and was caught in some debris. His buddies had to pick it up to get him inside. Woodville called out for a status of his men, "Is Joe (Casino) OK? Is Steve (SSG Stephen Moore) OK?"

"Sure, don't worry about it", was the answer. The men patched him up as best as possible. When Woodville was eventually taken out of the bunker to be medevaced he passed a body. "Is that Steve?" "Yes".

"He's dead right?"

"Yes"

"Why?"

Placed on the Medevac floor, Woodville was still choking with blood running down his face into his mouth. Someone was standing over him and bleeding on him. The other soldier, weak from pain and loss of blood stepped on Woodville. Nothing else mattered to Woodville but to stay awake until he reached the hospital. His comrades told him, "Don't fall asleep, stay awake!"

Staff Sergeant Tim Woodville lost both legs on Hill 76, the left leg above the knee and the right leg below the knee. He had planned to make the military a career but had no regrets for his sacrifice. Not then, not now as the reader reads his account, not ever.

Hill 270 had radioed Hill 76 at the start of the attack, reporting they were seeing mortar and small arms fire. Seven minutes later the recon grunts radioed back that sappers were now inside the perimeter using satchel charges and AK-47's. The attack was brief but deadly, just as sappers were trained to do. It was made all the more deadly by the speed with which the attackers reached the top of the hill totally unimpeded with the cooperation of the Vietnamese in the hamlet at the base of the hill. By 2:50AM the contact was broken off and dustoffs were called for the dead and wounded.

SP/4 Russell Printy was on the night shift at the battalion tactical operations center (TOC) in Chu Lai. He and his shift partner were playing Parcheesi and all was quiet. All of a sudden the main radio net came alive with screaming and explosion noises, "Help us! Help us! Oh God help us!" More screaming and uncanny noises filled the radio with lots of squelch noise. It was obvious to Printy someone was in severe danger but they were not using call signs and the man on the other end would not "Unkey" his radio mike. No one could talk to him.

Then Fire Support Base (FSB) Fat City radioed on the artillery frequency. They could see Hill 76 from their site and now they were screaming as well, "Hill 76 is getting hit! Hill 76 is fucking hit bad! Echo Recon is getting fucked up bad!" Finally the recon soldier on Hill 76 unkeyed his mike and the radio went silent. Printy kept trying to raise the recon group on Hill 76 but to no avail.

This all happened very quickly. He had his shift partner wake up the Battalions S-3 Operations Officer, Major Donald Van Enyde, who arrived in a few minutes with a short-timer medic in tow. Van Enyde, a two-tour Vietnam veteran instinctively knew there was carnage. Printy had already called Chu Lai Dustoff's for a medevac and brigade headquarters for gunships to fly to the hill. Van Eynde gave the battalion commander, LTC Passmore, the situation report and said, "I have to go in, there's no commo from the hill." Passmore agreed.

Delta Company's 2nd Platoon, operating east of Hill 76, was tasked to begin a night march to get to the hill as quick as possible. The first dustoff picked up wounded at 3:13AM and a second dustoff took the remaining dead and wounded at 3:35AM. All were taken to the 91st Evacuation Hospital at Chu Lai. The casualty toll was immense.

Five members of the recon platoon were killed and seven more seriously wounded. Only three members of the platoon remained on the hill after the dustoff's departed. Ten of the PF militia that also defended the hill were wounded.

The attack on Hill 76 was the last major firefight resulting in heavy casualties for the 5th/46th Infantry Battalion in Vietnam. It occurred with only three months before the battalion would permanently cease operations. Ironically, it was the battalion's reconnaissance platoon which also suffered the first major casualties in Vietnam, on April 21, 1968 on top of the heavily-mined Hill 56.

Those answering their final roll call that night were: Staff Sergeant Joseph Walter Casino age twenty-one and single from Drafter, Michigan; Sergeant Gordon Lee Crawford age twenty-four and married from Fort Wayne, Indiana; Staff Sergeant Stephen Alan Moore, age twenty-three and married from Nitro, West Virginia; Sergeant Richard Dale Randolph age twenty and single from St. Johns, Michigan and Specialist 4 Stephen Edward Warren age twenty and single from Rochester, New York.

Van Eynde was provided a Light Observation Helicopter (LOH) and flew to Hill 76 to try to make some order out of the chaos. Printy as the RTO and the medic, both volunteered to go in with him. To Printy, squeezed in the small chopper, the parachute flares floating in the sky made things on the ground look like the earth was moving. As his eyes fixed on the approaching hilltop the pilot kicked the chopper sideways and dropped it into a spiraling motion down to the top of the hill.

Printy saw "A scene that was a total cluster-fuck; very dark, people screaming, total chaos". As the RTO he tried to stay in radio contact with the battalion headquarters and dustoffs. As another example of the increased caution taken by soldiers as the war wound down, the dustoffs and gunships screamed into the radio, "Is the fucking

LZ secure or not? We are not coming in unless the LZ is secure! Pop smoke and flares!"

The medic with Van Eynde vanished into the darkness as he made his way towards the screaming to help the wounded. The PF's were running in all directions yelling and pointing, causing more mass confusion. Van Eynde and Printy, who stayed close to the Major, found some soldiers alive but covered with blood. Others were dead in their bunkers or just outside the entrances. Body parts were lying all around. As they helped load bodies on the Hueys a dustoff pilot screamed on Printy's radio, "No fucking dead...no fucking dead! Stop loading the dead, just the wounded!"

When the dustoffs were completed only eight Americans, including Van Enyde's team, remained on the hill. Van Eynde surveyed the scene with a flashlight. He found a couple of soldiers in good shape and several Popular Force (PF) militias allegedly in a shouting match with a few Vietcong who were supposed to still be in the small hamlet at the base of the hill. It remained a question as to just how genuine the argument was. The enemy was surely moving away from the area. Was the shouting done for a show? A pall of doubt hung over the PF's and the villagers in the hamlet. In retrospect it appeared the hamlet and/or some PF had allowed the VC to assault the hill from that direction. There was no other explanation to account for the speed with which the attackers were able to get inside the perimeter.

Van Enyde requested permission to call in artillery on the retreating attackers who scurried across the flat rice paddies beyond the hamlet. Permission was denied by division headquarters as there were too many civilians in small sub-hamlets in the area. The artillery was properly registered to place effective fire but memories of My Lai made the division extra cautious. The Americal could not tolerate another civilian disaster in the field. Van Eynde called for gunships to circle the area until daylight. As he surveyed the hilltop by flashlight he saw unexploded munitions lying everywhere. Some of the enemy's satchel charges had delayed fuses and occasionally exploded along the perimeter.

The soldiers on the hilltop could see enemy mortar rounds that landed, still unexploded, with their explosive noses buried into the ground and their tail fins sticking up for all to see. Despite the flares dropped from aircraft which illuminated the sky, the remaining defenders had no desire to walk around with unexploded munitions lying everywhere. The group's collective wisdom was to wait until daylight. Van Enyde agreed. Delta's 2nd Platoon was told to stop their march toward the hill and return to their assigned areas. There was nothing more to be done. Everyone was pulled off the hill in the morning. The newly assigned recon platoon leader was relieved of command and reportedly court-martialed for failing to heed the signs of the impending attack.

Later that day, seven miles farther northwest, Charlie Company in the Ky Thanh area found a large enemy hooch with several interconnecting bunkers just west of Thon Hoi(1). The bunkers contained a 60mm mortar round, M-16 ammunition, assorted equipment and food along with five pounds of marijuana.

The danger of mines and booby-traps continued to increase as the enemy applied the only defensive measure it could. When part of Alpha's 2nd Platoon moved into a night position in Dragon Valley, they found a small innocent-looking branch lying across a trail. Close inspection revealed it was connected to a 60mm mortar round. Close-by on the edge of a dry rice paddy next to a thicket, a trip wire device was connected to a C-ration can filled with explosives.

Alpha's 4th Squad, 2nd Platoon found an 81mm mortar round hooked to a trip wire in the middle of a rice paddy. It was positioned to catch American troops crossing the area to avoid using nearby trails. The mine was blown in place.

A battalion sniper team moved into a night ambush site one-half mile west of Thanh Hoa (1), escorted by PF Platoon 931. They found a booby-trapped 60mm mortar round with a trip wire across a trail. The next morning at 8:10AM the snipers spotted two Vietcong, killing one while wounding another who limped away. The dead VC yielded an AK-47.

An hour later, a Huey arrived with a six-man team to search a wider area with the snipers, who were too lightly armed to do it alone. They followed the blood trail and found clothing and food baskets along the way. The search discovered a small cultivated field by a network of three well-used trails. From there they picked up the blood trail again which led the patrol south to a fork in the trail, where the blood ended. Along the way they found five "campfire sites" with sleeping positions dug in prone holes below the ground. All five positions were well used. Another small cultivated field was found next to two wells and a tunnel.

Hand grenades were tossed in the tunnel before the soldiers were picked up by a Huey.

February 1 saw Charlie's 1st Platoon continue its search and clear patrols west of Thon Hoi (1). SP/4 Mike Crosby, a squad leader was mentoring a new soldier, a "FNG". Crosby peeled away some unnatural-looking brush which revealed a trip wire. He told the FNG "You never want to walk through this stuff." Crosby's platoon leader, however, wanted to keep going saying "We will neutralize the mine later." Crosby, walking point, was against it but was told to move on. He stepped high and slow to avoid tripping another wire. His FNG remained behind him, "walking drag" to observe. The FNG did not imitate Crosby's high steps and tripped another wire, setting off a booby-trap which wounded them both.

Late that afternoon Chu Lai was hit with fifteen 122mm rockets. Delta's 2nd Platoon saw the flashes from the launch site, which was just one mile west of Highway One and northwest of LZ Bayonet. Delta had focused on the usual areas for launch sites and the enemy chose to slip closer than normal to the Chu Lai base to launch its attack. Radar at Chu Lai pinpointed the launch site and counter-battery fire was placed on the suspected location. Delta also inserted a hunter-killer team into the area. Casualties in Chu Lai were limited to three wounded and none killed.

On the morning of February 3 Bravo Company was picked up from its standdown in Chu Lai and air assaulted far west into the terrain around LZ Bowman to search and clear the area. Its mission required an extension of the battalion's operational area into terrain controlled by the 196th Light Infantry Brigade. The extension was approved.

Charlie Company was lifted to Chu Lai on the backhaul of the choppers which had returned Bravo to the Bowman area. Alpha continued its operations in Dragon Valley while Delta continued to patrol the area south and southeast of Hill 76, including the northern and southern rocket pockets with squad-size patrols and Hunter-Killer teams.

That night at 2:05AM Delta's 1st Platoon, operating in the southern rocket pocket, was hit by two 4.2-inch mortar rounds which landed thirty feet from its position. The platoon quickly surmised it came from the heavy mortar position on LZ Chippewa one mile to their west. The Chippewa detachment denied it. The Fire Direction Officer (FDO) for the 1st/14th Artillery Battalion, which controlled indirect fires in the area wasn't buying the denial. He told the Chippewa outpost he would check-fire its position for the night, allowing no firing until morning and then conduct a crater analysis to determine the launch location of the rounds. The mortar position admitted its mistake. They had made a 3,200 mill directional error on one mortar tube.

Both Alpha Company (in Dragon Valley) and Bravo (near LZ Bowman) took special precautions with night ambushes and daytime patrols as Regional Force and Popular Force militia from Ky Tra and Tam Ky launched a major sweep that would cover part of the battalion's area. This caused a great amount of confusion.

Alpha spotted what they thought were three enemy soldiers in uniform but first checked with the PF commander at Ky Tra to insure they were not friendly militia. When the clearance came to fire the enemy had moved out of the area. Later that same afternoon Bravo Company also spotted three insurgents wearing black pajamas near Dong Dang (2). Clearance was given to engage the enemy but the time to get the clearance gave the enemy time to move farther away. Artillery was called instead of using small arms fire and, as it was getting dark, the grunts decided to sweep the area the next morning.

Despite the confusion coordinating with the Vietnamese RF's and PF's, their operations were proving effective. Insurgents were located and killed in small groups, just like the battalion's patrols. On February 6, RF Company 132 encountered a force of NVA/VC in dense terrain south of Thanh Hoa (4), east of Bravo Company. The militia engaged the enemy in heavy fighting, killing three Vietcong and retrieving their weapons.

Increased enemy activity occurred closer to Chu Lai as the enemy tried to infiltrate hamlets in the populated area near Highway One. At 4:55AM on the morning of February 6, two Americal Division Long Range Reconnaissance Patrol (LRRP) teams, "Texas" and "Maine" observed fifteen to twenty VC near their hidden position. They were located in dense terrain north of Hill 270 and three-quarters mile southwest of Fat City. The teams were working together, a rarity for LRRP's, but this exception may have saved them. The LRRP's spoke in muffled voices over the radio, keeping communications to an absolute minimum, as the enemy was a mere one hundred yards away.

At 5:47AM the LRRP's radioed for gunship support, reporting they were surrounded and in heavy contact with the enemy who was throwing Chicom grenades at close range and unleashing heavy automatic weapons fire. The brigade commander ordered Delta

Company south of Hill 76 and Charlie, on standdown in Chu Lai, to be ready to go as a reaction force. By 6:00AM the LRRP's were requesting a dustoff for eight soldiers, two of whom were seriously wounded.

By then Charlie Company was standing by, ready to go. By 6:35AM the LRRP's reported that contact with the enemy was broken. Shortly after, Charlie's 1st Platoon was inserted on the eastern edge of the dense ridges where contact had been made. The 2nd and 3rd Platoons were inserted just to the south of the contact site where the enemy was thought to have fled. By 9:10AM the 1st Platoon linked up with the LRRP teams who were extracted by Huey to Fat City while Charlie Company searched the heavily foliaged area for the enemy.

Charlie's grunts did not find any evidence of the elusive enemy and were picked up by Hueys in the afternoon and flown on eagle flights to cover a larger span of terrain. The 1st Platoon landed on the southern edge of the hill mass where the fighting had occurred. It climbed up and crossed over the crest of the hill, gazing at a large crater apparently created by an earlier air strike. Most of the platoon had crossed the hilltop and were descending on the other side when the rear element, now crossing over, detonated a landmine. The explosion took down four soldiers with a vengeance. The main body avoided being hit because the shrapnel passed over their heads. But some who had cleared the hilltop were wounded as well.

The soldier who detonated the mine lost his foot. Standing next to him was Sergeant Fred Brunson who was carrying a M-60 machinegun slung across his midsection. Brunson was laced with over one hundred slivers of shrapnel to his body which saturated his face, midsection, arms and legs. His condition was serious but one large shard of metal that would have killed him was stopped by the machinegun across his front. The shrapnel hit the gun with such force, it rendered it inoperable.

Brunson sunk to the ground with his stomach, face and arms bleeding heavily. Blood squirted out of his arm like a water fountain, leaping ten feet across the parched earth. He then realized he had sat down on another mine. PFC Steven Allen, the patrols point man climbed back up the hill and went to Brunson's assistance. He dug out the mine from under his wounded comrade and disposed of it.

LTC Passmore landed in his light observation helicopter and quickly took out two of the more seriously wounded on his bird while a dustoff airlifted the remainder. No sign of the quickly evading enemy was found in the area and by late afternoon the rest of Charlie's troops were taken to Fat City, then trucked back to Chu Lai. Delta Company was picked up to return to Chu Lai for a scheduled standdown.

The following day intelligence was received from the Vietnamese in Ly Tin indicating a battalion-size force of Vietcong were moving east in small groups from the Dragon Valley area to destroy three bridges. It was highly unlikely such a force could be assembled or get to the vicinity of Highway One without detection, even if moving in small groups. Nevertheless Charlie Company was placed on notice to be ready to react within thirty minutes of an attack.

But a different enemy situation was presented at the Ky Tra Outpost. A Vietcong from the V-14 Local Force Company surrendered to RF militia, bringing with him two AK-47 rifles. He wanted to give up because of the pressure from the battalion's patrols, rapid artillery fire, continuous air surveillance and the increased effectiveness of South Vietnamese RF and PF militia. He claimed his company was located near Thon Hoi (2) and was down in strength to thirty soldiers with Ak-47's and one 60mm mortar.

On February 8 Charlie Company, with sniper team "Travis" were lifted out from Fat City and air assaulted back out to the Ky Thanh region. Charlie's headquarters element and its 81mm mortars landed astride Provincial Road 532 one mile west of Trung Tin. The 1st Platoon landed just south of Trung Tin on Route 532. The 2nd Platoon was inserted one mile north of the headquarters element in the dense ridgelines near Hill 203. The 3rd Platoon set in one-half mile north of Trung Tin while the sniper team was inserted in the Phuoc Khach area to look for enemy movement.

At 7:45PM RF Company 132, while in a night ambush site spotted approximately forty-five insurgents near Thanh Hoa (4) north of Ky Tra. Both elements spotted each other at the same time but the enemy was entrenched and in a better position to fight it out. The RF's were hit with small arms, RPG and mortar fire. Artillery fire from the Ky Tra Outpost quickly answered the enemy's firepower after which the lightly-armed PF's swept the area and found six Vietcong bodies with weapons.

During the day another insurgent became a Chieu Hoi, surrendering to PF Company's 104 and 500 operating near Thanh Hoa (1). The insurgent led the RF's to a cache of fifty 60mm mortar rounds, one carbine, an AK-47, one can of anti-personnel mine fuses and a can of explosives.

The following morning RF Company 132 was hit again by enemy fire. This time it was pinned down in a rice paddy with the enemy hitting it from both the north and south of its position. Artillery fire from Ky Tra again supported the RF's and helicopter gunships nearby promptly came on station to rocket the enemy. The RF's swept the area and found three Vietcong killed at a cost of four RF's wounded.

After a long rest and refitting and receiving replacements from its losses on Hill 76, the battalion's recon platoon was sent to work off the Ky Tra Outpost on reconnaissance missions in the area. The battalion's widely-scattered patrols, some of which were squad-size which worked off of platoon patrol bases, continued to find evidence of an enemy on the run with occasional small-arms or sniper fire. Bravo's 1st Platoon operating near Dong Dang (7) found two hooch's with underground bunkers, cooking utensils and an elderly woman with medical supplies.

Later in the afternoon, Charlie's 2nd Platoon received ten rounds of small arms fire near Thon Hoi (2), wounding two soldiers, one in the leg and the other in the hip. The grunts returned fire while calling for artillery support. This response was becoming the standard mode of operation; try to fix the enemy in place with grunt firepower while calling for heavier fire support before sweeping the area. It was the same mode of operation the Vietnamese forces were getting accustomed to although their fire support would be greatly reduced once American forces departed their country. Four artillery white phosphorous rounds and eighty high explosive rounds pounded suspected enemy positions.

As the battalion operated in the field, artillery support was readily available and eager for fire missions. There were fewer contacts being made with a diminished enemy. The battalion's soldiers continued their work, searching and clearing areas of enemy movement, but charging headlong into enemy positions at this juncture of the war was out of the question. The soldiers knew their war was gradually standing down as the Vietnamese military was standing up.

In the afternoon of February 9, Alpha Company air assaulted to the rolling hills west of Fire Support Base Fat City. From there they walked east, clearing the terrain to Fat City and then were trucked to Chu Lai for a standdown. Delta left Chu Lai to air assault deep into the mountains between the lower reaches of Dragon Valley and then moved east to Hill 270. The area had not been searched on the ground for weeks and the Commander of the 198th Brigade still hoped to locate a sizable enemy force.

February 12 saw Charlie Company beating the bushes again, finding evidence of an evading enemy that was small in numbers but fleet of foot. It found abandoned hooch's, small cultivated potato fields and occasional sniper fire. Charlie's 1st Platoon on patrol was hit by three Chicom grenades thrown at close range and fifteen rounds of Ak-47 fire. One soldier was wounded in the foot with shrapnel. The grunts responded with small arms fire until 105mm Howitzer fire pounded the area. They swept the terrain and found several more cultivated fields and an enemy animal trap with a dead rat inside.

The next day the platoon found a warhead shot from a gunship's rocket pod that had not detonated, near Thon Hoi (1). It was booby-trapped inside a knee-high hedgerow and was blown in place. Bunkers and trenches were found nearby.

Later the platoon spotted two Vietcong several hundred yards away. Again artillery fire was summoned but the first marking round landed too close to the grunts and wounded one soldier with shrapnel to the head. Once the platoon reached the enemy site, they found two tunnels with fresh sandal tracks leading away. As they followed the tracks they spotted another insurgent who responded with small arms fire and a Chicom grenade. One soldier suffered gunshot wounds to his right wrist and arm pit. The insurgent vanished.

The end of the day saw Alpha continuing its standdown in Chu Lai. Bravo was extracted from the field for a rest in Chu Lai as well. Charlie, Delta and the Echo Recon Platoon continued operations in the field.

The next day, Charlie's 2nd Platoon on patrol heard voices from a small group of insurgents approximately one hundred and twenty yards away through a dense bamboo thicket. The platoon called for 81mm mortar and artillery fire to be placed beyond the voices to cover their retreat as they advanced through the heavy bamboo. After moving one hundred yards they heard more voices and directed artillery to that location as well while slowly thrashing their way through the bamboo. But again, the wily enemy disappeared.

If enemy booby-traps and mines were not enough of a hazard, Charlie's 1st Platoon was tasked late on February 14 to be air-lifted to the Phouc Khach area to search for dud five hundred-pound bombs from an air strike made earlier that day. The strike resulted in an unusually high number of dud rounds. An explosive ordnance demotion (EOD) team was also sent in.

The next morning Charlie's 2nd and 3rd Platoons were also sent in to help secure the dud bombs before the enemy could find them and carry them away. The soldiers found eight unexploded bombs in total, all burrowed into the ground. They were destroyed in place. It was all in a days work. Charlie's 1st Platoon Leader, Andy Ladek, placed his soldiers in a wood line while a light observation helicopter assisted in spotting the dud rounds. The pilot asked to confirm Ladek's position and promptly landed his bird in front of the grunts to seek protection, climbed out the bird to urinate, then climbed back in and flew on. By days end Charlie was lifted back to Chu Lai for a standdown.

When Charlie arrived in Chu Lai, Alpha moved out, landing in the Thuan An Tay hamlets south of Dragon Valley which had not been searched in several months. At 3:05PM, Alpha's 3rd Platoon heard movement twenty-five yards to its front and set up a hasty ambush. Three insurgents walked towards them but just before walking into the kill zone, they stopped, sensing something was wrong. The grunts opened fire killing one and wounding another who sprinted away with the third insurgent. The dead insurgent's AK-47 was retrieved. The grunts followed the blood trail but with no success.

Alpha's 2nd Platoon received small arms fire from six to seven insurgents while landing at its LZ. The gunships escorting the Hueys, pouring rocket fire into the dense foliage as the platoon moved out to search the area.

Delta Company continued its operations in the mountainous terrain both north and south of the lower reaches of the Quan River and Provincial Route 532 which ran from Hill 76 west into Dragon Valley and north to Ky Tra. Delta's 3rd Platoon found a small, recently abandoned camp one-half mile south of Tu Chanh. Four hooch's with pots and pans and piles of firewood were found in what appeared to be a resting station for the NVA and VC. Everything was destroyed.

Ever since Hill 76 was attacked by sappers on February 1, which caused the deaths of five recon soldiers, Americal Division LRRP teams hid in the ridges south of the hill to monitor enemy activity. It appeared that the populated hamlets in the expanse of open fields which stretched one mile between the hill and the ridges, was a rest stop for small groups of insurgents who could count on some families in the hamlets to shelter them as they moved through.

On February 16, LRRP team "Ohio" spotted three insurgents carrying a 60mm mortar base plate and two cylinder tubes resembling 122mm rockets across its front. The insurgents walked into a wood line and two elderly men exited empty handed. The LRRP's detained them while searching the area and found two rocket launch sites while catching some sniper fire. The third insurgent with the base plate melted away.

Both detainees were lifted out by Huey and sent to Chu Lai for questioning. Both claimed they were brutally beaten by the LRRP's but the interrogators found no marks or bruises. A young boy approached the LRRP's selling Cokes and trinkets, and undoubtedly trying to gather information about its strength, equipment and search techniques. The LRRP's told him to leave and the boy started yelling about brutality. It appeared he was coached well, seeking to gain some leverage because of the intense media scrutiny of the Calley My Lai trial.

The following day PF Platoon 202 joined the LRRP team in its search of the area. At 7:25PM, as the PF's moved to a night ambush position they came under small arms fire. The LRRP's nearby were also fired upon. Bravo Company was placed on alert. A light observation helicopter flew to the area and came under RPG fire but was not hit. At 8:30PM, the LRRP's requested a resupply of ammo. The insurgents who attacked them were estimated to be no more than five or six in number but had a machinegun which made them a considerable threat for the small recon team. Artillery was fired on the enemy position despite the presence of several hamlets located in the area. The arty fire caused the enemy to break contact and evade.

Delta continued its search and clear operation in dense and mountainous terrain. At 10:30AM on February 18, Delta's 3rd Platoon heard one of its mechanical ambushes detonate one mile south of Tu Chanh. Operations in this remote terrain did not require MA's be dismantled each morning, as no populated hamlets were in the area. A search of the ambush site revealed two dead Vietcong in black pajamas, one carrying an AK-47 and the other an AK-50.

On the same day, a Popular Force patrol found the graves of seven insurgents southeast of Fat City within a small complex of bunkers containing mines and booby-traps. Villagers nearby indicated the bodies were brought there for burial after the night attack on Hill 76 on February 1.

Bravo Company was trucked from Chu Lai to Tam Ky, then south on Provincial Route 531 where they off-loaded near the Ba Ky River. The mission was to search and clear an area four miles north of the Ky Tra Outpost, moving east for four miles in dense terrain, then south and west, to the Thanh Hoa hamlet area.

The morning of February 20 saw Charlie Company end its standdown and air assault deep into the Annamite Mountains two miles southwest of the lower reaches of Dragon Valley, a full seventeen miles due west from LZ Bayonet. Intelligence reports indicated a base camp was in the area and Charlie was sent in by itself to search for it. After the Hueys completed their lifts, they picked up Delta Company on its return flights to Chu Lai for a scheduled standdown.

By early afternoon, Charlie's 3rd Platoon found two ten foot by twelve foot military structures with bunkers, ten pigs, ten chickens and over three hundred pounds of rice along with bloodied clothing. Close by two other larger structures were found.

The next morning just before first light, Charlie's 1st Platoon, operating one mile south of the 3rd Platoon, had a trip flare go off beyond its night defensive position and blew the two claymores facing the flare. A patrol found two fifty-pound bags of rice dropped by the enemy when the claymores were detonated. Blood trails led away into the bush. Nearby the grunts discovered an abandoned "Field Expedient Hospital", more like an aid station. The area was littered with bags of rice, six pounds of tobacco, mess kits, bags of seeds and assorted medical supplies. Forty-five documents were also found.

On February 22, part of Bravos 2nd Platoon operated in the area south of Thanh Hoa (1) and spotted four Vietcong in black pajamas moving in its direction, five hundred yards away. But the VC suddenly halted, apparently to eat. The grunts spotted more enemy wearing green uniforms that linked up with the first group, for a total of fifteen insurgents. Bravo's grunts decided to let the enemy eat their meal and then continue to walk in their direction. But the VC split up, leaving the original four to eat while the others moved in different directions.

One group headed northwest where Bravo's 4th Squad of the 2nd Platoon was positioned. The two groups clashed with small arms fire and the enemy evaded from sight. The squad found a blood trail and requested a tracker dog to help search in the dense terrain. But, deciding not to wait, they took up the search and found an abandoned hooch which contained five rifle-propelled grenades, two carbines and a Browning Automatic Rifle (BAR). The soldiers continued the search with some aerial surveillance help from a light observation helicopter that came on station.

Later in the afternoon, Bravo's 3rd Platoon on patrol in isolated terrain one-mile farther south heard someone coming down a trail. They opened fire on a middle-aged male and killed him. He had no identification or a weapon. About the same time Bravo's 2nd Platoon heard one of its MA's detonating, wounding a Vietcong in a green uniform. He was found with one leg blown off. He had two papers in his shirt. The grunts bandaged him up as best as possible and dusted off for medical treatment and interrogation.

Charlie Company, deep in the mountains south of Dragon Valley continued to find evidence of an enemy presence. While on patrol, the 3rd Platoon discovered a dam which blocked the flow of a small river moving south off a steep set of ridges. The concrete dam measured seven feet high and ten feet wide. They attempted to destroy the dam with Light Anti-Tank Weapons (LAWS) which had no effect. They placed nine pounds of C-4 explosive on a crude door at the side of the dam. The explosion also had little effect.

Later in the evening while at a night ambush site, Charlie's 2nd Platoon spotted a lantern moving through the terrain. The 81mm mortars at the small company command post fired four white phosphorus and two high explosive rounds which quickly extinguished the light.

The next morning Alpha's 2nd Platoon near Dong Dang (2) spotted an NVA in uniform sixty yards away and opened fire, wounding him before he was able to evade into the bushes. The soldiers followed his blood trail to a clearing. Half of the patrol followed the small smudges of blood which led off into the foliage. The blood undoubtedly marked the final hours of a dying man they would not find. The other half searched the clearing and found a Vietcong insurgent sleeping. He awoke to see the grunts approaching and tried to flee but was cut down.

Both Alpha and Bravo continued to find evidence of small enemy camps throughout the day. At 8:40PM, Bravo's 3rd Platoon north of Hill 203 spotted a campfire about five hundred yards to their southeast. Knowing the insurgents would flee if they approached the position, they called for five rounds of 81mm mortar fire to extinguish the flames and cause casualties. The grunts heard a secondary explosion, indicating a cache of ammunition had been hit but a sweep of the area the next morning found no bodies.

On February 25, Charlie Company continued to find bunkers and small hooch's in the mountains southwest of Dragon Valley. One of the hooch's contained one hundred and fifty pounds of rock salt, pots and pans, a rice dipper and two flashlights.

The following day Alpha was extracted from the field for a standdown while Delta Company combat air assaulted deep into the mountains three miles west of Dragon Valley by the Bong Mieu River south of Hill 306. In recent days, elements of the 2nd/1st Infantry Battalion (196th Light Infantry Brigade) operating west and north of Hill 306, had reported considerable movement of NVA regulars moving from the north toward the area around the hill.

February 27 saw Bravo extracted from its area of operation in the Trung Tin terrain and moved farther east into the hilly terrain west of Hill 270 in response to intelligence reports of an enemy buildup, possibly to attack the hilltop position. On February 28, its 2nd Platoon, while patrolling one and one-quarter mile north of Hill 270 found a dead Vietcong, apparently killed by artillery fire. The corpse was approximately two weeks old. Bravo was also assigned the mission to plant additional motion sensors in the hilly terrain which could be monitored by radar sets on Hill 270 for more advance warning of any impending attacks.

Charlie Company continued to find hooch's and rice storage facilities deep in the mountains with signs of recent use. It found some storage bins which were built on stone stilts one foot above the ground, containing bags of rice with cooking utensils. These types of search operations would continue for two more months as rumors increased that the battalion's days in Vietnam were numbered. Increasingly the soldier's focus was to stay alive and retain all their body parts in the final weeks the battalion remained. But war is war and some more of the battalion's soldiers were destined to make the ultimate sacrifice.

18 – FINAL SACRIFICES

KILL OR BE KILLED

The 5th/46th Infantry Battalion continued its combat mission in its final weeks to sweep and clear the enemy in its large area of tactical responsibility. On March 1, 1971, Delta's 1st Platoon found a bunker with two sets of sandal tracks one mile south of Hill 306. Nearby they searched the site where their mechanical ambush had been detonated the night before but found nothing. Delta's 2nd Platoon also found fish traps and recent campfires one and one-half miles northwest of Hill 306.

The battalion's recon platoon continued its screening operations northwest of the Ky Tra Outpost in conjunction with some Provisional Reconnaissance Unit (PRU) Vietnamese Soldiers. Recon's Sp/4 John Hastings didn't like the PRU from the moment he saw them, thinking they had the "death squads" look written all over them.

The terrain where they operated was very dry but on March 1 the recon grunts found a trickle of water flowing down a ridge and surmised, where there's water there may be some enemy. There were rumors of an enemy base camp in the area and the PRU thought it was nearby. They pushed up the ridge through dense brush and suddenly walked into a small enemy base camp with bunkers. There were six VC/NVA soldiers in the camp who were as surprised at seeing the recon platoon as the recon was surprised at the sudden encounter with them. The enemy attempted to flee. The combatants briefly slugged it out with small arms fire at close range and the recon's new platoon leader, Lieutenant Kotes, was wounded in the shoulder. One young Vietcong female was wounded in the left arm as the rest of her comrades escaped.

After Kotes was stabilized the medic went to work on the teenage female insurgent, but internal bleeding from her wounds caused her to go into shock and there was nothing much he could do. She died before a dustoff could pick her up. Hastings pondered as he looked at the young female, "So this is what it has come down to, fighting teenagers". The enemy was conscripting younger males and females into its ranks. There was simply no one else to continue the insurgency.

One PRU started to remove the dead girl's pants and the recon grunts made him stop. Because of that that action, and the death squad attitude toward the PRU's, the recon soldiers would have had no problem at that moment with shooting their own "allies". The PRU men actually found their actions humorous.

The recon platoon found six military structures with assorted letters, clothing and medical supplies along with three blood trails leaving the site. The documents and medical supplies were evacuated by Huey. Sixteen rounds of artillery fire blanketed the enemy's escape route.

When the 5th/46th departed Vietnam, SP/4 Hastings served in the Division LRRP's until his Vietnam tour ended. One of the LRRP missions was to capture POW's for questioning. But his LRRP team's knowledge of ARVN questioning techniques, particularly of females, kept the team from ever sending prisoners to the ARVN.

On March 2, Bravo was extracted from its mission and moved to Chu Lai for a standdown. Alpha Company replaced Bravo on the west and northwest portions of Hill 270 to screen for any enemy that might threaten the hilltop position or try to push farther east in small groups to attack the Fat City or Ly Tin areas.

Out in the mountains Delta continued to find evidence of enemy movement, finding newly built hooch's, fresh tracks, and a concealed trail carved out in dense terrain that was wide-enough to support vehicles. Back at the battalion's headquarters at LZ Beach in Chu Lai, a fragging incident (exploding grenade) occurred on March 2 at 11:50PM in the headquarters mail room, but no one was injured.

The next day on March 3, Delta's 2nd Platoon found a bunker reinforced with steel and heavy logs located north of the Bong Mieu River one and one-half mile northwest of Hill 306. Delta's 3rd Platoon patrolled the dense mountains one and one-half miles farther east and discovered rest stations with fighting positions made of stone. Everything was destroyed. Delta's 2nd Squad of its 2nd Platoon found five bunkers with clothes, rice and cooking utensils. A search of the complex revealed enemy documents which were evacuated.

Later in the day the 2nd Platoon discovered twelve tunnels along a trail, honeycombed into a hillside. The entrances measured three feet in width and four feet in height which, once entered, dropped down fifteen feet into the tunnel system itself. The grunts also found burlap bags and warm campfires. Some tunnels were shored up with wood beams while others used steel rods. Nearby were fresh tracks.

For an infantry platoon to be patrolling in such dense terrain by itself, with such clear signs of an enemy presence, would have been unthinkable in 1968 or 1969. But this was 1971 and the enemy's strength had been greatly diminished. Combat fire support allowed platoon-size and squad-size patrols to be the normal mode of operation.

Pressure on the enemy continued. One and one-half miles north of the Ky Tra Outpost enemy activity was detected on a dense hill mass. An air-strike of thirty-two five hundred-pound bombs was dropped in the early afternoon.

On the afternoon of March 4, Charlie's 1st Platoon found an old military camp two miles from the platoon's original LZ as it continued to patrol the heavily forested and mountainous terrain by itself. The site was seventeen miles due west of the former LZ Gator. Empty 20mm cartridges, rusting rice knives and a small stove were all that remained of a once flourishing base camp. A two-page document dated in the fall of 1970 was found, perhaps the last time the camp was occupied.

By days end the 4th Squad of Charlie's 1st Platoon patrolled an area close to their designated pick-up zone (PZ) and was hit by enemy small arms fire. The two solders in the point element were crossing an open area when concealed enemy soldiers opened fire with AK-47's, wounding both. The squad immediately returned fire, shedding their heavy rucksacks at the same time to be able to maneuver as their machine gunner opened up a base of fire.

PFC Michael Brooks, the platoon's medic, was pumped with adrenaline and made a one hundred and fifty yard dash from his position to the two wounded men who were pinned down by the fire. He dragged them to a more concealed position. The platoon leader, Lt. John J. Robinson marveled at Brooks speed, "I've never seen someone run that fast, especially with a full pack on." Brooks looked at his jaunt under enemy fire as "just doing my job."

Charlie's 81mm mortars were brought to bear on the enemy and the soldiers searched the area but with no results. The two wounded soldiers were dusted off. Three days later Brooks had something else to think about, he was notified that he had just become the father of a baby girl.

While the battalion continued its search and sweep missions, the American withdrawal from Vietnam continued as well. On March 5, the 1st and 3rd Squadrons of the 11th Armored Cavalry Regiment departed from Vietnam. Throughout March and April the 5th Marine Regiment of the 1st Marine Division would also depart.

On March 5, Delta's 1st Platoon found another small camp with three structures and a small hospital complex, estimated to have been abandoned for many months. While on patrol the 4th Squad of the 3rd Platoon took sniper fire from two locations, a reminder some enemy remained in the area and could claim soldier's lives. Mortar and artillery fire was called on the sniper positions. Another Delta patrol found a hooch with three small tunnels alongside a well-cultivated field. The site had been recently used and everything was destroyed.

The next day it was more of the same. Delta's 3rd Squad of its 3rd Platoon, while linking up at the platoon patrol base received more sniper fire which was answered by 81mm mortar and artillery fire. Four hours later, at 4:40PM, a 3rd Platoon patrol approached a hidden hooch. Their Kit Carson Scout detonated a booby-trap. The Scout received lacerations to both legs from the shrapnel and another grunt received minor wounds. Both were dusted off.

Throughout the mountain searches being made by Charlie and Delta Companies, aerial reconnaissance flights scouted other areas for signs of enemy movement. Sightings that were close to one of the battalion's patrols were relayed to the grunts to check out. Other sites were destroyed by air strikes if aircraft were available.

The rugged mountains were laced with trails often carved out of dense foliage but no sign of a large enemy presence was found. The enemy in the mountains, as they did in Dragon Valley and the Piedmont area around Hill 270, operated in groups of two to ten soldiers, constantly on the move and constantly evading. With the American withdrawal from Vietnam now on full throttle, the enemy was willing to be patient. But it continued to provide mines and booby-traps to counter the aggressive patrolling of the battalion's soldiers.

PFC Thomas Smith with Charlie Company checked out a suspected enemy position when he stepped on a small mine, a "Toe Popper". The ensuing blast knocked him down but failed to put a dent in his steel-plated boot. Smith recalled, "At first I didn't know what happened, I was on my back before I could do anything." The Toe Popper consisted of an AK-47 rifle round which had been placed in a plastic container with a nail in the bottom of it. When a foot steps down on it, the nail strikes a primer, thus creating a rifle-shot effect from point blank range. Smith's platoon sergeant heard the round go off and looked at his foot with the boot off. There was no wound. He laughingly told Smith "Ah you're faking it. When you are ready you can go back to work!" Smith replied, "Those were the best words I'd ever heard in my life."

On another occasion, a Charlie pointman spotted a tripwire across a trail leading to a Russian made hand grenade. The soldiers set up a mechanical ambush of daisy-chained claymore mines, then tripped the enemy booby-trap, thinking the insurgents may come back to view their handiwork. The soldiers then moved away from the area. One half hour later they heard an explosion and returned to find they had nailed three enemy soldiers. The lower-half of their bodies were gone from the claymore's blast. For some unknown reason Charlie's Kit Carson Scout shouted at the enemy dead and placed tooth brushes in their mouths. It was "kill or be killed" and now there were three fewer enemy soldiers to contend with.

On March 6, a light observation helicopter (LOH) spotted five submerged sampans near Ngoc Nha (4), three miles northwest of the Ky Tra Outpost. The sampans had not been spotted there five days prior. Nearby the LOH pilot spotted a series of small cultivated fields. Delta's 3rd Platoon was tasked to move north and conduct a recon in the area.

On the afternoon of March 7, Bravo Company finished its standdown in Chu Lai and combat air assaulted into the area around Thanh Hoa (1) and (2) with a mission to push east into dense and hilly terrain to search for enemy movement. Shortly after Bravo landed on its LZ, a NVA Chieu Hoi appeared out of the bush and took Bravo's 2nd Platoon to a small camp just north of Thanh Hoa (1) which contained a campfire and baskets of potatoes and fish. The camp's occupants had just evaded to the east.

Charlie Company, after trudging through its assigned mountainous terrain finding abandoned camps but few enemy, was picked up for a scheduled standdown in Chu Lai.

Later that same day at 6:30PM Bravo's 2nd Platoon found five new hooch's, all with bunkers, one quarter mile south of Thanh Hoa (1) on ridges that had been heavily swept in the recent past. The camp now contained twelve chickens and signs of a quickly departed enemy.

Since the sapper attack on Hill 76 on February 1, hilltop outposts such as Hill 270 and Ky Tra were placed on extra alert with additional motion sensors planted around them. This was especially crucial at Ky Tra because many of the PF's assigned to the outpost were in the field on patrol and the perimeter defense was not at full strength. Perimeter sensors were activated several times at Ky Tra on the evening of March 7 and mortar fire was fired on defensive targets.

Alpha Company continued its operations in the heavy terrain west and north of Hill 270 since landing there on March 2. The Hill 270 position was the "Gateway" to Chu Lai and the Ly Tin District and it was crucial to prevent any major attack while the battalion finished its combat mission in Vietnam. On the evening of March 8, one of Alpha's MA's detonated and the following morning a patrol found empty sandals riddled by the blast with a large pool of blood next to them. A letter was found but no body.

Worrisome reports continued to surface over a period of several weeks about the growing threat of a major rocket attack on the Chu Lai base. Occasional sightings by division LRRP teams confirmed small groups of two to three insurgents carrying rockets through the area.

An intelligence report mentioned that twenty-two Vietcong of the 78th Rocket Battalion were located in the dense mountains six miles southwest of LZ Bayonet. They possessed seven 122mm rockets. Sixty Vietcong of the 402nd Battalion were located six miles farther west and south of Provincial Road 532. These reports had to be evaluated in terms of accuracy and compared to many other reports of enemy movement. The battalion sent its soldiers where it thought it had the best chance of making enemy contact.

While enemy contact was becoming more infrequent the danger from mines and booby-traps was a daily threat. On March 10, as Bravo's 1st Platoon secured an LZ for a resupply Huey, one soldier stepped on a pressure-release device which blew a foot-wide hole when detonated, mutilating his foot. He was quickly dusted off to the 27th Surgical Hospital. Another Bravo patrol found two more booby-traps, one a pressure release mine set between two rocks and the other, a C-ration can filled with explosives under a rock.

More soldiers were arriving at the 5th/46th Battalion from other departing units, which helped bolster the battalion's strength in the field. Between March 9-11 thirty-three new soldiers, all field soldiers from departing units, were placed on the battalion's rolls.

The battalion's sniper teams continued to be placed along routes of known enemy movement to apply additional pressure on the insurgents. Sniper Team "Yankee" worked the Thanh Hoa area near Bravo Company. On March 11 they spotted two Vietcong at a distance of four hundred and fifty yards and engaged them using their sniper scopes. The enemy quickly dashed into a wood line. The snipers called in artillery fire which chased the enemy back out in the open and one was wounded. His comrade tried dragging the body back into the wood line but the slow process allowed the snipers to wound the second insurgent. Artillery was summoned again as half of the sniper team (three soldiers) moved forward to look for bodies. While moving alongside a trail the snipers tripped a booby-trap which wounded one soldier with shrapnel in the lower legs and another in the head. Both were dusted off. The wounded enemy was left to limp away, presumably to die a slow death.

The afternoon of March 11 saw Charlie Company trucked from Chu Lai to Fat City, then air assaulted west into the mountains at three separate LZ's three miles south of LZ Bowman. Delta, which was operating farther south was picked up on the return lifts of Hueys and took its scheduled standdown in Chu Lai.

That evening on Hill 270 an explosion occurred at 10:15PM. Private Gary Cohen was found dead with a severe wound to his upper body. There had been no enemy fire. At first it was thought he had carelessly fired his M-79 grenade launcher but an inspection of his weapon revealed the round was still chambered. An investigation was immediately launched with everyone on the hill questioned. A close inspection of his body and the materials around him led to the conclusion that Cohen "committed suicide by blowing himself in place with C-4" explosive.

Cohen had extended his Vietnam tour to get an early release from active duty but he was still just a private, the rank of a recruit entering basic training. This suggests he had issues with authority and/or drugs and was a discipline problem. Gary Martin Cohen died three days before his twenty-second birthday. He was single from Dartmouth, Massachusetts.

The following day Charlie's 1st Platoon spotted four Vietcong crossing a small stream a half mile to its front. Artillery fire was called on the insurgents.

Bravo's 2nd Platoon, patrolling three-quarters mile southwest of Thanh Hoa (4), found five hooch's each measuring six feet by ten feet with well-constructed bunkers under them which measured three feet by six feet. The hooch's were destroyed. Close by was a new grave that was dug up, revealing a Vietcong in black pajamas. The corpse was believed to be two weeks old and was riddled with shrapnel.

A visual reconnaissance (VR) flight made by a light observation helicopter (LOH) three miles east of the lower reaches of Dragon Valley, spotted six large hooch's in dense terrain. When it swooped low and slow for a closer look, the bird came under small arms fire and took a number of hits. As the small bird pulled pitch to climb away the pilot spotted six Vietcong. The LOH returned to Chu Lai for inspection while helicopter gunships pounded rocket fire into the small camp destroying the hooch's. Artillery from Ky Tra pounded away with twenty-seven 105mm high explosive rounds in the area around the camp.

North of the Ky Tra Outpost Bravo's 4th Squad of its 3rd Platoon was returning from securing water at a small stream. Although they walked twenty feet off the side of the trail to avoid mines, one soldier hit a booby-trapped Chicom grenade that wounded five soldiers with shrapnel.

On another occasion a platoon from Bravo had moved into a night defensive position when Staff Sergeant Michael Gracey, the platoon sergeant, traveled down a trail to look for a pole for a makeshift poncho shelter. He found what he needed and as he tugged on the pole he felt pressure on the other end and let it go. A closer look revealed a wire tied to the end of the pole with the other end connected to a mortar round. The booby-trap was blown in place. But Gracey still need a pole for his improved shelter. Ten feet past the booby-trap he found another perfect pole but checked it first. It too was booby-trapped. The soldiers roped off the area, deciding to destroy it in the morning. When daylight came they found three more booby-traps, all constructed in the same manner.

The battalion's recon platoon patrolled the area west of the Thanh Hoa hamlets in support of Bravo. On March 13, a VR bird spotted three Vietcong in green uniforms carrying rice near Dong Dang (2). The bird received small arms fire and returned fire which scattered the insurgents. The recon platoon was tasked to search the area and found two enemy hooch's with underground bunkers. Inside were pots and pans, hammocks, ponchos and clothing. Nearby was a fighting trench carefully covered with foliage. The platoon's Kit Carson Scout spotted one VC and shot him in the shoulder as he evaded. The camp was destroyed.

That afternoon while moving to a night position, Bravo's grunts spotted two insurgents, wounding one in the arm and shoulder before capturing him. The other was shot in the back but managed to escape. The captive was dusted off for treatment and questioning. Later it learned the two were NVA regulars and the captured prisoner had been returning to his unit after treatment at a small field hospital. Bravo's 3rd Platoon, operating farther west along the Ngoc Nha hamlets spotted another lone VC carrying a pack and weapon three quarters of a mile away, too far for small arms fire. The grunts had no choice but to call artillery.

Some Bravo soldiers returned to a location where their 2nd Platoon had found some hooch's the prior day. Inside one partially destroyed hooch was a fireplace connected to what appeared to be a baking oven. It also appeared that crude Chicom grenades were being assembled there. NVA equipment was found nearby, including a letter introducing the bearer of the letter as a soldier who had been an NVA since 1967.

On March 14, Alpha was extracted from the field for a standdown in Chu Lai and Bravo was lifted out of its area of operations to move farther northwest by the Ba Ky River and LZ Bowman. Bravo's 2nd Platoon was inserted one-quarter mile north of LZ Bowman and came under heavy fire. Artillery support was delayed by the 5th ARVN Regiment Headquarters in Tam Ky due to pacified Vietnamese living in the area. The grunts were finally able to pull away from the hot LZ. Later at 5:50PM, the platoon spotted fifteen enemy soldiers along a trail. The enemy was too far for their small arms fire so they called artillery which again which had to be cleared by the ARVN. Ten minutes later clearance was granted but the enemy had escaped.

This frustration was one of the prices to be paid for increased Vietnamese Army involvement. When the 2nd Platoon operated just north of Bowman, the ARVN were west of the firebase and both elements were in direct line of fire from artillery at Tam Ky, which required additional precautions to avoid friendly fire incidents.

The learning curve for the ARVN to operate efficiently carried a heavy price. In early 1971 ARVN artillery was fired in support of its troops but the guns were poorly registered and the rounds landed on the small hamlet at the base of the hill of the Ky Tra outpost. The battalion's soldiers on Ky Tra heard the guns fired in the distance, then the sound of incoming rounds and the deafening explosion of artillery just outside their perimeter, the shrapnel flying through the air, cutting everything in its path. Fortunately the soldiers had bunkers and overhead cover but the villagers in the hamlet at the base of the hill were completely helpless. Hueys arrived to take out the many casualties from the hamlet while the dead were quickly buried along without any mention of the incident. An official investigation was not launched as it would be too inconvenient and an interruption for the takeover of the war by the ARVN.

On March 14, Delta finished its standdown and it was trucked to Fat City and then walked west to its newly assigned AO. The AO was to extend as far west as the Thanh Hoa hamlets and Trung Tin and run south to the dense terrain west of Hill 270. Delta's grunts were to react to any intelligence reports of enemy movement. By late afternoon, a Delta patrol found a small base camp one mile north of Hill 270 comprised of lean-to shelters. They found sweet chocolate, NVA rucksacks, Khaki uniforms, five Chicom grenades, Ak-47 ammo magazines and NVA propaganda but no enemy.

On the morning of March 15, Bravo's 2nd Platoon encountered nine Vietcong on the southeast side of LZ Bowman. The enemy took refuge between two large boulders which formed a cave. The grunts threw in two fragmentation grenades, both of which failed to detonate. A third grenade was thrown and the soldiers moved in with small arms fire but the dud grenades had provided the necessary time for the enemy to slip away. But one Vietcong was killed and his Ak-47 retrieved. The grunts also found six sandbags used to carry supplies, various documents and twelve rounds for a K-54 pistol, which indicated an NVA officer was one of the escapees.

Bravo Company continued to walk a tight-rope in the LZ Bowman area, spotting insurgents on the one hand but hampered in its effort to obtain immediate fire support because of nearby ARVN. To its west were various 5th ARVN Regiment patrols from Tam Ky and to its east were the RF's from Ky Tra conducting day patrols and night ambushes. North of Bravo between Bowman and Tam Ky were friendly hamlets over which artillery support could not be fired. Too many friendly units on different modes of operation and the presence of a pacified hamlet nearby made it difficult to achieve success in the area.

The next day, on March 16, the pointman for Bravo's 1st Platoon spotted three NVA with Ak-47's approaching him. The point opened up with M-16 fire but, as was often the case, the enemy quickly melted away. That evening, Bravo's 2nd Platoon while in its night ambush site received four rounds of 60mm mortar fire but drew no casualties. One 105mm White Phosphorous round and three high Explosive (HE) rounds were called to counter the mortar fire.

On March 17, Alpha concluded its standdown in Chu Lai and air assaulted out to the LZ Bowman area to take over from Bravo, which was lifted to Chu Lai. Continuous adjustments were made in the operating area for the battalion's soldiers around LZ Bowman, based on the movement of the ARVN and RF's from Tam Ky who were expanding their area of operations. Alpha was shifted farther northeast of Bowman.

Charlie Company, working south of LZ Bowman, spotted several Vietcong working in small garden patches, trying to sustain its small numbers with potatoes. As usual the enemy bolted into the bush before the soldiers could get within small arms range. That evening a platoon ambush spotted a small light moving up a hill towards its location, three miles southeast of Bowman. The grunts moved forward in the dark to intercept the light bearers but the enemy quickly disappeared.

In about the same time frame a Charlie Company platoon moved into a night defensive position. SP/4's George Fuentes and Earl Chaplin were assigned their spot to set up a defensive position on the small perimeter. There were no trees in the area, just a few bushes three to four feet high, so the two soldiers decided to use the branches of the bushes to conceal their position.

Fuentes got out his machete and went to work, finding a branch he liked and taking a good whack at it. The first swipe wasn't powerful enough so he raised his hand to swing at it again. Chaplin spotted a mortar round suspended in the same bush and grabbed Fuentes arm before he could set off the round. Both soldiers realized the first swipe of the machete had come within three inches of striking the mortar round. Chaplin yelled "Booby-trap" and the rest of the platoon cleared the area while the two soldiers set up an explosive charge and destroyed the mortar round.

The next day the 1st Squad of Alpha's 2nd Platoon spotted four Vietcong in green fatigues with backpacks. The grunts followed the enemy hoping to move up on them if they stopped for a rest. But the enemy moved forward into an area of "friendly" hamlets patrolled by the ARVN. The grunts backed off the hunt and relayed the information to the ARVN. Two hours later the patrol was hit with about one hundred rounds of AK-47 fire from a large (ten foot by ten foot) hooch. The soldiers fired and maneuvered against the position and spotted two Vietcong running into the dense brush. The hooch was destroyed. Later the patrol was fired on by snipers as the grunts were talking to villagers in another small hamlet. The fire came from hooch's on the edge of the hamlet which were searched but not destroyed because the hamlet was one the ARVN was trying to pacify.

With the battalion's soldiers moving farther west and north from their normal AO, which had Dragon Valley as its western boundary, the battalion moved it's forward tactical operations center (TOC) on March 18 from the Ky Tra Outpost to three miles farther northwest at LZ Donna (Nui Don Da). Donna was named after the battalion commander's wife (LTC James R. Henry's) before he was relieved in mid-December 1970.

That night the crew manning the battalion's heavy mortars (4.2-inch) on LZ Donna saw moving lights approaching its hilltop. Five mortar rounds were fired which promptly extinguished the lights. The next day Alpha's 2nd Platoon spotted an insurgent wearing black pajamas emerging from a small hooch just beyond the northeast slope of LZ Bowman. The insurgent attempted to evade but was wounded and captured. He was dusted off for questioning. His hooch contained an NVA mess kit and a poncho.

Alpha continued to have coordination problems with Army Republic of Vietnam (ARVN) soldiers who were increasing their presence in the battalion's area of operations (AO). On the evening of March 19, an Alpha night position was hit by mortar fire. The ARVN on Hill 94 were firing H&I (Harassment and Interdiction) fires, allegedly at targets one and one-quarter miles northeast of Alpha's position but the mortars had not been properly registered and the rounds fell on Alpha's position. With the luck of angels no Alpha grunts were wounded.

The battalions forward TOC at Donna spotted more lights three-quarters mile southwest of its position across the Ba Ky River. Four 81-mm mortar rounds extinguished the enemy lights.

Charlie Company continued its sweep in the area south of LZ Bowman. On March 20 near Ngoc Nha (3), its 1st Platoon found a small hooch with abandoned NVA equipment, Coke cans, pots and pans and chopsticks. One mile farther west the 3rd Platoon found another abandoned hooch and a small tunnel. Both were destroyed.

Nighttime brought more incidents of moving lights in the dark terrain, carried by inexperienced insurgents hoping to avoid mechanical ambushes while trying to hold together some resemblance of a guerilla movement. Alpha's 1st Platoon spotted lights moving in its direction several hundred yards away and extinguished the lights with artillery fire rather than give away its position.

The battalion's Forward TOC on Donna spotted small campfires where no friendly units or hamlets were located and pummeled the area with eleven 4.2-inch mortar rounds.

The following day at 10:30AM, Alpha's 3rd Platoon found more abandoned enemy hooch's in dense terrain three-quarters mile east of LZ Bowman. The dwellings revealed abandoned stocks of fish and rice, cooking utensils and clothes. An hour later two more abandoned hooch's yielded two-hundred pounds of rice, fifteen hundred pounds of potatoes, two notebooks, some khaki shirts, a pistol belt and two hand grenades.

Air assets became tight, except for the birds needed to return the troops to and from the field for standdowns when the distance was simply too far to walk. At times those lifts were delayed as well. For close to two weeks the battalion had planned air assaults for its rifle companies to rapidly shift from one location to another based on reliable intelligence of enemy platoon-size groups. The air assaults were repeatedly cancelled due to the lack of Hueys. Operation Lam Son 719, the ARVN invasion into Lao's had begun on February 8 and the ARVN was locked in heavy combat.

American Army and Marine units were heavily engaged in securing the Khe Sanh area and Route 9, to provide artillery support for the Vietnamese involved in Lam Son 719. Two Americal Division battalions were also brought north to participate in the operation. The priority for helicopters throughout the I Corps of Vietnam went to support the Lam Son operation.

The battalion's soldiers continued their search missions, being careful to avoid mines, booby-traps, and ambushes by small groups of insurgents. The soldiers pushed farther into terrain partially pacified by the ARVN who were trying to gain control of hamlets west and south of

Tam Ky. To do so the soldiers had to walk a tightrope. A "partially pacified" area was not totally free of the enemy, which made the grunts mission tougher than the free reign they had in the rugged terrain overlooking Dragon Valley.

At 3:00PM on March 21, Alpha's 2nd Platoon detected movement in the vicinity of some boulders. They fired and maneuvered their way against the enemy position capturing four males aged twenty to fifty, two women, one fifty and the other nineteen and three children under the age of ten. Two others evaded. The grunts captured one AK-47 and a pistol. While returning with their detainees to a patrol base, they were hit with six Chicom grenades from seven Vietcong forty yards away. The grunts returned the grenade attack with their M-60 machine gun and M-79 grenade launchers, killing five of the enemy. The detainees were evacuated to Hawk Hill north of Chu Lai.

That night at 8:20PM, Alpha's 1st Platoon in a night ambush site, heard some movement one-hundred yards away. It called for artillery illumination and swept the area with small arms fire. The battalion's forward TOC on LZ Donna also spotted lights beyond its small perimeter and responded with mortar fire.

On the morning of March 22, the same routine began again. Alpha's 2nd Platoon, before leaving its ambush position one mile southwest of Bowman, spotted three Vietcong in a field nine hundred yards away. The distance was too far to send out a patrol which would be spotted, so artillery fire was called. Two hours later they spotted two more enemy, both in uniforms with weapons, over one-half mile away. Artillery was called again.

At 2:30PM, the platoon found what its Kit Carson Scout believed to be an enemy pay station, a small hooch that extended out from under a large boulder. They found two paper tablets with ninety-four names and pieces of paper that appeared to be pay vouchers.

Charlie Company continued its sweep south of LZ Bowman. The heat was unrelenting. At 2:45PM, their second platoon called for an urgent dustoff near Phuoc Loi (1) for a soldier with heat stroke and a temperature of 106 degrees. He was dusted off after a wait of thirty minutes but survived.

At 3:30PM, while on patrol three-quarters mile farther north, the 1st Platoon's pointman, SP/4 Tom Ziegler was hit by sniper fire. The enemy bullet smashed into his M-16 then tumbled into to his stomach along with fragments of his weapon. The platoon medic immediately went to work patching his comrade. A resupply bird was diverted to pick up the critically wounded Ziegler but would not land out of fear of enemy fire, citing he was "too loaded down". It was a rare occurrence of cowardice from a Huey pilot.

Another bird was summoned. Ziegler was bleeding profusely despite the bandages and his lungs were filling with blood. But he held on, telling his comrades he was OK and that he would make it. After thirty-five minutes Ziegler was dusted off to the 91st Evacuation Hospital in Chu Lai. Helix, a forward observer aircraft flew in after the sniper attack. While providing cover for the dustoff he spotted two Vietcong and fired two marking rockets on their position and followed up by directing artillery fire.

SP/4 Ziegler's best friend, SP/4 Scott Longhurst took up a collection of C-ration pound cake from the platoon. The pound cake was cherished by Ziegler. He caught a Huey to take it to Ziegler in the hospital. When he arrived he found out his comrade had died. Charlie Company's First Sergeant was with Ziegler in his final moments. The First Sergeant told Longhurst his best friend knew he was dying in the field but didn't want to demoralize his comrades. SP/4 Thomas Lee Ziegler was age twenty and single, from Hamill, South Dakota.

Following Ziegler's death there was a replay of events and decisions among his comrades. It was the soul-searching that occurred hundreds of times in the battalion after a comrade was lost. Each soldier felt that the mortal wound or traumatic amputation of a fellow soldier should have been for them.

That day began like so many others. SP/4's Ziegler, Dennis Stevens, Scott Longhurst and Paul Rupp, all in the same squad got ready to "hook up" for another day of patrolling. Their squad would lead the platoon. The question came up between them whose turn it was to walk point. Stevens was lugging the M-60 machinegun so left it to the others to decide. There was no arguing, just confusion on whose turn it was. Ziegler stood up and in a matter-of-fact manner said he would do it. And so it was. A decision made that his comrades would find hard to live with the rest of their lives.

That evening Alpha's 3rd Platoon, patrolling one mile east of Bowman, heard movement one hundred yards to its east at 9:30PM. They fired M-79 grenades so as to not divulge their exact night position. Fifteen minutes later they heard more movement and mortar fire was ordered. One hour later more movement was heard accompanied by moving flashlights close to their perimeter. The platoon called for one white phosphorous on its DT (Defensive Target) closest to the flashlights. The lights went out. An illumination round was fired but no enemy were spotted.

Early into March 23 at 1:30AM, Chu Lai was hit by a rocket attack. Neither Hill 270 nor Fire Support Base Fat City could spot the launch site. At first light Alpha's 2nd Platoon spotted three enemy soldiers one mile southwest of its position. They could not order artillery fire because the enemy was too close to Charlie's 1st Platoon. The Charlie grunts were alerted and moved out to find the enemy.

North of the 1st Platoon Charlie's 3rd Platoon found NVA equipment stained with blood. Later the platoon's pointman, while taking a break, spotted a Vietcong walking towards him from around a bend. Fifty feet away the pointman opened up with his M-16, saw the insurgent fall and then scamper away, leaving his AK-47 and a notebook. The grunts followed the blood trail and found ten pounds of fish and twenty-five pounds of rice he or his comrades had been carrying. But the enemy disappeared.

Still farther north of that action Charlie's 2nd Platoon spotted another VC one-quarter mile away and called for artillery. Forty-five minutes later the platoon spotted another eleven Vietcong that were too far away for small arms fire. Artillery was again summoned with two white phosphorus rounds to mark the location, then twenty-four rounds of high explosive to blanket the area.

Alpha's 2nd Platoon on the southern edge of LZ Bowman spotted a enemy hooch just as two enemy soldiers, both in green uniform, sprinted out the front door and ran down a well-used trail to evade the approaching grunts. Shortly after, the grunts approached another hooch in the distance and spooked four more enemy who sprinted down a trail. The enemy's familiarity with the trail network made quick escapes relatively easy. Likewise Alpha's 1st Platoon spotted five enemy soldiers one-quarter mile east of Bowman but at a distance of six-hundred yards, out of effective range for small arms. Once again artillery was called.

On March 24, Bravo Company completed its standdown in Chu Lai and air assaulted by Huey to the terrain southwest of LZ Bowman to replace Charlie Company which was backhauled to Fat City, then trucked to Chu Lai for its standdown.

Alpha's 2nd Platoon, still patrolling the southern edge of Bowman spotted two enemy, killing one wearing a green uniform while the other in black pajamas managed to escape. Left behind were six NVA ponchos, a helmet and two hundred pounds of rice. Delta Company continued its mission to screen the hilly terrain west of Hill 270 and look for small groups of insurgents attempting to attack the pacified areas around Ly Tin, Fat City and Chu Lai.

March 25 saw more of the same, as the 5th ARVN Regiment continued its sweep operations southwest of Tam Ky in a heavily populated area four miles west of Bowman and south of LZ Young. The ARVN also covered the western corridor leading to Tam Ky from the mountains near the Pineapple Forest which had been the scene of heavy fighting with the America's 196th Light Infantry Brigade in 1967 and 1968.

Regional Force (RF) Vietnamese militia conducted company-size sweeps with American advisors in the Ky Tra and Duc Phu area (RF Company 131), and the Ba Ky River area north of LZ Bowman (RF Company 196). Popular Force (PF) militia saturated the populated areas in the Ly Tin District by Highway One, moving west into the densely vegetated foothills leading to the mountains. The PRU operated closely with the PF's and in some cases, RF Companies made special raids on hamlets known to hold Vietcong infrastructure.

Alpha continued to patrol the terrain near Bowman and encountered one to two enemy insurgents at a time. The enemy remained fleet of foot and hard to kill. The 1st Squad of Alpha's 2nd Platoon spooked three VC as it approached a small hooch. The insurgents wore grey uniforms. M-16 and M-79 fire chased them away and inside the hooch was a document relating to booby-traps in the area.

That afternoon Bravo's 2nd Platoon tripped a booby-trapped Coke can filled with explosives but suffered no casualties. Alphas 3rd Platoon detained twenty-seven women and children who had no identification. They were turned over to the PF's. Later they spotted seven Vietcong with weapons five hundred yards away. Small arms fire and M-60 machinegun fire was placed on the insurgents to fix them in place or draw some blood. A sweep of the area uncovered nothing.

On March 26, an NVA Chieu Hoi surrendered to RF Company 929 which was operating east of LZ Young. He indicated one hundred NVA were located in the dense terrain three-quarters mile southeast of its location. The 5th/46th Battalion requested and received an extension of its area of operations to go after them. Bravo Company was tasked to search for the enemy unit from March 27-29, then swing east and return to within six miles of the Ky Tra Outpost by March 30.

March 27 saw RF Platoon 19 linking up with Alpha's 3rd Platoon to assist in population control with the many undocumented villagers Alpha's grunts were detaining. A local female led the RF militia Platoon in its link-up with Alpha's patrol base and tripped a booby-trap on the way, which killed her instantly. The RF soldier behind her received multiple fragment wounds.

Charlie Company finished its standdown and was air assaulted to the terrain west of Hill 270 to replace Delta in its screening mission as Delta was scheduled for a standdown. The battalion's Echo Recon Platoon continued to retrain and refit, building its strength and morale after its bloodbath on Hill 76.

The following morning RF Platoon 19, after splitting with Alpha's 3rd Platoon, captured a Vietcong who had been sent to booby-trap a school in a hamlet under pacification. He was sent in for interrogation.

Bravo's 2nd Platoon, patrolling one and one-half miles east of LZ Young, spotted four enemy soldiers one-half mile away. Artillery was called. Bravo's 3rd Platoon searched one mile southeast of the area claimed by its Chieu Hoi prisoner as holding one hundred NVA. At 12:55PM the soldiers spotted two Vietcong three hundred yards to their east and quietly approached the enemy. After advancing one hundred yards they were hit by automatic weapons fire which wounded three soldiers, including one who suffered a gunshot wound in the neck. The soldiers swept through the area and found a military structure with two NVA rucksacks and an acetate-covered terrain map.

Alpha's 3rd Platoon continued its delicate task of apprehending unarmed and undocumented women and children who were supporting the Vietcong. The platoon spotted one male, a female and two children who were under the protection of the Vietcong. Their Kit Carson Scout yelled at them to stop. Ten rounds of AK-47 fire responded from a nearby hedgerow. The villagers were detained while a sweep of the area revealed nothing.

Earlier that day on March 28, the battalion was notified of a massive sapper attack that occurred on Fire Base Mary Ann on March 22 which killed thirty-three soldiers of the American's 1st/46th Infantry Battalion and wounded seventy-six more. Only ten sappers were killed out of an estimated fifty who entered the fire base. Detailed instructions were given to the Ky Tra Outpost, Hill 270 and Fire Support Base Fat City to place listening posts (LP's) beyond the perimeters at night, to reset all claymores and trip flares beyond the perimeters and conduct fifty-percent alerts at night. Aggressive daytime patrols were to be conducted beyond all perimeters.

The company commander responsible for security on LZ Mary Ann, Captain Richard V. Knight, was killed. He was well liked by his men as he was when he first came to Vietnam with the 5th/46th Infantry Battalion. Knight was one of the original platoon leaders who came over with the battalion from Fort Hood. During one incident Knight had walked through a minefield his men were in and personally dug out many mines while his men remained in place. He was seriously wounded from small arms fire early in 1968 and sent back to the states.

The American withdrawal from Vietnam continued. On March 27-28 the 5th/7th Cavalry, 1st/8th Cavalry and 2nd/12th Cavalry Battalions of the 1st Cavalry Division departed Vietnam.

The enemy attempted to try to maintain a viable presence against the dominating forces of the 5th/46th Infantry Battalion, ARVN, PF and RF militias. For a number of weeks, NVA assassination teams had been targeting pacified hamlets in an attempt to coerce villagers to support them with food and shelter when they passed through. They also increased their night attacks and mortar and rocket fire to shake the feeling of security among the pacified populace. Popular Force militia in many ways stymied the effort, especially through night ambushes in the Ly Tin area by Highway One and the terrain west for several miles.

This enemy effort to control the population was witnessed by the battalion's soldiers operating near LZ's Bowman and Young. Their encounters with women and children in remote areas were often met with sniper fire. Villagers seeking to maintain an identity with their ancestral hamlets were, as usual, caught in the middle. If not providing direct support to the insurgents their sympathies were still with the enemy, as a hedge, for the day when the American battalion would no longer be present. Security would then rest on government forces, which were seen with a mixed level of confidence in the mountainous areas. In late March the hamlet chief of Thanh My Trung (2) near Hill 76 was assassinated and nine children were taken into the mountains to work for the NVA.

In the early morning hours of March 29, a number of battalion night ambush sites saw moving lights beyond their perimeters. The enemy on the move at night still carried a healthy respect for the battalion's mechanical ambushes.

At 1:15AM, Bravo's 3rd Platoon heard movement beyond its perimeter and observed moving lights. Not wishing to divulge its exact location, artillery was called.

At 2:35AM, a listening post (LP) beyond Hill 270 observed four VC moving quickly across their front, heading in the direction of a Charlie Company patrol. Charlie's grunts were alerted. Once the insurgents cleared the LP, Hill 270 tried to call for artillery fire which was denied. Chu Lai had come under a rocket attack and artillery was being adjusted for counter-battery fire against the launch sites. One soldier from Echo Company in the battalion's rear was wounded by a rocket which exploded close to the battalion headquarters in Chu Lai. Hill 270 spotted rocket flashes coming from an area one-quarter mile southeast of its position.

At 3:00AM, LZ Donna also spotted moving lights beyond its perimeter. Snipers manning one of Donna's LP's heard enemy probes looking for the defenders' trip flares. The LP detonated their claymore mines and returned to the perimeter. From that point the LZ went to one hundred percent alert.

The day was marked with more enemy sightings, usually two-three insurgents at a time passing through and quickly evading when sensing Americans were close by. Charlie Company called for an urgent dustoff for a soldier with heat stroke, whose temperature had spiked to 108 degrees.

At 11:25AM, Bravo's 2nd Platoon, patrolling one and one-half mile from LZ Young to their west and Bowman to its east, engaged three Vietcong with small arms fire. The enemy quickly evaded into the bushes. The platoon swept the area and discovered some stone bunkers with people inside. After thirty minutes of coaxing, six females and four children emerged from one bunker which had partially collapsed, killing one female. One child was injured and dusted off. The dustoff received AK-47 fire from a distance of four hundred yards. More bunkers and hooch's were found in the area, which were located far from any established hamlet.

Later in the day both Hill 270 and some of Charlie Company's patrols reported what they believed were rocket launch sites. Charlie's 2nd Platoon patrolled south by Provincial Road 532 where the rockets were fired the previous night. The platoon's pointman heard voices in the brush and opened fire, wounding a Vietcong male and capturing a female and child, most likely the man's family. The couple was dressed with US soldier uniforms and equipment. A dustoff was called to take them in to Chu Lai for treatment and questioning.

Bravo's 1st Platoon settled into a night ambush site when at 7:30PM two enemy soldiers approached its position. Claymores were detonated and the grunts saw in the faint light one insurgent fall while the other dashed away. Darkness precluded a search of the area and the grunts decided a wounded insurgent was as good as a dead one.

The night brought more sightings of moving lights beyond a number of the battalions LZ's and ambush sites. Fire Support Base (FSB) Fat City reported several movements outside its perimeter wire. Small arms fire poured out to discourage any sapper attack and helicopter gunships were summoned to pour rocket fire in the area aided by night illumination. The Americal Division was determined to suffer no more Fire Support Base Mary Ann disasters.

During the day on March 30, Delta Company completed its standdown and was airlifted far west to LZ Pleasantville, twelve and one-half miles west of LZ Bowman, to secure the LZ in support of an operation by the 196th Light Infantry Brigade. The 5th/46th had not been on LZ Pleasantville since August 1968, when it was established as a battalion forward TOC during operations under Task Force Cooksey.

Bravo Company engaged the enemy in more shoot and run activity in the hills between LZ's Bowman and Young. The battalion's recon platoon, operating near Duc Phu (3) saw four Vietnamese talking to an old man. As they approached the group the Vietnamese fled. The elderly man identified them as Vietcong with weapons who told him they would return that night. At 7:00PM, division LRRP team "Oregon" made contact with the enemy on Hill 180 one mile southwest of Hill 270. The LRRP's were hit with small arms fire and Chicom grenades. After breaking contact they moved one hundred yards and were hit again. With the help of gunships the LRRP's were extracted. Charlie's headquarters element was in the area, heard enemy movement, and responded with 81mm mortar fire.

March 31 saw much of the same shoot and run encounters throughout the battalion. Bravo's 4th Platoon spotted insurgents in the distance while pulling security duty on LZ Donna. Again, artillery fire was the most effective way to deal with the rapidly evading enemy. In the last minutes of daylight a Huey flying visual reconnaissance spotted ten to fifteen enemy soldiers sitting around a campfire in a remote location one-quarter mile northwest of Thanh Hoa (2). The bird engaged the enemy with its two M-60 door gunners pouring out fire, killing two before the remainder took refuge. Artillery was then summoned.

Still later that evening Alpha's 2nd Platoon north of LZ Bowman heard one of their mechanical ambushes detonate approximately two hundred yards away. M-79 fire was placed on the site and plans were made to sweep it at first light.

At 2:10AM the morning of April 1, 1971, radar on LZ Donna detected a platoon-sized element one mile south moving towards the LZ. Sensing another FSB Mary Ann-type attack was underway, sixty rounds of 105mm high explosive artillery and twenty-one rounds of 4.2-inch mortar fire were placed on the area. Two secondary explosions were detected. Ky Tra Village at the base of the Ky Tra Outpost was also hit with enemy mortars wounding a women and her child. Ky Tra responded with 105mm Howitzer and 4.2-inch mortar fire on the suspected mortar position.

Charlie Company continued its patrols around the Hill 270 area. On some hilltops the rolling terrain offered spectacular views of the mountains to the west and the lowlands to the east, which flowed past the Chu Lai base to the South China Sea. Well-worn paths blanketed the area, leading down from the hills to dirt roads that crisscrossed the landscape in all directions, to Fat City, Hill 69, Hill 76, Ly Tin and Chu Lai.

The walk on footpaths from hamlets in the lowlands to the hilly terrain patrolled by the battalion's soldiers near Hill 270 could be as much as three to four miles distance. But it did not stop Vietnamese "soda girls" from bringing their wares to sell to the grunts when they were in static daytime positions. As SP/4 Dave Hammond recalled, "They were young, bright and pretty and could provide almost anything you might want for a price. "Holly", "Ann" and "Linda" were only a few of the American names they used. Their dark, sun-baked skin, black silky hair and friendly, but aggressive personalities made them welcome guests to take our minds off the war." The grunts never saw "soda boys", guessing the younger boys tended to the family water buffalo while the older boys were local militia, Vietcong or both.

Most hilltop locations in the Hill 270 area gave the grunts 360-degree observation with little chance for snipers or a surprise attack during the day. Mortar fire was never received when soda girls were present, supporting the belief that most girls were probably VC sympathizers or family members and the VC did not want to chance hurting one of their own. Also the sales to grunts were good for the local economy and whoever controlled it.

The soda girls, usually age ten to fifteen, brought flags, watches, hats, dope, cigarettes, dirty pictures, Coke and beer. A can of Coke or beer cost one dollar in Military Pay Certificates (MPC's) which was a large price to pay, except it was a "sellers market" when stranded on a barren hilltop in a war zone. A cool drink was a reminder of home. More often than not the girls brought a small block of ice for customers to roll their aluminum cans against, to chill their beverage.

A visit by soda girls usually included a "Boom-Boom Girl", slightly older, about eighteen, who carried an Army-issued poncho and a bucket of water for hygiene after each customer. There were plenty of bushes alongside any hilltop to offer privacy when conducting business.

If soda girls did not have the merchandise the soldiers wanted (Hammond wanted a hammock on one occasion) they would come back the next day with it. If the unit moved out of the immediate area the girls patiently waited until they returned days or weeks later. When the afternoon grew late, the soda girls packed their wares to return to their hamlets before night activities began for both the enemy and the battalion.

At 2:20PM on April 1, Charlie's 1st Platoon watched four children nine to ten years old walk into their patrol site, two and one-half miles north of Hill 270. They told Charlie's interpreter that about forty VC had detained them in a narrow valley by a stream one mile northwest of Hill 270. The children were paid by the VC to put up a VC flag on a pole near an American patrol base and then booby-trap it. The VC also threatened to stop soda girls from selling items to the soldiers.

Later in the afternoon by LZ Bowman, Alpha's 3rd Platoon spotted fourteen enemy soldiers in green uniforms carrying AK-47's and moving quickly at a distance of three hundred yards. The sighting was, once again, too far for effective small arms fire. The scrub brush and trees provided only fleeting glances of the enemy. Artillery fire was called.

Another Alpha platoon nearby hit a tripwire connected to a Chicom grenade which wounded a soldier with shrapnel to his arms and legs. Two more Chicom booby-traps were found nearby and destroyed.

That evening at 7:30PM, Hill 270 spotted five to eight more rockets being launched three miles south of Hill 270 toward the Chu Lai base. Ten minutes later another volley of five to seven rockets was fired. Artillery in Chu Lai responded with counter-battery fire as a third volley of four to six rockets were sent crashing into Chu Lai. The rockets landed in the vicinity of the 596th Maintenance and 62nd Signal Company, not far from division headquarters. There were no casualties.

The next afternoon on April 2, Hill 270 spotted three to four more rockets being launched towards Chu Lai. The launch site was again only three miles from their location. Artillery fire was called to saturate the launch site. The battalion's recon platoon was pulled back from its patrols to help defend the Ky Tra Outpost against an expected attack that night.

At 1:30AM on April 3, one of LZ Donna's LP's heard movement seventy-five feet in front of its position. The enemy was aware the grunts were close and probed for their position by scratching metal together and throwing rocks to prompt a response. The LP was not sure how many enemy were in front of them but decided they fulfilled their mission by detecting the enemy. They detonated their claymores and promptly moved back to Donna's perimeter. Mortar fire was placed on their position and the area around it. Radar on Donna detected a platoon-size element walking south to north across the front of the perimeter about three-quarters of a mile away. Thirty-six rounds of 105mm High Explosive rounds were fired to help them on their journey. The enemy patrol scattered on the radar screen and contact was lost.

The day was marked with a shifting of forces in response to the heavy rocket attacks on Chu Lai. Planned sweep operations further west would have to wait. Alpha returned to Chu Lai for a standdown and to act as a reaction force against more rocket attacks.

Bravo and Charlie Companies combat air assaulted into the hills south of Hill 76 and Route 532, due west of LZ Bayonet, where the rockets were launched. It was roughly a ten square-mile area that had to be searched. It was in hilly and dense vegetation which easily swallowed up the two rifle companies.

Although the enemy was greatly diminished in strength and equipment, the insurgents had the space and time to determine when to launch rocket attacks and create noticeable havoc. The battalion relocated its forward tactical operations center (TOC) from LZ Donna to Hill 270 for its shift in focus. Delta Company continued to pull security on LZ Pleasantville thirty miles west of Chu Lai in support of the 196th Brigade and ARVN operations.

Passing the Baton – Ready or Not

April 4, 1971 saw a continued effort of American and Vietnamese forces trying to flush out pockets of enemy forces throughout southern Quang Tin Province. The area stretched from Chu Lai west to LZ Bowman and south to the old rocket pockets located northwest of the former LZ Gator, and north to Hill 54 which sat seven miles north of Chu Lai astride Highway One.

RF Company 931 blanketed the contentious Ky Thanh area among the Thon Hoi and Trung Tin hamlets. ARVN (5th Regiment from Tam Ky) and other RF/PF Company's now covered the areas around LZ's Bowman, Young, Donna and Ky Tra while the 5th/46th maintained a small element on each LZ for communications and liaison.

The RF/PF militia also formed a combined operation north of Hill 270. Popular Force militias were especially effective in the populated hamlets east and west of Highway One in the Ly Tin District. The enemy continued efforts to infiltrate assassination teams to kill hamlet officials and launch sapper units to destroy bridges. But the PF's developed a reasonably effective early-warning system among the populace to counter these attacks. The primary threat was from the V18 Vietcong Local Force Company.

First Lieutenant Lawrence Kenney had a unique vantage point at this stage of the battalion's journey of war. Kenney was a platoon leader with Bravo Company from September 1970 until late March 1971. When it was time to leave the field for staff duty, he was assigned as the liaison officer for the 198th Brigade on LZ Bayonet and the 6th ARVN Regiment (2nd ARVN Division) which was also quartered at Bayonet. Kenny was billeted with the American advisors (MACV) at the ARVN compound.

The MACV team with the 6th ARVN was a combined 50/50 US Army and US Marine Corps group, commanded by an Army Lieutenant Colonel. Kenney did not observe the ARVN conducting many missions, and when they did, the missions were of short duration. The ARVN maneuvered in the same general area of Bayonet. One of the advisors who went to the field with the ARVN, a Marine Lieutenant, told Kenney he never saw any action with them.

From Kenney's view, the RF's and PF's appeared to do more and be more aggressive although their performance was erratic. Some units were much more effective than others. Working with the ARVN had been challenging for Kenney when he was a platoon leader in Bravo Company.

The idea of staying within assigned areas or boundaries was of little concern to the ARVN's he had worked with. One ARVN company called an area fire mission from an ARVN firebase after the ARVN had strayed about three miles into Kenney's assigned area. Kenney recalled, "Their Captain couldn't have given a shit less where he was."

On Bayonet Kenney still didn't trust the ARVN. When he was a platoon leader a "cowboy" ARVN Captain robbed Kenney's radio operator at pistol point. Kenney also didn't trust his Chieu Hoi Scout, an NVA defector. One night in the field he saw the Chieu Hoi literally whispering to someone outside the platoon's perimeter. Kenney thought about shooting him but transferred him out the next morning. Kenney recalled, "He should consider himself a very fortunate man."

Other platoons in the battalion felt the same as Kenney. But some platoons had competent and loyal Chieu Hoi scouts who put their lives on the line with the Americans and a number were killed or lost arms and legs to mines while working with the battalion. However, it was becoming obvious to the grunts as the battalions duty in Vietnam was drawing to an end, that many of the Chieu Hoi scouts did not like or trust the ARVN, and would most likely revert to the enemy once the battalion left.

Trust of the ARVN by Americans was also lacking. One night while on LZ Bayonet, the LZ came under an attack alert. The Lieutenant Colonel in charge of the American advisors, a group of about ten total, formed a tight defensive perimeter of their own within the ARVN's perimeter and kept round the clock watch because they didn't fully trust the ARVN.

In Kenney's view the ARVN officers on Bayonet felt they had a cushy job on the LZ with a "don't rock the boat" attitude. For sport Kenney would watch the ARVN helicopter pilots trying to land on Bayonet. He recalled, "It was hilarious. Some were decent but many were not. I used to kid the MACV guys about flying with those morons when they went to the field with the ARVN."

The 6th ARVN Regiment's area coincided with the 198th Brigade's area of operation, and the 6th ARVN was to receive the direct handoff of missions after the brigade left Vietnam. The 5th ARVN Regiment which the battalion patrolled with near LZ's Bowman and Young was headquartered in Tam Ky and was slated to replace the 196th Brigade when it left the area.

At 11:00AM on April 4, a visual reconnaissance aircraft spotted what appeared to be a tunnel system below a large black boulder in a heavily vegetated area three miles southeast of Hill 76. Charlie's 1st Platoon was picked up on an eagle flight and dropped into the area. They found three hooch's which measured eight by fifteen by six feet and were newly constructed. Lying around were ponchos, parts of rockets and M-60 ammo cans. Inside one bunker were the guts of a slaughtered pig. While the 1st Platoon checked the abandoned camp, which probably housed those who launched the rocket attacks on Chu Lai, the balance of Charlie Company shifted its operations west and north of Hill 270.

On the morning of April 5 at 5:45AM, the battalion lost another young soldier to the war. It would be their last mortal casualty. SP/4 James Alexander from Headquarters Company was assigned perimeter security duty on LZ Donna. Alexander's military occupation specialty (MOS) was a "Food Service Specialist". He worked in the mess hall to cook and feed troops but support personnel always helped with base security ever since the battalion had arrived in Vietnam three years prior.

In the early morning when it was still dark, Alexander apparently heard some movement beyond the perimeter. He pulled the pin on a fragmentation grenade and attempted to throw it, only to have it slip from his hand and fall into his fighting position. A field experienced soldier would have jumped away from his position, even if daylight afforded the opportunity to see the grenade. But it was still dark and Alexander's reaction was to find the grenade and throw it. The grenade exploded and killed the soldier. SP/4 James Patrick Alexander was age twenty and single from Green Rock, Illinois. Alexander's death came almost three years to the day the battalion suffered its first killed in action, PVT Richard Atwood, Company B, on April 11, 1968. The battalion lost one hundred and sixty-one of America's sons in the Vietnam War.

Later that afternoon, four under-strength Popular Force (PF) platoons were placed in two ambushes one and one-quarter miles north of FSB Fat City at about 6:55PM. Joining them was a team of Popular Self-Defense Force (PSDF) personnel with their hamlet chief. Fifteen Vietcong approached their position and the PF's opened up in a short but vigorous firefight. Three Vietcong were killed while one PF, one PSDF and the hamlet chief were wounded. The VC retreated back west to the mountains as they were pounded by artillery fire from Fat City.

During the day Vietnamese at the main gate to the Chu Lai base reported that approximately one hundred and thirty Vietcong were in the area of Fat City. Charlie Company was placed on a twenty-minute alert notice to air assault to the enemy if any sizable group could be found. Alpha Company had its standdown cut short and was sent north under the operational control of the 196th Brigade to support them in a mission.

The South Vietnamese military continued to step up in its own fashion as the American military continued to step down from the Vietnam War. On April 7, three of America's 1st Infantry Division's organic battalions departed South Vietnam.

Pressure continued on the widely-dispersed and diminished enemy with the Vietnamese forces, particularly the RF's and PF's, taking up an increased offensive role. At mid-morning on April 7, a combined platoon of PF's and Provisional Reconnaissance Unit (PRU) personnel on a mission to kill or capture Vietcong infrastructure personnel, were ambushed by a squad of Vietcong north of Chu Lai by Highway One. One PRU was killed and one wounded.

Delta was moved back to Dragon Valley from LZ Pleasantville and its 2nd Platoon encountered small arms fire just west of My Dong (2) on the low-lying ridges which overlooked the valley floor. A sweep of the area found bags of potatoes and surgical scissors which were recently used and covered with blood. Eighteen rounds of high explosive artillery were placed on the area of enemy fire. By days end, Alpha Company returned to Chu Lai to complete its standdown.

The next day, April 8, six more battalions of the 1st Infantry Division departed Vietnam, five were infantry and one was mechanized infantry. That morning the 5th/46th recon platoon air-assaulted south of Dragon Valley and Provincial Route 532 by Thuan An Tay (1) and landed next to a streambed. They were sent in response to reports of an enemy presence there. The last Huey bringing in the platoon took small arms fire. The gunship accompanying the air-assault poured rocket fire into the enemy position as the recon grunts moved off the LZ into the bushes. No enemy soldiers were found.

On April 9, Delta's 2nd Platoon found two well-constructed bunkers near Dong Dang (1) on the east side of the Quan River. The grunts were suitably impressed with what they saw. The bunkers were covered with three layers of timber and dirt to protect the insurgents from artillery fire. Inside were potatoes and a freshly cooked chicken with eating utensils and clothes. Everything was destroyed.

Alpha Company completed its standdown and combat air assaulted one and one-half miles west of Dragon Valley into dense terrain to search for enemy camps reportedly in the area. Bravo was returned to Chu Lai for a standdown.

That afternoon at 6:40PM, Charlie's 1st Platoon heard one of their MA's detonate in a small valley one and three-quarters miles northwest of Hill 270, the same area where the Vietnamese children said they were detained on April 1 by the Vietcong. One NVA was killed and his AK-47 rifle captured. Among his possessions were a green shirt, cut-off shorts, rubber sandals, an NVA poncho, ammo belt, wallet, tooth brush, canteen and a bag of marijuana. By days end on April 9, the 1st/5th Cavalry of the 1st Cavalry Division also departed from Vietnam.

On April 10, the battalion received twenty-three more soldiers from units departing Vietnam. Most of them were assigned to Bravo Company. The battalion continued to pursue intelligence reports which might lead to killing or capturing a larger cluster of enemy than the two or three insurgents they usually spotted. A "very reliable" intelligence source indicated an enemy headquarters was one and one-quarter mile southwest of Trung Tin and Delta Company was ordered to search the area along with the battalion's recon platoon. The day was concluded with two PF platoons ambushing fifteen VC one and one-quarter miles north of Hill 76. Four VC were killed.

On April 11, patrols continued to search for the enemy based on intelligence reports but few enemy were to be found. At 11:05AM, Alpha found the body of a NVA soldier in the mountains west of Dragon Valley. The soldier had been dead for at least a week, his body already in a state of decomposition with his green uniform riddled with bullets. It appeared to the grunts he was cut down by a gunship's mini-guns. By his side were eating utensils, two empty sandbags, five yards of black cloth and a rice knife.

Two hours later Alpha found the body of a female also apparently killed by a gunship. Her black pajama-clad body had not decomposed but rigor mortis had set in. She was only fifty feet from a trail. Alpha's Kit Carson Scout found a paper on her body that was a directive for the VC to leave the area as there was too much pressure being directed on them. The Scout, himself a former NVA, said the dead female was from North Vietnam, not a Vietcong.

Echo's Recon Platoon found four military-age Vietnamese, one female and three males, working in a rice paddy one-half mile southeast of Duc Phu (1). They carried four US Army canteens and had no identification and were extracted for questioning.

That evening PF Platoon 172 ambushed ten to fifteen Vietcong one and one-quarter mile south of Hill 54, north of Chu Lai. The PF's slugged it out with M-16's while the VC returned fire with B-40 Rockets. Two Vietcong were killed and three PF's wounded. Further south, one-quarter mile west of Fat City, PF Platoon 76 ambushed a squad of VC, killing two and capturing an AK-47. Artillery was not fired on the retreating enemy because of pacified hamlets in the area.

While the PF's and RF's continued to do what they did best, protect pacified areas where the militia had grass-roots familiarity with the populace, the battalion continued to air-assault into locations that intelligence reports suggested contained larger groups of the enemy.

It was increasingly unlikely that the enemy remained in any sizable force beyond a diminished platoon of fifteen to twenty insurgents at any location. The continued rice denial and interdiction missions of many months kept large main-force enemy units in Laos, rebuilding and refitting, waiting for the 5th/46th Infantry Battalion to depart Vietnam when the ARVN could be tested on its own.

On the morning of April 11 Delta, minus one platoon, left on the Ky Tra Outpost for security, combined forces with RF Company 931 to conduct a reconnaissance in force over the high ground west of Ky Tra.

The next day at noon a patrol of RF 931 spotted two VC and quickly engaged them. In their aggressiveness, one RF soldier tripped a booby-trapped mine which killed two of the Regional Force soldiers. Later one of Delta's soldiers stepped on a pressure-release mine, sustaining serious shrapnel wounds to his body.

That afternoon Bravo Company combat air assaulted to the high ground three miles south of the Ky Tra Outpost at Hill 271, with a mission to search and clear the dense hills two miles in all directions. This was again in reaction to reports of an enemy presence in the hills. No friendly forces had swept that area in a number of weeks. Charlie Company and the recon platoon returned to Chu Lai for a rest and refitting. The battalion's Forward TOC also shifted west from Hill 270 to the Ky Tra Outpost.

The next morning, April 13, Bravo's 2nd Platoon was hit with small arms fire which wounded one soldier in the stomach and arm. The dustoff took enemy fire as it lifted out with its casualty. In the early afternoon, the platoon again made contact with ten enemy soldiers only fifty feet away on a ridge one mile southwest of Hill 271. The enemy poured AK-47 and 30-Caliber machinegun fire into the soldiers. The platoon laid down a base of fire while calling for artillery support. Bravo's 1st and 3 platoons moved to the area to make contact but the enemy quickly slipped away.

Alpha's 2nd Platoon west of Dragon Valley found a small base camp with five hooch's and a bunker under each. They were all destroyed. Later the company found an old base camp consisting of thirty-two bunkers, all of which had deteriorated with the roofs caved in. It was a stark reminder of what once had been. The Valley was the scene of major combat with the US Marines in 1966 and 1967.

April 13 marked a landmark in the continuing withdrawal of American forces from Vietnam. The remainder of the 1st Marine Division officially ceased all operations. The next day it departed Vietnam.

On the morning of April 14 at 10:30AM, Bravo's 2nd Platoon heard one of its mechanical ambushes detonate. They found a blood trail at the site and in short order found a dead Vietcong. The platoon left a squad-size ambush to see if the enemy would return for the body while the remainder continued their patrol. Close by, they found ten hooch's with bunkers underneath containing assorted ammunition, Chicom grenades, rifle magazines, an AK-47 cleaning kit and clothing. Everything was destroyed, including the hooch's. From the fresh footprints found, it appeared there were from ten to fifteen insurgents who evaded to the southwest.

On the morning of April 15, Alpha Company suffered a casualty one-half mile west of Dragon Valley that was indicative of the challenges the terrain posed for the soldiers. While directing a light observation helicopter (LOH) landing at their patrol site, one soldier was hit in the head by its rotor blade. He was dusted off to the 91st Evacuation Hospital in Chu Lai.

To the east of Dragon Valley, Bravo's 2nd Platoon found a two-day old grave. The troops dug it up and found a young male NVA approximately twenty-five years of age in a green uniform. His body had been hit with small arms fire.

That same day Charlie Company completed its standdown in Chu Lai and was air assaulted to a new area of operations, the Tam Son hamlets three miles east of LZ Professional and four miles south of LZ

Bowman. Shortly after arriving at the LZ, the 2nd Platoon spotted a lone insurgent one-quarter mile in the distance. The platoons M-79 "Thump Gunners" fired at the insurgent while gunships worked over the area with miniguns and rockets. A sweep of the area found the dead soldier who wore green fatigues and carried a rain jacket, a hammock, an NVA medal, one-hundred Vietnamese Piasters, a pair of scissors and, mysteriously, an Americal Fortran Computer print-out sheet. Close by was a small tunnel used for quickly hiding lone insurgents on the move. It was searched and then destroyed.

By the end of the day Delta Company decoupled from its Reconnaissance In Force mission with RF Company 931 and returned to Chu Lai for a standdown.

On April 16, Charlie Company received sporadic automatic weapons fire as it patrolled its AO in the Tam Son hamlet area. Charlie's 2nd Platoon, while securing a LZ for a resupply Huey, spotted a Vietcong three-quarters of a mile away. It relayed the information to the resupply bird to fly over and take a look. The door gunners poured fire on the insurgent, watching him get hit before he crawled into a tunnel to face a slow and lonely death. Five more VC were spotted in the distance while the bird was unloading its supplies but they vanished before the Huey could take to the air.

Later that day Charlie's 1st Platoon found a booby-trapped beer can with a trip wire strung across a trail four inches above the ground. It was blown in place and the explosion left a mini-crater twelve inches wide and six inches deep.

Twenty-five feet away was a fresh grave judged to be just a few days old. It was getting dark so the patrol left the digging for the morning in order to prepare a night defensive position but the day was not over for the platoon. At 6:20PM, they heard one of their MA's detonate. After calling for mortar fire to work the area over, they swept through the foliage and found three dead Vietcong along with an Ak-47 and Ak-50. The dead bodies also yielded four Chicom grenades, two NVA-made fragmentation grenades, three pistol belts and documents with lists of American soldiers. Each weapon only had one full magazine of ammo. The insurgents wore grey and blue pants and shirts.

April 16 also saw Echo Recon air assault back into the Thon Hoi and Trung Tin area to check reports of enemy activity. Its Hueys received small arms fire when the platoon was inserted into the area.

Alpha Company west of Dragon Valley also received sporadic small arms fire from the evading enemy.

In the afternoon a patrol came upon a bunker and was hit with small arms fire. Artillery was fired after which the patrol once again swept the area but came under more fire. Again artillery pounded the area, as there was no stomach from the soldiers for fire and maneuver tactics which could cause unnecessary casualties. Three years earlier an assault would be routinely made when the concept of winning a war was still plausible. A subsequent sweep found a small camp of two hooch's measuring fourteen feet squared and another, larger hooch which was in the process of being built.

Bravo Company, patrolling east of the valley floor, found two more abandoned hooch's. The enemy's only hope of maintaining a presence in the valley area was to establish small, independent camps of two to three dwellings maximum, for easy cover and concealment. At this "camp" it appeared the grunts found an area-wide enemy aid station. One hooch, which measured ten feet by twenty feet contained twenty-two medical books, a medical records journal, two hundred pounds of rice, two NVA rucksacks, bottles of Novocain and assorted pills, hypodermic needles, plasma, penicillin, morphine and three bottles of glucose.

That night RF Company 820 from Tam Ky contributed to the day's enemy killed-in-action count by ambushing a platoon of Vietcong two miles north of LZ Donna at 10:15PM. Three VC were killed and one wounded. Two grenades and an Ak-47 were retrieved. ARVN artillery at Tam Ky fired on the retreating insurgents while US artillery from Ky Tra fired illumination rounds so the RF's could sweep the area. Elsewhere the end of the day, April 16, saw the 2nd/12th Infantry Battalion of the 4th Infantry Division depart Vietnam.

The 5th/46th Battalion's sniper teams continued to add their expertise to the pressure being placed on the enemy by the rifle companies. Sniper team "Travis" operated in the Thanh Hoa hamlet area one and one-half mile north of the Ky Tra Outpost. On April 17 at 1:50PM, the snipers spotted seven NVA in the open, all wearing camouflaged fatigues and carrying AK-47's. The snipers opened fire and killed four while calling in 4.2-inch mortar fire on the remaining insurgents as they tried to evade.

Charlie Company continued to find abandoned enemy dwellings east of LZ Professional. At 6:00PM, they found a tunnel that led to an underground room that was eight-foot squared. Nearby was a ten foot by twelve foot hooch recently abandoned. It yielded an NVA helmet, GI canteen and cooking pots. Close by was another hooch measuring eight by ten feet, with an NVA poncho, cooking pots and a newspaper dated March 11. Everything was destroyed.

At 6:15AM on April 18, Charlie's 1st Squad of its 3rd Platoon heard its night MA detonate. They found a dead Vietcong approximately eighteen years of age in a dark green uniform. The VC carried a rucksack which contained a hammock, bottle of malaria pills, extra shirts and pants and a baseball-style hat with an American name on it.

At noon, the 3rd Platoon found two more abandoned hooch's with a tunnel and bunkers. Some discarded clothing and fresh bananas indicated it was a recently-used way station for the enemy. The grunts set up two mechanical ambushes to welcome the next guests.

Bravo's 3rd Platoon operated in dense terrain three-quarters of a mile southeast of Hill 371. It tripped a booby-trap which seriously injured two soldiers with multiple fragment wounds to their lower bodies. The dense terrain required the use of a jungle penetrater to extract the wounded. Both men survived.

One hour later the platoon found another booby-trap, which was destroyed in place. One mile farther northwest the 2nd Platoon found a booby-trap by a grave that was several months old. In addition to booby-traps, high fevers continued to cause soldiers to be dusted off from the field. Three of the battalion's soldiers were dusted off that day with high temperatures from malaria.

At 9:00AM on April 19, another grunt from Bravo's 1st Platoon was dusted off for wounds caused by a booby-trap. Aerial reconnaissance flights continued to saturate the battalion's AO looking for targets of opportunity as the battalion completed its final weeks of field duty. Most grunts sensed their days of field duty were numbered but that uncertainty in an uncertain war held no promises. The possibility of death or serious injury from booby-traps now made them extra cautious. Soldiers continued their missions but the manner in which they carried them out had to make extraordinary sense. Aggressive searches in dense terrain for a diminished enemy only offered needless casualties while the enemy could slip away.

Charlie's 2nd Platoon found more structures, each recently occupied and abandoned with cooking utensils and assorted NVA equipment left behind. An Alpha patrol found another grave which contained a Vietcong male apparently killed by artillery fire. The grave was judged to be two months old. Throughout the vast area controlled by the 5th/46th many more enemy graves would never be found. But artillery fire consistently placed on enemy escape routes, air strikes on known positions and helicopter gunships constantly picking targets of opportunity, took a heavy toll on the VC and NVA remaining in the battalion's area of operations.

April 20, 1971 saw more of the same; a continued drawdown of American forces in Vietnam while the 5th/46th Battalion completed its final weeks of combat. These final weeks of field duty were performed against a backdrop of inconsistent performance of the Vietnamese military facing a small but nagging enemy presence. The battalion's soldiers in the field kept close counsel to themselves on what was reasonable to do and what was too risky, while commanders at higher levels continued to push the soldiers to gain higher enemy body counts.

On April 20, the 3rd/22nd Infantry Battalion of the 4th Infantry Division also departed Vietnam. That same day the Military Advisory Command Vietnam (MACV) publicly acknowledged that fragging incidents, the killing or injuring of unpopular officers or NCO's was on the rise, and for the first time admitted to thirty-four deaths in two hundred and nine fragging incidents in 1970.

Chu Lai remained a contentious base during standdowns for troops in the field. The atmosphere was poisoned, mainly from REMF's in support units who had not faced the same dangers that troops in the field did. Drugs were readily available, anything from marijuana to heroin. And by November 1970 more than half of incoming replacements to Vietnam had used marijuana or other drugs prior to entering the military or, at the least, prior to arriving in Vietnam.

Fights and drunkenness became daily occurrences. The causes usually stemmed from two realities of Vietnam duty in 1971: An awareness the troops would not see a clear victory and therefore remaining any longer to draw casualties was fruitless; and the foreboding Black Power movement which saw the real war to be waged in the United States over social injustice, with whites in general as the cause of that injustice. Their mantra was "there is no reason to become cannon fodder in a white man's war."

All of this placed the field soldier in an unenviable and irreconcilable position. There was also a growing sense that the Kit Carson Scouts and interpreters working in the battalion's companies in the field would change their loyalties after the battalion left. Already the actions of some of these Vietnamese drew strong suspicions and some officers, like LT. Kenney of Bravo Company, had released his scout out of total mistrust.

The performance of the Vietnamese ARVN, PF's and RF's was mixed, brought about by a MACV policy that began Vietnamization too late, with too little pacification emphasis in the Americal Division at the battalion level and below in 1969 and 1970. Now Vietnamization was being rushed to an uncertain conclusion. Moreover, Vietnamese forces were not being weaned off Americal firepower because the commanders of the 198th Brigade and the Americal Division still looked for body counts as long as they had troops in the field. For most commanders in 1971 at the battalion, company and platoon level, it was a tough time to lead soldiers.

The RF's and PF's in the battalions AO continued to do the "Heavy lifting" by assuming responsibility for the war. Their performance for the most part was acceptable and would have been stronger had the turn-over effort started much sooner with more time for a prolonged American phase-out.

Two small examples on April 20 offered a glimpse of hope if not a foreshadowing of what might have been. At 1:30AM, a PF Platoon engaged a Vietcong insurgent north of Chu Lai who quickly evaded into the populated Ly Tin area. The PF's with the advantage of common language and knowledge of the area, tracked the insurgent into a hamlet. He was killed and his Ak-47 captured. RF Company 931, continuing its sweeping operations in the Ky Tra area, established eight separate ambush positions for the night, a solid effort for its undermanned ranks.

Mines and booby-traps continued to take their toll in the battalion's final weeks of field duty with each casualty bringing anger and regret by troops who sensed the war would not be successfully concluded. Sniper Team "Travis" worked off LZ Professional. One of its soldiers tripped a Bouncing Betty, receiving lacerations to his legs and back. He was dusted off to the 91st Evacuation Hospital.

Echo's Recon Platoon also patrolled off LZ Professional, discovering recent enemy campfires with temporary fighting positions and other signs of enemy soldiers moving through the area. The battalion's focus in its final days now shifted far west to the LZ Professional area twenty miles west of Chu Lai. Everything in between Professional and Chu Lai, for the most part, was turned over to the

Vietnamese. Delta Company had air assaulted into the Professional area on April 19. The battalion's 4.2-inch heavy mortars were also relocated from Hill 270 to Professional to provide more indirect fire support.

April 21 saw Delta's 1st Platoon finding signs of enemy in the area. Spider holes and small tunnels by well-used trails provided quick concealment for small groups of enemy soldiers on the move. Four hours after discovering the tunnels the platoon's pointman heard voices one hundred feet to his front. He retreated a few feet to pick up three riflemen who advanced on line and poured fire into the area of voices. The platoon leader ordered mortar fire from LZ Professional into the presumed avenue of escape. The platoon moved in but found no bodies.

Alpha Company also air assaulted to the Professional AO and landed two and one-half miles east of the LZ. Alpha's 3rd Platoon observed VC in a wood line as it landed on its assigned LZ. The grunts quickly took them on with M-60 machinegun fire which sent the insurgents scurrying deeper into the brush. By 7:15PM the platoon started looking for a night ambush site near Long Son (3) when it spotted two more enemy one hundred yards away. The insurgents spotted the grunts first and evaded as small arms fire followed them into a bunker. There were occupied hamlets in the area so no artillery fire was called.

That day Alpha's headquarters element and its 2nd Platoon moved to a daytime ambush site at 3:15PM where their pointman encountered a Vietcong walking toward him. The pointman cut him down with his M-16. The insurgents backpack included five pounds of rice, Russian pills and a cooking pot but no weapon. That night, four rounds from a captured M-79 grenade launcher were fired into LZ Professional's perimeter on the portion manned by Delta's 2nd Platoon. One soldier was wounded with shrapnel to his thighs and hips and was dusted off to Chu Lai.

The following morning on April 22, one of the battalion's soldiers walking the perimeter on Professional, detonated a Bouncing Betty mine. No lives were lost but the mine accomplished its purpose and sent twelve soldiers from the recon platoon, sniper team and Echo Mortars back to Chu Lai to have shrapnel removed. Patrols in the area continued to find abandoned hooch's and bunkers but there were no sightings of the enemy.

The enemy remained ghost-like. Alpha's 2nd Platoon, patrolling four miles east of Professional heard movement across a draw at about two hundred yards. The platoon opened up with M-16 and M-60 machinegun fire, the M-16's having tracers in the magazines to help guide the grunts fire when used at night. The tracers started a small fire but when the grunts reached the area no bodies were found.

Charlie's 1st Platoon, patrolling one and one-quarter mile southeast of Professional by the Bong Miel River, discovered a hand-crafted bridge fifteen feet in width and length with three arches supported by culverts. The arches were also used as shelters. The bridge was so well camouflaged the grunts did not spot it until almost on top of it. It was impossible to detect from the air.

Charlie's patrols near the river spotted sandal tracks but the phantom enemy kept its distance. That night while on an ambush, Charlie's 3rd Squad of the 3rd Platoon had a trip flare ignite and immediately detonated the claymore mine which covered the flare. A short sweep of the flare site beyond its tight perimeter revealed nothing.

Patrols continued throughout April 23 with the scattered and diminished enemy remaining elusive. While on a listening post beyond LZ Professionals perimeter, Echo's Recon soldiers spotted a moving light that was promptly extinguished by eight 81mm mortar rounds.

The battalion's large area of operation since arriving to defend the greater Chu Lai Defense Area in early April 1970 was now, a year later, under the control of South Vietnamese forces. Regional Force (RF) and Popular Force (PF) militia were responsible for the bulk of the terrain handed off by the 5th/46th Infantry Battalion. The night of April 23-24 offers a good example. Five RF and PF Companies blanketed the Ky Tra, LZ Bowman and LZ Donna area with twenty-seven night defensive positions and ambushes in the field.

Elements of the 1st/6th Infantry Battalion, which had traded AO's with the 5th/46th in April 1970, were now operating near the area of the rocket launches that plagued the division headquarters in Chu Lai. The Americal Division did not want to depend upon Vietnamese militia to keep the rockets "off the general's backs" in Chu Lai while the 5th/46th operated elsewhere and intelligence reports continued to point to major rocket attacks aimed at Chu Lai.

Bravo's 2nd Platoon remained in the Hill 76 area to help mitigate rocket attacks. A trip flare ignited off its night position and a claymore mine was detonated in response. Night illumination was provided as the grunts swept the area but nothing was found.

April 25 saw Charlie Company continuing its patrols in the Bong Mieu River area east of LZ Professional. More evidence of an enemy presence was found. At 10:45AM, a NVA soldier in green fatigues with full field pack and AK-47 hit the grunts with a burst of AK fire before skirting into the dense brush. Gunships in the area made their way to the scene and spotted two insurgents coming out of a wood line along the river bank. The gunships opened up and killed both. Charlie's troops reached the dead bodies and recovered an AK-47 with two backpacks.

A wider sweep of the area uncovered two abandoned hooch's which yielded a potpourri of enemy materials: A wicker basket, two NVA shirts, bags of rice, buckets, a Seiko watch, two NVA poncho's, bush hats, pots and pans over a hot fire, rice knives, punji stakes and three bags of opium. One bunker nearby yielded thirty-four Chicom grenades and an NVA backpack. The backpack held three grams of marijuana, a fishing net, NVA canteen, bag of rice, small cooking pots and a homemade satchel charge made in an aluminum can which contained two Chicom grenades and a bottle of acid. The grunts followed a blood trail nearby which quickly evaporated.

Upriver north of LZ Professional, the battalion Commanders Command & Control helicopter (C&C) spotted a male and female with two children in civilian clothes crossing a sandbar along the river. Their presence was two miles south of a controlled fire zone far from populated hamlets, which meant they were in a free fire zone. No weapons were spotted so the male was not fired on. A short distance farther up river the C&C bird spotted a VC leaving the river and fleeing back into the wood line. The door gunner poured machinegun fire into the trees.

During the day Alpha Company was lifted back to Chu Lai for a standdown. The day's activities ended at 8:50PM when PF Platoon 140, in an ambush site one mile northeast of Hill 76, engaged a small group of Vietcong killing five and capturing an AK-47 at the cost of one PF wounded.

Early the next morning on April 26 one of Charlie's night positions heard a MA detonate. They swept the area and found one grey cat killed in action. As the battalion patrolled the terrain near LZ Professional and Hill 76, the PF's and RF's continued to control most of battalion's domain. RF Company 931 established fifteen patrol bases and ambush sites in the Ky Thanh and Ky Tra area. PF's from Tam Ky established eight patrol bases in the LZ Bowman area. And farther east in the populated Ly Tin District near highway One, Popular Force militia established sixty-one checkpoints, patrol bases and ambush sites.

Roles in the battalion's AO between the 5th/46th and Vietnamese military forces were now totally reversed. On April 26, three-quarters mile north of LZ Donna a soldier from RF Company 820 hit a mine and was killed. Close by another RF unit hit a mine wounding one of its militia. Farther north and west in the Tien Phouc area an RF outpost was hit in a day-long fight resulting in one RF killed and three wounded. The Vietcong lost forty-two dead by body count and the RF's captured fourteen Ak-47's along with three B-40 rockets and one 60mm mortar. Two miles west of Dragon Valley in dense terrain a RF soldier tripped another booby-trap and was killed. Northeast of Hill 54 a squad of VC were spotted in a hamlet and quickly fled when attacked by the RF's. A B-40 rocket was recovered.

Charlie's 2nd Platoon, operating two and one-half miles southeast of LZ Professional by the Bong Mieu River, heard two insurgents in a conversation in the bushes in front of them. Charlie's grunts were leery of an ambush and fired up the area before moving in. They found a blood trail which they followed until it ran dry. They doubled back from their pursuit and found sixteen abandoned rucksacks, each filled with supplies and each weighing approximately seventy-five pounds. The contents included clothes, cooking oil, hammocks, cans of food, twenty bars of soap, NVA poncho's, booby-trap devices, six drums of small fish and some children's toys. Charlie's Kit Carson Scout estimated at least eighteen insurgents had been scattered which included at least nine women who served as supply carriers.

The early morning hours of April 27 saw the provincial capital of Tam Ky, headquarters of the 5th ARVN Regiment, hit by four 122mm rockets. Only one building was hit and one civilian was wounded. At 7:00AM, Charlie Company's command post near the Bong Mieu River spotted two Vietcong walking through a small valley approximately one hundred and fifty yards away. They were walking directly towards a mechanical ambush. Five minutes later the MA exploded and the grunts found a dead female in her twenty's. She carried clothes, hammocks, writing pads and cooking pots but no weapon.

Later in the afternoon Charlie's 3rd Platoon heard another MA detonate and found two females killed, aged eighteen to twenty-two. They were dressed in black pants and NVA shirts, carrying watches, radios and rice. Neither female had any identification papers.

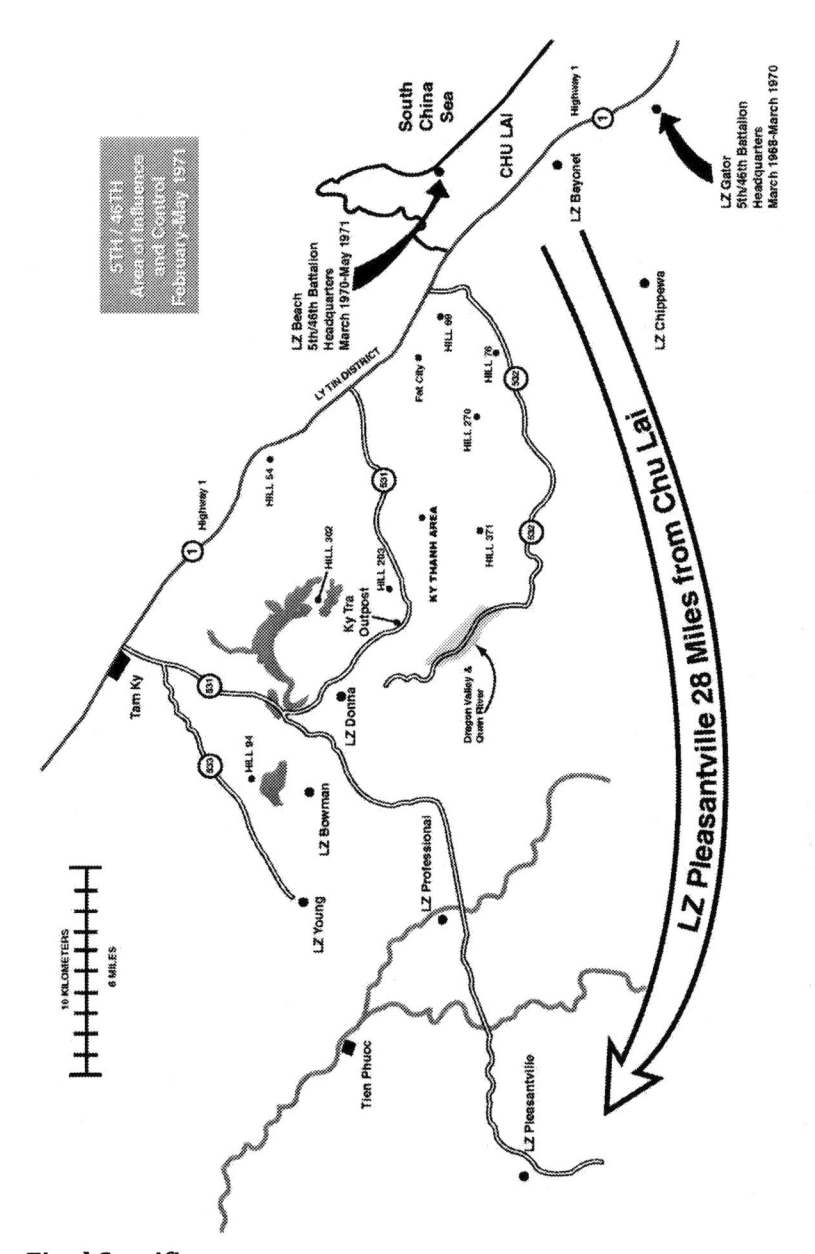

Final Sacrifices

Bravo's 2nd Platoon, patrolling north of Hill 270, required a dustoff early that evening for a soldier believed to have contracted hepatitis. The day ended for the battalion with Alpha in Chu Lai on standdown, Bravo south and north of Hill 270, Delta and Echo Recon on LZ Professional and patrolling the surrounding area. Charlie Company patrolled three miles east of the LZ, near the Bong Mieu River. The day also saw the 1st/502nd Infantry Battalion of the 173rd Airborne Brigade depart Vietnam.

At 11:15PM on April 27, PF Company 172 made contact with approximately fifteen Vietcong trying to enter a hamlet three miles northeast of Fat City. One VC was killed and four B-40 rockets were captured. US artillery at Fat City fired at the retreating enemy. The following morning at 2:30AM, PF Platoon 86 ambushed a squad of VC in the vicinity of Hill 76. One PF was killed. Enemy casualties were unknown.

At noon on April 28, Charlie's 3rd Platoon two and one-half miles south of the Bong Mieu, spotted two Vietcong moving west to east. The grunts opened fire at a distance of three hundred yards and swept the area. They found no blood trails but discarded sandals, a sandbag full of salt and a rucksack containing bandages, soap, ten pounds of rice, a mosquito net, potatoes, letters and assorted clothes.

Charlie's 1st Platoon was positioned close by at a designated pick-up zone (PZ) when it spotted another insurgent one hundred yards away. Small arms fire and a quick sweep of the area yielded negative results.

At mid-afternoon, Charlie Company was lifted out of the Bong Mieu River area by Huey and flown to LZ Professional. The same birds then took Delta off Professional two miles to the southwest with a mission to sweep the terrain while gradually moving east back to the LZ. Bravo moved by foot to Fat City to be trucked to Chu Lai for a standdown while Alpha trucked back out to Fat City to walk back into the Hill 270 area.

The month of April 1971 was closing fast and so too was the journey of war for the 5th/46th Infantry Battalion. But the enemy, in small numbers, was sticking around. An intelligence report on April 29 indicated possible sapper attacks would be launched on the 6th ARVN Regiment's portion of LZ Bayonet as well as the Americal Combat Center in Chu Lai. The sappers designated for the attack on Chu Lai would be dressed in ARVN uniforms wearing the 2nd Division patch but wearing no shoes so they could identify each other.

The 5th ARVN Regiment, headquartered in Tam Ky, moved some of its battalion's farther west to occupy LZ's Siberia, Pleasantville, West and Center as the 196th Infantry Brigade shifted its forces north to the Danang area to replace the departing 1st Marine Regiment. The brigade took on "Operation Caroline Hill" during May and June, a search and destroy operation into the mountains and lowlands west and south of Danang, still looking for body counts. The two-month operation would yield approximately one hundred and sixty NVA/VC killed with eleven enemy taken prisoners. This came at a cost of fifteen brigade soldiers killed in action and approximately one hundred and twenty-five wounded.

April 29 also saw the majority of the 1st Cavalry Division depart South Vietnam with one brigade remaining, the 3rd Brigade with four battalions, that became a separate command.

Delta Company of the 5th/46th continued its sweep of the terrain southwest of Professional finding the discarded refuse of a beaten enemy that operated in small groups to maintain a minimal presence. The grunts also found the refuse of previous American patrols that had grown sloppy with little enemy contact and a focus on going home. It was symbolic of what the war had come down to in the area, for both the enemy and the Americans.

A Delta patrol came across an old VC/NVA base camp with two tunnels that had partially collapsed and six destroyed hooch's where only the frames remained. Later the grunts found a small cave with four cooking pots and a few C-ration cans. Three hundred yards from the cave they discovered six tunnels and fourteen frames for constructing new hooch's. Vines were carefully interwoven around the beginnings of a new camp so that it was invisible from aerial observation.

On May 1, 1971 at 3:30PM, Alpha's 2nd Platoon, operating one and one-quarter mile northwest of Hill 270, requested a routine dustoff for a soldier with chills and fever, a possible case of malaria. In the meantime an increasing number of intelligence reports pointed to re-equipped enemy units with plans in the coming weeks to "Attack coastal areas and pacified hamlets with a combination of assassination teams, sappers, rockets and main-force soldiers heavily armed with mortars, RPG's, machineguns, individual weapons and grenades".

May 2 saw Delta Company still sweeping the terrain southwest of LZ Professional when it was alerted it would be picked up by Huey the morning of May 3 to return to LZ Professional. They would be lifted by Chinooks, along with Charlie Company, Echo's recon platoon and heavy mortars to Chu Lai for the battalion's final standdown.

At 2:00PM on May 2, Delta's 1st Platoon called for a routine dustoff for a soldier with a swollen right elbow. The dustoff was completed at 4:35PM. Alpha in the Hill 270 area also requested a routine dustoff for a soldier with a 102 degree fever. That dustoff was completed at 4:55PM and would be the final dustoff for the battalion in the Vietnam War.

The next day at 1:00PM, the first lifts of Chinooks left LZ Professional with the battalion's soldiers and flew back to their headquarters at LZ Beach in Chu Lai. Alpha Company walked from its terrain around Hill 270 to FSB Fat City and was picked up by trucks for the return trip to LZ Beach. By 4:00PM all of the battalion's soldiers were back in Chu Lai, never to return to the field as a battalion again. A battalion briefing was held at 5:30PM. For the 5th/46th Infantry Battalion the war was now over. For many of its soldiers who had time left to serve in Vietnam, the war would continue in other units, primarily the 196th Light Infantry Brigade.

For the next eighteen days equipment was inventoried and assigned elsewhere. Those soldiers with time still to be served were transferred to other units. Others were sent home. During those eighteen days, the 2nd/7th Cavalry of the 1st Cavalry Division departed on May 5. On May 7 all Marine forces of the III Marine Amphibious Force, which comprised the remaining Marines in South Vietnam, ceased combat operations and stood down. May 15 saw the 3rd/506th Infantry of the 101st Airborne Division depart Vietnam.

The battalion's headquarters held a small deactivation ceremony. On May 21 a small headquarters contingent in the 5th/46th Infantry Battalion's headquarters departed from South Vietnam to Fort Lewis, Washington, where the battalion's colors were retired.

The war in Vietnam was now over for the battalion but would live on in the memories of its soldiers for the rest of their lives.

19 – REVELATION

"I heard a loud voice from the throne saying,
'Behold, God's dwelling is with the human race.
He will dwell with them and they will be
His people and God himself will always be with them
(As their God).
He will wipe every tear from their eyes,
and there shall be no more death or mourning,
wailing or pain, (for) the older order has passed away."
Revelation 21: 3-4

On May 21, 1971, approximately twenty soldiers from the 5th/46th Infantry Battalion stood in formation at the Chu Lai runway, their tours of duty in Vietnam completed. They were designated to take the battalion's colors back to Fort Lewis, Washington for the deactivation of the battalion. The battalion's Sergeant Major gave each man in formation a small gift, thanked them for their service in the battalion and, with tears in his eyes, told them "When you get to Fort Lewis, get to a K-Mart, buy some civilian clothes so you won't be harassed, and go home."

At 1:00AM on May 22, they departed Cam Ranh Bay on flight C204 and flew to McChord Air Force Base, Seattle, Washington. Within three days the battalion was administratively deactivated as the American separation from the Vietnam War continued at a rapid pace. The Americal Army Division itself had only six months left before it too would be deactivated.

The remaining soldiers in the battalion were assigned to other Americal units to complete their Vietnam tours. Dennis Stevens had served with Charlie Company, 5th/46th from January to May 1971 and then was transferred to the 1st/1st Cavalry Squadron in Danang until the end of October. He hated riding around on Armored Personnel Carriers (APC). For Stevens, a foot soldier, the APC's were too restricted in their movements and too much of a target for mines.

Steven's unit worked a lot with the ARVN. He recalls, "It was hard to tell if they were with us or against us. I didn't trust them, that's for sure" Then, when the 1st/1st Cav went home, he was transferred to the 101st Airborne Division up near Hue, back in the field again as a foot soldier. He returned home a few days before Christmas, 1971.

Stevens remembers the duplicity of it all. "When I was there near Danang and Hue, politically, the people back home were told we were not in the 'field'; that the ARVN were taking over. There were times I would receive letters from home saying they were relieved that I was no longer in the 'field' and that I was 'safe'. As I was reading that letter I was getting shot at with RPG's and AK-47 fire. I didn't appreciate being lied to."

On November 1, 1971, a sister unit of the 5th/46th, the 1st/52nd Battalion of the 198th Brigade, departed Vietnam. Two weeks later the headquarters of the 198th and 11th Light Infantry Brigades departed Vietnam, and the last battalion of the 198th, the 1st/6th Infantry Battalion, departed Vietnam sixteen days after that.

The Americal Division headquarters was deactivated on November 29, 1971. This left only the 196th Light Infantry Brigade, which returned to its original status as a separate brigade. It had been merged into the Americal Division in 1967. By June 1972, the battalion's in the 196th also began departing until the brigade's 3rd/21st Infantry Battalion (the last U.S. ground combat unit in the Vietnam War) was deactivated on August 11 and departed Vietnam on August 23, 1972.

The tactical area of responsibility (TAOR) for the Americal Division was now left to the South Vietnamese military to defend. Part of this TAOR was the contentious terrain assigned to 5th/46th during its three years of operations. This included the large coastal plain east of Highway One from Chu Lai south to Quang Ngai City. This was an area approximately seventeen miles long (North to south) and ten miles wide at its widest point, which was from Highway One moving east to the notorious Batangan Peninsula.

The Batangan Peninsula covered approximately five square miles and was the most heavily mined piece of terrain in the Vietnam War. History will record the soldiers of the 5th/46th Infantry Battalion served the longest time and shed the most blood on the Batangan.

When the 5th/46th left the coastal plain in late March of 1970, the 48th Local Force Vietcong Battalion had been decimated by the battalion's continuous operations, with few enemy soldiers remaining. Indeed, prior to leaving the area, the 5th/46th had seen NVA reinforcements for the 48th Battalion moving west, back into the mountains, because the battalion's sweep operations in conjunction with ARVN, Regional Force (RF) and Popular Force (PF) militias had left the 48th Battalion with virtually no supplies, little support, and few personnel.

An analysis of intelligence reports at the Military Advisory Command Vietnam (MACV) showed that by early 1970, throughout South Vietnam, and most certainly in the 5th/46th area of responsibility, enemy casualties were exceeding both their infiltration rates from North Vietnam and local recruitment rates. Moreover the quality of enemy forces was steadily declining. It remains for history to contemplate those words uttered by a North Vietnamese Army Colonel after the war, "Our forces in the south were nearly wiped out by all the fighting in 1968. It took us until 1971 to re-establish our presence, but we had to use North Vietnamese troops as guerillas. If the American forces had not begun to withdraw under Nixon in 1969, they could have punished us severely. We suffered badly in 1969 and 1970 as it was."

After the battalion left the coastal plain the RF and PF militia, while far from perfect, took on the task of population control and pacification. Once the militia established permanence in the protected hamlets, there was a rapid increase in Chieu Hoi defectors. The experience of the 5th/46th Battalion mirrored the observation of one expert in pacification who noted, "The Chieu Hoi rate always goes up, not as a result of sweeps but as a result of getting in an area and staying in it."

Pacification was the "secret weapon" to winning the war in South Vietnam that most US military forces never fully embraced. But the importance of pacification was understood early in the war by the US Marines. Major General Lewis Walt, the original Marine Commander of the III Marine Amphibious Force in 1965, recognized that pacification was the most important role for an American presence in Vietnam. Yet "search and destroy" and "body counts" took over much of the Army's focus in the war. For the Americal Division, as well as other Army divisions, there was no clear demarcation between the various kinds of ground operations: "search and destroy", "clear and hold" and "accelerated pacification", all accomplished by "combat air assaults". Some operations included elements of all three.

When General Creighton Abrams took over the reigns of leadership of MACV and started emphasizing pacification, the division and brigade commanders he inherited found it hard to break with the "search and destroy" mentality of General William Westmoreland, the outgoing MACV commander. Consequently, body counts continued to occupy much of the attention of tactical commanders, particularly in Quang Ngai Province.

Quang Ngai Province was one of forty-four provinces in South Vietnam; but between 1967 and 1972, it proved to be one of the most hostile provinces, disproportionately accounting for six percent of all American combat deaths. Further, over one-half of all combat deaths in the Vietnam War occurred in the I Corps tactical zone.

One might ask, did the US Army and South Vietnamese government allow enough time for the pacification program to achieve the best possible results, or did the rapid American withdrawal leave our ally gravely vulnerable? President Nixon's political mandate to withdraw from Vietnam was at cross-purposes with General Abram's belief that the war was still winnable, via the new, less costly approach of pacification. While Abrams wanted to win, Nixon wanted out. As one historian noted, "Abrams wanted to use pacification to win the war, Nixon wanted to use pacification to help America withdraw from Vietnam."

For Abrams, Westmoreland's "war of the big battalions" had gone on too long without enough attention to securing and pacifying the populace and requiring the South Vietnamese to do more of the pacification and fighting. As was noted in previous chapters, in Southern Quang Ngai Province, the 2nd ARVN Division was judged to be one of the most lethargic ARVN divisions in South Vietnam. The Americal Division did most of the heavy fighting until the die was cast for withdrawal, creating for the 2nd ARVN Division the necessity to rapidly take on more responsibility for the ground war. Referring to the Vietnam War, one counter-insurgency expert noted, "You can't go in and win it for somebody, 'cuz you'll have nothing in the end."

Not lost on a savvy enemy was the realization that, if the US and its allies should persevere, General Abram's shift in emphasis to pacification would deal the most serious blow to their "War of National Liberation". Consequently, the enemy increasingly focused most of its attacks on the PF's and RF's protecting the pacified areas, which resulted in a much increased casualty rate for the militias. Some of the sad statistics of the war reflect this. In 1970 the combat death rates in South Vietnam for RF and PF militias were twenty-two per thousand. By contrast, the ARVN suffered sixteen deaths per thousand and American ground forces suffered eleven per thousand.

The mission of pacification was thrown on the RF and PF militia in haste by the Americal Division and the Quang Ngai and Quang Tin Provincial Governments. The "Accelerated Pacification" effort across South Vietnam officially ended in January 1969. But it was not until the 5th/46th "clear, hold & pacify" operations were conducted from October to December 1969, that a serious effort was directed by the brigade and division to pass the ball to the Vietnamese forces in the 5th/46th TAOR.

In late March 1970, when the 5th/46th Battalion bade farewell to the coastal plain, as beautiful as it was deadly, to trade areas with 1st/6th Infantry Battalion, the 48th Local Force Vietcong Battalion had by then been seriously depleted in strength. But, when the 1st/6th soldiers took up their positions and operated in and around the enemy-influenced hamlets that were so familiar to the 5th/46th, such as the Van Tuong's, Lac Son's and Nam Yen's, they too found themselves facing serious challenges from mines and booby-traps.

The 1st/6th Battalion's assigned missions were similar to the 5th/46th missions: To interdict enemy forces and supplies on the coast and along the waterways; support South Vietnam's pacification program, commit one company to the Infantry Company Intensified Pacification Program (then called the Combined Unit Pacification Program – CUPP) and conduct rice and salt denial operations against the Vietcong. The CUPP mission was the Army's version of Marine CAP teams.

The 1st/6th Battalion's involvement on the coast, like the 5th/46th, came at a high price. For example, on August 14, a rifle platoon tripped a mine which wounded five soldiers. The 198th Brigade Commander landed in his Huey to help with the medical evacuation. While the wounded were being loaded on Hueys, another mine was detonated wounding twelve more soldiers in the blast, including the brigade commander and his operations officer. Of the two hundred and forty-nine casualties suffered by the 1st/6th between March 22 and December 1, 1970, two hundred and three (eighty-two percent) were the result of mines and booby-traps.

Ultimately, one of the "Final Solutions" to controlling the large coastal plain was to bulldoze it into submission. Beginning in mid-May 1970, four engineer companies were brought in to improve roads for better farm-to-market support for the populace. In addition, land clearing was undertaken to level the miles of thick hedgerows, heavily wooded areas and hills that for many years had offered the enemy cover and concealment on the coast. One of the 1st/6th Battalion's most important missions was to secure the area of operations for the engineers. The engineer company responsible for clearing the land used large D7E bulldozer tractors that protected the operators from bombs that might be detonated by the main blade. Nevertheless, booby-trapped artillery shells hanging in trees were an ever present danger.

By the end of May 1970, just two months after the 5th/46th Battalion departed the coastal area, the engineers had cleared close to three thousand acres of land, destroyed seventy-eight bunkers, one thousand, four hundred and thirty tunnels and forty mines and booby-traps. In the following two months approximately one hundred and fifty enemy soldiers, mostly NVA who had infiltrated into the area to help the Vietcong, had moved west of Highway One back into the hills because of the lack of cover and concealment on the coast.

By the end of October, another one hundred and eighty-six bunkers, forty-eight mines and booby-traps and many more tunnels were destroyed. Between December 1970 and the end of January 1971 a Vietnamese surrender program of leaflet drops and aerial loudspeakers resulted in ninety-two Vietcong on the coast surrendering as Chieu Hoi's.

The change in areas of responsibility made by Colonel Joseph Clemons, the 198th Brigade commander at the time, between the 5th/46th Battalion and the 1st/6th Battalion in March 1970, requires some additional discussion. This is because of comments made by the 1st/6th Battalion commander at the time, Lieutenant Colonel H. Norman Schwarzkopf (Later General Schwarzkopf of "Desert Storm" fame) in his autobiography, "It doesn't Take a Hero."

There is a creed in the military, especially the combat arms, which says "Leave no man behind". This author feels compelled to address comments Schwarzkopf made in his book, which attack the integrity of the men of the 5th/46th Infantry Battalion and dishonor the memory of those in the battalion who died. I will not let their memory be unfairly tarnished.

In his book Schwarzkopf states: *"Supposedly the 5/46 had gone to the Batangan to fight a VC battalion known as the "Phantom 48th" – "phantom" because nobody actually found it – but the troops had become so demoralized by the mines and booby traps that they'd lost their will to fight. When patrols were sent out at night, they'd go two hundred yards outside their perimeter and stop, and the next morning they'd come in and report that they'd completed their mission and encountered nothing. Colonel Clemons called me in and said, 'The fifth of the Forty-Sixth isn't cutting it down there. They're scared to death. I want you and your unit to trade places with them."*

First is the statement, *"The phantom 48th that nobody ever found"*. This statement is a revelation to the soldiers of the 5th/46th Infantry Battalion who consistently encountered and defeated the soldiers of the 48th Vietcong Battalion, both VC regulars and their NVA reinforcements. The closely detailed pages in this book speak for themselves.

Further, several of the battalion's officers were told at the Americal Officers Club by division staff officers, (after the battalion relocated its headquarters to Chu Lai) that after January 1970, because of the battalions work, the 48th VC Battalion was "taken off the board" because the division believed it no longer had the capability to mount any kind of major offensive operation. The battalion's officers thought this assessment was a bit too optimistic, but it, nonetheless, was indicative of the official view of the enemy's strength on the coastal plains after the 5th/46th's departure.

Another statement, *"They lost their will to fight"* is an insult to the soldiers of the 5th/46th, who braved the dangers of firefights, mines, ambushes, booby-traps and the elements while Schwarzkopf and his battalion struggled with their own problems in the Chu Lai area.

Another Schwarzkopf statement needs to be addressed: *"When patrols were sent out at night ... they'd go two hundred yards and stop ... next morning they'd come in and report they completed their mission and encountered nothing."*

The detailed pages of this history, taken from official records and many eye-witness testimonies, chronicle the 5th/46th Battalion's numerous ambushes and firefights on the coastal plain that accounted for many enemy dead. They also candidly chronicle the hesitancy of some soldiers and their leaders at times to perform night patrols on the Batangan Peninsula - the Binh Duc Cape (Schwarzkopf mistakenly refers to the Batangan as the large coastal area from Chu Lai to Quang Ngai). As noted in the chapters of this book, patrolling the Batangan was extremely dangerous during the day but to move at night was suicidal.

Like other infantry battalions in the Americal Division, including the 1st/6th Battalion, phantom night ambushes did take place when the junior leadership allowed them to happen, particularly in mined areas. But it was the exception to the norm. Schwarzkopf, whether he took Clemmons' alleged comments at face value or not, owes an apology to the men of the 5th/46th Infantry Battalion. As one of the 5th/46th's platoon leaders (and later a company commander) remarked, "We have nothing to apologize for while operating on the Batangan. The men were all-American boys and had a tough job that few other battalions had to endure."

Schwarzkopf writes, *"Colonel Clemons said the Fifth of the Forty-Sixth isn't cutting it down there. I want you to trade places with them."* But a review of the circumstances surrounding the move of the 1st/6th to the coast after its performance in its Chu Lai defense assignment, suggests other reasons for the switch of battalions.

The division headquarters became increasingly impatient with rockets being fired into the Chu Lai base and the 1st/6th Battalion's difficulty in curtailing it. Moreover, on March 17, 1970, the command and control helicopter of the Americal Division's Commander, Major General Lloyd Ramsey, crashed in dense terrain approximately seven miles west of Chu Lai. This was Schwarzkopf's area of responsibility; but he couldn't find the downed helicopter. When it was eventually located by the 71st Assault Helicopter Company, division headquarters thought that Schwarzkopf was too slow in getting his troops to the site. For eighteen hours, the Division's Commanding General lay unconscious at the crash site.

Although weather conditions were very bad, which caused the crash in the first place and definitely hindered rescue efforts, the division headquarters was unsettled by the amount of time it took to rescue its commanding general. The area belonged to the 1st/6th Battalion, and given its performance in the field (Schwarzkopf in his book referred to the 1st/6th reputation as the "First of the Worst") his battalion's performance in this emergency was viewed as unacceptable.

During the time immediately following the aircraft crash, it was mentioned to some 5th/46th officers that some senior officers at the division headquarters talked of relieving Schwarzkopf. Schwarzkopf was also reeling from a contentious friendly fire incident in his battalion (which eventually became the subject of the motion picture, "Friendly Fire") and his battalion's failure to stop rockets from being fired on Chu Lai.

But Colonel Joe Clemons admired Schwarzkopf for his aggressive (some said "brutish") manner of commanding. It mirrored Clemons's own style, whose official radio call sign was "Grim Reaper." Clemons wanted to protect, what appeared to be, his favorite battalion commander.

An eye witness account offers more background. One of the 5th/46th Battalion's company commanders had finished his command time and was performing staff duty in the S-3 Section at the 198th Brigade headquarters during the period just before the battalions switched areas. The officer observed Clemons worrying and discussing options with the brigades S-3 Operations Officer of "What to do with the Schwarkopf problem." Clemons offered the division headquarters an option to move Schwarzkopf's battalion out of its current assignment and have his battalion trade areas with the 5th/46th Battalion.

Later, officers from the division headquarters told some of the 5th/46th's officers in Chu Lai that the switch was made "To give Schwarzkopf's battalion an easier mission to give him time to get his unit restructured and whipped into shape. They gave him ours (5th/46th) because we had pretty much cleaned it up".

Another comment from a battalion officer, "Division said it would allow him (Schwarzkopf) time to get his battalion reorganized and get their feet under them." The only reason the coastal area of operations was at that time characterized as "easy duty" was because the division headquarters had considered it, correctly or not, to be pretty much cleaned up by the 5th/46th.

Whether Schwarzkopf was aware of the division's dissatisfaction of his command, and/or took Clemons at his word about the 5th/46th, is conjecture at this point. The author of this book spoke to Clemons by phone in March 2010, informing him about this book and asking him if he had any observations about the enemy and the nature of the war in the 198th Brigade's area of operations. Clemons stated he didn't remember anything; but then, almost on queue, suddenly blurted "Yeah, I switched the 5th/46th with Schwarzkopf's battalion because they were not going out on ambushes."

It is this author's opinion that his response may well have been a "quick-think-on-your-feet" effort to keep a lid on a potentially embarrassing situation, forgotten until now, buried within Schwarzkopf's impressive military career. And to that end, the collective reputation and integrity of the 5th/46th Infantry Battalion may have unwillingly and unknowingly served as a sacrificial lamb.

Schwarzkopf's performance on the coastal plain can be debated as well. While the 5th/46th performed missions at the platoon and squad level, the 1st/6th made company-level movements against the small, nimble and widely dispersed Vietcong. His unit's movements were very predictable to the enemy. They performed mostly day operations with few night movements under Schwarzkopf's command. It is reported Schwarzkopf's rapport with his troops was not good. At one point while talking to one of his rifle companies at LZ Dottie, he was booed. As one lieutenant in the 1st/6th who retired as an Army Colonel opined, "Schwarzkopf made a much better general than a battalion commander in Vietnam."

Another disconnect from reality is Schwarzkopf's rather off-handed statement that Clemons insinuated the "*Fifth of the Forty-Sixth can't cut it.*" If this were truly the assessment of Colonel Clemons, the brigade commander, why did Clemons, almost immediately after switching areas of operation with the 1st/6th Battalion, send the 5th/46th Infantry Battalion into the mountains over fifteen miles from the coast, close to Laos, in a three-company sweep where the expectation of encountering an NVA Regiment was highly probable?

Add to this is what several 5th/46th officers have told this author, that when the battalion relocated its headquarters to LZ Beach in Chu Lai, they were congratulated by division staff officers for doing an outstanding job on the coastal plain.

Colonel Clemons was viewed by some officers in the brigade as "no whiz kid either". As one officer in the 5th/46th recalled, "His first 'innovation' as our brigade commander was to outlaw rucksacks and make us use the 40's-style little canvas butt packs on suspenders. We refused and showed him that the little butt packs wouldn't even begin to give us the basic load of ammunition that we needed and they absolutely killed our backs, for lack of the frame and lumbar strap."

Clemons apparently had other issues with the division command. Although he was a graduate of the US Military Academy and awarded the Distinguished Service Cross in the Korean War, he did not get promoted to the next rank, Brigadier General, after his brigade command in Vietnam.

Finally, Schwarzkopf writes in his book, "*It was a compliment for our unit finally to be handed a real assignment*" (the coastal area). However, the area of most strategic importance to division headquarters was the Chu Lai tactical area of responsibility (TAOR), which included the contentious rocket pockets which was taken from Schwarzkopf and given to the 5th/46th Battalion. The 5th/46th would eventually expand and control its new TAOR far beyond the original boundaries, penetrating deep into the mountains beyond Dragon Valley, which has been documented in Chapter 18.

The 5th/46th Battalion left Vietnam and its AO not as it had found it. Left behind, after its three-year long fight, was a population that had greatly benefited from uninterrupted gains in security. Now, security had to be backed up by the Vietnamese Army (ARVN) which would have to face any major attacks from main force North Vietnamese units.

The NVA launched a major offensive in early 1972 (The "Easter Offensive"), with the objective of cutting South Vietnam in half. This was the first test for the ARVN and RF/PF militias without American ground support. In the battalions old TAOR, Quang Ngai City was captured by the NVA in early May. Historical analysis shows that, for both the ARVN and the militia units, their performance was uneven in quality. Some units performed well and others did not. Overall the South Vietnamese, backed by American firepower, performed adequately enough to give some hope for the future if the South Vietnamese had time to build its forces. The 2nd ARVN Division finally regained control of Quang Ngai City from the NVA in September, about the same time the NVA offensive throughout South Vietnam was repulsed.

After the Easter Offensive, desertions in the RF/PF units increased due to long separations from families, low pay and benefits, and discontent with unit commanders, hurting RF/PF performance. The RF/PF militia in I Corps, the southern portion of which the 5th/46th had operated, was considered by senior MACV advisors to be the most effective in the country. But they still experienced deficiencies, primarily in leadership at the platoon and company levels. There was also a lack of direction from their district chiefs and, of course, there was persistent corruption in local governments.

Following the NVA offensive, population security fell sharply in those areas where the NVA Divisions had forced their way into South Vietnam. Every province in the I Corps suffered serious security declines. Quang Tin Province, including Dragon Valley, Tam Ky, etc., lost over thirty-four percent of territorial control and Quang Ngai Province, the coastal plain, Binh Son, Batangan, etc., lost forty-three percent control.

The ability of the South Vietnamese to increase its span of control through pacification after the enemy's Easter Offensive, was simply nonexistent. The blame should be laid at the feet of American military planners early in the war and the South Vietnamese government. The South Vietnamese and the Communist forces in the south had simply drained the pool of fighting-age men in South Vietnam. There were simply no more men to expand the number of RF/PF units to secure and hold the South. The South Vietnamese had little choice other than to expand the operational areas of the existing RF/PF units, which greatly limited their effectiveness.

The situation continued to worsen and, on March 10, 1975, in the absence of American artillery and air support anywhere in South Vietnam, the North Vietnamese Communists launched their spring offensive. In short order the NVA overran Ban Me Thuot in the Central Highlands, a pivotal capital. The highlands were abandoned to protect the cities along the coast. The withdrawal of ARVN from the highlands opened the floodgates to the NVA and the I Corps bastions of Hue, Chu Lai and Quang Ngai City fell to the enemy on March 25. All that remained in I Corps under ARVN control was Danang City, where the scene quickly became one of fire, murder, looting and rape. Shortly after, the North Vietnamese Army entered Saigon and it was over.

It was during these final days before South Vietnam collapsed that the author of this book, like many other 5th/46th Battalion vets, watched the collapse of South Vietnam unfold each night on the television news. The scene of the North Vietnamese tanks smashing through the iron gates of the South Vietnamese parliament in Saigon was, for the author, too much to bear. He fell to the floor and cried, then prayed. The next Sunday he returned to weekly church services which he had not attended since joining the Army eight years prior. There was nothing left to do but seek God to fill the void inside him. After receiving bullet holes and shrapnel, and knowing the sacrifices of so many others in the battalion, all seemed for naught.

Transitions back to civilian life after Vietnam were not easy for the battalion's vets. John Hastings had transferred from Echo's Recon Platoon to the Divisions Long Range Reconnaissance (LRRP) when the battalion stood down in Chu Lai. One of his close friends in Echo Recon, who had transferred to another unit, stepped on a mine and lost both legs at the knees. Hastings had gone to see him. He remembered, "I went to see him at the Evacuation Hospital in Chu Lai and he wasn't doing well. He was a big country boy and, like anyone else, was having a tough time."

By pure coincidence, Hastings ended up in a bed next to his friend after he was wounded in July, 1971. He continued to offer his friend encouragement. Both were sent to Camp Zama, Japan together and later to Scott Air Force Base in St. Louis (both soldiers were from Illinois and thus not to far from their families).

Hastings recalled, "My friend was doing better by the time we got to St. Louis, his spirits were up until the time his family came in. Everyone was crying as if it was a funeral and my friend quickly went 'way south'. It hit me like a lightening bolt how much I had changed, and I realized coming back was going to be a little harder than I thought. I did some searching years later for my friend and found nothing. I suspect he's long gone; one last heartbreak on the way out of Chu Lai."

For many, the mental adjustment from the war zone to home life took time. And for some, the adjustment still continues. One battalion soldier, a medic, wrote, "Many years after getting out of the service I thought I had dealt with all the issues of Vietnam and was over it. But then I realized all I did was try to forget and that worked for a while. But all those horrible memories were still there in the back of my mind, just waiting until the right time to show themselves."

"At first it was slow and gradual. I didn't even know what it was. At times I was irritable and argumentative. Other times I was stressed out and depressed. Then something happened that made it all clear."

"My mother gave me the uniform I had worn home after I got out and a newspaper clipping about me being wounded. When I got home that night I fell completely apart. All the guilt, remorse and awful memories came flooding back. Everything hit me at once. At first all I could do was cry. And then, after I was cried out, I was overcome with sadness."

This medic was present when a comrade was killed by a large mine. The medic was knocked out and his body rolled over several times from the concussion of the blast. He recalled, "When I came-to, for a few minutes I couldn't see or hear. A few minutes later my eyes and ears started working. What I saw and heard was terrible. One man was killed, blown up beyond recognition, another, a sergeant lost both legs from the blast. Another man had a sucking chest wound. Others were hit in various parts of their bodies. My arm was cut, both my eyes were black with more cuts on my face and over the rest of my body. Eleven of us in all were hit. I was the only medic at the scene when it happened".

A day later, when the medic was in the hospital he was told one of his company's Lieutenants, whom he admired, was killed. "I was lying in a hospital bed when I received the news, eating real food and enjoying clean sheets instead of being in the field where I was needed".

Now, seeing his uniform again after many years, "Everything seemed so dark and hopeless. There didn't seem to be a point to going on. There was not anything that was going to change what had happened so many years ago and nothing was going to take my guilt away. There was only one thing to do; only one way out. I thought about just driving into a bridge support at 70 MPH. That should do it. The only thing that stopped me was the thought of my family."

John Forshag, Echo's Recon Platoon Sergeant recalls, "I arrived in New Orleans in the early afternoon of January 12, 1970. I was met by my wife of one year and two months, my parents, her parents and her brother. After a brief visit my parents drove my wife and me back to my childhood home. Later that evening just about sundown, I was walking into a tree line at the edge of the pasture with my dad to feed the cows. I wondered if it was safe to be walking out in the closing dusk without a weapon and I worried about stepping on a mine. Although I had been out of the field for five months (working in the TOC) there was still that uneasy feeling of venturing into an area without a weapon. It didn't take me long to get over it however, and be comfortable again hunting in the woods near home."

Charlie Company's Dennis Stevens notes, "For me, I chose to hide my being a Vietnam vet from others. I threw out all my fatigues and hid my photos. There was nothing in my house that would show I was a Vietnam vet. I thought that was the way to handle it. I went back to college, got married, etc. Very seldom did I admit I was a veteran. When my oldest son was fifteen he asked me if I knew any Vietnam vets. He was doing a project at school and needed a vet to come and speak. He didn't know that I was a Vietnam vet. I told him I was a vet. He was shocked, he didn't know. It was the first time that I went public and talked about being in Vietnam. It was gut wrenching. I still have issues with allowing the public to know that I am a vet".

Sergeant Robert Wolf, AKA "BuddyWolf" from Alpha Company admits, "I dealt with the memory of Vietnam in my own fashion, I forgot everything. That is why I now examine each and every event in such great detail as I have located over one hundred comrades. When Dave Taylor contacted me in 2003 about the book he was writing, I didn't even remember what company I was in. When I asked Willie Lavender about the day Joe Barcus was shot, Willie said, 'BuddyWolf, you were standing right next to him when it happened'. Perhaps I was, but I didn't remember. I am still in the process of relearning events I have long-since forgotten."

Robert Wolf is circumspect about his country's handling of the war. "You know, President Johnson began the Paris Peace Talks before I was drafted and they were still discussing what kind of table to sit at after I was discharged from the Army. Bureaucracy is the reason why I opted out of the Army. Besides, I don't take orders well. I'm too independent."

Since 2003, Robert Wolf, like other vets, sought out his long-lost comrades and several small reunions have taken place. He has also spoken to the families of vets no longer living who were in his company. One of those is the daughter of Barry Sweigart, who died years later after returning from Vietnam. Communicating with one of her father's vet friends has brought his daughter some understanding of her father. "I had a bit of a problem coping with what my Dad had to do in Vietnam", she wrote to Wolf. "I now fully understand why my Dad was the way he was at times. Looking back, my responses to him would have been a lot different. (But) I always told him I loved him so that was never an issue."

Vets talking with family members of other vets often helps provide understanding. This author called a battalion vet for some information but he was not available at the time of the call to talk. The vet had lost his right arm and right leg to a mine. His wife asked me on the phone about the man in front of her husband who tripped the mine and was killed. She asked me, "How old was he? Where was he from?

What about his family?" I gave her as much information as I had. Her voice quivered on the phone, telling me "For the first time I am able to connect with a name and a hometown of someone who died next to my husband". It was an eternal question for her that was now answered. Knowledge was gained, followed by sorrow.

Robert Chappell, one of the original Lieutenants of Bravo Company when they formed at Fort Hood, who eventually commanded the company, recalls, "When I got home from Vietnam I was stationed at Fort Dix, New Jersey. I was summoned to the post S-1 office by a Lieutenant Colonel who offered me an 'early out'. I smelled a rat and asked twice if I would have any reserve obligation and he told me, twice, 'no'. A year later I received a letter from Uncle Sam stating I had missed three reserve drills and if I missed another I would be activated in the Regular Army".

Chappell continues, "I showed up at the 86th Reserve Training Division in Rhode Island. I told a Major (a finance officer in his 50's) that I was lied to and I would resign my commission. He replied, 'Son, you're gonna serve your reserve obligation as a Captain or a private but you will serve your obligation!' I reported to a Colonel (Transportation Corps) who was wearing three ribbons and had to be sixty-plus years in age. It seemed like he never left the drill hall during his Army reserve career. He seemed distracted, embarrassed and even afraid of me. He didn't ask me anything."

"I was eventually assigned to command the divisions drill sergeant school. On my first weekend drill I conducted an inspection of the cadre. I noticed a few soldiers' hair looked a little weird so I ordered them to remove their cover. These guys were wearing wigs. I pulled one off and this guy's hair fell down past his shoulders and he was pissed. He said something to me that would have gotten him an article 15 in Vietnam. I told them to get a haircut for next months inspection. Not the high and tight cut the active Army had but I wanted it short. The next thing I knew I was in front of the CO and he's chewing me out, telling me not to screw up a good thing, take it easy on the men, etc."

For the two years that Chappell was in the reserve unit, the officers would not talk to him. He got along well with the NCO's and really bonded with a few of them, answering their questions about Vietnam. He remembers, "I quit wearing my ribbons on my khakis or dress greens but I did wear my CIB. I honestly feel the officers were either intimidated, embarrassed, didn't trust me or all of the above because I was the only officer in the unit that had been to Vietnam and seen the elephant. My combat experience was too much for them. I loved my experiences in the Army but this unit was not the Army."

Chappell had completed two years at a junior college prior to the Army and wanted to complete his education at the University of Rhode Island (URI) for a bachelor's degree. There were approximately eight to ten Vietnam vets enrolled at URI at that time. Chappell says, "We all very quickly recognized each other by a boonie cap, fatigue shirt, field jacket, etc. We all hung out together in between classes and ate at the same table at the Student union every day. Nobody but nobody would come over to talk to us or even look at us. I admit we were scary looking and enjoyed it. We were also four to six years older than they were and one hundred years more mature. We would walk down the street and people walking toward us would cross the street before they got to us and then cross back after we passed them."

Chappell attended URI when the Nationwide Moratorium (student strike) took place. He recalls "One day a contingent of students accompanied by a couple of very big football players who looked really nervous, approached our table and asked us to speak on the quadrangle the next day against the Vietnam War because they were sure that we didn't support it. To a man we told them to fuck off and move away before they got hurt. I heard later they got some sorority girls' brother who was a REMF in Saigon to speak. We were not present that day."

This author's post-Vietnam college experience was different. I had completed two years of college before entering the Army to become an officer (OCS). Upon my return I enrolled in the University of South Carolina (Columbia) in 1971 while my wife finished her Army commitment as a nurse at nearby Fort Jackson. I remember that this was the south, and war protests were simply not tolerated on campus, or the police would knock heads. Besides, this was 1971 and the in-thing was females wearing washed out t-shirts and going braless. That kept the young students attention on other things.

There were a lot of Vietnam vets like me trying to get their degrees and get on with life. We had no time for frivolities, so we took early morning classes back to back to allow more study time and studied hard, getting high grade-point averages. The kids just out of high school started classes at noon after partying all night. It was like night and day between them and us.

Some battalion vets tried to reconnect with past comrades soon after leaving the Army. David Tunnell, one of the original members of Echo's recon platoon from Fort Hood, had developed a special friendship with SP/4 Richard Amick of the battalion's Headquarters Company when Tunnell came out of the field to work on LZ Gator as an electrician. Tunnell left Vietnam first, promising Amick they would stay in touch.

SP/4 Amick along with Charles Wilson had been killed on May 12, 1969 when sappers attacked LZ Gator. They were killed as they guarded Lieutenant Colonel Barnes, who also perished in the attack. Tunnell surmised that Amick would have finished his tour in late 1969, and so while passing through Nashville, Tennessee at that time, he decided to look up his good friend. He also wanted to meet Amick's wife and child, born while Amick was at LZ Gator.

Tunnell knocked on the door of Amick's house and waited. A few seconds later, he was greeted by a young woman with a child in her arms. He asked excitedly, "Is Richard Amick here? I'm his good buddy from Vietnam!" Looking confused, the woman simply announced "My husband died in Vietnam." Then she slowly turned and went back into the house, leaving Tunnell standing there by himself, in front of a closed door, shocked and in pain.

Ron Cannon was wounded severely on April 21, 1968 when the recon platoon was decimated by mines on Hill 56. Cannon still carried the emotional wounds of losing his best friend that day, Ron Van Avery. Van Avery was killed at his platoon leaders side when Lieutenant Mrdjenovich stepped on the first of many mines detonated on the Hill.

Both Cannon and Van Avery were Portland, Oregon natives, and for many years Cannon tried to find Van Avery's wife and two children; but to no avail. On April 21, 1998, the thirty year anniversary of that tragic event, Cannon drove to the Oregon Vietnam War Memorial to place a personal letter next to his buddy's name which was etched on a wall.

Someone picked up the letter and took it to the Oregonian Newspaper to be used in conjunction with a story honoring veterans. Van Avery's name was mentioned and a friend of his children saw the article and told them about Cannon, the letter writer. A search to find him began. Just after Memorial Day, five weeks later, Ron Cannon opened the front door to the house of Ron Van Avery's daughter, Debbie. Standing by her side was her brother, Bryan. Cannon remembers the moment well. "I could see my buddy Ron's eyes in the eyes of his children. I was amazed. I saw my buddy again." The children and the veteran remain close friends.

A full twenty-nine years after Ernie Hopkins plugged all of his fingers and one thumb into nine holes in a fellow soldier's body to save his life, Hopkins learned his comrade, Jesse Hill, had survived those wounds. It happened to Charlie Company on July 30, 1970. Using his hands was all Hopkins could do to save Hill, because following that horrific blast, which resulted in so many casualties; there was a shortage of available medical supplies. The two met again at an Americal Division Veterans Association (ADVA) annual reunion in St. Louis, Missouri. When he came face to face with Hill, Hopkins didn't think it was the same man. "I don't think you're the guy I saved. Show me your chest."

Hill unbuttoned his shirt and showed him the nine scars received on that jungle hill so many years ago. Jesse Hill's wife, sister-in-law and her husband were all there and profusely thanked Hopkins for saving Hill's life.

The next morning, Hopkins noticed Hill in the lobby, sitting alone, just staring ahead. Hopkins asked him what he was thinking. "Ernie", he replied, "Tell me what happened. I passed out after you loaded me on the chopper. The next thing I remember is waking up in a hospital in Okinawa."

Later as part of a tour, the group went to a casino. Hill, who worked as a grounds keeper and maintenance man at a large church, said he felt uncomfortable going into the casino. His wife and sister-in-law replied, "That's OK honey, Ernie's taking us in." And with that, they grabbed the five foot, six-inch Hopkins, one woman on each arm, and entered. They would have a very good time.

Wounded soldiers returning home carried not only the mental scars of war but physical scars as well, as a constant reminder of pain and sacrifice.

Michael Stachowiak (Delta Company) stepped on a pressure release mine on February 22, 1970. He credits his squad leader who was next to him, Dave Morton, for saving his life. He recalls, "His quick action in cutting me out of a big cactus I had been blown into, then bandaging me and getting me on a resupply chopper saved my life. I literally owe him everything."

Stachowiak lost both legs above the knees, his right arm and right eye. He continued on in life to raise a family with his wife and three children (one boy and two girls) and now boasts about his five grandchildren. If you talk to him in his Nanicote, Pennsylvania home or see him rolling by in his wheelchair in town, he will tell you, "I'm the luckiest and richest man alive." Stachowiak still receives some stares from time to time, but looks at others as not really understanding much about him or where he's been from or what's truly important in life. "Life can be tough" he says, "But if you cherish it, it's truly wonderful."

Earl Brannon, a medic for Alpha Company lost both legs in a mine field near Nghiem Quong (1) on March 2, 1970. Jim Pene moved among the mines and saved his life. Bill Wolski was his platoon leader. Brannon went on to settle in southeast Texas, got married and raised two children; a boy and a girl. With an ample amount of land to farm and hunt, Brannon got on with life's work, which included working at Shell Oil. But he always raised eyebrows when the "Legless Man" worked on his land, hoisting hay bales onto his pickup truck, changing tires or working on his house by the highway.

One of Brannon's friends had lost his only son in a boating accident. He became despondent and decided to drive his truck to the levy, with his pistol on the front seat, and end it all. While driving past Brannon's home he saw the legless Brannon pulling up a pack of shingles onto his roof to make some repairs. Brannon's friend thought to himself "If he can persevere like that, then I can try to stay alive" Another lady who was mentally depressed about her life's situation drove by and saw Brannon up on the roof the same day. She told him later by e-mail her problems had been brought down to size.

In 2009, at the Americal Division Veterans Association annual reunion in Shreveport, Louisiana, Brannon met up again with Jim Pene, the man who saved his life and Bill Wolksi, his platoon leader. They, with their spouses and close friends could be seen moving about in a close, tight circle of friends, Wolksi pushing Brannon in his wheelchair, the other vets clinging closely, the wives following the tight band of men. Brannon's wife told her husband's comrades, "Thank you for these last thirty-nine years of life with Earl"

Others who returned from Vietnam with serious wounds died years later as a direct result of those wounds. Joel Simpson and Kyle Holfeltz are two names added to the Vietnam Wall in Washington D.C.

PFC Joel Simpson was the recon platoon leader's RTO in early 1970. He took a sniper round to the base of his spine on February 7, 1970, paralyzing him at the age of twenty-one. In July, 1983 he died of complications from his paralysis at the age of thirty-four.

SP/4 Kyle Holfeltz, also in the recon platoon, was seriously wounded on February 1, 1971 during the attack on Hill 76. He died in November, 1994.

A few battalion vets, mercifully a few, could not contend with the anguished memories of Vietnam and took their lives. One was the brave and bold but erratic platoon leader of Alpha Company, who at one point collected the ears of his enemy dead. He took his life in Pennsylvania after marrying and having children. Another, Robert Whiteside, married with children, took his life in 1988. Whiteside had been a platoon leader in Charlie Company and remained on active duty several years after returning from Vietnam. He struggled with PTSD (Post Traumatic Stress Syndrome) and devoted himself to helping others who also struggled. The pamphlet at his funeral pronounced, "In death, he has found the peace he fought so hard to find here on earth."

The Vietnam Wall has become a catharsis for many of the battalion's vets, as it has for many other Vietnam veterans. One battalion vet from Alpha Company saw two soldiers in Vietnam die in separate incidents where he should have been. He recalls, "Two people died in my place. It took PTSD therapy and a couple visits to The Wall to help me deal with it and move on. I guess the Lord just wasn't through with me."

Those who suffer the longest are the families and friends of the men who were killed in Vietnam. Sergeant Mike Bastian (Alpha Company) was killed by mortar fire in the early morning hours of January 2, 1969. His company commander made a poor choice for a night defensive position deep in the mountains west of Quang Ngai city. He was subsequently relieved of command.

The neurosurgeon in Chu Lai who operated on Bastian's head wound felt compelled to write the parents a letter. The family's devastation was far-reaching and permanent. After the funeral service (Catholic Mass) Bastains sister remembered that her father "Never set foot inside the church again. He would leave my mother off each Sunday and wait for her in the car."

Bastian's girlfriend, Diane Rudderow whom he dated throughout high school, said they had planned to get married, even though they fought a lot. "I wanted to settle down and he wanted to play around with other girls while we dated" she recalls, "But if I dated anyone else he would get jealous. Our relationship was off and on as things tended to be as teenagers. But he always had my heart."

Bastian, with an "Adventurous spirit", enlisted in the Army in June 1967. Diane remembers, "He was one hundred percent Army." Diane became engaged to someone else, but Bastian's parents took her with them to visit Mike at Fort Dix, New Jersey at the completion of Basic Training, before he shipped out to Fort Polk, Louisiana. They had a picture taken together at the time.

Fort Polk was an Army training post most people remember with scorn. Bastian liked it and his tough Vietnam-oriented training. In a letter to his mother he wrote, "Training is rugged but I like it. I thought this place would be crawling with alligators. We haven't seen one yet. When we get our first pass, I got a couple of guys talked into going on an alligator hunt."

Diane was married in December 1967, but the marriage did not last. The picture of her with Mike Bastian taken at Fort Dix is still on her book shelf in her home. Mike was close to his mother and wrote her constantly but his mother would not share the letters with Diane, even though he often asked in his letters, "Have you seen Diane?" So, for her, there has never been closure.

Diane recalls, "The mother of my daughters friend came over about a year ago and took me into my kitchen. She said, 'I have to talk to you. Mike is in this house. He is always watching over you". Now, as Diane moves into her senior years, she is left to ponder what was, what is, and what could have been.

Amy Chadwick also planned to marry her fiancé, Stephen Warren, one of the Echo Recon soldiers killed on Hill 76 on February 1, 1971. In 2003 she wrote, "It's been thirty years and I can still remember the face, the shades worn when he boarded the plane in Rochester, NY. That was the last time I saw him alive. That was July 1970. I still have every single letter written to me. I have an 8 by 10 US Army picture, framed. He's 'frozen in time' within that frame. We were engaged, and planned on being married when he returned. That never happened. I asked him to remove the sunglasses and he only smiled. I now know why. Men didn't cry at that time, and he was. I still carry that memory and always will. He was my 'soulmate'. I still love you."

A soldier's death and the notification to the family brought extreme sorrow and pain. And that sorrow was marked in different ways, depending on the situations in the soldier's family, all different, because roads through life are different.

Jack Harra was the younger brother of Lee Harra, who was killed on January 30, 1969, by the horrific mine blast caused by an enemy insurgent pretending to be a "Chieu Hoi". Jack remembers, "I was six years younger than Lee so we were not close personally but he was a role model for me. My parents separated when I was age six, so Lee, rather than being a brother, became a father figure for me."

"My Dad was informed first by a military officer about Lee's death. He was divorced from my mother at that time. After the officer inquired, 'Are you going to be OK?' my father assured him he would be and then he went to the local Sears store where my mother worked to inform her. My father was an alcoholic and he went into a tail spin after that. A few years later he went into treatment. He died in February 1993. My sister and I remained in Minnesota but, after reading some of Lee's letters he mailed from Vietnam, I don't think he would have remained around town had he lived. He really wanted to travel when he got out of the Army, and not get tied down."

Lee's sister Pat, was one year younger than Lee and they were very close. She ended up with his medals and his Vietnam letters. Pat recalls, "When the notice came that Lee was killed, I was snowmobiling that weekend up north in a remote area. My parents were angry because they could not contact me, it was an understandable reaction, they knew how close I was to Lee. They put my name and picture on a local news channel and a friend saw my picture and notified me. I understand Lee suffered terrible wounds. The casket was closed."

"As time has gone on I think that Lee was lucky. When I have seen other people return from Vietnam with their wounds, I know Lee would not have wanted to live like that. I still have a photo album Lee and I made with pictures of us growing up, just him and me. Looking back at the time of his death, when his body was shipped home, I was in a fog. My questions have now been answered with the research on this book. It's good to know Lee was liked by his fellow soldiers. I am not surprised."

Cecil Olsen (Bravo Company) was walking point on January 8, 1971, pushing through the thick brush to avoid the mines hidden on trails. At 3:55PM he was hit by a burst of AK-47 fire and was killed instantly.

His nephew, David Olsen, wrote in 2004, "I never had a chance to meet my Uncle Cecil in person; he was killed in action before I was born. However, through family memories I have always felt he is still very much alive in spirit. Had he lived, I think we would have had a lot in common. Dad has often commented to me in recent years of how much I remind him of Cecil. Even though he passed away almost five years before I was born, I have always felt a special connection with Uncle Cecil".

He continues, "I wish to thank not only all veterans but especially those who were in his unit, or knew him just prior to him being sent to combat. In recent years my dad has come into correspondence with some of the men in his platoon who have helped dad receive some closure (as well as myself and our family). He and Cecil were close brothers, and I can't thank these guys enough for sharing their experiences. They have helped dad a lot".

Tom Markunas (Alpha Company) along with Alvin Merricks was killed in a horrific mine explosion on May 9, 1969. His wife, Lucille, who never remarried, found a poem many years ago that she reads often, reminding her of her husband:

Don't think of him as gone away -
his journey's just begun,
life holds so many facets
this earth is only one.
Just think of him as resting
from the sorrow and the tears,
in a place of warmth and comfort,
where there are no days and years.
Think how he must be wishing
that we could know that day,
how nothing but our sadness
can really pass away.
Think of him as living
in the hearts of those he touched ...
for nothing loved is ever lost ...
and he is loved so much.
(Author unknown)

William Jeffrey Hodges (Charlie Company) was killed on LZ Dottie on December 4, 1968, when a grenade exploded. His cousin wrote in 2004, "On this November 3, 2004, you are not forgotten dear Jeff. Your sacrifice for your country had been vindicated. I will see you on the other side, dear cousin."

Michael Dinda (Charlie Company) was killed by small arms fire on December 29, 1969. His younger sister Susan recalled in 2008, "Mike was my older brother and he was a real good guy. He was a kind soul and he had a great sense of humor. After 38 years (I was 10 when he died), there still isn't a day that goes by that I do not think about him and wish that I had been able to grow old together with him. I know God took him away for a reason and I want to believe that Mike is watching over me and my family every day. Thank you to all our brave men and women who have fought and continue to fight for our freedom. I love you Mike!"

Larry Burkholder (Bravo Company) was killed in the attack on his company's position during the dark and rainy night of October 5, 1969. A friend from his hometown of Portland, Indiana, Melodi, had these recollections in 2002:

"Larry and I graduated from Portland High School, Class of 1966, the best of friends. We had gone to school together since the third grade. The memory that prevails the most of those years is that Larry never learned to drive, thinking surely he would die in a violent auto accident. He either walked or gladly paid for the gas to go where he wanted."

"I spent the evening of my 21st birthday (8/11/69) celebrating it with Larry. He was to ship out the following morning and didn't want to go to sleep. When 'Bills' closed we headed to the country to go fishin' til the wee hours of the morning. I will never forget that day as long as I live. Larry was sure he wouldn't live to turn to 21. He was sure he would die and even told me that the Army would bring me a Christmas present in a green bag. He told me that I wouldn't be able to tell it was him, just his dog tags for recognition."

"Larry's life was taken in battle on October 5, 1969, just 31 days before his 21st birthday. The Army did bring him home as he thought, identified only by his tags."

"Larry I miss you and will always wonder what your life would have been like if you had survived Vietnam. You are still missed by many of us today, 33 years after your death".

Most of the battalion's vets returned home and integrated into civilian life, taking up their chosen professions and raised families. Some remained connected to the Army on active duty or in the Army Reserve or National Guard, and moved up in the enlisted and officer ranks.

They are black, white, oriental, Hispanic and American Indian. They are farmers, business leaders, work in the trades, business owners or otherwise self-employed; they are doctors, lawyers, Presidents and CEO's. Many are now reaching the decision to retire. Regardless of their life's work, Vietnam has stayed with them, each day reminded in some small way, a sound, a smell or an image.

Increasingly the battalion's vets are drawn to veterans groups such as the Americal Division Veterans Association or smaller groups of comrades, to reunite periodically and reminisce. Others still struggle with memories and find it hard to reunite.

And so dear reader, now the written account of "Our War" has come to an end, forty-three years after the battalion's first soldier stepped on the soil of South Vietnam. The foregoing "Revelations" are only a handful of many. The effect of each individual soldiers sacrifice in the Vietnam conflict with the 5th/46th Infantry Battalion continues to be lived today and into the future.

Lives were changed and continue to be changed. But when will the process of closure end? Perhaps, as one relative of the battalion's dead suggested above, only when we see each other again, "On the other side" - in Gods time.

Appendix A - Lest We Forget

Soldiers of the 5th/46th Infantry Battalion, Vietnam who made the ultimate sacrifice for their country

"Night will be no more, nor will they need light from lamp or sun, for the Lord God shall give them light, and they shall reign forever and ever."
Revelation 22:5

Rank	Name	Unit	Date	Home of Record
PVT	Richard Atwood	Co B	11 Apr 68	Cleveland, OH
PFC	Ronald F. Van Avery	Co E	21 Apr 68	Portland, OR
2LT	Charles Mrdjenovich	Co E	21 Apr 68	Ft. Bragg, NC
SP/4	James Wallace Rudd	Co E	21 Apr 68	Halifax, VA
PFC	Danny West	Co B	1 May 68	Fort Smith, AR
SP/4	Edwin Grant Newell	HHC	19 May 68	Xenia, OH
SP/4	Gerald Thomas Parmeter	Co A	24 May 68	Cazadero, CA
PFC	Daniel Lee Powell	Co B	26 May 68	Artesia, CA
PFC	Wayne Austin Decker	Co A	13 Jun 68	Elkhart, IN
PFC	Woodrow Davis	Co B	15 Jun 68	Holly Hill, SC
SP/4	Roosevelt Hurst	Co B	5 Jul 68	Saraland, AL
SSG	William Paul Webber	Co A	7 Jul 68	Denville, NJ
SP/4	Donald Charles Wilson	Co B	7 Jul 68	Portage, IN
SP/4	Charles Duane Bennett	Co A	7 Jul 68	Calhoun, GA
SP/4	Roland Mike Sheredos	Co B	8 Jul 68	Long Island, NY

Rank	Name	Unit	Date	Hometown
PFC	George Vander Dussen	Co B	10 Jul 68	Artesia, CA
PFC	Stephen Ryan Richards	Co A	28 Jul 68	Burlington, NC
PFC	Paul James Meaux	Co E	17 Aug 68	Kaplan, LA
PFC	Bruce William Poulson	Co A	18 Aug 68	Corona Del Mar, CA
CPT	Wilburn Chastain Gideon	HHC	23 Aug 68	Dilley, TX
SGT	Robert Salter	Co A	23 Aug 68	Parrish, AL
PFC	Joel Mitchell LaRoche	Co A	23 Aug 68	Huntington Beach, CA
PFC	Steven Charles Vinter	Co A	23 Aug 68	Sacramento, CA
SP/4	Roger Ralph Moll	HHC	23 Aug 68	Bay City, MI
PFC	Clay Holt Jr.	Co B	28 Aug 68	Marshall, MO
PFC	Tom Michael Thomas	Co B	28 Aug 68	New Philadelphia, OH
PFC	Edward Merl Jackson	Co E	1 Sep 68	Athens, TX
SP/4	Albert Eugene Rose	Co D	17 Sep 68	South Lyon, MI
PFC	Willie Ray Lay	Co B	22 Sep 68	Fairhope, AL
PFC	Teodoro Santellan	Co D	23 Sep 68	Grant, WI
PFC	Jerry Lee Halpenny	Co C	13 Oct 68	Enterprise, WV
SP/4	John Martin Horton Jr.	Co C	19 Oct 68	Suffern, NY
1LT	Donald Thomas Penney	Co E	28 Oct 68	Willseyville, NY
PFC	William Frederic Meinecke	Co C	7 Nov 68	Milwaukee, WI
PFC	John Ferdinand Schaffer	Co C	7 Nov 68	Altus, AR
PFC	Garryl David Cardinal	Co A	9 Nov 68	Montrose, MN
PFC	John Rufus Gaston Jr.	Co A	29 Nov 68	Washington, DC
SP/4	William Jeffrey Hodges	Co C	4 Dec 68	Silver Spring, MD
PFC	Frederico S. Matias-Santana	Co D	6 Dec 68	New York, NY
PFC	Grayson Craft	Co A	17 Dec 68	Magee, MS
SGT	Vincent Thomas Daiello	Co C	20 Dec 68	New York, NY
1LT	Thomas Gary Sikes	Co C	20 Dec 68	Jacksonville, FL
PFC	Ambrose P. Tanasso Jr.	Co C	24 Dec 68	Randolf, MA
SGT	Michael Francis Bastian	Co A	2 Jan 69	Sewell, NJ
PFC	Richard Clair Seely	Co A	2 Jan 69	Berwick, PA
SP/4	Matthew Winston Thornton	Co B	11 Jan 69	Alexandria, VA
PFC	Harry James Dorsey	Co D	13 Jan 69	Nesmith, SC
SSG	Freddie Allen Bonetti	HHC	18 Jan 69	Brady, TX

Rank	Name	Unit	Date	Hometown
SP/4	William Blaine Rollins Jr.	Co B	18 Jan 69	St. Marys, WV
PFC	Marvin LeRoy Erickson	Co A	22 Jan 69	Ashland, WI
PFC	Gary Lee Payne	Co A	22 Jan 69	Tucker, GA
PFC	Tyrone Melvin Wright	Co A	22 Jan 69	Philadelphia, PA
PFC	Thomas Graham Jr.	Co D	27 Jan 69	College Park, GA
SGT	Lewis Andres Callaway III	Co B	28 Jan 69	West Point, GA
SP/4	Lee Hamilton Harra	Co A	30 Jan 69	Owatonna, MN
PFC	Bobby Dean Anthony	Co C	31 Jan 69	Cherryville, NC
1LT	Irvin Willis Prosser Jr.	Co A	31 Jan 69	Saquoit, NY
SP/4	Albert Mc Cullough	HHC	22 Feb 69	Bridgeport, CT
SFC	Herbert Raymond Grant	HHC	23 Feb 69	San Rafael, CA
PFC	Gerald Wayne Gwaltney	Co C	23 Feb 69	Newport News, VA
PFC	Michael Ray Rommel	Co B	27 Feb 69	Clarksville, IN
SP/4	Edward Lee Gilliard	HHC	2 Mar 69	Heildelberg, MS
PFC	William Leroy McFarland	Co A	14 Mar 69	Lancaster, PA
SP/4	James John Lister	Co C	21 Mar 69	Burley, ID
1LT	Curtis Onchi	Co B	24 Mar 69	Portland, OR
PFC	Wayne Michael Randall	Co B	17 Apr 69	Passumpsic, VT
SP/4	Larry Dean Bleything	Co B	18 Apr 69	Ottumwa, IA
SGT	Larry Eugene Kigar	Co C	2 May 69	Baring, MO
SGT	Roy Lee Arnold	Co A	3 May 69	Holden, MO
SGT	Thomas William Markunas	Co A	9 May 69	New York, NY
SP/4	Alvin Merricks	Co A	9 May 69	Orlando, FL
PFC	Sam L. Eggert	Co C	10 May 69	Tucumcari, NM
PFC	Thomas Wayne Cummins	Co B	12 May 69	Marysville, CA
SP/4	Richard Michael Amick	HHC	12 May 69	Nashville, TN
LTC	Alfred Barnes	HHC	12 May 69	Montclair, NJ
SP/4	Charles E. Wilson Jr.	HHC	12 May 69	Greenwood, MS
SP/4	Roy Edward Clark	Co C	24 May 69	Culloden, WV
PFC	Tomas Gomez-Robles	Co B	3 Jun 69	Caguas, PR
PFC	Mitchell Harvey Sandman	Co C	3 Jun 69	Syosset, NY
SP/4	Harry Richard Italiano	Co C	3 Jun 69	Suitland, MD
SGT	Michael Gregory Scherf	Co C	3 Jun 69	Golden, CO
SP/4	David Allen Curtis	Co D	16 Jun 69	Greece, NY
SP/4	Robert Douglas Bittle	Co A	21 Jun 69	Arkansas City, KS
PFC	Danny G. Endicott	Co E	21 Jun 69	Columbus, OH

Rank	Name	Unit	Date	Hometown
PFC	Andrew Frank Kokesh	Co E	21 Jun 69	Aitkin, MN
PFC	Gordon Alan McMillan	Co A	21 Jun 69	East Meadow, NY
PFC	William Franklin Malone	Co E	21 Jun 69	Afton, TN
PFC	Robert Nozewski	Co E	21 Jun 69	Dearborn, MI
PFC	Larry Michael Bryan	Co D	2 Jul 69	Highland, MI
SSG	Melvin Shoichi Fujita	Co D	2 Jul 69	Honolulu, HI
PFC	Kenneth Arthur Mahl	Co D	2 Jul 69	New Orleans, LA
PFC	Timothy Craig Nunnally	Co D	2 Jul 69	Pico Rivera, CA
SP/4	Robert Walker Peterson	Co A	8 Jul 69	Jacksonville, FL
SGT	John D. Martin	Co A	13 Jul 69	Lamesa, TX
PFC	Roger McElhaney	Co A	16 Jul 69	Jamestown, PA
PFC	William C. Proctor Jr.	Co D	18 Jul 69	Burbank, CA
PFC	Myron Keith Renne	Co A	23 Jul 69	Glasgow, MO
PFC	Everett W. Brauburger	Co A	24 Jul 69	Soda Springs, ID
SP/4	Albert Vick Jr.	Co B	25 Jul 69	Goldsboro, NC
PFC	James Franklin Talbott	Co B	6 Aug 69	Kewanna, IN
PFC	Roosevelt Abraham Jr.	Co A	7 Aug 69	Wilmington, NC
PFC	Leo Joe Adakai	Co A	7 Aug 69	Blackfoot, ID
PFC	Charles Lenard Reefer	Co A	7 Aug 69	Jamestown, PA
PVT	Abelardo Rodriguez-Guzman	Co A	10 Aug 69	Hato Rey, PR
PFC	James Henry Brown Jr.	Co C	21 Aug 69	McClellanville, SC
SP4	Laurence Arthur Millett	Co B	31 Aug 69	Norway, ME
PFC	Thomas Glenn Cornwell	Co D	13 Sep 69	Port Huron, MI
PFC	Robert Lee Person	Co D	14 Sep 69	Richmond, IN
PFC	Eric Anthony Lord	Co C	22 Sep 69	Philadelphia, PA
PFC	James Irvin Yates	Co D	22 Sep 69	Mount Eden, KY
SP/4	Thomas Federick Lawler	Co C	24 Sept 69	Tampa, FL
PFC	Larry Gene Burkholder	Co B	5 Oct 69	Portland, IN
PFC	Shelby Gene Foster	Co B	5 Oct 69	Ohley, WV
SP/4	Robert Marion Haynes Jr.	Co B	5 Oct 69	Amarillo, TX
PFC	Ralph Ernest Piano Jr.	Co B	5 Oct 69	Madison, NJ
SP/4	Frank Davis Jr.	Co D	19 Oct 69	Logansport, LA
SGT	David Lawrence Napier	Co C	3 Nov 69	Glen Allen, VA
2LT	Larry Leroy Betts	Co B	21 Nov 69	Eagle River, AK
PFC	David G. Ritz	Co D	26 Nov 69	Croghan, NY
SGT	Russell Eugene Gedeon	Co C	7 Dec 69	River Grove, IL

Rank	Name	Unit	Date	Hometown
SP/4	Daryl Wayne Patrick	Co E	16 Dec 69	Murdock, KS
SP/4	Michael Joseph Dinda	Co C	29 Dec 69	Kensington, CT
SGT	Thomas Lee Blanks	Co A	4 Jan 70	Riverdale, GA
SP/4	Earl William Marlin Jr.	Co E	6 Jan 70	Keokuk, IA
PFC	Gilbert Albert Benaim	Co D	14 Jan 70	New Orleans, LA
2LT	Martin Sully Schiller Jr.	Co C	14 Jan 70	Memphis, TN
SP/4	Carlton F. Mc Cagg	Co C	16 Jan 70	Chatham, NY
2LT	Michael George Foutz	Co B	21 Jan 70	Roseburg, OR
SP/4	Michael Robert Glenn	Co A	11 Feb 70	Smyrna, GA
SP/4	Dickey Larue Cooley	Co D	19 Feb 70	Galax, GA
PFC	Daniel Aguilera	Co A	3 Mar 70	Cutler, CA
PFC	Richard Henry Durant	Co B	12 Mar 70	Vernon, NY
PFC	Robert Wayne Culver	Co D	17 Mar 70	Eureka, LA
SP/4	Oscar Allen Connell	Co D	31 Mar 70	Montevallo, AL
SGT	Clayton Donald Whitcher	Co D	7 Apr 70	Cuyahoga Falls, OH
SSG	Carl Timothy Bauer	Co B	21 Apr 70	Rock Island, IL
SGT	Ronald Eugene Dills	Co B	7 May 70	Valparaiso, IN
PFC	Larry Austin Foster	Co D	8 May 70	Gastonia, NC
SGT	Robert Joseph Huddleston	Co A	12 May 70	La Follette, TN
SGT	Guy Lynn Stokes Jr.	Co D	16 May 70	Commerce, GA
SP/4	Bruce Joseph Nichols	Co C	21 May 70	Lower Burrell, PA
1LT	Michael Stephen Mesich	Co C	21 May 70	Milwaukee, WI
1LT	Gary Ruel Mower	Co C	22 May 70	Fairview, UT
SP/4	David Concepcion-Nieves	Co C	10 Jun 70	Arecibo, PR
SGT	Stephen Edward Krajeski	Co C	12 Jun 70	Groveland, MA
SFC	Donald Eugene Auten	Co C	30 Jul 70	Cramerton, NC
PFC	Jerold Franklin	Co C	30 Jul 70	Greenville, MS
SSG	Dale Ervin Sathoff	Co C	30 Jul 70	St. Louis, MO
PFC	Edward James Whitton	Co C	30 Jul 70	Gaston, OR
PFC	Donald Dean Layton	Co C	4 Aug 70	Aberdeen, SD
PFC	Robert William Hart	Co C	17 Aug 70	Chicago, IL
SGT	James Brown Jr.	Co B	16 Sep 70	Port Allen, LA
PFC	Donald Lee Percy	Co B	16 Sep 70	Devers, TX
SP/4	Gary Lee Abrahamson	Co D	20 Sep 70	Albia, IA
PFC	Jerome Raymond Frilling	Co C	30 Sep 70	Sidney, OH
SGT	Larry Wayne Berkholtz	Co B	1 Oct 70	Sullivan, WI

PFC	Thomas Charles Schiess	Co A	10 Oct 70	Edgewater, NJ
SP/4	John Joseph Farnsworth Jr.	Co B	13 Nov 70	Frackville, PA
SP/4	Monroe Alan Powers	Co B	13 Nov 70	Newport News, VA
SP/4	Robert Carl Gottier	Co D	24 Nov 70	East Stroudsburg, PA
1LT	Michael James Petrashune	Co C	11 Dec 70	Lyon Mountain, NY
PFC	Dennis Ralph Moreno	Co D	14 Dec 70	Hay Springs, NE
PFC	Cecil Chancey Olsen	Co B	8 Jan 71	Rowley, IA
PFC	Edward Wayne Bethards	Co D	11 Jan 71	Novato, CA
PFC	Lee William Clore	Co B	11 Jan 71	Westchester, NY
PFC	Dennis Ray Easter	Co B	13 Jan 71	Brownsville, PA
SSG	Joseph Walter Casino	Co E	1 Feb 71	Dafter, MI
SGT	Gordon Lee Crawford	Co E	1 Feb 71	Ft. Wayne, IN
SSG	Stephen Alan Moore	Co E	1 Feb 71	Nitro, WV
SGT	Richard Dale Randolph	Co E	1 Feb 71	St. Johns, MI
SP/4	Stephen Edward Warren	Co E	1 Feb 71	Rochester, NY
SP/4	Joseph Lamar Stone	Co A	3 Feb 71	Desert Hot Springs, CA
PVT	Gary Martin Cohen	HHC	11 Mar 71	Dartmouth, MA
SP/4	Thomas Lee Zeigler	Co C	22 Mar 71	Hamill, SD
SP/4	James Patrick Alexander	HHC	5 Apr 71	Green Rock, IL

BIBLIOGRAPHY

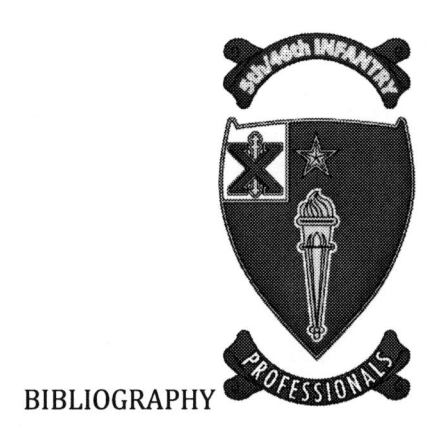

ARCHIVAL DOCUMENTS

Combat after Action Reports (National Archives, College Park, Maryland)

HQ, 198th Infantry Brigade, Americal Division, Combat after Action Report, Operation Muscatine, 20 December 1967 to 10 June 1968. Report dated 17 September 1968

HQ, 198th Infantry Brigade, Americal Division Combat after Action Report, Operation Binh Son Support, 3-5 December 1967. Report dated 15 February 1968

HQ, 198th Infantry Brigade, Americal Division Combat after Action Report, Operation Burlington Trail, 9 April – 11 November 1968. Report dated 9 January 1969

HQ, 198th Infantry Brigade, Americal Division Combat after Action Report, Night Movement and Engagement in Operation Burlington Trail, 081850 June 1968

HQ, 198th Infantry Brigade, Americal Division Combat after Action Report, Operation Gator, 140400-141700 Jan 1968

HQ, 198th Infantry Brigade, Americal Division, Combat after Action Report, Operation Russell Beach, 3 January 1969 – 21 July 1969. Report dated 6 September 1969

HQ, 198th Infantry Brigade, Americal Division, Combat after Action Report, Stability in Conjunction with a Combined Action Platoon. 201000 August – 131400 September 1969. Report dated 28 November 1969

HQ, 198th Infantry Brigade, Americal Division, Combat after Action Report, Operation Geneva Park, 18 March 1969 – 1 March 1971. Report dated 18 March 1971

HQ, 198th Infantry Brigade, 23rd Infantry Division, Combat after Action Report, Operation Middlesex Peak, 010601 March-011200 July 1971, 17 July 1971

HQ, 198th Infantry Brigade, Americal Division, Combat after Action Report, Operation Wheeler/Wallowa, 041200-281020 July 1968

HQ, 5th Battalion, 46th Infantry Battalion, 198th Light Infantry Brigade Combat after Action Report – Stability in Conjunction With A Combined Action Platoon, 201000 Aug to 131400 Sep 1969. Report dated 28 November 1969

HQ, 5th Battalion, 46th Infantry Battalion, 198th Light Infantry Brigade Combat after Action Report – Search and Clear 4 to 27 October 1969

5th/46th Infantry Battalion Daily Staff Journals (National Archives, College Park, Maryland)

S-1, S-2/S-3, S-4 & S-5 Daily Staff Journal (DA Form 1594), 5th/46th Infantry Battalion, 4 April 1968 - 3 May 1971 (Includes 3-page Journal entries covering sequence of events, in chronological order, of the battalions move from Fort Hood, Texas to Chu Lai Airbase, Americal Division) Approximate size of documentation is 23,000 pages of Journal entries.

Fragmentary Orders (FRAGORDS) (National Archives, College Park, Maryland)

FRAGORD 1-68, Confirmation of Verbal Orders Re: Task Force Roach) Task Force Roach – Chu Lai, 080800 22 April 1968

FRAGORD 2 (Reconnaissance) and FRAGORDS 3 through 20 to OPORD 2-68, Task Force Cooksey Operations, Burlington Trail, From CO, 198th Infantry Brigade

FRAGORD 7-69, Redeployment of the 5th/46th Infantry Battalion to Reinforce Heavy Contact Developed by the 196th Infantry Brigade Vicinity Hiep Duc District 220800 August 1969

FRAG ORD 1-70 (to OPORD 8-69) Nantucket Beach, HQ, 198th Infantry Brigade, 101200 March 1970

The History of the Joint Chiefs of Staff
The Joint Chiefs of Staff and the War in Vietnam 1971-1973, Webb, William. Part 1, The Conduct of the War, 1971-early 1972 PP 208-213, 225-226 (National Archives, College Park, Maryland)

Memorandums (National Archives, College Park, Maryland)

Mines and Booby Traps, HQ, Americal Division (AVDF-CG), October 1968

Headquarters, Americal Division (AVDF-BCZ) 10 November 1969 Subject: Daily Intsum #84-69 Enemy Tasks To Be Achieved in November 1969

Organizational History – The 198th Infantry Brigade 1967-1971, Undated

Request for additional US Forces, HQ 198th Infantry Brigade, 7 November 1969

Sample Plan – Defense of Northern Rocket Pocket, HQ, 198th Infantry Brigade, 25 June 1969

Termination of Operations Wheeler/Wallowa and Burlington Trail, Disposition Form dated 7 November 1968 to Chief of Staff, Americal Division, from Major Colin Powell, ACofS, G3

Operational Orders (OPORDS) (National Archives, College Park, Maryland)

OPORD 3-68 (Operation Golden Fleece) HQ, 198th Infantry Brigade, 270800 September 1968

OPORD 4-68 (Defense of Vital Installations and Offensive Operations) HQ, 198th Infantry Brigade, 301400 November 1968

OPORD 6-68 (Support of Specific Pacification Offensive) HQ, 198th Infantry Brigade, 191400 November 1968

OPORD 1-69 (Operation Russell Beach) Task Force Cooksey, LZ Bayonet, 07 January 1969

OPORD 2-69 (Realignment of Brigade Forces) HQ, 198th Infantry Brigade, 021200 March 1969

OPORD 4-69 (Recapitulation of Tactical Missions), Geneva Park Operations, HQ, 198th Infantry Brigade, 291600 April 1969

OPORD 5-69 (Defense Against Rocket/Mortar Attack) HQ, 198th Infantry Brigade, 301200 April 1969

OPORD 8-69 (Nantucket Beach) HQ, 198th Infantry Brigade, 161400 July 1969

OPORD 10-69 (Golden Fleece) HQ, 198th Infantry Brigade 241200 September 1969

OPORD 2-70 (Relocation of Brigade Forces), HQ 198th Infantry Brigade, 201200 March 1970

OPORD 3-70 (Recapitulation of Tactical Missions) HQ, 198th Infantry Brigade, 191500 March 1970

OPORD 4-70 (Defense Against Rocket/Mortar Attack) HQ, 198th Infantry Brigade, Undated with Reference to Americal Secret Division Message 230700 December 1969

OPORD 6-70 (Golden Fleece) – Annex A (Intelligence) HQ 198th Infantry Brigade, 211200 August 1970

OPORD 8-70 (Combined Fall-Winter Military Campaign Plan 1970-1971) HQ, 198th Infantry Brigade 240700 October 1970

OPORD 9-70 (Rice Denial) HQ, 198th Infantry Brigade 240800 November 1970

OPORD 1-71 (Adjustment of Battalion TAOR's with 6th ARVN Regiment) HQ, 198th Infantry Brigade 21 February 1971

Operational Plans (OPPLANS) (National Archives, College Park, Maryland)

OPLAN 1-68 Task Force Cooksey, HQ LZ Bowman (Interdiction of Enemy Forces in the Phuoc Chau Valley) 121800 August 1968

OPPLAN 2-68 Natural Disaster Relief Plan, HQ 198th INF BDE, 100800 July 1968

OPPLAN 1-69 Task Force Cooksey, HQ, 198th INF BDE, LZ Bayonet (Russell Beach) 231500H, January 1969

OPPLAN 10-69 Americal Division & 198th Brigade Redeployment, 200800 SEP 1969

OPPLAN 13-69 198th Brigade Secures My Lai (4) for operation with duration of two weeks. 281800 December 1969

OPPLAN 3-70 Noncombatant Emergency relocation and Evacuation, HQ, 198th INF BDE, 211400 March 1970

OPPLAN 10-70 PW Recovery Operations, HQ, 198th INF BDE, 24 Aug 70

OPPLAN 1-71 Anti-Demonstration Operations as Necessary to protect Personnel, Military property and to Restore Order, HQ, 198th INF BDE, 16 Jan 1971

Operational Summaries (National Archives, College Park, Maryland)

HQ, 198th Infantry Brigade, Americal Division

   SITREP #88-68 for Period 271900-281900 Mar 68
   SITREP #89-68 for period 281900-291900 Mar 68
   SITREP #90-68 for period 291900-301900 Mar 68
   SITREP #91-68 for period 301900-311900 Mar 68
   Summary 1-31 January 1971 23rd Div OPORD 9-70
   Quarterly Written Summary 4th Qtr 1970
   Half-Year Summary 1 January – 30 June 1971

Planning Directives
Reference to OPORD 2-68, 198th Infantry Brigade relinquishes responsibility for southern portion of Chu Lai TAOR to the 11th Brigade; realigns forces and continues combat operations in remainder of Chu Lai TAOR and in Burlington Trail AO 041200 August 1968 From: CO, 198th Infantry Brigade LZ Bayonet, RVN (National Archives, College Park, MD)

BOOKS

Carlock, Chuck, *Firebirds* (Bantam Books, New York, 1997) pp. 12-13, 227

Campbell, John, *They Were Ours. Gloucester County's Loss in Vietnam.* (They Were Ours, Glassboro, New Jersey, 2000) p. 223.

Dunn, Lt. General Carroll H., *Vietnam Studies: Base Development In South Vietnam 1965-1970* (Washington DC: Department of the Army, U.S. Government Printing Office 1972) pp. 32, 52, 136

Herrington, Stuart A. *Stalking the Vietcong. Inside Phoenix, a Personal Account* (Originally published as "Silence Was a Weapon"). (Presidio Press, New York 1982). pp. 2, 5-6, 17-18, 29, 47, 52

Hunt, Richard A. *Pacification. The American Struggle for Vietnams Hearts and Minds* (Westview Press, Inc. Boulder, Colorado 1995). PP. 3,5,7,10, 12,25, 39, 47, 63, 116-117, 138, 154, 172-173, 193, 203, 205, 209, 213-214, 217, 227, 245-246, 253, 257-258

Kelly, Col. Francis J., *Vietnam Studies: U.S. Army Special Forces, 1961-1971* (Washington DC: Department of the Army, U.S. Government Printing Office 1973)

Larson, Lt. General Stanley R. and Collins, BG James Lawton Jr., *Vietnam Studies: Allied Participation in Vietnam* (Washington, DC: Department of the Army, U.S. Government Printing Office 1975) Chapter VI – The Republic of Korea, pp. 120-159

Ledrack, Otto J., *The First Battle. Operation Starlite and the Beginning of the Blood Debt in Vietnam.* (Pennsylvania, Casemate, 2004). PP. 18, 20-22, 37, 50-51, 165-166

Nolan, William Keith, *Sappers in the Wire. The Life and Death of Firebase Mary Ann* (Texas A&M University Press, College Station, Texas, 1995) PP. 21, 24, 28-29, 49, 54, 99, 137, 226-227

Pearson, Lt. General Willard, *The War in the Northern Provinces: 1966-1968* (Washington, DC: Office of the Chief of Military History, U.S. Army, 1975) pp. 11-15, 26, 28, 99, 105

Peers, Lt. General William R., *Report of the Department of the Army review of the Preliminary Investigations Into The My Lai Incident, Volume I, The Report of the Investigation* (Washington, DC: Superintendent of Documents, U.S. Government Printing Office, 1970) pp. 3-1 – 3-6; 4-1 – 4-3; 5-15 – 5-21

Peterson, Michael E., *The Combined Action Platoons: The U.S. Marines' Other War In Vietnam* (New York, Praeger Publishers, 1989) pp. 33-36, 68-69, 78

Prados, John *The Blood Road. The Ho Chi Minh Trail and the Vietnam War* (New York, John Wiley & Sons, Inc., 1999) pp. 181, 190, 191, 212-213

Ramsey, Lloyd B, *Major General Lloyd B. Ramsey – A Memoir*, (Albany, Kentucky, Clinton County Historical Society 2006) pp 298-306

Schwarzkopf, General H. Norman, *It Doesn't Take A Hero (New York, Bantam Book paperback edition 1993) P.188.*

Sigler, David Burns, *Vietnam Battle Chronology, US Army and Marine Corps Combat Operations1965-1975* (North Carolina, McFarland & Company, Inc. 1992) pp. 122-123, 125-127, 131

Sorely, Lewis, *A Better War* (New York, Harcourt Brace & Company, 1999) pp. 4, 42, 43, 65, 69, 94, 170, 192, 292-293

Shulimson, Jack and Johnson, Charles M., *U.S. Marines in Vietnam. The Landing and Buildup 1965* (Washington, D.C. Superintendent of Documents, U.S. Government Printing Office 1978. P. 87

Shulimson, Jack, *U.S. Marines in Vietnam. An Expanding War 1966.* (Washington, D.C. Superintendent of Documents, U.S. Government Printing Office 1982. PP 239-247.

Thayer, Thomas C. *War Without Fronts* (Boulder Co. Westview Press 1985) PP 116, 119, 157

Valentine, Douglas, The Phoenix Program (Authors Guild back in print edition; universe.com inc. Lincoln, NE 2000) pp 161, 173, 181, 254-255, 267

West, Bing *The Village* (New York, Simon & Schuster, 1972) Pp. 8-9, 46, 90, 104

ELECTRONIC CORRESPONDENCE (E-MAIL CORRESPONDENCE)

Arruda, John (Charlie Company) April 15, May 7, 14, July 21, 2009.
Arndt, Edward (Charlie Company) July 16, December 10, 2009; March 10, 2010
Anderson, Ben (Alpha Company) December 9, 2009
Barbo, Chuck (Alpha Company) April 15, September 20, 2007; August 30, September 4, 2009
Bentley, Ron (Charlie Company) May 1, 2006
Brissey, Thomas (Echo Recon Platoon) May 15, August 1, 2009.
Care, Terry J., (Echo Recon Platoon) September 8, 2000; April 18, 2005

Chappell, Robert, (Bravo Company) February 15, September 26, November 2, 30, December 3, 2000; January 1, 2, 8, 2001.
Coate, Lewis (Echo Recon Platoon) May 10, 2009
Cummings, Robert, (Charlie Company) April 8, 2005, January 8, 21, 2010
Cummings, Len, April 10-11, 2005 (Cummings was a Special Forces A-Team Commander at Tien Phuoc).
Culver, David (Charlie Company) May 7, November 12, 2009
Dant, Steven (Charlie Company) April 17, 27, 2009
Davis, Howard (Echo Company 4.2-inch Mortar Platoon) April 19, 22, 23, 24, 2006
Dunn, Ronny (Alpha Company)
Ehret, Harry (Battalion Medical Platoon) April 19, 2009
Essemacher, Ray (Alpha Company), April 28, 2000
Forshag, John (Echo Recon) October 10, 2003 (Includes attached 17-page typed memo of Forshag diary of service with the battalion).
Fox, Jerry (Bravo Company) August 20, 2010
Fuller, Elbert E. (198th Brigade S-3 & Commander, 1st/52nd Infantry Battalion) August 10, 2000.
George, Sidney (Delta Company) November 9, 2007
Goorley, John (Delta Company) December 14-15, 2006; February 14-15, March 13 2007
Gunton, Lee (Charlie Company), September 30, March 21, 2003; April 10, 23, 2006.
Hammond, David (Charlie Company), January 5, 2010
Hastings, John (Echo Recon Platoon), February 5, 11, 22, March 2, 2010
Hendricks, Jim Oct 7, 2006
Herier, Doug (1/14th Artillery) April 22, 23, May 2, May 6, 2006
Hollmann, John (Alpha Company) Oct 16, 2009
Hugues, Dennis (Bravo Company), January 5, 2001 (Hugues served with Richard Atwood, 5th/46th Battalions' first killed in action).
Kannapel, Carl (Charlie Company) May 20, 2009
Kapp, Robert (Charlie Company) January 2, 2008
Kaseberg, William (Bravo Company) Numerous and detailed e-mail correspondences from November 27, 2009 to September 6, 2010
Kenney, Lawrence (Bravo Company) February 17-19, 2010
King, John (Charlie Company) March 23, 2005
Kotlas, Howard (Alpha Company) September 6, 2009
Krause, James (S-3, 5th/46th) October 11, December 15 2007

Loftis, L.D. (Alpha Company) June 20, August 11, September 5, 2006.
Lavender, Wilson (Alpha Company) November 15, 2009; March 13-14 2007
Longhurst, Scott (Charlie Company) February 11, 2010
Longgrear, Paul (Alpha Company) September 2, 6, 27, October 1, 2009.
Lyon, David K. (First Commander, 5th/46th Infantry Battalion) March 10, August 27, 31, September 4, October 6, 13, 2000.
Mackie, Ronald (Delta Company) May 1, 2008
Migacz, John (Bravo Company), March 9, 2004
Moles, Robert, April 5, 2005
Moriarty, Raymond (Alpha Company) January 8, July 16, December 3, 9, 11, 2009
O'Neil, Bill (Charlie Company Forward Observer) October 15, 23, 27, 2006
Phillips, Ray (Alpha Company) March 14, 2006
Printy, Russ (Headquarters Company) February 4, 27 2010
Samples, Mitchell (Bravo Company) February 1, 2007
Schulte, Daniel, (Battalion S-5) Nov 1, 2006
Schopp, Steve, (Bravo Company) March 8-9, February 13, September 28, October 3, November 1, 2007;
Stachowiak, Michael (Delta Company) December 9, 16, 2008
Starck, James (Charlie Company) December 27, 2009
Stanford, Roger e-mail to Harry Ehret (Both Battalion Medics) April 14, 2009
Stevens, Dennis (Charlie Company) February 11-12, 2010 via Charlie Company Yahoo® Web Chat site
Teglia, Kenneth (Charlie Company Forward Observer), April 19, 15, 18, 2009
Tittle, Grady (Headquarters Company), March 18, 2005
Totten, Richard (Charlie Company) March 3, 2010
Wolf, Robert, (Alpha Company) September 16, November 4, December 10 2003; October 2, 2006; February 25 2007; December 11, August 30, 2009; January 5, 2010
Wolski, Bill (Alpha Company) March 12, 2008
Woodworth, James (Headquarters Company) January 29, 2007

ELECTRONIC RESOURCES (WEBSITES)

WWW.a-1-6.org (1st/6th Infantry Battalion – Vietnam)
25thAviation.org (25th Aviation Battalion – Vietnam)
http://capmarine.com (Dedicated to USMC Combined Action platoons in Vietnam)

WWW.Virtualwall.org (The Coffelt Database – Virtual Wall ® of the Vietnam war's killed in action)

ORAL HISTORIES AND EXIT INTERVIEWS

Richard Ellashek, (Delta Company). October 31, 1974 Interview by David Costello, Youngstown State (Ohio) Oral History Program, YSU Veterans Project (Veterans Experience O.H. 354)

LTC Ronald R. Richardson, ACofS, G4, Former Battalion Commander, 5th Battalion, 46th Infantry, 198th Light Infantry Brigade, Americal Division. April 26,1969. Interview by Maj. James M. Hallinan, Americal Division, Vietnam for the US Army Center for Military History, FT. McNair, Washington (VNIT #449)

Col James R. Waldie, Commanding Officer, 198th Light Infantry Brigade, May 30, 1968. Interview by Captain James J. Armor, Americal Division, Vietnam for the US Army Center for Military History, FT. McNair, Washington (VNIT #190)

The Vietnam Archive (Oral History Project) Texas Tech University, Lubbock, Texas
   Dant, Stephen, C Company, 5th/46th Infantry Battalion
   Hammond, David, C Company, 5th/46th Infantry Battalion
   Taylor, David, C Company, 5th/46th Infantry Battalion

PERIODICALS, PUBLICATIONS AND NEWSLETTERS

Americal Division Magazine (Vietnam),
   "The Noose Around the Batangan" PP. 8-9, spring, 1971,
   "The Land" PP. 2-6; US Army Military History Institute (USAMHI), Carlisle, PA.

Americal Division Newsletter (Official newsletter of the Americal Division Veterans Association).

   "Task Force Oregon" July-August-September 1995. P.22
   "The Long Shot Warriors: Americal Snipers in Vietnam" David W. Taylor, October-November-December 2002. P.22
   "Proudly Served! The 23rd Military Police Company" David W. Taylor July-August-September 2003. P. 27

The Americal Journal (Official Magazine of the Americal Division Veterans Association),

"Nose to the Ground", Jim Pene, July-August-September 2008. PP 30-32
"Soda Girls", David Hammond, January-February-March2010. PP 30-31
"The Rocket Pockets", David W. Taylor, April-May-June 2007. PP 26-28

The Army Reporter (Authorized Unofficial Weekly Publication of the U.S. Army Information Office, Vietnam) (U.S. Army Military History Institute (USMHI), Carlisle, Pennsylvania)

"Close Shave with Machete" March 22, 1971 P.1
"Concealed Patrol Rips Up Badly Shaken Vietcong" January 20, 1969 P.7
"Happiness is a Booby-Trap That Fizzles" March 22, 1971 P.12
"Medic Sprints to his Job" March 8, 1971 P.12
"Toe Popper Flops" March 8, 1971 P.12

Ground Surveillance Radar and Military Intelligence. Lav Varshney. Technical Report by Syracuse Research Corporation, North Syracuse, New York. December 30, 2002 (Rev 2).

History of the 5th Battalion, 46th Infantry, prepared by the 3rd Military History Detachment (USAMHI – Carlisle, PA) 1967-1970 3 pages; 1967-1971 6 pages

Readers Digest, "Beyond the Call of Duty in Vietnam", Kenneth Y. Tomlinson June 1970 PP. 99-100

South Coast Today, "An American Patriot" (Gary Martin Cohen), Linda Andrade Rodriguez January 16, 2008

Southern Cross Newsletter (Published by the Americal Division in Vietnam). U.S. Army Military History Institute (USAMHI), Carlisle, PA

"A Hard Pillow" Vol. 3, No. 22, 19 June 1970 P. 8
"Buy Explosives and Ammunition" Vol. 1, No. 3, 8 December 1968 P.6
"Children Reveal Caches" Vol. 3, No. 23, 26 June 1970 P.1
"Geneva Park" Vol. 3 No. 20, 5 June 1970 P. 1
"Hidden SRP Baffles VC" Vol. 2, No. 2, 19 January 1969 P.6
"High Point of Malaria Cases" Vol. 3, No. 23, 26 June 1970 P. 2
"Infantrymen Play With Rubber Ducky" January 22, 1971
"NVA Hospital Found" Vol. 1, No. 7 15 September 1968 P. 1

"Rocket Attack Thwarted" Vol. 3, No 22. 19 June 1970 P. 6
"Russell Beach Task Force Sweeps to Sea" Vol. 2, No. 04, 16 February 1969. P.1.
"SRP's Collect 22 for Debut" Vol. 1, No. 13 8 December 1968 P. 1

The Falcon Newssheet of the 16th Combat Aviation Group (Vol. II, No. 6), March 18, 1969, Page 2 (Vietnam Helicopter Pilots Association).

The Manchester Star, "GI Describes First Bloody Battle", by PFC Tim O'Brien, July 4, 1969. P.7A.

The Marine War: III MAF in Vietnam 1965-1971. Jack Shumlinson, U.S. Marine Corps Historical Center. Paper delivered at The Vietnam Center (Texas Tech University) 1996 Symposium, Lubbock, Texas.

The Oregonian newspaper, Portland, Oregon. "Vietnam Casualty Lives On In Friend" Angela Cara Pancrazio May 25, 1998.

Vietnam Magazine, "The Claymore, A Combat Killer" Carl Shuster, Weider History Group, October 2009, P. 19

TELEPHONE INTERVIEWS

Ach, Joseph G. (Delta Company) October 28, 2008
Arruda, John P. (Charlie Company) May 5, 2009
Ashworth, Shelton (Bravo Company) July 28, 2009
Baxley, William G. (Commander, 1st/6th Infantry Battalion, 1968) 17 October, 2003
Bentley, Ron (Charlie Company) February 14, 2007
Father Berry, Barton D. Jr., (Battalion Chaplain in 1970) November 5, 2009
Beville, Richard D. (Alpha Company) December 14, 2008
Brannon, Earl (Alpha Company) November 5, 2010
Brewer, Thomas (Charlie Company) January 3, 2008
Brunson, Fred (Charlie Company) February 1, 2010
Cannon, Ron (Echo Recon Platoon) May 26, 2009
Castillo, Arthur (Echo Recon Platoon & C Company) May 17 & October 17 2009
Cherryholmes, Wayne (Echo Recon Platoon) December 4, 2008
Crawford, Bill (Alpha Company) July 17, 2009.
Crosby, Mike (Charlie Company) January 31, 2010
Culver, Dave (Charlie Company) April 9, 2009

Decker, Richard (Echo Recon Platoon Leader) October 15, 2009
Ehlke, Donald M. (Alpha Company) July 14, 2009
Esslinger, Michael (Alpha Company) October 1, 2009
Fossen, Pat (Sister of Lee Harra, killed in action January 30, 1969) (Alpha Company) November 5, 2010
Fultz, Al (Charlie Company) October 12, 2009
Greer, Ralph (Alpha Company) June 18, 2008
Hall, Steven (Alpha Company) August 3, 2009
Harra, Jack (Brother of Lee Harra, killed in action January 30, 1969)
Haubner, Frank (Delta Company) July 17, 2009
Herbert, Rick (Echo Company) May 25, 2009
Joseph, Robert (First Battalion Surgeon), April 14, 2009
Knisley, William R. (Bravo Company) May 2, 2009
Kucenic, John (Delta Company) April 8, 2009
Meiling, Ted (Charlie Company) October 12, 2009
Morton, David (Delta Company) December 10, 2008
Morrison, Robby (Charlie Company) July 29, 2009
Murray, Clyde E. (Charlie Company) December 16, 2008
Nichols, James "Jerry". (Charlie Company) May 6, 2009
Nolan, Eugene (Alpha Company July 19, 2009
Pfalzer, Timothy (Alpha Company) July 27, 2009
Pillow, Leo (Delta Company) February 15, 2007.
Renze, James (Alpha Company) July 28, 2009
Rudderow, Diane (High School girlfriend of Michael Bastian, killed in action January 2, 1969)
Schanke, Kenneth (Alpha Company) August 2, 2009
Schrier, David C. (Alpha Company) May 21, 2008
Stachowiak, Michael (Delta Company) December 8, 2008
Stretch, Kenneth (Charlie Company) August 18, 2009
Swek, John (Battalion S-2, October 2009-January 1970) August 4, 2009
Totten, Richard (Charlie Company) November 21, 2009
Tunnel, David (Echo Recon Platoon) May 26, 2009
Van Enyde, Donald (Battalion S-3 Operations Officer December 1970-May 1971) January 22, 2010
Wagner, James (Delta Company) December 3, 2007
Woody, Jason (Alpha Company) January 16, 2008

WRITTEN CORRESPONDENCE

Father Berry, Barton D. Jr., (Battalion Chaplain 1970) Letter to David Hammond dated April 17, 1996, relating the details of Charlie Company's tragedy on July 30, 1970).

Care, Terry J., letter to author dated March 30, 2000.

Chiofee, Alfred R., letter to author dated September 22, 2000.

Craig, Ray E., "Report of Captain Ray E. Craig" letter to author (letter undated, sent in August 2001)

Davis, Howard, reflections on duty with Echo Company's Heavy Mortars at CAP 133 and LZ Minuteman, September 1968-August 1969. Letter dated April 22, 2006.

Edwins, Mark (Echo Recon Platoon) Letter to author dated August 12, 2009 reviewing the activities of the Recon Platoon during July 1970.

Erb, Herbert E. II, letter to author (undated) in November, 2000.

Esslinger, Michael J. Letter to author dated September 27, 2009 with personal memorandum attached, dated June 15, 1970 relating to the Alpha Company incident of June 14, 1970.

Fuller, Elbert E. Letters to the author: August 20, 2000 and October 4, 2000. Also provided was a 27 page document previously prepared by Fuller (undated) titled: "Comment on Tet 68 Combat Actions, RVN Military Region 1, Chu Lai and Vicinity (Quang Tin and Quang Ngai Provinces) as Viewed by LTC Elbert E. Fuller Jr., then Brigade Operations Officer and later, Commander, 1st/52nd Infantry Battalion (10 April 68), 198th Light Infantry Brigade, 23rd (Americal) Infantry Division".

Hall, Steven J. (Alpha Company) Letter to author dated August 22, 2009 with Bronze Star citation attached.

Hammond, David (Charlie Company) Unpublished work, "Barroom Brawl", a vignette of a fight instigated by "Black Power" Soldiers at the Chu Lai Enlisted Club during a standdown in July 1970.

Hugues, Dennis, "The Pipes Are Calling", an unpublished work of personal vignettes of authors tour of duty with Bravo Company, 5th/46th Infantry Battalion. Wilmington, DE

Karr, Jerry, Letter dated April 27, 2007. Reflections of duty with Alpha Company, 3rd Platoon, 3rd Squad, 1969

Laughlin, Michael J. (Bravo Company), Letter (undated) received December 2009 detailing in a three-page typed memo incidents and experiences with Bravo Company 1969-1970

Mink, Kenneth (LTC, USA-Ret) Letter to author with review of draft chapter "Golden Fleece", received April 2006, and draft chapter "Russell Beach, dated May 15, 2006. Mink was the battalions S-3 Operations Officer, November 1968 – April 1969.

Pene, Jim, Personnel vignettes (unpublished) of his experience with Alpha Company

Rice, Everett, Undated memorandum received February 16, 2006 with personal memories of his service with Charlie Company, 1969.

Sanchez, Jeffrey (First Sergeant-Retired, Charlie Company) Written letter (Undated) regarding road-clearing operation 3 June 1969

Scurlock, William J. Personal memories dated November 26, 2007 and December 2007 after reviews of draft chapters #5 and #6. Scurlock was a medic with Charlie Company.

Sheffield, Donald (Battalion medic assigned to Alpha Company), twelve pages of handwritten notes written in 1998, reflecting on his experiences with the battalion.

Smith, Michael (Colonel-US Army Retired). Memorandum dated January 2007 containing four pages of recollections from his tenure as Commander of Delta Company, September 1968-March 1969.

Stephens, Albert (SFC, USA-Ret) Letter to author February 13, 2006. Stephens was the platoon Sergeant / Platoon Leader of the 4th Platoon, B Company, formed at Ft. Hood. Letter reviewed draft chapters 2-4-5.

Wagner, James (Delta Company) Letter to author December 21, 2007 detailing certain events as the RTO for Delta Company's commander

Wilson, Donald, personal reflections of duty with the 5th/46th at Fort Hood, Texas and Vietnam. Memorandum undated, received March 28, 2008.

Wolski, Bill, Undated 20-page, typed letter to the sister of SP/4 Michael Robert Glenn, killed by friendly fire on February 11, 1970. Letter details Alpha Company operations before, during and after friendly fire incident.

PERSONAL INTERVIEWS

Care, Terry J. (Charlie Company & Echo Recon Platoon) October 10, 2000. Las Vegas, Nevada
Dimsdale, Roger (Battalion S-2 Intelligence Officer upon arrival in Vietnam) June 21, 2000 Washington, D.C.
Fuller, Elbert E. (198th Brigade S-3 Operations Officer upon arrival in Vietnam, later Commander, 1st/52nd Infantry Battalion) November 24, 2000, Alexandria, VA
Lamb, James, (First Bravo Company Commander) May 20, 2000 Columbus, Georgia
Lyon, David K. (First Battalion Commander, 5th/46th Infantry)) Dec 2, 2000, Dallas, Texas
McCarley, Kenneth (Battalion S-4 Logistics Officer upon arrival in Vietnam) May 19, 2000
Mink, Kenneth, (5th/46th S-3 Operations Officer 1968-1969) November 3, 2005, Gettysburg, PA

INDEX

A

Abraham, Roosevelt, 322-323, 658
Abrahamson, Gary Lee, 499, 659
Abrams, Creighton, 40, 216, 235, 306, 632
Accelerated Pacification, 168, 216, 297, 330, 348, 355, 362, 366, 368, 376-377, 391, 409, 421, 424, 458, 481, 531, 632-633
Adakai, Leo Joe, 323, 658
Adams, Charles, 252-253
Adams, Dalton, 142
Agent Orange (Defoliation), 113, 125, 272, 274-275, 475, 489
Aguilera, Daniel, 413, 659
Ahern, Steven, 359
Aldrich, Harold, 110-111, 141
Alexander, James, 611
Allen, Steven, 576
Amick, Richard, 246, 646, 657
Anderson, Ben, 207, 230, 239-240, 279, 302
Anderson, Steven, 283
Annamite Mountains, 28, 41, 45, 62, 75, 143, 226, 422, 442, 461, 488, 530, 582

Area of Operations (AO)
  Babylon (My Lai Investigation), 387-388, 391, 394
  California, 380
  Clean Sweep, 374-376
  Custer, 374-375, 380, 426
  Diamond Head, 357, 361, 363, 368
  Eagle, 370, 372, 380, 398, 400, 402
  Falcon, 378-379, 387
  Florida, 375
  Razorback, 375
  Safeguard, 375
  Scythe, 415, 416
  Searchlight, 343
  Serene, 347, 357, 364, 366, 374, 379, 381, 384, 387-388, 397-399, 402, 406, 408, 410, 416, 420-421, 426, 479
  Texas, 375, 377, 380
Arndt, Ed, 67-68, 70, 81-82
Arruda, John, 448, 456-458
Ashworth, Shelton, 441-442
Atkins, Richard, 63
Atwood, Richard, 49, 611, 655
Auten, Donald, 478, 659
Ayers, Mike, 67-68
Avery, Ronald Van, 19, 53-56, 646, 655

B

Backovich, Randy, 262-264
Bahner, Thomas, 273
Barbo, Chuck, 304-305, 328
Barcus, Joe, 643
Barker, Jim, 266
Barnes, Alfred, 214-215, 220, 225, 228, 230-231, 234, 242, 244, 246-247, 249, 253, 268, 646, 657
Barney, Dave, 266
Bastian, Michael, 165, 649-650, 656
Batangan Peninsula, 28, 83, 85, 166-169, 177, 188, 202-203, 207, 213-214, 217, 220, 225, 233, 235, 241, 249, 252, 258, 265, 267, 290, 298, 300, 306, 316, 326, 343, 368, 370, 378, 394, 421, 508, 630-631, 636
Bauer, Carl, 398, 437, 659
Baun, Eddie, 117
Benaim, Gilbert, 393-394, 659
Bennett, Charles, 89, 655
Bentley, Ron, 264-265, 286
Berkholtz, Larry, 506, 659
Bethards, Edward Wayne, 555, 660
Betts, Larry Leroy, 370-371, 658
Bittle, Robert, 273, 657
Black Power, 21, 159, 242, 483, 561, 619
Blanks, Thomas, 389, 659
Bleything, Larry, 230, 657
Bonetti, Freddie, 185, 656
Borel, Nolan, 557
Brady, Patrick, 56
Brannon, Earl, 411-412, 648
Brauberger, Everett W., 312
Brayboy, Dennis, 156
Breedlove, Robert, 125, 398
Brenner, Oral, 55
Bridges, John, 89
Bright, David, 443
Brill, William, 436
Briscoe, James, 308
Brissey, Tom, 469-470
Brooks, Michael, 587-588

Brown Jr., James, 496, 659
Brown Jr., James Henry, 333, 658
Bruck, Kenneth, 451
Brunson, Fred, 233, 576
Bryan, Larry, 287-289, 658
Bryan, Reilly, 398
Burkholder, Larry Gene, 353, 653, 658
Bush, Bernard, 354
Byler, Gary L., 335

C

Cagie, Randal, 354
Callaway, Lewis, 196, 657
Calley, William, 390, 565
Camacho, Richard, 359
Cam Rahn Bay, 7
Cannon, Ron, 19, 54-56, 646
Cardinal, Garryl, 145-146, 656
Care, Terry J., 17, 19, 41, 56-57, 74, 75-76, 109-112
Casino, Joseph Walter, 568-569, 571, 660
Castillo, Arthur, 377, 456, 458
Chadwick, Amy, 650
Chaplin, Earl, 595
Chappell, Robert, 15-16, 72-73, 77-78, 89-93, 101, 105-106, 120-122, 644-645
Charnisky, John, 236
Cherryholmes, Wayne, 403, 405-406
Chioffe, Al, 16
CIA- Central Intelligence Agency, 59-60, 345
CIDG (Civilian Irregular Defense Group), 75-77, 104, 107, 111-113, 120-121, 139, 164, 344
CHIC (Combined Holding & Interrogation Center), 181-182, 188, 192-193, 196, 202-204, 207, 301
Citadel (near My Lai), 93, 303, 308, 349-351, 354-355, 357, 361, 367, 370, 374, 377, 399, 419
Clark, Danny, 175

Clark, Roy, 258, 657
CLDC (Chu Lai Defense Command), 462, 494
Clemons, Joseph, 634-639
Clore, Lee William, 557, 660
Coate, Lewis, 446-447
Cohen, Gary Martin, 591, 660
Collins, Gary, 125
Colon, Walter, 542
Combat Training Center (Americal Division), 41-42
Combined Action Platoons (Marine Corps)
   CAP 131, 211
   CAP 132, 48, 137
   CAP 133, 47, 128, 130, 134, 138, 147, 153, 163, 165, 168, 174, 208, 213, 216, 276, 320, 336, 346, 363, 368, 396, 408, 418-420
   CAP 134, 134, 139, 172-173, 357, 370, 376, 381
   CAP 135, 45, 140, 173-174, 193, 211-212, 253, 255, 337, 340, 344, 348, 356-357, 359, 376, 405, 409
   CAP 136, 139, 141, 211, 272
   CAP 137, 133, 139, 271-272, 331
   CAP 138, 211, 275, 330, 359, 420-422, 437
   CAP 142, 270, 290, 293, 295, 300, 302, 306, 308-309, 316, 319-320, 342-343, 346, 348, 364-366, 376, 378, 381, 388, 390, 394-397, 400, 418, 420
   CAP 143, 271, 290, 293-295, 301, 306, 369, 379, 390
   CAP 144, 318-319, 331, 333, 364, 366, 373, 379, 390, 399-400, 413
   CAP 146, 356, 364, 366-367, 373, 388
Connell, Oscar Allen, 408, 426, 659
Cook, Donald, 233
Cooksey, Howard, 97-98, 104, 124, 168, 184-185, 362

Cooley, Dickey, 393, 659
Concepcion-Nieves, David, 456, 659
CORDS – Civil Operations and Revolutionary Development Support, 340
Cornwell, Thomas Glenn, 343, 658
Cosner, James, 165, 259
Cotton, Charles, 22, 72-73
Coughenour, Frank, 507
Craft, Grayson, 160, 656
Craig, Ray, 49
Crawford, Gordon Lee, 571, 660
Crosby, Mike, 574
Culver, Robert Wayne, 418, 659
Cummings, Robert, 58, 86, 116
Cummins, Thomas, 247, 657
CUPP – (Combined Unit Pacification Program), 633
Curtis, Dennis, 270
Curtis, Paul A., 403, 405-406

D

Daiello, Vincent, 161, 656
Danang, 1, 9, 37, 255, 341, 366, 444, 480, 515, 523, 532, 627, 630
Daniels, Jim, 257, 273
Dant, Stephen, 474
Davidson, Francis, 135
Davis Jr., Frank, 358, 658
Davis, Howard, 134, 163
Davis, Woodrow, 63, 655
Decker, Richard, 378
Decker, Wayne, 70, 655
DeLorenzo, Thomas, 354
DeMott, Terry, 26-27, 52-53
Dills, Ronald Eugene, 441, 659
Dimsdale, Roger, 14, 46
Dinda, Michael, 380, 653, 659
Disney, Robert C.G., 346, 348, 353
DMZ – Demilitarized Zone, 5-7, 550
Donley, Stephen, 354
Dorsey, Harry, 178, 656

Doyle, Merrill, 354
Dragon Valley, 444-446, 450, 453-454, 458-459, 461-466, 468, 470-472, 475-476, 478-479, 481, 485, 490, 492-495, 497, 500, 502-504, 506, 508, 512-513, 518, 520, 523, 526, 528-529, 536-537, 539-541, 558-559, 562-563, 566, 573-575, 577-578, 580, 582-584, 588, 592, 596, 598, 612-613, 615, 617, 624, 639-640
Duncan, Donald F., 339, 370
Duncan, Terry, 445
Dunn, Ronny, 322
Durant, Richard, 417, 659

E

Eason, Freddy, 322
Easter, Dennis Ray, 588, 660
Edge, Walter, 117-118
Edwins, Mark, 468-469
Eggert, Sam L., 244, 657
Ehlke, Donald, 460
Ehret, Harry, 53
Eklund, James, 283
Ellashek, Richard, 178
Endicott, Danny, 273, 657
Erb, Herbert, 26, 46-47, 62, 80, 85-88
Erickson, Marvin, 189, 657
Esquilin, Lazu, 354
Essenmacher, Ray, 199, 201-202
Esslinger, Michael, 449
Eynde, Donald Van, 561, 571-572

F

Farnsworth, John Joseph, 527, 660
Fenhrenbach, Steven, 354
Fire Support Bases, 29, 37, 180
    Fat City, 425, 428, 434, 436, 438, 440, 442-443, 449, 452-455, 458, 461-464, 466, 470-473, 475, 478-479, 481-482, 484-485, 489-491, 494-496, 498, 506-507, 509, 513, 520, 522-523, 525-526, 528-530, 533, 535, 543-544, 558, 561, 570, 575-578, 581, 586, 591, 594, 600-602, 605-606, 611-612, 614, 626, 628
    Mary Ann, 58, 602, 605-606
    North, 180-181, 183
    South, 180-181, 184, 190-191, 193, 200, 204, 206, 227, 238, 363
Floyd, Edward, 175
Forshag, John, 225, 235, 241, 273, 388, 642
Fort Hood, Texas, 8-11, 12-14, 17-19, 21-22, 26, 36, 38-39, 41, 52, 57, 61, 80, 110, 126, 191, 216, 603, 644, 646
Foster, Larry, 442, 659
Foster, Shelby Gene, 353, 658
Foutz, Michael George, 397-398, 400, 659
Franklin, Jerold, 478, 659
Frilling, Jerome Raymond, 504-505, 659
Frye, Craig, 372
Fuentes, George, 595
Fujita, Melvin, 287-289, 658
Fuller, Elbert, 9-10, 74
Fultz, Al, 505

G

Gabbert, Edward, 141
Gallager, William, 268
Gallagher, Charles, 229
Gaston Jr., John Rufus, 153, 656
Gedeon, Russell, 374, 658
George, Christopher, 100
George, Sidney, 48
Gerace, Santo, 211-212
Gideon, Wilburn, 115-119, 656
Gilliard, Edward, 211-212, 657
Gilmore, Andrew, 140
Gingros, Ronald, 283
Glenn, Michael, 403, 405-406, 659

Gniadek, Joe, 390
Gomez-Robles, Thomas, 265, 657
Goodman, Benny, 72
Goorley, John, 256, 276, 285, 287-288
Gottier, Robert Carl, 534, 660
Gould, Richard, 411-412
Gracey, Michael, 592
Graham Jr., Thomas, 195, 657
Grant, Herbert, 210, 657
Green, Benjamin, 236-237
Greer, Ralph, 322
Gregory, Robert, 338, 354
Guilder, Thomas Van, 82-83
Gunton, Lee, 20, 110-111, 161
Gwaltney, Gerald, 209-210, 657

H

Hackett, James, 112
Hall, Steve, 466
Halpenny, Jerry Lee, 140, 656
Ham Giang River, 184, 233, 349, 351, 356, 358, 361, 370, 407-408, 416
Hammond, Dave, 606-607
Harmon, George, 188-189, 191
Harra, Jack, 651
Harra, Lee Hamilton, 198-199, 651, 657
Hart, Daryl, 542
Hart, Robert, 478, 659
Haas, John, 305
Hass, Jack, 315
Hastings, John, 585-586, 641
Haubner, Francis, 461-462
Hauck, Robin, 125
Haynes Jr., Robert Marion, 353, 658
Henry, James R., 540, 596
Herier, Doug, 180, 183-184, 200
Hernandez, Tony, 449
Hess, Donald, 88
Hiep Duc, 66, 97-100, 103-104, 232
Hill, Jesse, 477, 647

Hills (Defensive Positions)
   Hill 26, 213-214, 220, 225, 233, 250, 253, 260, 265, 271, 308, 331
   Hill 54, 123, 422, 471-472, 475, 485, 491, 493, 548, 609, 614, 624
   Hill 56, 54, 56-57, 571, 646
   Hill 61, 350
   Hill 69, 489-491, 606
   Hill 76, 421-422, 450, 461, 479, 494, 502, 516-517, 520-521, 525-526, 528-529, 535, 537-538, 547, 563-564, 566-571, 574, 576, 578, 580, 582, 590, 602-603, 606, 608, 611, 613, 622-623, 626, 649-650
   Hill 85, 89, 91, 93, 364, 366-367
   Hill 97, 120
   Hill 203, 533, 535, 547-548, 553, 558, 577, 583
   Hill 212, 127
   Hill 237, 104-105, 121
   Hill 270, 277, 284, 450, 464, 494-495, 498, 507, 528, 530, 543, 545, 564, 566, 569-570, 575, 579, 584, 586, 588, 590-591, 594, 600-602, 604-609, 611, 613-614, 621, 626-628
   Hill 294, 260
   Hill 302, 533, 535, 551
   Hill 306, 584-586
   Hill 371, 517-518, 521-522, 550, 618
Hodge, Acie, 354
Hodges, William Jeffrey, 155-156, 653, 656
Holfeltz, Kyle, 648-649
Holman, David, 92
Holt Jr., Clay, 122, 656
Hooker, Billy, 82-83
Hopkins, Ernie, 477-478, 647
Hopper, Robert, 390
Horne Jr., Richard, 86
Horton, John, 141, 656
Huddleston, Robert, 443-444, 659
Hughes, Dennis, 41, 52
Hurst, Roosevelt, 82-83, 655

I

ICIPP – (Infantry Company Intensified Pacification Program) 349, 633
Italiano, Harry, 262, 264, 657

J

Jackson, Edward, 123, 656
Johnson, Howard, 10
Johnson, Larry, 17, 45, 55-56, 70-71, 77, 111
Johnson, Lyndon B., 19-20, 22, 41, 643
Jones, Clyde, 450
Jordan, Martin, 77
Justiano, Victor, 233, 268

K

Kannapel, Carl, 451
Karr, Jerry, 239-240, 242, 250
Kaseberg, William, 337-338, 352, 367, 370
Kashuba, Michael, 354
Kenney, Larry, 555-557, 609-610, 620
Kester, Jon, 88
Kigar, Larry, 238, 657
King, John, 108-109
Kirk, John, 354
Kit Carson Scouts, 60, 181, 188, 291, 619
Klebau, James, 354, 390
Knight Jr., Richard, 58
Kokesh, Andrew, 273, 658
Koppeis, Carl, 45, 78
Korean (South) Marines, 32, 37, 54
Krajewski, Stephen, 458
Krause, James, 281, 313-314
Krulak, Victor, 1
Kucenic, John, 433-434
Kuhn, Michael, 49, 191
Kulchinsky, Harry, 469-470

L

Ladek, Andy, 580
Lamb, James, 16, 22, 47, 52-53, 62-63, 72-73, 96, 101
LaRoche, Joel, 119, 656
Laughlin, Mike, 425, 437, 441
Lavender, Wilson, 146, 643
Lawler, Thomas, 346, 658
Lawson, Kenneth, 381
Lay, Willie Ray, 131, 656
Layton, Donald Dean, 478, 659
LeBeau, Richard, 249
Lister, James, 218, 657
Loftis, Lonnie D., 118, 197-199
Longgrear, Paul, 327-329, 344, 369, 401
Longhurst, Scott, 599
Loop, Frederick, 304
Lucibello, John, 236-237
Lyon, David K., 10, 12-15, 17-21, 24-27, 40, 49, 55, 57, 62, 64, 68, 74-75, 77, 80, 85-86, 91-93, 95-96, 98-99, 103, 105-107, 109-110, 112-115, 117-119, 121, 125-126, 148, 175, 215, 224, 280, 368

LZ (Landing Zones)
LZ Ann, 45-47, 50-53, 62-63, 67, 70, 73, 94, 101
LZ Bayonet, 10, 35, 40, 60, 63, 66, 80, 87, 96, 129, 181, 189, 218, 228, 234, 242, 247, 253, 276, 282, 301, 306, 313, 316, 323, 374-375, 392, 398, 417, 420, 425, 433, 437-438, 440, 445, 453, 463, 515, 538, 543, 564, 574, 582, 590, 608-610, 626
LZ Bowman, 68, 71, 77, 113-114, 119, 124, 476, 480-482, 484-485, 489, 491-496, 500-501, 503-504, 507, 524-526, 528-529, 538, 543, 574-575, 591, 593-598, 600-601, 605-607, 609, 622-623
LZ Buff, 74, 81, 93, 130, 138, 142-144, 146, 153, 156, 158, 160, 163-166, 269, 308

LZ Chippewa, 35, 45, 55-56, 62, 70, 125, 128, 130, 135, 137-138, 168, 214, 260, 442, 450, 452-455, 461, 464, 480, 493, 574
LZ Craig, 99
LZ Creek, 426
LZ Donna, 596, 598, 604-606, 608, 611, 617, 622, 624
LZ Dottie, 37, 74, 81-82, 85-86, 95-96, 98, 130-131, 138, 141, 143-144, 152-153, 155, 157, 160, 162, 165, 170, 172, 180, 192, 204, 210-214, 218, 238, 247, 259, 265, 269, 272, 294, 339, 391, 396, 418, 420-421, 638, 653
LZ Gator, 33-35, 38, 40-42, 44-45, 48, 51, 53, 55-57, 62-64, 67, 71, 73-74, 100, 103, 113, 118, 125, 127-130, 133, 135-136, 138, 142, 145, 150, 153, 158-159, 162-167, 175, 180, 183, 191, 193, 201, 203, 207, 209, 212-213, 215, 218, 221, 224-229, 231-232, 234, 240, 242, 244-245, 247-248, 250-251, 253, 255-256, 258-261, 265-267, 269, 272, 274, 280, 290, 294, 306-309, 312-313, 327-330, 333, 336, 338-339, 343-344, 348, 355-356, 361-362, 366-369, 373, 377-378, 380-381, 384-385, 388-389, 396, 398-399, 402, 406-407, 409-410, 415-416, 418-426, 435, 445, 448, 453, 461-462, 502-503, 563-564, 587, 609, 646
LZ Grass, 76-77
LZ Hustler, 426, 428, 431-436
LZ Karen, 99
LZ Manchester, 75-77, 79
LZ Minuteman, 203, 207, 211, 213, 218, 220, 223-225, 228-229, 233, 237-238, 241-242, 244, 250, 256-257, 267-268, 272, 274, 276, 295, 301-302, 308-309, 324-325, 330, 332, 336, 342, 344, 346, 348, 363, 365, 372, 378, 381, 390, 392, 399, 400
LZ Paradise, 36, 44, 47, 53, 62, 71, 73, 130-131, 138, 153, 157, 180, 211, 357, 363
LZ Pleasantville, 105-107, 112, 605, 608, 612
LZ Polar Bear II, 99
LZ Professional, 541, 543, 615, 617, 620-624, 626, 628
LZ Sand, 76-77, 81
LZ Siberia, 627
LZ Sooner, 100
LZ Stinson, 74, 247, 269, 276, 281, 290, 308
LZ West, 96, 99
LZ Young, 113-116, 118, 120-127, 462, 524, 527, 601-602, 604

M

Mackie, Ronald, 394
Mahl, Kenneth, 288-289, 658
Mailloux, Raymond, 153
Malone, William, 273, 658
Markunas, Thomas, 242-244, 652, 657
Marlin Jr., Earl William, 390, 659
Martin, Dan, 315, 334
Martin, John, 294-295, 658
Martin, Robert, 267
Massey, Rick, 266
Mather, G.R., 20
Matias-Santana, Frederico, 156, 656
McCagg, Carlton F., 395, 400
McCarley, Kenneth W., 13, 25, 27, 41-42, 44
McChristian, Joseph A., 21
McClellan, David, 469-470
McConnell, Richard, 273
McCullough, Albert, 209
McElhaney, Roger, 303-305, 327, 658
McFarland, Vernon, 199
McFarland, William, 214, 657

McMillan, Gordon, 273, 658
McMullen, Tom, 153
McNamara Line, 5-6
McNamara, Robert, 5-6, 116
Medina, Ernest, 82
Meinecke, William, 145, 656
Meli, Francis, 268
Mennuti, Stephen, 175
Merricks, Alvin, 242-244, 652, 657
Mesich, Michael, 452, 659
Meter, Thomas Van, 533
Migacz, John, 26-27, 42, 52
Miller, Terry, 116-117
Millett, Lawrence Arthur, 337-338, 658
Mink, Ken, 158-159, 163, 185, 190
Mobley, Dennis, 287
Moheit, Ozzie, 417
Moll, Roger, 115-116, 119, 656
Moore, Hal, 214
Moore, Paul, 142
Moore, Stephen Alan, 569, 571, 660
Montagnard Tribesmen, 29
Moreno, Dennis Ralph, 583, 660
Moriarty, Raymond, 291-292, 321-322, 324-326
Morton, Dave, 408, 647
Mower, Gary, 452, 659
Mrdjenovich, Charles, 16, 45, 53-54, 56-57, 646, 655
Murdock, Dale, 354
Murphy, Tommie, 354
Murray, Clyde, 394-395

N

Napier, David, 237, 364, 374, 658
Nascimento, Alan, 237
Nelson, Max, 512-513
Nichols, Bruce, 451, 659
Nichols, James, 450-451
Nolan, Eugene, 442
Nozewski, Robert, 273, 658
Nunnally, Timothy, 288-289, 658

O

O'Brien, Tim, 239, 312
O'Conner, Jay, 268
O'Dea, Edward, 123
O'Neil, Michael, 469-470
O'Neill(or O'Neil), Bill, 173
Olsen, Cecil Chancey, 552, 651, 660
Olsen, Larry, 106
Olsen, Thomas, 435
Onchi, Curtis, 220, 657
Operations
    Bold Mariner, 168, 176, 178, 181-182, 193, 204
    Burlington Trail, 62-63, 66-67, 71, 74, 85, 96, 98, 102, 104, 107, 114, 125-126, 300
    Dewey Canyon II, 550
    Geneva Park, 217, 227, 254, 256, 267, 271, 282, 295, 298, 308, 425, 481
    Golden Fleece, 132, 135, 140, 157, 164, 167-168, 183
    Hammurabi (My Lai Investigation), 382, 387-388, 391, 394
    Lam Son 719, 545, 550, 597
    Muscatine, 35, 61, 80, 82
    Nantucket Beach, 296, 298-299, 301-302, 308-309, 313-314, 321, 323, 331, 333, 349, 391, 415, 419
    Piranha, 4-5, 177, 181, 204
    Pocahontas Forest, 98, 104
    Russell Beach, 168-169, 171-173, 176, 178-179, 181-183, 189, 192-194, 200, 204-209, 211-212, 214, 216, 224, 232, 242, 252-253, 256, 291, 295, 297-298, 300-301, 308, 314, 412
    Starlite, 4-5, 177
    Vance Canyon, 74-75, 85
    Wheeler/Wallowa, 66-67
Ortiz, Edward, 304

P

Page, Robert, 268
Paige, Irving, 304
Palmeri, Joseph, 305
Parkhurst, Murphy, 354
Parmeter, Gerald, 63, 655
Passmore, Edwin, 540, 555, 571, 576
Patrick, Darryl Wayne, 377-378, 659
Payne, Gary, 189, 657
Pene, Jim, 411-412, 648
Penney, Donald, 143, 656
Percy, Doland Lee, 496, 659
Person, Robert Lee, 343, 658
Peterson, Bob, 293, 658
Peterson, Dan, 237
Petrashune, Michael John, 533-534, 660
Pfalzer, Timothy, 443-444
Piano Jr., Ralph Ernest, 353, 658
Pillow, Leo, 256, 288-289
Pineapple Forest, 119-121, 601
Pinkville, 81, 83-86, 88-90, 92-96, 98, 168-169, 176-177, 183, 185-186, 213, 217, 223, 225, 238, 241, 253, 256, 258, 298, 300-301, 309, 341, 346, 355-356, 366, 368, 375-376, 388, 391, 406, 411
Porter, Dan, 218, 261-262, 264
Porter, Darrel, 197-198
Porter, Robert, 123-124
Potenza, Peter, 237
Poulson, Bruce, 112, 656
Powell, Daniel, 63, 655
Powers, Monroe Alan, 528, 660
Printy, Russell, 570-572
Proctor Jr., William C., 308, 658
Prosser Jr., Irvin, 201, 657
PRU-Provincial Reconnaissance Unit, 58-60, 186-187, 227, 229, 257, 270, 272, 274, 290-291, 302, 307, 311, 320, 331, 345, 348, 585-586, 601
Pudlas, Jim, 305
Pyle, Gomer, 266

R

Ramsey, Lloyd B., 281, 636
Randall, Wayne, 230, 657
Randolph, Richard Dale, 571, 660
Ray, Drexel, 117-118
Reefer, Charles, 322-323, 658
Reigles, Donald, 359
Renze, Jim, 444
Rice, Everette, 144, 160-161
Richards, Stephen, 88, 656
Richardson, Ronald, xi, 126, 139-142, 145, 148-150, 152, 155-156, 158, 160, 163-166, 172, 174-178, 180-183, 185, 188-190, 192-193, 195, 199, 202-203, 211, 214-215, 231-232, 248, 253
Riggs, Claude, 354
Ritz, David G., 372, 658
Riverboat North, 36
Riverboat South, 36, 47, 62, 73-74, 130, 138, 173-174
Robinson, John J., 587
Rocket Pocket/Rocket Valley, 34, 162, 164, 212, 217-218, 221, 225-226, 232-233, 235, 247, 250, 259, 265, 267, 269, 272, 274, 291, 295, 306-307, 309, 375, 399, 421-422, 435, 437-440, 444-445, 450, 453-455, 462, 489, 492-494, 563-564, 574, 609, 639
Rodriguez, Ronald, 354
Rodriguez-Guzman, Abelardo, 328-329, 658
Roegner, Carl, 88
Rollins Jr., William, 184, 657
Roman, Richard, 365, 381
Rose, Albert, 125-126, 656
Rosson, William, 7-8
Rowles, Everett, 237
Rudd, James, 18, 54, 56, 655
Rudderow, Diane, 649
Rupp, Paul, 599
Russell, Lawrence, 175, 230

S

Saal, David, 354
Saigon, 7, 60, 112, 221, 366, 421, 561, 640, 645
Salopek, Joseph, 198
Salter, Robert, 86, 119, 656
Samples, Mitchell, 90-92, 186
Sandman, Mitchell, 262, 264, 657
Santellan, Teodoro, 131, 656
Sathoff, Dale, 478, 659
Savoy, John, 117
Schaffer, John, 145, 656
Schanke, Kenneth, 463-464
Scherf, Michael, 262-264, 657
Schiess, Thomas Charles, 513, 660
Schiller Jr., Martin, 393, 659
Schopp, Steven, 269, 277-278, 280-282, 285, 332, 334-335, 337-338, 351-353, 366
Schrier, David, 389
Schuelke, Scott, 305
Schulte, Dan, 133, 138-139, 141, 188-189
Schwall, John, 196
Schwarzkopf, H. Norman, 634-639
Scurlock, William, 73, 77, 109
Secrest, Wayne, 175, 202
Seely, Richard, 165, 656
Selle, Ronald, 288-289
Sheffield, Donald W., 198
Shelk, John, 365-366
Shepler, Jimmie, 372
Sheredos, Roland, 94, 655
Shields, William, 354
Sikes, Thomas, 160-161, 164, 656
Sikora, Gregory, 198
Simpson, Joel, 648
Smith, Adolf, 173, 218
Smith, Michael, 124, 126, 164, 176, 178, 182, 195
Smith, Robert, 336
Smith, Thomas, 589
Smith, Tommy, 268

Snyder, Melvin C., 369, 396, 411, 443
Spaid, Jacob, 451-452
Spearing, Matthew, 117-118
Sprinkle, William, 354
St. Bernard, Kim, 72
Stachowiak, Michael, 358, 386, 408, 647-648
Stanford, Roger, 14
Starck, Jim, 236-238
Stauffer, Henry, 70
Steele, Kenneth, 88
Stephens, Albert, 82, 89
Stevens, Dennis, 599, 630, 642
Stogsdill, Ralph, 496
Stokes Jr., Guy, 445, 659
Stone, Harold, 233
Stone, Joseph Lamar, 562
Stotterboom, Gary, 457-458
Stretch, Kenneth, 18
Strieff, Wayne, 239
Sumner, Steven, 233
Sweigart, Barry, 153, 643
Swek, John, 345, 369

T

Talbott, James Franklin, 321, 658
Tam Ky, 10, 36, 66-71, 73, 94, 96-99, 104, 106-107, 114, 119-121, 153, 163, 280, 300, 306, 321, 461-462, 479-481, 488-489, 491-492, 494, 501, 503, 514, 518, 524, 540, 575, 582, 593-595, 598, 601, 609-610, 617, 623-624, 627, 640
Tannasso, Ambrose, 162
Task Force Cooksey, 96-98, 113-114, 163, 168, 174, 181, 202, 204, 214, 232, 279, 300, 605
Task Force Lizard, 426, 429, 435, 448
Task Force Roman (My Lai Investigation), 381, 383, 387-388, 391, 394
Task Force Saint, 507
Tatom, Phillip, 507, 547

Taylor, David, 232, 257-258, 261-264, 267, 643
Teglia, Kenneth, 395-396, 400, 428, 431-432
Templar, Roger, 542, 556-557
Terrell, Denton, 376
Thetford, Harold, 195
Thomas, Alfred, 257
Thomas, Larry, 110
Thomas, Tom, 122
Thorton, Matthew, 175
Tien Phuoc, 66, 71, 97, 104-107, 112-114
Tittle, Grady, 114-115, 117-118
Trapp, Steven, 245
Tucker, Jim, 94-95, 120-122
Tully, Robert, 214, 244, 248, 253
Tunnell, David, 55-56, 646
Turner, Kenneth, 121, 151
Typhoon Joan, 515
Typhoon Kate, 519-521
Typhoon Patsy, 532

U
Units, U.S. Army
    1st Cavalry Division, 214, 603, 613, 627-628
    1st Squadron/1st Cavalry, 67, 119-120, 190
    1st/6th Infantry Battalion, 8, 32-38, 42, 44-46, 67, 136, 217-218, 290-291, 306, 308, 375-376, 399, 415, 419, 622, 630, 633-634, 636-638
    1st/14th Artillery Battalion, 67, 76, 213, 426, 438, 574
    1st/46th Infantry Battalion, 8, 10,14, 36, 58, 62-63, 67, 94, 136, 524-525, 527, 602
    1st/52nd Infantry Battalion, 8, 35-38, 44, 46, 64, 74, 81, 125, 127, 130, 153, 163, 172, 209, 211, 217, 242, 245, 250, 256-258, 266, 268-269, 82, 308, 343, 480-481, 630

    2nd/1st Infantry Battalion, 550, 584
    4th/3rd Infantry Battalion, 98, 169, 176, 181, 183, 185, 190, 192-193, 197, 200, 202-204, 550
    4th/21st Infantry Battalion, 98
    4th/31st Infantry Battalion, 98
    4th Infantry Division, 7-8, 10, 474, 537, 617, 619
    9th Infantry Division, 514
    11th Armored Cavalry Regiment, 588
    25th Infantry Division, 7, 114, 508, 522, 537, 567
    26th Engineer Battalion, 181, 213, 260, 542
    27th Surgical Hospital, 109, 145, 147, 163, 196, 267, 304, 312, 317, 346, 390, 405, 516, 590
    71st Assault Helicopter Company, 72, 636
    91st Evacuation Hospital, 304, 312-313, 365, 393, 395, 419, 501, 532, 562, 571, 599, 615, 620
    101st Airborne Division, 7-8, 10, 628, 630
    196th Light Infantry Brigade, 7-8, 10, 36, 66, 68, 97-98, 119, 217, 476-477, 524, 545, 550, 574, 584, 601, 605, 608, 610, 612, 627-628, 630
    199th Light Infantry Brigade, 514
    312th Evacuation Hospital, 165, 184, 199-200, 208, 230, 249, 264
    F Troop / 8th Air Cavalry, 98, 227, 259, 309, 312, 450, 497, 500
    H Troop /17th Cavalry, 9, 36, 45, 62, 70, 81, 92-93, 96, 130, 138, 140, 173, 176, 180, 187, 193, 203, 209, 212, 220, 232-233, 248, 262, 302, 306, 334, 371-372, 381, 383, 391-392, 396, 405, 412, 435, 535

Units, Marine Corps
    1st Marine Regiment, 627
    2nd/26th Marine Shore Landing Battalion, 169, 190, 309
    3rd/26th Marine Shore Landing Battalion, 169, 176-177, 190, 193, 195, 197, 203

Units, South Vietnamese Army
    2nd ARVN Division, 67, 85, 98, 167, 169, 216, 480, 609, 632, 639
    2nd/6th ARVN Battalion, 217, 227, 259, 308, 391
    3rd/4th ARVN Cavalry, 119
    3rd/6th ARVN Battalion, 217, 240, 260, 361, 397
    4th/6th ARVN Battalion, 217, 260, 278, 281, 283, 387, 391
    5th ARVN Regiment, 114, 176, 593-594, 601, 610, 624, 627
    6th ARVN Regiment, 216-217, 234, 240, 259, 282, 298, 397, 425, 609-610, 626

Units, Enemy
    1st VC Regiment, 2, 4-5, 204
    21st NVA Regiment, 181, 262, 267, 272, 278, 282
    30th NVA Regiment, 503
    38th VC Local Force Company, 169, 181, 183, 192, 300
    40th NVA Battalion, 71
    48th VC Local Force Battalion, 5, 46, 83, 85, 167-169, 177, 181, 183, 186-188, 192-193, 195, 204, 206, 227, 300-301, 314-315, 318, 321, 331, 354, 356-357, 359, 368-369, 388, 390-392, 397, 399-401, 415, 418, 421-422, 508, 631, 633, 635
    60th NVA Battalion, 231
    60th VC Battalion, 4
    70th VC Main Force Battalion, 71, 121
    78th NVA/VC Rocket Battalion, 461, 567, 590
    80th VC Battalion, 4
    95th VC Sapper Company, 46, 300-301, 320, 361
    95B VC Sapper Company, 301, 407, 429, 461
    107th VC Anti-Aircraft Battalion, 300
    125th VC Battalion, 461
    406th VC Battalion, 409
    409th NVA/VC Sapper Battalion, 71, 375, 461, 502, 567
    K-51 VC Local Force Weapons Company, 300-301, 309, 345, 408
    P-31 VC Local Force Company, 301
    T-20 VC Local Force Company, 300-301
    V-14 VC Local Force Company, 567, 577
    V-20 VC Local Force Company, 553, 568

Utley, Ray, 197-198

V

Vander-Dussen, George, 26-27, 81, 656
Vater, Jack, 135
VCI – Vietcong Infrastructure, 58-60, 168, 170, 253, 298, 320, 331, 345, 356, 521, 523
Vest, John, 142
Vick Jr., Albert, 313, 658
Vietnam Wall, 648-649
Vinter, Steven, 119, 656
VIP – Vietnamese Informant Program, 140, 155, 238, 241, 272, 294, 339, 473
Vogelpohl, Rex Alan, 557-558

W

Wagner, James, 176, 178
Wagner, Jim, 123-124
Wagner, Julian F., 255-256, 262, 267-269, 276, 279-281, 290-291, 306, 309-312, 314-315, 322-323, 327-328, 330, 332, 337-338, 344, 353, 355, 369
Waldie, James R., 9-12, 40, 62, 670
Walt, Lewis, 1-2, 5, 36, 631
Warren, Stephen Edward, 571, 650, 660
Watkins, William, 258
Weber, William, 89
Welder, Russ, 110-111
Welsh, Thomas, 354
Wereszynski, Henry J., 443, 454
Westmoreland, William, 6-8, 40, 235, 306, 546, 632
Whitcher, Clayton, 433, 659
Whiteside, Robert, 649
Whitten, Edward, 478
Whittington, Jere, 281
Wight, Robert, 270-271, 274-275, 283-285, 287-289, 310, 339, 342-343, 350-351, 385-387
Williams, Carl, 55
Wilson Jr., Charles, 246, 646, 657
Wilson, Donald, 20, 26, 39, 77-78, 92, 655
Winn, Johnny, 56
Wolf, Robert, 196-197, 226, 266, 643
Wolski, Bill, 401, 403-406, 648
Woodville, Tim, 567-570
Woodworth, Jim, 244
Woody, Jason, 172-173, 357
Wright, Tyrone, 189, 657
Wyant, James, 147

Y

Yates, James I., 345, 658
Yeargin, Walter, 268

Z

Ziegler, Tom, 598-599
Zimmerman, Robert, 262-264